SOVIET U
Black Sea
Caspian Sea
TURKEY
CYPRUS
SYRIA
Iraq Petrol. Co.
LEBANON
ISRAEL
IRAQ
IRAN
Natl. Iranian Oil Co.
andria
Cairo
Suez Canal
JORDAN
Trans-Arabian Pipelines
Persian Gulf
EGYPT
SAUDI ARABIA
Aswan
Red Sea
TRUCIAL CST.
MUSCAT AND OMAN
SUDAN
YEMEN
HADHRAMAUT
Aden
ETHIOPIA
Gulf of Aden
Arabian Sea
△ Oil fields

DULLES OVER SUEZ

BOOKS BY HERMAN FINER

Political Philosophy and Institutions

THE THEORY AND PRACTICE OF MODERN GOVERNMENT
MUSSOLINI'S ITALY
GOVERNMENTS OF GREATER EUROPEAN POWERS
MAJOR GOVERNMENTS OF MODERN EUROPE
ROAD TO REACTION

World Politics

AMERICA'S DESTINY
THE TENNESSEE VALLEY AUTHORITY: LESSONS OF INTERNATIONAL APPLICATION
THE UNITED NATIONS ECONOMIC AND SOCIAL COUNCIL

Political Institutions

THE PRESIDENCY: CRISIS AND REGENERATION
THE BRITISH CIVIL SERVICE
REPRESENTATIVE GOVERNMENT AND A PARLIAMENT OF INDUSTRY

Public Administration

ENGLISH LOCAL GOVERNMENT
MUNICIPAL ENTERPRISE
ADMINISTRATION AND THE NURSING SERVICES

Secretary of State Dulles at an emergency White House conference following the Israeli thrust into Egypt, October 29, 1956.

French Foreign Minister Christian Pineau in London, August 17, 1956, where he proposed international management of the Suez Canal.

British Prime Minister Eden, before rejecting the United Nations call to halt the British-French invasion of Egypt, November 3, 1956.

President Eisenhower, just returned from a campaign swing through the South, pauses during the White House meeting, October 29.

Photos: Wide World

DULLES OVER SUEZ

THE THEORY AND PRACTICE OF HIS DIPLOMACY

by HERMAN FINER

QUADRANGLE BOOKS / *Chicago*

 For information, address: Quadrangle Books, Inc., 180 North Wacker Drive, Chicago 6.

Library of Congress Catalog Card Number: 64-10924

Manufactured in the United States of America

First Printing

With my gratitude to

Parker, *surgeon*
Golden, *internist*
Levinson, *pathologist*

Contents

Foreword

THE SUEZ CRISIS OF 1956, WHICH CAUSED A HOT WAR IN THE MIDDLE EAST and threatened an atomic World War III, was one of the most momentous and formative in United States foreign policy in the twentieth century.

This book attempts a close scrutiny of the diplomacy and action of those who represented the United States at that time, chiefly John Foster Dulles, who acted under the authority of President Eisenhower. The title of the book, in fact, expresses the decisive effect of Secretary Dulles's character and personality on the mighty world forces then in conflict. If the President had acted alone, or if some other man had been Secretary of State, the results would have been much different and, I think, more beneficial for America's national interests and for her moral influence with the rest of the world.

I have tried to reveal the progress of the Suez affair as though the reader were actually inside the State Department and the White House—day by day, sometimes almost minute by minute—taking part in the problems, anxieties, decisions, and actions. The work is thus, incidentally, also a study of the respective roles of the Secretary of State and the President. It watches them in action from the time when Dulles denied to Nasser a loan for the Aswan Dam and when the latter seized the Suez Canal in revenge. It carries them through the secret diplomatic battles, the scenes at the United Nations, and the swift events of invasion, sanctions, and withdrawal.

Thus, the study is one of diplomatic strategy and tactics, and of the confrontation of power by power—East and West; Washington, London, Paris, and Moscow; Afro-Asians and Communists and democracies—in a wild storm of world opinion and emotions.

The chief source of the work is the systematic interrogation of the thirty or so top men who, in and around the Suez affair, directly participated with Dulles and Eisenhower in developing and executing American policy decisions. In addition, the principal representatives of Britain and France, Prime Ministers Eden and Mollet and Foreign Ministers Selwyn Lloyd and Christian Pineau, as well as knowledgeable Israeli and Egyptian officials, were interviewed.

This process of close verbal questioning was essential, because the official papers, especially of the State Department, are not open for examination until 1970. Dulles's papers in the Princeton Library are affected by the same ban. It was therefore necessary to seek out the men who had personally helped to shape the Suez events and who had written, in some cases, the relevant papers, or had heard how the process of decision-making was developing. Of course, it is well known that some steps in the making of decisions are never recorded, and that even when records are kept, they are sometimes destroyed by accident or design. Moreover, perhaps the best-known truth about diplomacy from ancient times to our own, and in all countries, is that public documents disclose reasons more than they disclose motivations, the former coming to the public in virtuous terms, the latter, real and true, but often disconcerting, being kept private. But the historian and the political scientist are vitally interested in knowing the human mind in all its reality.

To my informants, I promised no attribution. But I have listed, immediately following this Foreword, those who so generously conversed with me, and I have indicated the office each held at that time. I also sought out some who knew Dulles before he became Secretary of State.

Former President Eisenhower allowed me a long and instructive discussion with him, in which he described various colloquies with Dulles and opened to me some of his correspondence with Sir Anthony Eden and Prime Minister Ben Gurion. I am most grateful to him for his generosity, as also for his spirited and eloquent vindication of his policy (and Dulles's). I am grateful also to his son, Colonel John S. D. Eisenhower, for two illuminating discussions of Suez and Dulles. He was in charge of the staff that prepared the President's memoirs. General Eisenhower himself graciously volunteered that I might state that he had given me the information that appears. So also with former Vice President Richard M. Nixon.

Since I know that men speak mainly in self-justification, I have made due allowance for this natural propensity. My informants were most generous to me, even when characterizing each other, and I very gratefully acknowledge their help.

Other sources were sometimes more persuasive: the official documents of the various nations and of the United Nations, various memoirs, and the facts as reported by the news media of several countries.

Dulles died in 1959, so that I missed the advantage of hearing his responses to my questions. But I all the more diligently sought out his closest associates and advocates. I have had to follow the facts where they led, and I regret if my own judgments should give any pain to the members of his family. A man is many men, especially when he holds high public office. Dulles's highly complicated and enigmatic character, his powerful will, his colossal self-esteem, his Wilsonian missionary passion, all these refracted and wrenched the mighty forces of the Middle East, Russia, the Western allies, and nationalism into a personally influenced torrent. Certain political circumstances devolved great authority to his hands.

Through the prism of the Suez affair, the reader may observe and assess the cardinal elements in contemporary world politics. Some of these deserve mention in the form of questions. What is the role of force among nations? What meaning has the phrase "the Rule of Law" in international politics? In what circumstances is the United Nations one of the nation's most valuable instruments in maintaining its security and leadership in the world, and when is it a hindrance thereto? What is sound and what is sick in the cry of "anticolonialism"? Was the Suez affair the first of the necessary collusions between Washington and Moscow to avoid atomic war, with the United States consequently abandoning justice for its allies? How far can sectarian moralism be taken in America's foreign policy without danger to its long-term interests? What is America's relationship to Europe and NATO, given her behavior in the Suez affair? It is perhaps permissible, too, to draw the attention of the reader to the realization on several occasions in the following pages of the implications of Suez for America's interest in the Panama Canal.

* * * * *

I have pleasure in acknowledging assistance from the Ford Foundation, the Carnegie Endowment for International Peace, and the American Council of Learned Societies. They gave me the means and time to identify, locate, and travel to converse with the persons I have mentioned, and did so in the finest traditions of American scholarship.

I thank three of my colleagues at the University of Chicago, Professor Morton A. Kaplan, Professor Leonard Binder, and Professor Tang Tsou, for their valuable comments on my first draft.

I also acknowledge the ready and capable help of these officials of the University of Chicago Library: Christine Reb, of the Reference Library; Joseph Gregg; Elizabeth Lundy; Barbara Hillman, periodicals and microfilms; Helen Smith, interlibrary loans; and Mrs. Ruth Foster, a genius at retrieving books from those who have long ago finished studying them. I also thank Dr. William Dix of the Princeton Library, as also his staff, for their kindness in making consultation of the Dulles papers convenient for me.

H. F.

Chicago, Illinois
January, 1964

Chronology

1955

September 24	Arms deal between Moscow and Nasser
December 19	U.S. government offers loan to Egypt to build High Aswan Dam

1956

July 19	Dulles rescinds offer of Aswan Dam loan
July 26	Nasser nationalizes Suez Canal with physical seizure of installations
July 29	Robert Murphy, U.S. Deputy Under Secretary of State, to London
August 1-2	Dulles to London, to confer with British and French leaders
August 2	Tripartite statement issued by U.S., Britain, and France
August 16-23	First London Conference of Maritime Powers, resulting in eighteen-power proposal for settlement of Suez dispute
September 3-10	Menzies leads committee of five to present proposals to Nasser; proposals rejected
September 12-13	Dulles's scheme for a Suez Canal Users' Association broached
September 19-21	Second London Conference of Maritime Powers to establish SCUA
September 26	British and French file complaint and Egypt enters countercomplaints at U.N.
October 5	Beginning of U.N. Security Council negotiations on Suez dispute
October 10	Israeli reprisals against Jordanian attacks at Qalqilya
October 13	Six Principles adopted by Security Council; administrative implementation vetoed by Moscow

October 16	Crucial meeting of British and French leaders in Paris on Middle East
October 16	Secretary General of U.N. seeks proposals from Egypt to satisfy allies
October 16	"Blackout" of news from allies to Washington begins
October 23	Hungarian anti-Communist revolt begins: U.N. seized with problem
October 23	Cairo announces joint Arab command of Egyptian and Syrian forces under Egyptian commander in chief
October 26-27	President Eisenhower warns Israel against military action
October 29	Israel invades Egypt via Sinai
October 30	U.S. initiates action in U.N. Security Council for cease-fire
October 30	British and French serve ultimatums on Israel and Egypt to cease fire
October 30	British and French veto U.S. and U.S.S.R. resolutions for cease-fire
October 31	Britain and France join in an assault on Suez
November 1	Dulles's resolution for cease-fire in emergency session of General Assembly adopted against Britain, France, and Israel
November 2	Israel's victory over Egypt in Sinai complete
November 4	United Nations Emergency Force voted for Suez
November 5	Moscow threatens intervention in Suez conflict with atomic bombs and "volunteers"
November 6	Britain, France, Israel, and Egypt accept cease-fire
November 7	U.N. adopts terms for action of U.N.E.F.
November 7	Israel demands peaceful regime at Gaza and Aqaba in return for withdrawal
November 14	First contingents of U.N.E.F. arrive in Suez
November 24	U.N. votes *forthwith* withdrawal of invaders
December 3	Under American pressure, British and French pledge withdrawal
December 22	British and French leave Suez completely

1957

January-February	U.N. puts pressure on Israel to withdraw totally and unconditionally; sanctions threatened in event of noncompliance
February 11	U.S. *aide-mémoire* promising Israel passage at Aqaba and protection by U.N.E.F. from Gaza attacks; U.S. threatens sanctions about same time
March 1	Israel accepts pledge of U.S. and other leading maritime powers; indicates willingness to withdraw
March 8	Israel complies by withdrawal of all troops
March 25	Suez Canal substantially cleared for passage

Personal Interviews

(PRINCIPAL SOURCES FOR THIS BOOK)

[I cannot name all those interviewed, or those who preferred to respond by letter or telephone. In some cases correspondence amplified the interviews. I have not sought specifically to *exclude* attribution in case, by elimination of possibilities, the specific personal sources could be identified.]

POLICY MAKERS	OFFICE HELD IN 1956
Dwight D. Eisenhower	U.S. President
Major J. S. D. Eisenhower	Son of the President, now in charge of Eisenhower *Memoirs*
Sir Anthony Eden	Prime Minister, Britain
Selwyn Lloyd	Foreign Secretary, Britain
Guy Mollet	Prime Minister, France
Christian Pineau	Foreign Minister, France
Henry Cabot Lodge	U.S. Ambassador to United Nations
Edward Heath	Lord Privy Seal, Britain; Conservative Chief Whip
Hugh Gaitskell	Leader of the Opposition in Parliament
Abba Eban	Israeli Ambassador to U.S.
Robert Murphy	Deputy Under Secretary of State
Dean Acheson	Former U.S. Secretary of State
Richard M. Nixon	U.S. Vice President

OTHER OFFICIALS AND PERSONAGES

Theodore Achilles	U.S. Ambassador to Peru
Winthrop Aldrich	U.S. Ambassador to Britain
George V. Allen	Assistant Secretary, Near Eastern Division, State Department
Hervé Alphand	French Ambassador to U.S.
Jean Beliard	Press Officer for Mollet and Pineau
John Bennett	Interchurch Commission for Peace, etc.
Andrew Berding	Press Officer, State Department
Phyllis Bernau	Secretary to J. F. Dulles
Eugene Black	Director of World Bank
R. R. Bowie	Chairman, Policy Planning Staff, State Department
Ralph Bunche	Secretary U.N.; Nobel Prize Winner
Henry A. Byroade	U.S. Ambassador to Egypt
Sir Harold Caccia	British Ambassador to U.S.
William Clark	Public Relations Secretary to Anthony Eden
Andrew Cordier	Executive Secretary to Dag Hammarskjold
Douglas Dillon	U.S. Ambassador to France
Allen Dulles	Director of CIA
Mrs. John Foster Dulles	Wife of John Foster Dulles
Walter Eytan	Israeli Foreign Office
Arthur Flemming	Director, Office of Defense Mobilization
Senator J. W. Fulbright	Foreign Relations Committee, U.S. Senate
Yehosafat Harkabi [vicariously]	Israeli Intelligence Service
Loy Henderson	Deputy Under Secretary of State for Administration; U.S. Delegate to Cairo, Menzies Mission
Christian Herter	Secretary of State (end of period)
Herbert Hoover, Jr.	Under Secretary of State
Emmet Hughes	White House Speech Writer
George M. Humphrey	U.S. Secretary of Treasury
J. E. Johnson	Carnegie Endowment, Middle East Expert

Senator William Knowland	Republican Leader, U.S. Senate
A. Laurie	Israeli Foreign Service
James Ludlow	Specialist in Middle East and U.N., State Department
Sir Roger Makins	British Ambassador to U.S.
Charles Malik	Lebanese Ambassador to U.S. and U.N.
Carl W. McCardle	Assistant Secretary for Public Affairs, State Department
Reinhold Niebuhr	Interchurch Commission for Peace, etc.
Bernard Noble	Historical Division, State Department
F. O. Nolde	Interchurch Commission for Peace, etc.
Lester Pearson	Foreign Secretary, Canada; Nobel Prize Winner
Herman Phleger	Legal Counsel, State Department
Maxwell Rabb	Secretary, Eisenhower's Cabinet
Admiral Arthur Radford	Chairman, Joint Chiefs of Staff
James Reston	*New York Times* White House Correspondent
Mahmoud Riad	Egyptian Ambassador to Syria
Mohammed Riad	Member Egyptian Delegation to United Nations
William M. Rountree	Assistant Secretary, Near East Division, State Department
Moshe Sharett	Former Prime Minister, Israel [by telephone]
J. J. Sisco	Chief, Bureau of U.N. Affairs, State Department
Donald Tyerman	Editor, *The Economist*, London
William Tyler	Chief, European Division, State Department

DULLES OVER SUEZ

1. DISASTER OVER SUEZ AND SINAI

TUESDAY, OCTOBER 30, 1956, WAS, PERHAPS, JOHN FOSTER DULLES'S MOST agonizing day as Secretary of State. At eight that morning he had hurried with special urgency to his office, to get a much firmer grip on the swift succession of calamitous events in the Middle East. The suspense and fury that tormented him had, in fact, begun some twenty-four hours earlier, when the news reached the State Department that the army of Israel had invaded the Sinai Peninsula.

By the early afternoon his remarkable emotional and nervous stamina was wearing thin, and he looked haggard. Since his arrival at the office, he had been chairman over five meetings of his staff. He had also pursued other consultations. The intense deliberations had focused on Israel and Egypt and the shocking news that arrived about 10:30 A.M. that Britain and France were about to attack Suez and Nasser. And interweaving these anxieties was the Hungarian people's uprising against the Communist regime of Budapest and its Soviet masters. Some of Dulles's advisers, in the tenseness of the moment, had actually urged American intervention in Hungary; others had instantly countered with the ghastly horrors of a thermonuclear war.

On the beige-lined wall of Dulles's handsome office, designed for majesty and quiet, hung, to his left, a large oil portrait of his grandfather, John W. Foster,[1] Secretary of State to President Benjamin Harrison. On his right was an oil portrait of his uncle, Robert Lansing,[2] Woodrow Wilson's Secretary of State, from whom he had learned the fundamental lesson of any Secretary, not to get at odds with his President. At hand was a white telephone, the direct line to President Eisenhower at the White House. In his grandfather's time, America hardly had need of a foreign policy; in his uncle's there had been no escaping one; today, America was present everywhere on earth to meet trouble head on.

On Dulles's desk, just to his left hand, lay his own well-thumbed family Bible, much studied. With it lay Joseph Stalin's *Problems of Leninism*, the Charter of the United Nations, and, close by, some copies of *The Federalist Papers*, which the Secretary would present to new foreign envoys in order that they might better comprehend America. It was Dulles's long-developed habit to seek comfort in the pages of the Bible, and also to select quotations apt to sustain his conscience and embellish his speeches, especially when these approximated the tone of homilies. His mood on this tragic day might well have been expressed by the scriptural prophecy that ranked high among his favorite apothegms: "Be not dismayed; God is not mocked: for whatever a man soweth, that shall he also reap!"

However, his much-agitated but self-assured mind did not interpret such a text to mean that the calamities were of his own making. It was rather Sir Anthony Eden, Prime Minister of Britain, and Guy Mollet, Prime Minister of France, and their respective foreign secretaries, and Ben Gurion, Prime Minister of Israel, who would now deservedly reap what they had sowed, just as he had predicted! To him, as much as to his President, these men were sinners against the light. They had chosen to wage war to assert their rights in the Suez Canal and for national survival, rights which Dulles himself had for some three months specifically acknowledged and strongly and officially advocated. But, in his opinion and that of his Chief Executive and client, President Eisenhower, these men sought redress by a means that was itself the primal iniquity—by war, by the use of force! Hovering over the White House and the State Department was that spirit so well reflected in President Eisenhower's observation to Ambassador Hervé Alphand of France, some nine days later than this day: "Mr. Ambassador, life is a grand staircase which rises to Heaven. I shall arrive at the top of that staircase and I wish to present myself before the Creator with a pure conscience."

Dulles's sense of outrages perpetrated on him was truly anguished. Since July 19, when he had brusquely rescinded his offer of a loan to finance Egypt's High Aswan Dam, the Middle East and his Western allies had subjected him to one shock after the other, and this was happening in a Presidential election year when it was imperative to hail the blessings of Peace and Prosperity!

On July 26, while on a ceremonial visit to Lima, Peru, he learned from Washington that Gamal Abdel Nasser, President of the Republic of Egypt, had seized the Suez Canal by physical force and legalistic nationalization. It was a totally unexpected revenge for Dulles's refusal of the loan a week before. But the revenge fell on Britain and France. Dulles had put his hand into a fire without realizing it *was* a fire. Nasser had turned the tables on the Secretary's own vaunted policy of pressing other nations to the brink of war until *they*

yielded. If he now retaliated effectively, the whole world might go up in flames. The Soviet might use missiles and send in "volunteers." But if he could not try another forceful thrust, how could Nasser possibly be compelled to do justice as Dulles's allies demanded?

Since that day, he had essayed every diplomatic gambit to discourage and deter any reaction by force by Britain and France. Only two weeks ago, he had again voiced optimism: "No one can say with certainty that there will be a peaceful solution. . . . Nevertheless, each difficulty overcome means one less difficulty remaining to be overcome, and we can thus take satisfaction from what occurred last week at the United Nations." [3] But the fundamental difficulty still remained, exactly as when he had first intervened: to secure practical guarantees not dependent on Nasser's mere word or whim.

He had, three days ago, at Dallas, Texas, claimed that before the Charter had been adopted, war over such a dispute as Suez would have already occurred. For three months, he said, peace had been "waged with intensity and imagination," even though the future was obscure.[4] But he did not share with his audience the probability that, had there been no Charter, Nasser might never have dared to seize the Canal by force; that, if there had been even an unvoiced old-fashioned expectation of retaliatory force, Nasser would have reckoned with its disciplinary effects; that the United Nations can be and had been a sanctuary for international evildoers. Nor did he confess that he had repeatedly evaded taking the Suez Canal conflict to the United Nations until the outlook had become desperate, and that even then he had tried to obstruct his allies' initiative in so doing. Nor could he say openly in Dallas that for the last three weeks he had suspected the very worst.

He had waged peace with intensity. But his claim to imagination must in all the pages that follow be painstakingly pondered.

The days immediately preceding October 30 had been abnormally busy ones in the State Department. Rumors had been coming in for some time of an uprising in Hungary against the Soviet-imposed Communist regime; these were confirmed on October 23 with the outbreak of armed rebellion in Budapest, to a crescendo of elation in official Washington. The rapturous and triumphant mood was dispelled, however, only forty-eight hours later, when American intelligence in Israel reported evidence of mobilization in that country. The next day, the U.S. military attaché there cabled that he thought the mobilization was general. Disturbed by these accounts, Dulles hurried to the White House on the morning of October 27 to discuss the unexpected and worrying news with the President, who was about to enter Walter Reed Hospital for his pre-election check-up. Dulles then flew off to make his speech at Dallas—and, in the circumstances, it took some nerve to leave the capital. About noon of the same day, as arranged with Dulles, the President sent a personal message to Prime Minister Ben Gurion, powerfully pleading that he take no action that might endanger peace. A second and even more pressing, indeed a menacing, appeal from Eisenhower was dispatched the following day. But when the Secretary's plane brought him back to Washington at 4 P.M. on the afternoon of Sunday, October 28, Dulles's Under Secretary of State, Herbert Hoover, Jr., met him at the stairs of the plane with fresh reports to the effect that Israel intended to attack Jordan, perhaps Egypt. This aroused suspicions that, if Egypt were the object of attack, Britain and France would join in.

The next day, October 29, the Israeli army did invade Egypt, via Sinai, not Jordan, and moved towards the Canal. The fires of war were ablaze!

Well, thought Dulles and Eisenhower in the midst of their agitation, surely we can stop the Israelis—by moral rebukes and appeals and stern practical measures? The State of Israel was highly dependent on American economic assistance and diplomatic support, and her leaders and people must certainly know that America was their most reliable final defense against extinction, so often and bloodily threatened by the Arab nations? The Secretary's indignation and principles were, to be sure, affected by a conflicting emotion. Suppose the Israeli army did "clean up Nasser" in their own war, and toppled the Egyptian leader and routed his Soviet friends? What a deliverance! Like so many others in the Pentagon and the State Department, Dulles rather hoped it might happen. But then, his protesting conscience warned, the victory would not be sanctified, according either to the Holy Writ of the United Nations Charter or to the pious and idealistic creed of the White House.

At any rate, Israel was not the only offender in Dulles's eyes, since he had obtained the news (first from the commercial news agencies) that Britain and France had given ultimatums to Israel and Egypt, implying intervention in the fighting. Since October 16, his allies had contrived an almost complete blackout of news. His men had not been able to penetrate it. (An exception to this is revealed in Chapter 13; this information may have been ignored through inefficiency or through disbelief in its veracity.) Both the Secretary and the President were bitterly exasperated with the secretiveness being practiced by Britain and France. Indeed, the assistants of the two highest leaders of the nation competed in their judgments of which man was showing the more furious anger. One of Dulles's intimates declared: "The Secretary was sore as Hell! And he kept asking, What can we do about it?" The allies had taken a step which, in the fearful state of mind of Dulles and Eisenhower. might well involve a third world war.

Dulles was undeniably in an embarrassing position. He had led the President to believe, by almost daily persuasion over the past three months, that he could manipulate the British and French *and* Nasser successfully. And it was particularly upsetting to have his diligently piled apple cart knocked over just at this moment, when he at last had the Soviet rulers exactly where he had wanted them, ever since 1945, when he had met Molotov and had been utterly revolted by him. All the opportunity of denouncing the Soviet government for its brutality, its carnage in Budapest, before the whole world was compromised. To demonstrate black and white in the morality of world politics had become a blurred enterprise. For some days now, as he had read the *New York Times*, the *New York Herald Tribune* (a very special and useful favorite), and the *Washington Post* during his early morning breakfast, the world had seemed to a benevolent man, wishing freedom, peace and welfare to all men everywhere, to glow with the promise of victory to those who deserved it. "God is not mocked!" It seemed as though the prediction he had made to the Senate Foreign Relations Committee in February that the Soviet system was about to collapse [5] was soon to be fulfilled. But now his own allies were threatening to use force against Egypt!

In his office on the afternoon of October 30, then, a harassed Secretary of State adjourned one of his vital staff discussions because Hervé Alphand, the French Ambassador, had requested time to call on him to explain his government's actions. It was a meeting the Secretary did not at all relish.

The French Ambassador entered the room at 3:15 P.M. It was now some five hours since Dulles had learned about the French and British ultimatums. They had required Egypt and Israel to cease fire within twelve hours and keep their forces from the banks of the Canal, or else the two European nations would intervene militarily at Suez and, in any case, they would temporarily occupy Port Said, Suez, and Ismailia.

The confrontation began in a tone of diplomatic civility. The Ambassador of France gently explained the course his government would pursue and what it expected to achieve. He said that France could not accept Egypt's *fait accompli* in Suez. His government believed that Nasser's nationalization had been the prelude to an attack by Egypt on Israel. France felt she must prevent fighting between these two countries to prevent the obstruction of free and secure passage of her ships through the Canal.

The Ambassador reminded the Secretary of the patience and cooperation France had shown, much against her better judgment, in joining Dulles's successive plans to achieve a Suez settlement with Nasser. France had agreed to these extended negotiations even though her material property in the Canal as well as her international rights of passage under the Constantinople Convention of 1888 had been seized by Nasser by an act of force. The result had been only a failure of diplomacy (that is, on Dulles's initiative), while Nasser maintained his physical and managerial possession of the Canal with impudence and impunity.

Dulles's face was flushed with anger. In a tone that was a mixture of grief, rebuke, and insult, he burst out in recrimination. "We are living in the gravest moments of Franco-American relations. You did not inform us of your military intentions and moves, although during the last three weeks I have suspected that something was brewing. This is the darkest day in the history of the Western alliance. It might even be the end of the alliance itself! This attack on Egypt incurs the risk of a general war. For the last twelve weeks your country and Britain and I have been trying to build a common front to secure our rights against Nasser's coup. The news blackout has done me the gravest personal damage and has put me in an impossible position."

Dulles concluded with a charge that transgressed the permissible. "The action and intervention of France and Britain is just the same as the behavior of the Soviet Union in Budapest!"

Alphand had known Dulles since 1947. The men had never yet exchanged an angry word. The present injury, even if it had been true, was more than the Ambassador could tolerate, as the caretaker of his country's dignity.

He responded, "I am bound to protest. Your accusation is not true!" He spoke with the air of one who expects the retraction of the offensive remarks.

The remonstrance brought back Dulles to his senses and momentarily checked his strong impulses of personal moralism that had produced the inability to admit the difference between Britain and France and Moscow. The ugly insult to an ally in the North Atlantic Treaty Organization and a venerable nation entitled to its pride had to be expunged.

"Then," Dulles answered, "I withdraw the comparison. I beg your pardon. You must understand that I am speaking under the stress of great emotion that such a terrible thing could have happened. This event is a horrible blow to the Western alliance, and I am laboring under the anxiety of how I can remedy the damage to the confidence between our governments."

The Ambassador left, and Dulles returned to resume his conferences with his staff experts at the table abutting on his own desk.

Over a week later, on November 8, Ambassador Alphand met with President Eisenhower. They talked over the terrible events that had occurred in the interval, events including Moscow's threats to use atomic bombardment of the allies in aid of Egypt. The President was at that moment in a mild mood, though when he had first heard about the Israeli invasion and the action of the British and French, "the White House rang with barracks-room language that had not been heard at 1600 Pennsylvania Avenue since the days of General Grant."[6] To Alphand, on this occasion, remembering that both were gentlemen and that a cease-fire had by now been imposed, he merely said, "Well, you've got the right to do as you want! I think you are wrong. History will tell!" It was as though neither he nor Dulles had been personally making the history of the event, or were continuing to do so. At any rate, he had never tolerated insubordination in all his career. Why should he start with Britain and France, even if they were particularly important allies, or Israel, indeed, which was but a suppliant?

The evidence is conclusive that, from October 29, Dulles was bent on action, swift and draconic, to extinguish the dangerous fires, and on condign correction of those who were the Breakers of the Law, the offenders against world peace and the organization established to uphold it. He resolved to compel Britain, France, and Israel (not Nasser's Egypt!) to obey the Law to its very last "jot and tittle," as the Bible said, by arraignment and moral condemnation and prosecution with tactics that may fairly be described as savage. For justice must not only be done, but the whole world must see that America was taking the lead in doing it.

From October 30 until a cease-fire was affected on November 6, and thenceforward until the armies were actually withdrawn (the allies by December 22, Israel not till March), Dulles, or his loyal assistants (for he became gravely ill on November 2), harried his allies unmercifully. His method was to wage a campaign of impassioned denunciations in the United Nations, as rough as and more elaborate than the outburst to the French Ambassador. And then he withheld the oil supplies on which almost all of their industrial systems and much of their agricultural produce depended, and the dollar credits that would have relieved the ruinous drain on their strength as world markets. This crusade resulted in the humiliation of the offending nations, to the signal advantage of Nasser and his constant, instigating friend in need, the Soviet government. The prosecution was undertaken, even if unjoyously, in the spirit of a Pharisee—and some may, understandably, believe that the Pharisee is valuable in the world of men if not among men of the world—in order tc justify the ways of the United Nations to Man, and to punish not only the sin committed, but the sinners, so severely that no nation would ever dare undertake such an offense again. It was not likely to remedy the blow to the Western alliance which Dulles had lamented in his session with the French Ambassador. Britain and France could not forget that in three months of negotiations and opportunity he had never once point-blank

and explicitly described to them what his United Nations tactics would be if they used force; nor did they glean this from him by so much as a pattern of hints, anxiously as they hung on his every word.

It is hardly surprising, therefore, that later both Prime Minister Harold Macmillan (as well as his successors in his party and men in the Labour Party also) and, even more, General Charles de Gaulle, should remember these humiliating and harmful days when Dulles cracked the righteous and painful whip in an affair in which their vital interests were in jeopardy, not to help them (whatever he believed his intentions and policy were), but to sap their strength. Never again could they wish to be so much at the mercy of an ally —however benevolent he claimed to be, however powerful he was— in that interval of seeming peace between one war and another. Millions of citizens in Britain and France came to similar conclusions, making up their own minds on the meaning of events independently of what their leaders might tell them. Their attitude, too, would increase America's future burdens.

Nevertheless, in examining Dulles's actions throughout the Suez affair, it would be not only inhuman, but unrealistic, not to feel sympathy for the United States Secretary of State. To hold this office in the middle of the twentieth century is to bear the most onerous responsibility a man can hold in any governmental office in the whole world, even if we include in the comparison the Premiership of the Soviet Union or the First Secretaryship of its Communist Party. To have yearned and worked, as Dulles had done, for at least a decade to win the office, must make its holder even more sensitive to the uses of power and the afflictions of Fate, meaning the tough, independent action of the scores of other countries with whom America is entangled in friendly, neutral, or hostile relationship. For, as the long record shows, Dulles was a human being of zealous, even missionary dedication to his conception of man's welfare. Sympathy is one's natural response when a valiant, potently Christian man is troubled, even if it should be demonstrable that the trouble was quite substantially of his own making and that his policies, even his virtues, contributed to disaster on an international scale and to serious damage to other nations. Yet if he made mistakes, as we believe he did, they cannot be condoned. America had forced its allies to step out of the Middle East, and henceforth she would be forced to step in. The evidence of her own egoism in her relations with her allies was bound to stimulate theirs in reprisal and self-protection: it is a natural consequence.

Every nation is a corporate personality composed of a moral creed and material power and needs. Of this corporate personality, the American nation, the Secretary of State is the trustee and plenary manipulator in the conflicts among nations, for the life and death, the moral ascendency or the degradation, of his own country, and of its services to mankind. His mind, conscience, and character are the master of the nation's fate, supported by all the nation's might and capacity for self-sacrifice—the master, that is, under whatever assertion of guidance and responsibility the President may think he himself owes the nation. In the affair of Suez and Sinai, what benefits or injuries did the partnership produce for the United States and the world at large, especially the free world? Can what happened happen again, more or less?

In investigating the available facts for clues to an answer, we may note in passing that the dramatic action seems to fall into the traditional form of five acts. The first is a fairly quiet but decisive opening: Dulles's refusal to Egypt of the Aswan loan. The second is the rape of the Canal by the military dictator, Nasser. The third comprises three ineffectual conferences in London and one in Cairo, under Dulles's leadership and "intensity," to enact a settlement, which, if it were to be successful, must be both peaceful and just. He does not face force with force in this act; he flinches at the brink imposed by Nasser. The fourth is played at the United Nations, which also fails to establish a just solution to the conflict or solve the problem of the hostility of the Arab states towards Israel. In the fifth act, the aggrieved nations make war to achieve justice, but are impeached before the United Nations by the United States under Dulles and are forced to terminate their action by the unilateral sanctions of oil and dollars imposed by the United States. Force fails and justice does not triumph, since Dulles is insufficiently skillful to manipulate the former and does not exact the latter. Nasser, with Moscow's resolute aid, succeeds in intimidating America, Britain, and France. Justice is abandoned and peace becomes more precarious than ever.

2. DULLES AND THE MIDDLE EAST

IN TIME, EVERY MAN ACQUIRES A CHARACTERISTIC POSTURE. THE MORE pointed word, perhaps, is *stance*, a position taken up to deliver a stroke. John Foster Dulles was physically quite an imposing man, about six feet tall and 190 pounds in weight. He almost invariably stood talking or thinking or striding about with his hands thrust deep and firmly into his trousers pockets, with his jacket pushed back like wings from his broad shoulders and his large head slightly bent forward. The posture expressed determination and self-assurance. Dulles is said to have acquired this habitual and decided master-of-the-house stance at Princeton, when a student. But his unprecedently swift success in law practice in the famous New York firm of Sullivan and Cromwell may well have engendered the attitudes of a man supremely, some have said colossally, confident of achievement and whose next success is ever imminent, however tricky and tough the men and circumstances. Dulles liked to dress the part also. His suits were tailored at Brooks Brothers in New York, usually of well-cut light tweed with a brown or gray background, and his silk shirts were made to order in Tokyo.

Dulles's face was elegant and spare and big. It was surmounted by shining, silver hair, short and well brushed from a parting on the left. His brow was fairly broad, high, and bony, giving an impression of force and intelligence. The jaw and chin were strong; the nose fairly large, slightly aquiline, with neat nostrils, and outthrust. His blue-gray eyes were large and bright and not deep-set, and peering, always peering. They were slightly crossed, the effect of an overdose of quinine during an almost fatal attack of malaria he had suffered in Latin America as a young man. They were also subject to a slight but noticeable tic.

What gave all of Dulles's features a definite cast was his mouth, rather thin and stern: on the right side, due to a slight stroke, it was sharply turned down. Habitually now, at the age of sixty-eight, the Secretary wore a look that was grave, indeed mournful, even censorious. He could laugh and joke, but cerebrally, not viscerally, and even so this was no dominant mood. Laughter is a release into irresponsibility, while Dulles was extremely conscientious. The general impression given by his face, as by his stance, was one of resolute will power, self-confidence, and determination to have his own way, even, some said, to hector his way through complexities. He was a cocksure man, and many said he had the right to be.

Of course, as United States Secretary of State, he had very good reason to be so self-confident: President Eisenhower was not assertive as a statesman, and consequently had chosen Dulles so that he could leave in his hands almost all of the direct and daily responsibilities for guiding this nation in her multitudinous and complex dealings with the other nations of the world. Dulles alone was in the driver's seat, as few other American Secretaries have been, of by far the most formidable apparatus of power politics ever known in history, incorporating the power and will, in 1956, of 170 million people. "Little" or "big," the first surveys and approaches to decision were taken by him, and the execution of the authorized decision was also undertaken by him.

One of these decisions, deceptively small at first glance, occurred on July 19, 1956, when Dulles informed the Egyptian Ambassador, Dr. Ahmed Hussein, that the United States would not finance Egypt's construction of the High Aswan Dam, which that country had hoped would significantly improve its backward economy and raise its international prestige. This decision, it may be said at once, caused the Suez crisis, since Nasser grasped it as the opportunity for seizing the Canal. The Secretary's decision was based on his comprehension of the Middle East in general and Egypt in particular, and, of course, on consideration of the United States' best interests in the complex world-political relationships in the maelstrom of that part of the world. The situation was far from simple.

The Middle East (sometimes called the Near East) is that group of nations consisting of Egypt, Syria, Iraq, Jordan, Lebanon, Saudi Arabia, and Yemen—all Arab—and Israel. Neighboring areas often closely involved are Turkey to the northwest, Iran (Persia) to the northeast, and various coastal areas like Kuwait, the Bahrein Islands, and Libya. It is a region of extremely complicated problems and passions and hostilities within each country (not so Israel), among the Moslem nations themselves, and among all the Arab nations on the one side and the Jewish nation of Israel on the other.

When Dulles became Secretary of State in 1953, he, like anyone else, could count only some ten years since the United States had become officially interested in the Middle East. The connection had begun with Anglo-American cooperation during World War II in lend-lease operations to supply the Soviet Union via Iran and to support Britain in the joint Middle East Supply Center.[1] Thenceforward, there was no extrication. Four factors, of a mixed geopolitical and moral kind, had been developing to link the area's fortune with the destiny of this country, and eventually to compel American involvement, deeply indeed, in Middle Eastern politics.

First, in the event of another world war America's physical survival itself might depend on the strategic location of the Middle East. The more bases the United States could have scattered around the world, the less likely it would be to suffer a complete knockout in the first atomic strike by a hostile power. In particular, the maximum number of friendly square miles in the vicinity of the most powerful potential enemy, Russia, could well make the difference between survival and extinction. The United States might need air passage across the Middle East and the use of its airfields. As in World War II, this country would also probably want overland access to friendly nations. Naval forces would need to move into and out of the Mediterranean via Gibraltar and the Suez Canal. The Dardanelles could bottle up Russia's Black Sea, and of that narrow channel, Turkey was the guardian. From bases in the Middle East, America could contain the U.S.S.R. and could assert a continuous threat over her sources of oil in Baku and Batum, as well as over all her major industrial installations as far north as Leningrad and west to the Urals. And, furthermore, the Middle East was especially close to the soft underbelly of Russia, soft in loyalty and soft with her richest harvests of grain—the Ukraine.

Secondly, Americans had a most substantial interest in the oil resources of the Middle East. Some day (prospectors were always putting it off), home oil reserves might give out and those of the Middle East were no less than two-thirds of all the known supplies in the world. American investments in them were large—in 1956, about $1.5 billion.[2] It could be granted that with a gross national product, at that time, of some $500 billion a year, the loss of these investments would not ruin the American economy, even considering also that American businessmen gained a billion dollars a year from the profits of production. What must not be lost was the oil itself, which would be especially important during a war. As for the investments and the annual income, the oilmen were the most powerful single influence in American policy in the Middle East: they pressed on the State Department an insistent pro-Arab policy.

The Soviet Union was well endowed with oil deposits and about to become an exporter of this commodity. In sharp contrast, Western Europe could not supply its own needs from native supplies, and, indeed, would find its industrial machinery stopped dead without Middle

East oil. That very threat had been shouted in Nasser's booklet, *The Philosophy of the Revolution.*[3] A prudent Secretary of State had to reckon with the possibility that Arab politicians might sometime, quite suddenly, cause their governments to cut off oil supplies in order to injure the West politically, even if this meant a financial loss to them. The Western nations that might be thus blackmailed were hosts to American missile and airplane bases, and these helped to contain the Soviet Union in the West. In particular, oil had a critical significance for France and Britain, America's chief European and world allies. Britain obtained 15 per cent of her total energy requirements from oil; for Continental Europe, the figure was 17 per cent. Even more important was the fact that oil was used as a fuel for machinery and processes that only petroleum could serve, or, at any rate, it would be very many years before atomic energy could replace it. The need for oil fuel was increasing rapidly year by year. Western Europe, including Britain, needed 87 million metric tons of oil in 1955; by 1975, it would need 310 million metric tons.

The third factor, the Suez Canal itself, was thus inseparably linked with the supply of oil. Through the Suez Canal, included in the amounts mentioned above, were 27 million metric tons for British account; outside those figures, were 40 million to North America. Some 75 per cent of Europe's oil came from the Middle East, one-half of it via the Canal; a good deal of the other 25 per cent reached the Mediterranean exit ports via pipe lines from Saudi Arabia and Iraq. If Europe's oil were forced to travel from the oil fields by way of South Africa, the tankers would need to sail five times the distance compared with the Suez route, and more so than the pipe line supplies. It might be added that no less than a quarter of all British exports and imports moved through the Canal. In all, forty or fifty ships passed through it every day, carrying one-sixth of the cargoes of the whole world. Whoever held the Canal held the life of nations in his power—and that is why, in 1888, the Constantinople Convention was drawn up by the major maritime powers and Egypt, to provide a system of administration whereby no single nation should have so mortal a monopoly.

The fourth consideration was more immediately human and charged with passion: Israel. Arab and Pan-Arab nationalism were so highly inflamed that any spark in the region could produce a high explosion. Dulles had not been responsible for America's recognition of Israel in 1949. He even thought there was some truth in the Arab recriminations that President Truman had traded the Jewish vote to elect him President for America's vote to recognize Israel at the United Nations.[4] Sometime in 1954, President Eisenhower had said in private at an American Jewish convention in Washington: "I don't know what I would have done had I been President when the question of Israel's independence came up . . . but Israel is now a sovereign nation to which we do have obligations. We shall keep them." However, the pressing and dangerous questions were: to what extent? at what cost?

The Arab nations had never ceased to attack America's conscience on Israel: that America had given away the Arab land of Palestine to Jews; had made its Arabs into refugees; had created a beachhead of "imperialism" in their midst. Of course, it suited them to ignore the fact that the Soviet Union had recognized Israel simultaneously with America. In an attempt to placate the Arab countries, Dulles and Eisenhower instituted a policy called "impartiality." However, as Dulles said to a Jewish delegation, America could hardly allow the "Land of the Prophets" to be wiped out, as the Arabs were threatening. The Arabs raided and murdered the Israelis; the Israelis retaliated; both sides wanted arms from America, the Israelis more desperately than ever since September, 1955, when Nasser had made a massive arms deal with the Soviet Union. It was a difficult, taxing problem, and no one knew where it would end.

Dulles's diplomatic legacy in the Middle East, which of course had to be taken into account along with the four factors outlined above, consisted for the most part of policies instituted by Truman, and these were acknowledged by Dulles to be of considerable advantage to American interests. In 1946, the United States had supported Iran against Stalin's attempt to absorb that country by occupation, fake rebellion, and the creation of a northern "autonomous" republic. The following year, it had aided the replacement of British power, which was on a substantial decline, in Greece and Turkey (the Truman Doctrine of 1947).[5] These moves had "contained" Russia's efforts to extend her power around and in the Middle East.

Dulles also accepted the Truman engagement in the Tripartite Pact of May 25, 1950[6] (with Britain and France), to maintain peace in the Middle East. According to this agreement, the three nations pledged themselves to regulate the supply of arms on a basis of parity between Israel on the one hand and the Arab states combined on the other. They would not permit armed aggression across the lines drawn up in 1949 in the armistice agreements signed by the Arab nations (not including Iraq) and Israel under the aegis of the United Nations, and should such aggression occur, would act against the aggressor within and without the United Nations. The existing situation, the *status quo*, would thus be preserved and an arms race prevented. For this balanced position, the Arabs bitterly hated the United States; their wish was to secure enough weapons and freedom to exterminate Israel.

One further circumstance was crucial in determining America's relationship to the Middle East. Arab feeling was vehement against the vestiges of colonialism, mainly represented by Britain, which remained in the region. The tactics of Mossadegh in Iran, seizing the

Abadan refinery from the British in 1951, inspired and incited the Egyptians, for example, as no other modern act of rebellion had, to non-stop violence and total nationalistic intransigence. It was to the interest of the United States, if she wished to align these nations on her side against Russia, to smooth over any such hostility towards her allies. In the Arab anticolonial cause the Egyptians had most often been in the forefront. They had come to resent, most furiously, the British base in the Suez Canal Zone, which had been granted Britain in the Anglo-Egyptian Treaty of 1936, a treaty which had practically brought to an end the occupation of Egypt by Britain begun in 1882. Before Dulles became Secretary of State, in October, 1951, Egyptian politicians had attempted to abrogate that treaty. The British Foreign Secretary, Anthony Eden, had reproached the State Department for supporting the Egyptians in this affair, and had tried to pacify Egypt by inviting her to participate in a Middle East Command alliance, as an equal founder, with America, Britain and France.[7] The Egyptian masses who were politically minded, as well as their leaders, had furiously rejected this proposal. Egypt denounced the treaty (which all her political parties had solemnly signed in 1936) and started guerrilla warfare against the British in the Canal Zone.

Just before Eisenhower and Dulles took office, in 1953, the Russians protested against the idea of a Middle East Command with great force. They charged that it would be a deposit for arms against the Soviet Union; it would draw the Middle East into a new world war; it would produce the encirclement of Russia; it was an explosive on their very frontiers!

Dulles was the first Secretary of State ever to visit the Middle East; he spent twenty-one days with an entourage of State Department and other officials, including Harold Stassen (Director of the Mutual Security Program), in the Middle East, India, and Pakistan, in May and June, 1953. When he returned, he spoke (June 1) on television of his findings, and he gave the impression that he now clearly understood the wisest policy for the United States to pursue.[8]. The Middle Eastern countries must themselves *initiate* common defense efforts: Western efforts in the past had failed simply because the initiative and interests were Western and therefore suspect. America herself had been "unnecessarily ambiguous" about colonialism. He believed the West would gain immensely if an orderly development of self-government occurred in those countries, and (or *but*) he himself emphasized the word *orderly*. Dulles also enunciated his doctrine of "impartiality" between Arab nations and Israel. The Arabs were entitled to more friendship than in the past, especially assistance in attaining a higher standard of living. He reaffirmed the Tripartite Pact. Then he mooted the idea of a military alliance between the nations of the "Northern Tier," just beneath the Russian bulge southwards into the Middle East.

But he did not then state which these countries would be, though it was easy to guess.

It was Dulles's policy to press the British to evacuate their Suez Canal Zone base. In this he had been preceded by Dean Acheson, who had begun pourparlers with King Farouk on the subject in 1952. Dulles diligently pursued these beginnings, especially anxious to give to Egyptian politicians, first General Naguib and then Colonel Nasser, the heads of the Free Officers' Revolution against the King, a political present in the hope that it would lead to their participation in or friendly acceptance of his Northern Tier alliance. He set himself out to win over General Naguib with small but gracious acts, one of which was the presentation to that military leader of a pearl-handled revolver inscribed: "To General Naguib from his friend Dwight D. Eisenhower." A diplomatic maxim runs: *Pas trop de zèle*, or, Don't be excessive in your zeal! His political critics and his friends in the Interchurch Commission on a Just and Durable Peace loudly deplored this gesture by so pious a Christian.

Dulles pressed forward with the diplomatic maneuvers and promises with the result that an Anglo-Egyptian Agreement was signed on July 27, 1954, concerning the Canal base. It was achieved only after the strongest pressure on the British by Dulles and Eisenhower; persuasion is hardly the word.[9] At one time Dulles had let it be known that if the Egyptians attacked the British, the U.S.A. would not go to the help of Britain. The British had maintained 80,000 troops at the base in vast installations. Naguib and Nasser had declared this area an Egyptian battlefield, with guerrilla not formal war. It had cost them a dozen or so casualties a day from Egyptian snipers and saboteurs. The Conservative Government, and before them, the Labour Government, had thought this not too expensive for the protection of the military and maritime stability the base afforded. British withdrawal from the base was nevertheless duly completed by June 13, 1956, rather ahead of time. They were most punctilious in meeting their promises, believing that their good faith would be met by good faith from Nasser. June 13 was only one month before the Egyptian Ambassador came from Cairo to Washington to obtain the loan for the Aswan Dam.

Dulles's British, French, and American (Democratic Party) critics observed with apprehension that the West had lost a mighty military base. The White House and State Department argument was that nuclear weapons made it untenable. The Soviet Union had exploded a hydrogen bomb in August, 1953. To this the critics responded that by such reasoning Cyprus, Malta, and even Britain herself were untenable! Should Arab good will be bought at so high a price?

Dulles believed he had made a good deal with Nasser. Without

Egyptian good will, Dulles argued, the base could not be held. He might expect happy cooperation from him now that this residue of colonialism was disposed of. He thought the British had come well out of it, also. The Agreement gave them the right to return to the base at any time during the next seven years, if a "foreign power" should attack any member of the Arab League or Turkey, though in such a case they were to withdraw once the emergency was over. Also during that period of seven years, British technicians would assist the Egyptians in maintaining and repairing the installations. The Agreement contained a further clause regarding the Suez Canal: the Canal was recognized as an integral part of Egypt, but also as a maritime connection of international, commercial, and strategic importance, and the parties pledged themselves to respect the Constantinople Convention of 1888 guaranteeing perpetual freedom of navigation.

Egypt's obligations under that Convention, however, now depended only on the word of the military revolutionists who had ousted their original leader, Naguib, and especially on that of Nasser, a ruthless and power-lusting nationalist who had intrigued Naguib into the front place and then thrown him out to take that place himself.[10] The Arabs were as violently hostile to the West as ever: they held that they had merely obtained their due, and very tardily at that! Their nationalist hysteria mounted; it did not diminish. And as no Western nation was close enough, with arms at hand, to restrain any bloody adventures in which they might indulge, Israel more than ever feared the future. She felt that the evacuation of the base had betrayed her existence. When Dulles was queried why he did not ask Egypt for a *quid pro quo*, he proferred the noble, Christian answer that America was engaged in demonstrating to the whole world her moral disapproval of colonialism and seeking the trust of the peoples who had been subject to it. Actually, the *quid* was to be Egypt's entrance into the alliance of the Northern Tier, soon to become the Baghdad Pact: Nasser did not give it as Dulles expected for his *pro quo*. To sweeten the way to the alliance, the United States appropriated $40 million as a first stage in economic aid to Egypt. It made no difference: Nasser was not selling any of his assets.

With vigor and persistence, Dulles continued to thrust forward his plan for a military alliance between Britain and the northern Middle East countries, in which it was widely understood America would participate. The Tier was Dulles's invention and initiative. In making his overtures to the various nations, he offered them, as he had Egypt, aid for economic and military purposes. (The "neutrals" India and Afghanistan strongly protested his efforts to bring in Pakistan.) By October, 1955, Turkey, Iraq, Iran, Pakistan, and Britain were linked by treaty, known as the Baghdad Pact, with, in Prime Minister Anthony Eden's words, "a frontier stretching from the Mediterranean to the Himalayas."

This was no unqualified gain for Dulles. Only Turkey had substantial military strength. Iran was militarily weak; was politically unstable; and was always likely to frighten the near-by claws of the Russian bear. Nasser had not only not entered the Pact (though he had pocketed his price!), but fomented an enraged public opinion against Iraq as an Arab nation that had joined the "imperialists." Indeed, Egyptian denunciation of Nuri Es Said, Prime Minister of Iraq, had been so virulently effective as almost to cause his downfall at the hand of the street mobs; he had needed to call together nine former Prime Ministers to convince King Faisal that he should sign the treaty. Nasser feared Iraq as leader of Pan-Arabism in the Fertile Crescent, including Iraq, Syria, Lebanon, even Jordan; it was a threat to the creation of any Arab federation headed by Nasser and Egypt.

It had been expected that Dulles would join the Pact. But at the summit conference in Geneva, June, 1955, he informed Eden he would not do so. The British government was filled with desperation and anger after what it felt had been America's promise. The British especially resented the rumors that the American Ambassador in Cairo, Jefferson Caffery, was making capital there with Nasser with the fact that America had not joined the Pact. Dulles responded to Eden's complaints and pleas with the singular suggestion that better than join and then, perhaps, have to withdraw, it was better not to join at all! [11]

Dulles had been intimidated by the ferocious uproar in the Middle East against Iraq, for he was afraid that if he offended Nasserite Arabism, he might lose the potential assistance of Egypt and Saudi Arabia against the Soviet Union. Perhaps Ben Gurion, too, would be further annoyed if Iraq's strength were enhanced by American membership. Israel had reason to fear an increase in the power of any Arab country. And Iran must not seem to be too intrusively supported by America, or Russia might make some forcible retort.

At the end of April, 1956, the Secretary of State told some Washington correspondents in a private "background" session that the British had "perverted" *his* idea of a pact which would include only nations facing north, when they brought in Iraq, and in doing so had aroused the hostility of the other Arab nations. The people present declare that they had never until that moment heard such a view of the Pact from Dulles, who spoke so often, and always, as his close associates put it, "exhaustively," or from anyone else. The alleged "perversion" was declared by Dulles to be one among several mistakes made by the British in the Middle East, and he added ominously, "I say that charitably!" It is true that the British obtained some advantage by entering the Pact: they would be losing their air bases in Iraq in spring, 1955, as the treaty of 1930 with Iraq would expire then. The Pact would give them bases and radar sites for the east flank of NATO. Nasser was in no hurry for a Pact, but Eden was. He had visited Nasser in Cairo in February, 1955, and no love was lost between the two men.

Many critics hold that Dulles's manipulations in the Middle East were the cause, now, of Russia's increased interest in the region. Mysteriously she had been almost an absentee since the end of World War II, except for Stalin's effort, thwarted by the West in 1946, to settle down in Iran. But Stalin died in March, 1953, and a new course was evidently being set. On April 16, 1955, just after Turkey and Iran joined the Pact, Moscow issued a very grim warning to the U.S.A. Moscow insisted that military blocs against the Soviet Union were unnecessary; that Russia had a special interest in the Middle East; that the region was close to Russia but thousands of miles away from America.[12] But Dulles remained unperturbed. It was his intense conviction that the way to make Russia's rulers recede was by continuous forceful pressures.

It may be added that Dulles took a 10 per cent interest in the Pact: he sent an observer to the Pact meetings of November, 1955, and April, 1956, and became a member of the Economic and Counter-Subversion Committees of the Pact, and he set up a military liaison office in Baghdad.

This experience of diplomatic joint ventures on the part of Dulles and Eden, involving Britain's evacuation of the Suez Canal Base and America's refusal to enter the Baghdad Pact, increased Eden's already existing distrust of Dulles and added to Dulles's already existing aversion for Eden. It was not a beneficial prologue to the business of the Aswan Dam Dulles was about to transact.

3. A LOAN REFUSED: THE CANAL SEIZED

AMERICAN FOREIGN POLICY IS COMPOUNDED OF THE GENERAL PRINCIPLES established by the President and the Secretary of State, and, for each specific application to area and case, of the knowledge provided by the experts. In considering each problem or circumstance affecting the foreign affairs of the nation, the Secretary must, of course, ponder the raw facts that come in from embassies, from secret intelligence sources (such as the CIA), and from the commercial press agencies. Before action is decided on and taken, he must also take into account whatever facts are pertinent—he must determine, for example, whether the nation's economy will readily stand the drain on it required by an otherwise desirable policy. He must weigh the effect the policy is likely to have on the Western alliances, on neutrals, on the Soviet Union. No country or region can nowadays possibly be treated by a foreign policy based on life within its own frontiers alone. Yet the local facts are essential to the local decision. If the Secretary has these wrong, his decision can be right only by accident.

John Foster Dulles's information about the Middle East was channeled to him by his Assistant Secretary for Near Eastern Affairs. (Middle Eastern affairs, in 1956, were the province of the Near Eastern, South Asian and African Division of the State Department.) This Assistant Secretary was at the head of several score of career officials in Washington, D.C., and was in correspondence with the Ambassadors stationed abroad. Every day at about eight-thirty A.M., he attended a meeting lasting an hour or so in Dulles's office, along with other Assistant Secretaries and with Intelligence. On Tuesdays and Thursdays this group was joined by the person responsible for Congressional relations and by three or four others especially called in to participate. All the top-priority wires were reproduced in a report given to every participant in these confidential meetings. Other information discussed there would have reached the Secretary from the CIA—the director of which happened to be his brother, Allen W. Dulles—sometimes communicated directly to him at their residences.

In other words, the brains surveying the whole world were at hand and busy thinking and talking. Dulles, himself adept in the efficient dispatch of business as the result of his law career, and driven by immense, indeed prodigious, mental and physical energy and determination to do his best in the most virile way to justify American leadership in the politics of the world, had instituted a (fairly) regular program for energizing his staff—sometimes beyond their liking.

He first reviewed the general news of the day, with which he had been familiarizing himself since his usual hour of rising, six-thirty: by the time he arrived at his office he had, as already mentioned, mastered two New York newspapers and the most important one in Washington. Since, however, not all members of the staff were as Calvinistically zealous as Dulles, the considerate and prudent Assistant Secretary for Public Affairs, a former newspaperman, had two of his staff (unknown to the Secretary) prepare for the late risers a very brief digest of each day's newspapers. Thus, when Dulles cross-examined his subordinates, they were not flunked, while he continued to delight in their constant dutifulness.

After the news was disposed of, a digest of foreign intelligence, cables, and similar information was read aloud, and a discussion ensued in which Dulles invited all present to speak up. The evidence, though it varies a good deal from informant to informant, is that conversation with Dulles was fairly free. In fact, in the case of Robert Bowie, then chairman of the Policy Planning Committee, the "speaking up" is reported to have been tenacious and gadflyish—at least in the early months of Dulles's tenure. But as time went on the participants apparently became rather intimidated by the Secretary's claims to conclusive knowledge and experience. He was able to remember some instance far back, ten or twenty or thirty years, or some book, or some earlier conviction of his, to cite in support of a present opinion. As time went on, the staff conversations and exchanges of view lost their biting edge. Yet one can never know for certain how much was lost or gained: no technique available to political scientists or sociologists or psychologists, now or in the foreseeable future, can help to determine this.

One further circumstance is pertinent in considering Dulles's relation to his State Department staff and other sources of information and advice: he was very often away from Washington. Dulles was a most vigorous advocate and practitioner of "diplomacy at the summit," personal diplomacy, the hob-nobbing of Secretaries of State and Chiefs of State. Indeed, as we shall see presently, for this reason he was away at certain crucial times in the Suez affair when contact with his staff was truly vital to a rational comprehension and interpretation of all the facts.

The business of an ambassador is to be, as one of that craft once said, an "in-between" man: to make clear his country's interests to the nation to which he is accredited, and to send back to his government as perfect as possible a representation of the other nation's interests, needs, intentions, and power to benefit or injure his own. Some ambassadors do not become involved enough in the life of their host country to serve the needs of their own government. Other envoys immerse themselves profoundly in making acquaintance with their host and achieve a high degree of identification. There is little doubt that occasionally such identification becomes so close as to cause an ambassador to pass beyond the role of a knowledgeable observer and to adopt the general outlook of his host. His country suffers a loss of knowledge as a consequence, because his ability to make evaluations by the standard of his own nation's interests has diminished. This situation —labeled "localitis" in the State Department—arises especially with a culture that is rather mysterious, and therefore fascinating, to the foreign envoy, and it is furthered by the readiness of the host to be (or seem to be) hospitable, intimate, and informative. This appears to have been the fate of one of the two American Ambassadors to Egypt in the period preceding the Suez affair, less so of the other.

In any such case, of course, the Secretary of State is very much involved. In the end the decision is his, and in the beginning too it is his, as the initiator and director of policy. He also has had a hand in the selection of men to fill State Department and ambassadorial posts. During the events under consideration, Dulles's Assistant Secretaries for the Near East were, successively, Henry A. Byroade, George V. Allen, and William M. Rountree. I have had the privilege of talking with each of these men, and with others who knew them during this time. Rountree was not in a position to influence decisions prior to July, 1956. Before that date, which begins the period crucial to this study, his views are excluded. The Ambassadors in Cairo with whom we will be concerned were Jefferson Caffery, until January, 1955, and then Byroade, who arrived in Cairo on February 27, 1955.

Caffery has been described as an Irish-American among several who caused trouble for the British.[1] Actually he descended from Orangemen! He served the interests of the United States as commanded by the State Department. His mission required that he accommodate the harshly inimical interests of British and Arabs in Egypt. This above all demanded the exit of the British from the Suez Canal Base.

Caffery had entered the diplomatic service in 1911, and in the years until 1949, when he was assigned to Egypt, most of his career had been spent in Latin American countries, except for the previous five years as Ambassador to Paris, and spells of duty in the State Department. Resident in Cairo, Caffery was deeply affected by Arab nationalist emotions. He was also distressed by the corruption and inefficiency of King Farouk's regime. Later, in July, 1952, he helped Farouk escape with his life when the Palace appealed to the American Embassy for protection against possible murder by the Naguib-Nasser officers' revolution. He befriended Naguib, the leader of that revolution, so far as the public were aware, and when Nasser ruthlessly and cunningly usurped the leadership of Naguib, Caffery developed a warm relationship with Nasser.

Caffery told the State Department that the Egyptian revolutionists' general purposes must be assisted. The British must be induced to leave the Suez Canal Base, a proposal which had already been in negotiation since 1952, initiated in Secretary Dean Acheson's time, even, if necessary, without compensatory conditions, since no Egyptian leader could politically afford to make any concessions to the "imperialists." He sought American economic aid to help the social ideals of the Free Officers to raise the conditions of the Egyptian masses—mainly peasants plus some members of the industrial and commercial proletariat—from their thousand-year long illiteracy, hunger, poverty, dirt, disease, and general wretchedness. When Nasser appealed to the Western powers for arms, Caffery was of divided mind [2] whether the United States should supply him except on the usual conditions, which under the Mutual Defense Act of 1949 meant that the arms must not be used for "offensive" or "aggressive" purposes and that a U.S. military mission must be accepted by Cairo. On the whole, he thought it rather dangerous without these limitations. Subject to the conditions, his reasoning seems to have been that some arms might be supplied to Nasser, for otherwise he would get them from other supplying nations, that Nasser was piqued by American bias towards Israel, and that some appeasement of Nasser might ultimately lead towards a settlement of the Arab-Israeli dispute which would otherwise continue to keep the Middle East in dangerous turmoil.

Concerning economic aid, Caffery particularly favored United States participation in the long-contemplated construction of the High Dam at Aswan. This would substantially increase the area irrigated by the Nile waters, and so raise the Egyptian standard of living. Although the people of the Middle Eastern nations, as Moslems, were infused with the ethics of the Koran, this would not stop them from going Communist if they remained in economic misery and despair and without some appeasement of their anti-imperialist and pro-Arab frenzy. Something had to give—it should be the U.S.A. and Britain. When Caffery talked of Communism, he did not necessarily mean that the Egyptian government would be composed of men of the Communist Party or that Soviet stooges would take over, but that the masses and the colonels and the biggest colonel of them all, the *Bikbashi*, the Boss, Nasser, might follow policies pleasing to the Soviet Union. Something had to give!

The State Department must do business with Nasser, then, because he had become the hero of the glorious streets and it was hardly possible to conceive of anyone who could take his place among the mobs. (The present author must ask, Why should it be anyone?) Furthermore, Caffery had held many long conversations with Nasser, and Nasser, he reported, had never turned him down on anything "I asked him to do of importance." [3] He meant such things as the British right of re-entry to the Base.

The State Department Near Eastern experts thus formed the impression that, though Nasser was rather a violent fellow and quite a ruffian and a rogue, still there was something of Mustafa Kemal about him, as when the latter had led in the modernization of Turkey, a patriot bent on getting his people a New Deal, raising their standard of living, and vanquishing their illiteracy. In the light of America's own way of life, was this not good? And was not also Nasser's independence, his hostility to colonialism, meritorious?

Hence, in part, the support of that policy of "impartiality" by Dulles and his Near Eastern adviser, Byroade, to which we have already referred, a policy that jeopardized the fate of Israel because it under-estimated the intensity of Arab hatred of that nation.

In private conversations with newspapermen he especially trusted, Dulles had revealed his tactics regarding Israel. He averred that the real hope for Israel and America's relationship with her was in the United Nations. (This implied, not quite in the State Department or with full American responsibility and initiative.) He thought Israel had been created by the U.N.; the truce under which it lived and the agency supervising this had been established by the world organization. If Israel (and her Arab neighbors) were entrusted to the U.N., then the Soviet Union would have a say in that forum, and only there, and would not be allowed any concession by the United States of a special position in the Near East. Dulles conceded he might have to fall back on the Tripartite Pact, with its provision for action by the United States, France, and Britain in the Middle East, outside the U.N. if necessary, but he hoped not: everyone could have a say in the U.N. He did not believe (April, 1956) that the Soviet Union would back the Arabs and Nasser all the way, in spite of the recent arms deal.

The State Department, its Near East Office, Dulles, President Eisenhower, and Henry Cabot Lodge in the United Nations virtually turned a blind eye on the Arab use of force when it occurred merely against the Israelis and in the night, retail, rather than in the daytime and all at once, when it surely would have been "war" or "aggression." Of course, they publicly deplored the killing and the sabotage, but after all they had not created the state of Israel, had they? According to their ambassadors there was something to be said for the Arab states, was there not? Losing a few people every couple of days was far better for Israel than losing its national home altogether, was it not? Virtually ignoring Israel's continual pleas for peace and a final treaty with the Arabs, Byroade laid Arab violence to fears of Israeli expansion, the proffered evidence for which was that Israel called for Jewish immigrants.

When Byroade came to Cairo as Caffery's successor in February, 1955, he was treated most entertainingly. He was thirty-seven and Nasser was thirty-seven. On a "colonel-to-colonel" basis, it was thought that Byroade, affable, vivacious, expressive, highly intelligent, with experience in military government in Germany, might help solve the Egyptian problem. He believed that if only he could really understand Nasser's problems he could win him over to the West. For hours and hours and frequently he conversed with Nasser at the latter's house. But the doses of truth given Byroade, after about May, 1955, steadily diminished and the small talk increased. Byroade gathered the baseless belief that after the Anglo-Egyptian Agreement, "the position of the British in Egypt came back surprisingly fast." [4] Byroade did learn about the sensitiveness and totally ruthless nature of Egyptian nationalism. He did learn the implacable hatred of Israel —implacable, he should have reported, by any concession at all short of extinction. He did learn about the economic wretchedness of the masses and the aspirations of the high school and college graduates for jobs, business, professional, and administrative opportunity, and the army's appetite for total political authority. Like Caffery, he conveyed to the State Department his belief that Americans must bow to Arab nationalism.

But what of Nasser himself—the momentary embodiment of that nationalism? No one was ever so deceived by Arab charm as were Caffery and Byroade, and also some Congressmen and Senators who paid Nasser casual and brief visits. These men failed to probe him sufficiently, to ransack his career for its portents and its black and bloody stains. They did send in mountains of information, microscopic, intimate, about this flamboyant patriot in his well-cut Western suits. But the most significant revelations were made by Nasser himself in his *Philosophy of the Revolution*, first appearing in April and May of 1954, in a Cairo newspaper, and translated daily by the major foreign embassies.

What were the substantial features of these expressions of Nasser's state of mind and character? To put it with the most desperate brevity, Nasser made these claims: (1) Eventually he would unite under one rule all Arab countries; and he would do this as soon as possible, joining them from the Persian Gulf to Gibraltar, whatever the native opposition in each Arab nation. (2) He would extend his influence through Africa wherever Islam had spread its religion and culture, certainly in the Sudan, and call for people in Africa to rise in violence against the colonial regimes rather than come to peaceful terms with them. (3) He would use the oil resources of the Arab nations to bring Western industries to a dead stop.

More important than all these concrete aims was the spirit—the "style," as the academic jargon now runs—in which they should be accomplished. What Caffery and Byroade and Dulles and Eisenhower did not seem to take seriously was that Nasser had been an assassin even though his attempt at murder had failed,[5] and would be an assassin, whatever the number of victims, Arab or non-Arab, whenever he believed the national interest of Egypt required it. He had begun his political life as a believer in assassination; he had, at the age of thirty-four, cooperated in an attempt at assassinating an important Egyptian political leader. He wrote later that the episode hurt his feelings, and that, in any case, assassination was inexpedient. And thenceforward he prescribed assassination day in and day out for all Arab leaders who opposed his ambitions.[6] This kind of knowledge would have been the finest quality of "localitis."

It was the *malice prepense* with a murderous conclusion, whenever it should be considered necessary in Nasser's sole judgment, that the State Department should have recognized and challenged. Dulles, in his speech of June, 1953, had advocated a self-determination for the Middle Eastern nations that was *orderly*. Such a policy, surely, could not condone giving a potential assassin the freedom to do harm whenever it should please his whim? Dulles must have known of the incitements to the people of Jordan to kill King Hussein that emanated from Nasser's policy and propaganda apparatus, and even of Nasser's false assertions that he knew nothing about assassination plots. Only six months before the day of the Aswan Dam loan appointment, Jordan's royal regime was almost destroyed by Nasser's agents!

Having been granted $40 million in aid after the signing of the Anglo-Egyptian Agreement in 1954, Nasser asked Byroade (then Assistant Secretary) for American arms. Dulles insisted that the arms must be bought with dollar payments, that they should not be used for aggression, and that an office of U.S. military aid should be opened in Cairo to supervise the use of the arms. Nasser rejected the aid. No strings for a hero who was, as he declared, moving in on the six Arab nations who needed one! Byroade had recommended that arms be given Nasser with few strings.[7] Having failed to obtain arms from the United States, Nasser still felt the need of arms from somewhere—anywhere. His permanent ascendency in Egypt was as yet far from entirely assured. An especially sharp reprisal by Israel, a counterattack, in February, 1955, against Gaza, the center of Nasser's commando organization whence *fedayeen* had infiltrated Israel as far as Tel Aviv, caused the death of sixty Arabs.[8] This Israeli raid again exposed Egyptian national military weakness.

At the Bandung Conference in April, 1955, Nasser, for the first time in his life, was to mingle with the "big shots" of the world, in this case Nehru, Chou En Lai, Sukarno, and U Nu. He came away more than ever convinced of the personal and public value of "positive neutralism," the doctrine developed by Nehru and Krishna Menon of which he had been an exponent for some time. To India, still a member of the British Commonwealth, this policy meant nonalignment with either Russia or America, Communism or democracy. Nasser, however, applied it in another form that resembled but corrupted it. He played off the fears and envies of one great power against the other to secure the maximum advantage from each with the minimum commitment to either: the "double-cross," the not-so-secret weapon of the weak.

Beginning in February, 1955, about the date when Byroade was sent to Cairo, Daniel Semenovich Solod, the Russian Ambassador to Egypt, had begun steadfastly and subtly to court Nasser. In the first place, both he and his host detested the Baghdad Pact. Previously, the Egyptian Communist Party had been vociferous against the "bourgeois" Nasser, and the Soviet press had fulminated against him as a reactionary. Now the Communist wolf pack was called off. A month or so later, the Ambassador and Nasser began talks on supplying Soviet technicians to Egypt, encouraging trade between the two countries, and the possibility of Nasser's recognition of Red China.

In May, 1955, Solod made Nasser a point-blank offer of arms. (Chou En Lai, at Bandung, had indicated to Nasser this source of weapons.) In June, Dulles and Eisenhower met Bulganin and Khrushchev at Geneva in the first of the futile summit meetings. By this time Dulles certainly surmised what was afoot between Russia and Nasser, but he made no forceful protest about it as Moscow had when offended by rumors of a Middle East Command. Indeed, Dulles ignored the rumors. In July, Dimitri Shepilov, then editor of *Pravda* (and later to be Russia's Foreign Secretary for a brief period), visited Cairo and it was then, most probably, that the arms deal was clinched.

Gradually the news leaked out, and on September 27, 1955, Nasser publicly confirmed it. He had arms from Russia (*pro forma*, Czechoslovakia) to be paid for by barter, without any conditions or negotiations for their use. Nasser explained that he had first sought arms from the U.S.A., Britain, and France. These, by the terms of the Tripartite Pact of 1950, had set down conditions, or, as he expressed it, "demands," which would have cost Egypt "our freedom." He blandly observed that his deal with Russia was merely a "commercial transaction." Some of these armaments were deployed in phases on the frontiers of Israel.

The actual arms deal hit Dulles and other State Department officials with the force of a thunderbolt, in spite of the previous rumors. It was humiliating to be outsmarted. It was a blow that kindly and considerate action toward Egypt had met with ingratitude and contempt and derision. In one single stroke, in one adept thrust, the Soviet Union had vaulted over the Baghdad Pact, over the Northern Tier of countries, and after centuries of unsuccessful effort had jumped, brazen and powerful, plumb into the Middle East! Dulles confided to a member of an American Jewish delegation which met him shortly afterward that the Egyptian arms deal was "the most serious development since Korea, if not since World War II." It had, among other effects, nullified Dulles's attempts to discover a foundation for peace in the Middle East. Although his impulse, as he said to some of his State Department entourage, was "to do something about" the arms deal, all he did immediately was to send George V. Allen to Cairo to lodge a protest and seek an explanation. That mission will be described presently.

Arms and technicians from the Iron Curtain countries flowed into Cairo. Arabs everywhere gave Nasser frantic hero worship. His ability to "double-cross" was gloatingly admired. His prestige sent tremors of hope and fear through every Arab nation. His head became swollen at Bandung; the arms deal meant he had won the Soviet Union as an ally for almost anything he planned to do with the weapons they had sold him. He became, in the famous phrase used by Stalin, "dizzy with success," and acquired the idea that every such stroke of cunning and ruthlessness would bring additional and cumulative success. No one could teach the dictator a lesson in moderation within his own country, for he had silenced all critics; and no one outside, least of all Dulles, had tried to teach him a lesson by the use of a power from outside. He was, however, still on trial as Egypt's leader, and hypersensitive to whatsoever might threaten his status or prestige.

We must examine the fairly immediate consequences of this arms deal. It has highest relevance to Dulles's policy on the loan for the Aswan Dam and all the fearful consequences that followed. Let it be reiterated that the deal implied Soviet diplomatic help in any of Nasser's enterprises. Some of these might well be adverse to the national interests of the countries allied in NATO, America's principal defense creation since World War II and a bastion of Western containment of the Soviet Union. Another likely possibility was an all-out attempt to destroy Israel. The Israelis did react in Moscow with a most vigorous diplomatic protest, but, of course, to no avail. The Israeli government also pleaded with the Secretary of State of the United States for a supply of arms to match those that Egypt now had. The plea was rejected, as on several previous occasions, with the habitual cliché that it was not the policy of the United States government to contribute to an arms race.

The wisdom of this decision is questionable. Under the circumstances, the phrase "arms race" was false, self-defeating, and sanctimonious. An arms race is not in the power of the innocent nation to stop; the race is already on when the aggressive party has been supplied or supplies itself. The race is evened and ceases to be a race when the supplies are counterbalanced. Moreover, given a true appreciation of Nasser's inordinate objectives and the ruthlessness of his greed, what could more effectively have called him to order than the knowledge that, however vast the supply of arms he acquired, Israel would always have access to a more than matching supply? Heartbreak is not seldom an antidote to the swelling of the head, and Nasser certainly needed it. It might be answered that such a course would inflame Arab feeling against America. Surely nothing could inflame it more than Nasser's propaganda, regularly issuing from the Voice of Cairo.

Politics had committed to Dulles the power to stop or slow down Nasser. He did not use it. He had, three years earlier, committed himself to the general strategy of "massive retaliation," by nuclear power if necessary, against the Soviet Union.[9] But now the issue was the application of a small dose of power, but a dose of power nevertheless, to a small man who intended to make himself a bigger and bigger pest, even to deploying the threat, sometimes open, always implied, that he would be the catalyst of a third world war between the U.S.A. and the U.S.S.R. Dulles had insufficient conventional forces to embark on a series of "brush-fire" wars, and at any rate no military-political doctrine about their use in such contingencies.[10] The Secretary stuck to the formula of the Tripartite Pact of 1950: Israel would be allowed to buy arms wherever she could, but she would *not* get financial aid for this specific purpose from the United States. He thus appears to have ignored a very crucial fact. Egypt's purchase of arms from the Czechs and Russians in quantities limited only by the payments Nasser was prepared dictatorially to confiscate from the Egyptian peasants' subsistence (barely above survival level) had smashed the Arab-Israeli balance of arms predicated in that Pact.

It is true, however, that America had supplied Israel with substantial financial aid from 1949 onward.[11] The amount to the end of 1955 was $240 million in grants, plus $143 million in credits. This aid continued, enabling Israel to divert some funds from its ordinary budget to buy arms. Arab nations were also being assisted by the United

States, but on a much smaller scale. Egypt, Jordan, Lebanon, and Syria had together received over a longer period $100 million (Egypt $59 million in 1951). Some Saudi Arabian amounts are classified. One must also add into the Arab account the fact that American oil enterprise in the Arab countries brought them in total close to a billion dollars a year, and that Israel was an exceedingly poor country. The Arabs were well aware of the trick of diverting the budget for military purposes: Dulles earned no good will from them by employing this indirect method of helping Israel secure weapons. An out-and-out arms assistance would have been a bold act, tending to curb, if to enrage, Nasser.

But Dulles stuck to his policy, which did not permit action against the growing belligerence of Egypt. He reiterated the policy, as late as February 6, 1956, in a letter to forty Congressmen.[12] The security of Israel could be assured better by means other than an arms race. The U.N. was "capable of providing many forms of protection." The Tripartite Pact could help. Yet the ineffectiveness of the world organization was plain in its history; and he himself had refused to concert measures with Britain and France to meet dangerous situations by means of the Pact. Once again he told the Congressmen of his overriding obsession: "the larger context of the free world's unceasing struggle against international Communism." It was an obsession, and it was a diversion.

Later on, trying to explain this period, Dulles displayed the same state of mind. This is what he said to the United States Senate Foreign Relations Committee when, in January, 1957, he went before it to ask for $200 million and the authority to use it in military aid to stop "international Communist" subversive activities or open attacks on Middle Eastern states.[13] "We all know it was the Soviet arms to Egypt which began, at least, a series of events which have led to serious trouble in the area, and the whole conduct of the Soviet Union throughout the last couple of years in particular—of course the story goes way back beyond that—has been to stir up trouble to put one country against another. . . ." But the man who sought the arms and bought them was Nasser. He should have been the Secretary's target.

The other practical policy open to arrest a dangerous deteriorating situation was for the United States to propose a defense pact with Middle Eastern countries. Many people suggested this, and it is even said that the Secretary pondered it. It would have amounted to a more elaborate variant of arms aid to Israel. The main features of such a plan would have been expressed something like this: the United States offers a treaty of friendship and defense of existing territory and political independence to all nations of the Middle East. Bona fide, it will accept even any one of them which cares to join.

Almost certainly the only one that would have joined would have been Israel. This situation could not possibly have alienated the Arab countries any more than they were alienated already, though it would have aggravated the vociferation of the Egyptian press and the leaders of the mobs. Such a pact would have had certain dangers for Israel. But, once again, such a pact would have been an American *fait accompli*, a local and immediate presence extolling the *status quo* and demanding from Israel also the repudiation of any intention (which the overwhelming majority of its citizens never had) of territorial expansion. Dulles was afraid to take this step, however, because he underestimated Nasser's ruthlessness, calling for strong counteraction, and was intimidated by what Moscow *might* do.

So far we have recited what Dulles decided not to do. Now we must consider what he did do. He sent his Assistant Secretary for Near Eastern Affairs, George V. Allen, to protest to Nasser. The details of the mission must have been known to Dulles more vividly than they are at present in any published form: but even the written accounts are full of information that should have taught him a thing or two about Nasser's unscrupulousness and helped produce the proper counteraction. (One of the most significant factors in political behavior is the intensity of emotion and passion involved, apart from the intellectual apprehension of the circumstances, but it is one of the least studied and observed in the course of policy-making.)

The day before making the public announcement of the arms deal, on September 24, 1955, Nasser phoned Byroade, the friend of the long, long nocturnal conversations, and disclosed his deed. Byroade had already been tipped off by the British that the deal was rumored to be in the offing. Later the British Ambassador, very upset, made an urgent call on Nasser. To him also, Nasser confirmed the dreadful news.

Soon after Allen's arrival in Cairo, he was granted an audience with Nasser. He was accompanied by Ambassador Byroade, and Nasser saw fit to keep both of them waiting for an hour and a half before admitting Allen to his presence, although the Americans had arrived rather ahead of the appointed time. It is worth adding, since foreign policy so often is a question of contending tempers and temperaments, that in 1959, the Egyptian secretary in the office when the Americans announced their presence explained, "We kept Mr. Allen waiting because we heard he was bringing from Washington an indignant letter and that he intended to bang the table and give us a lecture. We kept him waiting to cool him off. We kept him waiting until he agreed not to present the note he had been sent to deliver." [14]

Allen expounded the American case to Nasser. He said that the American government did not in any way deny Egypt's sovereign right to acquire arms wherever it wished and could. But, he observed, the U.S.A. is also a sovereign nation, and, faced with Nasser's action, it had to make up its mind what to do about it. Therefore, he asked Nasser to make clear to him what course his relationship with Czechoslovakia was to take. Allen then would be able to inform Nasser of America's reaction to it. Nasser responded that he did not *know* what he would do in the future. It depended on the course of international events and on America's behavior whether the arms deal he had already consummated would be a one-shot affair or whether he would continue to do business for more armaments with Czechoslovakia.

Allen patiently explained that the United States was opposed to an arms race in the Middle East. He pointed out that Israel had asked the U.S.A. for a supply of P-80 and P-81 planes and that if such a request had been granted, it would be likely to lead to further Egyptian armament and this to further Israeli appeals, ad infinitum. He pressed the point on Nasser that America was trying to help him with economic aid and that it would be most unpleasant for the donor to see the recipient nation spend the funds on armaments and military enterprises. Allen also expressed the government's unhappiness about Nasser's purchase of MIG's from Russia. Paraphrased, his discourse concluded, "If you intend to continue to acquire armaments, let us have an understanding that you intend to, but my government cannot be happy if you say that this is the road you are going to take."

This surely most reasonable message, put in a reasonable tone, with no "banging of the table," was met by Nasser with a spontaneous or assumed outburst of rage. He became fidgety and agitated and rolled his eyes, much as Mussolini used to do in the heyday of his Fascist dictatorship. Nasser launched into a hysterical tirade against Israel. "We are accustomed to imperialism," he shouted. "We have had five hundred years from the Turks and eighty of it from the British! But—under them, at least, we had our own Arab schools and local administration. And now that we can call our nation free from that imperialism, you Americans are the *worst* of all imperialists. Why? You want to know why? I'll tell you! Because it was you, America, who established the state of Israel. That, my dear Mr. Allen, means that in Arab lands you introduced not merely a foreign administration but a completely *foreign people*! You also saddled us with Arab refugees! This American imperialism is the worst kind we Arabs have ever experienced!"

In other words, Nasser was totally intransigent. His state of mind was duly reported, of course, to Dulles. Dulles's reaction is described by Sherman Adams in his book, *First Hand Report*.[15] Adams reports that on September 30, 1955, at the first business-as-usual Cabinet meeting after President Eisenhower's heart attack, six days before, "Dulles gave a scheduled report on current world affairs." The Secretary told his colleagues that for the first time the Russians were making a determined effort to move into the Middle East, where two-thirds of the world's known oil reserves were located. He explained that Russia could cause trouble there by sending massive shipments of their obsolete weapons to the Arabs, "who were suspicious and uneasy about United States policy because of our friendship with Israel." Now, this speech was *not* the whole truth, by any means, as we have seen, about American-Egyptian relations. It was not even the most significant part of the political truth about Nasser.

Adams further says that on November 9, 1955, Dulles sent his Under Secretary, Herbert Hoover, Jr., to the President at Denver, with a statement for the President to make: "Americans will not contribute to an arms race." On December 13, Dulles talked with Congressional leaders of both parties. He said (and again the explanation was incomplete) that in 1950, when Israel and Egypt had made their armistice, they had seen no need to build arms strength. He continued: "But now, since the Russians have intervened, they say they want to bargain from positions of strength. They learned that expression from us." "Us" meant Dulles; the phrase was probably borrowed from Winston Churchill, who may have invented it.

Robert J. Donovan also has reported on the Cabinet meeting of September 30. His words square with Sherman Adams'. He adds, "Without giving any details he [Dulles] assured the Cabinet that the United States was not without plans for dealing with the situation." [16] None, however, were in evidence.

On November 9, the British Prime Minister, Sir Anthony Eden, profoundly alarmed by the Soviet move, proposed peace between Israel and her Arab neighbors based on an accommodation of frontiers. His purpose was to restore confidence and security in the Middle East. The United States supported this initiative. But the suggested frontier adjustment would have been a drastic request to make of Israel, who would have had to give up more territory, and to do so even *after* the arms from Russia were already flowing to Nasser.

Partly because of the hurricane clouds in the Middle East, Eden decided that talks with President Eisenhower and Dulles in Washington had become more urgently necessary than ever. As an immediate measure, Eden approved of the sale of fighter planes by Canada and France to Israel (to challenge the fast bombers that Russia was selling to Egypt), and England and France delivered Meteors and Mystères respectively. Dulles assented to these deliveries; he did *not* assist them. He would not risk Arab disapproval.

The meeting in Washington occurred in early February, 1956. Eden strongly urged that preparatory plans of action visible to all nations should be undertaken to make the Tripartite Pact of 1950 effective—that is, to prevent violation of the Arab-Israeli frontiers.

Dulles and the President refused to cooperate in such a measure. The excuses that Dulles put forward were that no commitments to use force could be given without Congressional approval. (Any American President, when he deems the occasion proper in terms of American interests, can, as Commander in Chief, dispose American military forces accordingly. The American Sixth Fleet was, even then, deployed in the Mediterranean!) Where there is no will in American diplomacy, Congress can always be dragged in as an alibi.

Eden begged Dulles for help to quench the mischievous incitements to rebellion conducted all over the Arab countries, for example, in Iraq and Lebanon, by agents paid by Saudi Arabia and instigated and briefed by Nasser. The Saudi funds for subversion and violence were drawn from the million dollars a day received by King Saud from Aramco, the Arabian-American oil company; he was especially interested in undermining the Baghdad Pact. The English had, moreover, a particular quarrel with Saudi Arabia because the royal despotism, even though it was already dropsical with oil revenues, laid claim also to the oil-rich sheikdoms on the coast which had long been under treaty arrangements with the British.[17] Dulles refused to join the British in any sedative action. For, of course, American oil interests were very important, and so was the air base at Dhahran, leased from King Saud. Furthermore, King Saud might become a political counterweight to Nasser in the Arab world; the fact that the holy places, Mecca and Medina, were in his keeping was one force likely to attract Moslem peoples to his side.

No great chasm seemed to divide Dulles and Eden on the question of Egypt—not openly. But if Eden had eavesdropped on some of Dulles's private briefings of some Washington correspondents, he might have heard Dulles resolutely assert that he had withheld aid to Egypt only to avoid embarrassing Britain, but against his better judgment. (This in mid-June, 1954.) At any rate, now the damage had already been done, and Nasser had Russian weapons and Russian diplomatic support. Dulles seemed to be pleased with the conference with the British, for Sherman Adams reports that at a Cabinet meeting about that time, "the trouble in the Middle East seemed to have brought Eden closer to us because it made the Prime Minister more willing to stand up against the Russians. A few months earlier Dulles said Eden had been acting like an impartial mediator in disputes between the United States and the Soviets." This incident at the Cabinet, the language and the thoughts, strikingly reveals Dulles's state of mind. He suffered from a dazzling and blinding obsession to bring every problem into the lens, into the exclusive burning glass, of that steadfast glowing hatred—justified as some may believe it to have been—of the Soviet Union, whether it fitted the circumstances or not. And hatred is, in some respects, an extinguisher of the light.

It is true that Eden, following his own instincts and the wisdom of Winston Churchill, was ready to talk with the Russians. After all, the Russian frontier (since 1945, at the River Elbe) is very much closer to Plymouth, England, than to Plymouth, Massachusetts. But Eden talked far more sternly to Bulganin and Khrushchev than Dulles ever did to Molotov. When the Russian pair (allowing us to anticipate chronology) visited England at Eden's invitation in July, 1956, Eden minced no words about British interest. As he later recounted, he told the Russians: "The uninterrupted supply of oil was literally vital to our economy. . . . I said I must be absolutely blunt about the oil, because we would fight for it. . . . Khrushchev answered that the area was close to Soviet frontiers. If my statement was intended as a threat they [the Russians] must reject it. I repeated that what I had said was that we could not live without oil and that we had no intention of being strangled to death."[18] Eden must have voiced similar concern over oil supplies in his Washington talks of February, 1956, though Dulles's subsequent actions reflect little awareness of the intensity of British anxieties about their fuel supply.

At the conclusion of the British-American meeting, Eden appeared generally satisfied by the discussion with Dulles and Eisenhower on the Middle East. In his words:

> We agreed that the future of our policy in the Middle East depended to a considerable extent on Nasser. If he showed himself willing to cooperate with us, we should reciprocate. The Americans thought that the present talks about the Aswan Dam with Mr. Black might indicate his state of mind. If his attitude on this and other matters was that he would not cooperate, we would both have to reconsider our policy towards him.

Sherman Adams, however, perhaps representing the view of Dulles and Eisenhower, but perhaps representing the bias of wider circles of the Administration and the American people, observed that a crucial difference still existed between the two countries after the Washington meeting:

> But Eden's visit to Washington did not resolve one serious difference between the American and British positions on the Middle East question; our firm opposition to colonialism made us sympathetic to the struggles which Egypt and the other Arab states were making to free themselves of the political and economic control that the British felt they had to maintain in the Middle East in their own self-interest.

The truth is that, behind the scenes, Dulles was more often emphasizing American differences of interest from the British than any common interest and fate. On the other hand, the arms deal was making it awkward for him to continue to treat Nasser with loving kindness, as, in a sense, enjoined by one of his favorite Biblical passages, perhaps the one closest to his heart. It is from Hebrews, 11:1 and it says, "Now faith is the substance of things hoped for, the evidence of things not seen."

Meanwhile, a vast project of economic assistance to Egypt had been before the State Department for some years.[19] This proposed undertaking was the building of the largest dam in the world at Aswan, on the Nile, to replace an existent smaller one. To be called the High Dam, the new structure would be 250 feet high at the center, and three miles wide. The lake formed by the Dam would be some three hundred miles long and run into the Sudan. The project would add one-third to Egypt's irrigated land and multiply her electric power resources eight times. Provided that the birth rate in Egypt could be appropriately reduced, the Dam would greatly benefit the undernourished, diseased, and wretched peasantry and begin to provide industry for those who had moved or would move to the urban centers. The additional agricultural production would assist industrial development and the power would spur on industrialization.

Engineers of the British "colonial power" had first broached such a project in the 1880's, and between 1889 and 1902 they had, with the use of Western money, science, and technology, constructed the first Aswan Dam. Its contemporary engineering triumphs and its continuing benefits were obvious even to the prejudiced "anticolonial" eye. It stimulated Egyptian hopes that the country could progress still further if the Nile waters, the one sustainer of life in that arid and sandy tract, could be conserved by a far bigger and higher reservoir to give not merely annual but perennial water conservation and electric power. This project was the Egyptian revolutionists' most beloved symbol of the Egypt of their hearts' desires. As such, of course, it was also that of the late-comer, Nasser, and especially so since it offered the most spectacular and sensational, as well as the most substantial, promise of heroic personal triumph: a clear and shining means of attaining economic prosperity, national military strength, and the enhancement of the dignity of the Egyptian people. As Nasser's publicity advisers had counseled him, he adopted the slogan: *Seventeen Times Larger than the Greatest Pyramid!*

About 1947, that is, in King Farouk's times, an Egyptian engineer of Greek origin had drawn plans for a High Dam, and in 1952, the Naguib government took the plans out of the desk. Henry Byroade, in the State Department, and Jefferson Caffery, Ambassador in Cairo, vigorously counseled American support for the construction of the Dam. By an agreement of November 6, 1954, the United States even assigned money to Egypt for another engineering survey.

Then came the Egyptian-Czech-Russian arms deal. Christian ethics, as well as everyday prudence and national interest, were now distinctly on trial in the mind of Dulles and the State Department.

Nevertheless, George V. Allen and George Wadsworth, Ambassador to Saudi Arabia, now joined Byroade and Caffery in advocating aid for the Dam. They felt that such aid was particularly needed to offset the defeat the U.S.A. had suffered from the Russian intrusion into the Middle East with arms for Nasser. They still believed that fundamentally, deep down in his heart, if you only had the patience to converse with him long enough to arrive there, Nasser was "a good boy," anxious only to bring welfare to his ailing and beloved people. Here was a sphere of action, financial and engineering, where the United States could in every respect outshine Russia. Bygones should be bygones. Perhaps the carrot would be more efficacious with Nasser and the Arabs than the stick. Thick and fast, the cables and memoranda went back and forth between Cairo and Washington and all around the diverse offices of the State Department. The International Cooperation Administration supported the project. So did Eric Johnston, who had served the Administration (1953-55) in devising a Jordan River Plan, to share the waters more productively between Israel, Syria, and Jordan, an engineering project technically brilliant and acceptable to all parties, but aborted by Syrian political objections egged on by Egypt.

Dulles, even if not with any special enthusiasm, yet quite *deliberately*, thought that the Aswan Dam should be assisted.[20] He reflected that the cost would not be so very great; but if the work committed Nasser for fifteen years or more, he might not be so restless and bellicose elsewhere. Peace would very probably be promoted by the building of the Dam; for "the Egyptian people" would demand that there be no delays in its completion.

In December, 1955, Dulles attended the annual NATO conference and discussed the Aswan Dam with his British and French colleagues. They endorsed the principle of making a loan. On December 16, he announced that the U.S.A. and Britain had agreed to associate themselves with the International Bank of Reconstruction and Development (colloquially the World Bank) in assisting Egypt to build the Dam. That is, Dulles initiated a positive offer to Egypt.

After protracted negotiations between officials of Egypt, the United States, and Britain, it was agreed that the financing would be borne in this way. The total investment during the fifteen years of construction on the Dam would be about $1.3 billion. The first stage of coffer-dams, taking about four years to build, would cost about $70 million. This sum would be given to Egypt as a free grant: $56 million would come from the U.S.A. and $14 million from Britain. The second stage would be furthered by a loan of $200 million from the World Bank plus a loan of $130 million from the United States and $80 million from Britain. These sums would be advanced in annual installments. The remaining $760 million would be furnished by Egypt herself, in man power, materials, and currency. The amounts furnished by the Bank were to be repaid over 40 years at an interest of 5 per cent annually; those by the United States and Britain on approximately similar terms.

Dulles, as usual, rightly made the maximum possible moral capital out of his decision. One principle of diplomacy runs something like this: When affairs are going your way and you are compelled to take action in any case, let everybody believe that you are the one and effective cause of progress. He was entitled to the credit for forgiveness, faith, and patience. At a press conference of December 20, 1955,[21] he told a questioner that the American-British offer had not been made as a counteraction to Russian offers of aid for the same purpose, as had been rumored. He strove to make the proposal look a mere, almost routine, continuation of matters under active consideration for years. He said that he had discussed the subject during his visit to Cairo in May, 1953. The program did not involve "a burdensome expenditure" (let this be noticed, in view of later troubles and arguments!), as it was to be spread over several years. (The reader might have noticed that it would mean about $13 million a year provided by American aid over a period of fourteen or fifteen years.)

Then came Dulles at his best: "This, after all, is a cheap price to pay for peace and progress." His assertion was true—if these goods were duly delivered. He warned, however, that the United States would not let itself be placed "in a position where the Soviets, by just making paper offers, can require us to make real offers to top them. That would mean that the Soviets would be spending nothing except a piece of paper but could require us to spend a great deal of money."

The Secretary was, in this last passage, referring to two aspects of Soviet foreign policy that had been agitating certain political and economic connoisseurs, and especially some mendacious and misanthropic newspapers and their hasty readers, for the last two years. One was the irruption of the U.S.S.R. into the area of foreign aid, called "ruble diplomacy." This policy was alleged by some center and right-of-center Republicans as being likely "to spend the U.S.A. into bankruptcy." This, of course, was nonsense, for America was far too wealthy compared with Russia. Yet it was nonsense that politically needed a cogent answer, especially from a Republican Secretary of State. The second aspect was the common American attitude that the U.S.S.R., being absolutely unscrupulous about the means it employed to gain the ends required by the Communist Party, could make promises of aid in larger amounts and on easier conditions, if it wished to, than the U.S.A., and then simply welsh on its promises. The United States, of course, could not play the game of falseness so long as it respected the principles of its own way of life. Therefore the U.S.S.R. could outdo the U.S.A. until its deceit was exposed, and that might take a long time.

Actually, the tactics of the Soviet Union and Nasser introduced complications over and beyond those normally to be expected in cases where the World Bank makes loans of sums like $200 million. The Bank's money belongs to its member states and most of the economically considerable of these have democratic governments responsible to their people, who, in the end, charge their budgets with grants and loans. The Soviet government had announced, in October, 1955, that it was ready to help in financing the Aswan Dam: hence Dulles's disclaimer at his press conference. Then, on December 18, two days after Dulles had made the first announcement of the offer of the United States-British loan, the Soviet Ambassador to Egypt, Daniel S. Solod, who had set in motion the arms deal, let it be known that the U.S.S.R. hoped to participate in the project, unless Egypt's agreement with the West specifically excluded Russia. The State Department at once retorted that the American offer of a loan implied that the U.S.S.R. would not be included in the deal. In November, 1955, Marshal Tito had paid a nine-day visit to Nasser. Tito had advised Nasser not to take the money from the U.S.S.R., as Nasser was already leaning too far over towards Russia by reason of the arms deal. But—he also advised that Nasser could use the Russian offer as a bargaining tactic, to obtain more from the U.S.A., and on better terms. Nasser may have broached the subject of using such tactics of double-cross to Tito, instead of the other way around; the Egyptian leader prided himself on his own political divination that the Russian arms deal would succeed, when many of his more level-headed and scrupulous advisers had warned otherwise.

Among the conditions laid down by the State Department for the making of the loan were these two: all contracts must be on a competitive basis; and Egypt's internal resources must be so managed as to avoid further inflation, now and during the years when she would be applying her share of the resources needed to build the Dam. Furthermore, the World Bank supported this latter condition. It went further, according to its statutes and regulations: it would review the investment program and propose to Egypt how she should adjust her total public expenditures to her financial resources.

In the background, the World Bank had been making its regular routine inquiries and reports in consultation with Egyptian officials, and conferring with Herbert Hoover, Jr., Sir Roger Makins, the British Ambassador, Egyptian Minister of Finance Kassouni, Eugene Black, Director of the World Bank, and United States Secretary of the Treasury, George M. Humphrey, who played quite a part in the negotiations and in the ultimate decision. Nasser raised objections to the normal conditions accepted by all nations who borrowed from the

Bank, great nations or small, empires or colonies. The Bank, as indicated above, required the right to watch Egypt's economic policy, in order to judge whether it might expect the recovery of its capital and the payment of the agreed interest. In order to expedite the loan, Eugene Black himself even traveled to Cairo. His discussions with Nasser were businesslike and, on his side, astute. Black is not only one of the world's most intelligent political economists, but also a man of open and agreeable character, of praiseworthy probity, and of immense practical ingenuity mixed with a devotion to the essential object of the World Bank, that is, to foster economic development wherever it is needed.

It was not possible to get into Nasser's head the understanding that the loan was economic rather than political, and that the conditions also fell into the former category. Nasser's rancor was far too murky for comprehension, though he himself throws a sharp light on his own bigotry. He boasted to the giant mob at Alexandria on July 26, 1956:

> Black said he was independent, and expressed views he believed it. I told him that the managing board represented nations. How could it represent nations without being a political bank? It was naturally a political bank, because he could not take any decision without approval by the managing board, which represented nations. This managing board is composed mainly of Western countries moving in the orbit of the U.S.A. I started to look at Mr. Black, who was sitting on a chair, and I saw him in my imagination as Ferdinand de Lesseps.[22]

Of course, both Nasser's imagination and his reminiscences were paranoiac. The world (except for the Soviet Union and Fascism in the interwar years) has tried hard to develop, and to some extent has succeeded in developing, international officials whose loyalty is to a service, a function, and not a nation or nations. How could a juvenile from the primitive Nile village of Beni Mer, not anxious to study hard at school, and nurtured all his life in nationalist vendettas in army barracks and in the streets rise to such a civilized conception? The world's progress, achieved at such terrible costs, seems always doomed to fall down again to its beginnings whenever a barbarian attains sovereign national power and thrusts his weight into the precarious balance of power among nations.

It took all of Black's ingenuity and good will to persuade Nasser that the loan was, for him, a pure and simple commercial transaction—banking, not foreign aid. The issue was resolved when Black, going far towards yielding to Nasser's frantic fears of offenses against the "dignity" and "sovereignty" of Egypt and Nasser, accepted Nasser's *voluntary* production of the government's accounts for the Bank's perusal. The "details" remained to be settled; but the true reason for Nasser's delay seems to have been the manipulation of the mind of American officials by the possibility of a rival offer from Russia.

Now two months had passed since December 16, 1955, the day when the American-British offer had been made. Nasser let the offer hang fire. Rumors were circulated in Cairo that the Russians had made bigger and better offers to build the dam. The most fantastic stories of Russian assistance became the fervent gossip of the Cairo and Alexandrian bazaars. When, in mid-March, Nasser mentioned to Ambassador Byroade that Egypt might barter 45,000 tons of cotton for 10,000 tons of Soviet steel, Dulles grew more dismayed and annoyed at the possibility that Nasser was playing off the East against the West. One of the most horrible anxieties of the American man is that he may "be played for a sucker," and the ex-lawyer Dulles was very much on his guard against being gypped. Dulles did not hurry the loan along at this stage. The offer had been made. He waited for Cairo. America had its dignity and national pride as well as any of the Nassers of the contemporary world. Since his inauguration, President Eisenhower had on several occasions warned foreign nations not to try to blackmail the United States by playing off aid from other countries against that offered by this nation.

Meanwhile, other important international events were occurring. Selwyn Lloyd, British Foreign Minister, had in October, 1955, visited Cairo. He agreed, it is reported from Egyptian sources, not to enlist more Arab nations in the Baghdad Pact if Egypt would stop anti-British propaganda, which was widespread and of the most homicidal character. Yet General Templer had been a little later sent to enlist Jordan, and had failed. Then Nasser had instigated, if indirectly, the instant dismissal of the British military expert, Lieutenant-General Sir John Bagot Glubb, known as Glubb Pasha, builder of Jordan's crack army units, the Arab Legion.[23] It happened that on that same day Selwyn Lloyd was on a second visit to Nasser, and Nasser flaunted the Glubb Pasha trump card in his face. Prime Minister Eden was urged by a group of right-wing Conservative M.P.'s to reply by denying the Aswan Loan to Egypt. He did not commit himself.

By the hour, Nasser became bolder. He and King Saud and President Shukri el Kuwatley of Syria met in Cairo to pledge the aloofness of the Arab world from the cold war (!). When French Foreign Minister Pineau visited Cairo in March, 1956, and promised Nasser never to join the Baghdad Pact, to permit elections in Algeria, and to reduce the supply of arms to Israel, he was given in return Nasser's promise not to train officers of the Algerian rebels in the Egyptian Army. Of course, Nasser's promise was broken, while

Pineau's promises, and Nasser's failure to promise to stop any other form of aid to the Algerian rebels, were exploited by the French Right Wing against the Mollet-Pineau Cabinet.

The Soviet Union was now wildly popular with all the Arab peoples, offering to build an atomic reactor in Egypt, to furnish uranium, and to train Egyptian physicists. In April, 1956, Nasser gave an interview to a New York newspaper. Had he made an exhaustive search to discover language especially styled to revolt Dulles, he could hardly have improved on it. "I have in my pocket a Soviet offer to help finance the Aswan Dam, and I will consider accepting it if there is any breakdown in negotiating with Washington." He continued with the taunt: "You can have military bases, but around each one of them are thousands of nationalistic bases and the Communists are winning them one by one." The taunt was directed to "America."

On May 15, 1956, in opposition to warnings from Egypt's Revolutionary Council of possible international consequences, Nasser arranged to barter 45,000 tons of Egyptian cotton for 60,000 tons of Chinese steel—and the Egyptian Government recognized Communist China. Under characteristic compulsion to boast about his triumphs and his state of mind, he then inspired the government-owned daily, *Al Gomhouria,* to say that he had recognized Communist China so that he should be able to acquire unlimited supplies of arms from that country, because British Prime Minister Eden (it was rumored) had obtained an agreement in principle with the Soviet Union to stop the Middle East arms race. And since China was not a member of the United Nations, she could not be bound by any arms embargo established by its resolutions. The Egyptian Government did not inform the State Department of its intention to recognize Communist China: the news was given to American Ambassador Henry Byroade by the Chinese Nationalist Minister in Egypt.

It was a very nasty slap in the face for Dulles. He offered merely a mild rebuke after the lapse of a week.[24] The President, in also expressing his regrets about Nasser's action, signaled that it was an error, though he still said it did not jeopardize American-Egyptian friendship. But "friendship" is a curiously elastic term in international politics: it stretches every way, length, breadth, and thickness, to a point where it becomes transparent, so that one can see that nothing at all exists there.

Egypt was insisting on its "neutrality," and Dulles's hatred of "neutrals" was the counterpart of his defiance of Communism. "Who is not with me, is against me!" In June, 1956, he broke out against neutral countries with severe reproaches. On June 6, the President spoke with Dulles's words: "Neutral doesn't mean neutral as between right and wrong, or decency and indecency." It meant only neutral as between contending military forces. The explanation became confused; an international uproar was provoked. After a talk with Dulles, the President issued an explanation: it allowed for special conditions that might justify *political* neutrality—but still "no nation has the right to be indifferent to the fate of another, or as he [Dulles] put it, to be neutral as between right and wrong or decency and indecency." On June 12, Dulles himself asserted that he and the President thought alike. In between, at Iowa State College on June 8,[25] Dulles proclaimed again that the doctrine "that a nation can best gain safety for itself by being indifferent to the fate of others . . . except under very exceptional circumstances . . . is an immoral and short-sighted conception."

And Dulles had before him a Nasser who not only had embraced the Soviet Union, but had recognized *Red China!*

During this month of June, 1956, the Secretary's office, and even the President's, were extremely busy with the reassessment of Nasser and the Middle East. The politically active-minded part of the nation—Congress, the newspaper editors, the columnists, and Republican and Democratic party leaders—became more and more annoyed with Nasser. These citizens were, in part, stimulated by the press conferences of Dulles and Eisenhower, which on this subject, to be absolutely frank, were the press conferences of Dulles and Dulles. And, in part, they founded their judgments on Nasser's provocative and, it seemed, deliberate public insults and hostility towards the United States. It goes without saying that the vast majority of the American Jewish community especially resented Nasser's belligerence and the casualties and economic injuries being wrought daily on the people of Israel. They appealed to their Representatives and Senators to correct the situation. The common State Department phrase, "fed up to the teeth," with Nasser's "antics," aptly represents the general state of mind.

Some time in June, Ambassador Hussein of Egypt warned Nasser to clinch the loan from America before opposition sentiment in that country should snowball uncontrollably. On June 15, 1956, Dimitri Shepilov, who a year before had visited Cairo "to herald the approaching storm" of the arms deal, and was now Foreign Minister of the Soviet Union, again arrived in the Eygptian capital. Nasser and he, along with their respective henchmen, entered into long and deep sessions. "Off-the-record" news was disseminated that the Soviet Union had offered to lend Egypt the total cost of the Dam at a very low rate of interest and for a very long span of time for repayment of the capital. Then, June 18, Shepilov joined Nasser at Port Said to celebrate the departure of the last British soldier from the Suez base, in accordance with the agreement of 1954. (The British had actually slipped away unnoticed on June 13, to avoid humiliation.)

Adoring crowds by the hundred thousands acclaimed the *Bikbashi;* two weeks earlier he had been elected President by 99.1 per cent of the voters. Russian weapons paraded through the streets and Russian warplanes swooped through the skies; token military forces from Jordan, Lebanon, Yemen, Lybia, the Sudan, Saudi Arabia, and Syria (but none from Iraq) were on hand; trade contracts with the Russian satellites were celebrated; arms from Sweden (but not for Israel from that country), from France, and even from Britain were displayed! Nasser's feral smile was turned gratefully on Shepilov: "Our policy is frank. We shall cooperate with anybody or any country ready to cooperate with us." Eugene Black would be in shortly to see Nasser again, since Nasser had not yet concluded the details of the loan with him.

The United States budget for 1956-57, announced on July 4, included the first appropriations for the Aswan High Dam. On July 10, however, Dulles told a press conference that it was "improbable" Egypt would get the loan. A week later he and Eisenhower objected to the demand by the Senate Appropriations Committee that the money it had provided for the Aswan project could not be used until the Administration had first consulted the Committee. As the President and the Secretary told some Republican Senators at that time, they were opposed to this proviso because the British and the World Bank were also involved as partners in the project.

On Monday, July 16, the ferment in the State Department produced by the Egyptian-Russian moves came to a head. George V. Allen was replaced by a comparatively unknown career man, W. M. Rountree, and it was announced that Henry Byroade would be withdrawn from Cairo. The changes, as usual, had been the subject of leaks to the newspapers several days before.

Allen was transferred to the Embassy at Athens. He was moved, it is said, because he inclined towards Israel, because he was at odds with Herbert Hoover, Jr., the Under Secretary (a man with whom very many in the State Department were at odds even though he did not realize it, for his very strong pro-Arab and pro-Aswan inclinations); because Dulles had got tired of the repetitive nature of Allen's Middle East advice; and because Allen was, perhaps, excessively fond of making public speeches. Although Dulles warmly regretted in private that "Allen wished a change and especially to go to Athens," the move was a move of policy. Dulles was out of his depth in Middle Eastern affairs. He had an uneasy feeling that he was not master of the situation. He was trying to find an alternative to the policies of the past. Whatever G. V. Allen had done or not done, he had not been an uncompromising rejector of Nasser.

The situation of Byroade was clearer: he had all along been an Arab friend, and as already remarked: "more Nasser than Nasser."

He had not prevented the arms deal; he had not stopped Nasser's anti-Western campaign. Byroade was at that very time begging Dulles not to jilt Nasser in regard to the loan for the Dam, even though Nasser was a nuisance. After all he had *now* turned to the U.S.A. and not the U.S.S.R. for help, and it was important not to push him further into Russia's arms. (Byroade remained in Cairo until September, 1956, until he was replaced by Raymond Hare.)

The moment these signs of shifting American policy became evident in Cairo, the Egyptian Ambassador to the United States, Dr. Ahmed Hussein, was suddenly sent back to Washington to accept the offer of a loan by the consortium of the U.S.A., Britain, and the World Bank. He arrived on July 16, 1956. Meanwhile, the Egyptian press carried the story of his mission in banner headlines. The most fantastic expectations were aroused, coupled with the name of the miracle worker, Nasser.

The Ambassador arrived shortly after an adverse current to Egypt had set in fairly strongly in Congress. The Senate Appropriations Committee, as noted, wished to impede the grant of money for the Dam. This prohibition had come about because some Southern Democratic senators, led by Holland of Florida, expressed fears that the Dam would promote irrigation in Egypt, that irrigation would increase cotton acreage, and that this would mean competition for markets by Egypt against the Southern cotton growers. Furthermore, pro-Israeli senators supported Holland's move as a curb on Egypt's strength and belligerency.

About the time that the Egyptian Ambassador was on his way from Cairo to Washington, Nasser was on his way to Belgrade on a state visit to Marshall Tito. The two dictators were to be joined by the Marcus Aurelius of Asia, Pandit Jawaharlal Nehru, with whom Dulles had had a recent public quarrel about "the immorality" of nations that were "neutral."

Dulles now had several substantial reasons why he should not grant the loan in the American national interest. But just as many good reasons could be prudently advanced why he should grant it. If his decision eventually turned out to be favorable, then he needed no special preparations. If, on the other hand, his decision should finally be negative—and *the Secretary was still not fully decided between July 16 and July 19*, the day Hussein was to call—then a communiqué would need to be made to the press. Dulles's top staff, including the chairman of the Policy Planning Committee, were charged with preparing such a communiqué. (It is not known whether this was at Dulles's order or not.) The statement was drafted with the maximum circumspection and with the studied purpose of reducing the potential offense to the Egyptian government. For the U.S.A. itself had, after all, taken the initiative in making the offer and it undertakes such initiatives in the first place for America's own interests. It was only in this period, since Nasser had announced that his Ambassador was on the way from Cairo, that the staff meeting in Dulles's office surveyed all the facets of the problem. One of his most important policy-planning advisers answered Dulles's question whether to tell Hussein the bad news (if it were so) at once, by counseling him to temporize. Robert Murphy, the Deputy Secretary, was not informed.

Still unsure of his and America's decision, about July 16, Dulles discussed the issue cursorily with President Eisenhower. He informed the President of the reasons for deciding as he himself, Dulles, should consider wise. The President did not, for his part, positively order the Secretary to withhold the loan. He was annoyed, he said, because, while he was working for peace in the Middle East, Nasser was acquiring arms that might be used against Israel. Where, then, was the point of finding money for the Dam? If the Secretary should come down on that side, then he would concur in the denial of the loan.

Two days later the British Ambassador, Sir Roger Makins, was called to the State Department: the British were in partnership in the proposed loan for the Dam, and both had an interest, each for itself, in the Middle East in general. Dulles informed Makins that he was *dubious* about making the loan, not that he was definitely about to refuse it. Sir Roger urged the Secretary to consider his ultimate decision with utmost care. Dulles then asked Sir Roger to consult Eden about it, because the Egyptian Ambassador was coming in the following day, that is, July 19. Dulles exploited his trouble with the Senate as a means of spurring the Ambassador and Eden on to agree with him to drop the loan. He pressed Makins with a plea that he, Dulles, must avoid the Senate rider hindering the loan. He pleaded that he was under intolerable pressure and time was of the essence. Makins, as already said, replied that the tactics would have to be "*playing it long*." London was as embarrassed as Dulles to learn that Nasser now positively wanted the loan, and that his Ambassador was on the way to get it, for they also had reason to be chagrined by Nasser's recent acts of arrogance. But they knew that Nasser was violent in temper and unreliable in his reactions. They also counselled, "Play it long." When Sir Roger consulted London, he came back with further express words of caution from Eden and Selwyn Lloyd, the British Foreign Secretary. Their opinion was "We leave the decision to your [Dulles's] judgment whether you grant or rescind the offer of the loan. But we do not wish you to be precipitate; we wish you to play it long." The tactics of delay were then the tactics agreed upon by the United States and Britain, in preference to any unceremonious refusal of the loan. Eden and Selwyn Lloyd had begged Dulles not to act, to use diplomatic classical language, *brusqué*, that is to say, abruptly-cum-roughly.

Only a couple of days previously the French Ambassador in Washington, Couve de Murville, had given the State Department a serious warning. He said in so many words, "To deny the loan for the Aswan Dam to Nasser is a very dangerous action; it can affect the Suez Canal. I know Nasser: as you know, I was Ambassador for my government in Cairo for several years. Beware how you handle the situation with the loan, because a most likely consequence of a refusal is the seizure of the Suez Canal!" The warning was laughed at by officials. It should not have been, for another reason altogether: Egyptian politicians had for decades been jealous of the Suez Canal Company's status and it was a favorite subject of attack, juridically and politically.

On July 19, 1956, Dulles was in the office at work, as usual, at shortly after 8:00 A.M. He repeated his consultation with the President, the issue not closed. At about 11:00 his phone rang and he was told that Ambassador Hussein was on his way up to the office. Two very high State Department career officials were present in the room with Dulles. The Ambassador entered with his aide. He himself was a not unwelcome figure. He had held his position since long before Nasser's deposition of Naguib and, according to some State Department officials, was not an idolator of Nasser. Indeed, he was said to be rather inclined toward the Western point of view in the struggle for mastery in the Middle East and the world in general. Dulles did not dislike him personally.

Dulles began to explain the many difficulties he was encountering in clinching the loan. This took him a little time, as he always spoke very carefully, in rather pedantic language and syntax.

The Ambassador began to advance questions on certain matters. The Aswan Dam scheme, if it was to be helped, was, as the Ambassador had long known, to follow on an agreement between Egypt and the Sudan whereby Sudan's share of the upper waters of the Nile would be assigned satisfactorily to that country. But this had not yet been concluded? He was anxious about this. Dulles in each case put the other point of view. It seemed that Hussein, by the proper demeanor and rhetoric, might have an indefinite postponement or an alibi, rather than a complete refusal.

Then, as Dulles appeared to be bringing the various reasons against the loan to a head, all in tones rather sad and firm, the Ambassador became excited. He was sitting on the divan near the coffee table, while Dulles was sitting just on the other side of that same table in an armchair with his legs stretched out onto the table. At a certain point, Ambassador Hussein, perhaps remembering the instructions received in Cairo, became worried and agitated. He leaned forward over the table, gesticulating. "Don't please say," he blurted out, "you are going to withdraw the offer, because . . ." (and he pointed to his pocket) "we have the Russian offer to finance the Dam right here in my pocket!"

No nerve was so raw in all of Dulles's sensitive composition as Russia. He at once retorted, "Well, as you have the money already, you don't need any from us! My offer is withdrawn!" The Egyptian Ambassador left, terribly unhappy, and at once the press services became extremely active. Serious things began to happen—irreversible deeds, deeds with widespread and disastrous repercussions.

Why did Dulles rescind the offer of the loan? In every action men take there are both reasons and motivations. Sometimes men are really motivated by the reasons. Very frequently, however, an individual can list perfectly sound reasons for a decision he has made, whereas the real motive for it has been something else altogether: the reasons have simply been adduced as accomplices of the impulse. It is important to try to distinguish between reasons and motivations, for we may thus obtain a clue to the relationship between cause and effect in foreign policy, especially in the Suez affair and the disasters that ensued. In this case, we may also obtain a clue to the enigma of Dulles's character. How very pertinent such an analysis is may be judged from the fact that one of the most gifted of America's career State Department officials, Robert Murphy, a trouble-shooter of veritable genius, twice confessed perplexedly to me that in spite of all of Dulles's explanations to the staff and to him, he still does not know truly why Dulles refused to make the Aswan Dam loan at that time, unless it were that Dulles did not like the ultimatum tone in Hussein's message.

The reasons for denying a loan to Nasser were amply paraded in the press and in the State Department's communiqué. The pertinent part of the latter said:

> Developments within the succeeding months have not been favorable to the success of the project, and the United States government has concluded that it is not feasible in the present circumstances to participate in the project. Agreement by the riparian states [the Sudan, above all] has not been achieved, and the ability of Egypt to devote adequate resources to assure the project's success has become more uncertain than at the time the offer was made. . . . The United States is prepared to consider at an appropriate time, and at the request of the riparian states, what steps might be taken toward a more effective utilization of the water resources of the Nile for the benefit of the people of the region. Furthermore, the United States remains ready to

assist Egypt in its efforts to improve the economic conditions of its people and is prepared through its appropriate agencies to discuss these matters within the context of funds appropriated by Congress.[26]

Let us evaluate Dulles's reasons, as presented in this statement and in the other official remarks of which we have taken notice.

(1) The Senate was reluctant to help increase the production of cotton in Egypt. But, as Senator J. W. Fulbright pointed out in a Senate debate some months later, very few states and Senators were affected, and the Secretary could either have persuaded the opponents to abstain, or could have overridden them by the votes of other Senators had he wished to.[27] It is true that Dulles always strove especially hard to avoid the difficulties suffered by his predecessor, Secretary of State Dean Acheson, that stemmed from his unpopularity with Congress. Nevertheless, Dulles recognized limits to his becoming obsequious. Supported by Eisenhower, he could get what he wanted in this matter, and the ruffled feathers of the Senators would soon settle back to their normal sleekness. Yet another point is made by the Director of the World Bank: cotton would not begin to grow in the two million new irrigated acres for at least another eighteen years—since the Dam itself would not be ready for fifteen. Moreover, it had been made perfectly clear in the Egyptian economic plan that the area was not going to be used for cotton; it was believed that the world market for cotton was already too well supplied.

(2) The repayment of the loans and the investment that Egypt herself was to make in the Dam were altogether jeopardized by the mortgaging of Egyptian cotton to Czechoslovakia over many years for the arms she had supplied. No one in Washington or London knew exactly what was the total cost of the arms. The guesses ranged from $100 million to $250 million. Dulles's point that the repayment of the loans was uncertain was, in fact, valid. But suppose all the American investment had been lost? It would have amounted to the first $50 million and then about $15 million for say twelve or fifteen years. This amount is practically negligible compared to America's annual wealth. Eugene Black, who had negotiated the consortium plan, is a hard-headed man and he had based the loan of the Bank's $200 million on full knowledge of Egypt's financial condition, including its obligations to Czechoslovakia for the arms. The Aswan proposal was made on December 16, 1955, by America and Britain *after* the arms deal in September of the same year, therefore with prior knowledge of it, and it was even made because Nasser seemed to be moving altogether into the Russian camp, in the hope of a reversal of this course.

One of the American policy makers during the episode of the

Dam was not a State Department official at all, or anybody directly vested with responsibility for America's foreign policy. He was George M. Humphrey, Secretary of the Treasury. He had been consulted on the issue of the loan by Dulles around the middle of 1955. Then at one of the early meetings at Camp David, shortly after Eisenhower's heart attack, he was called in to review the question with the President and Dulles. The Secretary of the Treasury bluntly and powerfully made clear his opposition to the loan from a financial point of view. If the loan were not repaid, not only would the United States lose its direct contribution, but the World Bank would be compelled to recoup its losses from America's contribution to the Bank. Humphrey believed the project was impossible because the Egyptian population was too unskilled to build the dam and operate its installations and the various industries that would be developed when electric power had become available. He calculated that in the certain eventuality of Egyptian failure, the U.S. government would foot a bill of over $500 million. When Dulles had joined Eisenhower's Cabinet early in 1953, the President had given him a general commission: "George is synonymous with money! If it is a question of money, then you must clear the policy with George!" By "pursuing" the matter of the Dam with Dulles, Humphrey believed he had brought him to realize the project would fall of its own weight. Certainly Black, among others, was nonplussed at the sudden and amazing change that occurred in Dulles's readiness to make the loan. Perhaps Humphrey's sheer personality, clever, powerful, swift, and witty, could and did make rings round a ponderous man like Dulles, and forced itself into Dulles's mind as he conversed with Ambassador Ahmed Hussein.

(3) Many Senators were antagonistic toward aid to "neutrals." It is hard not to sympathize with them. They were being asked, as often happens, to provide money taken from people who earn it by hard labor to give to "nonaligned" nations who condone the brutalities of the Soviet Union at home and abroad. On the other hand, it is perfectly right for America to use wealth as an instrument of policy, if it is admitted that force may be so used. Dulles's error on Aswan was less the object of his policy than its manner—manner may ruin purpose. When all the cards were his, he committed a very clumsy diplomatic mistake.

Nasser had driven Dulles into the quandary of turning a Christian cheek towards him, since Dulles constantly and earnestly claimed Christian virtue for his policies, and at the same time of being less than kind to his friends. Dulles observed later (April, 1957, after the event) that Pakistan, Turkey, Iran, the Sudan and Libya, all friends, had complained of the proposed loan to Egypt. Dulles recounted their anxiety thus: "Do nations which play both sides get better treatment than nations which are stalwart and work with us? That question was posed by the manner in which the Egyptians presented their fund request to us. . . ." [28]

(4) Some State Department officials—George V. Allen was one of them—looked askance at America's assumption of an obligation to cooperate in Egypt in an economic plan lasting for over ten years. It must necessarily impose a burden on the manpower and other resources of that country. Diplomatic experience had shown him (while he served in Yugoslavia, for example) that friction was bound to develop between donor and beneficiary. It was even likely that economic aid would not merely not improve relations, but actually worsen them.

(5) When we notice the anger Dulles felt, the *personal* affront, when Egypt became the first Arab country to recognize Peking—when all of his anxious efforts were bent on containing Communism—we come nearer to Dulles's motivations. It was scorn and anger at being jilted by a nonentity like Nasser who preferred all the Soviet black iniquities to all the shining moral achievements and potentialities of the West and of Dulles.

The truth seems to be that, on the spur of the moment, all the resentment of a man who had monumental self-righteousness, a reborn Calvinist who was a deeply committed lay pillar of the Christian church—all this boiled up and was visited on Nasser. Dulles did not play it long; he could not play it long; his feelings got the better of him. He could have said, "Let us wait!" He could have said, "Let us talk it over again in a couple of weeks' time!" He might have replied: "I'm still thinking it over!" Instead of this, he said, "No!" in very brusque terms.

Now, on that day, July 19, 1956, waiting for Dulles to finish his crucial interview with Ambassador Hussein, two men sat in his sanctum—a small office to which he could repair to meditate or rest or meet special guests. They were Henry Luce of *Time*, *Life*, and *Fortune*, and C. D. Jackson, editor of *Fortune*, formerly special assistant to President Eisenhower for Psychological Warfare; both of these men had been valiant campaigners for Eisenhower in 1952.

Dulles was already rather late for lunch. Suddenly he burst in, apologized for his unpunctuality, and explained that he had just told the Egyptian Ambassador that the United States government would not make the loan to Egypt for the Aswan Dam. Dulles looked thoroughly pleased with himself, beaming as much as his personality permitted. Indeed, he was exultant. He still had about him the aura of his remark to the Ambassador: "Okay! You can go to Moscow for your money!" The talk veered to whether Nasser might retaliate, and someone speculated that he might seize the Suez Canal. But this idea was an insignificant aside and quickly dropped out of sight.

What Jackson did learn of hard fact from Dulles's victorious demeanor and from conversations with the Secretary was that the latter felt he was being blackmailed by Nasser with the alleged counterbids from Russia. Dulles had decided to meet the economic counteroffensive of the Soviet Union there and then, especially as it concerned a large sum of money. If the Russians had made an offer and if it were seriously meant, the fulfillment of it would bleed the Russian economy to some extent, for he (erroneously) believed that economy was failing. And perhaps in the long run, if they made the loan, the transaction would embroil them with the Egyptians in the many years the construction of the Dam would require. On the other hand, if they had not been serious, his move would expose the hollowness of Communist promises and would leave Nasser flat on his back.

Later on, Jackson spoke at a meeting of businessmen in Toronto and told them the story of this lunch. A reporter quoted Jackson as saying that Secretary Dulles had deliberately used the Aswan Dam as a way of precipitating a showdown with Nasser over Suez! (*The Toronto Globe and Mail*, Wednesday, March 13, 1957.) This was only sophisticated and titivating name-dropping on Jackson's part. But the motive of thwarting and taunting Russia, while humiliating Nasser, is accurate. This was the motivation of Dulles, as distinct from his reasons. The effective cause was Dulles's character, not the cost of the Dam or the opposition of a few Senators. This judgment is fully confirmed by two other pieces of evidence, one from the "semiofficial" biography, *John Foster Dulles*,[29] by J. F. Beal, and the other from a remark made later by Dulles himself before the Senate Foreign Relations Committee. At the very next meeting of the National Security Council after July 9, Vice President Nixon observed how deeply Dulles was moved over the rescinding of the loan. He told those present over and over again that he did not intend to be "blackmailed." "Blackmail! Blackmail!" he muttered and grumbled victoriously and indignantly. "Blackmailed by Nasser! Not me."

If, indeed, Dulles did foresee consequences, never was a man so blind to what they might be. For Dulles "got what was coming to him," or, rather, unfortunately it was actually America's allies who got what was coming to Dulles, while he very cleverly evaded the punitive consequences. It is perfectly possible for a statesman in the office of Secretary to be clever enough to make moves over short distances, and yet to be lacking in far-sighted wisdom. Two quotations will make this a little clearer. The first is from an unusual and, it may be thought, a most irrelevant and even sacrilegious source. It is from an article written about Joseph Stalin by Leon Trotsky for *Life* magazine, October 2, 1939. Trotsky says this of Stalin: "He sees clearly for a short distance, but on the historical scale he is blind. A shrewd tactician, he is not a strategist."

The second quotation comes from the memoirs of Field Marshal Montgomery.[30] Montgomery is offering some thoughts on high command in war:

> To exercise high command successfully one has to have an infinite capacity for taking pains and for careful preparation; and one has also to have an inner conviction which at times will transcend reason. Having fought, possibly over a prolonged period, for the advantage and gained it, there comes the moment for boldness. When that moment comes, will you throw your bonnet over the mill [or, as Montgomery puts it a page earlier, "over the moon"] and soar from the known to seize the unknown? In the answer to this question lies the supreme test of generalship in high command.

The conduct of the office of Secretary of State has many analogies to the exercise of high command in the field. Dulles did have infinite capacity for taking pains and for careful preparation, and he had, as well, inner convictions that transcended reason. He also had a certain boldness. He demonstrated in the affair of the Aswan Dam that he could throw his bonnet over the mill and soar from the known to seize the unknown. But the crucial question is whether the imagination is adequate to seizing upon the lineaments of the unknown accurately as they will be in the more distant future. This is the point at which Dulles's conduct inspires doubts. Another doubt arises, but it must be considered at a later stage of the Suez affair: it is one thing to be an eloquent and persuasive theoretician and quite another to take action when live bullets are flying at you or your friends.

Hence, when Dulles was defending himself before the Senate Foreign Relations Committee against a charge of having triggered the seizure of the Suez Canal by Nasser, he was emphatic in his responses to Senator Case. He said:

> There is one thing I want to make clear, Senator. I do not believe in the U.S. being blackmailed, and any time I sense a purpose on the part of any country to try to get money out of us by threatening that if we don't pay it money it will do something, at that point I say, "Nothing doing." . . .

And again Dulles said:

> We would never have gone through with the plans for the Aswan Dam as a way of getting insurance for the non-seizure of the Suez Canal Company. As I made clear, I just do not believe in doing business that way.[31]

If Secretary Dulles had had even a minor gift of imagination and a far-sighted regard for America's security and the vital interests of her principal allies, Britain and France, would not he have given the loan for the Dam to insure against the non-seizure of the Canal?

Trenchancy and truculence are two separate qualities of mind and character. Dulles was almost always trenchant, and that did no great harm: but he was also often truculent, hectoring, and that is quite another matter in the relationships between states. Henry Cabot Lodge, at a special vantage point, the Embassy of the United States to the United Nations, thought the brusque denial of the loan to be a terrible mistake.

The Secretary's precipitancy met with a bad press almost universally in the U.S.A., in Britain, in Continental Europe, and in the Asian countries. He had been unwise and heavy-handed. The abrupt action shocked Eugene Black, because he knew the financial realities and had not the slightest inkling that Dulles would withdraw the loan he had himself initiated. These were immediate commentaries, not the product of hindsight; they thought the action was unwise in itself, apart from the train of consequences we have yet to narrate. On April 7, 1957, the *Washington Post*, reviewing Beal's book about Dulles, severely rebuked the Secretary on learning his motives. It said, "Now Mr. Dulles is portrayed as the champion of purposeful irresponsibility, the inventor of the calculated blunder. . . . All this serves to paint Mr. Dulles as the most reckless sort of gambler."

The men who were Dulles's devotees are always at considerable pains to vindicate his reputation as one who never, never acted from pique. Interrogation reveals that they mean that he never made or carried out a decision from animosity against a person: his decisions were the exclusive product of a rational consideration of the real ingredients in the circumstances, disregarding the person or persons who were their bearers in negotiations. But the other evidence points to a different conclusion. Dulles was not impersonal. He had ardent hates and loves among the human beings with whom he dealt, and they were not manifested exclusively as responses to the real factors in the policy. Nasser had piqued him; he felt piqued toward Nasser. It was one of many times that personal resentment interfused with moral righteousness played a crucial part in Dulles's foreign policy. In the words of an extremely close participant in Middle East diplomacy at that moment, "Mr. Dulles kicked Nasser in the teeth, with a missionary twist."

The Washington correspondent of the London *Times* dwelt on the "political" motives, as distinct from the economic—that is, the deflation of Nasser. He said, "But it is also clear that Mr. Dulles, a master of evasion when he chooses, has deliberately taken the opportunity to force the issue with Nasser, incidentally at the moment of the Brioni exchanges—perhaps out of his new concept of 'the immorality of neutralism.' " [32]

On July 20, 1956, the British government also withdrew its offer to finance the Aswan Dam. All it said was, "We have concluded that in present circumstances it would not be feasible to participate in the project." Laconic.

While these drastic events were coming to a head in Washington and London, Nasser had been in gala-like conferences with Marshal Tito in Belgrade and on the beautiful island of Brioni in the Asiatic. The two were joined by a third chaste neutral, Nehru of India. For Nasser, this was the second conspicuous international recognition, the Bandung Conference having been the first. His kept press in Cairo sang his praises—the new Saladin of all the Arabs. On July 20, the three composed and signed their declaration on the thirteen chief problems of world policy (with the sageness of the calmly non-aligned) including the Middle East, central Europe, Germany, the peaceful use of atomic energy, aid to underdeveloped countries, the admission of Red China to the United Nations, the Algerian rebellion against France, and disarmament, as well as some others.

Nasser was on his way back by plane to Cairo on the evening of July 20. When he reached Cairo at three A.M., the news of the refusal of the loan was broken to him by the waiting officials.

Meanwhile, the Egyptian newspapers had already burst into savage recriminations. The news came as a tremendous shock, and surprise and anger swept the city. Dulles was accused of showing bad faith, of breaking a promise, of being a cheat. Imperialism and imperialistic plots against the welfare of Egypt were charged against the U.S.A. and Britain. The clamoring multitudes, led by the editors, alleged that the West was intent on undermining Nasser. Of course, they blamed Israel for stimulating the American Zionists to injure Egypt, since this year—1956—was a Presidential election year and, they argued, the President needed the "Jewish vote." Nevertheless, the Egyptian press defiantly cried out, somehow the Dam would be built.

Nasser was staggered by the news and went into immediate and long conferences with his Cabinet. He examined the dispatch from his Ambassador and the comments of the American newspapers. What galled him most was (1) the peremptory and contemptuous attitude of Dulles, and (2) more than anything, the disparagements of the health of the Egyptian economy. As one Near Eastern informant in a very high place in Washington asked me, "Would you like to hear it spread all round the world that your credit was no good?" High Egyptian diplomats were echoing or swelling Nasser's words: "If you did not want to make the loan all that you needed to do was to say 'No!' plainly. Why add the excuses, and the insults about our economy? You just wanted to teach us a lesson before everybody in the world because we disagreed with a good deal of your policy—as we had every right to do! We are sensitive; we like nice words!"

To Nasser, the sense that Dulles had punished *him*, not necessarily Egypt—of course he put it in the first person plural, *us*—was insufferable! The next day, as recounted, the blow was repeated when the British withdrew their offer to participate. Even the British manner was considered by Nasser as an additional insult: the newspapers in Britain, he complained, were told about it some hours before the Egyptian Ambassador was. On July 22 came the newspaper reports of some remarks by Shepilov, to the effect that Moscow had *not* offered to build the Aswan Dam, though the Soviet Union would help other economic projects. Now Nasser had been made to look like a liar! Worse, perhaps, this insinuation had been circulated all over the world!

On July 24, Nasser began his counterattack. Eyewitnesses report that he spoke with an anger so intense and sustained as almost to produce a bursting of his blood vessels. He vented his savage fury almost exclusively on Washington. What he found most wounding, as already suggested, was the suggestion that his economy was insolvent. He produced statistics purporting to prove that Egypt's national income had increased by about 30 per cent since the Officers' Revolution of 1952. Then he began to curse:

> If an uproar in Washington creates false and misleading announcements, without shame and with disregard for the principles of international relations [notice this—after the recognition of Red China and the arms deal and the rumor-mongering about a loan from the U.S.S.R. about a loan for the Dam!], that the Egyptian economy is unsound and throwing shadows of doubt on Egypt's economy, I look at the Americans and say, "May you choke to death on your fury!" [33]

In the audience was the new Soviet Ambassador, Yevgeni O. Kiselev. At these remarks of Nasser's, he thoughtfully nodded Soviet approval.

Nasser's language is a clear, overt indication of his own personal savagery and despotic temperament. Some newspaper commentators, having become flatterers of persons they persuade themselves are great men, often try to exculpate such virulence of language. In this case they said, "After all, the language was only for home consumption, and you must remember that he was speaking to Arabs whose daily language and thought, as T. E. Lawrence has taught us, are very poetic and fiery. He must speak to them in the way they understand." To condone a dictator's rhetoric of war because he needs it to maintain his popularity is to assist a nationalistic militant to evade the sobriety and self-control necessary for world peace. It is not only policies that are inimical to America's national interests that one is asked to swallow but an enemy's very "style." Nehru, some have said, had purposes similar to those of Nasser, but his "style" was polished and sanctimonious. It makes a difference.

Nasser, on July 24, promised that he would give a detailed answer to the West in two days' time.

Dulles, having purged himself of his reasons and resentments, joined President Eisenhower and a large party in a round of visits to Latin American countries. He was exercising the capacity, as one of his official associates is fond of saying, of "switching his mind off one thing and giving it a rest—using his mind like a well-honed tool that needs consciously undertaken periods of repose." He had, it is asserted with adulation, "a wonderful capacity beyond any other man or statesman to Shut Off." He emplaned without a care in the world on July 21. First the two leaders, with their entourage, attended an Organization of American States meeting in Panama, Dulles then proceeded to Bogotá, Colombia, on July 24, and to Quito, Ecuador, on July 25.

On July 26, he flew off at 10 A.M. to Lima, Peru, to be the personal representative of President Eisenhower at the inauguration ceremonies of the President-elect, Dr. Manuel Prado. These ceremonies were to last from July 27 to August 1, though Dulles planned to depart from Lima on the evening of July 28. Arriving at Lima at 4 P.M. on July 26, Dulles stayed with the United States Ambassador, Theodore Achilles, who had formerly been his capable handyman in Paris to solidify NATO after the failure of E.D.C.

Dulles asked Achilles for the latest news of world events since he had been in the air. Achilles had nothing special to report. Then Dulles and his wife graciously attended a reception for Embassy officials.

Nasser's speech announcing the seizure of the Canal ended in Alexandria at about 5:40 P.M. Washington time, identical to Lima time. At 8:56 P.M. Herbert Hoover, Jr., in the State Department and Dulles spoke by telephone, but it is almost certain that Dulles had the news from cables sent him by Hoover a couple of hours earlier.

"Nasser has seized the Suez Canal!" he was told by Hoover and Allen Dulles, his brother, head of the CIA. Dulles's Acting Secretary had been on tenterhooks to reach his chief and had already reported the bad news to President Eisenhower, now back in Washington. Eisenhower also talked on the phone with Dulles, repeating the story, which he had discussed with Allen Dulles, Hoover, and his intimate personal assistant, Colonel Andrew Goodpaster.

Dulles sustained the shock of his life, and it was clearly

registered on his face. He had not expected any reaction, except that Nasser would stay suitably rebuked. No one had taken serious notice of the French Ambassador's warning, for, among other things, the Secretary's mind was turned on Latin America. It had just finished with one case, flushed with victory, and it was now turning to the next. Yet in the section of the State Department concerned with United Nations affairs, some praiseworthy minds had made "contingency plans" of how to approach the United Nations if ever the Canal should be seized. The plans had, however, never reached the Secretary.

Of course there ought to be, and usually are, "contingency" or "position" papers, foreseeing and making preparation for events. But the most important feature of a "contingency" plan is that the "contingency" be recognized to have occurred. The plans cannot be used unless one has the imagination, the reflexes, to realize that the moment has arrived. And, even so, as everybody who has ever had the responsibility of handling even simple situations in human relationships knows very well, even the best imagination may go awry as compared with the reality that abruptly appears in all its unexpected subtlety of complication.

Dulles's first reaction to the unanticipated calamity was a combination of disappointment and anger that suddenly another Middle East crisis had boiled up, and of fury that Nasser had seized the Canal without due process of law and negotiations, and, as far as the Secretary could tell, with ridicule and insults hurled at the United States!

The question did not arise in Dulles's mind and among his entourage during July 27 whether he should return to Washington at once. He apparently decided that his frequent telephone conversations with Hoover, Robert Murphy, career Deputy Secretary of State (that is, the principal career official in the State Department), Allen Dulles, and Eisenhower, through July 27, would suffice because (a) "nothing was going to happen while he was out of the country," and (b) if war was going to come, America couldn't run the risk of losing the sympathy of the Latin American countries—they would be needed! However, testimony from the embassy in Lima says that Dulles did did not take the news from Suez seriously until the morning of July 28. The night before, that is of July 27, a long cable in which Robert Murphy had a hand had come from Washington embodying one from Eden in London to Eisenhower. (The cable from Eden is dealt with in the next chapter.) But Dulles had already gone to bed. He was given it on waking next morning. At about 8 A.M. Dulles himself knocked at the bedroom door of the Ambassador, extremely agitated. He asked whether it would be unforgiveable if he left for Washington immediately. The Ambassador observed how long it had taken to improve relations between the United States and Peru. Dulles, consulting Eisenhower and Hoover by phone, decided to stay until the ribbon of office was placed on President Prado. He would not stay for the late evening reception. Nasser was beginning to have a distinct effect.

The narration of the diplomatic action will be deferred to a new chapter. A few general observations about Dulles's course thus far are apposite at this point.

Surely, it must be accounted as extraordinary lack of perception and empathy that for nine days after revoking the loan for Aswan, Dulles was away from the State Department and contact with his important ambassadors, and that little or no notice was taken of Nasser's violent speech of July 24! It must betoken, surely, that the Secretary and the President were not realistically in touch with conditions in the Middle East?

The withdrawal of the loan offer was more than a mistake of tactics; it was a political disaster. Did Dulles's action "trigger" the seizure of the Canal? Indubitably, the answer is Yes! Dulles's idolators attempt to rebut this categorical conclusion with the point that the lease was to have expired in 1968. They contend that Nasser and other Arab politicians had even two years before the events of 1956 suggested that the Canal should be nationalized before 1968. It is, of course, quite possible that plans of this kind existed. In the wake of a military, revolutionary seizure of government, especially in the present age of economic planning for a higher standard of living, it would be surprising if such plans for nationalizing industries and other economic resources were not pondered and carefully elaborated with all the attendant blueprints.[34] Indeed, for decades, the status of the Suez Canal, and Egyptian grievances over the fact that it belonged to others, had been an everyday feature of antiforeign, anticolonial agitation. As a matter of fact, early in 1954, Nasser felt out the United States about a conference of signatories on the revision of the status of the Canal. Ambassador Caffery advised against it lest it bring Moscow, a signatory, into the affairs of the Middle East.

But the nationalization of the Suez Canal, let alone the forcible nature of the seizure, was not planned for July 26, 1956, or anywhere near it. Thus, at some other time, in some other circumstances, the Canal might have been acquired by Egypt by such procedures as not to provoke war. Coming when it did, and as a berserk act of defiance, the seizure led directly to war. Dulles's diplomacy was the immediate cause. Defenders of Dulles retort that "the withdrawal of the loan was not the underlying *cause* of the seizure: it only *triggered* it!" As though a trigger were not a cause!

When the shooting was over, but when, also, Nasser, Dulles's bugbear, had been handed one of the most considerable political triumphs of the twentieth century by Dulles, the Secretary admitted to a State Department admirer his "diplomatic" mistake in his timing and manner of rescinding the loan. Dulles had not been able to resist the possibility of a reverberating victory against a "neutral" and the U.S.S.R. But the reverberation was graver than he had bargained for. Even more, the record will show, he would not take the consequences of his own mistake, but tried to thrust them from his own nation onto the shoulders of its much-needed allies. He tried hard to wash his hands of the affair. As some commentator has observed: Egypt was not a principal piece but only a pawn in the game, but, unfortunately, it was forgotten that a pawn can capture the queen and checkmate the king.

Senator J. W. Fulbright had much more prescience than the Secretary of State. He said, on July 28, 1956, "The situation is dangerous and ominous. . . . Our entire civilization is based on respect for international agreements and contracts, and Egypt's action constitutes a real threat to peace." He was not only prescient: he put his finger on the quintessential issue, the sanctity of treaties.

The President's Secretary of State, being put in full charge of decision in everyday incidents by the President, in charge of what some may regard as "trivial" matters—a mere loan—committed the President to a world-shaking series of unpleasant, onerous, and finally extremely dangerous consequences, so dangerous that these two men themselves shrank before them in patent fear. Can a responsible President avoid immersion in the details of foreign policy; and, if not, what kind of man ought to be chosen to handle these matters in his stead?

Now, Dulles liked to score, to play a trump, and to relish and tell about it. It went along with his "brinkmanship." He vaunted in January, 1956, of this "brinkmanship." [35] Those who have accepted his claim—to frown as terrifyingly and as effectively as Mars—whether his flatterers or his critics, are, most probably, making a bad mistake. He was overbearing. He was truculent. He fulminated. But was he bold? It is open to serious debate. Nasser had now taken Dulles to the brink. He flinched. Nasser had seized the Canal as the retort to a diplomatic error committed by Dulles.[36] What would Dulles do about it? Many a staff college general has talked a good battle, but when the live bullets have begun to fly on a real battlefield, has collapsed. Many a teacher of naval tactics has been superb in dictating the tactics of victory in imaginary naval encounters, but has not dared to risk his ship when the enemy's guns have opened up. It was now Dulles's turn: he had talked a policy of action from strength. He now had his chance. The battle was real.

4. DULLES'S FIRST CRUNCH OVER SUEZ

THE NEWS OF NASSER'S SEIZURE OF THE SUEZ CANAL REACHED PRIME Minister Sir Anthony Eden at an unfortunate time. No Greek classic could have more ironically contrived the debut of Fate. He was at dinner, entertaining the young King Faisal of Iraq, and his elderly, wise, and tough Prime Minister, Nuri Es Said, both friends of the West, the builders of the Baghdad Pact, the rivals of Nasser for Pan-Arab leadership if there was to be Pan-Arabism at all. The lives of these two men were under momentary menace from pro-Nasser Iraqi and Iraqi Communist politicians parasitical of Arab nationalism. At the dinner table were seated other Ministers, military chiefs, the leader of the Opposition, Hugh Gaitskell, and a Labour Party legal luminary, Sir Hartley Shawcross.

At about 9:00 P.M., London time, on this July 26, a secretary entered the dining room and brought Eden the evil and ominous news. The Prime Minister at once related it to his guests. All realized, with the deepest misgiving, that a critical change in the world balance of power and in their respective political positions was in the making. Although they could not know it, a train of events had been set in motion which would result in the murder of two of them, King Faisal and his Prime Minister, and in the destruction of Eden's health and career.

Prime Minister Eden moved with impressive energy, decisiveness, and deliberate judgment. Within an hour or so he gathered a Cabinet meeting.[1] The issue of whose world political authority was to prevail in the Middle East, that of Nasser or that of the Western nations, was clearly at stake. Nasser's action was judged by the Cabinet to be the retort to Dulles's refusal of the loan for the Aswan Dam. Eden and his Ministers felt a profound and immediate anxiety to cooperate with the United States.

Prime Minister Eden invited Ambassador Winthrop Aldrich and French Ambassador Chauvel to the Cabinet meeting. But Aldrich was then en route by air to the U.S.A. on leave. Hence his chargé d'affaires, Andrew B. Foster, attended in his place. The meeting lasted two and a half hours, taking stock of "a sudden, unexpected, and highly dangerous situation." Neither the Frenchman nor the American said much, since they had not yet been instructed by their governments, but Eden, Foreign Secretary Selwyn Lloyd, Lord Salisbury, and Lord Home conducted a full review of the incidents of the Canal seizure and the dire effect it would have on the economic life of Western Europe, which depended on the Canal for oil and other cargoes. The military position was analyzed, the Chiefs of Staff were present, among them Lord Mountbatten, First Sea Lord. Above all, now, at the very beginning, Eden stressed the fact that a solemn international agreement had been crudely violated. He urged the need for a concert of action between the three governments, the U.S.A., Britain, and France. He gave Chauvel and Foster the terms of the statement he intended to make to the House of Commons the next day, July 27. They promised to ask their governments to make statements also. The British Embassies in Paris and Washington were alerted. Andrew Foster's account reached the State Department by 5 A.M. on July 27.

President Eisenhower held a Cabinet meeting at 9:30 A.M. on July 27. The seizure of the Canal was discussed. Herbert Hoover, Jr., reported what Dulles had told him on the telephone —mainly "Hold everything until I get back." The meeting also had before it a full account of Eden's statement in the House of Commons, for that statement was made about noon in London, which was 6:00 A.M., Washington time. Washington knew that a grave and somber moment had arrived; Eden considered it intolerable for a man with Nasser's record "to have his thumb on our windpipe." Shortly after the Cabinet meeting was concluded, statements were issued by the State Department. The first, on July 27, was made by Lincoln White, the Department's official spokesman: the United States government had been taken by surprise. Then the Department issued a press release observing that the seizure of the Canal had far-reaching implications for the economies of many nations and that the United States government was consulting urgently with other governments concerned.[2] This reaction was much cooler than Dulles's feeling over the Aswan Dam loan.

In Eden's statement in the Commons, which had helped shape the American pronouncements, he had said, "The unilateral decision of the Egyptian government to expropriate The Suez Canal Company, without notice and in breach of the concession agreements, affects the rights and interests of many nations. . . ." To this, Hugh

Gaitskell, Leader of the Opposition, responded: "On this side of the House, we deeply deplore this high-handed and totally unjustifiable step by the Egyptian government." The reader may notice the phrase "*totally unjustifiable*." The English newspapers were unanimous in their furious resentment at the aggression and in their determination to seek redress and punishment of the culprit. The state of mind of the House of Commons was described by the Parliamentary correspondent of the *Manchester Guardian*, perhaps the most intelligent observer on the scene: "Indignation was the unanimous verdict at Westminster . . . there were no recriminations, no blame from the Opposition. . . ." [3]

Shortly after Eden made his statement to the House of Commons, he called a Cabinet meeting. Among other decisions, it was resolved to invite President Eisenhower to send a representative of the American government to London to discuss the situation and work out a joint policy with the Foreign Secretary and the French Foreign Minister, Christian Pineau, who would get to London on Sunday, July 29. The military chiefs were called into consultation and instructed to prepare a plan for military action to occupy and secure the Canal, if economic and political pressures should fail to stop Nasser's actions and assure the continued international operation of the Canal. Then Selwyn Lloyd saw both Chauvel and Foster once again. The Prime Ministers of the British Dominions were informed of the events.

Another most important and crucial action was taken. Eden sent a telegram on July 27 to President Eisenhower. It arrived at the White House about 4 P.M., Washington time. It is most probable that shortly thereafter the President gave the gist of this wire, and perhaps even read the whole verbatim, to Secretary Dulles, then in Lima, Peru. Until then the President does not seem to have understood the gravity of the situation. It is essential that the telegram be read word for word, as Eden has published it.[4]

> This morning I have reviewed the whole position with my Cabinet colleagues and Chiefs of Staff. We are all agreed that we cannot allow Nasser to seize control of the Canal in this way, in defiance of international agreements. If we take a firm stand over this now we shall have the support of all the maritime powers. If we do not, our influence and yours throughout the Middle East will, we are all convinced, be finally destroyed.
>
> The immediate threat is to the oil supplies of Western Europe, a great part of which flows through the Canal. . . . If the Canal were closed we should have to ask you to help us by reducing the amount which you draw from the pipeline terminals in the Eastern Mediterranean and possibly by sending us supplementary supplies for a time from your side of the world.
>
> It is, however, the outlook for the longer term which is more

threatening. The Canal is an international asset and facility which is vital to the world. The maritime powers cannot allow Egypt to expropriate it and to exploit it by using the revenues for her own internal purposes irrespective of the interests of the Canal and of the Canal users. . . .

We should not allow ourselves to become involved in legal quibbles about the rights of the Egyptian government to nationalize what is technically an Egyptian company, or in financial arguments about their capacity to pay the compensation which they have offered. I feel sure that we should take issue with Nasser on the broader international grounds.

As we see it we are unlikely to attain our objectives by economic pressures alone. I gather that Egypt is not due to receive any further aid from you. No large payments from her sterling balances here are due before January. We ought in the first instance to bring the maximum political pressure to bear on Egypt. For this, apart from our own action, we should invoke the support of all the interested powers. My colleagues and I believe we must be ready, in the last resort, to use force to bring Nasser to his senses. For our part we are prepared to do so. I have this morning instructed our Chiefs of Staff to prepare a military plan accordingly.

However, the first step must be for you and us and France to exchange views, align our policies and concert together how we can best bring the maximum pressure to bear on the Egyptian government.

About this time, the President asked Robert Murphy to fly to London and discover what was happening and "to hold the fort."

On July 28, Hoover had a talk with Hussein in which his main point was *not* that Nasser had committed an act of violence, but that "the U.S. government was shocked by the many intemperate and inaccurate and misleading statements made with respect to the United States by the President of Egypt during the past few days, and particularly in his Alexandria speech on July 26 . . . entirely inconsistent with the friendly relations that had existed between the two governments and peoples and were alien to the frank and cordial relationships which had prevailed among American and Egyptian officials." Therefore, the United States "had no alternative but to protest vigorously the tone and content of these statements." [5]

What an extraordinary response to the injury which had been inflicted on Britain and France! This was, in the words of Edmund Burke, "to pity the plumage and forget the dying bird." Britain and France were incensed about the loss, by force, of a vital artery the shares in which belonged to them and the administration of which was internationally directed. They were alarmed at the further reduction that this meant of their strategic position in the world as middle-sized powers compared with the Soviet Union and America. Herbert Hoover, Jr., and President Eisenhower, instead of expressing a truly powerful objection to the grave injury done to their friends in World War II and now in NATO, and committed in violation of the rule of law, merely sniffed at being insulted! Dulles, on the telephone, was party to this frame of mind. They didn't like the way Nasser talked about them. Their initial nonchalance was most conspicuous. In fact, as the indignation poured in from London, the State Department and the White House began to feel resentfully that the United States was a victim, undeservedly, of other people's troubles! Meanwhile, Prime Minister Guy Mollet sent a strong telegram to the White House requesting Dulles's presence in London.[6]

Dulles was still in Peru. At 7 A.M. on July 28 he was already arrayed in full dress, white tie and tails, and high collar, and in that costume he sweltered through the tropical day. He participated in a Mass for the incoming President, in processions, and in a ceremonial lunch. His face was set with worry. He sat for hours in his seat in the Peruvian Senate. He couldn't avoid taking a furtive look at his watch from time to time—a thin platinum pocket watch on a chain, bequeathed to him by his uncle, Robert Lansing, Secretary of State under President Wilson. He had been on the phone to Hoover and Eisenhower before Mass and had urged them to send Robert Murphy to London at once "just to listen."

At 7 P.M., the ceremonies were ended and Dulles and party left the Senate for the airport. A very heavy rain storm had broken. Dressed as they had been all day, they were rushed to the airport where the plane stood ready to fly. Rather damp about the heels and the bottom of the coattails, Dulles changed dress in the plane. He turned his mind on Suez and began jotting notes on a yellow legal-sized writing pad (he was never without one) which had been fished out for him from some locker. The President had let him know that he should try to find a way out of the difficulty with Nasser; he should persuade the British and French to make a statement on the legal validity of their position and propose to them that they should go to the World Court about it, while keeping payments of the Canal tolls in escrow. Nothing of the nature of an ultimatum must be given Nasser at this moment: he would not back down; war might break out!

The plane touched down in Washington at noon the next day, Sunday, July 29. Dulles sped to the State Department, and called a staff meeting immediately to assemble at his own home. This meeting lasted until nearly eight in the evening. This was physical and mental energy, indeed.

On arrival at the airport, Dulles had announced that he had been on the telephone with Hoover and that (as was usual with him) the incoming cables from the American Embassies abroad had been relayed to him. He said, "The Egyptian action purporting to nationalize the Suez Canal Company strikes a grievous blow at international confidence. The action could affect not only the shareholders who, so far as I know, are not Americans [sic!] but it could affect the operation of the Canal itself and that would be a matter of great concern to the United States as one of the maritime nations."

This statement was made before the Secretary had spoken to President Eisenhower. The President happened to be at Gettysburg for the weekend, though he had delayed his departure a little to talk with Robert Murphy. Dulles called the President on the phone and talked with him for a very long time. Perhaps it did not matter that the President was not in town and would not return until Tuesday, July 31.

In State Department staff meetings before Dulles arrived in Washington, and then, with him, it had been decided to *avoid* the United Nations, for fear of the Soviet Union.

Robert Murphy arrived in London late July 28. On July 29, he met with Sir Harold Caccia, permanent Deputy Under Secretary in the British Foreign Office and Ambassador-Designate to the United States, for a preliminary review of the entire situation. Then he conferred with Andrew B. Foster, the American chargé d'affaires who, the reader will remember, had been called in on July 26 when Prime Minister Eden had heard the news that Nasser had seized the Canal. Murphy was accompanied by various civil and military aides, among them Admiral Walter S. Bone, Commander in Chief of the American Naval Forces in the Eastern Atlantic and in the Mediterranean, where the United States Sixth Fleet was on constant patrol.

Later the British, headed by Selwyn Lloyd, the French, headed by Christian Pineau, and Murphy and his assistants conferred for over five hours beginning in late afternoon, with a break for dinner, and ventilated the main issues, military, economic, financial, and legal. It being Sunday, Eden was away for the weekend.

Robert Murphy's position was to give no engagement whatever at this stage, except the benevolent interest of his country within the general framework of Dulles's statement of July 28, to observe that the governments had not reached the point of considering the use of force, and to explore the legal situation. This last, the legal situation, was a subject highly proper for examination—and it was also most ominous from the standpoint of Britain and France. It was proper because the juridical situation was involved, especially with a legalistic-minded Secretary as Dulles, supported in this by his Legal Counsel, Herman Phleger, was. It was most ominous because legalities could be used to trip up the momentum of Eden and Lloyd, and even the French government, which was rather rougher in impetus in meeting the political realities. Harold Macmillan, Chancellor of the Exchequer, protested to Murphy that the legality was subordinate to the political problems. Pineau later told the National Assembly, disappointedly, that though Murphy was in the highest class of officials he was, nevertheless, unable to undertake commitments. Pineau was extremely suspicious of Murphy's presence and attitude; indeed, he accused him (wrongly) of telling the press about the conversations.

On July 29, a stag dinner was given for Murphy by some of his English colleagues known as the "North Africa crowd," the men with whom Murphy had worked to overcome the opposition to Admiral Darlan when the American forces were to land in Algeria in November, 1942. Murphy is a big man of remarkable charm, humor, and wit, and is a brilliant statesman. Of Irish descent, he used his wisdom henceforth for the interests of NATO and never to spite the English or French. At the party, then, were Harold Macmillan, General Alexander, Sir Harold Caccia, and Sir Roger Makins. At this dinner, Macmillan disclosed to Murphy that the British and French were planning and intended military action in Suez, and they would not yield possession of the Suez Canal to Nasser without it. The two allies refused to be despoiled of their rights and property and above all would not tolerate a *fait accompli* that cut the artery through which their vital oil supplies flowed, through which so much of their normal commerce was shipped, on which their strategic interests depended. and on the basis of which their prestige and influence among the Middle Eastern nations, whether of the Baghdad Pact or others, to so large a degree rested. If necessary, they would fight. This statement of intentions was put in the strongest possible militant form. It was "Munich all over again!" Nasser must now be chased out of Egypt!

Eden was not present at the dinner. Macmillan could not possibly have been making a disclosure merely casually or garrulously or simply as an "inside dopester" to an old friend. Prime Minister Eden must have authorized it, even perhaps urged it, and Dulles got to know it, as no doubt it was the intention that he should. It should be added that, resolute as Eden was to obtain redress for the seizure of the Canal, Macmillan was equal with him in zeal; perhaps Macmillan was even more determined than Eden, from the beginning and all along through the arduous ventures that followed.[7]

Robert Murphy's cable to Eisenhower direct at 9 P.M., Washington time, on Sunday, put the fear of the Lord into Dulles. Rather, let us say, it intensified his fear, since that had already been engendered by his discussion with Eisenhower. The President answered Murphy at once: Dulles would come over. But Dulles was most reluctant to go. He tried to avoid it. He further conferred with the President on Tuesday morning, July 31; after an hour and a half of it, Eisenhower urged him to go at once to London. Dulles himself had by now decided that he must hurry to London for fear of an early war or some immediate military course of action that might lead step by step to war involving the U.S.A. The unison of British voices and the tone in the Commons and the press were particularly alarming. The tone of Pineau's speech of August 3 is evidence of the fact that, at first, Dulles believed he could stay in Washington out of reach and trouble!

Murphy sympathized with the British point of view. But he had to remember, if not express, the Eisenhower-Dulles attitude that force, as in the nineteenth century, would make for trouble. At a lunch for him given by Eden on July 31, with Salisbury, Lloyd, and Macmillan present, he did not encourage their apparent assumption that the U.S. had a common identity of interest in the Canal seizure with the British and French. The latter assumed that in case of trouble (says Murphy), the United States would "take care of the Bear," that is, Russia, but they asked for no other practical help.

Dulles's plane left at about 2 P.M. and arrived early next morning in London. Robert Murphy met him at the airport, and quickly added pungent details and color on what had passed in the last few hours. The two went into conference with Selwyn Lloyd and Christian Pineau, and their various advisers. Dulles had already planned his next step. It was to temporize, to stall, to sense forces and magnitudes, but not without some activity and progress designed to get a grip on the movement of events, to decide better what America ought to do and could do.

On the plane, he drafted a statement for the calling of a conference of the maritime nations interested in the status and operation of the Suez Canal. The only change from this original formulation to his final draft, and almost even to the communiqué finally issued by the three powers, was that Dulles initially recommended that such a conference meet in Geneva, but the British and French insisted that London should be the venue. Their firmness was designed to make it clear that they had been injured, indeed robbed, and that if the despoliator, Nasser, were to be invited (and he was) then he or his representative must be made aware of the austerity confronting him. Dulles did not really mind the change; in fact, he may never have expected that his allies would accept Geneva, though he had hoped Nasser might come to Geneva, if not to London. The change from Geneva to London gave him the occasion to exhibit one of his very, very rare flashes of his peculiar kind of humor: "I'm outvoted," he said, "two to one, by Selwyn Lloyd and Pineau. And in my country, the majority wins."

Meanwhile, Ambassador Henry Byroade was sounding out Nasser and Nasser was sounding out Byroade.

Dulles was now about to begin negotiating the Suez affair with

America's allies in World War II, since then in NATO. These nations, also, just then were further developing the unity of Europe, a movement of cardinal significance for United States foreign policy. Much, perhaps all, of his achievement was inevitably to depend on his convictions and his character, the basic components of his policy, his skills of intellect and exertions of personality. To learn lessons from a story which was mainly one of melancholy, the outcome of which Americans are paying for today and will continue to do for many years yet to come, we need a proper circumspection. Therefore, before confronting the cataract of events, it is essential to assess briefly the character of the unique John Foster Dulles, who now and for the whole crucial period, embodied and deployed the might of America.

First, in spite of numerous treatises and reports that attempt to delineate the status of Secretary of State as it is or ought to be,[8] it varies and always will vary with the character and abilities of the President and the character and abilities of the Secretary. These variables bear no identity, and only an extremely distant similarity, with those of any other pair comprising President and Secretary. In the history of the American Republic there had been fifty-three individual Secretaries and thirty-three Presidents to Dulles's time. When we call each of them "a unique human being," we are simplifying the problem, because the assortment of the qualities of mind, conscience, and character that makes up the personality is multitudinous and subtle. These two unique human beings, holding the offices of President and Secretary of State at any given time, are related to each other and to the events, forces, problems, and opportunities of their own few years together, in the nation and in the world, all in diurnal movement. They are also associated with other people, colleagues in the Administration, friends, foes, idolators, critics, and rivals, and both are men who must enlist the will of several hundred Congressmen and Senators.

What was the relationship between Dulles and Eisenhower? Dulles, under the final mandate of the President, insisted on the exclusive and absolute command of every policy, every decision, and every action that concerned foreign affairs. He demanded it, and he contrived it. He demanded it: on January 21, 1953, he cleared the situation with the President in the afternoon directly following the inauguration. The foreign policy of the United States of America was lodged with Eisenhower and Dulles and with no third person. (But U.S. Secretary of the Treasury, George M. Humphrey, sometimes jogged their elbows!)

He contrived that this understanding should be totally fulfilled. In the course of events, he had Nelson Rockefeller excluded as the President's adviser on Latin American affairs. This act was maneuvered by Herbert Hoover, Jr., since Dulles himself was reluctant to oust a fellow Republican from New York State. For his service Hoover was assured of high place in the State Department, as deputy to Dulles, although Dulles (and few others) had any valuable substantive use for him at this high level. Dulles also had Harold Stassen ousted from his advisership to the President on disarmament. He employed one other man in a position of marked importance very close to him in the department, to the consternation of many men of judgment, merely because he could rely on his total loyalty and his will and ability to ward off any encroachment on the Secretary's supremacy of status and triumph of ideas and his chosen personnel.

Rarely, then, was the Secretaryship so concentrated in the one man. This state of affairs, of course, came about for two reasons already implied: determination that it should be so, and monumental self-esteem, supreme self-confidence. This we must examine again in a moment.

Before we do so, it is necessary to consider the contribution of President Eisenhower to Secretary of State Dulles's hegemony in foreign policy. The Presidency was not the ideal office in which Eisenhower's positive qualities could be valuably deployed. He knew little about the economy, American social conditions, the culture of the nation, the history of the world and of international relations. Some people believed, or for election campaign purposes argued, that his ability to conduct the foreign policy of the country was considerable because "he had met and dealt with all the great leaders of our time." Such observers were referring to Eisenhower's semidiplomatic role as Commander in Chief in Europe and then in NATO (1952-54). However, this situation was hardly a school where the complex and subtle power relationships, traditions, and expectations of over a hundred sovereign nations—all different—could be adequately learned.

Hence, Eisenhower was inevitably and exceptionally reliant on Secretary of State Dulles. He had to be very sedulously briefed in the simplest elements of fact and interpretation, historical and contemporary, if he was to fulfill his constitutional function of assuming responsibility for decisions in foreign policy, and that still in a rather formal and exiguous sense.

For this function, Dulles, the very learned and astute lawyer, was his man. Dulles had the ideal combination of religiosity (even piety), forcefulness, knowledge in scope and depth, energy, stamina, and negotiating skills to produce reverence, acquiescence, and marvel in a President who was himself pious, out of his depth, and overwhelmed almost to enforced passivity by the burden for which he was unprepared in 1952.

What Eisenhower could and did contribute was his world prestige and a general wisdom and prudence which enabled him to exert a twofold influence on his Secretary of State. He had a natural shrewdness capable of spawning questions quasi-critical of Dulles's recommendations. Above all, he had convictions in the light of which he could impart to Dulles the anxieties or pleasure the proper policies gave him and to command what was his will. They were simple convictions, the rule of law in the world; in the United Nations; in America's national interest pursued with some generosity; in the American way of life as the criterion of a good society everywhere.

What Eisenhower lacked Dulles had, and it was almost always decisive in their relationship. For the President's attention was, as it is always compelled to be, dispersed among domestic affairs, executive direction, Congressional relationships, party politics, social functions—and foreign affairs.

Two observations made to me by those intimately connected with the Eisenhower household are pertinent at this point. One observation comes from a person who served the Eisenhower Cabinet in very close relationship with the President. On one of the occasions when Dulles addressed the Cabinet, Eisenhower commented, "He seems to me like a patriarch from the Old Testament." Another comment on Dulles by the President, from a source even more intimate, is this: that when it should come to the writing of the President's autobiography, it would be impossible for the President not to identify himself, "all the way down the line," with Dulles's policies even if some should be regarded as errors. When doubt was expressed of the wisdom of this attitude, the response was that, after all, the President regarded John Foster Dulles as St. Peter.

The Constitution of the United States vests in the President, on the executive side, the exclusive responsibility for decisions on foreign policy. But supposing he does not know what to decide without the prompting of his Secretary of State? Then to all intents and purposes, the power granted by the Constitution to the President becomes devolved upon the Secretary.

Dulles venerated the historic constitutional primacy of President Eisenhower; he respected the fact that the office was filled by popular election. But the question is: How did he, in practice, interpret and implement this respect? The answer is graphically illustrated in his determination never to make the mistake made by his uncle, Robert Lansing, when he was Secretary of State to President Woodrow Wilson. Lansing, who had already served Wilson as a counselor of the State Department, was appointed Secretary of State in June, 1915, and held the office until February, 1920. He had on several occasions been seriously at odds with Wilson, especially on the peace aims of World War I and on the League of Nations, and on the tactics to be employed to secure the support of the Republican party for the Treaty of Versailles. But the break came when Lansing, during the most serious period of Wilson's incapacity through a cerebral thrombosis, called and presided over Cabinet meetings and conducted a high-handed individual foreign policy. Wilson, partly recovered, demanded his resignation. "It would relieve me of embarrassment, Mr. Secretary," President Woodrow Wilson had written to Dulles's uncle, "the embarrassment of feeling your reluctance and divergence of judgment, if you would give up your present office and afford me the opportunity to select someone whose mind would more willingly go along with mine." [9]

Dulles learned the lesson; he made up his mind not to arrive at any decision without talking the matter over with the President first. The memory of Byrnes' dismissal from the Secretaryship by Truman for not reporting frequently enough on his actions was more recent and also vivid. Moreover, Dulles not only respected the President just because he occupied the Presidency; he also admired this particular President. He did not intend to let down either the majestic office or the renowned and likable man. Both office and man added up to Dulles's country. They were the components of his patriotism.

Therefore Dulles always busied himself, in his own fashion, with the education of the President in foreign affairs, who was glad to be informed. He called on him at least every other day—though he was often away from Washington. He had immediate, open, and around-the-clock access, or rather welcome, to the President's office. He was the only Cabinet member who could speak with the President at the White House without a witness being present. Dulles telephoned the President several times a day at need from office to office or home to home, always explaining, expostulating, arguing, asking opinions, making recommendations.[10] He would get up from the conference table wherever a meeting was being held abroad, perhaps several times during a session, and acquaint the President by telephone with the march of the proceedings and the problems the conferees had debated, and he might ask for the President's judgment. He was a diligent and eloquent, if a slow-paced teacher, who often bored his pupil with his prolixity and pedantry.

Dulles's pedagogy assumed a regular pattern. The President had acquired, both as a child in the home of a beloved Mennonite matriarch in Abilene, Kansas, and in recent years, an idealistic, perhaps sentimental, and one could even say sanctimonious, belief in pacifism.* There are some who might prefer to replace the word *sanctimonious* with the word *sanctified*. It cannot be said, in truth, that his attitude meant peace at any price, but the facts and utterances show that it came very close to it. Dulles's own position was in outline similar, except that he was the daily executant of a policy, and, therefore, the price of peace bore more heavily on him, and he was every day, every moment, in motion in the clash of nations and destinies, in intercourse with men who represented the tough corporate interests

* Until he became President, Eisenhower belonged to no religious congregation. Once in office, he joined the church in Washington where Dulles went to Holy Communion, the National Presbyterian Church.

of *their* nations. The President was his client, and he was the President's executive lawyer; the relationship of client and trustee, or board chairman and executive director. Given the President's status as ultimate and sole authority, Dulles had to apply the President's benevolent simplicisms in the conduct, willful, and sometimes wicked, of affairs among power-deploying, egoistic nations. Also he had to advise the President that his interpretation of his simple brief was what the President really ought to want if the nation was to be properly served. And so, for his client's good, he sometimes gave the impression that he himself was the principal, and he took some actions without first telling his client.

Generally speaking, two ways are open to a Secretary of State, in his advisory approach to his President. In the first, he would state the problem, for example, what shall we do about the seizure of the Canal by Nasser, and he would then set out all the facts and the alternative options of action with their merits and demerits; and he would ask the President what policy he chose for the Secretary to carry out. The decision, the choice, would be a creative act of the President. The second way was Dulles's way, and it was as follows: he stated to the President the predicament the nation was in, but he rarely offered open alternative answers which would demand that the President choose and decide. He made a recommendation for a decision for action, and then supported the recommendation with the arguments in favor. It would have required years of private study on Eisenhower's part, impossibly vast and time-consuming in the circumstances, to be able to pick valid holes in the web of Dulles's meticulous and often pedagogical monologue, and even more to offer his own independent pattern instead, consisting of the melding of his convictions with his comprehension of the facts. As we shall see later, there were occasional impulsive divergencies, divergencies by the President, and the President's will prevailed in certain important matters.[11] Usually, however, he was soon induced to follow the path Dulles had prospected, the only path the Secretary had prospected.*

The predominance of the Secretary in relationship to the President had its deep roots in the process of Dulles's arrival in this high office. He had reached it via his friendship with Thomas E. Dewey, his short period as a replacement Senator in 1949, his advisership to Dewey thereafter. He was obsessively ambitious for the office of Secretary of State. He took the opportunity of giving a lecture at the Institut des Études Politiques in Paris, May 5, 1952, in order to seek out Eisenhower, then Commander in Chief of NATO. Lucius

* The letters of gratitude and admiration that passed between the two men, "Foster" and "Ike," or "D.E.," on birthdays, anniversaries of taking office, special occasions, expressed the deep satisfaction and reward each found in working with the other. The President even complained that, by reason of his Germanic origin, he was too tongue-tied to put in words the gratitude he felt.

Clay had suggested this move. Dulles was impressed by Eisenhower's knowledge of Europe; Eisenhower by Dulles's knowledge of the Far East—for example, his part in the negotiation of the Japanese Peace Treaty. Both were agreed on the necessity for containment of Communism and for European unity. Henceforward, Dulles abandoned Taft for Eisenhower. Dewey himself and Henry Cabot Lodge were no match for Dulles as candidates to be Eisenhower's Secretary of State.

It was often said that Dulles was the "best prepared" Secretary of State the United States has ever had. This is an interesting compliment, because it is mysterious. How can its truth or even its meaning, since it is comparative, possibly be weighed? The real problem is "best prepared" for what? For the issues of which era in America's relationships with the rest of the world? For which President? Let us leave this insoluble problem and turn to another: not to unravel the meaning of "best prepared," but to answer the question whether Dulles was "well prepared." Again we must ask, "For what?" Now there is a general *what* and a special *what*. A man may be prepared for the totality of the tasks of the Secretaryship in our own era, as compared with some other man of our own time. Yet he may be as dismally inept for a *specific predicament* that confronts him during his tenure. It is the second aspect that is the truly important one to us; not was Dulles well prepared in 1953 to be Secretary of State in general, but was he in July, 1956, and the following months endowed with the talents and character to meet that specific set of circumstances, those particular momentous forces, the unique men with, for, and against whom he had to deal? The testimony of Dulles's friends regarding his participation in the Suez affair is largely concordant with that of those who manifestly disliked him.

Dulles never forgot or let others forget he had a more than first-class intellect, because he had victoriously matched it against that of others in his law practice and in international politics when on bipartisan missions for the United States government before 1953, and since then as Secretary. He had attended The Hague Conference, as a young man; and then, at thirty, he was in the close circle of Woodrow Wilson's consultants at Versailles during the preparation of the peace treaty of 1919, giving much of his attention to problems of reparations. He had subsequently been an American agent for the fulfillment and modification of the reparations imposed on Germany. From 1937, he had given all of his leisure and more to the Inter-Church Commission on a Just and Durable Peace. From 1940 onwards he had been engaged in bipartisan politics leading to the drafting of the United Nations Charter, and in this he played a substantial part at the San Francisco Conference in 1945. In 1951 he had negotiated the highly complicated and difficult Japanese treaty, though the decision on that treaty was not his but Truman's and Acheson's. And by 1953, he had a vast experience in the practice of law for his firm in many countries, especially those of Latin America, pre-World War II Germany, and France.

Thus—and it is the barest outline of scores of ventures [12]—he was chock-full of the knowledge of events, practices, and the lessons of recent world events. So was his principal negotiator on the "other side" in the Suez affair, Prime Minister Eden. But whereas Dulles bristled with his knowledge, Eden, as an English gentleman who did not like to "talk shop," did not. Dulles most diligently briefed himself for each tactic, each gambit, each conversation beforehand, in rather the same way as he had at the George Washington University Law School boned up on his law cases the night before his exams well into the dawn. He despised Eden for taking his own learning so very lightly, even frivolously (though others would say vainly), since Eden displayed a discreet amusement at Dulles's sermons and speeches to him. In contemplating this relationship one is reminded of some lines from Oliver Goldsmith's *Deserted Village:*

> In arguing too, the parson showed his skill,
> For even though vanquished, he could argue still;
> While words of learned length, and thundering sound
> Amazed the gazing rustics ranged around,
> And still they gazed, and still the wonder grew,
> That one small head could carry all he knew.

Could Eden have done a better job by the very fact of being more pedantically self-briefed? It is very doubtful. He was able to rely fully on the loyal, devoted, and superbly educated career officials of the Foreign Office. Dulles probably understood the Middle East far less realistically than Eden, whose education at Oxford had been in Persian literature and civilization and whose long and immersed experience with the region far outweighed Dulles's few days' trip in May, 1953.

Though Dulles knew France fairly well and Germany fairly well, he knew England much less substantially. Too much can be made of the former, too little of the latter. We come down to two important questions about the preparation of a Secretary of State. First, did he like the country with which he was doing business, not did he know it? Secondly, not what did he know, important as that is, but what part does knowledge play, what part does the power of intellect alone play in the creation of foreign policy and the successful conduct of diplomacy? Dulles came to like Adenauer first, Frenchmen second, and Englishmen last, or, perhaps, the Israelis last, for they were his problem too, although by the time the Suez affair was over perhaps the French leaders had been demoted to the last place in rivalry with the Israelis. Dulles, of course, liked America first. So did Eisenhower, but after that, England.

One of the most critical problems in foreign policy and diplomacy now confronts us. What is the most important talent in this field, the relation with other sovereign nations at a time of tension and conflict, of hope of a more perfect union or fears of war and trouble? It is not knowledge. It is not logic. It is not memory. It is not likes or dislikes. It is the capacity for original, creative, and inventive ideas that solve an impasse, that prevent men and nations from falling over a chasm (a brink) that one has had the insight to perceive sufficiently well ahead of time to avoid death or failure.

This talent is the talent of an artist, and Dulles did not possess it, or rather, was not possessed by it.[13] On this role of distinction, Eden stood far higher than Dulles, and Acheson perhaps higher than Eden. It may be commented when the narrative of the Suez affair is completely recounted here, that Eden showed his failures. Yes, his ventures in this were a failure, though, perhaps, in the short rather than the long run.

Dulles's character was dominated by three elements, his religion or religiosity; his personal and national self-righteousness; and a certain deviousness, characterized by some even, I think unjustly, as conscious duplicity. These three elements he never harmonized; they were at war with each other; he was confused; now one, now the other triumphed in action. He became a mixture between Yankee shrewdness and theological rectitude, in doctrine and in behavior.

Dulles was thoroughly imbued at home and in his father's Presbyterian church at Watertown, New York, with Christianity, though perhaps with rather less of the New than the Old Testament. He was persuaded by the Yankee-type Victorian family despotism of his parents, especially of his forceful mother, to learn the Bible lessons by heart. His parents had hoped that he would become a minister of the church, like his father. He grew up in a liberalized but devout Calvinist creed. His association with church affairs was loose, however, until his visit to the Oxford Conference on Peace in the year 1939.

The proceedings of the learned and practicing theologians,[14] marked by devoutness and some knowledge of world politics, produced in Dulles a profound moral conversion or reversion. Of this there is no doubt. In a sense, he did become a minister and preacher of religion without being ordained, preaching not from a pulpit but from the State Department, and uttering prophecy not in a church but at international political conferences, an Isaiah among world statesmen. In 1943 he was chairman of a church conference which produced a report called "A Christian Message on World Order." The men with whom he was associated were church personages, convened by the Inter-Church Commission, of whose editorial committee he was chairman. Here, in this report, Dulles's attitude is manifested clearly and strongly as Gabriel's triumpet blast, from the very first sentence:

> The Christian church believes and declares to the world that there is a moral order which is fundamental and eternal, and that if mankind is to escape chaos and recurrent war, social and political institutions must be brought into conformity with this moral order. This moral order is the will of God, the Creator of mankind. Basic in it are the love of justice, and the principle that man should love his neighbor as himself.

This prophetic tone already pervades his book, *War, Peace and Change*, published in 1939. By 1950, when a new edition of the book was published, as *War or Peace*, it must be said, with all respect to religion and to Dulles, his ideas of the relationship between nations had become mawkish with the odor of the confessional and his personal salvation, as all may appreciate from reading these works.

Now religion acts upon political behavior in two ways: by the content of its morality, what is believed to be Good and what Evil, what Godlike and what Satanic, and by the fervor of its righteousness. Dulles either had temper and drive and belief as a result of his religion, or he used his religion because it was congenial to his inborn dispositions. Dulles was the only American Secretary of State who had anything resembling a confessor: Doctor of Divinity Roswell Barnes, his Presbyterian pastor.[15]

Some who were associated for many years with Dulles in the church, reflecting on the presbyter within him, and Suez outside him, have wished me to believe that a product of his religion was casuistry of a Jesuitical character. This casuistry, that is to say, caused him to be overzealous, overforceful with his friends, until he compelled them as a reaction to become hostile. But it also alienated them because it simply was casuistry, for this means quibbling, the drawing of fine but suspicious distinctions, the adducing of arguments close to the spurious in cunning interweavement, whereas direct and frank disclosure of ends and means instead was essential to the justice and peace which constituted his Godlike ends. Such characteristics are clearly discernible in Dulles's behavior as Secretary of State. But, as Mary McCarthy has wisely said, "I am driven to the conclusion that religion is only good for good people. . . . For the others, it is too great a temptation to the deadly sins of pride and anger chiefly, but one might also add sloth."[16] Dulles was not slothful.

Religion did not create him out of some baser clay: he was born very much the way he grew up. It made him all the more powerful as a Secretary of State, at least in his ambition for the office, in the purposes he intended it to serve, and the single-minded, dedicated, potent salvationist impetus with which he went about his functions. Dulles's religious feeling burst out especially on the day when the Israelis invaded Sinai, October 29, 1956, and when the British and the French declared they would invade Suez in the days following. As we shall have occasion to note, the exercise of his religious piety on that occasion, as on all others, was not without an admixture of grosser psychological elements. It is a well-attested characteristic of such religious commitment, that when problems are complicated and action difficult, the mind reverts to the simplicities, although they are only remotely relevant.[17]

Everybody who did ecclesiastical and political business with Dulles found his self-righteousness striking. Even his Presbyterian churchmen friends came to demur at his excessive self-righteousness, especially when he did not follow the commandment to "turn the other cheek." They noted with dismay that, on becoming Secretary of State, he preached "massive retaliation" with atom bombs; was adamant against Communist China's entrance into the United Nations and would not even permit American journalists to visit that country; fulminated against neutralism; was reluctant to have a summit meeting with the Russians; and protested that diplomacy must proceed from "positions of strength." His friends in the church believed that strength lay not in arms but in the love of justice, the love of God, and prayers.

This self-esteem, this attitude of exclusive knowledge of eternal things coupled with a sense of moral superiority, is attested to by scores of witnesses. It alienated many people in Congress and the press, and it irritated and antagonized foreign statesmen. It is almost like the temper of Lenin, whom Dulles detested perhaps above all other men excepting Stalin; it is the temper of exclusive salvation. It easily leads to bullying others, even foreign statesmen, if they are deemed too slow, too unzealous, too wrong-headed—in other words, damned! This is what close and quite sober observers during the Suez crisis from the refusal of the Aswan loan to the end of 1956 have said: "A Calvinist atmosphere had come to prevail in the State Department, with the advent of Dulles," and again, "Dulles had the illusion of moral superiority over everybody else, with a pipeline to God." And once again, "He talked as though he had received a special message from on high—from the Almighty." Deep down in his heart, Dulles was of the stuff of the martyrs of the church.

Does not a Secretary of State need moral purpose and drive to fulfill his purpose? Of course he does. A nation is not merely a band of logrollers, or, as St. Augustine phrased it: "A state without a principle of justice is nothing but a band of robbers." A nation ought to play its part in the world to the full extent of its power to produce a better moral order. But the moral order may be ruined by the very man who has vowed his commitment to it if he uses too swift, too brutal, too early, too ambitious, too condescending, and too crafty an approach to the statesmen and peoples of other nations not yet convinced that his principles are in their interests. Above all—and this is where Dulles erred—to argue, browbeat, threaten other nations' leaders as though there were *only one possible moral system*, of which he was the certain and exclusive repositor, is to invite trouble. It is to introduce the temper of the crusade, the religious war, into a world which has outgrown these and adopted a more liberal creed that says, in the words of Tennyson, "God fulfills himself in many ways!"

Every foreign statesman at some time or another felt the lash of Dulles's religion and self-righteousness: in France, Bidault and Mendès-France; in Germany, even Adenauer;[18] in India, Nehru; in Britain, Eden and Selwyn Lloyd, as we shall see; and in the Soviet Union, "One Thousand and Three."

Dulles had been converted to his hatred of the Soviet Union by the usurpation of Czechoslovakia by Russian-inspired Czechoslovaks in 1948. Before this, he had regarded the Soviet Union as just one more nation seeking survival, security, opportunity, and peace. Even in January, 1948, he advocated the inclusion of Russia in a four-power government of the Ruhr! He then became an avid student of Stalin's *Problems of Leninism* and other such literature, whereupon he stigmatized the Soviet Union as the leader of a conspiracy, an international fanatical movement, to take over the world. In doing this, it would replace the Christian way of life by its own Marxist-Leninist-Stalinist creed of atheistic, anti-Christian materialism by any method, including force, available to it. This was the leaders' relentless purpose.[19]

This view introduced an urge for consistency in Dulles's thinking about Russia which did not correspond to Russian realities, especially in a time of rapid change for the Soviet Union and for the rest of the world. He was wrong in his calculations that the Russian people were not loyal to their leaders; at any rate they were not disloyal. He believed that antagonistic pressure was the only way to curb the leaders and to bring about a rift between them and their people. He believed, or said so, that the leadership was about to collapse because of the essential moral unsoundness of the regime. He objected to negotiation with the Russian leaders as Eden proposed; he objected to disarmament talks with them as Stassen proposed; he objected to the summit meeting of 1955; he objected to the "open skies" proposal. However, he believed the leaders of Russia were shrewd, calculating, rational. Therefore he developed the policy of massive deterrence (assisted by Admiral Radford) to curb them, but he hoped to do so without the expense of local wars fought with conventional weapons: he believed the threat would be sufficient. He did not believe their word could be trusted. Whenever they retreated, he inveighed that it was due to their relative weakness, but not to a "change of heart"—to necessity, not virtue.

Having ascribed these characteristics to Russian policy, he was blind, or closed his heart, to the actual geopolitical Russian, its state of mind and purpose. Here, Eisenhower was the more pragmatic. Dulles held to the belief that Russia's economy was in a state of deadly weakness at a time when it was, in fact, fast rising in productivity; and he continued to talk and act anti-Stalinism when the ruler was Khrushchev, an anti-Stalinist himself, preparing for a new look in Moscow's world relations. In the matter of the Aswan Dam, Dulles believed Russian economic weakness would make Russia abandon economic aid to Egypt. And when it came to the point, as we shall show, Dulles could not measure whether Russia was a military threat or not, and therefore, he acted as though she was: in the beginning of November, 1956, he flinched and retreated.

One other trait of Dulles's character in action in foreign policy is variously called deviousness or duplicity. The only divergence on the evidence about this is whether it proceeded from malice aforethought or an innocent defect or mere overfertility of ideas; the consensus is there. The fact is simply that Dulles did not mean what he said, that therefore he did not live up to his promises, that he whittled away his commitments, that he seemed to deceive.

One of Washington's most distinguished journalists asserts: "Since we need news we make many friends at the embassies. The envoys call on us from time to time to give or ask us for help. The most astounding and general reaction to anything Dulles said or did was almost always this: the embassies would call our office and anxiously ask, 'What do you think he meant by what he said? What is there behind it? Does he really mean it?' "

Some ancient philosophers of politics and diplomacy considered deviousness to be a valuable trait, to enable one to deceive the enemy or the other party. Has that not sometimes been accepted as the very definition of diplomacy, especially by the school of Machiavelli—Old Nick, the devil himself? All, of course, for the good of mankind, and only because mankind does not readily see for itself what is its own good? However, Harold Nicolson holds that the better course for the diplomatist is *truth.* He says, "First among these virtues [of a diplomat] is truthfulness." [20] But, on reflection truthfulness is openness and candor of the ends and the means, unless you are actually at war. Yet what is war? A Secretary of State may have warlike feelings even to preserve peace if he is imbued with the sense that he represents God.

It was Hegel who said, "The State is the March of God in the World," but it sometimes seemed as though it was Mr. Dulles who was saying, "The Secretary of State is the march of God in the World."

The attitude antagonized other nations. These traits plus Dulles's knowledge and brilliant and powerful mind were in the service of America and of Dulles's America, not of Britain, not of France, not of Germany, not of any other country in the wide, wide world, but of America with all her virtues—the closest transcription, at the earthly political level, of a Christian Commonwealth. He deployed America's might with corresponding sanctified zealousness and coercive conscientiousness.

Partly in consequence of his missionary zeal, his aggressive evangelism, Dulles grasped at the role of teacher of the public and of Congress. It may, perhaps, be exaggerated to say that he was the most garrulous Secretary of State since the foundation of the Republic, but, with fairly close rivalry from Bryan and Cordell Hull (who served for some twelve years against Dulles's seven), he was the most talkative and self-advocating, in volume and pride. His outpouring of explanation and advocacy did not always serve his cause well, because it was too obviously self-serving and was based on unsound premises and evasions. It did not always advance the public's knowledge of the truth, for his perceptions were often erroneous and he was suspected of going beyond the office of education to manipulation of his audience on behalf of his purposes. Nor did it win over the newspaper world or wash away Congressional mistrust: men in these quarters did not like his domineering conceit or his trickiness in evading commitment.

Dulles was an America Firster [21] in the sense that America's interests and America's will in world affairs—"We want it this way!"—came overbearingly in his mind as soon as any practical problem presented itself. Anyone who couched the Republican platform of 1952 in its heavily distorted denunciation of the Acheson-Truman foreign policy record as Dulles did, in its words, its intent, and its temper, merits that designation.[22] Is it an extenuation to say that, after all, he was only participating in a campaign where hard knocks are in order, are even necessary? If it is, where then is the man of God, the Calvinist, the churchman, and the "moral law"?

Deliberately, he sought the primacy, the hegemony and domination of American leadership and American ethics in the world. He believed in foreign aid; in American responsibilities and burdens everywhere in the world; above all, in the contest with the Soviet Union; in the unity of Europe (on American terms and under American pressure); in the union of America, Britain, and France against the Soviet Union (and therefore he was an anti-neutralist). All these purposes were to be furthered by American strength, supplied with the deterrent of nuclear weapons and using a strategy of "massive retaliation." Thus he pursued a peaceful world of sovereign nations leading an American-patterned way of life and kept peaceful by American assistance and American power and American advice. From the 1930's he had so espoused the idea of "peaceful change" to adjust conflict situations by negotiation, discussion, conciliation, retreat before the rising forces as actually to defend Nazi Germany's claims! [23] One new instrument was now available for this process of "peaceful change," the United Nations, which would lead, he thought, to a Rule of Law that is peace.

It is of prime interest to notice here a view that constituted a most dangerous tenet for a future Secretary of State: that the international law principle, indeed, the fundamental one, the sanctity of treaties, *pacta sunt servanda*, was simply a device of satisfied nations to maintain their dominance.

Dulles was deeply imbued with anti-imperialism, and, as an anticolonialist, committed to remove existing dominations so that all countries might enjoy their full independence and sovereignty. This was an intense *motif* in the American tradition. Every American has it bred in his bones from infancy. We always remember July 4, 1776, and we cannot forget Bunker Hill and the Boston Tea Party. Nor can the immigrant groups forget the oppressions their forefathers suffered at the hands of Britain or France or Russia or Poland or Germany. "The sins of the fathers are visited on the children to the third and fourth generation."

The Secretary disliked the British. What was England to him? Yes, it had given birth to his church, his Bill of Rights, his Constitution, it had even given birth to his nation. It was at a conference at Oxford in 1937 that he had "got religion" for the second time in his life. But he did not like England's ancient predominance in the world. He found England's imperialism and colonialism distasteful, especially when he talked to the envoys of other nations behind the backs of Englishmen. These envoys have apprised me of this, some of them with great anti-British glee. The English had been first in the world, and Dulles remembered how obstinate her leaders were in their interpretation of the freedom of the seas, in World War I, against the claims of America and Woodrow Wilson. He recalled the canny, clever tricks of that old rogue, Lloyd George, when he (with the assistance of Clemenceau of France) had made rings around his revered chief at the Versailles Peace Conference in Paris, martyred him until they perverted the holy Fourteen Points of the New World into a piece of Old World Revenge! It was now America's time to be first, by reason of her ideals, by reason of her powers, by reason of her clean-cut ability not only to bear moral responsibilities but to go out and seek them.

The shape of the world was to be made in America's vision, not England's. For centuries the world had been regulated by the *Pax Britannica*, the British Peace, supposedly supported by the British navy; now in the twentieth century Dulles projected the *Pax Americana*, and nuclear weapons would be its rod.

It is not useful to respond to this that Dulles considered, as he often proclaimed, the Anglo-American alliance as a keystone of his foreign policy. In an alliance, everything depends on your conceit about the eminence of your own nation in the world, what others owe to it, and the value you place on your partner. Dulles did not like Britain or Eden. He liked Dulles's and Eisenhower's America.

He mistrusted the urbanity, the polish, the aristocratic glamor, even if now dimmed, of its society, which was still class-ridden as compared with American society. He rather distrusted the fact that Englishmen liked Ike and that Ike liked the English! Look at the way Eden sat at international conferences—as though he were being photographed by Karsh and posed by Otto Preminger! Just like Dean Acheson—you couldn't tell them apart!

The most serious disqualification suffered by Dulles in the actual negotiations over Suez was that the transactions had to be carried through with Sir Anthony Eden, even though the intermediary was often Selwyn Lloyd, his Foreign Secretary. All of Dulles's preparation for the "fulfillment" of his foreign-relations function broke down on this stone. He detested Eden and Eden detested Dulles. The direct and almost universal evidence of those who knew both of them is clear, direct, and incontrovertible. This mutual aversion is an important fact and the reasons for it must be briefly stated.

Since our principal theme is the role of Dulles in the Suez affair, Eden's character and qualifications need not be appraised in so direct and methodical a way as Dulles's: his weaknesses and strengths will become amply apparent. Eden had enjoyed many years of high office as Britain's Foreign Secretary and then as Prime Minister. He was a handsome and polished figure with beautiful, even extravagant, Oxford diction. Although ten years younger than Dulles, he had some historic successes to his credit, including his participation in the decisive policies made during World War II when Dulles was only a distant off-stage theorist. Dulles would gladly have accepted the applause that had come to Eden for his leadership in the League of Nations and for his resignation from the British Cabinet in 1936 when Neville Chamberlain over-appeased the dictators. Here was for Dulles a world rival running the foreign policy of a country that was on the downgrade in world power. Eden had had the first place; now the first place belonged to America, represented by Dulles, with all his character and principles.

What might have commenced as merely emulation or rivalry, perhaps theoretical criticism, or mere captiousness, was transformed into damaging antipathy, aversion—a state of mind which connotes a refusal to listen closely and a determination to outreach, or at least not to be outreached by, each other. This situation came about as a result of Eden's successes in some diplomatic transactions where Dulles was unable to succeed and where his failure was caused by his own personal deficiencies. In one matter which is mentioned below, it will be seen that an action by Eden contributed to the trouble.

The mutual repugnance began before Dulles became Secretary of State; in fact, Eden made an appeal to Eisenhower, early in 1952, not to appoint Dulles if he became President. Eden's attitude probably stemmed from the Japanese Peace Treaty negotiations between the U.S. and Great Britain in 1951, when Dulles left a reputation for calculated duplicity. The action resented was not a transgression against Eden but against one of his predecessors in the Foreign Office, Herbert Morrison of the Labour Party. In the briefest possible compass the issue was this. Dulles had promised Herbert Morrison that he would bring no pressure on Japan to recognize the regime of Chiang Kai-shek. Dulles asked Morrison not to announce this publicly for the time being. Morrison agreed. The question of recognition was to be left as a free matter for the Japanese government. These were the terms of an agreement between Britain and the United States. The commitment was unmistakable. But when Dulles returned to the U.S.A. he bowed to Senatorial pressure (he said). He strongly urged Japanese Premier Yoshida to recognize Chiang Kai-shek, and gave the impression that Morrison had previously agreed to his action. This was untrue. It was a matter of some moment to Britain that she had recognized Communist China and the United States had not, and Dulles had strongly objected to British policy. Dulles even squeezed a letter out of Yoshida that he would recognize Nationalist China. Morrison said of this tactic: "I may be forgiven if I resolved there and then not fully to trust Dulles again." [24] Dulles evidently would not either face the forum of the Senate or face Morrison with his own grinding political necessity. Dulles won his Japanese case. But in politics among nations there is no "open-and-shut case," which, alone, when closed off, closes off the interests of the parties or of third parties and other related concerns of the participating nations. Actually, I cannot even repeat the epithets Morrison himself applied to Dulles, and he thought them just. It is beyond doubt that Eden heard Morrison's actual words, since Foreign Secretaries of the same generation, even if leaders of rival British political parties, are on friendly terms. Foreign offices, chancelleries, preserve the record of the trustworthiness of foreign diplomats and statesmen. When Eden returned to office, he was always reminded of Dulles's deception.

Furthermore, when Dulles was preparing the Japanese Treaty, he called on Eden in London, since Britain had an important stake in the Far East and had made substantial contributions in World War II in that region. Dulles, to his great credit, was determined not to repeat the damaging severities of the Treaty of Versailles against a conquered people. Of course, as a Wilsonian he was inclined to idealism in the treatment of post-war Japan and up to a point he was not only right in this, but most laudably right. Eden, who had achieved a hero's distinction in the trenches in France during World War I and had lived through the disillusionment of Wilsonianism and had worked (but in vain) to get the American government to obstruct the Japanese invasion of China in the 1930's, was not so tender-hearted. At dinner with Eden, Dulles explained that he was not seeking to be vindictive. A very heated five minutes was suffered by both when Eden asked, "What do you want to do, tear up Versailles and all the other treaties that went along with it?" It is said that out of this there grew up a fable of the aversion of Dulles for Eden. It was no fable. The altercation fed the aversion.

Thus, Eden had been so anxious about Anglo-American relations, that on hearing the rumor that Dulles might possibly be appointed as Secretary of State, he had been considerably alarmed. Early in 1952, at NATO headquarters in France, he had visited Eisenhower, with whom he had had long and warm and heroic relations (in World War II and its aftermath). This meeting, perhaps, occurred after Dulles had paid his call on Eisenhower in the same place to sound out the possibilities of his becoming Secretary of State. Eden confided to Eisenhower that if he became President he hoped he would not appoint Dulles to be Secretary, "because I do not think I would be able to work with him"; [25] but he had no luck. On the other hand, some of Dulles's own more sensitive officials testify that, although Eden was a Prime Minister, Dulles talked down to him, and some add that he "despised" him. Of course, it could not have been long before Dulles learned of Eden's attempt to thwart his ambition, though not necessarily from Eisenhower directly.

In 1954, Dulles tried to induce Britain and Eden into military action in Indo-China, to save the French regime there and its soldiers at Dien-bien-phu. Eden and Churchill did not wish to participate in such a venture. But, above all, Dulles was utterly vague about his intentions. What military action did he wish to take—naval action, assault from the air, the use of troops on land? In what magnitude? Over how long a period of time? Exactly when would it start? Eden simply could not get a commitment from Dulles. The Secretary of State was constantly zigzagging from what he personally proposed or hoped, when pressed by Eden, to what the Joint Chiefs of Staff might recommend, back to what the President would endorse, back to what Congress would permit, since the President had repeatedly declared, when faced with decisions for military action, that he must consult Congress! This may have been a genuine reason for vagueness or it may have been an alibi; or possibly Dulles, as very frequently happened, had not thought his course through thoroughly. But Eden and Churchill balked at such imprecision and inconstancy.

How then was the Indo-Chinese affair solved? By Eden's energy and tenacity in negotiating with the Russians and Chinese at Geneva. From this conference, Dulles actually *fled* back to Washington, sending Bedell Smith to represent America. Yet while he sulked and barked, Eden and Mendès-France fashioned a settlement at the seventeenth parallel. This partitioning of Vietnam at least saved South Vietnam from being altogether overwhelmed by the communists, and allowed for the possibility of tolerable independent regimes for Laos, Cambodia, and Thailand. All this happened, too, after the State Department and White House had shouted across the world: (1) that they would not allow a single free man to become subject to communist rule (in Indo-China), and (2) that if Vietnam went, then all the countries in that part of the world would fall one after the other like a row of dominoes! Eden managed, at any rate, to save many millions from communist rule, and to limit the loss to about one-half of a domino. A truly amusing touch, *pour rire*, to this indeed important episode is provided by a certain idolator of Dulles. He said, "The relations of Dulles with Eden were good until the Indo-Chinese affair, when Anthony decided to go off on his own!"

Dulles had wished to set up the South East Asia Treaty (SEATO) as a leverage over North Vietnamese Communist Ho Chi Minh and his Chinese supporters; Eden postponed the treaty lest it might make any Indo-Chinese solution impossible. Dulles claimed Eden had promised him the former; Eden completely denied any obligation. The spectacle was unpleasant.[26]

Next Dulles was most laudably concerned, as other Americans had been, notably Truman and Marshall and Acheson, with the unification of Europe. The questions have always been, how far, how fast, by what institutions? When the French, in 1950, developed the plan of a European Defense Community, a long step indeed was projected. It was nothing less than the merging of the armies of the Western European nations, above all of West Germany and France, in one defense force. Its fundamental purpose, besides protecting Europe from the Soviet Union, a matter of supreme interest to the United States, was to overcome at last the millennial enmity between France and Germany. Other steps, economic and cultural, had already been taken along what are called "functional" lines; that is, preparations had been made for a monetary union, a tariff union, other defense alliances, an organization for economic cooperation. But the EDC, as it came to be called popularly, would make a vast contribution to the external strength and internal peace of Europe.

It happened that Mendès-France became Prime Minister at the crucial time for decision on this issue, and he knew, as Dulles could not possibly know, even though he had bicycled in France as a boy, that the Assembly would not provide a majority for ratification. He knew that if he pressed it to do so, the inevitable negative vote would overthrow his cabinet with all the good it could do in other paths of legislation and executive policy. Dulles bullied and insulted him and insulted France, in a sulky manner, with the threat of an "agonizing reappraisal," referring perhaps to the withdrawal of economic and military aid. That very phrase is quintessentially characteristic of Dulles. He returned to the United States, and the EDC collapsed. He did nothing substantial to put the pieces together again, nor could he carry out his threat of "agonizing reappraisal."

Eden, however, by a remarkable diplomatic *tour de force*, found a way to bring Western Germany into the comity of Western Europe through an arrangement falling short of EDC, but nevertheless linking the European armies in defense policy and tactics and again linking this association with NATO. Part of the arrangement was the commitment, for the first time in British history, of a substantial contingent of British troops to be stationed in Europe in peacetime.

Dulles had failed; Eden had succeeded. The rough and clumsy tactics of a courtroom trial had collapsed. Rather than nothing at all, the second best, pursued with energy of enterprise and delicateness of diplomacy, had succeeded. Even Dulles could not avoid, for his own purposes, hailing Eden's achievement as a hard blow to Soviet hopes of world domination.

Thus, it was difficult for Dulles to communicate with Eden with any engaging candor or to concede successes to him. Eden, for his part, could not easily trust Dulles and he could not understand either his conversation or his writing. It is well to bear in mind the judgment of Harold Nicolson, to rebut a potential charge that the personal element in the settlement of international conflict is being exaggerated, as well as to challenge the view that impersonal forces, even expressible in mathematical equations, determine the issues. He says:

> Yet it must be realised that the texture of any international negotiation is formed of diverse strands, some stretching back into the remoter recesses of national tradition, some being derived from previous commitments, and some owing their presence within the fabric to personal antipathies, chance misunderstandings, and sudden improvisations. The structure of any international crisis is organic rather than artificial; it is the result of gradual growth; and however much one may seek to detach and mount the specimens for purposes of exposition, it must never be forgotten that at the time they were part of the thought, feeling, and action of sentient beings, exposed to all the impulses and fallibility of human nature.[27]

How true, too true, of Dulles and Eden over Suez.

If, then, considering all we have said about Dulles's talents and character, we find that it was difficult for him to do business openly and equally and candidly, trustworthily or trustingly, with Eden, it is also both deplorable and significant that when Dulles's article on "brinkmanship," distasteful if true, and vexing if merely cocky, appeared, Eden was compelled to exclaim, "That terrible man, that terrible man!"

To solve a conflict that affected them in common, gravely though not equally, required especially easy sympathetic and sensitive communication. All signs point to this conclusion: well prepared as Dulles may have been for anything or anybody else, he was ill equipped to handle Nasser's seizure of the Canal and Eden was not minded to surrender it. A Cordell Hull, a Marshall, an Acheson might have contrived the way of justice and peace, offering a choice that Eden could have accepted. For none of these men would have identified America and the world with himself as Dulles did. Identification with one's office being essential, each would have identified, but by subordinating his personality to the demands of the office, not elevating his personality above it.

* * * * *

Thus intellectually equipped and by character disposed, Dulles arrived in London Wednesday morning, August 1, 1956, with a very small staff including his Legal Counsel, Herman Phleger. Robert Murphy left shortly after the arrival of Dulles. Almost immediately Dulles went into session with Selwyn Lloyd and Christian Pineau. Lloyd and Eden claimed forthrightly that this maritime powers' conference being held was at their initiative. They did not wish Dulles to claim sole credit for it, as he was doing, for this made them look like warmongers, anxious to win back Suez only by force.

The situation Dulles faced was as follows. The British and French were angry, resolute, and even menacing. Eden's telegram to Eisenhower shows this temper. Macmillan's declaration to Robert Murphy attests it further. Public opinion in Britain was aroused with strong emotion against Nasser's act, described as "brigandage." In France the revulsion of feeling and determination to get redress was perhaps even angrier and sterner, because Nasser, who had committed the outrage, was an active accessory and sponsor of the Algerian rebellion. The reactions of Britain and France were probably all the more exacerbated because official Washington responded so slowly and so mildly to the indignity and injury visited upon them. Washington reacted, indeed, as though it were in a torpor.

By August 1, the British and French had undertaken some measures of economic reprisal against Egypt (the freezing of Egyptian funds), and Dulles knew, also, that orders were being carried out for a show of British and French naval force in the Mediterranean.

About the same time, American Ambassador Byroade, in Cairo, had seen Nasser, and whether as a result of the conversation with him or by reason of advice of wiser and more liberal Egyptians such as Foreign Minister Mahmoud Fawzi, Nasser had begun to croon a conciliatory song. Byroade took no threats to Nasser from Dulles, but he was instructed by him to make clear to Nasser some possible consequences of his act of force. Most importantly, as a result of considered and resolute policy, Byroade's efforts were directed to keeping the Canal open because: (1) the closing or abuse of it would weaken the commerce of Western Europe; and (2) if the Canal were closed or not efficiently run, the British and French might have a clear concrete cause of war on the grounds that the Convention of 1888 had been violated. So long as the Canal remained open, Dulles's problem, to avert war and to secure justice, was still not insoluble. Byroade reinforced Nasser's own cleverness and that of Fawzi in the realization that Egypt dared not do otherwise than keep the Canal in proper operation. What Byroade sought, in many conversations, was to bring home to Nasser what he, a fanatical nationalist, had entirely missed in the calculation he and his advisers had made of British and French reactions to the seizure of the Canal. They had expected the response to be quite strong, even extreme, but to be concerned only with recovery of the economic losses of the shareholders and the assets of the British and French governments. Nasser and they had utterly miscalculated, as with Israel, the deep emotions that were to burst out in Britain and France, the national feelings of dignity and honor and the concern for their power position in the world related to their rights in the Canal and the fact and manner of their dispossession.

The noise of the international reactions, as well as second thoughts about what Egypt could gain by good behavior and lose by bad, caused Nasser to announce in a conciliatory tone that the Canal would be kept in proper operation according to the Convention of 1888.[28] This move did not solve the problem he had raised by his seizure. But it gave Dulles hope and latitude, and he proceeded to use the principle as a means of checking any act of war by his allies.

Dulles entered into vehement discussions with Lloyd and Pineau and their respective advisers. Pineau was so powerful in his pleading for strong measures against Nasser, that an American official present went so far as to disbelieve that his eloquence could be caused by anything but the Foreign Minister's ownership of Suez Canal shares, as though there were no other causes, such as patriotism!

On August 2, Dulles lunched with Eden at Downing Street and reviewed the problems in depth.

This brings us to a crucial point upon which very much hinges. Eden had for some hours been in possession of a letter from President Eisenhower, evidently in answer to the telegram Eden had sent to him on July 27, in addition to the serious, warlike tidings Murphy had reported and Dulles had interpreted. The discussion between Eden and Dulles revolved about the telegram and the letter, which were the first fairly full statements of British and American policy on the Suez affair.

The cardinal issue was the use of force *some time, eventually* against Nasser. For the solution to the problem of the violation of the Convention of 1888 was made to depend, by Britain and France, on whether a mere unilateral promise by Nasser to respect the spirit and letter of the Convention could be relied on. If not, reliance must be sought in some kind of international government of the day-by-day *use* of the Canal. Then the issue of some kind of coercion or pressure upon him became the core of the problem, their problem and America's problem also. Did Dulles refuse to face this problem, some form of coercion on Nasser in order to establish a regime to replace the one he had torn down for his own national and personal purposes, or possibly to re-establish the shaken system? Up against the brink himself, forced by Nasser, of all people, at last, what was Dulles prepared to do? We shall see.

As Dulles mounted the stairs of his plane in Washington on July 31 to fly to London, a messenger from the White House handed him a letter from President Eisenhower. An aide, taking out the letter from the unsealed envelope, glanced over it. It was typewritten and covered three and a half smallish pages, but it was superscribed "My dear Prime Minister," and signed "Dwight D. Eisenhower," whereas the correspondence between these two was usually superscribed "My dear Anthony" and signed "Ike E." (It is possible, then, that this letter was not composed by the President, but by Dulles.)

First, this is what Eden reported to be the gist of the letter.

> Mr. Dulles brought with him a message from the President, who was emphatic upon the importance of negotiation. *The President did not rule out the use of force.* He recognized the transcendent worth of the Canal to the free world and the possibility that *the eventual use of force* might become necessary in order to protect international rights. But he felt that every possibility of peaceful settlement must be exhausted before this was done.[29]

General Eisenhower, who graciously accorded me a longish and animated conversation on June 5, 1962 (supported by discussions with Colonel John D. S. Eisenhower, in charge of preparing his father's *Memoirs*), said that I might repeat what he had told me. This includes the letter he sent to Eden by Dulles, the letter, that is to say, of which the gist as expressed by Eden appears above. (I took notes as the General read the letter itself twice for my convenience and his emphasis, and again when he read me a letter he sent to Churchill some four months later, embodying the same terms as this letter of July 31. It is almost sure that when the original is published by General Eisenhower himself there will be some discrepancies, because I was not able to take the whole text down word for word. I believe, however, that I have all of the significant and critical phrases in this account.) The message was as follows:

> I have news through Murphy, you, and Macmillan, about the Canal seizure and your views thereon. I cannot overemphasize my conviction that before any action is taken, you must have a conference of maritime powers at the very least. This should be educational to the whole world. This is a must.
>
> We (the U.S.A.) are committed to the United Nations organization. You must avoid the use of force—at least *until* we have proved to the world that the United Nations organization cannot handle the problem. We must keep our eye on Russia, so that our action must be especially lawful. Thus by logic and tactics we will win the world over to our side. We must remember the resentment that force will produce everywhere, and even if Nasser were overthrown, we would be faced with the problem of guerrilla warfare.
>
> Now your initial victory might be easy, but eventually the situation would be very different. [This refers to eventual guerrilla warfare by the Egyptians.] I emphasize the unwisdom of force *now*. If you are to use force *later*—then you must think of other ways to solve it to have a clearly acceptable justification; otherwise the Russian and world reaction would be severe.
>
> Therefore, to review the problem all over again, I am asking Foster to fly over and meet you. Every peaceful means must be exhausted *first*. *If* those fail—the world will understand.
>
> Any war would cause bad feelings and harm the standard of living of all nations. So one must be fearful lest his actions should lead to this.

To these notes, there is a supplement in a letter Eisenhower sent to Churchill on November 23, 1956, evidently in answer to Churchill's plea that the British and French, being in position at Suez, should not be compelled to withdraw under pressure by the United States. Eisenhower in his answer recalled the letter of July 31 to Eden.

> I asked him to avoid the use of force *until* it was proved to the world that the U.N. could not achieve a settlement. We must be especially aware of the position that Russia would take in the world situation if we invaded Nasser. It would be *power politics*, and we are not in favor of that. Nasser is an Egyptian Mussolini and we shall have to curb him somehow. But force, invasion, is not the way to correct the situation.

It is abundantly clear that Eisenhower did not rule out the use of force altogether. If Eden's précis of Eisenhower's letter is a little bleak, it is perfectly truthful. President Eisenhower seemed later to believe that he forbade the use of force *altogether*, or he may be wrong about his memory of it, but the letter shows that although force was not to be used at once, a time might come when it would have to be used. Deliberation, conference, negotiation, and recourse to the U.N. must come first. Eisenhower and Dulles may have made up *their* minds that they would never agree to force under any circumstances; but *they did not say so*. Yet if they had so made up their minds this was their crucial decision. The words italicized in the two letters as given above are the critical, conditional words; the italics are mine in order to bring out their full significance. Once again: if they had made up their minds that force was not to be used, then they did not say so candidly and immediately.

It must be added at this point, for unmistakable emphasis, that the President took a more active part in the Suez affair than in other diplomatic conflicts, since the principles to be applied seemed to him more than usually simple and self-evident. But the President seemed to believe it not necessary to count their cost to the nation and the world, while his Secretary was caught halfway between this *sancta simplicitas* and the brutalities of *realpolitik*.

The heart of the problem for Dulles consisted of four responsibilities: (1) to clarify the legality of the situation; (2) to set up conferences to find a negotiated way out of the conflict; (3) to postpone the use of force as long as possible; (4) to avoid the use of force altogether if possible. Courses 1, 2, and 3 were procedures of temporization, postponement, in the hope that some solution could be found, that some answer would "turn up." That is an appropriate phrase, seeing the difficulty of satisfying the maritime powers' demands for their rights as well as Nasser's fierce and intransigent claims of Egyptian sovereignty. Course 4 tended to become the one which Dulles took in precedence above 1, 2, and 3.

Now whatever Eisenhower may have had in his mind about the exclusion of force (and we have seen that his expression of such exclusion was very far from being absolute), his spokesman and plenipotentiary, Dulles, went forward, day after day, week after week, directly in conversation with Selwyn Lloyd, Christian Pineau, Anthony Eden, and Guy Mollet, and indirectly through the American Ambassadors in London, Washington, and Paris, saying something else markedly different.

It would have seemed to be incumbent on Sir Anthony Eden, on receipt of the letter from Eisenhower, to have taken its temper to require his own immediate personal visit to Eisenhower and a colloquy with him, Dulles, and Selwyn Lloyd. He should not have left Washington until he had a private binational agreement on paper to take the place of Eden's telegram of July 27 and Eisenhower's letter of July 31. Dulles and his experts in the United Nations Division of the State Department knew that, for revenge and chauvinism, Nasser and his friends of the Afro-Asian bloc would vote down any claim for justice by the British and the French in the General Assembly and that Russia for mischief and spite would veto it and thereby further her own purposes of power politics. Any agreement about the future management of the Suez Canal satisfactory to Britain and France would never be acceptable to the United Nations for these two reasons. In other words, for Dulles to say, "Do not use force unless the U.N. says you may coerce Nasser!" was tantamount to a submission to Nasser. This point, then, Eden should have clarified, especially recalling the Japanese Treaty!

Let us turn now to Eden's account of this period of negotiations. He had noticed that neither in the initial reaction between July 27 and July 30 in Washington, nor in the messages received from Eisenhower, nor in reports from the British Ambassador in Washington was there any American suggestion of applying *political pressure on Nasser*. The U.S.A. seemed bent on legality and conferences in order, as Eden says, "to bring the moral pressure of combined opinion to bear upon Colonel Nasser . . . but it took no account of the probability that Nasser would show himself impervious to such pressure." [30] The State Department's course, partly out of ordinary prudence—that is to say, to win its case on grounds of argument and law—and partly to undermine the case for any coercive measures against Nasser, was to raise the issue of the legality of Nasser's seizure and the legality of any riposte thereto by the Western powers.

The search for legality was especially a product of the fact that Dulles was by profession a lawyer, experienced in varied and devoted practice of the law, who fancied himself an authority on international law. His Legal Counsel, Herman Phleger of San Francisco, who was very intimately involved in making policy with Dulles, was, of course, a lawyer too. Phleger had met Dulles by chance during the United Nations Charter Founding Conference in San Francisco in 1945. They grew to like each other. Dulles took long before he confided in other people (for example, Herbert Hoover, Jr.): he confided in Herman Phleger very soon and very deeply—in my opinion, as far as legal acumen and general judgment go, rightly. But two lawyers, devising the foreign policy of a nation, are apt to give legal technicalities and attitudes the primacy over diplomatic necessities and forces and opportunities, even if they do not deliberately prefer the former as a means of stalling. But the law of the matter, especially seeing that the United Nations might be called on some day to take a hand, had, of course, to be discovered. Eisenhower even mentioned an appeal to the World Court.

When this process of searching for the law was undertaken in

Washington two dicta became common. One was Eisenhower's. It ran somewhat thus. "You, Eden and Mollet, will never get the United States to support you where your legal position is so flimsy. We in the U.S.A. are accustomed to the idea of eminent domain, that is the taking over by the government of private property for public purposes with compensation established by an arbitration tribunal or court. Unless you can prove you are not going to get compensation from Nasser, we can hardly go to war on that basis. The American people would not understand it. If you, the British, assert, leaving the property issue aside and regarding simply the management of the Canal, that Nasser cannot keep the Canal open—well, we think he can. And until it becomes actual, until it is proved true, that he cannot keep the Canal in operation, there is nothing we, the United States, Britain, and France, can do. If he should fail to keep the Canal open, a different situation would arise."

Dulles and his legal friends came to take a different though a related stand. It was connected with the British position as stated by Eden in the House of Commons on July 30. The statement was the foundation and heart of the British policy as it was of British rights under the Convention of 1888. It asserted a position which Dulles had to wrestle with; unless he could cause Eden to surrender or Nasser to submit, there might well be war. Eden had said:

> No arrangements for the future of this great international waterway could be acceptable to Her Majesty's Government which would leave it in the unfettered control of a single power which could, as recent events have shown, exploit it merely for purposes of national policy.[31]

This position he made clear beyond any doubt to Dulles, and Dulles knew also that the House of Commons, in which at that time there was a practical unanimity of all three political parties, heartily agreed with Prime Minister Eden. The rights of nations in international law are not limited to the rights they enjoy within their own geographical territory; they have rights outside their boundaries also, by treaty and by the customary law of international relations.

Therefore, the legal officers of the State Department and Dulles evolved the second dictum: by the Convention of 1888 and by universal usage since that time, that is for almost seventy years, custom has confirmed the benefits and rights of all nations moving ships through the Canal; the Canal is thus established as an international public utility. Some time later, Dulles used the language of which American constitutional and administrative law has become so enamored, referring to the Canal as "a utility *impressed* with a public interest." This was a variant of "a utility *affected* with a public interest," the present public being "all maritime powers" and especially "the signatories of the Convention of 1888 including Egypt." Dulles and his friends may have remembered their law school days when they had read the classic case of *Munn vs. Illinois* (1891) and the Supreme Court's decision about public utilities affected with a public interest. They reflected, certainly, that on the basis of the free passage internationally guaranteed by the Convention, the commerce of the world, the prices of goods, the rates for freight, even the size and type of ship that had been developed—a whole pattern of trade and living—had taken shape.

It was this legalistic aspect that Robert Murphy had been instructed to maneuver with, to the misgiving of the British and French. For they saw from the outset, as perhaps Dulles did, though pretending not to, that the issue was to compel Nasser to restore the supra-Egyptian rights of other nations. Murphy and his aides suggested that a special agency of the United Nations be entrusted with control of the Canal. Eden was not averse to such a solution. But the American spokesmen were in no hurry. Then Dulles reinforced the American view that legality was a basic issue, because, if it became impossible to avoid military action against Egypt, then President Eisenhower would need Congress' authority for any participation therein, and Congress would have to be convinced that the allies were on legal ground. However, for the moment, consideration of the relationship of the United Nations to the Suez dispute, important as it was, must be deferred. This was Dulles's policy.

The stand taken by the United States of America in its argument with Britain and France, with Dulles as the agent of American power, responsibility, and honor, can be summed up in five stages: (1) his views expressed to Selwyn Lloyd and Christian Pineau on August 1, 1956; (2) these views plus a supplementary statement, constituting his remarks to Eden during lunch on August 2; (3) the communiqué agreed upon by the three powers; (4) a television statement he made on August 2; (5) a statement made to President Eisenhower's Cabinet by Dulles on his return from London. Let us look at these several phases.

Eden reports that at lunch Dulles summed up his views as follows. "It was intolerable that the Canal should be under the domination of any single country without any international control." The key words, as the reader may note, "intolerable," "domination," "international," are either legal or casuistical. "We should use the 1888 Convention as a basis for discussion in order to avoid complications that might arise in regard to the Panama Canal."

From the very beginning, Dulles's attitude toward the international interests of Britain and France in the Suez Canal was affected, most adversely to them, by his determination to permit nothing to question, still less to diminish, America's rights in the Panama Canal, deemed a military and economic vital interest of the United States. Here was a plain clash of interests, let us never forget or misunderstand, *not* an issue of the Rule of Law or the status and role in the world of the United Nations. And Dulles preferred American interests to these ideals and to the claims of his allies.

The fact of the matter is that the United States' possession of Panama put Dulles in a grave moral dilemma, which was also a political and diplomatic dilemma. If he demanded that the Suez Canal should be internationally managed on the grounds that so many nations had an interest in it (including Britain and France), he could hardly resist, on the same reasoning, an argument that the Panama Canal should also be managed internationally. Thus, for the sake of American national interests, he did not wish to dwell on the issue of international management. If, in order to get the British and French to recede from their demands in some degree or another, he were to use the implicit or explicit reason that they had assisted in the establishment of an international regime of the Suez Canal by duress of a "colonialist" kind, then he would risk a much severer reprimand by his allies and all impartial onlookers. They might remind him that the process by which the United States had fomented the severance of Panama from Colombia in 1904—in order that the United States might circumvent the objections and terms of the Colombian government concerning American access to the Isthmus and possession of the Canal when built—was morally reprehensible in the extreme,[32] in spite of the divine claim of President Theodore Roosevelt: "I have a mandate from civilization to take Panama!" His mind would have either to ignore, or be exceedingly casuistical about, the contentions of some Panamanian political leaders that Panama had never relinquished sovereignty over the Canal Zone. All the Hay-Bunau-Varilla Treaty of 1903 had said was that "perpetual rights" were granted to the United States, "*as if* it were sovereign," so that Panama could claim never to have relinquished that sovereignty. Dulles in a news conference (sometime later) called forth protests from Panama when he declared that by the Treaty of 1903 the United States government had acquired "perpetual rights *equivalent* to sovereignty," making the United States *solely* responsible over the Panama Canal. So long as Dulles did not inject into the conflict over the rights claimed by Britain and France in the Suez Canal a rebuke to them for "colonialism," his allies might close their eyes to the moral flaw in American policy; but should he raise the issue, or others raise it, it would surely be a source of bitterness. His position would be hard if he should lift his voice in lofty moral sermons to the world reproving their colonialism and requiring them to surrender their economic and strategic assets in the name of anticolonial morality.

Other views which Eden quotes Dulles as expressing at the luncheon are these: "Force was the *last* method to be tried, but the United States did not exclude the use of force *if all other methods failed.*" (My italics.) And, "We should mobilize world opinion in favor of international control of the Canal. . . . We should attempt to get our tripartite views accepted by at least a two-thirds majority of the Conference of Maritime Powers that was to be called." The congruity of Dulles's views about the contingent use of force with Eden's summary of Eisenhower's letter and my own reported notes of Eisenhower's letter, is clear: force is conditional, not excluded.

But, although international, far more than domestic, policies need to be expressed with precision, the clause regarding the eventual and contingent use of force, "if all other methods failed," is vague, imprecise. *"Failed" to do what?* Dulles was a most ardent supporter and preacher of the doctrine that wars may be caused by miscalculation, that potential enemies may take the offensive because they are not certain about the intention of their victim.[33] But the word "failed" is a vague one, about which there could be, about which there ultimately was, a miscalculation that resulted in a war over Suez. Miscalculation began with the Eisenhower letter to Eden: Eisenhower claims to have wanted it to mean no force at all under any circumstances ever.

Here are men using the English language as their mother tongue, trained (not Eisenhower) in all the niceties of English literature in its many forms, and yet neither side is bound beyond a peradventure (to use a favorite expression of Dulles's idol, Woodrow Wilson) of a miscalculation or misunderstanding.

Dulles went along much further to meet the rights of Britain and France and the interests of the U.S.A. The Foreign Minister, Selwyn Lloyd, reported to Eden this supplement to the discussion on August 1. Dulles then added:

> A way had to be found to make Nasser disgorge what he was attempting to swallow . . . we must make a genuine effort to bring world opinion to favor international operation of the canal . . . it should be possible to create a world opinion so aghast to Nasser that he should be isolated. Then if a military operation had to be undertaken it would be more apt to succeed and have less grave repercussions than if it had been undertaken precipitantly.[34]

Eden's immediate comment is interesting. "Nasser must be made, as Mr. Dulles put it to me, 'to disgorge.' *These were forthright words.* They rang in my ears for months." [My italics.]

But were they "forthright" words? Dulles was a master of imprecision, well known for this propensity. It is almost universally attested (we, too, shall demonstrate this as we proceed with the narrative) that he was too often super-rhetorical, without quite knowing what he really, concretely and practically, did mean by the useful, the ready, the expedient word; that he often was merely experimental with a word or device like "disgorge." It is an evocative word, calculated to give tremendous comfort to a man whose relative has just been swallowed by a boa constrictor. In this metaphorical twist, one can almost see Nasser retching and finally and painfully belching out the Canal so that all those who were entitled to repossess it could do so. Many witnesses will attest to the truth of a remark once made by Anthony Eden: "My difficulty in working with Dulles was to determine what he really meant and in consequence the significance to be attached to his words and actions. I know I was not alone in this, but the consequences were unfortunate for Britain, the weaker partner." [35]

Men who have had business relationships with Dulles, not as adversaries but as partners, have reported that he carried to an extreme, indeed a pathological extreme, a lawyer's practice of making mental reservations, not committing himself, but meanwhile not allowing his partner into the true confidential grounds of seeking his freedom from commitment. Even the clauses about "international control" and the 1888 Convention "as a basis" were shot through with ambiguity and grounds for misunderstanding.

On August 1, in the absence of Dulles, but perhaps as a result of intensive coaching received from him before he departed for London, and perhaps with a little advice from Herbert Hoover, Jr., President Eisenhower made some remarks at a press conference to anxious reporters. He evaded a question assimilating the Panama Canal to the Suez problem. (And legalistically, of course, they were not quite the same. But politically?) He said, "Well, of course, the conditions aren't the same." He reverted to the Convention of 1888 and said:

> The Suez Canal will always be an international waterway, free for use to all nations of the world in peace and war. So the conditions aren't quite the same [as in the case of Panama]. But right now the great problem is to make certain of the continued efficient use of this great waterway whose importance is not confined to the neighboring countries or Europe, but *indeed it is vital* to our economy and our welfare . . . the only thing I can say is, we are manifestly faced with a very grave issue, important to every country that has a sea coast, and maybe even all the rest. So it is something to be handled with care to make sure we are just and fair; but we must make certain that the rights of the world are not abused. [My italics.] [36]

The term *vital* appears often in writings and speeches on politics among nations, as for example in the phrase "vital interests." In plain language, it would seem that this must mean, "My life depends on it."

Sometimes it has this meaning fully. But it can be used loosely. Usually men and nations will fight for their lives and the word; or they mean that, failing to take action, they fear they would die. What degree of importance had Eisenhower invested in this drastic word? Was he using it to signify a "clear and present danger" of the loss of life, or merely to express a much milder eventuality? We shall see that he misused this word—he thought other things were vital, not the Canal, to America.

At any rate, Dulles was playing for time: an interval to look about him so that he could better assess the various forces converging on him. How swift, how astute he was, already—at once, indeed—to have made the Panama Canal an exception (to avoid complications) to the basis of discussion about the other international waterway, the Suez Canal. Whereas Eden says, "Pineau and I did not want to lose momentum, or to allow discussion to drag on from conference to conference," the sense of urgency was much less pressing on Dulles. What Eden and Pineau did not want was almost exactly what Dulles did want.

One other theme must be introduced now, sinister, and ultimately a disaster to the allied powers: the attitude of the Soviet Union. By the time Dulles arrived in London, he certainly had news of Russia's support of Nasser's violent act. On July 31, Khrushchev approved, before a crowd of 100,000 at the Lenin Sports Stadium, Nasser's seizure of the Canal, declaring that the action appeared to be completely legal. In a tone of "butter will not melt in my mouth," he explained that he found it difficult to understand the furor being raised by France and Britain. In his opinion, the nationalization of Suez did not affect the interests of the people of "Britain and France, but only small groups of 'profiteering monopolists.'" The West ought not to get excited over Suez. The situation would not be exacerbated unless the West artificially exacerbated it. "We, too, are interested in free navigation of the Suez Canal," he said. *Pravda* similarly expressed the view that the nationalization should be accepted by London, Paris, and Washington, declaring that it was "a fully legal act." [37] How interesting that both the U.S.A. and the U.S.S.R. almost by parallel action gave a legalistic turn to the discussion! Dulles thought he had no vital world power territory or prestige to defend in this case and Khrushchev knew that he had one to win. Whose ox was gored? Only the ox of Britain and France, not ours.

Khrushchev also had the gall, combined with blandness, to praise the withdrawal of the British from the Suez Canal Zone, as well as Britain's reasonableness in granting independence to India and Burma. He hoped that British and French public opinion would "understand us" when he proposed that the Suez problem should be regulated peacefully, with no ground for the sharpening of relations in the

Mediterranean, and less for influencing hostility between states. As if the oil and food and fiber that came through the Canal, the crews that worked the ships, were not of direct benefit to every human being in England and France!

The three powers agreed on a communiqué. It ran as follows:

> . . . . The Universal Suez Canal Company has always had an international character in terms of its shareholders, directors, and operating personnel and in terms of its responsibility to assure the efficient functioning as an international waterway of the Suez Canal. In 1888 all the Great Powers then principally concerned with the international character of the Canal and its free, open and secure use without discrimination joined in the Treaty and Convention of Constantinople.
>
> This provided for the benefit of all the world that the international character of the Canal would be perpetuated for all time. . . .
>
> They [the governments of France, the United Kingdom and the United States] do not question the right of Egypt to enjoy and exercise all powers of a fully sovereign and independent nation, including the generally recognized right, under appropriate conditions, to nationalize assets, not impressed with an international interest, which are subject to its political authority. But the present action involves far more than a simple act of nationalization. It involves the arbitrary and unilateral seizure by one nation of an international agency [upon which] the economy, commerce, and security of much of the world depends. This seizure is the more serious in its implications because it avowedly was made for the purpose of enabling the government of Egypt to make the Canal serve the purely national purposes of the Egyptian government, rather than the international purpose established by the Convention of 1888.
>
> . . . the action taken by the government of Egypt, having regard to all the attendant circumstances, threatens the freedom and security of the Canal as guaranteed by the Convention of 1888.
>
> . . . .
>
> They consider that steps should be taken to establish operating arrangements under an international system designed to assure the continuity of operation of the Canal as guaranteed by the Convention of October 29, 1888, consistently with legitimate Egyptian interests.
>
> To this end they propose that a conference should promptly be held of parties to the Convention and other nations largely concerned with the use of the Canal. . . .[38]

Now Dulles and his immediate assistants, as well as Ambassador Winthrop Aldrich, were exceedingly alert for expressions of British public opinion in addition to the accounts they heard of it from the

Foreign Secretary and the Prime Minister and their assistants. This is wise and proper. The CIA assists this work of evaluating and discovering public opinion in foreign nations. There is a steady liaison betwen the local CIA agencies and the local embassies. Every morning in an American embassy, the ambassador, or chargé d'affaires, if the former is absent, meets with his six or seven top advisers: political counselor, political attaché, cultural attaché, military liaison, etc., and in this session the local state of affairs, as well as the cables from the U.S.A., are pondered and evaluated for America's interests.

Especially in a very open society like that of Britain is public opinion ascertainable. Cabinet ministers must meet opposition from the other party and from their own, face to face, every day for a considerable time, answering questions or debate. It is much harder to know or guess what America thinks and feels, for reasons that can be inferred from what has just been said, but above all, because it is vast and regionalized and the two assemblies of Congress are at odds, and both are at odds with the Executive, erratically and fluctuatingly.

All along, then, Dulles knew British public opinion and could use his knowledge for American advantage, or, if one wishes to speak in Dulles's own more idealistic vein, for the sake of world peace and justice. As soon as British public opinion split on what should be done about Suez, Dulles knew it and could use it, as we shall see.

On this occasion, when Dulles's representatives went to see Selwyn Lloyd on August 1 at the Foreign Office, the latter said, "Well! This is it! I've never seen our people so united as at this business over the Canal and Nasser!" Any examination of the newspapers and the brief debate in the House of Commons on July 30 would amply have confirmed this viewpoint. But people close to Dulles did not want to see it, and tended to persuade Dulles that he should not see it either. Dulles was the more easily persuaded because, as he entered or alighted from his car at the Foreign Office, the American Embassy, or Downing Street, he was cheered by the passers-by and the lookers-on, those good, dutiful cockneys, the descendants of A. E. Housman's "army of mercenaries" who, in 1914, had held the pillars of heaven on their shoulders, some of whom cried out, "You gonna save us from a war?" They hoped, of course, he was an envoy of peace and justice. But it was wrong to assume that they were therefore at odds with Eden's policy. Many British families had sons and fathers who had since 1945 served in the Suez Canal area. Almost every family had some relative or acquaintance who had been a soldier or a technician there, and they detested the Egyptians, referring to them with ignominious nicknames.

The solidarity of British opinion at that time should have been realized by Dulles, surely, as soon as he received an account of the first long debate on Suez in the House of Commons on August 2.

The debate had lasted from 12:21 P.M. to 6:30 P.M., with Eden speaking for twenty-one minutes and Mr. Gaitskell, leader of the Opposition, for over thirty-five minutes. It was a tense, steady, coherent give-and-take. After he had spoken Eden returned to Downing Street to have lunch with Dulles, the lunch to which we have already referred.

Indeed, Gaitskell's speech was far more belligerent in tone than Prime Minister Eden's. Naturally, given his own character by birth and nurture and his Labour Party beliefs, he did not advocate the use of force at once. But he was very severe in his denunciation of Nasser's behavior and Nasser's political and personal demeanor. He supported the "precautionary" measures which the government was taking, that is to say, the deployment of the armed forces. Nor did he absolutely rule out the use of force. He, not Eden, was the first English political leader to liken Nasser to Hitler and Mussolini. The Conservatives differed from Gaitskell and from the Prime Minister only in that some of their extremist spokesmen were more bellicose in tone and ready for more immediate action involving the use of force against Nasser.

Later Gaitskell and the largest part of his party changed their attitude radically and, in the case of Gaitskell, unaccountably.

About the time this debate came to an end, the last before the summer adjournment of the House (which would be called back again if events became urgent, as Eden promised), Dulles and company flew back to Washington, arriving at 12 noon on Friday, August 3. He went home for lunch, but was back at the State Department by 3 P.M., having reported to Eisenhower and worked on a television address to be given that evening.

While in England Dulles had believed, or said he believed, the British and French were about to take immediate military action, though he was unaware of their timetable, if any. Prime Minister Eden had been quite frank with Dulles about the allied military moves. The United States naval attaché had been asking for information. Eden asked Dulles, "Does the U.S.A. really wish to have it?" Dulles answered that his government perfectly well understood the purpose of the allied preparations, to keep Nasser sober and on tenterhooks and keep the Canal open, and ventured even to say he thought the military moves had had a good effect. But he did not want "detailed information." The tentativeness on this subject between statesmen at that stage was good for both sides. For Eden offered to be frank; yet Dulles did not press Eden, though perhaps he should have. By not getting to know all that was available to him, his involvement was reduced; he was left with less worry and responsibility to act in ways that may have been dictated if he had known.

Did Dulles not also reflect that the British government was taking *him* to the brink of war, too? That its show of force was not merely to impress Nasser, but to make it clear that Britain had been despoiled of something precious and that therefore her American ally must take her grievances and claims seriously?

Returned to Washington, Dulles was still anxious, but glad for the moment that the situation had neither blown up nor sharply deteriorated. He had achieved at least a two-week stay of execution before the Conference of Maritime Powers, perhaps a long enough period for all to cool off. He made two statements on his return, both on August 3, 1956. One was a short monologue, the other a radio and television appearance with President Eisenhower. They must be reviewed, for in contemporary conditions official utterances of this kind are diplomatic acts, and statesmen read them as such.

In his first statement, Dulles called the Suez situation "dangerous." [39] He recalled that Nasser had "suddenly and arbitrarily" seized the Canal. He added that Nasser had announced "he would turn this *vital* international waterway into an Egyptian operation designed to promote, as he put it, the 'grandeur' of Egypt." (The italics are mine.) Then Dulles turned to a statement of policy:

> We do not, however, want to meet violence with violence. We want, first of all, to find out the opinion of the many nations vitally interested because we believe that all nations concerned, including Egypt, will respect the sober opinion of the nations which are party to the internationalizing treaty of 1888, or, by its terms, entitled to its benefits. . . . We would hope that out of this [the conference of twenty-four nations that had been called] would come a solution which all the nations, including Egypt, will respect so that the danger of violence may be averted.

Thus, in the phrase "to meet violence with violence," Dulles was plainly admitting that Nasser had committed violence. It is a crucial point, moral and legal.

It is, furthermore, important to notice that Dulles was expecting, or pretending to expect, that Egypt would respect "the sober opinion" of the parties to the 1888 Convention, after a conference. He still did not exclude the possibility that violence would be used, and that the U.S.A., on the terms stated, would be by its word obliged to support it, but he hoped it would be averted by a conference-made solution. Egypt was still, in the context of his statement, open to an attack, and Dulles may well have deliberately worded his statement to keep this possibility open, so that Nasser would be sobered and made pliable by its coercive anticipatory effect.

That evening, Eisenhower and Dulles appeared together on television and radio, the President as the introducer of Dulles, Dulles as the principal speaker.[40] This session had been arranged by telephone from Dulles's plane as it winged its way across the Atlantic. It took place in the President's office in the White House. The public saw only the familiar office and Dulles and Eisenhower. But outside the camera's scope were visitors, among them Vice President Nixon.

This was a moment, of course, of some national emergency. For no one could then be certain whether or when there might be a military explosion in the Middle East, or whether, if there were, somehow or another the Soviet Union would not interfere in such a way as to require the American government to honor its far-reaching obligations to its NATO allies.

It was also a moment of domestic political emergency. The Democratic National Convention was to meet from August 13 to 17 and the Republican National Convention from August 20 to 24, after which the 1956 Presidential campaign would start in earnest. International affairs were bound to affect the outcome of the election. At any rate, they had played a tremendous part in 1952. Nobody will forget that stunning slogan, "I will go to Korea!" The 100,000,000 voters must be confronted and informed, in view of the coming campaign. The President's campaign managers did not think that victory was "in the bag." Voters are fickle: something might always slip up. The electoral strength of Eisenhower, aside from the fact that he had been a war hero when so many of the voters were in high school, was that he deployed the famous old slogan, the voters' anesthetic, "Peace and Prosperity."

The U.S.A. had as its Ambassador at the United Nations—the Cave of the Winds, where all the gusts of "world opinion" might be known—Henry Cabot Lodge, Jr. He was the "politician" of the United Nations *par excellence,* a politician in the United Nations, for he had himself been a United States Senator from 1946 to 1952. Lodge had a seat in the Cabinet; he was Eisenhower's and Dulles's spokesman in the U.N. and the conduit through which they received opinion from within it. He had a ready entrée to the White House. He was among the foremost of those who warned the White House and Dulles to bear constantly in mind what effect their moves in regard to Suez would have on the domestic situation November 6, 1956.

Eisenhower would never have done what he believed to be against American interests for the sake of winning an election. The President would not seek a war or avoid a necessary war to win a second term. But any President, in rationally choosing courses of action between these two extremes, given the many diverse solutions conceivable and practicable in any situation in which the issue of using force ever arises, naturally has feelings about the effect his choice will have on his chances of being voted out of or being kept in the White House. We cannot gauge this by any weights and measures or by Gallup polls, but it is sure that electoral instincts will guide his decision among several possible tactics.

What people such as Lodge feared was that public opinion, which was being nursed along in favor of Eisenhower and Nixon, might be incalculably disturbed if some sudden emotional landslide should occur among the masses through fear of war, imminent or actual. No one was ready to say whether this might take the form of "Ike has failed; so out with him," or, on the other hand, "War has come; keep the General in his place for another term!" Eisenhower had bound himself tightly to a policy of and reputation for pacifism. Furthermore, on many occasions the Administration spokesmen had boasted complacently that "there is not a single American boy anywhere in the world fighting in a war!" The electoral preoccupation became even more influential with the passage of the weeks toward the denouement of the election. Dulles wanted to go on being Secretary of State, since, seriously, of course, the Moral Order of the World depended on it, in his opinion. To this Vice President Nixon is witness.

The Secretary explained to the American public that this "dangerous, critical Suez situation" had been caused by interference with the Canal and the operating company, both of which were "international" in character. This word "international," spoken by Dulles to millions, and voluntarily, has a tremendous bearing on the outcome of the crisis and the sincerity of Dulles. Dulles, in fact, insisted on the full international character of the Canal. He rebuked Nasser for taking over the Canal, not to improve the various services it rendered, but for his Egyptian political triumphs, the enhancement of Egypt's grandeur, the intent to extend his sway from the Atlantic to the Persian Gulf. Also, Nasser had boasted that with the Canal in his hands he would be able to strike a blow at what he called "Western imperialism." And Nasser thought also that he could exploit the Canal to produce bigger revenues for Egypt, and so retaliate for the failure of the United States and Britain to give Egypt the money to get started on the billion-dollar-plus Aswan Dam. He also needed foreign currency.[41]

Dulles said, in his televised colloquy with the President:

> We believe that out of this conference will come a plan for the international operation of the Canal which will give assurance that the objectives of the 1888 treaty will in fact be realized and that the Canal will continue to be operated by those who feel that it is their duty to serve the international community and not to serve the special interests of any one nation.
>
> This plan should both give security to the nations principally concerned with the Canal and also fully protect the legitimate interests of Egypt. Egypt, we believe, should be adequately represented on this operating authority and be assured, also, of a fair and reasonable income for the use of the property, because the Canal, although it is internationalized, is on Egyptian territory.
>
> There is every desire that Egypt shall be treated with the

utmost fairness. And, also, the owners and the employees of the now dispossessed Universal Canal Company should also, of course, be fairly treated.

If these principles are accepted by the conference, then we believe that they will also be accepted by Egypt.

As you know, Mr. President, it is one thing for a nation to defy just one or two other nations. But it's quite a different thing to defy the considered and sober judgment of many nations—nations which have treaty rights in the Canal and which in large part depend for their economic livelihood upon the operation of the Canal in accordance with the 1888 treaty.

Now, I've been asked, "What will we do if the conference fails?" My answer to that is that we are not thinking in terms of the conference's failing. But I can say this: We have given no commitments at any time as to what the United States would do in that unhappy contingency.

I repeat, we assume, Mr. President—with you—that the conference will not fail but will succeed. And I believe that by the conference method we will invoke moral forces which are bound to prevail.

Now all the arguments and sentiments in this speech are sound and lucidly phrased. It is admirable; it nourishes a sense of justice to come. It is Dulles's intellect in play at its best. Yet, in the circumstances, namely of Nasser's rapine and defiance, and Russian diplomatic support of Nasser, was it altogether flawless?

The statement was diplomatically in error at certain very important points: in summary, it lacked a sharp enough feeling of injury and indication of imminent justice to be visited on Nasser. No doubt there is almost always something to be said for using a tone of conciliation, and President Eisenhower in particular was naturally inclined this way. But Nasser had seized the Canal by violence, according to Dulles himself. Suppose we concede Dulles's assurances (later in his remarks) to Egypt of "terms which would respect, and generously respect, all the legitimate rights of Egypt," and again, that the decision of the conference would "fully protect the legitimate interests of Egypt," and, again, "that Egypt shall be treated with the utmost fairness. . . ."

Yet the Secretary omitted all mention of the punitive, the coercive, the sanctioning, from his statement of policy. He was to rely on the *avoidance* of violence, according to the passage about the United Nations; the belief that Egypt would *not* "defy the considered judgment of many nations"; the conviction "that by the conference method we will invoke moral forces which are bound to prevail."

What? Moral forces? Sober judgment of many nations? When the culprit had been an assassin, and had become a hero (though not so highly popular until that time) by the very act of seizing the Canal and boasting about his misdeed, utterly regardless of moral forces and all the rest? Did Dulles believe that even in Egypt everyday life proceeded upon a pure Christian basis? In scores of articles and lectures since 1937 Dulles had developed his creed that moral forces could gain political victory in conflict among nations and should be utilized for that purpose.[42]

The Secretary of State committed a far more serious fault still in including the passage, "What shall we do if a conference fails?" He need not have asked this question. He certainly should not have given the answer he did. The trouble is that he could not stop talking long enough to deploy the clever and wise and "moral forces" he believed in. His answer weakened any intended effect on Nasser. For this is what he had said:

> But I can say this: we have given no commitments at any time as to what the United States would do in that unhappy contingency.

This assertion, plus the subsequent point that "we will invoke moral forces which are bound to prevail" was a dreadful weakening of Western position. Instead of the phrase about "no commitments," Dulles could have said something like this: "There are many ways available to those who have been injured (and we in the U.S.A. number among these nations) to induce an international breaker of treaties and malefactor to repair his wrongdoing." Also, the reference to the United Nations could have been couched to show that Nasser had, violating Egypt's pledge to the Charter, used not only the threat of force, but force itself, to endanger the peace, and that if Nasser expected the Charter's protection it was his obligation to respect its demands.

It is alleged in the *New York Times* (August 4, 1956) that the "no commitments" phrase was added by Dulles to his prepared text, in order to dispel any idea that the U.S.A. might support the use of force. I add this allegation for what it is worth.

To whom did Dulles believe he was appealing when on that Friday night, August 3, 1956, self-satisfied and ponderous, he invoked the noble words of the Declaration of Independence: "I believe, Mr. President, that most people pay decent respect for the opinions of mankind when these are soberly, carefully, and deliberately formulated"?

Was he talking about individuals, persons? If so, in what country? In Africa? India? Korea? Iceland? China, Communist or Nationalist? Individuals in the U.S.A., where justice was protected by an authoritative legislature, an effective and continuously operating executive, including detectives and police and chairs for electrocution, and law courts that could summon men to listen and take heed by subpoena? And where one must compulsorily attend court for hearing verdict and sentence; and where verdict and sentence were carried out by the court and the executive? Did he think he was appealing to meek and mild English, French, German individuals under a common and nonvetoable government's formulation of the opinion of mankind? Or was he thinking of nations? And above all Middle Eastern nations? And above all, Nasser, a despot in his nation, a despot who had wiped out the voice of the nation and replaced it exclusively by his own?

It must have been somewhat before this time, on August 1 or 2, when Dulles had suggested a conference of nations to gain time and perspective, that an intimate associate suggested some other course to him, and received the answer, "No, I will do it my way; you see, I have *faith*, whereas you are only a sinner." This act of faith, that he could get two weeks' respite before the conference opened—on August 16—plus the time the conference would take, say a week, plus a little time for digestion or action on its recommendations, was justified, and Dulles felt happy and grateful.

On Eden's part, but much more suspiciously on that of Pineau and Mollet, there was always an honorable disposition to enter into the first London Conference of Maritime Powers. Eden was persuaded by Dulles that Nasser could be made "to disgorge." If this could be done, while sparing the bloodshed of his country, indeed, of any nation, he would be glad. This was ingrained in Eden's thirty years of practice in Britain's foreign policy. But he now suffered from additional qualms about Dulles, for specific causes.

First, when the idea of a conference was agreed upon between America, Britain, and France, Dulles suggested not that it be held within two weeks, but that it be preceded by "several weeks of preparation." Eden says, "In the end we compromised and August 16 was the date set." Secondly, "there then arose the question of a little immediate coercion on Nasser and evidence from Dulles of a resolution to discipline him." Eden and Pineau wished to keep to the minimum the money paid in tolls to Egypt by ships using the Suez Canal. Normally, British shipowners paid their dues into the account of the Suez Canal Company in London; the French paid in Paris. Other countries, including the U.S.A., paid in Egypt. In London 55 per cent of the total was collected annually; in Paris, 10 per cent; in Egypt, 35 per cent. The British government wished to continue British payments as hitherto, in London, until a new international authority was established. If the Egyptians now tried to exact payments, British ships might be refused passage through the Canal by Nasser and have to be rerouted via the Cape of Good Hope, South Africa.

What Nasser desperately needed was *foreign* currency, and this Eden and Mollet wished to deny him. Eden could *not* get cooperation from Dulles on the payment of tolls. Dulles explained that he could not say how American shipowners might respond to any advice the American government gave them on this subject! Nor had the American government the power to instruct the many American-owned ships that were registered as flying the flags of Panama, Liberia, and other countries to avoid regulation by the U.S.A. Dulles gave not the slightest sign of exerting himself in this matter, although the issue was one of major public policy for the government of the U.S.A., in addition to the "moral forces" involved.

The facts of the relationship between American-flag vessels and American-*owned* vessels using the Suez Canal route at that time are these. American-flag vessels constituted 3 per cent of the total traffic. But 12 per cent, over and above this, while under U.S. ownership or control, was under Panamanian and Liberian registry. Thus, adding American-owned shipping together, of whatever registries, it constituted 15 per cent of all Suez traffic. After the seizure of the Canal, the Egyptian authority was receiving only about one-third of the Canal tolls from all users, including the 3 per cent of American-flag vessels. To have subtracted another 12 per cent, roughly, would have left Nasser with only a little over one-fifth of all the usual receipts from tolls. In other words, Egypt would be bearing all the expenses of running the Canal, while recovering only one-fifth the tolls. This is the experience of hardship which Eden and Mollet wished Dulles to bring about. He evaded the obligation to his allies. They wished for more than this: American refusal to pay tolls to an illegitimate authority for the explicit purpose of demonstrating its illegitimacy and of exhibiting the moral solidarity of the Western nations. Dulles refused to do this also.

I am of the judgment that, by this time, Dulles and Eisenhower had privately resolved between themselves—or each had concluded in his own heart, without full disclosure to the other, or even full admission of it in clear consciousness to himself—not to use force under any circumstances or to condone its use. They had not yet faced the further question: How would we openly oppose it? I believe they did not consider that the Canal was of sufficient significance to American interests to warrant the use of force, and that even if it remained in Nasser's hands, they could still sweeten him or threaten him in some other ways, not yet precisely and concretely formulated.

It is most probable that the attitude of Dulles and Eisenhower at this point, and all along to the very end, regarding the seizure of the Suez Canal was practically identical with the attitude of Bismarck on the nineteenth century's Eastern question, that is, the Balkans and Turkey. "It was not worth the healthy bones of the tiniest single Pomeranian grenadier," Bismarck said of the latter issue in December, 1876. I believe that Dulles and Eisenhower, in their hearts, thought that the Suez Canal was not worth the bones of the smallest single American G.I.

Now their problem was for the time being not Nasser. And he

was not their problem even in the long run, because Dulles's self-confidence and America's power could handle him if America's *vital* interests should ever be affected, and the time was not yet. The problem was Britain and France. How to stop them from going to war and by that action converting the problem into a vital one for the U.S.A.? For if they engaged in war in the Middle East, it would mean the weakening, in Europe, of the strength and prestige of these allies of America in NATO, America's shield against the Soviet Union in the West. Or what if, in some cunning way, that John Foster Dulles and Allen W. Dulles could forecast, the Soviet Union should take a hand in any fighting, by means of volunteers or submarines, or arms supplies, especially fighting planes and bombers?

Now, if this was the attitude of Dulles and Eisenhower, and I have formed the judgment from their words and demeanor that it was, it was absolutely essential that they should frankly tell their allies at once, but they were afraid to do so for two reasons. If they had at once explicitly excluded force *absolutely*, under any circumstances, then Britain and France, realizing that they were alone, might in all probability have used force as early as an attack could be mounted, and Dulles's and Eisenhower's fat would have been in the fire throughout the whole of the Middle East. Israel surely would have been involved at once also. Furthermore, it is very difficult, but it is not impossible, to command sovereign nations, with noble histories and eminent cultural traditions, absolutely not to use force in order to defend what they consider to be their vital interests. The answer to Dulles and Eisenhower could have been a rebuff.

The avoidance of war in the Middle East, not international justice, became, in my considered judgment, the cardinal and decisive value of Dulles and Eisenhower. All the rest was moral commentary and diplomatic tergiversation, useful, good, most desirable, if it could be reliably utilized, but otherwise to be abandoned. While there is life there is hope—and war is death. It is an arguable proposition.

Hence, Dulles's problem was to defer the day of reckoning. This could not be done without insincerity towards his allies and concealment of his motives. It could not be done without dishonesty and betrayal.

It has been reported that a former Secretary of State, far more distinguished than Dulles, more brilliant in conception and execution of American foreign policy, Dean Acheson, laments that Eden was foolish to have been inveigled by Dulles into a conference and then later on to have agreed to another. An eminent and comprehending lawyer himself, he believes (according to those who have conversed with him intimately on this subject) that trouble arose in the Suez affair because a man like Eden, nurtured in English traditions, had never hitherto become encoiled in the wiles of a Wall Street lawyer, fertile in expedients, astute in traps—in this case a man who firmly believed that there was no point in telling the other lawyer or party where his case was weak or what strength, unknown to the opposition, it really possessed. Eden was putty in Dulles's hands once he had agreed, against his own judgment, to slow down momentum.

Furthermore, Dulles never at these early stages, decisive for justice and peace, fully disclosed America's position to his allies. Some of his associates defend this evasion on the grounds that there was no general and comprehensive strategy planned at the beginning of the Suez affair and that it was therefore not possible to have disclosed it. All that could be done, they allege, was to apply certain general principles and then "play it by ear," responding to the new circumstances and facts as they arose every day. Or, as other collaborators with and admirers of Dulles are reported to argue, perhaps from the beginning it was Dulles's policy to avoid being drawn by the British and French into an involvement in interests which, moving along day after day, could become irreversible, so that at some given incident, Dulles and the President would find it impossible to extricate themselves from the use of force or from the practical or moral support of force used by their allies. Whatever the excuses or reasons, the Secretary was simply not frank.

He was asked in London about that time by two, and perhaps more, important Englishmen to be completely frank with Eden. One of these was a high political leader opposed to Eden, another the editor of a very important weekly journal. They almost begged him to do this, to disclose American policy in full, her intentions and hopes and determination, especially as it related to the use of force. He answered them, "No! I will do it some other way."

If a disaster were to be avoided, then Dulles needed to make up his mind clearly and firmly on his dilemma, and to tell his allies clearly and firmly what he had decided his course was to be. He would have to say that the United States government was in this predicament: it needed its Atlantic alliance and, simultaneously, it was obliged to demonstrate that it was the friend of nationalist self-determination all over the world—a movement that included Arab nationalism in the Middle East.

Could a policy be discovered that permitted both options to the United States?

One solution was for the United States to wash its hands of Britain and France and to let Nasser have his own way. If this were the choice, then, at the earliest possible moment, it was imperative for Dulles to apprise his allies that the United States would under no circumstances or for whatever reasoning tolerate their use of force at all. If, in spite of this warning, they did use force, then the United States would act in opposition to them in the United Nations.

It was important that the action to be taken in the United Nations by Dulles, Lodge, and Eisenhower be disclosed and explained in concrete detail to their allies. Such an option was not expressed clearly and firmly by Dulles. His oblique or indirect methods allowed miscalculation of America's intentions.

An alternative was possible. Dulles could have said that the United States would keep the ring (as in the Chinese Civil War), while Britain and France chastised Nasser. They could have been warned, however, that they would face more trouble than they expected from guerrilla war in Egypt, and that the United States would not give them help. Neither would the U.S.A. hinder them. It would act as a neutral, unhappy, but resigned, and explain its moral position in a manner to maintain credit with the Afro-Asians yet not harm the Western allies. It was a difficult course, but not impossible. Dulles did not take this course, either, though he appreciated the injustice done to Britain and France—up to a point.

Why was no decisiveness manifested from the very beginning? Two broad reasons dominated Dulles and his advisers, though within these two, there were other, lesser, ones enwrapped. For Dulles the main issue was his adversary in global conflict, the Soviet Union. Therefore, he did not tell his allies that he would keep his hands out of the Middle East while they went to work. He feared the growth of Soviet strength in that area of the world as a consequence of forceful action there by his allies. He would not look at the problem as merely one of British and French national interests in the Middle East. Secondly, the United States, in all its foreign policy troubles since 1931 (the date of the Japanese invasion of Manchuria), has shown a marked reluctance to take a decisive stand, supported by force, except in an extremity, such as Pearl Harbor, or in the case of Communist offensives, like those in Greece in 1947, or the attack on Korea. It will not face the need for decision and the threat of force earlier than a situation *in extremis*. It tends to seek a "middle" course.

Dulles evaded complete frankness. It is probable that he was not a man either of far-reaching historic vision or of fearlessness. He lacked the courage, it may be, to cause pain in others by being frank and refusing them comfort, or to accept the burden of hearing from them the drastic steps they would take if he disclosed his real intentions. It is one thing to conduct cases in a law court, say, over a railroad reorganization, or even over the title of a Polish government to gold which has been deposited in an American bank, and quite another to conduct negotiations with sovereign countries with armies at their disposal that might be used if you were frank and trusting. Dulles was brave to bravado in his orations; whether he had intrepidity in action is quite another question. "Now faith is the substance of things hoped for, the evidence of things not seen." He was waiting for something to turn up.

Neither Britain nor France could at once make war on Nasser. Egypt was a long way from the nearest British base of any magnitude, Malta. British and French forces were to a considerable extent tangled up in NATO military defenses. Their withdrawal was a complicated affair if they were to gather a balanced striking force, and this would require considerable time. As usual, in the piping times of peace among peaceful governments, when Eden asked the chiefs of staff how soon they could act, the reply was a recital of the difficulties of assembling the men, the planes, the vessels from all the oceans and continents—and the need for time! Movements toward Cyprus began. Hence, on this practical ground, Eden was not averse to a two weeks' delay. Washington, London, and Paris prepared for the first London Conference on the Suez affair.

5. DULLES STUDIES THE FORCES

THE FIRST LONDON CONFERENCE OF MARITIME POWERS WAS DESTINED TO be a stage for the triumph of Dulles's peculiar character and skills. His plane took off from Washington at 2:30 P.M. on August 14. As usual on such flights, Dulles changed into pull-over, slacks, and slippers. He and the staff reviewed and recrystallized the diplomatic situation, as they had been doing since August 3 in continuous staff meetings and conferences with foreign envoys in Washington and American envoys abroad. They continued until dinner time.

What was in Dulles's mind? A kaleidoscope of forces and persons in violent motion. To group these vibrating changelings is to do some violence to the succession of events; but not to group them is to invite incomprehension.

1. His allies, Britain and France, with their military preparations, frightened him and convinced him of the gravity and tenacity of their claims for justice. For big countries experience this need for justice as well as the clamorous small countries, since if they do not obtain it they lose their magnitude; and, if Britain and France were now but "middle" countries, even more did they dread additional attrition.

2. Nasser was alternately making peaceful conciliatory gestures and threatening war. All the Arab nations applauded his deed, his claims, and his defiance: even Iraq and Jordan, which hated him, also were Arabs and Moslems. Almost all the African and Asian countries, except Japan, supported him. He had refused to attend the London Conference.

3. The U.S.S.R. was resolved to be the champion of Egypt; so was the India of Pandit Nehru and V. K. Krishna Menon.

4. The United Nations organization was consciously evaded by

Dulles; it was avoided by Britain and France at his behest and for their military precautions; it was flirted with by Nasser.

5. A serious rift had appeared in British political solidarity, the Labour Party now having assumed a highly charged emotional opposition to Eden's Government, fearful that it would use force against Nasser.

It is necessary to unravel these skeins, as briefly as possible.

Both Britain and France were dispatching naval and air forces towards the Middle East, to Malta and Cyprus and Libya. An operation of considerable size was being planned and mounted: Operation *Hamilcar*.[1] If the issue came to force the two nations wanted and needed and expected no assistance from Eisenhower and Dulles. What they did expect was that there would be no obstruction from them, and that if the Soviet Union should offer to fight for Nasser the U.S.A. would "take care of the Bear," meaning that America's deterrent might would cause Moscow to confine its reaction only to shouts, threats, and boasts. Feeling against Nasser was still very strong in Britain, despite the growing opposition of the Labour Party. A *Christian Science Monitor* reporter had written[2] that the mood of the House of Commons on August 2 had been like that in September, 1939, when the deliberate and impassioned opinion had been that Hitler had gone too far and must be stopped, whatever the means necessary. British ministers expected American generosity in return for British acceptance of America's policy of quitting the Suez Canal base.

In Paris, the determination to deal Nasser a blow was even more intense, partly by reason of the nation's excitability, but also because in that country the Cabinet happened to be mainly Socialist, with a Socialist Prime Minister, Guy Mollet, flanked by a Socialist Foreign Minister, Christian Pineau, and otherwise chiefly composed of Defense Minister Bourgès-Manoury, a Radical, and Vice Prime Minister Chaban-Delmas, a de Gaullist. All French political parties supported the Government's policy of attempting to secure redress from Nasser —all except the Communist Party. Its newspaper *Humanité* seems to have been joined in opposition by only the *Libération*, the *Manchester Guardian* of France. After a remarkable speech by Guy Mollet at the Press Club on July 30, the National Assembly and Cabinet had voted by a majority of 416 to 150 its disgust with and distrust of Nasser and demanded a severe riposte by a speedy operation against Nasser. It was a matter of special alarm for Dulles that *Socialists* were prepared to make war! The most significant phrases of Guy Mollet's oration rang out with terrifying implications. Nasser was described as a "would-be dictator," whose ambitions were clearly and openly described in his *Philosophy of the Revolution;* this book, said Mollet, might be more properly called *Mein Kampf*. The parallel was resented in Cairo, and deprecated by those people in Britain and America who quailed before the moral burdens imposed on their conscience by such a description. It was extenuated by the politicians of the Afro-Asian countries who had become ready to tolerate despotism if they believed their hunger could be appeased by it, their sense of social inferiority relieved, their government placed totally in their own hands, and practically unbridled power opened up to their own appetites.

Mollet pointed to the insulting terms, like Hitler's, addressed to the democracies by Nasser on and about July 26. He denounced Nasser's policy of "alternating between blackmail and violation of agreements." He appealed for "a common policy by the Western powers [Dulles knew that this included America] for the Middle East in order to guarantee the equilibrium of the whole zone of the Mediterranean." The area included Algeria, where a fierce rebellion against France was being sponsored, counseled, and armed by Nasser.

On August 2, by the majority already cited, the Assembly [3] passed its resolution expressing indignation over Nasser's *coup de force*, and over the gravity of the situation created "brutally and unilaterally" by him. It declared that he had broken his promises and the rules of international law by discriminating in the use of the Canal (that is, against Israel), and by proclaiming his will to establish his hegemony over the Arab world, and that thus he was a continuing threat to peace. "Confident that it is interpreting the will of the nation, the Assembly reaffirms its determination not to bow before the *fait accompli;* and demands to this end the most energetic measures and appeals to the solidarity of the allies."

What worried Dulles, and certainly worried those of his staff who were responsible for European affairs and world policy in general, was that some British and French politicians and journalists were already declaring that America's actions regarding Suez were a test of the North Atlantic Treaty Organization. As a matter of fact, during luncheon on August 2, in London, Pineau had warned Dulles of the danger he faced in the Atlantic alliance unless there were a complete understanding among the three powers on the Middle Eastern conflict. Oblique references were made in the European press to the fact that when the U.S.A. had been in trouble in Berlin (during the Soviet blockade) in 1948 and in Korea in 1951, Britain and France had unconditionally joined America in resisting the aggressor. Before the Foreign Relations Committee of the National Assembly, the French Government said that it would take all measures, including force, if Nasser failed to accept the principles or rules established in the tripartite communiqué of August 3 and especially the results arrived at in the coming conference of August 16.

These disturbing events and a television and radio speech by Sir Anthony Eden on August 8 had so alarmed Dulles that he had persuaded President Eisenhower to consult Congressional leaders of both parties, so that he could go to London with the evidence of national solidarity in his support. He was also concerned lest a sudden turn of events for the worse, that is, towards force, should need Congressional support.

The British Parliament had risen for the summer on August 2. Eden had promised to recall it before its normal autumn reopening if international events made it necessary. In the interim, especially considering the rather sudden volte-face of the Labour Party, he needed to keep the nation informed and to maintain a continuous reminder to Dulles and Eisenhower that America had obligations to her allies. His fifteen-minute speech was delivered in almost academic tones of explanation and in the most elementary English: without incitement, without provocation. The firmness of his posture was all the more evident.

He said, among other things:

> For Britain the Canal has always been the main artery to and from the Commonwealth, bringing to us the supplies we need. . . . World commerce depends upon it. It is, in fact, the greatest international waterway in the world and what Colonel Nasser has just done is to seize it for his own ends. Nobody should be surprised that this has created a very grave situation. The whole trend in the world today is against taking selfish action for purely national ends. Hitherto the Canal has been international. . . . True, it runs through Egypt, but it is not vital to Egypt as to other countries in all parts of the world. . . . This is a matter of life and death to us. . . . Some people say Colonel Nasser promised not to interfere with shipping passing through the Canal. Why therefore don't we trust him? The answer is simple. Look at his record. Our quarrel is not with Egypt, still less with the Arab world. It is with Colonel Nasser. . . . instead of meeting us with friendship Colonel Nasser conducted a vicious propaganda campaign against our country. He has shown he is not a man who can be trusted to keep an agreement. . . . We all know it is how Fascist governments behave and we all remember only too well what the cost can be in giving in to fascism. . . . If Colonel Nasser's action were to succeed, each one of us would be at the mercy of one man for the supplies upon which we live. We could never accept that. With dictators you always have to pay a higher price later on—for their appetite grows with feeding. Just now Colonel Nasser is soft pedalling. His threats are being modified, but how can we be sure that the next time he has a quarrel with any country he won't interfere with that nation's shipping or that the next time he is short of money he won't raise the dues on the ships that pass through the Canal? If he is given a chance, of course he will. . . . It is just that the Canal must be run efficiently and kept open, as it always has been in the past as a free and sure international water-

> way for the ships of all nations. It must be run in the interests not of one country but of all. In our view this can only be secured by an international body. That is our purpose.[4]

The speech posed quite a problem for Dulles. However much he would have preferred it otherwise, he was forced to pay attention to the wounds of his allies. He was already in difficulties with them, because he seemed to be putting himself into the detached position of a neutral and "honest broker" between them and Nasser, a neutral among equal parties to a dispute, a neutral now after having two months earlier declared that neutralism was immoral.

The Secretary had, of course, briefed the President frequently and at length between August 3 and his departure for London on August 14. What was so difficult for Dulles was that he had no authority to dissuade the President from answering questions at press conferences, conferences which had long become an institution. A confusing duality of tongue and mind became troublesome to America's allies (as it had over neutralism only two months before). But the duality also offered the Secretary a ready alibi—that is, the opportunity of maneuver by ascribing the last word to the President and so gaining time, saving face, and retreating from his own apparent commitments.

On August 8, the President was badgered by reporters at his press conference. He was asked, "How do you feel about the use or threat of military force in the Suez dispute?" He answered: "The United States has every hope that this very serious difficulty will be settled by peaceful means. We have stood for the conference method, not only as a solution to this problem but in all similar ones. . . . Now, I can't conceive of military force being a good solution, certainly under conditions as we know them now, and in view of our hopes that things are going to be settled peacefully."

Later he was asked, "Do you think, sir, on the basis of what you know and the reports you have received from Secretary Dulles, that there is a danger that the two sides have committed themselves so deeply that a peaceful solution would be very difficult or virtually impossible?" The President replied with a typical allocution of unfounded optimism: "Not yet. I think that there is—I think there is good reason to hope that good sense will prevail. Here is something that is so important to the whole world that I think a little sober second thinking is going to prevail in a good many quarters, and it is one of those things that just has to be settled, and I would like to point out that damage and destruction is no settlement when you are trying to build and construct."

London and Paris complained that they found it ominous that the President had deprecated "damage and destruction." Did this exclude the use of force to make good sense prevail? If so, the President was telegraphing to Nasser that there were to be no punches against him, not even a feint, and that the Western allies were divided. Such a division was exactly what had occurred over the question of withdrawal from the Canal Zone by the British under American nudging and nagging, and it was exactly the divorce conspicuous when the United States, having initiated the movement for the Baghdad Pact, made the *gran rifiuto*—jilted her partner, Britain.

Dulles had read the entire transcript of the reporters' interrogation of the President. The President's view now—and he had not stressed this to Eden in his letter of July 31st, though it was most material to the course of action Britain wished to take—was that the veto power (that is, Russia's) would be obstructive in the U.N. But here was a matter, he now said, "that seemed to demand not a hurried solution, but a prompt one," so that at the moment the better method was to get the maritime nations together. The appeal to the U.N. would be troubled by its slowness.

At this point the President was dealt a question which, in the words of Dana Adams Schmidt of the *New York Times*, caused him to "stiffen and flush."

A British correspondent (of Reuters) asked: "Mr. President, your earlier remarks on the Suez Canal might be interpreted as meaning that you were opposed to the use of military force under any circumstances—" "I didn't say that," interjected the President. The questioner continued, ". . . in a crisis." The President answered, "I was very careful not to say that. I said every important question in the world in which more than one nation is interested should be settled by negotiation. We have tried to substitute the conference table for the battlefield. Now I don't mean to say that anyone has to surrender rights without using everything they can to preserve their rights." [5]

Certainly, if the last sentence carried its ordinary meaning, Secretary Dulles would need to make the Conference to which he was flying a genuine success—for it implied force, if Dulles did not. The President had refused altogether to comment on another question the Reuters' correspondent put to him, whether British and French military precautions in the Mediterranean and presumably the presence of the United States Sixth Fleet there were "justified in a defensive sense."

Those precautionary moves by Britain and France and many statements from Cairo along with the rumors, confirmed on August 12, that Egypt would not attend the Conference, caused the Secretary intense misgiving. He had felt the need to unburden himself to Congressional leaders. On August 9, the President summoned these leaders to meet with him and Dulles on August 12. It was an awkward date for Democratic leaders, since their National Convention was getting under way. They were brought in by Presidential plane.

On August 10, Dulles explained that no special session of Congress was in view, but that the President felt strongly about sharing responsibility with Congress, if there should be a risk of hostilities. It was an astute move!

The meeting at the White House on August 12, a Sunday, has, fortunately, been described by Sherman Adams.[6] The Senators and Representatives in the Cabinet Room "saw facing them a serious President and a grim Secretary of State." The news had already arrived that day that Nasser would not attend the London Conference. The President opened the meeting with this news and the observation that "at the moment there was no unbounded hope for a peaceful solution." Then Dulles took over the proceedings. He faced the politicians with the gravity of the conflict: "The British and the French under these circumstances could not allow Nasser to get a stranglehold on Suez."

Dulles then proceeded to explain his actions on August 1 to 3 in London in terms which were self-servingly exaggerated. He told the Congressmen that "the British and French were ready at that time to attack Egypt." This was not true. Dulles knew that they were without the capability of action immediately or even of action soon. Dulles claimed he had finally managed to hold the British and French in check by warning them that an immediate use of force would turn world opinion and especially American opinion against them, and that such a move would be regarded by the United States as a violation of their commitments to the United Nations.

The Secretary was speaking in this wise about the United Nations at exactly the same time as he was maneuvering to prevent the Suez dispute from coming before it. He did *not* want the United Nations to play its designed role until he had exhausted all other means and perhaps exhausted all other persons and nations involved. Dulles explained to the Congressmen that he shared the British and French feeling that Nasser was a dangerous threat to the West and his action much more than a demonstration of nationalism. "I believe Nasser intends to unite the Arab world, and if possible, the Moslem world, and then to use Mideast oil and the Canal as weapons against the West." This assessment of Nasser's policy was almost identical with that of Eden and Mollet. *If* the Secretary meant it honestly, rather than as a mere boast of his personal prowess and as a means of giving the Congressmen a dose of the shakes, then his kid-glove handling of Nasser and simultaneous rough handling of his Western allies become difficult to understand.

Dulles was asked by Speaker Sam Rayburn how much provocation would be needed to make the British and the French take action against Egypt.

"Dulles stared through his glasses at Rayburn with surprise

[Adams reports]. 'They think there has been sufficient provocation already,' the Secretary said. 'They have only agreed to bide their time until the conference. They call Nasser a wild man brandishing an ax.' "

The President took part in the subsequent discussion. In view of Dulles's admonition to Eden that he must heed the United Nations, it is interesting to read the President's words. He said that in such an emergency as the one in being, he did not think the United Nations would be effective, because the British and French had a veto power in the Security Council and the General Assembly would be dilatory and inconclusive. He continued on this theme in an answer to Senator Saltonstall, asserting that in a "fast-breaking crisis," there might be times when we could not rely entirely on the slow United Nations machinery.

The President concluded in words which, on August 14, in his roaring plane, must still have been vibrating in the ears of Secretary Dulles. "There are so many possibilities involved that I shudder to think of them. The most important thing is that we must explore every peaceful means of getting to a settlement and the world must know that we are doing so."

Certain other things had been occurring in the relationship between Britain and France on the one hand and America on the other. The three nations were bound to each other in the North Atlantic Treaty Organization. This was the bulwark of Western strength in a policy of containment of Russia, a continued policy, first announced by Churchill and Dean Acheson, in 1950, of "negotiation from strength" with the Soviet government. This allied policy was welcomed with both hands by Dulles—and by Eisenhower—in 1952 and onwards. America's own security depended on the continued and enhanced strength of this alliance. Without it, any Far Eastern policy to contain Communist China and to sustain Japan and the Pacific nations, as well as the western coasts of the U.S.A., would be impossible. For Europe outflanked the Far East, just as the Far East outflanked NATO. It was an alliance that had been engendered in the Grand Alliance, the profound comradeship in arms in World War II, proof against Hitler, Japan, and Stalin. It had been nourished to hold back the imperialism of the Communist empire, known as the Soviet Union, and to hold down any Nazi-type insurgency in Germany. It was the bedrock of survival of all the free peoples of the world, the democracies and those other nations unwilling to be swept under and drowned by the Soviet currents.

Now, Eisenhower, whose personal involvement in World War II and in NATO was peculiarly intimate, and Dulles, more the "theoretician" (as his Soviet bugbears would put it) of NATO than the practitioner as compared with Eisenhower, looked with dismay on the effect of Suez on NATO. On August 7, General Grunther had visited London to look into the problem of the withdrawal of British troops from the NATO military establishment for use in the Middle East. He reported the results to the President and then met the National Security Council in a long session on August 9. Dulles was present. A long discussion assessed the chances of war. The next day, or perhaps a day after that, additional information came in from the U.S. Secretary of the Navy, Charles S. Thomas, who had visited the U.S. Sixth Fleet and then gone on to London for a four days' visit, including conferences with the British Chiefs of Staff and ministers of the various armed forces departments. British NATO units were soon to leave their stations in Germany for the Middle East.

Robert Menzies, Prime Minister of Australia, a Conservative Party leader with a point of view much like that of Eden and Macmillan, had been in Washington in July, 1956; he had stayed on to see Dulles after the Secretary's return from Lima and later from London. He had pressed the British claims against Nasser with forceful persuasiveness on Dulles. Australia was especially concerned for the passage of her vessels from and to Europe and its Mediterranean countries through the Canal. He was concerned even more for the British strategic position in the Middle East, Britain's relationship to the Arab countries large and small, for that position and the prestige that went with it were part of Australia's assets of security, as they were also of New Zealand's. And there were the bonds of British nationality, the sentiments of patriotism and proud tradition. Furthermore, when Menzies was talking with Dulles, Dulles was reminded that Australia, New Zealand, and the U.S.A. were allies in the ANZUS Pact of 1952 and SEATO, both designed for joint defense in the Pacific and Southeast Asia. Menzies then preceded Dulles to London, in order to confer with Eden. Whatever astonishment and shock Dulles had experienced over the extreme sternness of the British and French determination to obtain redress, it could not possibly have been mitigated by Menzies' persuasions. Menzies possesses a cogent mind, a virile character, and a personality that can be just as tough as Dulles's was.

About the time that Dulles was getting into his plane on August 14, the French Cabinet was in session. It was not only unanimous, but fervid, in its support of Prime Minister Mollet's plan for international control of the Canal.

A little later, in the evening of the same day, Selwyn Lloyd, the British Foreign Secretary, spoke to the British people on radio. He claimed that British action on Suez lived up to the United Nations Charter, in that the Government were pursuing a course validated by Article 33, which requires that the parties to any dispute likely to endanger peace and security shall first of all seek a solution by negotiation, arbitration, judicial settlements, and so on, or by other peaceful means of their own choice. His claim was valid. He insisted that Nasser had used *force,* and that he had violated international law in substance, if not technically. He singled out Nasser as an evildoer distinct from the Egyptian people. He publicly claimed that Britain had originated the idea of the Conference that was about to take place. Thus, by implication, he denied Dulles's boast to have suggested the meeting.

The demeanor of Nasser and his military clique of colonels and commanders continued to oscillate rather consciously, as tactics, between truculence and wheedling. They were in possession of the Canal. Punishment by force was far away. It is much easier to maintain peace and justice by the presence of a small number of troops in a disputed territory than it is to restore them by ten times the number against a hostile force already in occupation. The war in Korea, in its origins and its course, had demonstrated that truth, if it needed demonstration at so late a date in the history of war and peace in this harsh world.

On July 28, Nasser had repeated his violent abuse of the Western powers, thus keeping up the pressure on Dulles as well as on Britain and France. He had screamed defiant and vulgar insults almost to the breaking of his blood vessels, whipping up the crowd into war cries and war dances, in celebration of the fact that "We [Egypt] know the meaning of independence and sovereignty." The people of Egypt had proclaimed of their own accord, he shouted, a general mobilization, that they were under arms! They had done this because Egypt knew imperialism and imperialists and their tricks! Why had the British raised such an uproar? Egypt was free to nationalize as the British had nationalized *their* industries. How dared they interfere with a purely internal affair of Egypt? Hence, the British government's protest had been rejected. The Algerians would teach France a lesson, too, especially as the French Foreign Minister had been rude to the Egyptian Ambassador in Paris!

Like every culprit, self-conscious and self-defensive, he roundly offered his affidavit that the responsibility for interference with shipping in the Canal would henceforth lie on the shoulders of Britain and France, for he was facilitating transit, wasn't he? And shipping had been normal since the nationalization, hadn't it? Egypt had always physically protected the Canal and would continue to do so. (A falsity. The British Fleet and, later, air arm were the Canal's protection, certainly from 1882 to 1956.) "But I announce today to the entire world that Britain and France are today attempting to convert the internal question of nationalization into a political problem—the problem of impeding shipping in the Canal." As though he had not already done so! "We shall meet aggression with aggression and evil with evil. We shall not be lenient where our rights are concerned. They know this all too well. We are ready and have much up our sleeve to meet aggression with aggression and evil with evil." Yes, "aggression"! Nasser had all the language and the tactics ready for the United Nations, language and tactics that might be of use to any of the smaller nations of the world, especially when they had violated their pacts and were in danger of being brought to justice. Did Dulles notice this and draw the proper conclusion that the United Nations may too easily become a sanctuary for transgressors? Or was he intimidated, as Nasser purposely intended?

However, in a press conference three days later, Wing Commander Ali-Sabry, Chief of the Egyptian President's Office for Political Affairs, toned down Nasser's tirade. He assured his listeners that the nationalization did not in any way or to any extent affect the international commitments of Egypt. "We are, as ever, determined to honor all our international obligations; and both the Convention of 1888 and the assurance concerning it given in the Anglo-Egyptian Agreement of 1954 are and will be fully maintained. The freedom of navigation in the Suez Canal is neither affected nor involved in any manner or degree." Notes to this effect were sent to every government and to Dag Hammarskjold, the Secretary General of the United Nations.[7] In the ensuing days, the Egyptian Embassy in Washington had driven the point home to Dulles; and from time to time the Indian Ambassador to Washington had endorsed the Egyptian point of view, adding the Indian government's support of Nasser from the angle of India's own national interests. On the same day as the Sabry declaration, Nehru, who had occupied the state of Kashmir in 1950 and was in continued defiance of the United Nations resolutions to hold a plebiscite there, made his first pronouncement: "Egypt's nationalization of the Canal is a sign of the weakening of European domination of Asia and the Middle East which has lasted more than a hundred years."

Day after day, the Arab nations and the African and Asian nations announced their alignment with Nasser, and not merely formally. They did so with cruel enthusiasm, for they were satisfying their revenge for the outrages, genuine or imaginary, inflicted on them in the past; the reckoning had been only too long delayed! Wherever there were pipelines from the oil fields of the Arabian Peninsula to the Mediterranean or to the Persian Gulf, Arab political parties and Arab workers' unions made ever bolder threats that in the event of trouble for Egypt the pipelines would be cut.

The Egyptian pressure on America was maintained conspicuously by the many conferences between Nasser and the Soviet and Indian Ambassadors in Cairo, plus Krishna Menon, and by appeals to the representatives in Cairo of all the nations invited to the London Conference. The Egyptian-Soviet-Indian liaison was particularly disturbing and mortifying to Dulles. It resulted either in the initiative to refuse to attend the Conference, or in a reinforcement of Nasser's own original decision not to attend—though, even if he had accepted, he would most probably not have attended in person.

Rumors of the refusal reached Dulles by August 3 or 4, for Nasser called in Ambassador Byroade on August 3. Byroade had been instructed to bring home to Nasser all the unfortunate *economic* consequences that might befall Egypt, if he would make no settlement satisfactory to the maritime powers; that more serious consequences than the economic ones might ensue; that he had much to gain by good behavior. Nasser, in response, fulminated against the pressure being put on Egypt by the military preparations and diplomatic offensive being undertaken by Britain and France. He reiterated all the complaints against colonialism and imperialism and lamented the wounds his country had suffered from them. As he had been doing for some time in his controlled press, he tried on Byroade the gainful tactic of separating America from her Western allies by praising the "moderation" of the U.S. government.

It was evident, from the discussion, how Nasser would meet any attempt to find a settlement that bound his will in the slightest, as the restitution of an international authority for managing the Canal would be sure to do: he would display complete intransigence, to the point of war. His political director, Wing Commander Sabry, said so explicitly, at about the same time. On August 4, Nasser publicly threatened to fight if the West pressed its demands for international control of the Canal. He probed the soft spot in the hearts of Dulles, of Eisenhower, and of a large part of the American people, and, of course, of all the newly emancipated peoples beyond the Western Hemisphere, when he said: "It would be like trading one kind of colonialism for another." This is an argument that Dulles should have resolutely rebutted from the very beginning and with all his power: it should have been met head on and argued down. Dulles should have declared that the keeping of international treaties is *not* colonialism; that a treaty is an agreement among sovereign nations, *not* colonial subjection; that the Convention of 1888 was *not* colonialism to begin with; that its breach by Nasser was an international crime; that colonialism was not the issue, except in Nasser's perfervid and ambitious inciter's brain. Dulles's failure to do so ended in war.

Nasser also brought to bear upon Dulles's mind, and on Eisenhower's, the very arguments his Political Affairs Office was gleaning from the Western newspapers, most of all those in America, that the Arab would wage a guerrilla war against the allies. He threatened a long-drawn-out guerrilla war such as was being waged in Algeria, a war that would spread throughout the entire Middle East. The U.S.

government itself had manipulated this very effect when it had induced the British to abandon the Suez Canal base. The idea of a guerrilla war had a potent inhibiting and enfeebling effect on the Near Eastern advisers in the State Department as well as upon some in its Division of United Nations Affairs—and in the Pentagon, whose strategy and tactics had been reshaped by Dulles and Eisenhower and their addiction to "massive deterrence." This policy of massive deterrence was more a budgetary measure sponsored by the Secretary of the Treasury, George M. Humphrey, than a proper policy of military and political decision. Now, and in similar cases later, it was to plague Dulles, but, far more, his poor allies, because the Pentagon was not equipped for less than all-out war. Hence, the inclination to do nothing.

What State Department officials and the Pentagon overestimated was the capacity of the Arabs, at that time, to fight a guerrilla war of any duration and weight in the midst of the certain complete disruption of their economy, including a complete economic blockade, that could be effectively undertaken by the Western powers if the laws of war were applied. France did not blockade Algeria, as in a war between sovereign states, for a very good reason: the one million European settlers who lived in Algeria. But no such inhibition applied to Egypt. It is a point that I shall consider again later; it has immense pertinence for future policy towards small nations who violate international law and treaties.

Nasser understood exactly how to frighten Dulles and Eisenhower, and he did it. It was in a conference of August 6, of about three-quarters of an hour at the White House, that Dulles had recited his fears of war and sabotage in the Middle East, the fears that Nasser proceeded to exploit against him. In this conference, too, another error was made—the assumption that all Arab nations would actually fight on Nasser's side, when so far all that they were doing was only to join the applause and to shout threats.

Now, oil supplies for America and Europe had at once been seized upon by the President as a first concern. Admiral Radford, Chairman of the Joint Chiefs of Staff, was also fearful of an interruption of supply. The oil interests of American businessmen were in jeopardy. All wrongly believed that the oil-producing Moslem nations, Iraq, Iran, and Saudi Arabia, would reduce their production for the sake of Nasser, as though they would not wish to continue to collect their vast oil revenues. Astutely conscious of the political leverage which the oil industry offered in the United States, Nasser on August 6 met one of the Western charges against him. He stated that he intended to devote a large share of the revenues from the Canal to modernizing and widening the Canal, to make the passage of larger oil tankers possible. "It is in Egypt's interest to facilitate the navigation of the Canal." What could be fairer than that? The Canal always open and operating, the Canal modernized?

The day afterwards another maneuver issued from Cairo, calculated to wring the heartstrings of the Administration. A threat was made to bring Britain and France before the Security Council on charges that they intended to use force and thereby imperil world peace! Such an imbroglio is exactly what Dulles did *not* want to happen, for reasons to be explained shortly.

A meeting between U.S. Ambassador Byroade and Egypt's Foreign Minister Mahmoud Fawzi on August 7, at the former's request, foreshadowed the imminent bad news that Egypt would not attend the London Conference. On that day, Dulles had the economic aid to Egypt ($33 million had been appropriated) suspended "pending the settlement of the Suez crisis." After all, his Western allies were pressing hard for practical evidence of serious intentions, and furthermore, he now personally detested Nasser. It was not surprising that next day Cairo let it be leaked out that it was beneath Egypt's dignity to attend the Conference "under present circumstances." The day after, Cairo both hailed India's statement that India would attend, and, simultaneously, established a Liberation Army for training the whole population in guerrilla tactics. Then, a day or so beyond this, perhaps merely as exploration, the Egyptian government asked the U.S. government for supplies of wheat and flour on purchase—and received no answer.

The Egyptian statement rejecting the invitation [8] was issued on August 12. It was one-half legal wrangling, the other half polemics, deftly interwoven with keening recriminations and, at the end, heavy and abusive defiance. Both parts were as displeasing to Dulles as they were joyful to Moscow. Nasser had taken Dulles's measure; being hammered, Dulles would give way, while making verbose objections.

The main point on which the Egyptian government insisted was that the Suez Canal Company was an Egyptian corporation fully created and unilaterally amendable by Egypt at any time, and in its full discretion a totally internal affair of Egypt. To this end, Egypt heavily brought to the foreground the character of the original concession by the Egyptian government, and the fact that the concession was, in any case, to last only another twelve years, to 1968. In doing this, it claimed that it rebutted any other effect of the Convention of 1888, which provided in its preamble that the purpose of the Convention was "to establish a *definite system* designed to guarantee to all states the free usage of the Canal." A "system" was set up in perpetuity, even though the particular administrative arrangement that had actually been evolved since 1888 was not necessarily the only conceivable one. But the Egyptian statement perverted the provisions of the Convention to mean that once the Suez Canal Company and the system of management it represented lapsed in twelve years' time, management of the Canal would be left to Egypt's sovereign will. So, if in 1968, why not in 1956? All one had to do, to represent Nasser's seizure and the new regime as legal, was, it would seem, to ignore the Convention of 1888 and the "definite system" which had grown up to fulfill it since that time. This the Egyptian lawyers had attempted to do, though they found it a very sticky problem.[9] Since they started from the political premise that the *only* problem was Egypt's sovereignty, the right to do as she liked so long as no one interfered to stop her, it was on Egyptian sovereignty that they obstinately insisted.

It was, tactically, a very difficult claim for Dulles to resist, because so much of American foreign policy, particularly in its world struggle with Communism, was a continuous and raucous insistence on the right of nations to self-determination and sovereignty. If nations were seeking to become sovereign states, or to preserve their independence if they had it, then they would beware of and resist Soviet attacks, subversion, and seductions, and they would range themselves on Dulles's side. As it was already clear, Nasser's military and diplomatic revolutionaries had learned in every note the lullaby or lamentation or lashing language that would touch the just heart of Dulles and many other Americans.

In the more polemical part of the statement, Nasser challenged the alleged "confusion between the Suez Canal Company and the freedom of navigation" as "but another illustration of a deliberate attempt to find excuses for interfering in the internal affairs and sovereignty of Egypt. . . . The Egyptian government considers the proposal for the creation of an international authority is but a mild word for what should be called collective colonialism." This was a most ominous warning note for the U.S. Secretary of State. Then, having exhibited his clean hands, legally, and proclaimed himself as a keeper of promises and treaties, and asserted his sense of injury at being juridically assailed by the wicked breakers of the law, Britain and France (this is what his allegation amounted to), the Egyptian ruler used a very familiar diplomatic technique. He claimed that Egypt was being treated aggressively, by "a planned conspiracy [associated with the three powers' communiqué] aiming at starving and threatening the Egyptian people." This conspiracy included the freezing of Egyptian assets, the mobilization of reserves, and the movements of military forces. America was included in the charges of economic pressure, while Britain and France were denounced for military pressure as well. Britain and France were, in fact, accused of taking a course inconsistent with the United Nations Charter, which they had bound themselves to respect! This arrogant accusation came from a government which had defied the Security Council's resolutions and the

Convention of 1888 by closing the Canal to Israeli ships, the vessels of a sovereign nation! It claimed all rights, admitted no obligations! The statement then denied that the coming Conference was competent to make decisions. For Egypt, "the country whom the matter directly concerns," had not been in any way consulted about preparations for the Conference. Therefore, the invitation could not be accepted.

However, being peaceful, being devoted to the United Nations Charter (how Egypt was to bless devotion to it by others than herself later in this crisis!) and to the decisions of the Bandung Conference, the government declared itself willing to sponsor with the signatories a more widely attended conference to review the Convention of 1888 and to reach an agreement of all countries concerned guaranteeing the freedom of navigation of the Canal. The agreement would be registered with the United Nations. But this Egyptian proposal failed to include any hint of an agency, an institution, a regime which should implement the said guarantee of freedom of navigation.

The second paragraph of the Egyptian statement—which could well have been inserted after much else had already been drafted—contained this clause: "The administration of the Canal was transferred to an independent authority with an independent budget. The authority was empowered with all the necessary powers without being limited by government rules and systems." The Egyptian intelligentsia was instantaneously demonstrating that it could exclude politics from the management of the Canal!

The Secretary had left himself open to this kind of crafty hoax, for he had been a leading spirit, backed by his policy-planning staff, in trying "to take the politics out of" the Suez conflict. He and his assistants had envisioned *not* an international political authority to run the Canal, installed if necessary after pressure was put on Nasser to restore what he had seized, but instead a kind of technical administration-cum-juridical-cum-fiscal robot, to manage or supervise the management of the Canal. Dulles got what he seemed to be asking for—as we shall see.

It is essential to the understanding of all that follows to apprehend that the Egyptian leaders henceforward were exploiting the letter of the law cynically, that they were not seriously concerned with obeying it. For four years they had been seeking a legal loophole in the Suez Canal treaties of concession and in the Convention of 1888. If a nation dislikes a treaty, it can always find a quibble (as with any civil contract, but more surely in a document of international obligation) to evade its responsibility. If the quibble is slippery, it retreats to a quarrel with the conditions under which the treaty was made. The Egyptian leaders now made such a retreat. Their attitude is well reflected in a letter written by the London correspondent (an Egyptian) of the *Akhbar El Yom* newspapers, to the *Times* from his London office, on August 6.

> But can you honestly ask us or expect us to agree to, or approve of, all that is in the Convention [of 1888], which no Egyptian Government in the proper sense of the word ever accepted or endorsed; nor were Egyptians participant to this Convention. In 1888 we were not a nation in the proper sense, we had no Government to reflect our feelings; we were victims of foreign domination and intrigues. Not until the Egyptian revolution [he meant 1952] did we have a free and independent Egyptian Government. Those who talk about this old [sic] document should bear this in mind.

This kind of philosophy directly attacks the sanctity of treaties. It does not even accept their renegotiation by peaceful procedure. It sends the world back into an infinite regression to the never-existent day of imaginary beginnings when pacts were made in all innocence, or forward to the day when pacts are to be abrogated by the dissatisfied party, or re-established by the party whose rights have been violated thereby. It offends against the rule of international law that successor states (Egypt was a successor to the Turkish Empire) must keep previously established obligations.

From August 3, Russian intentions opened out. The Soviet Union, successor to Tsarist Russia, was the custodian of Russia's rights and obligations in the Canal. She, like Communist China, claimed an interest in the maintenance of free passage through the Canal. But she had another interest, superior to this: to buffet and cripple the economic and strategic power assets of the United States and the NATO alliance, of which Britain and France were principal members, and to infiltrate her own power and personnel into the lands of the Middle East. Hence, her almost immediate support of the righteousness of the seizure of the Canal and continual fulminations against the military measures being taken by the Western powers. Soon, another theme entered into the stream of Soviet tactical propaganda being poured out to the four corners of the earth. It was a theme that the Egyptian government press and spokesmen had sounded. It must have surged up into the minds of Nasser and Soviet Ambassador Kiselev in their frequent and lengthy conferences. If the Suez Canal needed international management because it served the shipping of so many nations, why not *an international regime for the Panama Canal?* Yes, why not Panama, and the Kiel Canal, leading to the North Atlantic from the Baltic and Russian waters? Why not the Dardanelles? And, if not these, then why the Suez Canal? Of course, the Russian press would not want this internationalization of management to go too far, to rule the orifices of the land mass held or dominated by Russia. For example, it ought not to apply to the Baltic and White Sea Canal; or the Volga-Don system; or the Danube. Perhaps, even, the Dardanelles was rather dubious, because it was better from Russia's strategic point of view to have the Straits administered by Turkey alone (a country which, after all, could be wiped out by the Soviet Union quite easily), rather than have all the other nations of the world joined together in the management of a passageway to and from the Black Sea.

As a matter of fact, Dulles viewed with considerable vexation the Panama problem. Dropped heavily on his doorstep by Nasser, Bulganin, and Khrushchev, and *by the British Conservatives*, and by British left-wingers in the Labour Party, it presented him with a nice problem in side-stepping. It had come up unpleasantly at a meeting he had called, August 7, of Latin American nations. He hoped this conference would assist him in winning over the support of anti-colonial nations for eventual use at the United Nations. All the Latin-American countries were invited—with the exception of Panama. This was a remarkably brusque display of United States power when acting in her own immediate interests. Dulles believed the tactic was morally good. He explained to the Latin Americans his conception of the dispute, and then expressed his concern that Britain and France might regard Egypt's use of force in seizing the Canal as grounds for intervention, under Article 51 of the Charter, which allows nations the inherent right of self-defense immediately when they are attacked with arms.

Dulles's exposition of the crisis to the Latin American envoys (it is among his papers at Princeton) contained very serious apprehensions of the damage that Nasser had done, and confessions of the inability to bring him to order other than by force. He repeated the anxiety of his allies that Egypt would be master over their very life, that Nasser entertained very deep hatred of them, and that they refused to accept the position of being second-rate powers. Dulles admitted to his audience that economic and financial pressures could not be adequate. Therefore, he thought Britain and France would use force. His Legal Counsel, Herman Phleger, concurred. They would use force on the plea that they were acting in self-defense.

Colombia's Ambassador to the U.S.A.* asked Dulles to explain what he meant. He answered with some hesitation, apparently mental as well as elocutionary:

> I don't know what would happen. The British and French maintain that their economic lives can be threatened at any

* A curious error is contained in the State Department private memorandum on the colloquy between Dulles and the Latin American ambassadors on August 7, 1956, starting at 10:36 A.M. It attributes to the *Panamanian* Ambassador the questions asked by the Colombian Ambassador. The Panamanian Ambassador was not present; he had not been invited. This is gleaned from Dulles's papers in the Princeton University Library.

> moment by the closing of the Canal. Maybe they would act under the Treaty of 1888. . . . Maybe they would consider the military occupation of the Canal that had already taken place would give them grounds for that.

It was later explained by the State Department's press officer that the Secretary of State had not meant to imply that the seizure of the Canal *was* grounds for the use of force, but only that Britain and France might *consider* it as "a *juridical* basis for the use of force." [10]

However, the main point here was that Panama was not invited. And Panama asked Dulles why she had not been invited. What the answer was is not reported, but the reason for the omission is known to Dulles's closest associates: "Very inconvenient questions would have been asked by the Panamanian representative, and the Panamanians would be prejudiced about how to treat Nasser." The next day, at the President's press conference, Eisenhower was heckled on this point, the Associated Press correspondent observing that Panama had not been invited to the London Conference either, despite the fact that she was one of the biggest shipping countries in the world. The answer caused smiles. "I didn't know they were irritated, and I can't comment on it because this is the first time I have thought about it."

At any rate, the Soviet Union pressed the issue of the Panama Canal in the hope of weakening American power in the Western Hemisphere. Having leapt over the Mediterranean in the summer of the summit meeting, 1955, bearing arms into the Middle East, she now sought an opportunity to leap over the Atlantic and scotch the Monroe Doctrine. Also, on August 7, the Syrian Ambassador in Washington was brazen enough to support Nasser's position by suggesting that the recipe for the international management of the Suez Canal might be extended to the Panama Canal! The have-not nations know the jugular of those nations that have.

The United States needed Russia's attendance at the Conference, by reason of Russia's power in the world and her ability to sway other nations, and in order to find the maximum attainable consensus on a settlement with Nasser. Charles E. Bohlen, United States Ambassador to Moscow, called on Soviet Foreign Minister Dimitri I. Shepilov on August 7 to find out how matters stood. The Russian press already foreshadowed attendance, that is, Shepilov's attendance, but suggested strong, unconceding support for Nasser.

When it came on August 9, 1956, the Soviet acceptance of the invitation, as expected, took the offensive all along the line against the Western position as expressed in the tripartite communiqué of August 3.[11] Since these arguments are repeated in the first London Conference, they will be deferred until the next chapter.

Russia would, however, attend the Conference. Why? For the

noblest reasons, of course: "as a champion of the peaceful settlement of international issues," and as a "determined supporter of further reduction of international tension, including tension in the Near and Middle East." But the Soviet government would not be committed to any restrictions or obligations arising from the principles the Western powers had stated in their communiqué; no harm must be done to Egypt's sovereign rights and dignity. "Dignity!" The Soviet government had picked up one of Nasser's most frequently trumpeted slogans.

India, too, was to attend the Conference; and it seemed that she would, like Russia, be an adversary of the Western powers there. Secretary of State Dulles was not fond of Pandit Nehru or Krishna Menon. Perhaps the witticism about these two men current in the diplomatic corps had not yet reached him. It ran, "While Nehru is Dorian Gray, Menon is the Picture of Dorian Gray." In any case, he was not fond of them. He knew how deep and contemptuous was the hatred Menon bore towards the United States, a sour, corrosive hatred of what he regarded as an inferior civilization, if a civilization at all. Menon had tried to influence Nehru with this disparagement when the latter was on his way to his first visit in the United States. Menon must have been born that way, *malin;* and he developed in England the belief that he had better ability and soul to rule England or the world than, say, Prime Minister Stanley Baldwin, or the Marquis of Salisbury, or Anthony Eden, or the rest of them, had it not been for the land of his origin and the color of his skin. Whatever the truth of this belief, the strategic balance of the world now placed him in a position of cardinal moral influence in the United Nations.

The moralizing of Nehru, which Menon shared, was as firm, as well-based, as articulately expressed, and as pontifical as Dulles's United States Christianity. The conclusions were, of course, quite different, especially in foreign affairs, for Nehru and Menon were India Firsters. Nehru remained unshaken by the possibility of losing the grants and gifts from the U.S.A. which meant life and death for his plan for the economic development of India—a plan which at best would in ten years raise the per capita income from about $58 per head to $60. The swift increase of the population ate up so much of the actual increase in productivity. He dared Dulles on his conscience—took him to the brink of his conscience, we might say—to refuse him aid, whatever he did. It was a kind of readiness to commit national hara-kiri on Dulles's moral doorstep. The aid was continued, and so was the dislike at being caught in the coils of one's own Christian conscience, so very often affirmed in the hearing of all. It is said that later on, Nehru, in several talks with Dulles, convinced him of the positive value of neutralism.[12] At any rate, in the year of Suez, Dulles was unreconstructed in the matter of neutralism *à la Nehru.*

The Indian Ambassadors in Cairo (N.A.Y.J. Bahabur) and Washington (G. L. Mehta) were busy with Nasser and Dulles respectively. Above all, Menon, minister without portfolio in Nehru's Cabinet, and Chairman of the Indian Delegation to the United Nations General Assembly, took an advocate's, even a champion's interest in Nasser's side of the question. Prime Minister Nehru, too, had great sympathy with Nasser for at least two reasons over and above Nehru's normal intention to do the best for the interests of India as his first priority. He had had some influence with Nasser at the Bandung Conference, and he had been with him in the parleys with Tito of Yugoslavia, another neutral, in the days just prior to the retraction of the offer of the loan for Aswan. At Brioni, as we have recounted, these three had reasserted their leadership among the neutrals of the world. They did not intend to let each other down.

On August 8 Nehru declared that India would attend the London Conference. His announcement differed in its emphasis from the Soviet's view that Egyptian sovereignty was the principal issue. Nehru, of course, heavily stressed this point, but also made mention of Egypt's international obligations: "The character of the waterway as of 'international importance' is recognized in the solemn agreement of 1954 in which the determination to uphold the Convention of 1888 was expressed by both Egypt and Britain."

The Indian government was worried because the Western powers were concerned not to surrender these assets of the Company "not impressed with an international interest," for the Canal Company had many other investments beyond the Canal itself.[13] What worried India most of all was the military preparations being made by Britain and France. For this produced a "grave crisis" with a mounting of passions, whereas a calmer atmosphere and rational outlook must be the foremost consideration. An additional source of anxiety was the fact that, in the background of the immediate alleged offense, other issues arose: "the upsurge and conflict of mighty forces." It is not difficult to realize to what Nehru was referring—nationalism, colonialism, anticolonialism, and so on. Nehru thought that the manner of the withdrawal of the Aswan Dam loan "hurt Egypt's pride and self-respect." But Nehru had not directly discussed this with Nasser. He thought that the seizure of the Canal and the matters dealt with in the tripartite communiqué of August 3 were not in themselves sufficient to cause "the violence of the reactions and the warlike gestures." The latter, the allies' economic and military actions, had been grievous in their results.

The government of India, then, would participate in the Conference—for this "is how best they could serve the cause of averting conflict and obtaining a peaceful settlement before it is too late." But India could not beforehand be bound by the conclusions to be reached, and would not take part in war preparations or any other pressures which challenged the sovereign rights of Egypt. The British government had assured India that it was not bound by the principles set out in the tripartite communiqué. Also, India recognized that Egypt could not participate in a conference in which she was merely an invitee. Nehru thought Burma and Yugoslavia should have been invited as well.

What was strange was that, while India was a member of the British Commonwealth, Nehru omitted mention of this fact. He was satisfied with the phrase "India has also good relations with the principal Western powers." India had kept in close contact with Indonesia and Ceylon and with others who had a broadly similar approach to hers. There would be no final decision, for that required the agreement of Egypt. Nehru underlined India's own self-interest in the proper running of the Canal: she is "not a disinterested party. She is a principal user of this waterway, and her economic life and development are not unaffected by disputes, not to speak of worse developments, in regard to it."

Thus, if Dulles thought to bend Nasser away from the strictest interpretation of his sovereignty, he would find he had an implacable adversary in India's representative. And yet—who knows but that he secretly relished the fact that India, also, was a drag on British and French determination, a domesticated Trojan Horse? Opinion in India was that the West had better accept Nasser's stroke peacefully and that if they wanted redress they should go to the United Nations, a curious view for those who held Kashmir by the most tenuous of legalisms and in defiance of the United Nations.

Two or three days afterwards the Indian Ambassador to Washington called on Dulles and told him that the Indian government did not like Dulles's plan for international management of the Canal. Meanwhile, Krishna Menon, en route from New Delhi to London, stopped off for lengthy conferences with Nasser, and it was rumored that his role at the Conference would be that of spokesman for the absentee Egyptians.

At this point, it was still unclear whether the dispute over the Suez Canal would be taken before the U.N. If ever there was a dispute or a situation threatening peace, it was the seizure of the Canal. It could even raise the possibility of action in "self-defense." [14] By August 2, Gaitskell, leader of the Opposition in Parliament, had asked that the United Nations be the forum of decision of the dispute. This was at the end of a speech otherwise extremely militant against Nasser.

At first sight, it would seem to have been a moral obligation of Dulles as a good world citizen, which he incessantly claimed, in varying language, to be, to take the matter to the United Nations. To my surprise, even to my shock, I learned from the highest source possible how very cool the State Department, which means Dulles, was to this course. When I asked, "Why did you not take this matter to the United Nations straight away?" I received the answer: "Why should we? It was no business of ours. There was no issue for the U.S.A. to take action on." I reminded my informant of Article 34: "The Security Council may investigate any dispute, or any situation which might lead to international friction or give rise to a dispute"—if the situation is "likely to endanger the maintenance of international peace and security." He still evinced and defended American detachment: "Britain could have done this; why ask it of the United States?" After further interrogation he ventured, "Dulles was unsure of Britain's legal position on the Canal." Now this was true; Dulles *was* unsure of the law relating to the Canal, and so was everybody else. But this unsureness was not the ground of his masterly care to avoid going to the United Nations.

On this occasion, especially because the Middle Eastern troubles had been put before the United Nations some months earlier [15] in the hope that Hammarskjold could bring some tranquillity into the relationship between Egypt and Israel, there were earnest colloquies in the State Department on the attitude to be taken now that force might be used over Suez. It was a situation that was vexatious and dangerous. Would an immediate appeal to the United Nations work best for peace and the just settlement of the issue? Dulles soon made up his mind to work in accordance with Article 33 of the Charter (already quoted), which charged that the parties should attempt to settle their dispute by *other* modalities than in the bosom of the United Nations itself. He decided to try to exhaust all the other resources, especially direct ambassadorial diplomacy and conferences, first. For usually the United Nations procedure was slow, while now events were moving fast. And, furthermore, the Russians could make havoc of the appeals by Britain and France in the United Nations. Long before a clear picture of the possibilities in a more direct approach had become manifest, the matter would be embroiled, obscured, torn to pieces by all the other disputes in the world, including the question of internationalizing every important waterway. If the United Nations ruled altogether against the Western claims, or so adversely as to preclude any further hope in the United Nations, then the moment for the use of force would arrive all the earlier. Dulles also put faith, far too much faith as events later demonstrated, in the pressure of "world opinion" on Nasser, and perhaps also on Britain and France. But for world opinion to mature and be effective, years were needed.

Therefore, Dulles asked Hammarskjold to come to Washington, because the Secretary General, it was rumored, wanted to have the Suez affair on the agenda of the General Assembly when its normal annual session convened on November 12. Hammarskjold wanted a declaration by the Assembly upholding the Convention of 1888—and seemed to believe that this would suffice to satisfy the respective claims of the aggrieved users and Egypt. It could readily be foreseen that if the West put the matter on the agenda, it would be counterattacked on Panama, Gibraltar, Aden, Singapore, Hong Kong, etc., etc. If Egypt raised this "colonial" issue, then the West would raise the question of Egypt's blockade of the Suez to Israel—and then, a dreadful event would have occurred in Dulles's judgment, that is to say, *the Israeli-Arab dispute would have been brought into an already tangled and overwrought situation.* On August 10, after some reflection and staff work, Dulles went to see Hammarskjold in New York, with the purpose of blocking Egypt's rumored desire to bring the Suez crisis to the United Nations by accusing Britain and France of disturbing the peace!

By the time the Secretary left for London, he had his way, and damped down any appeals to the United Nations for the time being. Indeed, he had managed to overcome in his own mind a criticism that had been advanced in various quarters, to the effect that he had made a diplomatic error in inducing the British and French ministers in London on August 2 to *omit* the reference to the U.N. from their own drafts of the tripartite communiqué before that document was finally accepted for publication. At that time he had strongly pressed the point that there had better be *no mention* of the United Nations, because the Soviet veto there would make any desirable settlement impossible. It suited the Anglo-French military pressure on Nasser.

One other factor in the situation Dulles had to assess in London was the Labour Party's growing opposition to the British Government (and even more, possibly, to the French Government of Socialist Prime Minister Guy Mollet). It had reversed its first patriotic outburst against Nasser, its insistence on no force. It now demanded recourse to the United Nations.

It is possible that Dulles was tipped off to the likelihood of a sharp change in the attitude of the Labour Party by one of Sir Anthony Eden's confidential and immediate official assistants, who saw Dulles on August 2, had talked with him on many earlier occasions, and was reputed to be a connoisseur of American public and official opinion. At any rate, the day after he had made his strongly anti-Nasser and vigorously pro-British speech in the House of Commons, Hugh Gaitskell, the leader of the party, was heavily assailed by many of his associates. These men bore down on him for not curbing the belligerent attitude of the Conservative Party, bent, as they thought it was, on the use of force. They claimed that had they not worried away at Gaitskell through the Labour Party's Foreign Affairs Committee, he would not have modified his blasts against Nasser in his peroration admonishing the Government (August 2) to beware lest it use force outside the United Nations Charter.

As the August days went on, the Labour Party became increasingly vehement in its opposition to Eden's Government and its Suez policy. It believed, or said it did, that force was intended, and that attendance at a conference or two was a mere blind to the public on the way to war.

Now, the Labour Party is for the most part, though the generalization does not usually apply to the highest three or four of its leadership, pacifist, and this in varying degrees. The Party is also anti-colonialist. Three brands of pacifism can be discerned in the English body politic, and all find a home in the Labour Party. One can be called *Tribune* pacifism; a second, *Manchester Guardian* pacifism; and a third, *New Statesman* pacifism. The *Tribune*, a weekly magazine, is in the hands of left-wing Labour members or their friends, but these are diverse in their pacifism, its absoluteness and its rationale. Some, like Brockway, Silverman, Warbey, and Koni Zilliacus, are out-and-out socialist pacifists. Zilliacus and a few who follow him are almost indistinguishable from Muscovite Communists in their domestic and foreign policy. Less radical was Aneurin Bevan.

The men of this persuasion soon organized a kind of petition by twenty-four Labour M.P.'s to Gaitskell and the Press and the Prime Minister, opposing forceful intervention against Egypt's action, which they considered as not justifying force. Nationalizers themselves, they accepted the legality of nationalization, and cared less for action, other than that in the United Nations, to guarantee the Convention of 1888. They never clearly stated whether they would accept *any* solution the United Nations voted as just, for they had no immediate responsibility, as the Cabinet had, for England's safety and welfare. They were in a position to indulge all their fantasies about the sweetness of human nature, their rancor against England unregenerate—that is, England not in their personal image—and their delirium at being the champions of the noble (a category that excluded British Conservatives, the "Establishment," employers of labor, and Americans). They hated the Eden Government, and they organized committees and public meetings to work up the public and other M.P.'s against Gaitskell's stand of August 2, as being too belligerent and insufficiently socialist. They praised Dulles (temporarily) for being a leader of the "peace forces" of the world, for helping to impede the Government's movement towards war. They organized the writing of letters to the *Times* and the *Manchester Guardian* and brought argument to bear on the *Daily Mirror*, with its daily circulation of 5,000,000 and its leftward and demagogic tendency, already disposed to belabor Eden and his Cabinet. Some among these organizers of pacifism are properly referred to by their contemporary, the *Economist*, as the "lunatic fringe," for their views of world politics, noble as they may have been in seeking to herald the day of Isaiah's prophecy, which we all may hope will be fulfilled, almost totally disregarded the actual state of relationships between nations and between man and man within them.

The *Manchester Guardian*, of relatively small circulation (100,-000 per day), but very influential among those of influential opinion—the second and third tiers of what is called the "Establishment"—took, from the earliest days, a stand which not unfairly may be called the "commercial view" of the Suez seizure. It advocated surrendering to the United Nations anything that Britain might claim as its rights in Suez. "Commercial breaches," it said, "are a cause for energetic action short of war; they cannot remotely justify going into battle" (August 9, 1956). If oil has to cost more, then it just has to cost more. (It all seemed very reasonable to accept the *fait accompli*, and abjure force. The cost of going via the Cape rather than through Suez would add some $207 million per year to the British bill for oil, compared with a gross national product of $50 billion.[16] Who would go to war for that?)

The editorial leaders of the *Guardian* canvassed every pessimistic possibility about securing redress from Nasser. The paper had risen to influence by its leadership of the Liberal Party in its heyday, by its sobriety in crises, and by its power with the written word, as well as by the comfort it gave to the country clergymen—those who liked a sweet world, no struggle, abiding mercy, compassion without limit, the mild, unrobust, but conscience-stricken and fractious Christianity of the country parsonage. It continued this vein of rational contemplation, of stoic surrender to the United Nations, in the face of all that institution's impossibilities, and of the quest of "Little Englandism."

The *New Statesman* leadership in the Suez crisis was rather like the *Guardian's* except that it appealed more to those who were socialist, as the *Guardian* is not; peevish and splenetic, whereas the *Guardian* tends rather to be mawkish; and caustically anti-American, whereas with America, the *Guardian* is but mildly and condescendingly admonitory. The *New Statesman* preached that force was illegal, immoral, and impossible, to solve the transgressions of Nasser.

At any rate, by August 13 the anti-Government groups, and even those that were anti-Gaitskell, had mobilized their opposition to the strong measures being taken, and the further ones apparently being contemplated, by the Government to the point where England was now seriously divided. On August 13 the Shadow Cabinet met: this is the journalists' term for the leading figures of the Opposition in Parliament. It was headed, of course, by the leader, Gaitskell. The Shadow Cabinet brought together all the protests being voiced against the policy of the Government and incorporated them into a statement; this was taken by Gaitskell to the Prime Minister the next day, August 14. He also requested the Prime Minister to disclaim publicly any intention of resorting to force should the coming London Conference fail. This the Prime Minister refused to do. That evening Labour Party- and Communist-inspired crowds converged on 10 Downing Street, chanting, "We want peace!" and "Go to the United Nations!"

This rift in England's official political hierarchy was a factor in Dulles's policy. It was something he banked on, once it appeared. The moral elements in his own speeches fed it, not unintentionally. At the August 12 meeting at the White House, President Eisenhower had been apprised of it, and he, too, proceeded to make use of it. "Closing the meeting," reports Sherman Adams, an eye-witness, "Eisenhower tried to express some of his usual optimism by telling the Congressmen that he had been greatly encouraged by the stand taken in England by Hugh Gaitskell in opposing the use of military force against Nasser until all possible attempts to reach a peaceful settlement had been exhausted." [17] The President worded this statement, it may be noted, *not* as a man who had absolutely excluded the use of force might have done.

Dulles might have been a little more worried than Eisenhower was, or as he himself was, if he had digested the results of the Gallup poll in England about August 4.[18] In that poll, 68 per cent of all voters denied Egypt's right to nationalize the Suez Canal; 65 per cent asserted Nasser could not be trusted to keep his international engagements; 33 per cent favored the use of military force if Egypt should refuse to accept the decisions of the London Conference; 47 per cent favored the use of further economic and political sanctions. Of course, the percentages in the case of Conservative voters were much higher. But 30 per cent of Labour voters were in favor of force, in the context mentioned above, and 52 per cent for economic and political sanctions (a course that might lead to war). When the "no opinion" figures are set aside, the statistics are substantial support of a strong policy against Nasser, and thus of the Government's position. The *Times* supported the Government *in toto;* so did the *Daily Telegraph*, the *Daily Mail*, and the *Daily Express*, these with greater vehemence. The *Sunday Times*, though conservative, opposed the use of force.

Still, looking at the hand that had been dealt him, Dulles saw in his first card the grim determination of Britain and France, led by statesmen with agile minds, to make war, if necessary, to secure redress and to vindicate the sanctity of treaties, and the resolution behind this of shoring up their respective positions in the Middle East and Algeria. The second showed the solidarity of half the world in support of Nasser's defiance. The third showed more particularly the physical and moral power of the Soviet Union and the moral power of India backing Nasser's ideas of legality and nationalist force. The fourth was one of mixed potential, displaying both the appeal and the unreliability and snares of the United Nations. And, finally, the fifth card contained something promising—Britain was divided, and about half of the British political leaders (admittedly a motley crew, some of whom he detested at all ordinary times), along with a large part of the British people, favored a peaceful conclusion to the conflict. Some Britons were already cheering Dulles, a most unusual gratification for him.

Now, how was he to play his hand? First, he must appear to go along with his allies and the maritime powers, but he must avoid a war which would cause his own country to suffer: as the President had required. Why should the United States be injured? Secondly, he must show respect for Nasser's sovereignty, and while making some threatening gestures, do nothing that would push Nasser totally into Russia's plot against the free world. Thirdly, he must argue with Russia and India before the whole world, in the hope of demonstrating that their attitude and interests were inimical to a peaceful settlement —then write these off as impossible. Fourth, he must keep away from the United Nations. Fifth, he must follow a policy of justice with peace, for this, as well as being right, was, fortunately, what one-half of the British people wanted, and they would bring pressure to bear on Eden: in short, he must see to the restoration of practical guarantees of the universal right to free passage of the Canal. Delay, and hope for something to turn up after the Conference had played its timely part, would hopefully obviate the use of force, especially since its use by Britain and France would almost certainly provoke Russia to violent retort.

The formidable question, however, was this: Would such a policy satisfy the intense feeling of the British that Nasser, with the opportunistic help of the Soviet Union, was bent on making himself master of the Middle East? There was much concern whether the arms and technicians the Russians had supplied were for nothing more adventurous in world strategy than a local war game and a vexation. So far, Eisenhower had shown no sympathy for Eden's fears of Russian designs, in spite of his Secretary's almost pathologically expressed hatred of Soviet Communism and imperialism. Dulles now neared a confrontation with the realities. He inspired in President Eisenhower the confidence that his negotiating virtuosity could succeed, and he had purveyed to the President an account of the facts that enabled both the President and himself to be sanguine about success: "Leave it to me!"

6. DULLES'S FINEST HOUR—AND STRANGE DEFAULT

FORCE, IN A SENSE, WAS NOW IN THE HANDS OF NASSER, FOR HE HAD BY force dispossessed the owners and rightful claimants to free and open passage and held the Canal by his arms. The problem was to dislodge him. But, by what means? Would argument do it? Would reason do it? With some other person in the U.S. Presidency, or in the chief leadership of Egypt, an arrangement short of force might have been feasible. Under existing circumstances the question was, could Nasser be brought to contribute his part to a peaceful solution? Dulles's puzzle, as he conceived it, was whether the issue of sanctions on Nasser, some kind of coercive action, could be avoided, evaded, averted. He acted as though he believed it could. By the end of the first London Conference, it seemed that he was right. It was his finest hour.

The American delegation, with Dulles at the head, arrived in London at 10 A.M. on Wednesday, August 15, 1956. At 11 A.M., with indefatigable energy and hopes, Dulles met at the Embassy with his senior advisers, nine in number,[1] including Winthrop W. Aldrich, Ambassador to Britain; Charles Bohlen, Ambassador to the Soviet Union; and C. Douglas Dillon, Ambassador to France. The others were the Legal Adviser to the State Department, Herman Phleger; the Assistant Secretary of Defense, Gordon Gray; Robert Bowie, of the Policy Planning Staff; William Rountree, Deputy Assistant Secretary of State for Near Eastern, South Asian and African Affairs; Walworth Barbour, Deputy Chief of Mission, American Embassy, London; and Carl McCardle, Assistant Secretary of State for Public Affairs.

At noon Dulles went over to the British Foreign Office to speak with Foreign Minister Selwyn Lloyd. He and his staff members secluded themselves in a corridor to avoid running into Shepilov, who was talking with Lloyd. Having been primed by the Foreign Office, he then went to lunch with the British and French Foreign Ministers. Here Pineau stressed that the French were insistent on a Suez authority vested with operating authority rather than mere international supervision to make sure that certain principles of passage were carried out. For news from Washington, ever since the President's meeting with Congressional leaders on August 12, had indicated that Dulles had weakened on what Eden and Pineau thought was his resolve of August 3. They had believed the Secretary supported the idea of some kind of managerial agency that would become the instrument of guarantees for the open and free use of the Canal—not to mention for efficiency and economy of operation.

Now, Pineau was highly suspicious of Dulles's intentions, far more so than Eden. A report in the *Washington Post* of August 13 seemed to let the cat out of the bag. In its report on the meeting with the President on August 12, the newspaper had said:

> The United States at London will not back the British-French idea of a new international agency to run the Canal. Instead, Mr. Dulles will propose that Egypt alone will run the Canal and that a new international body be created to hear appeals on such matters as toll rates, management efficiency, provisions for expanding the Canal, and unhindered passage for ships of all nations; in short, to see that the Canal is run equitably and fairly on behalf of all maritime nations rather than actually run it.

We have to ponder whether this was one of those kites, inspired by the Secretary of State, the kind so often used in the past by the bad old diplomacy of the Western world, used now just to get a rise out of Britain and France. It seemed to weaken, by contradicting, the tripartite communiqué of two weeks before; it seemed to be an abandonment of Britain and France. It even sounded like Menon! The State Department felt obliged that same day, August 13, to repudiate this view of Dulles's policy: "It was not aware of any change in this fundamental agreement [the tripartite communiqué]." The agreement had been on "the necessity of practical measures to guarantee the free, open, and secure use of the Suez Canal as an international waterway." Rumors circulated that Dulles had changed position from a device for "operation" of the Canal to a contrivance for mere "supervision." The latter was the Indian government's view of a right and feasible solution, and Dulles surmised that it was also the maximum control to which Nasser would submit. Perhaps it was even beyond, maybe *far* beyond, the Egyptian leader's amenability. Indeed, Washington rumors had it that the Secretary was dubious whether he could even rise to the promise of the tripartite communiqué. But nobody really knew what was in the Secretary's mind on such a precarious balance of possibilities as existed among these: Nasser's stubbornness about his sovereignty, his readiness to accept some kind of supervision (not management), and the use of military force by America's Western allies. Was the whole business—the rumor and the denial—a probing of Dulles's allies?

Dulles came away from lunch with Lloyd and Pineau with the harsh realization that he would be *obliged* to side with the British and French in favor of an international managing body; and that, at any rate, he must propose this at the Conference and discover the response it would get. Of course, his decision to do this was not made all at once. It was made only after consultation with the British and French, and soundings of the mind and will of all the powers who were to be present at the Conference through the U.S. Ambassadors to those nations and their Ambassadors to Washington. The French and the British, too, had their own poll of nations to display before the Secretary. Dulles gathered that the chances were good that a large majority would go along with him in a proposal for some kind of Suez international managerial board. Whatever his private doubts about its ultimate acceptability, he must try for this solution now. For he was caught in the toils of two of his own moral principles: "a decent respect for the opinions of mankind" (and quite a large part of mankind was coming to the Conference); and the conviction that the Suez Canal was an international waterway so established by a solemn treaty, requiring that good faith be observed by all signatories, including Nasser.

After this lunch of the Western leaders, the Soviet Foreign Minister, Dimitri Shepilov, visited the American Embassy, at his own request, to talk matters over with Dulles, at 3:45 P.M. When Shepilov left the Embassy after an hour and a half, the strong and hostile views of the U.S.S.R. being well-known and incapable of moving from the fixed position, he volunteered to the reporters that "there was no reason to despair."

Dulles next talked with the Italian and the Spanish delegates, and with Krishna Menon. At dinner with Ambassadors Aldrich and Dillon, he reviewed the American approach to the Conference and the attitudes of Britain and France. By this time, he judged the Indian plan of merely instituting supervision over a Canal authority, which would be altogether and exclusively Egyptian, as inadequate as his present approach. He resolved that, though he could not condone an ultimatum to Nasser based on whatever plan the Conference should believe to be proper, he nevertheless was in no position to compromise on the principle of international participation in an operating authority for the Canal. Of course, if he had done so, he might just as well have gone home to Washington at once, so far as the British and French were concerned, and quite a few other countries also, some of them, like the Netherlands and Belgium, members of the North Atlantic Treaty Organization. But then, it may be asked, why not go home?

The First London Conference met at Lancaster House on Thursday, August 16, at 11:15 A.M. France, Italy, the Netherlands, Spain, Turkey, the United Kingdom, and the U.S.S.R. were present as the nations that had been party to the Convention of 1888. From this category, Egypt was missing. The United States had never been a signatory. The other class of nations invited were those "largely concerned in the use of the Canal either through ownership of tonnage or pattern of trade." They were: Australia, Ceylon, Denmark, Ethiopia, India, Indonesia, Iran, Japan, New Zealand, Norway, Pakistan, Portugal, Sweden, the United States, and the German Federal Republic (West Germany). Greece had refused to attend: she was at odds with Britain concerning British "colonial" rule of Cyprus.

A word here, at once, may be offered on the attendance of Bonn. The *Frankfurter Allgemeiner Zeitung* (August 4 and 7) made it clear that Bonn suffered agonies of hesitation before accepting the invitation, for Adenauer's principal anxiety was that Nasser should not obtain a pretext for recognizing the East German Communist regime. This is a most instructive commentary on "justice" between nations. Almost at once on the seizure of the Canal, Adenauer, head of a government then devoted to the "economic miracle," had taken the cool, long-run view that the heavens were not going to fall just because the concession passed to Egypt in 1956 instead of 1968. But, of course, Bonn was also anxious for American support of its growing status in the world—a status, in fact, that it owed chiefly to America, and in personal terms, supremely to Dulles. It bowed to the inevitable, shrugging off the matter of the legality of the seizure ("an internal Egyptian affair"), and claiming that, in attending, it would be chiefly motivated by achieving a settlement without the use of military force of any kind. Indeed, Bonn's presence, like that of several other nations, was a tribute to Dulles's clever persuasions, as well as to the desire of all to avert an explosion, and, as in the case of Japan, to the desire of many to preserve their economic interests by free and inexpensive passage simultaneous with staying out of any political embroilments.

Although Nasser had refused the invitation extended to Egypt to participate in the First London Conference, he sent to London, as his "observer," his closest political confidante, Wing Commander Ali-Sabry. Sabry did not, of course, attend the sessions, but from the vantage point of the Egyptian Embassy in London, he was able to obtain an immediate and intimate account of the proceedings in them and in the private conversations, and to be a lobbyist for Egypt's interests by phone and personal meetings with the envoys he could hope to influence.

* * * * *

Eden took two minutes to welcome the Conference. "The occasion must rank among the gravest that any of us have had to face since the Second World War. . . . Each one of the nations represented here is deeply concerned, either by reason of its shipping or of its trade; all have a common interest in the sanctity of agreements. . . . Many of you who are listening to me are friends and colleagues of many years' standing. The result of your work together has never mattered more. With sincerity I bid you welcome; with conviction I express the confidence that good will result from your counsel. I wish Godspeed to all your efforts. Good morning, and good luck!" He left, as Selwyn Lloyd took charge of the proceedings.

The Conference worked from August 16 to August 23, omitting Sunday. Its eight plenary sessions took place in the afternoon; the mornings were open, according to Selwyn Lloyd, for "other discussions which often form a very important part of a conference such as this."

I will follow the contention over policies, not in strictly chronological order. They were:

What was to be the future management of the Canal?

What authority had the Conference to establish a solution?

What was to be the next step after the Conference?

The record of the Conference (240 verbatim pages) has been studied to reveal, in particular, the motives in Dulles's diplomacy and the characteristics of the opposition he had to face. His principal speech, that of August 16 in the second plenary session, will be given in full, for three reasons. It represents the position of the United States at that time. Hence, the British and the French thenceforward assumed, and had the right to assume, that this was a genuinely solemn American commitment, the engagement of Secretary Dulles and President Eisenhower, substantially and in constancy. They entrusted their faith and hopes in their American ally on the foundation of this speech and on Dulles's subsequent tactics at this Conference designed to support by firm and precise resolutions the policy he therein advocated and thereafter defended. Secondly, the speech is a demonstration of Dulles's best accomplishments in advocacy. It is purposeful, cogent, winning, displaying the end and the means in admirable and efficient interweft, lucid in phrase, powerful and pungent in striking force, muscular without bullying. It is designed to find a solution with Nasser, and dexterously contrived to convince Dulles's allies that he was doing his very best, fighting with all his power, to assure that their grievances were accorded full justice. Thirdly, the speech states the law of the Canal and its seizure as the United States Government asserted it.

At the very beginning of the Conference, a wrangle occurred about the chairmanship. Shepilov objected to its being vested in Selwyn Lloyd, the inviting government (as usual), on the grounds that the British had a "particular interest." He suggested that "from our point of view such a role might be suitably assumed by, for instance, the representative of India, the greatly respected Mr. Menon." At this suggestion, one of Dulles's intimates could not forbear the subdued but expressive comment, "Jesus!" But Menon and the Pakistani delegate supported the chairmanship of Selwyn Lloyd.

The first important clash came a moment afterwards. Menon and Shepilov were anxious to avoid anything in the nature of a *decision* by the Conference. They said that, in the United Nations, *all* were bound by a majority, because the principle of universality of membership, with each member having an equal vote, prevailed. But at this Conference there was no universality; it was a selected group only. In the eyes of Shepilov it was even a planted and corrupt group (capitalists!); and it had not been deputed by anyone to have authority, but the allies had seized it. And one nation was missing, one with a fundamental interest in the development of the Conference's will: Egypt. Shepilov even challenged, as in the Russian note accepting the invitation, the composition of the Conference, and demanded that it be considered as only of "preliminary nature." Delay and mischief was Russia's purpose—this, and the diplomatic support of Egypt and the Arab states and the preparation of another, later conference where Russia would bring forward all her cohorts, satellites and others in the Eastern Hemisphere.

Dulles sat out this discussion. The discussants agreed, without a vote, that no vote should be taken on the substantial decisions, since a majority would have no authority to bind dissident nations to any point of view or course of action. There was general acceptance of the statement by Christian Pineau of France: "If we can reach a unanimous approval, that will be for the best. But I think it is a frank expression of opinion on the best possible solution for the freedom of transit through the Canal which interests us all. . . . You cannot stop those countries, whether they are twelve or fifteen (out of twenty-two), if they have declared themselves in favor of a good solution and that is the solution which they wish to support, which they wish to apply by the most appropriate means." [2]

The nations present, of course, constituted a vast majority of Canal users, whether computed by the count of nations, or by their total tonnage passing through the Canal (in the neighborhood of 90 per cent of the world's total). Still, the Conference had no *authority* to impose a solution. It had not received authority from on high; it had not received it from the United Nations, which might have found within the folds of the Charter some legitimized way of offering (but hardly *imposing*) a solution; it had not received it, let us say, from the maritime nations signatory to the 1888 Convention, including Egypt. The powers inviting to the Conference had taken it upon themselves to call the meeting to try to reach some consensus as to what was best. Its sponsors, and in chief Dulles, hoped that this would have *moral* authority with the culprit Nasser, that the opinion of most countries or most people (it is difficult to know what Dulles meant by "world" in "world opinion") would influence him, as well as the British and French, to accept that *kind* of authority. The atmosphere was easier than with a binding vote in view.

Some discussion about the agenda and procedure and the need for maximum private conversations further took up the first session. (When Dulles left his seat at 12:45 P.M., he left a considerable heap of pencil shavings on the table, produced by whittling with his big pocketknife. While talking for a moment with a few delegates who came to his side, he took the stub of a cigar crushed into the ash tray by one of his officials. He put it under his nose and sniffed the tobacco with keen relish. Until a year and a half before becoming Secretary, he had been a heavy pipe smoker. Then his physicians had persuaded him to give it up, as they thought his vascular and gouty condition was not helped by smoking.)

During the luncheon recess, Dulles prepared his major speech. When the Conference reconvened, he was recognized. It was a decisive moment. The ambiance and the opportunity were made for him, as, in a way, he had made them. He spoke in a firm and even tone, fairly slowly, as usual masticating his words, and occasionally patting the table for emphasis. His speech constituted a formal proposal; a resolution was circulated and was made in full on Monday, August 20 by the American delegation. It was modeled and remodeled in the interval, often in private conversations between the American and other delegates. It remained essentially and firmly that which Dulles asserted he believed was justice for Britain, France, and the maritime powers of the world, and, quite in the foreground, Egypt. The speech of August 16 introduced and advocated it.

Let us notice its main points. The gravest issue facing the Conference, the one most stinging to France and Britain, the one which Dulles felt must be resolved on pain of a possible war, was this: Is there to be *international management* of the Suez Canal in the future? Or, is the Canal to be not only under Egypt's ownership, but also under her sole and exclusive management? If this issue was not resolved by Dulles, then, sooner or later, he would be morally obliged to fulfill his implied commitment to condone the use of force as a last resort, a resort if all else failed, as implied in his and Eisenhower's previous verbal and written statements. Was Egyptian ownership and control tolerable, with only an international consultative and supervisory board at long distance to watch the Egyptian everyday management, and to voice complaints to and ask redress from the United Nations and/or the World Court? On this point, the Secretary of State had to make up his mind. And it ought to have been made up once and for all at this stage. By his assurances in private discussions, he had given the British and French every reason to believe that he had done so and was committed thenceforward to hold to the principle of international control of the Canal. Above all, the substance and tone of the Secretary's supporting speeches on August 16 and subsequently encouraged them in this view.

An international board would be vested with the rights of the maritime powers as stated in the Convention of 1888. Egypt was and would be, of course, one of the powers. This Suez Canal Board would, then, operate, maintain, develop, and enlarge the Canal. A machinery of government for these purposes would be set up between Egypt and other nations to safeguard their respective interests in it. The Board would make periodic reports to the United Nations. Sanctions would be instituted for any violation of the Convention by *any* party to it or by any other nation, in accordance with the principles of the United Nations. "*The operation of the Canal would be insulated from the influence of the politics of any one nation.*" Egypt's sovereignty would be respected. Egypt would obtain a fair return from the organization for the use of the Canal. Apart from these sums to Egypt, the tolls would be as low as consistent with the payment of fair compensation to the Suez Canal Company that had been dispossessed, and with the costs of management and enlargement of the Canal. And apart from the fair share of moneys to be paid to Egypt, Egypt would not make a profit.

Now the central issues raised by the U.S. proposal were (a) whether or not the establishment of such an international board vested with the authority established by the Convention of 1888 for perpetual validity was compatible with Egyptian sovereignty, and (b) if Egypt and her supporters, say, India and Russia (above all, Russia), did not think it was, whether the proposal had any chance of being executed —*except by exerting coercion over Egypt.* It is always possible for a nation to define its sovereignty in such a way as to do absolutely as it likes in disregard of obligations that it or its public ancestors in authority have engaged to uphold. The definer was Nasser. His definition was the origin of the conflict. Dulles offered a way of answering it; this was the core of all the discussion for seven days, in public and private session, in groups and in parties of two.

Here is what Dulles said; his emphases fell at the words and places italicized, marked by his raising his voice and patting the table. (The text is from the verbatim record taken down by British Foreign Office stenographers. The brackets represent their emendations of punctuation, meaning, and grammar.)

> We have met here to deal with a grave situation. I am sure I do not need to labour that point because if it were not so we would not have come here at such short notice from so many distant parts of the world. If we cannot deal with the problem before us constructively [,] immeasurable ills may descend upon much of the world. On the other hand, if we can deal with it constructively all of the world will benefit and particularly the peoples of Asia and of Europe.
>
> I would like first of all to make a few observations about the Suez Canal itself. That is of course a waterway of supreme importance to all the nations. For many of the nations in Europe and in Asia *it is in an almost literal sense the lifeline* that it has so often been called. From its beginning a century ago the Suez Canal and its operations had been indelibly stamped with an international character. The canal was built under international auspices with international capital and for international purposes. The building and operation were conducted by the Universal Suez Canal Company formed in 1856. The relations between the company and the Government of Egypt were habitually regulated by what were called conventions. The basic convention and a ratifying decree is that of February 22nd, 1866.
>
> In 1888 the nations principally concerned made a treaty respecting the free navigation of the Suez maritime canal. *That treaty is of perpetual duration.* It is by its terms for the benefit of all nations and was made open to adherence by any nation. The preamble to the treaty expressed the purpose as being, and I quote [,] "To establish by a conventional act *a definite system designed to guarantee at all times and for all powers* the free use of the Suez Maritime Canal, and thus to complete the system under which the navigation of this canal had been placed by the Firman of His Imperial Majesty the Sultan, dated 22nd February, 1866." Thus the decree of February 22nd, 1866 certifying the convention of that date between the Government of Egypt and the Universal Suez Canal Company has been by reference incorporated into and made part of what is called the definite system set up by the 1888 treaty. Egypt was not an initial signatory of the treaty, being bound by the signature of the Ottoman Empire of which it was then a part. Since becoming an independent nation Egypt has accepted the treaty as binding upon it. Out of the system thus established in 1888 there have occurred no doubt some abuses. National politics were not wholly excluded even by the treaty of 1888, but by and large the operation of the canal has been competent and even-handed, and has led to a steadily increas-

ing movement of general world trade through the canal, which has been beneficial to all the nations, and which increasingly makes them dependent upon the canal. About one-sixth of all the world's sea-borne commerce now passes through the Suez Canal. The canal plays a special role in the close relationship between the economy of Europe and the petroleum products of the Middle East. Europe received through the canal in 1955 67 million tons of oil, and from this oil the producing countries received a large part of their national incomes. The economies of each of these areas are thus largely dependent upon, and serve the economies of, the others, and the resultant advantages to all largely depend upon the permanent international system called for by the 1888 Treaty.

Now let me refer to the events which bring us here. On 26th July 1956 the Egyptian Government, *acting unilaterally and without any prior international consultation* of which we are aware, issued a decree purporting to nationalise the Universal Suez Canal Company, and to take over all its property and rights pertaining thereto, and to terminate its rights affirmed by the 1866 decree to operate the canal until 1968. The installations of the Suez Canal Company were then physically taken over by the Egyptian Government. Its employees were prevented from leaving their work without Egyptian Government permission under penalty of imprisonment. President Nasser at the same time made a public declaration of the reasons for his actions. He said that the timing and immediate occasion for the nationalisation was the fact that the Governments of the United States and of the United Kingdom had shown themselves unwilling to commit themselves to finance the foreign exchange costs of the vast programme to construct the Aswan high dam and related works. But President Nasser made clear that *his action was not merely an act of retaliation.* Speaking on August 12th, 1956, he said he had been thinking about it for 2½ years, and the announcement was timed to coincide with the fifth anniversary of the Revolution and to demonstrate, he said, its capacity for action. In his July 26th speech proclaiming the seizure of the Canal Company rights, President Nasser said: "We shall, God willing, score one triumph after another." He has made clear his desire to use the canal for *Egyptian national purposes.* He has described as one source of Egyptian strength the strategic position of Egypt, which embraces the crossroads of the world, the thoroughfare of its traders, and he has described as another source of Egyptian strength, oil, a sinew of material civilisation without which all of its machines would cease to function and rust would overcome every iron part beyond hope of motion and life. "So," he says, "we are strong when we measure the extent of our ability to act." Now there is every reason why the Government of Egypt should by every proper means build up and strengthen its country both materially and morally. The United States has been and is wholly sympathetic with that goal, and we have contributed in no small measure towards its realisation. However, the grandeur of a nation is not rightly measured by its ability to hurt or to threaten others. *Whenever there is interdependence, which is a characteristic of our times*, one of the parties can hurt the other, and the greater the interdependence the greater the power to hurt. But that aspect of interdependence cannot properly be used for national aggrandisement. Particularly is that the case when the interdependence has been built up in reliance on solemn governmental obligations. In the Suez Canal the interdependence of nations achieves perhaps its highest point. The economic life of many nations has been shaped by reliance on the Suez Canal system, which, as I have pointed out, has treaty sanction. To shake and perhaps shatter that system or to seek gains from threatening to do so is not a triumph, nor does it augment grandeur. The Suez Canal, by reason of its internationalised character both in law and in fact, is the last place wherein to seek the means of gaining national triumphs and promoting national ambitions. I realise that President Nasser, taking note of the world-wide reaction to his action, now says that Egypt will accord freedom of transit through the canal, that operations will be efficient and that tolls will continue to be reasonable. But we are bound to compare those words with other words which have perhaps a more authentic ring. We are also bound to notice the difference between what the Treaty of 1888 calls a definite system, designed to guarantee *at all times* and for all Powers the free use of the Suez Maritime Canal, to compare that with an Egyptian national operation which puts other nations in the role of petitioners. *One thing is certain, whatever may be the present intentions of the Egyptian Government, the trading nations of the world know that President Nasser's action means that their use of the canal is now at Egypt's sufferance*. Egypt can in many subtle ways slow down, burden and make unprofitable the passage through the canal of the ships and cargoes of those against whom Egypt might desire for national, political reasons to discriminate. Thus Egypt seizes hold of a sword with which it could cut into the economic vitals of many nations. Some of these nations are now especially disturbed because the present Government of Egypt does not conceal its antagonism towards them. To these the new situation, understandably, seems unacceptable, but even those nations which may at the moment enjoy Egypt's favour cannot but realise that the operations of the canal are in the long run less dependable even for them. That is bound to be the case whenever operations can be influenced by the fear or by the favour of any single nation. The international confidence which rested upon the Convention of 1866 with the Suez Canal Company and the Treaty of 1888 have been grievously assaulted. It is for us to consider whether that confidence can peacefully be repaired. *If not, then we face a future of the utmost gravity, the possibilities of which we hesitate even to contemplate*. It is an encouraging fact that all concerned recognise that there is need for remedial action. The Egyptian Government, although it declines to participate in this conference, recognises that what it has done has created a need for corrective action. On August 12th, 1956, President Nasser proposed the drafting of a new international treaty, which would reaffirm and guarantee freedom of navigation on the Suez Canal. That is the Egyptian Government's formula for undoing the harm that has been done and for restoring the confidence which its actions have so gravely impaired. The Soviet Government, in its statement of August 9th, 1956, recognised that this conference—and I quote—"May provide an opportunity for finding a peaceful approach to a settlement of questions connected with the freedom of navigation within the Suez Canal which, taking into account the new circumstances, may be acceptable to the Egyptian State as well as to the other countries concerned." All the Governments represented here, plus the Government of Egypt, recognise the need for international action. And indeed our presence here is the beginning of such action. The question is therefore not whether something needs to be done; as to that we are all agreed. The question is what should be done. Now the solution of the problem we face is difficult enough to find and to apply. But let us not exaggerate the difficulties which are inherent in the problem, and let us not create new difficulties by creating false issues. What is required is a permanent operation of the canal under an international system which will in fact give confidence to those who would normally wish to use the canal. Those in Asia and elsewhere who depend upon the canal for the movement of their exports and imports should be assured that their economies will not be disrupted. Those who provide oil out of the sands of the Middle East should be confident that they can ship the oil to its only advantageous market. Those in Europe who convert their industries from coal to oil, or who manufacture, buy or drive automobiles, to use only one of many possible illustrations, must be confident that fuel will be dependably forthcoming.

Those who build, charter or operate tankers and general cargo and passenger boats must have confidence that their ships can move through the canal on schedule, for even a day's delay can turn a shipping operation from one of profit to one of loss. Insurers of ships and of cargoes must feel confident that there will not be obstructions or maritime disasters. Confidence is what we seek; and for this it is indispensable that there there should be an administration of the Canal which is non-political in its operation. *That, I think, is the key to the problem, an operation which is non-political in character. The Canal should not be allowed to become an instrument of the policy of any nation or any group of nations, whether of Europe, or Asia or Africa.*

How to achieve this will, as I say, be hard enough. But let us not unnecessarily make it harder. We do not have here to measure our actions in terms of that elusive quality which is called prestige, whether it be the prestige of a single nation or of a group of nations. If we allow ourselves to be swayed by such factors we shall not worthily discharge the grave responsibilities which fate has imposed upon us. *We have to solve a practical problem; it is simply how to give effective practical expression to the principles of the 1888 Treaty.*

Now, a first thought which inevitably suggests itself is, should we seek a solution in terms of reinstating for the remainder of its term the Convention of 1866 between Egypt and the Universal Canal Co.? As I say, that thought naturally occurs. I feel I should say this. *The United States does not believe the Egyptian Government had the right to wipe out that Convention* establishing the rights of the Universal Suez Co. until 1968. This arrangement had the status of an international compact; many relied upon it. The operating rights and assets of that company were impressed with an international interest. The Government of the United States questions that the Government of Egypt had the right unilaterally to take its action of July 26th last. Nevertheless, while the United States reserved its legal position in this respect, we are quite prepared to explore the new situation which has been created, seeking a solution which is fair to all and generally acceptable.

We must, of course, start with the Treaty of 1888, which provides in perpetuity that (I quote from the Treaty) "Suez Maritime Canal shall always be free and open in times of war [, *in time of war as*] in time of peace [,] to every vessel of commerce or war without distinction or [*of*] flag," and which Treaty calls for a system (again I quote the words) "a system to assure that." What shall that system be if the Convention of 1866 is not to be restored to life? The United States believe[s] that a fair and equitable plan can be devised which will recognise the legitimate interests of all. They further believe that it is in the interests of world peace that the nations gathered here should agree on such a plan, that it should be accepted by all necessary parties and promptly put into operation.

What are the principles which should underlie such a plan? First, the canal should be operated efficiently as a free, secure, international waterway in accordance with the principles of the Suez Canal Convention of 1888. Second, the operation should be divorced from the influence of national politics, from whatever source derived. Third, there should be recognition and satisfaction of all legitimate rights and interests of Egypt in the canal and in its operation, including an equitable and fair return. Fourth, provision should be made for the payment of fair compensation to the Universal Suez Canal Co. Those, we believe, are the principles; and under those principles what might be a plan?

We suggest a plan along the following lines will satisfy all these requirements of principle. First; the operation of the Suez Canal in accordance with the 1888 Treaty and the principles therein set forth would be made the responsibility of an international board to be established by treaty and associated with the United Nations. Egypt would be represented on such a board, but no single nation would dominate it, and its composition would be such as to assure that its responsibilities would be discharged solely with a view to achieving the best possible operating results, without political motivation in favour of or in prejudice against any user of the canal. Two; Egypt would, by appropriate arrangement, have the right to an equitable return which would take into account all legitimate Egyptian rights and sovereignty. Three; the arrangement would make provision for payment to the Universal Suez Canal Co. a fair compensation; and four, any differences upon the last two points—that is, the right of Egypt to an appropriate return and the amount of compensation to the Suez Canal Co.—any differences upon these two points would be settled by an arbitral commission to be named by the International Court of Justice.

I may be asked: Does such a plan infringe upon Egypt's sovereignty? *The answer is clearly that it does not.* Egyptian sovereignty is, and always has been, and always will be under the 1888 Treaty, qualified by that Treaty, which makes the canal an international and not an Egyptian waterway. Egypt has always recognised, and recognises to-day, the binding effect of that Treaty. What we consider and suggest here are merely ways to effectuate rights in relation to the Canal which are possessed by those nations which are parties to the Treaty or for whose benefit the Treaty is avowedly made. We recognise of course that at this stage any proposal should be flexible, within the limits of such basic principles as we have outlined. And of course Egypt's views should be ascertained. But we believe that the principles set forth and a plan such as that we have outlined contain the basic elements needed to restore confidence and to assure that the Suez Canal will be operated in accordance with the Treaty of 1888. Thus it may increasingly serve the vital interests of all the world, to which that Treaty is solemnly and perpetually dedicated.[3]

Dulles pushed aside his papers, put his head on one side, pouted his lips in finality and enjoyment, and nodded his head a few times, staccato, to indicate to the conference and the chairman that he had finished. He was pleased, indeed, at the tense quiet and evident enjoyment with which his words had been listened to during the twenty-five minutes for which he had spoken. He had made a very marked impression by his moderation, his sound practical sense, his sympathy for Egypt's difficulties and problems and needs, as well as his firm demand that treaties be respected. His listeners reflected how well briefed he was, and how well all the facts of the subject were covered and integrated in his argument. They were affected by his benevolence.

That afternoon, he was supported by Sweden, Portugal, Italy. His views were not yet treated with complete hostility by Indonesia, although that country was to fall on the side of India and Ceylon. It was a good day for the Secretary. But the battle was still ahead.

As he began to shuffle out of the room in conversation with other delegates, his secretaries and his Assistant Secretary for Public Affairs rushed to his seat at the table to pick up the papers on which he had been doodling, his inveterate habit while he measured his colleagues' arguments. They were terrified lest any of these be collected by journalists and shown to a psychiatrist: even if the diagnosis was complimentary, it would only cause trouble in the press and be turned into a joke by all his opponents. Dulles was acutely aware that newspapermen disliked him and that not much love was stored up on Capitol Hill for him either, in spite of his anxious attempts to win it. After his speech, he had produced some most complicated and grotesque patterns, and all the way across the most involuted and weird scribbles was written, in enormous placard letters, the phrase "THE PRESIDENT WANTS PEACE."

Immediately following the meeting, Dulles telephoned the President to inform him in detail what had happened, what he expected to happen next, what he recommended ought to be done (the message was elaborated in cables). And the President answered, "Foster! Good! Ok! Go ahead! We must keep the peace!" "No!" he said in answer to a question, "Menon has not spoken yet—he's reserving himself for the big occasion!"

It is essential to set out the Indian position, because it was the reasoning that pleased three other powers at the conference, Indonesia, Ceylon, and Russia, and in part attracted Spain. And, although Dulles was then its fierce opponent, on the surface, his ultimate policy and behavior were hypnotically influenced by India's appeal. India thought that the Ancient World of Asia would redress the balance of the Old World of Europe by the moral weight of the New World of America.

In India's arguments and her proposal for a settlement, the primary clause advocated "the recognition of the sovereign rights of Egypt." This was not the *first* clause of Dulles's draft. India, and those who were with her, insisted on the sovereignty of Egypt in the physical possession of the Canal and in the assets which it had taken over from the Universal Suez Canal Company, and on her right to do with the Canal as she wished—subject only to certain minimal restraints. But the recognition of Egyptian sovereignty was their cardinal and decisive basis for further talk and negotiation. This point was involved in the legality of the nationalization. About this there was considerable difference of opinion in the Conference, as among international lawyers all over the world. The unfettered right to do whatever a government liked in its own land without restraint or submission legally to anybody inside or outside its borders—which is sovereignty—commended itself to all nations, but for different reasons. The newly emancipated nations, formerly colonial, like Indonesia and Ceylon and, say, the Philippines, wanted no doubt about their right to push ahead and act exactly as they found profitable and convenient, whatever the consequences, or up to the point where the forceful wrath of other countries might fall on them (e.g., as in the boundary disputes between —in their own estimation—two of the purest countries in the world, India and Communist China). And they especially wanted no legal or moral doubt about their right to manhandle by their own national legislative and executive processes foreign and domestic entrepreneurs and owners of property as it suited their plans of economic development. The older nations, like Britain and France and the U.S.A., like Spain and Portugal and Italy, also, of course, wanted these rights. In addition, they demanded respect for the treaty obligations into which they, as sovereign nations, had entered and from which, having fulfilled *their* obligations, they expected to derive the covenanted benefits.

In order to save time and abate recrimination, the nations of the West, especially Britain and the U.S.A., but *less so France*, were willing to sidetrack any elaborate debate on the question of the legality of the seizure of the Canal and push on to consider how the Canal was to be run from that moment on. Specifically, they wished to settle the issue of what would be the safeguards against the unfettered control of the Canal by one country in the interests of its own politics, or as Dulles now put it, of how "to insulate from the politics of any one country" the running of the Canal, and make the interests of all maritime powers the overarching rule.

The Indian argument therefore emphasized these points. First, "It is proposed in these ideas [those of Dulles and his supporters] that an international corporation or unit should take its place [that is, the place of the Suez Canal Company]. The effect of that is to repeal the act of nationalization; not to repeal it in the sense of replacing what was before, but to substitute an international body." This plan would not work, for the following reason: "The factual position is that the rulers of Egypt, whoever has sovereign power in Egypt, are really the people who can guarantee freedom of navigation. It would be the government that had physical possession of the Canal that would be the power that in reality guaranteed freedom of navigation and the security of properties of the Canal." Therefore, and because Egypt had properly acted to protect its sovereignty in nationalizing the Canal, the appropriate solution was to leave the possession of the land and the water and the various installations, etc., etc., from now on in the sovereign hands of Egypt, and merely to make sure, through the United Nations and the World Court and an international body of user interests charged with advisory, consultative, and liaison functions, that the rights of free and open passage and of fair levels of tolls and improved efficiency should be observed.[4]

Menon claimed that Nasser's principles and the fears of the formerly colonial peoples were sound; that they must ineluctably be satisfied by the big powers. Yet, he admitted, "That does not mean we are to pander to every kind of mob opinion that turns up from everywhere." [5]

Menon hit at the root of the practical need for some kind of international reservation on the full sovereignty of Egypt: the reliability of the government of Egypt to fulfill its obligations. Nehru, the cultivated aristocrat, who had twice met Nasser, at Bandung and Brioni, well understood the need for some, if minimal curbs, on the uncouth dictator's power. Holding Suez, Nasser had a stranglehold over India also.

It is, of course, clear that the modern age is the age of feverish, even pathological nationalism. The worst aspects of this phenomenon are seen in frenzied, almost insane action. The men who control the nationalist governments, especially in nations ruled by one man at the head of one monopolistic and dictatorial political party, are the sole embodiment of their country's nationalism. In these circumstances, nationalism assumes the personal idiosyncrasies of the one man. A most unstable and unreliable situation results. The personification of Egyptian, and alleged Arab, nationalism in Nasser is what had produced the Suez crisis, more than any other one factor. Nasser was Egyptian nationalism; he desired to be Arab nationalism; and he reached out to be the nationalism of all Moslems everywhere.

Menon sought to transmute the apprehensions about this fearful force into some international arrangement for curbing the excesses and injuries committed by such wild nationalists. Yet how could the Suez crisis be solved if Nasser, who had started it, was still in power? Menon was in a dilemma. He could find an exit from it only by condoning the dictator. He said: "We could also say that, in international affairs, when we have to deal with countries, it is the approach of my Government that we have to take their internal structures and their administration, and their Governments as they are; it is not possible for us to approach problems by first desiring a change of government or constitution or personnel in another country." How convenient, in various ways, for the Indian occupiers of Kashmir and recipients of aid from America.

Menon went on:

> They [the Egyptian Government] have already stated they will not permit an infringement of their sovereign right, as they consider it, and they are quite competent to carry out the work of the Canal. Therefore, since our interest in this Canal is not a

political one, it is a user interest, and that user interest can best be served by negotiation, by trying to make the interest a mutual one, by persuasion, by making Egypt a party to a solemn agreement which comes under the obligations of international law and of the Charter of the United Nations.[6]

Menon well understood Dulles's view that the observance of treaties should be assured by international partnership in actual management. (Though there are many examples of this kind in the world, the representatives of India did not want another in this case: it came too close to India's own bones. Suppose somebody proposed to India, "We will help you with a billion dollars towards your economic development plans, but we want an *executive* part in a corporation that is in charge of the job."?) What, then, continued Menon, would give the users their rightful guarantee? The United Nations! "We have made progress towards some sort of world obligations in matters of this kind. Egypt is a member of the United Nations bound by provisions of the Charter and with this treaty, a treaty that is of this character, registered with the United Nations, the violation would become a major matter and ensurement in this case is at the treaty level." [7]

Was the United Nations sufficiently reliable? Did Menon not confess in his heart that India had been able to make use of the United Nations to cover her usurpation of Kashmir? It was now six years since her representative in New York had promised solemnly to take a plebiscite on the wishes of the vast majority of Moslems who lived there. The Security Council's resolution of September, 1951, requiring Egypt to cease the closure of the Canal to Israeli ships and later to ships of other nations carrying cargoes to and fro for Israel had been flouted. India had not protested. Israel had not been invited to Bandung. India had no ambassador in Jerusalem. India's foreign policy, especially since Pakistan is on both her eastern and western borders with 100 million Moslems, had sacrificed Israel's interests and rights to avert the hostility of Arab Moslems.[8] Menon had proposed that Israel should go to the World Court for a judgment on her claims under the Convention of 1888, to rebut the Egyptian claim, which Menon parroted, that being in a state of self-defense against Israel, Egypt had the right to close the Canal to her.[9] But Menon knew, surely, that the Security Council had rejected this claim of Egypt's, and he also knew the hazards not only of getting a decision from the Court, but even if it was ever obtained, of getting it carried out.[10]

Now, every nation at the Conference had a self-serving personality. Not that none in any degree never transcended that egoistic outlook by generosity towards others or a conscience that sought the good of all mankind. But each man bore in mind powerfully the interests of his own country, those interests being, as in the case of all men everywhere at all times, a mixture of the material and the ethical. The Indian representative who spoke as though he had been commissioned by all History and the Lord to lead men in the paths of pure altruism, himself averred the actual immediate interests of his country in attaining free passage through the Canal. He wished to be a world political leader, especially in the Eastern Hemisphere; to lead a bloc against both the Soviet and American powers, for disarmament; to reduce their power in order to increase that of the middle and small nations to shape events as they desired. He would have abolished every atom of power, in both senses of the phrase, in order that India might triumph at Commonwealth, United Nations, and other international councils. An imperial superiority lurked in these sentiments, like that former British point of view expressed in the phrase "the white man's burden." Furthermore, India was grossly displeased that Pakistan, as a member of the Baghdad Pact, had been armed by the United States—as some return, she permitted the U.S.A. to use bases against the power of Russia to the north.

India's support of Egypt was also partly motivated by her need for votes in the United Nations: the Arab nations' votes would go in favor of India if India upheld the Arab nations' claims to nationalize how and whenever they liked. Menon did not know for sure that he could get Nasser to accept even his mild scheme of a consultative board when it came to the final point: Nasser may or may not have promised to go along with him on this. But it is also possible that without British and French and American clamor a commitment would not have been Menon's and Nehru's for the asking. All Menon would have obtained, like anyone else, would have been a promise from a man who, he knew, had been an assassin and was a reckless breaker of promises.

On Sunday, August 19, the Conference was in recess. The whole gamut of emotions and ideas was now spread before Dulles. He was beset by the militant firmness of Lloyd and Pineau, and he was harassed by the ferocity of the anticolonial passions evinced by several nations during the private talks he and his American assistants had held with them.

He was to lunch with the Marquess of Salisbury, whom he preferred to Eden for his intellectuality. Before this, he went to the morning service at St. Paul's Cathedral. There he noticed the repairs that had been made where bombs had damaged the cathedral during World War II, repairs that had been assisted by donations from the United States. During almost the whole of the service, his Assistant Secretary for Public Affairs, who had accompanied him, noticed that he was on his knees with a hand covering his eyes. "Well, Jesus," he thought, "he's so tired out with all those meetings, he's gone to sleep!" Then, in the great cathedral cavern whose roof reached almost to the firmament of the Divine, Dulles stirred, and at the closing hymn, removed his hand from his eyes and brow, and said to his servitor, as though answering the only question *he* could think of asking, "I've been praying for the success of the Conference; may God grant it!"

That evening he dined with Sir Anthony and Lady Eden. Eden's firmness, though expressed with the maximum courtesy due to a guest and to the Secretary of State of the United States of America, re-emphasized the gravity of the conflict they must resolve.

Menon had posed the dividing issue. And on Monday Dulles, refreshed by the freedom and spiritual recreation of Sunday, rose to answer it and that of all the other delegates who had now spoken. He masterfully made these points and commitments.[11]

1. The Conference could not make binding decisions for those who did not agree. The majority would not bind the minority. 2. The Conference was not in negotiation with Egypt, because she was not present. This was said to side-step Menon's assumption of speaking for Nasser. Dulles wanted to keep the way open for a direct approach to Nasser, once the Conference had freely made up its mind. 3. He touched on a subject, which had, of course, been first raised by Russia, the mischief-making, self-appointed champion of all nations of "the East." This was not a conference which would deliver any kind of *ultimatum* to Egypt. 4. If the United States did *not* seek some new regime to safeguard international interests, it still did not mean that America's private citizens would have confidence in the Egyptian management of the Canal! 5. The nations present should in all honesty express their views of what was expedient for the future, and then, later, communicate them to Egypt, leaving the government of that country to make up its mind what to do about them then. 6. If Egypt should not think fit to proceed on a basis that seemed indispensable to other countries, then a new situation would have arisen. 7. It was very important to get the maximum degree of unanimity on what was right at the Conference, and not try to speculate what Egypt would or would not accept. Therefore, he set out the proposals already referred to "which takes into account to an appreciable extent expressions of opinion" around the table. It read:

> 1. They affirm, that, as stated in the Preamble of the Convention of 1888, there should be established "a definite system designed to guarantee at all times, and for all the Powers, the free use of the Suez Maritime Canal."
>
> 2. Such a system should assure:
>
> (a) Efficient and dependable operation, maintenance and

development of the Canal as a free, open and secure international waterway in accordance with the principles of the Convention of 1888.

(b) Insulation of the operation of the Canal from the influence of the politics of any nation.

(c) Respect for the sovereignty of Egypt.

(d) A return to Egypt for the use of the Suez Canal which will be fair and equitable and increasing with enlargement of the canal's capacity and greater use.

(e) Payment to the Universal Suez Canal Company of such sums as may be found its due by way of fair compensation.

(f) Canal tolls as low as is consistent with the foregoing requirements, and except for (d) above (that is the return to Egypt), no profit.

3. To achieve these results on a permanent and reliable basis there should be established by Convention:

(a) Institutional arrangements for co-operation between Egypt and other interested nations in the operation, maintenance and development of the Canal and for harmonizing and safeguarding their respective interests in the Canal. To this end, operating, maintaining and developing the Canal and enlarging it so as to increase the volume of traffic in the interests of the world trade and of Egypt, would be *the responsibility of a Suez Canal Board*. Egypt would grant this Board all rights and facilities appropriate to its functioning as here outlined.

The members of the Board, in addition to Egypt, would be other States chosen in a manner to be agreed upon from among the States parties to the Convention, with due regard to use, pattern of trade and geographical distribution; the composition of the Board to be such as to assure that its responsibilities would be discharged solely with the view to achieving the best possible operating results without political motivation in favour of, or in prejudice against, any user of the Canal.

The Board would make periodic reports to the United Nations.

Dulles concluded with a cogent appeal for candor among themselves and towards Egypt:

Perhaps there may not be complete unanimity among us on this point, but I believe it is very important to have the maximum possible degree of unanimity. But if there are different views, these also should be stated and communicated to Egypt. The paper which I have just read, submitted by the United States Delegation, constitutes an honest effort in the light of observations which have been made at this Conference to set forth what it seems are judged by most of us to be the necessary requirements of the situation. Just as I believe that no one should, for political reasons, ask for more than is actually required by the hard facts of

> economic life, *so I do not believe that we should ask for less as a result merely of speculating—and it can now only be speculating —as a result of speculating as to what Egypt will or will not accept.* There is here no disregard of Egypt's sovereignty. What is suggested is that Egypt should make a treaty. It is true that every treaty involves a certain surrender of sovereignty, but execution of a treaty is in itself an exercise of the highest sovereignty. What we are proposing is courteously to inform Egypt of certain facts, and to ask Egypt whether or not she is prepared to enter into negotiations for a convention which will take account of those facts. If she will do so, then she is exercising her sovereignty in a situation deeply impressed with an international interest.

Dulles's statement was a brilliant *tour de force,* in advocacy and inventiveness.

Shepilov, envoy of Dulles's Villain, armed with nuclear bombs ready as weapons of blackmail, rose to disrupt the growing harmony of the Conference. First, he contended that "world public opinion" had toned down the bellicose cries of the advocates of "positions of strength." Secondly, "Nobody now disputes the legality of the nationalization." Both of these observations were false. Third, equally false: the only lawful owner of the Canal was Egypt. Fourth, the Canal was operating normally—which was practically true. He then totally rejected the American proposal because it suggested "a definite decision of the Conference." This was a spurious play on the word "decision." He sneeringly added that if the principle of an international board of management were formulated, then, "Egypt is kindly allowed a place in her own home." Even the idea advanced by Menzies, the Australian delegate, that Egyptian rights might be purchased was too peaceful for Shepilov, for "The national sovereignty of no state can be the object of a commercial transaction. It can be neither bought nor sold. A proposal of this kind is an expression of colonialism in a somewhat modernized form." What a perfect argument for use by Nasser and the radio outlet for his propaganda, Voice of Cairo! But what a sin against Karl Marx's ideology!

Shepilov then drew a line, which Menzies was warm in refuting, between the nations of the West and "the East": those latter poor bodies were being threatened with the old colonialist policy under the guise of nonpolitical action. Menzies observed that Australia and New Zealand were both in the "Eastern" hemisphere, not the West.

Shepilov produced another apple of discord: the Soviet government, he said, possessed information that the Suez Canal Company, with approval and support in certain British and French quarters, was attempting to disrupt navigation in the Canal by calling out the pilots and other technical personnel. On Egypt's behalf and for Russia's benefit, Shepilov was trying to provoke the very act of which he was affecting to accuse others.

Russia was willing to accept the Indian proposals, but what Russia herself suggested was the appointment of a commission to consider these proposals, and then the convening of another much larger conference to draft final proposals. The preparatory commission, as one might have guessed, would be composed of Egypt, India, the United States, Britain, France, and the Soviet Union: three nations versus three nations, with, no doubt, the veto power of Russia in full play. The present writer does not wish to give the impression that the Soviet Union wanted a war over Suez; it wanted free navigation, but also the maximum loss to and provocation of the West.

Dulles now approached the conclusion of the Conference. He needed a resolution of some kind, something firm and operable. Therefore, he accepted an amendment to his original proposal offered by Pakistan, and supported by Ethiopia, Iran, and Turkey. These were African and Middle Eastern nations, emotionally inclined to the apprehensions of the small and new nations. But they were not unqualified and totally blind friends of Egypt, and they had their own national interests. Turkey belonged to both the NATO alliance and the Baghdad Pact; Iran and Pakistan were members of the Baghdad Pact and each had treaties with the U.S.A.; and Pakistan was also a member of SEATO. Ethiopia had no cause to feel happy about Nasser's restive and ambitious energies so close to her borders, or the constant screams broadcast from the Voice of Cairo calling for war, assassination of rulers, anticolonial and occasionally "socialistic" rebellions. Turkey looked sourly on Nasser's engagement to Russia. Iran was concerned for free passage of the oil produced by her territories. Pakistan, a Moslem country, bound to the West by the culture of its small governing class and by trade and financial aid, was afraid of the ambitions of India, two-thirds of whose armed forces were concentrated on her frontiers, and was aggrieved over the fate that had befallen Kashmir, also a Moslem area: thus she was particularly inclined to Dulles's proposal.

The Pakistanis leaned toward a board that would manage the Canal, and away from India's mere consultative body. Their main amendment made Egyptian sovereignty the primary clause; and stipulated that the nature of the international board would be the subject of negotiation between Egypt and all affected nations.

Dulles not only accepted these changes, as furthering his own idea of stressing Egyptian sovereignty,[12] but shrewdly suggested calling the amended resolution the Five Nations' Proposal—hoping that before "we are through it can be known as the Twenty-Two Nations' Proposal."

How could the proposal be conveyed to Nasser with the maximum chance of success? On August 22, by arrangement behind the scenes with Dulles and Selwyn Lloyd, New Zealand's Foreign Minister, Thomas L. Macdonald, proposed a committee of the assenting powers to call on Nasser.[13] He urged that this proposal be accepted, since otherwise a dangerous situation would continue to exist, with a rise of belligerent passions. To take the wind out of the sails of predictable opponents, Dulles proposed (he said it was implicit in the New Zealander's recommendation) "that in the course of the explanations of the five-power resolution, there would be given a rather complete résumé of what has taken place here so that we can get the spirit of it." He added: ". . . and particularly that any such statement as that made by the honorable delegate of Spain should be included. I think a very full record should go as part of this explanation."[14] By this last gambit, regarding Spain, the supporters of the five-power proposal, though with some qualification by Spain, numbered no less than eighteen, some officials crying facetiously seventeen and three-quarters!

Faced with a practical *fait accompli*, Krishna Menon's rage knew no bounds, because it was now openly being said that the U.S. proposals had seventeen supporters, and more. That is, something like a vote had occurred! There was a majority and a minority, and Menon was in the minority! He did not like it at all; it seemed to raise a moral hand of retribution over Nasser.

"Well," inveighed the frustrated Menon, "if that is to be the decision of the Conference, then we have to put up our hands when we walk into the lobby, *we have taken a vote;* that is to say the Conference is asked to accept this majority view and to submit it to Egypt. It is very difficult to see, if that is the position, what those who do not agree with this proposition have to do in this Conference. . . . I cannot see how the proposal can go from this Conference representing only part of the composition. . . . Well, that at once cuts this Conference into two pieces, and if that is the desire then I think it is only fair that it should be stated beforehand, so that other delegations can consider their position."[15]

Shepilov, whose first big foreign conference this was, saw himself and Russia on the losing end of the struggle. He needed to have as many on his side as could be. If several dissentients coalesced into a bloc on their own account, so long as they dissented, he could then sidle up to them, whereupon Moscow's propaganda organs could claim that he had led them, on behalf of Egypt, to justice and world peace. He charged that the procedure was not democratic because the populations of Russia, India, Indonesia, and Ceylon outnumbered those of the other eighteen powers! As one delegate interjected, this argument was not democracy but "demography." Dulles quickly and joyfully intervened too: If Shepilov were sincerely interested in democracy then he should have been prepared to accept a vote, based on the number of states voting.

Once again, Dulles rose and spoke briefly, after having measured the way events were going. As one of his intimates, perhaps too inclined to say that everything Dulles did had genius about it, commented, "How quickly he could cut these boys down to size! I mean —really—he just gives these boys a lecture!" But the boys Dulles really needed to "cut down to size" were Nasser and Khrushchev. And a lecture, even a sermon, is not successful foreign policy (as his illustrious mentor and idol Woodrow Wilson learned): for could it win back the Canal? However, allowing for these rather disturbing reservations, Dulles's intervention was masterly. He begged for speed, because the conference was taking risks in an urgently developing and emotional situation.

> The Soviet Foreign Minister talks about the desirability of our proceeding here in democratic ways. Of course, to most of us that would mean that we would take a vote. That is what most of us mean by democratic ways, but because we do not all agree as to the definition of democracy we accept here the view that I expressed that no majority however large can bind any minority however small.
>
> That is not a democratic procedure, but it is a procedure which we accept here because of the strong views in that respect which were expressed by some of the delegations. It results from that that we cannot act in a corporate capacity as a conference because, if we adopt the rule that we cannot bind any minority however small by a vote however large, the result would be that *a minority of one could prevent us from taking any action at all*, because the proposition seems to be that we cannot act in a corporate capacity as a conference because we cannot take votes. Yet also it is objected to when it is proposed that we act as governments, so the result would be to *immobilise* entirely this conference. . . .
>
> While naturally we want to respect the views of everybody here as to procedure, and moving deliberately, and not precipitating matters, I think also we must be aware of the fact that every day that we wait after having concluded our general debate and having come to a consensus of views—every day we wait after that is a day which can be full of grave import, and that we assume a serious responsibility in delaying for procedural reasons after there has been, as I say, a completion of the discussion of this matter on its merits, and after 18 nations have agreed on the desirability of presenting certain views to the Egyptian Government.
>
> Naturally other governments either here or who are not here have full liberty to present their views to the Egyptian Government also. We are not claiming any monopoly on the right to present views to the Egyptian Government, but certain views are

held here by governments whose interest in the canal is so overwhelmingly great that views which ran wholly counter to those, even though they obtained some agreement elsewhere, would not in fact solve the problem which confronts us.

Now I certainly would be the last to suggest acting here tonight when [one of the Governments, or] two of the Governments[,] or more[,] who are with us have asked that we should not conclude our deliberations tonight, but should wait until tomorrow. Perhaps we can safely wait until tomorrow. I realise we are taking risks in doing so but for myself I would go along if it be the view of most that we should take that risk and postpone for another 24 hours the approach to the Egyptian Government, which I think is extremely urgent under all the circumstances.[16]

Shepilov again tried to make capital by slanderously labeling the proposal to take the eighteen-power proposals to Cairo as an "ultimatum," a word that strikes a violent and plangent chord in the Russian diplomatic vocabulary, whether given or received. In the midst of a heated and stormy wrangle at the eighth and last session on August 23, Indonesian Foreign Minister Abdulgani found a solution in the form of a conference communiqué, which would authorize *all* governments to approach Nasser. It required the verbatim record of the Conference (which would include *all* proposals before it) to be sent to the Government of Egypt. Even to this, also, Shepilov demurred.

The usual afternoon recess followed. Various delegates met with the Indonesian representative. He was unhappy at the prospect of seeming to be in the tow of Russia, if the Conference should end in a split between two groups. Menon saw this possibility also, which India, as a leader of nonalignment, would not like. It was realized that all might support the proposal, except Russia. When it came to a kind of vote, or, if one likes, a voice, on this Indonesian communiqué, *as edited by the American delegation in the recess*, Shepilov tried to meddle with some irrelevant suggestion intruded by Christian Pineau. But Dulles firmly refocused attention on Indonesia's proposal. He cleverly pinned it on Shepilov that the only objector was Russia. Chairman Selwyn Lloyd asked whether it was true that the delegate of the Soviet Union could *not* support the revised Indonesian text? Shepilov fell into Dulles's diplomatic trap: "I confirm that you, Mr. Chairman, were quite correct in your understanding." He was branded as the lone dissenter to the communiqué. Dulles had made him look a fool.

"Therefore," said Dulles, "I do not see what more we have to do, really."

Really! What had been accomplished? A very substantial advance, from Dulles's point of view and policy. Eighteen powers had been persuaded to accept, as a solution of the Egyptian-British-French embroilment, proposals regarded as just to the chief powers in conflict and as fair and valuable to all maritime powers. It had been accepted by the eighteen that a committee from among them should go to Cairo and negotiate on this basis. I repeat, *negotiate*, and I mean to open the way for discussion of the proposals, not to dictate them word for word to Egypt. Russia had been put into an ignominious minority of one! A slight relaxation of world tension over Suez had occurred during the Conference, in spite of some ominous moves and noise.

This was Dulles's finest hour, for his forensic and close-up-to-events diplomatic and procedural talents had triumphed to establish, among (as he was so fond of repeating) over 90 per cent of the users of the Canal, an actual set of principles that ought to be applied to the future control and management of the Canal. And—he had won more time in his effort to postpone, perhaps entirely to avert, the use of force.

It was Dulles's finest hour—but was it enough? It was good for him, but what were the portents for a just solution without the exercise of force upon Nasser's Egypt? This was the problem from the beginning. It was still the problem. Did Dulles ever realize it? Did he ever face the agonizing actions it would seem he inevitably must take if he did realize it? It is rather difficult to believe that he did. He needed to find a way of convincing Nasser. He had not yet done it, not yet, perhaps, even made up his mind to do it. He and Eisenhower may already, indeed, have made up their minds to absolve Nasser of obligations, if it meant force to act otherwise.

The evidence that his finest hour was still far from enough could be found in the speeches of Selwyn Lloyd, Christian Pineau, and Robert G. Menzies of Australia. These men were anything but complaisant about what they had lost, what they were losing, and what they had to recapture from Nasser's violent hands. Although Dulles regarded him as a "lightweight," Lloyd shrewdly understood Dulles and his tactics. He surmised that Dulles wished that the British and French should renounce their claims on Nasser, and that Dulles was willing, seeing the imbroglio in the Middle East, to give something belonging to Britain and France to Nasser in the hope that he would then behave himself. He did not misunderstand Dulles's determination to show who was "boss" in the world.

Lloyd brought the Conference back to the fact that "a situation of the utmost gravity" had been created by Colonel Nasser's action in Suez. Britain wanted a peaceful settlement. Her governments and people "do not like the use of force. It is for us always a last resort." He went on to say, "As a nation we are very slow to anger, but when it is clear that vital interests are threatened by acts of deliberate hostility we are in the habit of standing fast whatever the odds."

Since, in the end, the British and the French did use force, this was a point for Dulles to note! The *vital* interests of Britain, implied her Foreign Secretary, were threatened by deliberately hostile acts. He then reiterated Eden's arguments expressed in his speech of August 8 (p. 117, above).

Selwyn Lloyd's admonition on the nature of national sovereignty deserves to be taken to heart by those whose minds are engaged in the anxiety of developing just and peaceful relations among the nations of the world. It is especially relevant in an age when scores of new nations and new and untutored men have arisen to possess sovereignty over the might of their resources in men and material, as well as the geopolitical leverage of territorial position, whether within or without the United Nations. Lloyd said:

> Sovereignty does not mean the right to do exactly what you please within your own territory. Sovereign government is the right in a general way to organise and govern the national territory and economy according to the wishes of the government of that territory. But the doctrine of sovereignty gives no right to use the national territory or to do things within the national territory which are of an internationally harmful character. We all know the maxim, "So use your own that you do not hurt that which belongs to another," and that is one which has been accepted by every legal system in the world; it is a principle of international law and of domestic law.[17]

Of course, we may reflect, if men like Nasser and Khrushchev did not heed the telling, someone would someday break out and fight.

"We have to produce a solution which will obviate the risk of war," continued the British Foreign Secretary. Dulles, in a "masterly speech," had set out the principles of a kind of international management that would satisfy Britain's basic position, "that this international waterway cannot be subject to the political control of one government, however constituted."

He stressed another theme. "It is common ground between us, and I think has been present in our minds throughout this discussion (now the seventh day of the Conference) that the standard of living of countless millions east *and* west of Suez depends to no small extent upon this international waterway." [18]

It was a valid and weighty point. But the non-European hundreds of millions east of Suez were, through their governments, and incited by their governments, saying in their hearts, with some vindictive satisfaction, "Yes, but Nasser's not going to hurt *us!*" Pineau deplored the fact that Egypt was not present. "It would have been extremely normal for Egypt to be here to state its case." [19]

Christian Pineau, the French Foreign Minister, a Socialist leader, a former political scientist and bankworker's union secretary, is a voluble and vehement speaker. He irritated some of the American delegation at the Conference because he so forcefully presented the policy and injuries of his own country, even more forcefully, more zealously than the British. The American delegation thought of Pineau, in the elegant expression of one of them, as "gumming up the works," or in other words as being an obstacle to the carrying out of 100-percent American policy (as represented by Dulles) and American tactics and procedure. The French distrusted Dulles more than the British did from the outset. Dulles believed it would be easier to handle and lead the British than the French: he remembered the French defiance of his dark threat of "agonizing reappraisal."

Pineau shot at Shepilov. He, like most of the other delegates, even Krishna Menon, was disgusted at the standard crocodile tears shed by the Russian, in keeping with his colored crocodile leather shoes. He was right in drawing attention to the fact that Frenchmen had conceived, planned, and built the Canal! He turned to the theme of colonialism and anticolonialism: "We must see that on the part of certain countries the protest of anticolonialism might become too easy a means of repudiating undertakings which one does not feel inclined to observe." [20] Shepilov had spoken as though cooperation between countries in economic development was the same as colonialism. This was confusion. "If all international solutions must be subordinated to considerations of prestige, pride, and xenophobia they merely prove we have not been able to adapt ourselves to the needs of the atomic age." [21] If the new nations were to achieve economic development, they needed capital: could it be obtained if confidence were shaken by acts like those of Nasser?

(Yes, some of the delegations admitted in private. Yes, alas! Because the might of Russia will force us to give it to them, whatever they do! Yes! if they play it right!)

Pineau twisted the conscience and outraged the feelings of Dulles by disturbingly reminding the Conference of a matter that its deliberations had avoided: Nasser's booklet called *The Philosophy of the Revolution.* He, Pineau, had very much hoped it was a mistake of Nasser's youth. But only on August 7, ten days before Pineau's speech here at the Conference, Nasser laid claim to the work as his own. "I must say," continued Pineau, "I should be very pleased to know, if, amongst the members of the Conference, or if amongst those who approve the action that has recently been done, there are certain people who are at the same time in agreement with the principles which are mentioned in that interesting work?" [22] Of course, the trouble was that politics in Ceylon and in Indonesia, international and domestic, had followed, and still vindicated, the principles of violence expressed by Nasser. The "anticolonial" nations wanted everything: independence, their own way in everything, and grants of money from those they assailed as well; and they were getting them!

Menzies of Australia, who was to play a most important role in attempting to get Nasser to negotiate on the basis of the proposals of the eighteen powers, also thought the debate between East and West was artificial.[23] In the long future, even, most of the Suez traffic would grow to be between nations of the East—nations like his own. He emphasized the fact that the conflict was not one simply or chiefly between governments, but primarily a matter involving "the interests of the ordinary people of our own country, and I have no disposition whatever, on behalf of my own country, to submit my own people to all the chances and uncertainties that would arise from their having immense trading interests through this Canal made subject to the whim of the moment, to the judgment of one country or to the judgment of one man."[24] Menzies was reasoning with Nasser, 3000 miles away. "We are not in an ultimatum mood, but we have made it perfectly clear that there are vital interests belonging to the rest of the world which we believe must be taken into account, and can be taken into account in a manner quite consistent with the sovereignty of Egypt. . . ."

The tone of Menzies' remarks, stark and challenging and demanding justice, was not to the taste of Dulles. It sounded like the British Empire at bay! The Suez affair was getting him into trouble again. Since this is so, it is strange to notice a startling turn that occurred in the middle days of the Conference, concerning Menzies and Dulles —a turn that presently will be revealed and discussed for the first time since the Suez affair occurred.

But, at this point, it must be repeated that Dulles's part in the Conference had been a most successful one. The very proposal he had put forward, *we must hope in good faith* (though, prudently, we cannot be sure it was in good faith), had been accepted as the basis for negotiations to secure justice to the despoiled. He had carried eighteen powers with him. Again and again, when each had recited the very large proportion of its supplies and products that were carried to and fro from its shores through the Canal, Dulles and his supporters had repeated that it totaled something over 90 per cent of the traffic going through the Canal. And again and again, one or other of Dulles's associates had asked, "Why does he keep repeating the 90 per cent?" The answer was, "Because the Soviet Union cannot say the same thing: we've got one over Russia in this!" Russia obsessed him.

* * * * *

Criticisms have somewhere been made—they must have stemmed from Russian and Arab sources, and some American and British congenital carpers—that the proposal was an attempt to dictate to Nasser; that he was being asked to accept a decision. *This is a falsehood.* The

Conference records prove its intention was that the proposals should be submitted for uninhibited consideration by Nasser.

Not much is to be gained by further reviewing the course of the Conference. But two problems encountered by Dulles in the course of the proceedings must be re-emphasized. They posed serious difficulties for him, of a moral nature; that is, they affected his personal view, the burden on his own conscience, and his duty as a statesman, working for the interests of his country. Briefly, they concerned the anticolonialism of some nations, and the implacable, brutal hostility to the West of Soviet Russia.

Helped by India, Indonesia, and Ceylon, the Soviet Union never ceased to pound upon the theme that Britain and France bore guilt for their past occupation of lands in Africa and Asia. The former three nations pretended they might be reoccupied, as some people were threatening to do to Egypt, and once again lose their freedom. Compared with this, what use was the appeal by Sir Anthony Eden that they should respect the sanctity of international law? Abdulgani of Indonesia asserted that "most of the international treaties which are a reflection of international law do not respect the sanctity of men as equal human beings irrespective of their race, or their creed or locality. Most of the existing laws between Asian and African countries and the old-established Western world are more or less outmoded and should be regarded as a burden of modern life." "Emancipation" should come about gracefully, or it "creates explosive repercussions," leading possibly to an armed conflagration or "at least to the verge of a third world war with all its terrible consequences." Before Dulles's very eyes, these men, not altogether innocently, were perverting a conflict between free and sovereign nations, over the violation of a treaty by Egypt, into accusations of colonialism. Tragic events in the world would depend on whether Dulles would succumb to this falsely labeled substitution. And he might do it by politic connivance or by undiscerning prejudice, or, perhaps, by a little of both.

Such ideas and passions were fully calculated to strike terror into the very bones of Dulles. This statement is no exaggeration. Such talk was to be reckoned with. Since 1956, one kind of modern war has come to be dubbed "catalytic," the kind, that is, that might occur between the Soviet Union and the U.S.A. precipitated by some third state, e.g., an Egypt or a Syria or an Indonesia, for its own egoistic purposes. In practice, the threat of war is designed to secure for the catalyst state, by a kind of blackmail, whatever it may demand in the name of anticolonialism or emancipation or national self-determination. Yes, the man from Indonesia went on to argue, "We understand the right and the duty of the Egyptian people to find the ways and means to serve the interest of their people with a due respect for international obligations based upon equality and mutual benefit." In the uproar, a few days after the seizure of Suez, on August 4, his government had blatantly repudiated debts of almost one billion dollars owed to the Netherlands, acknowledged by the newly independent Indonesian Government at the conference at which the Dutch had conceded Indonesia's national independence. Dulles knew all about it. The U.N. had facilitated the independence agreement!

Dulles's blood froze when he pondered the implications of such feelings for a peaceful settlement of the Canal dispute. He could not, in any case, hope to persuade such advocates to be lawful wherever it did not suit their interests. To them, their national interests had the sanctity of "natural rights."

* * * * *

Now the question arose of who should present to Nasser the proposals and the verbatim record of the Conference. The conferees in their meetings and conversations outside the sessions gave attention to the problem. The British had a brilliant political flash. This is what occurred.

On the evening of August 20, Dulles's party was entertained by Sir Anthony Eden at 10 Downing Street. As they walked up the steps, "Anthony" came out to greet them. Some desultory conversation and small talk occurred. Then, Sir Anthony put his arm through that of Carl McCardle (an intimate and unquestioning admirer of Dulles), and said in a low, urgent voice, "Listen! You *must* convince Foster [Dulles] that he is the only one, the only man, who is capable of handling the matter in Cairo! He has demonstrated tremendous powers of leadership!" Since McCardle claims that he, also, had thought of this idea, he was only too glad to carry out the mission. Eden spoke to Dulles, it may be, with much the same phrasing. Furthermore, Harold Macmillan (at that moment Chancellor of the Exchequer, but until quite recently, himself Foreign Secretary), not second to Eden in his vigorous prosecution of the policy of making Nasser "disgorge," was pressed into the pleading also. Particularly forceful in this, he fervently pleaded with Dulles to lead the mission.

This was Dulles's most propitious opportunity of solving the crisis on his terms or something close to it, of managing his allies as well as Nasser. DULLES REFUSED TO LEAD THE MISSION. The maximum that McCardle or anyone else could elicit from him was, "I've been away from Washington too long! But. . . ."

One can find reasons why the English asked him to undertake the mission in the regions of the cunning and crafty, if one wishes. One can find reasons why, in the realm of the shy and the astute, Dulles refused to be the bearer of the will of his allies and their many friends.

Perhaps Eden and Macmillan wished to involve the United States in Cairo itself so that they could thereafter say to Dulles, "Now you can see for yourself what kind of a rogue Nasser is, and that there is nothing to be done with him but force him to disgorge!"

The excuse that Dulles would have been absent from the State Department for a few days after an absence already of over a week is too feeble to stand. He could have gone back to Washington for a few days, and then traveled to Cairo. Perhaps Dulles declined because the risk of failure was considerable. That he inferred from the behavior of Cairo during the Conference. After all, apart from the reports from the news agencies, he had his own reports morning after morning from Washington and direct from all the Arab capitals, since the ambassadors sent their cables to be available for the morning staff meetings. He did not put his reasons for declining in writing or tell his advisers what they were. Dulles may have felt it to be beneath his dignity and that of America to wait on Nasser in Cairo. He may have thought that Nasser was too petty a tyrant to be met as a suppliant. Yes, as a suppliant: for partly by the Secretary of State's own behavior he had helped to furnish Nasser with unusual strategic strength which now required a more than equal strength to dislodge him. Dulles did not wish the United States to use the power necessary, which, given America's might, was very little in proportion to the amount it had at its command. If he was not ready to use power, what had he left to take to Cairo? Promises of "advantages" that would come, if Nasser behaved himself? Nasser already had the advantages—he had the Canal. Further "advantages in the future"? Nasser already had it good! Dulles had broken one promise, the Aswan loan—he thought. Talk of penalties? Dulles could only offer them as possibilities of pressure, of some kind of coercion. He would not take the risk. He did not have it in him to take the risk. If he had not already put himself into the position of a nonaligned nation, a neutral, he was on the verge of doing so.

Dulles's refusal was a tremendous mistake and misfortune for everybody concerned. It was his business to have considered whether there was another nominee to accomplish the present mission with his own likelihood of effectiveness. The next in line as leader was Menzies of Australia—a man as able as Dulles in every way and in addition a boisterous and master politician, with a warmth of oratory that Dulles always longed to have but altogether lacked. However, Menzies had two defects from the point of view of successfully persuading Nasser to accept the views of the vast majority of the London conferees. He was, in a way, a direct spokesman of Britain, and as such was anathema to the Arabs. He was also quite forceful in speech and demeanor, without having the world power and prestige of the United States.

In the end, Menzies led the mission, and to represent the United States Dulles sent Loy Henderson, a very capable career diplomat with a long and illustrious record of service in the Middle East, but only a career diplomat. What was needed for this delicate and complicated mission of persuasion and power was a statesman directly associated with the President of the United States—in other words, the Secretary of State. Dulles turned his back on an unusual opportunity, as he had much sought to escape the London meetings of early August by sending Robert Murphy in his stead.

Dulles's decision to refuse, his repudiation of opportunity, was a terrible error, pregnant with mortal troubles. To gain much, a statesman must dare much. Dulles's imagination and daring fell short of the soaring, promising, inexorable necessity. A Churchill, a Roosevelt, would not have refused: they would have said, If you want peace as well as justice, you must go and get it!

What was to happen next? President Eisenhower is under the impression that the Secretary had made it clear to Eden that force would not be a tolerable move; the Secretary had told the President that he had done so. But, as we have seen already, the qualifications and conditions were many. Would the meeting in Cairo bring a peaceful and just settlement? The composition of the Committee of Five to go to Cairo was designed to be conciliatory and fair: only one British Dominion, Australia; Sweden, the well-known European neutral; Ethiopia, a small African country; Iran, a Moslem and anticolonial nation; and the United States. Could fairness and a conciliatory approach prevail?

7. DULLES'S SOLUTION FAILS IN CAIRO

WHEN LOY HENDERSON ARRIVED IN LONDON, AT DULLES'S URGENT CALL, early on August 24, Dulles told him he was to go to Cairo with Menzies. He replied that the mission appalled him, that he did not think it could possibly succeed. He was sixty-four years of age, the physical and sartorial picture of a career diplomat. He had spent thirty-four years in the diplomatic service. In the late 1940's he had become head of the Office of Near Eastern and African Affairs. He had implemented the Truman Doctrine in Greece and Yugoslavia. He had skillfully assisted the negotiations between Britain, America, and the Iranian government at the time of Mossadegh's seizure of the British refineries at Abadan, and had been praised for his services by Anthony Eden. He had, however, objected to the recognition of Israel by President Truman, emphasizing the trouble to be expected to America from this act.

On the afternoon of August 24, Dulles chatted with various people at the American Embassy. Among his callers, at 3 P.M. that Friday afternoon was Hugh Gaitskell, leader of Her Majesty's Opposition in the House of Commons, and by now a fierce and redoubtable foe of the Prime Minister's on the Suez affair. On that very day, indeed, the Opposition had itself published a five-point proposal for dealing with the British claims on Suez. Its main features were recommendations to proceed by conference and to go to the United Nations.

A faint note of complaint pervades the context of Eden's reference to Dulles's meeting with his chief official opponent. Apparently Gaitskell had requested the meeting; and then Dulles had followed the protocol of asking Eden whether he had any objection. Eden replies that he certainly had none. Eden continues: [1]

It had always been a principle with me . . . to encourage meetings

> between foreign visitors and the Opposition or other leading figures in our country.

But then, after some more comment in this same liberal vein, he adds:

> On an informal occasion Mr. Dulles spoke several times to me of the state of public opinion in Britain, which he maintained was not in support of the Government's policies over Suez. In the end I had to contest this myself. I still believe that American opinion underestimated the firm sentiments of our country at that time, and that this underestimate had a debilitating influence on their policies.

It seems strange that a nation should seek to bolster itself at the expense of an associated power by thriving on the divisions within that associate, and even encouraging them. But Dulles wished to slough off any obligation in the Suez affair to the maximum feasible extent. His speeches were calculated to encourage, even as he drew comfort from, the Opposition. Gaitskell was not, of course, unpatriotic.

Gaitskell tried to get Dulles to tell Sir Anthony Eden America's point of view fully and frankly and comprehensively. This, indeed, was now close to that of Gaitskell, except that Gaitskell put reliance more confidently and immediately on the United Nations—to which Dulles calculatingly refused to commit himself. But Dulles only answered that he would make America's views known, "in another way."

In a jovial mood, at 6:30 P.M. on August 24, Dulles boarded the plane that would return him to the United States. Before getting a really long sleep, he picked a hand in the bridge game after the first bid, and made his habitual "fantastic" guess where every card was, and teased the life out of the poorest player. He had just invested an enormous amount of nervous and intellectual energy in the London Conference, during ten very hard days.

* * * * *

Meanwhile, national, militant passions were developing dangerously over Suez.

A storm was already brewing about the personnel of the Suez Canal who had been compelled by the Egyptian government, under severe penalty, to stay at their posts. The pilots were in the employ of the Company, but the British and French held most of its shares and majority membership on the board of directors. Many pilots did not want to work under the coercion of a foreign dictator who was hostile to the interests of their own nation. Why should they? They were private employees. But it was essential to Egypt to keep the technical engineering and other staff, and particularly the pilots. The Egyptian government feared that if any interruption in passage through the Canal occurred, then the maritime powers would have a cause for some kind of military intervention. If a clash occurred between Egyptian police or military personnel and, say, British merchant seamen and their officers, then force might be used and a *casus belli,* a right to make war, might exist. The Universal Suez Canal Company, assisted by the French and British governments' private advice and demeanor, refrained from calling its personnel, including pilots, off the job. The British and French governments announced they would await the outcome of the Cairo conference before the Company absolved the pilots from their service obligations. Nasser regarded even this as a threat.

The British and French governments wrongly believed the special assurances of the Canal Company that when the pilots were withdrawn or left, passage through the Canal would cease and Egyptian incompetence to manage the Canal would be openly exposed. The idea was erroneous; not owing to deliberate deception, but because the professional pride which men develop in their job tends to become a conceit that no one else can learn the craft easily or soon. There were 205 pilots on the books: British, 61; French, 53; Dutch, 14; Greek, 12; Norwegian, 11; Danish, 3; Italian, American, Belgian, and Swedish, 2 each; Spanish, Yugoslav, and Polish, 1 each. The remaining 40 were Egyptian. They were men who had been master mariners for at least two years. The Company had asked the 165 non-Egyptian pilots on August 6 whether they would stay with the Company or join the Egyptian authority. By August 12, all had said they would do the former. As counter-pressure on Nasser, the 58 on leave were instructed by the Company, about August 23, not to return. Because those on leave were not to return, the Egyptian government canceled the leave of those on duty. Others were not to leave without a month's notice. The British government asserted that the keeping of the personnel against their will was a violation of human rights (Article 23 of the Universal Declaration of Human Rights). Such a meek and mild protest made unscrupulous nations merely smile or shrug their shoulders or spit, and at the U.N. nobody made a fuss about the virtually imprisoned men.

Meanwhile the Egyptian government was seeking all over the world to recruit men able to pilot vessels, and was getting satisfactory responses, especially from Soviet volunteers. Salaries were up to $1,294 per month.

So, in a sense, a race was on between, on the one hand, the Egyptian collection of personnel to replace the Company's and, on the other, the British and French pressing of negotiations to a point where they could say, "We have in good faith tried to reach a just settlement; Nasser is still refractory; we must release our personnel from their obligations. And now that passage through the Canal has ceased or slowed down insufferably we are going in to manage it ourselves!" Dulles and his advisers believed that the British and the French were wrong: that enough pilots could be found, or quickly trained, or used in continuous shifts, to keep the Canal going. Therefore, American policy for the time being had two strings to its bow: the protraction of negotiations, and confidence that force could not be invoked on the ground that Canal transit was blocked.

The Egyptian government did not hold up ships that refused to pay the tolls at Suez when summoned to do so. The British and French still paid to the account of the Company in London and Paris. The American ships (flying the American flag) at the suggestion of the State Department *paid tolls to the Egyptian government*, "under protest." Virginity preserved, allies deserted. By paying, they supported Nasser and weakened their allies, who declined to use this typical Dulles compromise, this pitiful form of leverage on Nasser—"under protest."

The Egyptian government was rumored to have said that if the French and British pilots were induced to leave, then the Egyptian management would give priority of transit service to other nationalities. This report may or may not have been true. The play of near-force and near-counterforce was continuously exploited.

On August 27, the Suez Canal Company did announce to the interested powers that it could no longer control the safety of its staff and could not take responsibility if that staff were constrained to remain in Egypt any longer. This action seems to have been taken in some kind of association with the British and French governments: throughout the second week of the Conference, Georges Picot, the managing director of the Company, had been in touch with Selwyn Lloyd. The Company desired the governments to take responsibility for the personnel in a situation the Company was not designed to handle or equipped with authority to do.

The Russians continued their provocations and incitement to keep Egypt from negotiating. At a diplomatic party on August 27 in Moscow, Khrushchev ominously remarked to the British and French Ambassadors that if war broke out over Suez the Arabs would not stand alone: "It will be a just war for the Arabs, and there will be volunteers." [2] Elsewhere the Russians described the Conference as a "fiasco."

The French government and press were pessimistic concerning the prospects of success for the proposals of the Conference. The members of the Government were particularly irate with Nasser's interference, for it strengthened the Right against them, domestically and in Algeria.

As the Conference ended, the British more steadily organized their forces for potential Middle East trouble, focusing on Cyprus;

and by August 29 French troops were also moving to Cyprus. These actions gave Nasser's spokesmen the opportunity to decry the rattling of sabers when the Western powers were claiming that they were seeking a peaceful way out of the crisis. The Egyptian leaders themselves were glad to have events occur which enabled them to fire the belligerence of their own people. On August 29, the Egyptian government employed a gambit typical of its ruthless character: it accused certain persons of cooperating in a British plot to overthrow Nasser's government. It alleged the "ring" had been directed by two First Secretaries of the British Embassy, who were named. Egyptians and some British businessmen were involved. Three Britons were imprisoned, with the usual provision made on such occasions by dictatorships protecting their "dignity"—the Embassy was not permitted to see the men. Further, the Embassy officials were ordered to leave Egypt almost immediately; they were withdrawn under strong protest by the British government. Five British newspaper correspondents and two officials of the Shell Oil Company were also expelled. The correspondent of the *Manchester Guardian* was *not* among them, for he was useful to Nasser. The tension was not decreasing; just the contrary.

Menzies set himself to the task of making the Conference a success by correspondence with Nasser and briefings for his colleagues.[3] He met with the Egyptian Ambassador in London to discuss arrangements for a confrontation with Nasser. After a lapse of four days, Nasser agreed to meet the delegation bearing the proposals of the Conference. The Soviet government, Menon, and the Indonesian Foreign Minister had encouraged Nasser to accept the meeting. Shortly after the Egyptian Ambassador notified him that Nasser would do so, Menzies despatched a second message to Nasser. He suggested, as the matter was very urgent, that if Nasser (His Excellency, the President of the Republic of Egypt) could not conveniently meet except in Egypt, the delegation would go to Egypt, and would arrive on Friday afternoon, that is, August 31. Nasser replied that he would meet the committee in Cairo on Monday, September 3.

* * * * *

It is now necessary to follow Secretary of State Dulles's diplomatic progress from his arrival back in Washington on August 25. At that time, he had made a statement about the Conference:

> The London Conference on the Suez Canal set in motion processes designed to lead to a fair and peaceful solution of the grave problems raised by the action of the Egyptian Government. . . .
>
> We hope that the Government of Egypt will respect the opinions thus soberly but firmly expressed and responsively make its own indispensable contribution to the peaceful solution which is enjoined by the principles and purposes of the United Nations.[4]

Dulles did not see President Eisenhower until Tuesday morning, August 28, since the latter was out of town. Then he briefed him on the progress that had been made and the line he intended to take that afternoon at the press conference he had set up.

It was a crowded meeting in the State Department auditorium, with standing room only. As he walked down the aisle with his aides Dulles murmured to one of them in a rare and curious excursion into humor: "We should begin charging admission to these shows, and use the cash to help out the State Department's budget!"

The answers on Suez, to the *Christian Science Monitor* reporter who called Dulles, "the conciliator, the arbiter, the peacemaker right down the line," [5] at once took an extremely strange, even a wanton turn. It must have seemed to Eden and Mollet that their countries were being abandoned by Dulles, after they had apparently been befriended, even championed by him, in what Lloyd had hailed as a "masterly speech." One or the other treatment seemed hollow, since a substantial and disconcerting inconsistency was immediately noticed. The inconsistency was also dangerous. Sir Roger Makins did report home at this time that it was out of the question that Washington would support the use of force—or, rather, that Washington would not contemplate such a move until after November 6.

A reporter asked Dulles if "physical possession" of the Canal by Egypt along with Egyptian guarantees of freedom of navigation to the users individually or collectively would be acceptable to him. He could have answered this question in some such way: "I do not think that that arrangement would quite answer the problem that confronts us. But I prefer to wait for the results of the negotiations in Cairo and would not wish at this time to vary, or add to or subtract from, the eighteen-power proposal."

Instead of this, he made a very disturbing statement. It must be remembered that Egypt and Britain and France were listening and analyzing every word, every gap between the words. He said:

> As I say, that is not a matter which is primarily of United States concern but primarily of concern to the many countries—about 20—whose economies are vitally dependent upon the Canal.[6]

The points that provoked worry and remonstrance were: (1) that it was not *primarily* a question for the U.S.A., and (2) that the economy of the U.S.A. was not dependent to any appreciable degree on the Canal.

These points were true. However, the occasion and context gave Dulles's words disconcerting diplomatic meaning. Could the progenitor of the eighteen-power proposal be trusted?

The play on the words "primary" and "vital" may not have been at all intended as a stroke of foreign policy to express withdrawal of American concern, the involvement of which had been so markedly, and it was believed so genuinely, demonstrated by Dulles between July 29 and August 24. If this was not the intention, however, the remark should never have been made. It was *playing* with fire power. But was it clearly such? To Eden, to Selwyn Lloyd, to Guy Mollet, to Christian Pineau—to Nasser? If the United States was not so dependent on the Canal why such an ardent and anguished interest in it until now? Why all that talk at London?

Dulles was further pressed by the reporters on this matter—for his precise view of the value of collective or of individual guarantees: which would he deem satisfactory?

He evaded this question. In doing so, he revealed that he *recoiled* from facing the fundamental question, that of the conflict of political will, that is to say, the mixture of power, ethics, and rights, which was actually the core of this dispute between nations. He repeated the thesis which the United States' advisers had hugged to their breasts with hoops of steel, that is to say, the idea of a "nonpolitical," purely administrative, purely technical body to manage the Canal. And he discussed again the possibility of devising such, so cut down to the bone of mere managerial instrumentation, that, as it were, even the most fanatical nationalist (the "political man" in his most extreme form) could live happily with it. This idea had been expounded a hundred times in ingenious memoranda full of legal and administrative gadgets by Dulles's Policy Planning Staff and Legal Counsel and other experts. With their suggestions at hand, he had reflected how much like his greatest corporation reorganization cases this reorganization case was, *in essence*. ("In essence" is the *ignis fatuus* of political science and the most artful misleader of statesmen.)

Dulles expressed his attitude thus:

> I don't think that question can be answered, or ought to be answered, in the abstract. You have to break this problem down into its ingredients. You have certain practical problems of operation. You have the question of pilots, who has the right of hiring and firing the pilots; who determines the traffic pattern for passage through the Canal—that is a very important aspect of the matter. Just as in the case of a busy airfield, the question of the competence of, and impartiality of, the man in the tower who makes the pattern of traffic in, particularly on a bad day—that is a position of great responsibility. So similarly the question of the pattern of traffic through the Canal is a great responsibility. Then there is the question of who has the responsibility of keeping the Canal properly dredged so that the sand doesn't fill it in. When you begin to think of the thing in terms of its detailed ingredients, then I think the problem does become soluble, at least I certainly hope so. I don't think it's necessary to think of the problem in terms of those very great issues, those great slogans, such as the slogans of

> "nationalism versus internationalism," or "nationalism versus colonialism" or "Asia versus Europe," or any such things. Then the problem becomes almost insoluble. But when you begin to think of the concrete practical things you have to do to establish confidence that there will be an impartial, competent and efficient operation of the Canal, then I think the matter should be soluble. I don't say it will be, but I think it should be.[7]

Was he not pushing reality away from him as hard as he could? Could he complain when the harsh realities of international politics eventually caught up with him, if he himself lived or pretended to live in such a Cloud Cuckoo Land? But he could express optimism now, partly in order to blandish Nasser.

> We move forward, I think, steadily. And while the end is not yet in sight, I do believe that the steps which have been taken indicate a certain desire on both sides to reach a peaceful solution.

Dulles thought, he went on to say, that Nasser's reception of the Menzies mission demonstrated that "We have moved forward, for when the Conference adjourned there was still no sense of certainty that he would see the delegation."

Alas! He did not yet comprehend the masterly political shrewdness and unscrupulousness of his adversary, Nasser.

Dulles severely castigated the mischievousness of the Soviet Union during and since the Conference: it had instituted a propaganda barrage to exacerbate feelings to the point where Nasser would reject the mission; it had especially promoted the idea that whatever the Conference proposed would be imperialism and colonialism. It is difficult to know what public purpose in America's national interest was served by this diatribe. It did not make Nasser or Moscow any more amenable.

Questioned on the effect of the refusal of the loan for the Aswan Dam, Dulles stuck firmly to the story he had held to since that time, that it had not caused the seizure of the Canal.[8] Britain and France and Egypt and the Soviet Union and India and all other nations, even American statesmen in the Democratic Party, had insisted that a moral responsibility for the seizure lay with Dulles for his timing and above all for his *manner* of withdrawing the offer of the loan. It was to his interest to deny this charge. For if he had conceded a moral responsibility, a political responsibility would have followed to take action and make sacrifices to correct his mistake, or he would be proven a poltroon. He rejected the implied burden. Yet he admitted something more serious by far: that Nasser had seized the Canal for "grandeur" and "triumph after triumph."

Then a very awkward question, indeed, was asked. It raised an issue at odds with Dulles's optimism and his seeming belief that the conflict over Suez could be depoliticized, so to speak, though he had just admitted the political motive *par excellence*: "grandeur" and "triumphs." The day before the present press conference, the Egyptian press had carried a protest by Nasser over an alleged remark of Dulles's that the Convention of 1888 had given "an international character" to the Suez Canal. He was now questioned on this point.

"Without undertaking to answer [the allegation], would you care to dilate for our benefit on the meaning of "international" in that connection?" Of course, Dulles was ready to dilate. Here he was on the safest ground. "I did not realize that there was any question but what the Suez Canal *was* an international waterway." And he explained it, correctly and normally (to a nationalist complainant who was incorrect and abnormal) thus: "Well, the Suez Canal was, of course, built before Egypt was an independent state, when it was still part of the Ottoman (Turkish) Empire, and at that period it was internationalized by the Treaty of 1888, which provides that it shall be a waterway freely open in time of peace and war to the traffic of all nations. That Treaty was signed by the nations at that time principally interested in the Canal and then constituting the 'great powers' of the world. It was open for adherence by all countries of the world."

A newspaper correspondent pressed: "If I am correct, in your statements today you didn't use the term 'internationalization' of the *operation* [of the Canal]. Is there any change whatsoever on this question of the United States' attitude?"

Actually, Dulles had not used the word, though he came close to it. He now explained why he did not use it.

> I am not sure that I used the word "internationalization." If I did not use it, it was because perhaps instinctively I was trying to follow the advice which I gave earlier of trying to avoid using these grandiose terms which create conflicts which are perhaps unnecessary. Certainly, I did, I think, say that basically the Canal is internationalized by the Treaty of 1888.
>
> Now when you go to the question of what are the essential operating functions; how do you assure that those functions are performed in an efficient and impartial way free from the political influence of any government, then you may get a result which some people may call "international operations," and other people may prefer not to call it that. I think it is better to think of these things in terms of what you actually do.[9]

After this, he continued on a note that could not possibly impress Nasser or London, Paris, or Moscow; not because of a difference in their interests and purposes, but simply because the analogy he composed was untenable. He said:

> Now you have got the United Nations at New York. I don't suppose anybody would claim that, because of our arrangement with the United Nations, the City of New York has been "internationalized." We don't exercise a voice on who are the janitors, and what not, who perform the functions in the buildings there of the United Nations. We don't think that is in any respect a derogation of our sovereignty; it is merely a practical problem. The Secretary General has certain responsibilities which he exercises there, and we consider them entirely compatible with the full sovereignty and dignity of the United States. We don't get into these great terms about whether or not we have "internationalized" and given up our "sovereignty" over a vital portion of New York territory. And I think if you can get this problem down, as I say, to terms of the concrete, practical things, and get away from these big terms which raise issues of psychological and prestige character, we are much more apt to get to a solution.

Did he expect world-level statesmen vested with the responsibility for the security and welfare of their nations to *trust* him as at once serious, dedicated to them, and wise, if he talked such absurdities?

The Secretary was once again taxed with the annoying analogy—far more applicable than the one he had just elaborated—of the Panama Canal. What is interesting in the Secretary's explanation is again the use of this phrase: "The Suez Canal by the Treaty of 1888 is internationalized." *But* the "Panama Canal is a waterway in a zone where, by treaty, the United States has all the rights which it would possess if it were sovereign, to the entire exclusion of the exercise by the Republic of Panama of any such sovereign rights, power or authority." [10] No other country had an international treaty giving it any rights at all in the Panama Canal, except Britain, which was entitled to the same tolls for its vessels as those of the United States.

This was only the legal situation. But the Secretary wished to rub in the significance of the difference in the practical situation.

> In the case of the Suez Canal a large number of countries, whose very livelihood, almost, depends upon the free and efficient and impartial operation of the Canal, are in fact gravely disturbed because they fear that there will not be the kind of operation and that their lifeline—and to them it is almost literally a lifeline—that their lifeline may be cut. As far as I am aware, no country anywhere in the world fears that its economy is jeopardized by possible misuse, abuse, of our rights in the Panama Canal.

What, then, did the Secretary of State, wielding all the power of the most mighty nation in the world, intend to do about Suez and the lifeline of his partners in NATO? The reader must notice that he gave himself a loophole for defection from his allies by the word "almost." Also, he implied that the U.S.A. could be trusted not to abuse its rights. The issue, however, was Nasser's unreliability, not America's.

Nasser soon let Dulles know he had a prickly problem on his hands. The brash optimism of the Secretary of State was proven unjustified. Reality was altogether different in politics among nations from what he seemed to imagine. It happened this way. On August 29, 1956, President Eisenhower returned from California after convalescing from his ileitis operation, looking, the press said, "deeply tanned and fit, although somewhat thinner." He had a two-hour conference with Dulles. During the second hour, Admiral Arthur Radford, Chairman of the Joint Chiefs of Staff, took part in the colloquy, providing his assessment of the possible military consequences of the Suez policy and the precautionary activities of the British, French, and Russian military forces. The President was then supplied by Dulles with a statement—that is, the composition was totally Dulles's—which was delivered to the public as the President's statement. It was read to the press by the Secretary in the office of Press Secretary James C. Hagerty at the White House. Before Dulles began to read, Hagerty observed that the President had asked him to express publicly "his appreciation to the Secretary of State for the fine and wonderful job he did at the London Conference for the United States and for the peace of the world."

Then came the Dulles-into-Eisenhower statement:

> I have just received from Secretary Dulles a full report upon the London Suez conference. This supplements the daily messages which I received from him while he was in London.
>
> It is, I think, of great significance that eighteen of twenty-two nations assembled in London, the shipping of which represents over 95 per cent of the traffic through the Suez Canal, have agreed upon conditions which in their opinion are indispensable to give confidence that this waterway, internationalized by the Treaty of 1888, will be operated so as dependably to serve its appointed purpose.
>
> I am glad that President Nasser is prepared to meet to discuss this program.
>
> This program was conceived in an atmosphere of friendly conciliation and, in my opinion, ought to rally behind it the support of all the nations and peoples that believe in the processes of international justice and conciliation.
>
> The United States Government and, I believe, the American nation, completely support the eighteen-nation proposal thus arrived at in London, which, fully respecting the sovereignty of Egypt, would assure a peaceful solution of this great problem.[11]

It was a pity, and it later became a disaster, that the President had not been able himself to master fully and immediately the forces and passions and interests in contention, including that of the United States. He spoke with the voice of Dulles, but he thought with a mind much less technically skilled than Dulles's, and even less did he approach matters with Dulles's strange conscience. Eisenhower did not study the documents of the First London Conference. He relied on Dulles to tell him what had happened. How could he possibly at any later stage, when quick and crucial decisions had to be taken, make an independent decision, that is, a decision not colored almost entirely by Dulles's account of facts of which he himself had no personal direct knowledge? What substitute for responsibility, even if it had been sought, could the President find in his own testimony that Dulles kept very careful notes and diaries of the conferences at which he represented the might and conscience and interests of the United States? The final word, surely, was said by the man who decided what to include in his notes, who separated the significant from the insignificant. The President would have to act on second-hand information, on facts refracted through the vessel, Dulles.

Almost immediately Nasser showed his fangs. "Friendly conciliation," indeed! As soon as he read the word "internationalization" in the "President's statement," he summoned Ambassador Henry Byroade —by now made the scapegoat by all for his difficult actions in a precarious situation with a touchy dictator. Nasser verbally protested about the use of the word. Egyptian Ambassador Ahmed Hussein—also a scapegoat for similar reasons—called at the State Department to inform Dulles that Nasser objected. He told Dulles that "All historic facts and documents prove the Suez Canal was never internationalized and was always Egyptian territory under Egyptian sovereignty." Dulles answered Hussein that "I did not mean at all to impugn Egyptian sovereignty. I had in fact said in the same news conference, 'The Canal is Egyptian territory. That fact is not disputed.' Nor do I mean that any kind of international operation has been established. When I said internationalized I was thinking merely of the international right of freedom of passage." [12] (In these remarks, the third person, indirect reporting, has been changed into the first person.)

Soon afterwards, the Secretary went to the White House to discuss the matter with the President. This was the third conversation with him on Suez in two days. And at a National Security Council meeting that morning, the military implications of Suez were considered in preparation for a North Atlantic Treaty Organization Council meeting in Paris during the first week of September.

Nasser followed up his "lecture" to Byroade with a formal communiqué of protest. The President and Dulles were thrown into a mood of annoyance mixed with alarm and some impatient confusion. They wanted peace and a just settlement. They dared not have Nasser rubbed the wrong way. A kite was flown that the difference was only a question of "semantics"—one of the most potent and demoralizing escapist words to have been provided by the linguistic research workers of America in the last twenty years. The difference was substantial, not verbal. But it was now necessary to play it down diplomatically. Hence, at his news conference of August 31, President Eisenhower said:

> The other announcement I have has to do with an apparent misunderstanding that's arisen about my use of the word "internationalize" with respect to the Suez Canal.
>
> I want to make this statement: We are, I think, talking at cross-purposes. I referred to the Suez Canal as a waterway internationalized by the Treaty of 1888. That treaty gives many nations rights in and to the Canal in perpetuity.
>
> Now, of course, that does not mean that these nations own the Canal. It does mean that under the treaty, Egypt cannot now or in the future jeopardize those rights of other nations. Therefore, in the sense of the usage of the Canal, it is internationalized.
>
> Now, in the formal statement of two days ago, I expressed the hope that the eighteen-power proposal would prove acceptable to all concerned, and in that statement I noted specifically that the proposal fully respected the sovereignty of Egypt.[13]

The voice was the voice of Eisenhower but the hand was the hand of Dulles. And it was deft. It did not, however, adequately rebuke Nasser's pretensions.

As soon as the President was left on his own, that is to say, outside his written statement, to the tender mercies of the newspapermen, he ran his allies into serious trouble. Charles W. Roberts of *Newsweek* asked him: "You have expressed the hope that the Suez settlement could be made in an atmosphere of calm deliberation. Do you regard the French movement of ships and troops into Cyprus as consistent with that aim?"

Eisenhower then seriously weakened the power of his allies to get redress. He gave aid and comfort to Nasser. He derogated from the firm front that Dulles had presented in London and even his press conference of two days earlier. This is what he said:

> Well, I am not going to comment on the actions of any other government. For ourselves we are determined to exhaust every possible, every feasible method of peaceful settlement . . . and we believe it can be done, and I am not going to comment on what other people are doing. I am very hopeful that this particular proposal will be accepted but, in any event, not to give up, even if we do run into other obstacles.

So far the President had done no harm, except that he might have reasserted his faith in Dulles's eighteen-power proposal, so that a constructive firmness could be heard. He had merely slightly enfeebled Dulles's tone.

Then came the disastrous and irreparable *gaffe*. The reporter from the *Washington Post and Times Herald* (Chalmers M. Roberts) asked, "Mr. President, in that connection, sir, can you tell us whether, since the Egyptian nationalization of the Canal, you have given any orders to our own military forces in the area in connection with this act?"

"Well, I can tell you this: I have done nothing that isn't absolutely consistent with what I have just said."

The President had no obligation to continue his remarks on this extremely sensitive and dangerous matter. But he could not govern his impulse: "*We are committed to a peaceful settlement of this dispute, nothing else*."

With these words he put himself and his allies into the hands of Nasser and the Soviet Union. He had shown his hand and dashed the cards of influence and intimidation from the hands of Britain and France. As far as their part in the affair was concerned, he might just as well have destroyed their armies, navies, and air forces. He still did not understand Nasser or Moscow, their homicidal insatiability, or their readiness to retreat under resolute and serious challenge.

Eisenhower had left his allies with less power than Nasser had in his physical possession of the Canal. His words had destroyed the strength of the Menzies mission. If Eisenhower truly thought that "nothing else" but a peaceful course was the way to reach a settlement, whatever its nature, however unjust to his allies in NATO, then he should have told them this privately, directly and with complete candor, and Dulles should have done the same thing exactly and explicitly. And if, in case force were to be used, the U.S. government intended to oppose Britain and France in the United Nations, the tactics it would adopt there should have been described. This was not done. Furthermore, if "We are committed to a peaceful settlement of this dispute, *nothing else*," was an absolute principle, not subject to qualification or reservation *now*, then it was *not* the same as the policy stated in Eisenhower's letter of July 31, which hoped for, looked to, advised a peaceful settlement, but did *not* totally exclude the use of force.

Force (artillery, as Richelieu said) is the *ultima ratio regum* of international change, the final reasoning of kings, the highest rule of the state, so often the amending clause of the relationship of power among nations in the constitution of the world. The United States has never disavowed it. The United States has often used it—sometimes, as in the acquisition of Texas, in ways hard to justify by decent ethics. It was at this moment using it in containing China and the Soviet Union. Force need not be used; it need not always be paraded; but can be held in reserve. And one of the ways to employ it in the interests of securing justice, especially against brutal interference with the rights of other nations, is to refrain from saying "I will not use it." Silence about the immense forces possessed by an aggrieved nation or nations is itself a force. It is not sound statesmanship publicly to throw away one's assets in the pursuit of justice, and merely intone maternal lullabies. If one wishes to do this, the minimum standards of statesmanlike conduct require informing one's allies first, in private. To trumpet such a surrender of one's weapons across the world invites, as this act did, the continuance of injustice and the eventual use of force.

Of course, the *gaffe* caused immediate consternation in London and Paris, and triumphant laughter in Moscow and Cairo. In Britain and France, the American abdication of force helped to develop a feeling that these nations had been betrayed. What on earth, they said, could all of Dulles's eloquence of belief and optimism mean, if this was how he advised the President when he returned home, or if this was how the President advised him?

Was this relinquishment of force the result of the reports from Admiral Radford and others at the National Security Council meeting? Was it a loss of nerve? For the kind of nerve required in contemporary cold-war foreign politics over a protracted time, with nuclear weapons ready for final solutions, is a different kind of nerve from that needed by a Commander in Chief in the midst of the tumult of hot war, supported by his staff and the coming and going of generals and colonels. Was the phrase "discarding force" an irrelevant, impermissible shot in the war for votes in this election year of 1956? Not in deliberate calculation or foreconsciousness, but as part of the emotional momentum of the Republican Party's platform: "Peace and Prosperity!"?

Perhaps the President *and* Dulles were responding to the British and French concentration of forces on Cyprus. But those Western military movements themselves arose from the distrust which the British and French felt towards Dulles and in a different way towards Eisenhower. The European countries believed that America's emphasis on international management of the Canal was not as resolute or sincere as that on mere freedom of passage without international authority to guarantee it. The State Department needed to bear in mind that the allies' ability to maintain diplomatic pressure and economic sanctions was a wasting asset in view of Nasser's physical possession of the Canal and his exploitation of it. Dulles's deliberations were wracking their nerves, for they were reaching a point where, in default of a settlement or military coercion, they would have lost their battle.

In England the Labour Party mass organizations and the Trade

Union Congress were putting pressure on Sir Anthony Eden, especially since Parliament was not in session. On the very day that the Menzies mission arrived in Cairo, the Trade Union Congress's resolutions on Suez were submitted.[14] They expressed the hope that the eighteen-power proposal would lead to a satisfactory settlement (without saying what it should be); that if the talks at Cairo should break down, force should not be used until the question had been referred to the United Nations and the United Nations had consented to the use of it. The implication, clearly, was that Britain should accept any solution the United Nations decided was right. But this would throw British interests into the egoistic hands of Russia in the Security Council and of a majority of Afro-Asian nations. Accordingly, 4 of the 30 members of the Congress dissented, favoring force if Egypt offered provocation.

On August 31, Gaitskell called on R. A. Butler, senior Cabinet minister in London while Eden was resting for the week end. He asked that Parliament be called not later than September 14 to discuss Suez. Butler answered that a date could not be fixed until after the Cabinet had been able to ponder the result of the Cairo mission. But this date became something of a deadline. Of course, Eden needed the rest, for as Prime Minister his burdens were, at times, as weighty as those of the President and Secretary of State of the United States added together.

The French government was more openly militant than the British. A Cabinet meeting on September 2 reiterated the determination to secure redress from Nasser, and announced that military preparations would be continued. Pineau even reasserted that France would use force, if necessary, against Egypt. He declared again that Nasser was a dictator with inclinations no less dangerous than Hitler's. "Is it not our duty to stop him right away? If we say No [to Nasser] with the very firm will to use force if necessary, that will be better than the international situation that our hesitations would lead to, a situation that would perhaps constitute a greater danger to peace." This statement was, in part, a response to the pacifist remarks made by Eisenhower at his press conference. Pineau also severely attacked the Soviet Union for egging on Nasser to refuse a peaceful solution of the kind proposed by the eighteen powers.

The British government meanwhile arranged for the families of its Embassy officials to quit Egypt.

* * * * *

Dulles's diplomacy was a subtle blend of immersion and detachment: immersion to secure a solution without force if possible, and detachment to keep the United States chaste, in case it ever needed to come before the United Nations. The strategy was subtle, its ingredients as fragile as porcelain. The question is, could it hold the forces in contention to little but a storm in a teacup, or would the mere pressure of Dulles's hand on the vessel break it and release the forces to fight each other? He was not sure himself, in spite of his Biblical quotation from Hebrews about the need of faith. In foreign policy, the only faith one can confidently entertain is that which concerns one's own conscience and will and one's own power to meet the consequences of that faith if it should prove to be, in reality, unfounded. But Dulles was pursuing a foreign policy that brought American interests into actual *conflict,* though they were in apparent cooperation, with the interests of his allies—in a struggle with a dictator he had mortified to commit a rash and perfidious act.

Dulles's next gambit was to have Loy Henderson, the American member of the Menzies mission, *not* take the same plane to Cairo as the others! A close observer has privately commented that, "It [American participation and its unpublicized, inarticulate major premises, which were 'under Dulles's own hat'] was a delicate and mixed situation." Henderson was to be "genuinely a member of the team," but there was to be no doubt that Dulles wished to avoid any involvement, any commitment, any sense of "ganging up" on Nasser. But the reverse of this stand was that Nasser's moral influence, his force of character, his intransigence, had thereby divided the allies. The picture was not lost on Nasser.

Before Henderson left London for Cairo, he had lunch with Sir Anthony Eden. Eden said to Henderson: "We are determined to secure our just rights in Suez, and if necessary we will use force, because I would rather have the British Empire fall in one crash than have it nibbled away as it seems is happening now." His mood was serious and determined. Henderson reported this to Dulles at once. Dulles was hearing almost word for word the expression of purpose that had been reported to him from Harold Macmillan by way of Robert Murphy's reports on July 29 to July 31, a month before. It was one more answer to Eisenhower's easy way with British interests.

The Menzies mission arrived in Cairo on September 2, a submission to Nasser's "dignity." They spent the morning of Monday, September 3, drafting plans for their meeting with Nasser, which was to take place at their headquarters, the Australian Legation. They were, besides Menzies and Loy Henderson: Oesten Unden, Swedish Foreign Minister; Sayed Aly Ardalan, Iranian Foreign Minister; and Akilou Abtewold, Ethiopian Foreign Minister.

The day before, Nasser had already put out a sharp jabbing left fist, declaring that "internationalization would be a reverse of nationalization and therefore unacceptable to Egypt." The mission was informed of the statement. Indeed, for several days now, Nasser had taken a firm posture in this respect, always in an astute manner. At a news conference of Western journalists, he had declared:

> I don't know about any compromise, but I will accept any solution that does not affect our sovereignty. International control would affect our sovereignty. It is a matter of interpretation, I know, but we interpret international control to be a form of collective colonialism. The Suez Canal is Egypt's and the company that runs it is Egyptian. We are willing to sign any agreement demanded by countries using the Canal that would guarantee free navigation through the Canal.[15]

He fastened on Eisenhower's recent conciliatory definition of the word "internationalization," and said he thought that now Eisenhower's was "the same general point of view as that of Egypt." Nasser added that Eisenhower's explanation had "lifted the worry we had about the American stand on international justice." What a crafty conclusion to have drawn so far as American support of Britain and France was concerned, and at the same time how lamentably debilitating to their position! He cleverly avoided direct and open reference to the President's declaration that he would not use force under any circumstances. He did not need to refer to it. His own statement that the President "had lifted the worry we had . . ." was sufficient to represent the strength that had been donated to him by Eisenhower.

Nasser continued that he would do everything in his power to keep the Canal open to world shipping. He expressed assurance that even if all the British and French pilots were to quit their jobs, Egyptian pilots could keep the Canal in operation. He defended the rounding-up of alleged spies as a military necessity in view of British and French threats. He refused to comment on the talks he had been having with Soviet Ambassador Kiselev. No mention was made of his conversations with Krishna Menon, who had stopped off at Cairo on his way back to New Delhi to talk with Nasser.

As for the United Nations, Nasser and his advisers had set their wits to work on this matter also. They claimed that Egypt was faced by a threat of war from two big powers, England and France. Hence, Nasser's government was watching and waiting. Was there a plan to take the threats being made by these governments to the Security Council? Nasser said he was not prepared to take this step yet, because the British and French each had the veto in the Security Council. "I would prefer to go before world opinion than to face these two aggressive powers in the Security Council." No decision on whether to go to the General Assembly had been made. He was willing to do everything to keep the talks going, regardless of the outcome of the presently convening mission.

That same day Nasser had also put his case forcefully to the world through an interview given to Frank Moraes,[16] editor of the *Times of India*. He claimed that he was keeping open the Canal, while Britain and France, by their talk of getting the pilots to quit, were interfering with free passage! He challenged these powers to go to the International Court in search of a remedy for their grievances. "Let them try it." The editor came away with the inference that Nasser would concede no more than the Indian proposal, even if as much: that is, the establishment of a consultative body, consultative but without the right to make mandatory recommendations.

Nasser later made the sky more lurid with war flames by his invocation of Soviet assistance. Nasser was asked by some Western journalists (Chapter 10), "If Egypt were attacked would you expect to receive military assistance from the Soviet Union?" Nasser answered, "It is natural that if we are attacked we shall ask anybody to help us." And he emphasized "*anybody*."

That reply was a clever and robust thrust at Dulles and Eisenhower! It was one of several indications that the dictator would go to the lengths of World War III to keep the rights of others he had usurped by force. What harm would Egypt suffer if they incinerated each other?

It is essential to realize that the Menzies mission treated Nasser with every gentlemanly consideration, not with condescension, not *de haut en bas*, but in a spirit of maximum conciliation, equality, and equity. It is material to the assessment of the quality of Dulles's foreign policy and diplomacy. The committee handed Nasser the Dulles proposals and a memorandum, the character of which was expressed in one of its phrases: "to conduct discussions in an objective manner and not in a spirit of hostility." [17]

Rumors have had it that there was a split in the mission, especially between Menzies and Henderson. In fact, no difference arose on the proposals that were finally put to Nasser as the discussion developed them. But the feelings of the various envoys were not identical. We mention the less serious differences first. The Ethiopian was very worried lest Nasser maintain his sole grasp on the Canal, because he could then, at some date suitable to himself, hold his small nation, to ransom; Ethiopia was dependent on access to the world via the Canal. He did not trust Nasser to be reasonable or fair. The Swedish Foreign Minister differed from Menzies in that the latter was a robust, Churchillian-type conservative, whereas the Swede was a mild, democratic socialist always inclined to tone down disagreements in the committee and to pour tranquilizing unction over emotional debate.

Henderson was constantly on his guard lest Menzies' manner evince a readiness to threaten force against Nasser. He took the stand that any indication of a threat of force would do more harm than good. Menzies believed that Nasser could not be brought to reason without a clear realization that he was confronted with the possibility of force. He had made this attitude quite clear to Dulles (who nevertheless supported him as chairman and refused that role himself!). When Menzies heard (still in London) of Eisenhower's observation that he was not going to use any but peaceful means, after having heard all that Dulles had said or left unsaid on this subject at the London Conference, he commented to Henderson, "We [that is, the Menzies committee] are finished!" Henderson was very wary in these sessions of any hint of the use of force, because if force should be used by the Western European powers, they might ultimately have to be backed up by the United States. Any use of force on either side could lead to war, and this is what the United States was trying to avoid.

Now, the sessions with Nasser began on September 4. This is a very important date in the Suez affair. By September 6, that is, after three sessions, the members of the mission had reached the conclusion that in all probability the eighteen-power proposals had not the ghost of a chance of acceptance, and that Nasser's temper inclined him not merely to defend his position, but to take the offensive against the proposals and Britain and France.

Before Henderson arrived in Cairo, and all the time he was there, daily, sometimes two or more times a day, he sent very long and detailed accounts to Dulles of what happened at the meetings of the Menzies mission, and especially at the negotiations with Nasser. Dulles was in possession of the dismal truth that the mission had not only failed, but abjectly failed, that, indeed, Nasser was militant, not penitent. Thus he was confronted with a terrible, agonizing problem. He saw the face of war looming before him. He realized that the situation he had laid down as the one under which force could *not* be avoided, namely, the collapse of conference and negotiations, had indeed occurred.

The bad news came to Dulles during the Labor Day week end. After Monday, September 3, the Presidential campaign would take on vigor and move uninterruptedly to its climax on November 6. His President, Dwight David Eisenhower, must win. And the President was mentally, neurologically, and physically tired.

Dulles had gone for the week end to his rural retreat, his old Indian cabin on Duck Island, Ontario, where he stayed, lounging, washing dishes, whittling, until September 3. He arrived back in his Washington office on Tuesday, September 4. But having taken refuge from business at Duck Island, he found beachcombing, as so many of us do, more attractive in prospect than as a long-run occupation. His conscience would not let him resist the impulse to cogitate arduously what next steps must be taken about the Suez dispute, if, as Henderson was indicating would happen, the Menzies mission failed.

Dulles did invent a new Suez scheme, all written out by him in longhand on his yellow pad with arabesques, the appropriate word in so many senses, one being Nasser's tactics that needed to be matched curve for curve. What happened to this over-ingenious scheme is discussed fully after consideration of the results of the Menzies mission.

Nasser was on top of the world. He guessed America would not touch him, and that Britain and France could not because they and so many other nations were committed to the United Nations Charter. He was also sustained by assurances from the Russian Ambassador, and by the attitude of Labour and Liberals in Britain. At the meetings he held fast to every iota of the principles and rights that he had proclaimed from the very beginning. He did not bluster, acted with the courtesy of a host; but then from time to time varied this by making faces and striking poses like Mussolini. Then as another variation, he would act as though he were afraid of the forces he had offended, and then he began to talk like a human being, instead of a *poseur*. Yet it all came back to the same *motif*: I will not give up one scrap of what I have seized: it's all mine!

By September 6, the committee realized that failure was probable. It nevertheless made one more attempt to secure justice by preparing a unanimous letter to be addressed by Prime Minister Menzies [18] to Nasser. Delivered on September 7, this summed up the results of the talks so far and asked for another meeting, the final one, before the committee left Cairo. It is not possible to print the whole of the document here. But the main points must be set out, to illustrate how tenderly Nasser was treated and how brutally he reacted.

The substance of the letter amounted to this: "Our discussions . . . have in our opinion disclosed deep differences of approach and principle which it seems clear that no repetition of debate can affect." Nasser had "with complete frankness made it clear to us that the existence of such a [financially and politically independent] body operating the Suez Canal would, in the view of Egypt, be a derogation from Egyptian sovereignty; that it would in substance represent a reversal of the policy announced by you [Nasser] on July 26."

The mission did not agree with Nasser's view. It submitted to Nasser in a homely and not inappropriate analogy that he was in the position of a landlord who would grant an international tenant a lease for use of the property—the lease being an expression of his ownership and conditional upon it. Nasser would get the rent; and since the tenantry would include Egypt also, Egypt's status would be even stronger than that of landlord.

The members plied him with another analogy, that of the International Bank for Reconstruction and Development (rather unfortunate considering his animadversions against Eugene Black, its director, unjust though they were!). No nation lost its sovereignty because it (as Egypt had) joined this international finance corporation.

The committee "frankly and objectively" tried to get him to accept their view that the efficient running of the Canal required skilled personnel. Those who used it had no confidence that Egypt could provide the skill. They also tried the inducement of forecasting that traffic would double or treble in a few years, with so much advantage to Egypt—and that this must depend on the users having confidence in the Canal's management.

Thus they returned, again and again, to the issue of confidence in Egypt's political intentions and technical competence, and therefore to the necessity of an international body for administration of the Canal. The men comprising the body could be appointed in such a way as to be immune from the political instructions of any country. "It is essential . . . that there should be no politics in the Suez Canal, whether those of Egypt or of any other nation." ("Ah!" Nasser and his political advisers are said to have commented among themselves, "This means the Suez Canal Board *would let Israeli ships through!* Do they think we are fools, with the Canal, this power, in our hands?")

Nasser had previously told the committee "with clarity and frankness" that he did not believe the Canal could be "excluded from the politics of Egypt, since it is part of Egyptian territory and assets." (*What a diametrically opposed view to that of Dulles in his expressed optimism! Would he take Nasser seriously?*) The Menzies committee now answered that, if such were the case, all kinds of discriminations in traffic and marshaling of control could be exploited for political purposes that *did not fall foul of the Convention.* They were saying that a treaty or other form of unilateral guarantee, or declaration, could be cunningly interpreted for Egypt's political benefit, without a clear breach for which the sufferers of such discriminations could claim redress. And there would be disputes about tolls, which could be raised to the maximum the traffic would bear.

Nasser's response ("repeatedly and vigorously") was that a Suez Canal body such as they envisaged would, "to the eyes of the world [meaning, in all probability, all Arabs] represent either foreign domination or seizure." They responded that, if Egypt freely agreed to the arrangement, such a representation would not be true.

And so, the arguments wound about and about and about. Nasser stuck to his guns. The committee members appealed to him that such a settlement would bring about the relaxation of the existing dangerous tension between nations, and that a world contribution would be made to the peaceful solution of international problems. (Did they think they were appealing to a philanthropist?)

They then asked him whether, since he had rebuffed all these persuasions, their understanding was correct that he was "unable to accept the basic proposals" put before him? By this day, the fourth after the beginning (that is, September 7), Wilton Wynn reports: "A person very close to Nasser confirmed to me the bad news: 'It's all over. The talks have failed. The answer is no. Now only strong American intervention can prevent the British and French from using force against us.' "[19]

Nasser replied in a note on September 9. It was truculent and brutal, and even rang with impudent amusement.[20] He described the claim that the eighteen countries making the proposal represented over 90 per cent of the users of the Canal as "distinctly a statistical exaggeration," since this reckoning did not take account of other countries that had no shipping, yet used the Canal for the bulk of their foreign trade.

Then he got down to business. "Furthermore, the principle of sovereignty, the right of ownership, and the dignity of nations are all deeply involved in this problem." He thus directly contradicted the terms and spirit of Secretary Dulles's optimistic contention that the Canal operating board could be "insulated" from politics. Nasser knew the conflict over the Canal was politics; he was deep to his elbows in politics. He knew, and he played, the game of politics: the contest over whose will should prevail, whose interests should have priority, and who should make the commanding decisions about these matters. That is the stuff of politics. And that is what he rubbed in to anybody who cared to listen. The truth is that, economically, he could have obtained from the Canal under international management, with the Convention fully observed, all that he could obtain by the seizure he had undertaken. It was not economic advantage he was principally seeking, though that was not excluded: he sought *power*, added power to Egypt, added power to himself, added power to the Arab peoples. The Canal was an instrument of such power, to be used as and when he liked to satisfy in unfettered freedom whatever the interests of Egypt at any time should require. This was *raison d'état* in the millennial, classical form. What stakes did Dulles think Nasser was playing for? Just a few more dimes? The more power one wins, the more power can be won! The Canal his alone, he could even stop Iraq and Saudi Arabia from easy export of their oil and pound their internal politics to suit his own whims!

Nasser made various claims in a trenchant form, and in a style of braggadocio, that Egypt had never violated any of its agreements concerning the Canal. The "grave situation" was artificially created by statements threatening force; by the mobilization of troops by France and Britain; by the incitement of Canal employees to leave their posts; by hostile economic measures against Egypt. He insolently sneered at the references, therefore, to a "peaceful solution" (Dulles's!). It was the Western powers who were violating the letter and spirit of the United Nations Charter.

Nasser's note accepted the solution of the eighteen countries so far as five principles were concerned. These were: respect for the sovereign rights of Egypt; safeguard of the freedom of passage through the Canal according to the Convention of 1888; respect of Egypt's right of ownership; ensurance of efficient and dependable operation; the importance of maintenance and development of the Canal.

However, Egypt entirely repudiated the ways and means proposed by the committee for securing these principles. Such a system, it was argued, would produce incalculable strife and would plunge the Suez Canal into the turmoil of politics instead of, as the committee "professed" to want, insulating it from politics. (The word "professed" was a quite gratuitous slur.) Nasser argued that he had in mind "the vital importance of genuine international cooperation as distinct from domination by any country, be it single domination as the one which Egypt just got rid of *or collective domination* as would inevitably be considered the system proposed by the committee."

He took the offensive with a vengeance, against the proposers of the Dulles system: jibing at "insulation," Dulles's favorite word in this matter; at "internationalization," the term Eisenhower had used at the prompting of Dulles; at the conveners of the London Conference; at the "tactical" selection and delegating of the Committee that had been sent to him. "What are all of these if not politics?"

Thus, root and branch, he rejected the pride of Dulles's intellect and conscience, which had been presented to him with the endorsement of the other seventeen powers. He threw back the matter of international confidence in the teeth of these powers: the real question, he said, was whether Egypt had confidence in *them*. He believed that the essence of the tripartite statement of August 2 was the intention of taking the Suez Canal out of the hands of Egypt and putting it into some other hands. "It is difficult to imagine anything more provocative to the people of Egypt than this."

Nasser offered to consider the principles he had himself set out (as above) "to negotiate a peaceful solution in conformity with the purpose and principles of the Charter of the United Nations." Egypt now, as earlier, was willing to sponsor with other governments signatory to the Convention of 1888 a conference to which would be invited the other governments whose ships used the Canal—"for the purpose of reviewing the Constantinople Convention and considering the conclusion of an agreement between all those governments reaffirming and guaranteeing the freedom of passage through the Suez Canal."

Now, when one adds together this last statement (which included no reference to an international agency of management) and the list of principles set out as basic for Egypt, it can be seen that such a conference could have done nothing but confirm Egypt in the position she had adopted; the Canal users still would have reliance only on Egypt's politics.

Thus, the Menzies mission departed from its visit to Cairo with nothing except a flea in its ear and dysentery. It is not possible to place the exact date of a characteristically vulgar and insolent act of Nasser's, but it most probably occurred on September 5. It is reported by Robert St. John.[21] "The conflict reached a climax one afternoon when he decided that Menzies was threatening him. 'This I refused to tolerate,' he explained later, 'so I brought the whole conference to an end. I was so angry that I even decided to cancel a dinner party I was supposed to give for the committee that night, but Loy Henderson, the American on the committee, and the Ethiopian Foreign Minister, who was in Cairo at the time, persuaded me to reconsider.' "

The committee had even tried the alternative proposals made by Spain. Nasser had rejected these also. He was on top of the world. He had acquired an immense strategic and economic resource for nothing at all. "I'm here, and here I stay! Get me out, if you can; I dare you!" As the Menzies report, signed by all the committee members, including, of course, Loy Henderson, summed it up:

> We encountered with regret an immovable resistance to any control or management other than the Government of Egypt itself. In spite of our best and most patient efforts, we constantly came up against such phrases as "collective colonialism," "domination," and "seizure" and what seemed to be an unwillingness to meet reason with reason. In the result, therefore, the central proposals of the eighteen powers were completely rejected.[22]

The supreme and very grave question for Dulles now, since he *had* intervened in the Suez Canal dispute, was: Am I going to condone the violation of a treaty, the treaty of 1888? This was the bare fundamental of the problem that faced him. Furthermore, all the evidence I have gathered leaves an apparent gap in Dulles's evaluation of Nasser. He never seemed to realize that in asking Nasser to accept his proposals he was inferentially asking Nasser to reverse the act by which he had become a hero to the delirious Arab masses. If Nasser did so he would, for one thing, be surrendering a tremendous asset which might add to his power to exterminate the Jews in Israel, as he and the Arab potentates often threatened in a variety of bloodcurdling curses.

Would the United States support its allies? They were bound together by the tribulations and triumphs of World War II and the current necessities of NATO. Would Dulles and Eisenhower give Britain and France military help, or, at least, not interfere with their determination to compel Nasser to restore the Canal to international management? The United States had a fundamental interest in the outcome. It now had to decide whether to allow a major treaty to be violated, whether to allow the might and vindictive arrogance of a small Middle Eastern nation to grow at the expense of its middle-sized allies' power and rights.

To onlookers, their sight fixed on the State Department and the White House, it was obvious that Dulles had the means to quell Nasser, if he wished to try them. They would be explicit or implied threats, and they would require common accord with Britain and France. A boycott of the Canal could have been firmly established, with full publicity as to its purpose and justifiability. It would have required from America substantial but not backbreaking economic aid to her allies. The Canal could have been blockaded, with the risk implied in the stranglehold such a move might have had on Soviet shipping—which was not substantial. Its cost to the United States would have been the odium of the Afro-Asian world, for the time being, and this could have been counteracted by forthright and eloquent American public explanations. The United States might have applied pressure involved in Britain's control (by an agreement it honored) of an important tributary of the Nile at its headwaters.[23] The United States, under Dulles's guidance, did none of these things: it was pusillanimous.

Yet, what of Dulles's idea, developed in the interwar years, that treaties were not totally sacrosanct in an age of change, if one wanted peaceful change? Did that notion, expounded in his *War or Peace*, remain prevalent in his consciousness and impulses? Was it not unction to his soul to observe peaceful change in process so long as only Britain and France lost by the change, while, in Panama, for example, America's position remained intact? It is a pity that the notion was not brought out into the open with his allies, for their edification and guidance. As for Nasser, he had realized that if he hammered at Dulles, Dulles could be kneaded like putty.

8. THE POISONED APPLE: THE USERS' CLUB

EDEN AND HIS CABINET AND THEIR FRENCH ALLY REALIZED MOST PAINfully that if the Menzies mission should fail they must at once undertake some bold new action. Britain had thousands of military reserves on duty, men and women taken away from their families, their work, and the nation's economy. The course of trade was disturbed and the public finances of the nation were being strained. Eden and his colleagues felt obliged to exert continuous diplomatic persuasion, perhaps in some cases pressure, on the maximum number of powers, certainly of the eighteen, in order to sustain their support of Britain's stand against Nasser's seizure. Some of these countries were the so-called neutrals. Britain was doing this, it should be noted, at a time when Nasser, Khrushchev, and Nehru were exerting their maximum effort in the opposite direction. Above all, Nasser was fomenting unrest, even revolution, in the Arab and African countries. This last was neither a joke nor an abstraction. It was an immediate reality, attested by the British government's intelligence services abroad and by messages from Arab friends in those lands. These men were Arabists, many being "Arab socialists," but they regarded Nasser as an imperialist towards them, as a mischief-maker, even as a madman, destructive of the serene and progressive future of the Arab peoples.

For all of Dulles's talk and efforts Nasser had been now in possession of the Canal for over a month. Within six or eight weeks, weather conditions would deteriorate in the Mediterranean; and *if*, we repeat *if*, and again, so there is no mistake about the attitude of the British government, *if* no pacific and just solution were soon found, then the issue whether to use force for redress must arise. To plan, let alone prepare, militarily, and to have a moral basis for keeping the reserve army away from home, Eden was compelled to decide on the next step at once.

In a thoroughly responsible mood, Eden and the whole Cabinet, supported by Selwyn Lloyd, who had received from all sides warm encomiums for his conduct of the London Conference, decided now —August 28—that they ought to be ready to appeal for their rights to the U.N. What possible objection to this straightforward course could they have expected from Dulles, who had impressed himself upon them as the zealous supporter of the United Nations, the dutiful memorizer of its involved clauses, the preacher of its virtues in so many books and articles—the Christian advocate of peaceful change?

While Dulles was still in London, that is, on August 23 or 24, Eden had broached this matter to him. He also raised the question of getting Dulles to have the Canal dues from American ships *not* paid to Nasser's account. Eden had French, Dutch, Norwegian, and German support for this. He wanted Nasser to feel the pinch of running the Canal out of his own budget. Dulles answered, "No! You've got alternatives. If the Canal is closed because we refuse to pay tolls, you know that it's going to cost *you* a lot of money to go round by the Cape! Besides, you can get some relief by rationing gasoline!" It was an unpleasant answer to a nation, an ally, dependent for its standard of living on every nickel it could economize in the cost of production. It was a particular shock coming from the American government, whose people were on the average about *three times* as wealthy (annual income per capita) as the English people—and not because English men and women and adolescents worked any less industriously than Dulles's own people. Being Prime Minister, Eden was responsible for the British budget. All that Dulles did was to promise to consider the matter. To the very end, he never did anything to satisfy Eden's plea.

Eden, of course, with his herculean weight of responsibilities, could *not* let the matter rest in the mood of Dulles's apparently lackadaisical manner (Senator Fulbright called it "vacillating"). His country had more to lose than it could bear. He felt that if military action should ever seem unavoidable he must go to the United Nations and place Britain's and France's case before the Security Council. He hoped that the United States Secretary of State and President would agree to join Britain and France, and would concert arrangements to avoid the long dragging-out of procedure usual in that arena of merciless nationalist egoisms, as well as supporting measures to fulfill whatever resolutions the U.N. might be induced to pass. It was Eden's idea that such a course would serve to keep the eighteen powers marching together.

The French, with less fear of the risks involved, assented to the approach to the Security Council.

BUT DULLES OPPOSED IT.

As Eden asserts, "One of Dulles's advisers described the Security

Council to us as a quicksand. Once in it, one did not know how deep it would prove, or whether one would ever get out."[1] True! But international politics, especially in a risky situation, is an affair of risks: only daring to act will open the door to knowledge of where one actually stands. The British and the French, not more than the Americans, were pledged not to take military action without first going to the United Nations. "We were pledged," says Eden, "and we intended to keep our word." The Cabinet decided on August 28 to go to the United Nations as soon as they had heard from Menzies, for then, too, the Cabinet would have something concrete for Parliament to debate. Dulles was informed of this decision on the day it was taken. This was the day of his press conference already described (Chapter 7). The British Cabinet also decided to sustain pressure on Nasser when the NATO powers met in Paris, September 5.

Eden complains that America did not at this juncture (perhaps at any point) approach the issue in the spirit of an ally. He expected from Dulles and Eisenhower that in view of the alliance with Britain (and France) they would support them in every way "short of the use of force"; closely plan their policies with their allies and stoutly uphold the decisions; insist on the restoration of international authority to insulate (Dulles's precious term) the Canal from the politics of any one country. He makes the charge:

> It is now clear that this was never the attitude of the United States Government. Rather did they try to gain time, coast along over difficulties as they arose and improvise policies, each following on the failure of its immediate predecessor. None of these was geared to the long term purpose of serving a joint cause.

Dulles, cognizant of British and French intentions, now used his various editions of the Charter, including the one he always fingered in his vest pocket, to entangle them in every kind of legal obstacle. Was the Suez affair a "dispute" or a "situation"? If the first, the allies might find themselves in a considerable minority. If the second, perhaps they could never get the Security Council to render an effective resolution. The British labored hard to satisfy these well-selected doubts, the Dulles-ventilated technicalities, and thus, incidentally, to expose the hollowness of the messages to Eden from Dulles and Eisenhower maintaining that recourse to the United Nations must precede military action.

To the British arguments, Dulles responded spinsterishly. He pretended to worry about the number of votes obtainable in the Security Council. He would be bold enough to agree to support the allies in the Council—BUT—"on the understanding that our [the British and French] move was an honest attempt to reach a solution and not 'a device for obtaining cover' "! To advance the matter and make its position crystal clear, Eden sent the draft resolution he thought to put before the Security Council to Dulles on August 30. It ran:

> Recognizing that the arbitrary and unilateral action of the Government of Egypt in relation to the operation of the Suez Canal has disturbed the *status quo* and has created a situation which may endanger the free and open passage of shipping through the Canal, without distinction of flag, as laid down by the Suez Canal Convention of 1888, and has given rise to a threat to the peace. . . .
> [The record of the first London Conference and the Cairo mission's rejection by Nasser were then recounted.]
> Considering that such a refusal constitutes an aggravation of the situation;
> Recalling the Egyptian Government's failure to comply with the Security Council's resolution of September 1, 1951 (requiring freedom of passage for all, including Israel);
> 1. Finds that a threat to the peace exists;
> 2. Reminds the Government of Egypt of its continuing obligation, under Article 25 of the Charter, to accept and carry out the above-mentioned resolution;
> 3. Reaffirms the principle of the freedom of navigation of the Suez Canal in accordance with the Suez Canal Convention of 1888;
> 4. Considers it essential that, in order to guarantee this principle, the Canal should be operated on the basis of the above-mentioned five-power proposals;
> 5. Calls on the Government of Egypt to negotiate on the basis of these proposals.[2]

Dulles replied that he thought the draft resolution implied the possible use of force. He did not want the United States *necessarily* (my italics) to be committed to this. The actual draft does not contain the implication Dulles suggested. But, as a lawyer of so much experience, a defender of the President's aversion to the use of force, Dulles quibbled at every possible circumstance. What nettled Dulles most was that the draft resolution bluntly condemned Nasser's action and firmly called on him to negotiate on Dulles's own eighteen-power proposals. For if the resolution passed, the onus of action would be put on Dulles. He had called for a condemnation of Nasser's seizure —no one so forcibly. He had invented the proposals. The British and French were fulfilling his own proposed course of peaceful negotiation. He was now being taken at his word, and at the United Nations he would have to support or turn his back on his own pronouncements and moral position. Dulles actually became fickle on his advocacy at the London Conference and elsewhere that the allies had a strong legal case! He equivocated that by asking the Egyptian government to accept a new treaty (namely, the eighteen-power proposals), the British and French were threatening force if Egypt refused! If this was the British and French attitude, argued Dulles, it implied that they did not possess adequate rights under existing treaties and needed to get them!

Then, when it seemed that he could not honestly find fault with the draft resolution (assuming that all Dulles and Eisenhower had said and written had been sincere, that they had been making a genuine attempt to get justice in the crisis), Dulles began to haggle with Eden over how long the Security Council debate might take. A week? A little more? Eden's answer was that it must depend on the concerted measures the Western allies took with other powers, e.g., Belgium, to discuss and to defeat amendments.

At this, Dulles and his advisers became coy about what Eden said they called "ganging up." (They had not let Henderson "gang up" with Menzies by traveling on the same plane with him to Cairo.) Dulles's tactics simply opened the allied ranks to rifts fomented by Nasser and calculated to result in his advantage only. "Nobody," says Eden justly, "suggested, for instance, that acquiescence by Britain and France in the repeated refusal to admit Communist China to the United Nations was in any sense ganging up." But Dulles knew that he must outwit Eden, if America's interests, as he judged, were to be preserved and Eisenhower gratified.

With the British and French position completely revealed to him by these exchanges, Dulles went off to his Duck Island Labor Day week end to ponder a way through his difficulties and obligations.

First, he was afraid of a breakdown in the operation of the Canal and of some incident, like the withdrawal of the pilots, that would provoke an immediate act of force by his allies against Nasser. Second, Eden had warned him that early in September he would have to recall Parliament, when the Opposition would harry the Government to go to the U.N. But Dulles's mind was fixed on the hazard that more than one-third of the General Assembly's votes were in the hands of the Afro-Asian and some other delegations, sufficient strength to block a recommendation against Nasser. The U.N. was an uncertain card to be preserved for a less uncertain future. Third, he needed time during which to impress on Nasser a sense of international obligation and a readiness to negotiate, if necessary, on more lenient terms than Dulles's own proposal.

Fourthly, Dulles was beset by troubles from another quarter, all the more tormenting because it could not be made public: President Eisenhower. The President was deeply enwrapped in a gentle euphoria of pacific piety. He had recently become confirmed as a Man of Peace, more so, indeed, than in his earlier days of the Moral Crusade. In a sense, he had just experienced a new baptism: renomination for a second term, on an enormous wave of cordiality from the vast majority of the people, because he was ready to serve for another onerous four years in spite of his heart attack. Even more: while Eugene Black and Nasser were haggling about the Aswan Dam, June 9, he had undergone surgery for ileitis. He soon rose from his sickbed and plunged into work. He even made the trip to Panama, as already narrated, to demonstrate his national fatherhood. Then, on August 22, while Dulles was bringing to a close his engagements at the London Conference, the Republican National Convention renominated the President unanimously. With his ingrained, simple, confident faith, the President may have endorsed the classical maxim that the Voice of the People is the Voice of God, although it was only Charles A. Halleck who nominated him as "the most universally respected, the most profoundly dedicated man of our times."

When Eisenhower returned to his office from his vacation on Tuesday, August 28, Dulles conveyed to him Loy Henderson's misgivings about the coming Menzies mission. At this moment, the President seems to have reverted to the doctrine of "no force" as adumbrated in his (?) letter to Eden on July 31, except that in that letter the use of force by Britain (and France) had been not forbidden provided all other courses had first been tried. Faced with Nasser's intransigence and insolence and the reports of the allies' military preparations, he seems to have leapt over his own provisos, minimizing the issue of international justice, and to have privately endorsed "only peaceful means." While peace still reigned, Europe and the Middle East were rather theoretical and remote to the President's mind, which was congested with more immediate business and preparations for the coming election.

We must now observe what Dulles did to try to satisfy the simple pacifism of his President and to offer his allies so much evidence of his apparent support of their demands and needs that they would hearken unto him and not at once use their armed forces, which were now nearing operative readiness.

Briefly, at Duck Island the Secretary invented a practical alternative to his international board for the management of the Suez Canal. Later, when more fully elaborated, the arrangement was named the Suez Canal Users' Association. It is henceforth called this, or Eden's synonym, the Users' Club, or simply SCUA. In the State Department, it was called the Duck Island plan. The essence of it was this: Britain and France and the U.S.A., and as many of the other London Conference Powers as possible, would join together in an association, whose ships would in concert sail through the Canal in accordance with their usual individual needs, employing its own pilots and other personnel to secure proper passage, and receiving the dues for passage. From the moneys received Nasser would be paid the share that they felt Egypt ought justly to have. They would seek Egyptian cooperation. If it were forthcoming, good; if not, they would pass through the Canal with the aid of their own pilots.

The evidence is incontrovertible that Dulles was the sole originator of the plan and that he assumed the responsibility of persuading Britain and France to accept it, and President Eisenhower, simultaneously, to acquiesce in it. The invention of the plan and its advocacy sprang from Dulles's conscience, the recognition of the political responsibility that he assumed since, by his own consent, he had first gone to London, or even had Murphy sent there, on July 29. Then, by the end of the week, September 7, he was deep in eager, and more than merely pleading conferences with the British and French Ambassadors that they should urge their governments to accept SCUA as the next step in securing their rights in the Canal.

The timing and the smoke screen regarding the identity of the inventor were designed by Dulles to make the world believe that perhaps Eden himself had devised the plan. This is what those who were closest to Dulles have asserted. For they were consulted by Dulles as soon as he returned to the State Department on Tuesday, September 4. All that week, Dulles formulated and reformulated his scheme with an obsessive and desperate zeal and with the inventor's gleam in his eye. By Monday, September 10, two days before Eden was to speak in Parliament, men like Ambassador Winthrop Aldrich and Herman Phleger, the State Department's Legal Counsel and a close confidant of Dulles, and other advisers, like Henry Cabot Lodge, had sought to demonstrate to him that his idea was inefficacious *unless he was ready to enforce* the passage of the Association's ships through the Canal. It was all very well to chatter delightedly about the tolls being paid by all users in escrow, and about the ships carrying their own pilots. But the main issue still was this: unless Dulles was ready to enforce free passage, the scheme was a meaningless provocation. The question on the tongues of everybody except Dulles was: "If the association's ships are stopped, what are the powers going to do? Turn back?"

Dulles would *not* face this issue at the end of the week, by which time he was close to persuading his principal allies to accept SCUA. To his advisers he confided (or boasted) his purpose: "The Canal is not Egypt's, but an international system set up in 1888 and usurped by Nasser. I'll find a substitute for it, and I'll make a *dry ditch* out of the Canal! And I will help to keep the West's lifeline going. Our experts show that we can find enough oil out of surplus and also by deflecting tankers for the needs of the West. We must not deal a body blow at NATO."

Here is Eden's account of the way Dulles put the matter to the

British Ambassador; it is based on the Ambassador's cable to the Prime Minister:

> If we could show that, in the event of Nasser refusing our proposals, we had an alternative to war, we would be in a far stronger position. The Convention gave Nasser no right to make a profit out of the operation of the canal. He would now see the money vanishing from his grasp and this, so Dulles argued, would deflate him more effectively than the threat or use of force. By thus relying on the rights which we possessed, rather than asserting fresh ones, we would be much better placed in regard to the United Nations.[3]

Can such a master stroke of pleading as this argument of Dulles's ever succeed? In the long run, if not in the short run? Its language was such as might have been directed at an enemy. In the politics of nations, men have reflected, an ally is sometimes, in some transactions, an enemy. Dulles had acted in this case as though he believed the maxim.

This was Dulles's *n*th mistake in his foreign policy and diplomacy in the Suez affair: to have fostered a scheme, all his own, all within his own power to propose, without having thought out its ultimate problems. Above all, he would not face the one issue he had so far balked at whenever it had arisen: "What sanctions am I prepared to use and assist my allies in using, if what I think to be a just and reasonable proposal is obstructed by Nasser?" No one can truly say whether the criticisms of his expert staff sank in or not. No one can be absolutely dogmatic in saying that he acknowledged them, being a man of reason, but then flinched from the practical political consequences of their acceptance. But it appeared to everybody around him who was consulted or who heard the confidential report of the consultations that Dulles realized the scheme's weakness, but concluded, "Well, we haven't any better at the moment. Sufficient for the moment is the evil thereof. Let us try this way. At least we will gain time for further thought, and something may turn up to help us that we do not clearly see now. Let's see!"

His error, even wrongdoing, from the standpoint of America's national interest in keeping respect for treaties inviolate, and in sustaining the rights and strength of his closest allies, was not to be frank with himself and not to be frank with them. He put them in a false position. And he did so by forceful, overpowering persuasion in which he promised them success. The avoidance of war is not the *only* factor in the national interest; maintaining respect for treaties is one also, and there are still others.

One of Dulles's idolators has observed, "He never thought it his business to tell the other party to a transaction the weaknesses of the case he was selling them." But Dulles was now engaged not in a transaction between buyers and sellers of goods in a domestic market place, but in cooperation with allies, sorely needed by the U.S.A. now —*and in the future*. By inference from his own doctrine that neutrals were not to get assistance, presumably allies were. Dulles misled his allies.

Dulles was sharply spurred on to winning acceptance for his contrivance by two further events, one during the week of his first persuasions of his allies and the other shortly afterwards. The NATO powers met in Paris on September 5. Dulles, of course, did not attend. But at the meeting, Selwyn Lloyd urged that NATO should refuse to recognize the seizure of the Canal, should withhold dues from Egypt, and should join in the approach to the Security Council. He was supported by the Dutch and by the Canadian Foreign Minister, Lester Pearson, who played an extremely important part in the final stages, yet to come, of this Suez crisis. Lloyd was also strongly backed by Foreign Minister Paul-Henri Spaak of Belgium. This kind of Eden-like maneuvering was, of course, fully reported to Dulles by the American delegation, and it pleased him not one whit.

On September 6, the day after Dulles's plan of SCUA had been put before the British Ambassador, Eden learned from Cairo that Menzies had definitely failed. The British Cabinet therefore decided both to appeal to the United Nations and to explore Dulles's proposition. It also induced the French government to join in a message to the Security Council to summon a meeting. Eden asked the United States to note this. Eden's view was that though the discussions at the United Nations would take time, they would produce some clarity about the respective intentions of the various parties—including the United States. Meanwhile, SCUA would make it possible to deny to Nasser the profit from his usurpation. Selwyn Lloyd kept insisting, in his cables to Washington, that Dulles was expected to see that the Canal tolls, including those for American ships, were paid into the SCUA treasury. In Eden's words, "This was the key to the whole business." [4] Eden's inclination at this point to consider SCUA was tremendous, because he believed that the United States would be *fully committed* by its own project. He still believed in Dulles's promise "to make Nasser disgorge." If this were a genuine commitment, it was only right—a typical British example of fair play and administrative-political procedure *among friends*—that the U.S.A. should be free to choose the method, in this case, the Users' Club. As the plan would take some time to clarify in respect to its organizational—and, it must be added, effectuating—institutions, Britain and France would go straight to the United Nations while they were being worked out. What was fairer than that?

Yet, if Eden had two forks to work with, so had Dulles. One was the Users' Club, the other was Eisenhower's club. On September 3 Eisenhower had sent Eden a message. In this the emphasis of the earlier messages regarding the use of force was reversed.

> Now the President told me that American public opinion flatly rejected force. He admitted that the procedures of negotiation on which we were then engaged would probably not give Nasser the set-back he deserved. But he advised that we should sharply separate the question of the Canal from our general attitude towards the Egyptian dictatorship and the menace under which Africa and the Middle East lay. The latter he considered a long-term problem.[5]

Now, (1) American public opinion was in a mass sense never consulted by Dulles or Eisenhower on the use of force. The American people were never asked to ponder the problems of the Middle East, the balance of power between the West and Russia and her satellites, especially Communist China, or the facts about Nasser's seizure of the Canal. If this observation by the President was not clumsiness, or merely Dulles's tactics for diplomatic purposes, what could it be called?

Actually, the State Department about this time must have received, from the agency it secretly employed, the preliminary results of its first public-opinion poll on the Suez crisis. This showed that 53 per cent of those interrogated believed Egypt was not justified in seizing the Canal (30 per cent "did not know"). It showed that 40 per cent did not believe Egypt could be trusted to use the Canal on fair terms (29 per cent "did not know"). *No less than 47 per cent* thought that Britain and France were justified in threatening to use armed force against Egypt to protect their interests in Suez (20 per cent ("did not know"). Among those 47 per cent who believed in the validity of the British and French threat to use force, 16 per cent went so far as to endorse American military help if they decided to use it, while 28 per cent believed America should stay out (3 per cent said they did not know). But the American people so questioned were not asked the only diplomatic question at issue: Should the U.S.A. support Britain and France *diplomatically*, not by armed force, for these two countries are not asking American armed help? The Administration was not being candid either in posing the questions or in interpreting the answers.

(2) How could the question of the Canal possibly be *sharply* separated from the general policy towards dictatorship in Egypt and its threats to Africa and the Middle East? Was this one more of those State Department and White House blunders that had cost so much at Yalta and Potsdam and in the concession of Berlin by Eisenhower on

the spot and Franklin D. Roosevelt in Washington—one more example of inability to see a few miles ahead of immediate military trouble?

(3) The tenor of Eisenhower's letter was disparagement of British and French claims on Suez. He was in reality requiring his allies to take some second-best alternative that would give them a noninternational guarantee of free passage and mere reliance on Nasser's word.

Eden, deeply dismayed, almost immediately answered this letter (it was sent on September 6), and Dulles had the advantage of studying the careful and considerate firmness of the reply. Eden's letter was the one that received President Eisenhower's answer on September 8.[6] It is a major state paper. I can only put its main points in the briefest compass, and end with its own prelude.

Eden held that Nasser's actions were like those of Hitler in the 1930's. Now, Eden did not say ever that Nasser *was* Hitler (it would have been folly to do so). What he told Eisenhower and the public was that he believed Nasser's course of foreign policy was like Hitler's in these particular ways: it was infinitely expansionist; and it had ulterior designs, which Nasser, of course, like the Nazis and Russians, did not disclose beforehand, but which unfolded with ever more vigor and craft with each successful coup. Eden believed the seizure of the Canal was an opening gambit in a campaign designed to expel all Western influence and interests from Arab countries. The plan was well on its way to execution, and every success brought Nasser more allies or intimidated more neutrals. In the end, it could mean that Nasser would deny oil to Western Europe and have that region at his mercy.

Eden gave the President direct and authentic alarming information about Nasser's subversion in the Middle East. Britain and France were not prepared to wait, as Eisenhower appeared to be willing to do, "until Nasser has unmistakably unveiled his intentions." That kind of argument had prevailed over most of the democratic world in regard to Hitler and his reoccupation of the Rhineland in 1936—with disaster; it had been rejected by Britain and America in their resistance against Russia's attempt to rape Berlin in 1948. It would cost far more to reverse Nasser's future revolutions throughout the whole African continent than to stop him now—which must be done unless he accepted the eighteen-power proposals. In the end, if the argument that Russia might come into the Middle East were put forward as an excuse for not taking action against Nasser, the world might well see Western Europe held up to ransom by Egypt acting at Russia's behest.

Eden's letter had begun:

> There is no doubt as to where we are agreed and have been agreed from the very beginning, namely that we should do everything we can to get a peaceful settlement. It is in this spirit that we

favored calling the twenty-two power conference and that we have worked in the closest cooperation with you about this business since. There has never been any question of our suddenly or without further provocation resorting to arms, while these processes were at work. In any event, as your own wide knowledge would confirm, we could not have done this without extensive preparation lasting several weeks.

. . . In this connection [giving the Suez committee every chance to fulfill their mission] we are attracted by Foster's suggestion, if I understand it rightly, for the running of the Canal by the users in virtue of their rights under the 1888 Convention. . . . But unless we can proceed with this, or something very like it, what should the next step be? [If Menzies should fail.]

You suggest that this is where we diverge. If that is so I think the divergence springs from a difference in our assessment of Nasser's plans and intentions. . . .

To Dulles's SCUA-cum-U.N. plans, in their entirety, the President was privy. Laying his plans well, Dulles had the day before Eden's letter arrived (September 6) had Henry Cabot Lodge come from his post as head of the American mission to the United Nations to talk matters over privately with the President. The three then went on to the meeting of the National Security Council, where the Suez problem was again reconsidered. They had, they thought, plenty of time, so far as the United Nations was concerned, because, owing to the coming Presidential election, the General Assembly meeting had been most conveniently postponed from about the middle of September to November. Also, on this same day, Dulles met with a bipartisan group of Congressional leaders to give them a review of the Suez situation. It was rumored that Dulles told them he was determined to prevent the use of force and that he had weakened on internationalizing the Canal.

Turning his attention back to British policy, Dulles spoiled the British and French purpose before the Security Council by *rejecting* the two conditions they regarded as necessary: (1) that America and they should agree in advance not to accept any solution that fell short of the eighteen-power proposals (even if they were defeated), and (2) that they would jointly resist moves by any unfriendly powers to limit the allies' future freedom of action. Dulles urged Eden then, for the time being, merely to *inform* the Security Council in a letter, without asking for action. As a French political leader said, with contempt, in doing so Eden was "leaving a visiting card."

Is Eden to be blamed for respecting America's power, and the presumed friendship of an ally? Yes! It might have been far better in the long run for him, and for America's future relationship to Europe, if he had pursued his own conviction, especially since it took him into the sublime sanctum of the Charter, and if he had done so by subjecting Dulles to all the obduracy which Nasser was inflicting on

Dulles *with success*. Eden had no business being kinder to Dulles and Eisenhower than Nasser was to them or him.

Dulles even refused to co-sign the letter to the Security Council! The excuse Dulles gave is astounding: "The United States government did not wish to create an identity of interest with Britain and France, which *might prove embarrassing to them, the British and French!*" What the British and French really felt at American policy was desperation and frustration. And these reactions ultimately impelled them to take violent courses, courses met by Dulles and Eisenhower with noble-sounding wrath and most devout appeals to the United Nations to chastise Britain and France, and by sanctions of oil and credits applied *unilaterally* by the United States against them.

If Dulles had been the most crafty and conscienceless of Machiavellians, and not a devout Christian, he could not have contrived a more enticing and deadly trap than the one he had just invented, SCUA. It was, in fact, a device, intended or not, to keep his closest allies from appealing to the United Nations. The Secretary was not always Simple Simon. As one of Dulles's advisers, very closely connected with these events, has reminisced, Eden thought that by now he had Dulles boxed in, but Dulles found the trap-door!

Selwyn Lloyd, the British Foreign Secretary, who was in continuous common business with Dulles, confessed to Dulles British misgivings over America's attitude. He said, on September 8, that now the United States and Britain seemed farther apart in their ideas than at any time since July 26. He expressed grave anxiety about this, and asked for effective action. Since Nasser was strengthening his hold on the Canal, the Western powers would lose face, and the Arab states were under dangerous strain from Nasser's subversive activities.

About this date, September 7, Dulles conferred separately with the British and French Ambassadors, and then jointly with George Humphrey of the Treasury and Arthur Flemming. Flemming's contribution was the prospects of the mobilization of oil resources for Europe if the Canal were closed or not used. Humphrey was needed because he would be asked to find a way to finance oil supplies that the allies might buy from the Western Hemisphere if the Suez passage was obstructed. This was some evidence that Dulles meant to pass through the Canal on his own terms or divert ships from it. He applied the heaviest persuasive tactics to convince the Ambassadors that they should induce their governments to accept his plan. He could hardly have done this without making them see that he was in earnest.

On the evening of September 6 and on September 7, Dulles took the matter to the President. (He may have dropped a few hints to the President a little earlier in the week.) As usual, there were no witnesses. My source is direct.

Before entering into the details of their colloquies, I should say at once that Dulles proposed SCUA to his President as a *very mild measure* but almost simultaneously to his allies as a *very strong measure*. He involved the President in the belief that he had found an easy and feasible way to settle the Suez issue by peaceful methods, while he represented to his allies that they need not yet contemplate the use of force because he had found a forceful, sanctioning, but non-violent means, with all America's resolution behind it, of getting satisfaction for them. When the allies finally became desperate enough to react against Nasser (and American diplomacy) by force, their move was all the more unexpected and seemed to the President to be all the more without justification, an act, almost, of brutal insult and injury to him personally.

As we have seen, on September 6 the President received a letter from Prime Minister Eden. Let us add some further points from it. It was full of foreboding observations on a message Eden had received from the British Ambassador, Sir Roger Makins, that day or the day before concerning talks with Dulles at the State Department about a scheme called SCUA. Eden wrote that he felt he might be able to go along with it *if* the plan were in practical shape and ready to be put into effect immediately after Menzies' failure with Nasser was made public. As earlier, in 1956, Eden insisted that the Western allies should have a definite program for Middle East policy. He begged that action should be taken before the situation in the Middle East and especially around Suez was rigid. Again, he reiterated British necessities in Suez. He concluded that Britain had many times led Europe against tyrants, and Britain would not wish the ignobility of perishing by degrees as she might by blows like the seizure of Suez. The letter was urgent and pathetic.

Eisenhower needed to answer Eden's letter. Therefore, on Saturday night, September 8, he discussed the SCUA proposal with its author, Dulles. Dulles advocated the SCUA scheme to the President as simply an extension of the eighteen-power proposal and its attendant formula for a settlement. SCUA was a device for *collective* bargaining with Nasser. Fantastic as it might sound to the President, Dulles argued that it could work because the Canal was an *open* waterway. All that SCUA needed to do, he expounded, was to place one ship at one end of the wide and open Canal, and one ship at the other end, and then proceed to transact the technical business of routing ships through with pilots supplied by SCUA. That is all. Simple. Then, he went on, Egypt could not stop this plan from working, except by force. No, SCUA would not take over the Canal. Its ships would merely pass through it. Dulles expected, he told the President, to get cooperation from the Egyptians. Suppose, he was asked, Nasser used force to stop ships attempting to pass through the Canal under this arrangement? Why, then, the answer was simple: Each ship would decide for itself what it would do.

The President and Dulles were not over-optimistic about the scheme, the President, using plain common sense, perhaps more skeptical than Dulles. The plan was founded on a belief that Dulles alone seemed to entertain with obsessive confidence, that there could be successful *de facto* negotiations on the spot with the Egyptian technicians on the banks of the Canal. The two men foresaw another advantage of SCUA—men have a practice of finding more reasons for a weak idea than they had originally thought of, caught up in a mood of self-persuasion—that it would be a face-saver for Nasser. (But why save his face?) They had one other purpose in mind, though the President thinks it was only a side benefit: it would allow time for tempers to cool among America's friends!

As a result of these conversations, Dulles and Eisenhower composed a long letter to Eden, dispatched September 9. It began by asking Eden not to worry over the loss of oil supplies if there should be trouble in Suez. It pleaded that the United States had every sympathy for the British and French position and needs, but that Eisenhower did not want the European powers to use force, since this would cause much of the world to turn against them. The letter suggested that the reference to Hitler in Eden's letter, and the expressed fear of the "ignobility" of going down by degrees, were too much like Churchill's temper and flamboyance. (I do not say this last word was used.) Again, the letter warned Eden not to compare Nasser with Hitler: he was far less significant. The United States did not agree with the British on the disruptive effects of Pan-Arabism. Whereas the British thought that drawn-out negotiations with Nasser would strengthen Nasser, and all Islam would grow more powerful and be lined up against Britain, the United States believed that the application of force would be most likely to cause the Arabs to become more pro-Arabist and hostile. (These are not the only alternatives in this situation.) The President used a phrase that appears from time to time elsewhere in his correspondence with Eden: "to re-examine the situation with some 'soul searching.'" *Force might be needful,* but every effort must be made to settle the conflict otherwise. If Nasser was not demonstrated to be the aggressor, the Arabs would be even more pro-Nasser. (Thus, force was still *not* ruled out; and Nasser had been an aggressor ever since July 26.) Yet, if force were used because Eden could not accept capitulation to Nasser, such action might cause a serious misunderstanding between America and Britain. Hence, the President was worried about the military preparations Britain was making. Nasser might ask the U.N. for a resolution to blame Britain for such action, and, if that happened, the U.S.A. would be thrust into an awkward predicament.

The letter continued by suggesting slower and less dramatic methods to defeat Nasser, such as SCUA. This would be a semipermanent organization to provide pilots, arrange traffic patterns (who goes through first, etc., etc.), collect dues to meet expenses, and make other *de facto* arrangements. Then economic pressure would grind Nasser down. At the same time, Arab national rivalries could be exploited. (How, was not specified.) Tankers could be used to avoid the use of the Canal. New ones could be built to take more fuel. Additional pipelines could be laid down to reach Mediterranean exits via Turkey.

Nasser throve on drama, reasoned the letter. Therefore, we should deflate him gradually. Such a course would be less costly, now and in the future. But—if Nasser should resort to violence, then he would be in trouble. *Eventually there might be no way out with Nasser except force.* To start and use it, however, when "the world" believed the dispute could *still* be settled in a peaceful way, would be wrong.

There the letter ended. The reader himself, already acquainted with the seizure of the Canal, Nasser's arrogance, Russian diplomatic support of his act, British and French feelings at despoliation, can appraise its adequacy as an act of policy—dependent as it all was on two assumptions: that SCUA was feasible and that *time* was unlimited. At the basis of the relationship between Dulles and Eden and Mollet was an issue of time, and Eden had begged the American Secretary not to lose momentum. Dulles would like to forget, but the allies could not forgive.

Now, not infrequently, Dulles put on an exhibition of cute cleverness before Eisenhower. He did so now. Eden's letter had referred to the fact that England had saved Europe in several struggles with dictators, from Louis XIV and Napoleon onwards. Dulles proposed to the President that they insert a little heavy-handed humor sneering about how long it had taken to accomplish this—e.g., eighteen years had been required to vanquish Napoleon, and then the period had grown shorter in World War I, and so on. The President, being more a man of the world than Dulles, simply discarded this exhibitionist affront.

Dulles's task with France was tougher than with Britain, because France had a more militant reason (Algeria) than Britain to ignore counsels of peace from Dulles. He conveyed to the French Ambassador, who is very experienced and quite alert and sagacious, the unmistakable conviction that he truly intended to put sanctions on Nasser for the passage of the Association ships, or to compel negotiation along the lines of the eighteen-power proposals, or to turn all their ships together away from the Canal, and make American provision in money and oil to assist this action. On September 11, when the Ambassador brought the affirmative reply of the French government in regard to the SCUA proposal, Dulles once again gave his assurance that the

United States would *do* everything required to assert the authority of the Suez Canal Users Association. Moreover, to emphasize his idea of going to the length of putting the Canal out of use except on the Association's terms, he conveyed the indubitable impression that the United States would apply *at least* economic sanctions, effective ones. Dulles was so enamored of his own scheme, so sure that it would be effective, that he could make it effective, that he triumphantly declared to the Ambassador: "This plan is certain to make Nasser a laughingstock throughout the world!"

When Dulles asked British Ambassador Makins to commend SCUA to Prime Minister Eden, he represented it unreservedly as a way of putting pressure on Nasser. The Ambassador then spoke to Eden by phone, and Eden asked, as the reader may have by now learned to expect he might, "Is it serious?" To this the Ambassador, who is a wise and prudent man, felt Dulles had given him the authority to answer: "Yes! It is a *genuinely* meant plan." Dulles, in his quite desperate anxiety to satisfy all the demands converging upon him, was more incontinent in private assurances and hints than he was later on in his public explanatory and exculpatory statements.

Now, Nasser took the diplomatic offensive as soon as the Menzies mission had closed, in an invitation to all nations using the Canal to send representatives to enter into negotiations with him. The invitation,[7] carefully drafted, must have been prepared before the final session with Menzies. The Canal's freedom and safety of navigation, its development, and tolls were questions that could be solved by peaceful negotiation.

The British and French governments brusquely rejected this ploy. Their own proposal had just been turned down flat.

On September 10, some little time after Nasser's note was available in Washington, but with no immediate relationship between the two documents, Dulles issued a statement on the failure of the Cairo talks. It expressed his deep disappointment at the rejection; thanked the committee and Menzies; declared that "only such cooperation as that detailed in the proposals of the eighteen would enable the Suez waterway to serve fully its intended purpose." Then he concluded:

> . . . the beneficiaries of the 1888 convention have rights which, in the words of the preamble of that treaty, are designed to "guarantee at all times and for all the powers the free use of the Suez Maritime Canal." Their rights remain, and they should be pursued consistently with the spirit of the United Nations Charter, a primary purpose of which is to "establish conditions under which justice and respect for obligations arising from treaties and other sources of international law can be maintained.[8]

However, all the news that was flowing into the State Department, and flying in a storm to Dulles's own desk, suggested this thought: Nasser hasn't any respect for justice and for international obligations except insofar as they redound to his advantage, and are put into practical terms in the resolutions of the many nations which, like his, are now overturning the present structure of international law and justice. This is the revolution of the nationalists, and they have no ethic that stands above their own uninhibited will. We have respect for Christian principles, but do all these other nations? * It was a hard world in which the Secretary lived and operated. Menzies had said the aftermath of the Conference was "very, very grave."

Dulles's statement was read by the Department's spokesman, Lincoln White. By a coincidence, Hervé Alphand, recently arrived as French Ambassador, had seen Dulles a little earlier that day. The text of the SCUA proposal had been presented to him, with a most earnest and pressing plea that he persuade his government to accept this newly devised way out. Alphand was waylaid by reporters as he was leaving, and he told them that France could not exclude the use of force. He referred to Eisenhower's news conference of August 8, in which the President had implied that *military force might conceivably be used* for the preservation of vital rights. The Ambassador dropped a hint, but too veiled to be taken advantage of as a "leak": "There are other routes to a peaceful solution." But he did not say what they were, or what he had just learned from Dulles. Dulles was extremely angry that Alphand had used the word *force!*

On that day also, the diplomatic grapevine was at work. The Pakistani Ambassador saw Dulles in the morning, urging him to prevail on England and France to avoid the use of force. Nasser's pressure never let up, and it was beginning to tell. He had already let out the news that he thought the Pakistani delegate to London had betrayed *him*, Nasser, an obviously unforgivable thing, by looking first to his own nation's interests and not Nasser's. And he knew that Pakistan, as a Moslem nation, could probably be made to side with Egypt the moment the West actually used force.

The first full text of SCUA thus was presented to the British and French Ambassadors on September 10. A rumor had meanwhile arisen that week end in Washington that somehow the Canal might be bypassed. An intense interchange of messages between Washington and

* Did he remember at this moment a conversation he had had with Christian Pineau, then just entered on his job as Foreign Minister, at a SEATO Council at Karachi, in March, 1956? Dulles tried to draw the younger man, the newcomer to world diplomacy, into his crusade against the Soviet Union, on the grounds that it was Communist and that it was anti-Christian. But Pineau had demurred. He had said, "Karachi is hardly the place to find acceptance for your attitude. The Asians are not Christian; and they are not idolators of capitalism; and they see in the collectivist efforts of the Soviet Union a path which they may themselves have to take in order to achieve swift and massive improvement in their standard of living."

London and Paris took place between September 8 and 12, when Eden faced Parliament. That was the day of the first official public acknowledgment of the plan, which was made by Eden in the House of Commons.

On September 11, Loy Henderson reached Washington via Libya and London from Cairo. In Libya, the day before, he had realized with full vividness the threat of war in the Middle East. He saw British paratroopers landing, all equipped, evidently fully trained and ready to go at command. Fully and even more forcefully he brought home to Dulles what a Tartar he had to deal with in Nasser.

The first leakage of a new scheme was made by Marguerite Higgins in the *New York Herald Tribune* of September 11. She was given the tip on September 10. There is much internal evidence that she was the confidante of somebody at the State Department, in being given information of future policy as well as present facts, for her forecasts are the most accurate this writer has seen, closely in accordance with later occurrences. Her headline was *U.S. For Suez Bypass if Passage Blocked.* She was told by an "economic" specialist in the Administration: "Egyptian interference in the Canal could be countered by concerted Western action that would result in the Canal's customers being diverted away. In this case, Egypt would get no profits because it would get no business."

The plan was not telephoned by Dulles to Eden across the Atlantic in the first place, as other authors have declared.[9] On September 10, Eden called Mollet and Pineau to come to London. Their joint communiqué [10] of September 11 did not contain any new ideas for resolving the Suez crisis, but expressed faith in the eighteen-power proposal and insisted strongly on Franco-British cooperation to resist arbitrary interference with treaty rights. While the British and French leaders had been in session, Dulles's almost complete drafts of SCUA had been brought in by officials, urging acceptance of the proposal as the answer to their immediate needs.

It was not until 1:30 A.M., London time, September 12, that the plan was in a shape acceptable to the British and French (and Dulles). It was now a joint endeavor. Eden was to speak in the House of Commons at about 4 P.M. on September 12, so that the plan was ready only about fourteen hours before he made his address. By this time, both the French and the British governments firmly, even confidently, believed that they were guaranteed a constructive plan with the will and power of the U.S.A. fully behind it.

The full formulation of the SCUA scheme by Dulles's own staff is to be found in Sir Anthony Eden's *Memoirs*.[11] Nobody in the State Department or elsewhere has ever contradicted Eden's account in any particular. Such a record is not, unfortunately, and inexplicably, to be found in the State Department's own publication of the *Suez*

Canal Problem, July 26 to September 22, 1956: A Documentary Publication.

Eden induced the reluctant and cynical French to waive their dislike and distrust. For Dulles was still saying to Eden on September 10 that SCUA was something "Egypt would like *much less*" than the eighteen-power proposals. He even used that famous old lawyer's line of peremptory and hectoring argument that (according to Eden) "the Egyptians having refused these (the eighteen-power proposals) *could not expect such good terms again.*" [12] One is entitled to extreme skepticism whether Dulles knew exactly what he expected SCUA could accomplish in fact, and whether he had the measure of Nasser. Or perhaps the explanation is that he was now very much frightened and also conceited beyond good sense, or that, being frightened, he was not candid. Of course, he pressed the additional argument on his allies that Nasser would not get the Canal dues, because SCUA would withhold them. That argument, the record later shows, had no conviction in it.

In the intense and frequent negotiations across the Atlantic, Dulles was an undaunted and dogged advocate, ever fertile, perhaps overfertile, in suggesting expedients and offering inducements. What a picture he painted! The British and French would be pressing Nasser by their already-established financial sanctions. Dulles dangled before Eden and Mollet the glittering revenge they would have on Nasser if they would reroute their ships bringing oil from the Middle East around by the Cape of Good Hope. Thus Nasser would lose the tolls for something like one-half of the 1.5 million barrels of oil that usually passed daily through the Canal. He, Dulles, would help Britain and France make up any lag in supply from the Caribbean and the Gulf of Mexico.

Just a moment, thought Eden: Doesn't this mean that England and France would have to find millions of dollars to pay for the oil to be supplied by the Western Hemisphere? Yes, replied the American government; but we'll help you to get a loan from the United States Import-Export Bank. But, thought Eden again: Does it not mean that eventually we would have made a large debt and need to find dollars to repay this *with interest?* Yes, replied the State Department (coached by the Secretary of the Treasury); of course a loan is a loan is a loan, and, naturally (how otherwise?), loans bear interest. Well, then, said Eden and Mollet: We are not paying dues to Nasser anyway at the moment, so that to send our oil round the Cape would hurt us, not Nasser, though it would please *you!* They rejected this bargain offer by Dulles. Eden's colleagues were not uniformly confident about the merits of the SCUA scheme either. The plan was riddled with doubtful components. Even the sleep of the Foreign Secretary, loyal to Eden's policy and Eden's person, was broken during the night before the Commons' debate on September 12. He was riven with doubts about the Users' Club. Therefore, while Eden was preparing the notes of his speech for 2:30 that afternoon, Selwyn Lloyd called at No. 10 Downing Street, and begged Eden not to go ahead with the scheme, as he believed it was *not* workable. Eden was a good deal shaken. The two talked it over. But they eventually decided to take the risks, now more conscious than ever of what these were, and to go ahead with the Cabinet decisions of the night before.

As if this were not enough, at the very same time that Dulles was pursuing his path of pressure and cajoling on Britain and France, Eisenhower appeared at a press conference on September 10.[13]

In answer to a question whether the United States "would back" Britain and France if they should eventually resort to force, Eisenhower's first side-stepping was: "I don't know exactly what you mean by 'backing' them." He then reassured the watchful Nasser, and did not harm his electoral prospects, by continuing:

> As you know, this country will not go to war ever while I am occupying my present post unless the Congress is called into session, and Congress declares such a war; . . .

(In July, 1958, as a direct result of America's policy of letting Nasser get a swelled head by not disciplining him as Eden and Mollet proposed, the United States government, led by Dulles and Eisenhower, did put troops ashore in Lebanon (Chapter 18), *without* a declaration of war by Congress, and without the conditions which Eisenhower set down as he continued his answer.)

> . . . and the only exception to that would be in the case of unexpected and unwarranted attack on this nation, where self-defense would dictate some quick response while you call Congress into action.
>
> So, as far as going into any kind of military action under present conditions, of course, we are not.
>
> Now, if after all peaceful means are exhausted, there is some kind of aggression on the part of Egypt against a peaceful use of the Canal, you might say that we would recognize that Britain and France had no other recourse than to continue to use it even if they had to be more forceful than merely sailing through it.

But, someone asked, suppose there is a long period, during which the peaceful means *are* exhausted, and there is still not on Nasser's part "some kind of aggression against a peaceful use of the Canal," would the claims of Britain and France be satisfied then? Menzies, the President said, had been a model of tact and patient diplomacy. His mission had failed. Nasser had then offered to participate in another conference, on his own terms. But the President said, "There is no substantive point on which to base a conference." Thus, the President seemed to be quite nonchalant and to have all the century in his perspective, as though time did not matter, in spite of the letter from Eden five days before explaining the need for some momentum.

Of course, he evaded a truthful answer to a question on submission of the trouble to the United Nations.

> I am certain that it will be referred to the United Nations before anything which you would call more positive, material—physical, positive steps are taken. I don't know whether this is the exact time. . . . We are consulting with all our associates throughout the world on this to see what is the very best next thing. . . .
>
> A program of economic sanctions has never been placed before me as of this moment, never.

But Dulles *had* been urged by his allies to consider various economic actions. Had he not told the President? Or did the President not understand what his questioner must mean? Or what the situation required? Or what he could conceivably do about it? Eisenhower was entirely at sea on the very proposals which Dulles had got accepted at the London Conference, and on Dulles's justification thereof, and on what he had already heard about SCUA—*if* the colloquies between him and Dulles were as frequent as they were said to be and as candid as they should have been. He was asked if force would be justified in the event that such measures as the quitting of the pilots should slow down or stop Canal traffic. He skipped the crux of the question, and answered in words for anyone to understand, as follows:

> I don't know about management. [NOBODY ASKED HIM THAT!] All that the Treaty says, the 1888 Treaty says, these nations are guaranteed the free use of the Canal.
>
> Now, if they are guaranteed the free use, then it—and it says—and then provides methods by which cooperation with Egypt may be achieved, I think they are justified probably in taking steps and conferring with President Nasser looking toward the free use of the Canal. But I don't—that doesn't mean that they are justified *at that moment* in using force. I don't think that—I think this: We established the United Nations to abolish aggression, and I am not going to be a party to aggression if it is humanly possible or likely to—lead—to avoid or I can detect it before it occurs.

At that very moment, and for days before and after this observation on the relationship between force and aggression and the United Nations, his own Secretary of State was putting intolerable pressure on Britain and France not to go to the United Nations. For there both Dulles and Eisenhower would have been obliged to disclose their intentions and policy in public and on record.

Eden, Selwyn Lloyd, Mollet, and Pineau must have shaken their heads in lamentation about the lack of crispness in the President's declarations. In the Suez affair, they, and especially Eden, were confronted with Box and Cox: American policy was double-tongued, double-willed, double-minded. Eden was confused between Dulles and Eisenhower, and so were Eisenhower and Dulles.

Now a political tragedy at once befell Eden. If Eden had not heeded Dulles, but had gone to the House of Commons on September 12 with the statement that Britain and France were appealing immediately to the United Nations Security Council, he would have had practically the entire membership of the House with him, and enthusiastically. The dissentients would have been a handful of Labour members on the extreme left, who can always find some abortion of reason to attack the government in the interests of the Soviet Union, and a handful of Conservatives on the extreme right who disliked the United Nations and feared that Britain could not get justice there, and therefore would not consent even to an attempt. Eden took the Dulles scheme to the House, and it was greeted, as we shall see, with derision and contempt. The promise that, at some future time, Britain would go to the Security Council appeared, by the accident of debate, to be forced from him as he encountered heavy onslaught by the Labour Opposition. The result was that the Commons divided against him, Labour demanding a division (roll call). This great rift was later to be used by Dulles and Eisenhower as a reproach against Eden that he did not represent a united country!

If the figure of speech may be changed for a moment, in producing SCUA, Dulles produced an ace, and it was deeply ingrained in his character to believe that God had dealt it to him in the weekend meditation on Duck Island. "Away from the U.N.!" he had demanded, and "Join this Users' Club I have thought out!"

Eden was tempted by the possibilities as colored by Dulles, and he fell. He fell from the most honorable motive a man could have in the circumstances: to maintain what had been the keystone of Churchill's British policy since one of the darkest moments of World War II (August 20, 1940): "the more we [Britain and America] are mixed up together, the better for the world." Eden fell because he was a man of conscience and a man of peace, and because, therefore, his *reason* could be engaged. He was faced with the problem of appeasing Nasser by appeasing Dulles and Eisenhower, a singular paradox. But the paradox was posed by two men who wielded enormous power for the good or ill of Britain and all Europe. Later on, Eden had to resist the forces to which he now bowed. Perhaps he should have resisted earlier, and with rudeness. In the long future, the crisis magnified his impulses of resistance.

9. EDEN VANQUISHED

WE MUST NOW NARRATE EDEN'S TRIALS IN THE HOUSE OF COMMONS during the two long days of debate, September 12 and 13. We must also ponder the manner in which the Prime Minister was mauled so cruelly by Dulles in a press conference that a momentous disaster was inevitable.

In a temperate speech lasting some forty minutes, Eden told the very excited House that Britain had still not obtained redress from Nasser for his seizure of the Canal. He hoped to maintain the substantial unity of the House that had prevailed on August 2. He submitted that to rely on detouring around the Cape of Good Hope was impossible, because the big oil tankers that would be required were not yet built. Hence, his Government were compelled to face a clear and present issue. "I must repeat what was said by the Foreign Secretary weeks ago; that it was from the first our intention that there should be such a Conference [the first London Conference]. *It is ludicrous to pretend that we were dragged into it;* we promoted it." [1] Eden, however, paid tribute to Dulles's "effective and vigorous advocacy" during the London Conference. He then developed the case for the eighteen-power proposals to the House. No voices, Government or Opposition, dissented throughout the two-day debate.

So far, the House was attentive and absorbed. Then, Eden submitted to the Commons the first intimation of what was now to be done to redress the injustice. It was the SCUA scheme.

> That offer [the eighteen-power proposals] has failed. In consequence, we have carefully considered, in consultation with our French and American allies, what our next step should be. We have decided, in agreement with them, that an organisation shall be set up without delay to enable the users of the Canal to exercise their rights.

It would be provisional until a permanent scheme was established.

> Although discussions are still proceeding between the three Governments . . . about the details of this plan, I can now give the House the broad outline, by accord with the other countries.

The Commons at once sprang to virile and critical alertness, focused on the Prime Minister. The Opposition, in a sense to their shame, now that they confronted a practical plan that was an alternative to immediate involvement in war, broke into an unruly uproar the instant that Eden referred to the consequences of interference by Nasser with the operations of SCUA. He was saying:

> . . . and we also recognise that the attitude of the Egyptian Government will have an important bearing on the capacity of the association to fulfil its functions.

Sarcastic laughter broke out from the Back Benches of the Opposition, while its Front Bench, led by Hugh Gaitskell, just managed to hold in check sarcastic smiles. It was rather like the attitude of Dulles's State Department advisers when he came to them with his ingenious but motorless gadget.

> Yes [continued Eden], but I must make it clear that if the Egyptian Government should seek to interfere . . .

Bedlam broke loose! Cries arose of "Deliberate provocation!" and, as he continued, "Resign! Resign!" and "What a peacemaker!" He continued in the din:

> . . . with the operation of the association, or refuse to extend to it the essential minimum of co-operation, then that Government will once more be in breach of the Convention of 1888. I must remind the House that what I am saying *is the result of exchanges of views between three Governments.* In that event Her Majesty's Government and others concerned will be free to take such further steps . . .

A member cried out, "What do you mean by that?"

> . . . as seem to be required . . .

The same member, "You are talking about war!"

> . . . either through the United Nations, or by other means, for the assertion of their rights.

Some members shouted, "Oh!"

> I think that the honorable Members might let me develop this. There is more to come.

The Prime Minister then said he did not exclude the reference of the dispute to the United Nations. "Quite the contrary, it might well be necessary." Meanwhile, he and the French government had by letter informed the President of the Security Council of their intention, so that if urgent action should become necessary he would be ready for it.

He then explained to the House some of the difficulties facing the Government. In the Abadan affair, when Iran, under Mossadegh, had seized the British-owned oil refinery, the reference of the British case to the Security Council had been met by Yugoslavia's whittling down of the resolution, followed, even so, by its rejection by the Soviet government. Britain was then required to take its resolution to the International Court. After many months, the Court declared it had no jurisdiction. The British resolution lapsed. The Security Council had been an impasse for the British Government. At that time, the Government was Labour: it warned that the failure of the Security Council to act effectively might create a most serious precedent for the future. Eden now said, "They were right!"

He defended the right of the pilots to leave: Egypt had used force to keep them. He defended Britain's military movements, reminding the House of the appalling government-tolerated massacre of foreigners that had occurred in Cairo in 1952.

Now, since both Secretary Dulles and President Eisenhower mistook the nature of Her Majesty's Opposition in the British Parliament, it is appropriate here to offer a comment on it. The largest party in the minority faces the Government with a well-defined status as the recognized concerted ranks that may one day be the Government, should it win a majority at the elections. The Opposition assumes the bearing of an alternative government. It has traditional and legal rights of debate and opposition. And it conducts itself, usually, in a responsible frame of mind.

However, the tradition is that *opposition* is its designed and accepted role. Part of the unity of the nation is the principle that the Opposition should divide it in the Commons when it believes that the Government is in the wrong. In all, this function renders the mass electorate and the Cabinet ministers themselves a remarkable service: it has an educative, clarifying, restraining, and remedial value.

Yet the role the Opposition plays is not unadulterated. Its ranks also include a number of men who want their side to win the next elections and who wish to overthrow the Government at once. They therefore from time to time throw themselves into a state of frenzied self-righteousness, which savors of hypocrisy because they are asking the Government to do what they may in their hearts know they themselves would not or could not do, and also savors of cynicism because their emotions are given free rein far beyond their intentions to see a proper policy followed by the Government. This side of the status of the Opposition has never been properly studied and evaluated.

In the Suez crisis, the pacifist element in the Labour Party assumed the ascendency over the more "realist" members. It even drove many of the latter into being advocates of Nasser. The question has never been settled, for example, whether some of the party, a majority of the party, all of the party, even its leader alone, would have accepted anything the United Nations might eventually have considered just—however allied claims had been manhandled by Russia and its satellites and the Afro-Asian Bloc. They have never been absolutely candid about this. For, while in Opposition, they bore no responsibility for action to assert the rights of the British people. One cannot learn from Gaitskell's speech, made after Eden's, whether he would have expected to get from the United Nations the kind of arrangement he thought was worth avoiding a war for: "an agreement [with Nasser] under which there is a supervisory board of the users concerned" which would "*negotiate* with Nasser the tolls" and the development plan and the disposal of the Suez Canal revenues. "On what grounds [asked Gaitskell] do the Government refuse to do so? Why should they not go to the Security Council immediately? That is surely the clear answer." Gaitskell concluded with that *ignis fatuus*, fine ground for an Opposition argument: "Upholding the rule of law means allowing other people, independent persons, to decide for us and not deciding for ourselves." But, it is fair to ask, where could such people be found and what authority would they have over Nasser as well as Eden and Dulles? The day before, September 11, Gaitskell had conversed with Guy Mollet, Prime Minister of France, leader of the French Socialist Party and for many years a leading figure in the European socialist movement. Mollet had taken the same position as Eden. Gaitskell could not convince Mollet otherwise.

Almost every element of Dulles's Users' Club was subject to injurious criticism in the Commons debate: the important matter being, what if it falls foul of Nasser's obstruction? Would the U.S.A. support force, a member asked, to back up the righteousness of this expedient? Of course, the Government could not say Yes to that.

In the debate on the second day, September 13, the brunt of the proceedings was borne by Selwyn Lloyd. A large part of his burden was to explain why the Government did not go to the United Nations at once. It must have been with bitterness of heart, all the greater because he could not confess the real reason (Eden had engaged not to do so, under Dulles's assurances and browbeating), that Lloyd went through the process of considering how the Soviet Union would be likely to distort and obstruct the Security Council's action thereon. But the Opposition conjectured every action the Government proposed in its most suspicious, indeed, pathologically suspicious, shape. For example, the possibility of using force. It suspected that submission to the Security Council would be only a matter of form.

Now, shortly after Dulles had the facts of Eden's speech of September 12 before him in Washington—and he would have had all of it by 9:22 A.M. on September 12, and all of Gaitskell's criticism by 10:17 A.M.—he was bothered enough to issue a public statement.

It was the very first official United States government statement on the subject of SCUA! It ran:

> If the United Kingdom alone or in association with others should propose a users' association to be organized by the 18 sponsors of the London proposals, or such of them as were so disposed, and perhaps others, the United States would participate in such a users' association. We assume that such an organization would act as agent for the users and would exercise on their behalf the rights which are theirs under the 1888 Convention and seek such cooperation with Egypt as would achieve the results designed to be guaranteed by that Convention.[2]

During the Commons debate on the next day, too, Dulles kept in close touch with the proceedings. At 3:10 P.M. in Washington on September 13, Dulles was in the midst of a press conference. It was 9:10 P.M. in London. Gaitskell had the floor in the House of Commons. He was handed the ticker-tape message from Dulles's conference bearing the notorious and fateful slogan by Dulles: "*We do not intend to shoot our way through!*" the Canal if Egypt should block the passage of American ships sailing under the auspices of SCUA. Dulles's announcement countered Eden's earlier speech. Gaitskell now used this American pronouncement to rub his own policy into the Cabinet: Go round the Cape! Get large tankers! Bear the extra cost! And, as Dulles had also said: Get down to practical details "taken out of the realm of national pride and emotions." [3] Eden's followers at once cried out, "This applies to Egypt!" since Gaitskell had commended the phrase to Eden. Gaitskell agreed they applied to Nasser. Yes: but, we have to ask, would Nasser agree? That had always been the question; he had sent the Menzies mission packing.

Gaitskell pressed strongly for submission of the dispute to the United Nations and reminded the Prime Minister that when the Charter was ratified by the Commons in 1945, Eden had said that the United Nations was humanity's last hope. One piece from Eden's reply, reflects the spirit in which both his first and this concluding speech were delivered.

> It sometimes seems to me, and I dare say it does to others of my generation, that ever since the first years when one was very young and in uniform and in war right up to the present time, one has always had war or the threat of war as the background to one's whole life. I would beg the House to believe that, that being so, there can be no conceivable thought in our minds that that is the kind of thing we want to repeat in one way or another. I know it is true of every part of the House of that generation and of others. I think we may start by accepting that peace is the aim of all parties.
>
> But I must add this. If my long—someone generously said

> the other night my too long—span of public life has taught me anything it has taught me this. I do not believe that true and lasting peace can be bought at the price of the surrender of rights and legitimate interests to outside pressure and force. I have found that before.[4]

He pleaded with the House to consider the question (which he had discussed with Eisenhower, it will be remembered, in his letter of a week before) of what might befall British interests and obligations in the Middle East if Nasser "got away with it." He stated that the eighteen-power proposals still stood as a basis of negotiation. He then repeated Dulles's remarks, made in Washington about the same time, on what would happen if the Egyptian government sought to interfere with the operation of SCUA or failed to take the necessary measures for ensuring the execution of the 1888 Convention.

"In this event," Dulles had said, "the parties to or beneficiaries of the Convention would be free to take steps to assure their rights through the United Nations or other action appropriate to the circumstances."

At this the Opposition, having invoked the authority of Dulles, and finding it at this point going against them, began to howl and jeer. They were, of course, taking a mark at the probability, they thought, that the "other action" would be shooting.

Eden continued: "If that happens, Egypt will be once again, according to our view, in breach of the Convention, and the case to be brought against her at the Security Council, or by a similar method, will thereby be infinitely strengthened. [More howls and jeers!] That is certainly one of the purposes which Mr. Dulles and we have had in mind."

The leader of the Opposition, Gaitskell, rose and moved forward a few paces, very red in the face, so that he was only an arm's distance from Prime Minister Eden. The House was shouting from all sides.

"Is he [Eden] prepared to say on behalf of Her Majesty's Government that they will not shoot their way through the Canal?"

Eden answered that they were in complete agreement with the U.S. government about what to do. If the Egyptian government were in default, after asking for their cooperation "We should take them to the Security Council." Eden was in a predicament because his arrangement with Dulles could not then be honorably disclosed. He submitted that the issue between the Government and the Opposition was not one of substance (which was hardly true) but of timing, which was fully true.

> I should like to remind the House that we are not handling this problem entirely on our own. We are dealing with it in

association with allies and with a number of other countries too. I believe that it is the wish of the House that we should act in concert with them. . . . I must therefore ask the House to allow the Government to judge, in the light of their continuing consultations with other Governments, what is the best moment at which it may become advisable to have recourse to the Security Council.[5]

Thus, the Opposition had obtained from Eden a pledge to go to the Security Council, but at the Government's judgment of the proper time and circumstances. Eden had intended to do this in any case, as the reader already knows. But the Prime Minister kept the Government free to deal with the most serious question of all, if it should arise. His peroration shows it.

I want to deal with the question: would Her Majesty's Government give a pledge not to use force except after reference to the Security Council? If such a pledge or guarantee is to be absolute, then neither I nor any British Minister standing at this Box could give it. No one can possibly tell what will be Colonel Nasser's action, either in the Canal or in Egypt.

Nevertheless, I will give this reply, which is as far as any Government can go; it would certainly be our intention, if circumstances allowed, or in other words, except in an emergency, to refer a matter of that kind to the Security Council. Beyond that I do not think that any Government can possibly go.

But I repeat that the Government must be the judge of the circumstances. That is something that no Government, no Executive, can share with anybody else, Parliament, or any other. I am confident that Parliament itself, on reflection, will believe that to be sound doctrine.

The Opposition divided the House: on the main question the Government majority was 317 to 248, a majority of 69, bigger than usual, in a straight party vote.

It was literally tragic that Eden had felt he could NOT reveal to the House that the Government had been ready then to go to the United Nations but had been diverted by Dulles's tactics. In the Commons one of the leading Conservatives, Sir Lionel Heald, formerly Attorney General and a highly reputable international lawyer (he had at one time represented Britain at the United Nations and the International Court) had recommended that the Government's best course, legally as well as practically, was to go to the United Nations at that time. A debate that occurred simultaneously in the House of Lords found legal luminaries like Lord McNair (formerly judge on the Permanent Court of International Justice at The Hague) and divines like the Bishop of Chichester and the Archbishop of Canterbury recommending this course. Furthermore, it would have been better for Eden to have declared his intention of going to the Security Council before force was ever used against Nasser (barring unforeseen accidents). This had been his policy, before it *appeared* to have been torn out of him (a falsehood disseminated to the public and perpetuated by the Labour Party, especially its left-wingers and their momentary hero, Gaitskell). If Eden had plainly stated his position, which was actually quite strong, it would have had the public reputation of being strong.

On the whole, the more responsible and less partisan newspapers condemned the Labour leadership for giving way to their left-wingers' passions and insensate exaggerations and pathological suspicions. Let us merely cite the *Economist* of September 15, 1956. "Gaitskell was evidently hurrying away from an original attitude of too much bipartisanship and visibly stumbling down an avenue of cheers [from his Labour followers], too far towards a neurotic wing with whom he was too responsible ever quite to catch up."[6] But he almost reached them.

Although the vote upheld Eden, the Opposition had tasted blood. Dulles must have believed he had a powerful and reliable moral and political asset in the Labour Opposition, and as we shall see, Eisenhower ignorantly, but usefully to him and Dulles, made play with the division later on (Chapter 14). There was opened to the watchful eyes of Nasser, Sabry, and Fawzi, and their envenomed henchmen, the heart, mind, and conscience of their enemy, and above all, the fact that they had many friends in Britain, so that they could continue their truculence with confidence that they would never be punished.[7] The *Washington Post*, on September 13, called SCUA "Eden's Plan"; and on September 14 (not knowing that Dulles had prevented Eden from going to the United Nations) it pictured Eden as "leading a dance on the brink"! Generally, Americans were induced by their press to believe that there must be something wrong with a policy that was reluctant to go before the world forum. It was Dulles, not Eden, who was reluctant, and much more, forbidding.

Henceforward, force was, somehow, in the offing; force was, at any rate, conceivable. When this realization came home to Dulles, he felt an alarm that knew no bounds. It was not merely that the House of Commons had uncovered and driven home the critical questions about SCUA, as his experts should have done to jolt him into consciousness. Nehru and Egypt spoke up. Nehru declared he had read Eden's speech of September 12 with "surprise and regret." "The consequences that may follow from it [SCUA] may well be grave." It would be an imposed solution, and make peaceful settlement more difficult. He had written to Eden and Eisenhower that Nasser's statement following the Menzies mission had opened a way; but now Eden's speech had closed it.[8]

The Director General of Information in Cairo issued a protest that was repeated formally to Dulles by the Egyptian Ambassador, the same who had been turned away without the Aswan loan. He spoke urgently. "The scheme which Sir Anthony Eden wants to impose on Egypt is an open and flagrant aggression on Egyptian sovereignty and its implementation means war." If the United States desired to work for a peaceful solution the scheme *must* be abandoned. How insolent and warlike compared with Eden's amenability towards Dulles and Eisenhower! What irony for Dulles to hear his scheme ascribed to Eden, and to hear from Nasser that it meant *war!* It was precisely the treatment to make him flinch.

Nasser's was the classic autocratic policy of empire, so well enunciated in the eighteenth century by Frederick the Great: "First I grab, and then I find a jurist who will prove I had a right to it!"

As for Dulles's tactics, Homer Bigart of the *New York Times* reported that diplomatic sources thought the plan was Dulles's and was "a smart lawyer's ploy . . . a canny maneuver." [9] In his press conference of September 13,[10] Dulles's performance was masterly, misleading, and lethal. By now he had heard the ominous possibilities as Eden had put them. In staff meetings, he gave the impression that Eden had spoken as though after a draught of heavy vintage. But Dulles had fermented it; and Dulles had compelled the hasty gulp.

To the newsmen, Dulles at the outset accomplished a remarkable evasion. "Prime Minister Eden in his speech yesterday set forth the concept of an association of users of the Suez Canal." This sounded as though Eden had begotten the scheme, not Dulles. He continued to say that, prior to the speech, the U.S. government had told Eden it would join the association. But Dulles still had not acknowledged his initiating and persuading responsibility.

He then set out the main elements of SCUA, and, citing the legal rights of the users, contended that "these rights cannot legally be nullified by unilateral Egyptian action." To safeguard their rights adequately, each nation, each ship, not being able to do it for itself, needed joint action. He proceeded to explain the proposed Association.

The reporters began to ask questions. Did the United States intend to go ahead with the Association in spite of the Egyptian protest?

Dulles answered that this initial Egyptian reaction would not deter him from proceeding with the program. He thought that the Egyptians did not really understand it, so far; but that they would "recognize it as an honest effort to try to achieve on a practical day-to-day working basis a solution of the problem of getting ships through the Canal." (Could his tongue have been in his cheek?) He then repeated his own remarks of August 28, about the insolubility of the dispute if the situation was considered in terms of the "great concepts" involved instead of problems being broken down to "concrete things" like pilots, their qualifications, their location, the pattern of traffic. We already know that Menzies and Henderson had not been able to reach a settlement on such a concrete basis. Yet the Secretary continued stubbornly, and with, apparently, all seriousness:

> But perhaps—and this is our hope—if we get operating problems out of the hands of the diplomats, the statesmen, and get it down perhaps into a situation where practical ship operators are dealing with practical people on the part of Egypt, maybe some of these problems will be solvable.

How did Dulles expect Nasser to make room for "practical people on the part of Egypt"? He continued to beg *the* question. In what world of ideas, if he was not merely joking, was he living, where he, a diplomat and statesman, declared that his hope lay in taking the problems out of the hands of diplomats and statesmen? His allies were bound to question his sincerity and make preparation for his defection.

He was faced, at once, however, with the question of what *peaceful* alternatives there were if Egypt resisted the plan. He saw two *if*'s: *if* a program could not be worked out for going through the Canal on acceptable terms, and *if* physical force should be used to prevent passage, "*the alternative for us at least would be to send our vessels around the Cape.*" It would involve inconvenience, cost, delays. "But we have given a very careful study to that whole problem, and we believe that it is solvable." But his allies had told him it was *not* solvable that way, because the careful study had showed that the cost to them was *too high* given their resources. For Britain and France, as for the U.S.A., the course Dulles suggested was not the substantiation of their rights to pass through the Canal, but to abandon them altogether and go by another and more expensive route! This was an abdication of the allied rights, even though in the way Dulles phrased it, he seemed to be speaking only for the U.S.A. ("for *us* at least").

A further question probed the use of force. If the U.S.A. sent vessels around by the Cape would it expect other nations to do so rather than resort to force?

Here Dulles reverted to the President's policies. He had spoken with him that morning, he said, and the President had approved the statement with which the press conference had opened. "Well, we have often said, and the President has most authoritatively said, that in his opinion force, if justifiable at all, is only justifiable as a last resort."

Only justifiable as a *last resort,* if at all; BUT NOT NEVER, and perhaps, then, as a last resort? Eden, Selwyn Lloyd, Mollet, Pineau,

Nasser, and Ben Gurion were microscopically scrutinizing this language.

"So," continued the Secretary, "if there are alternatives to the use of force, we believe that they should be fully explored and exhausted." But the Secretary did not then declare in public what "exploration" or "exhaustion" might be. Sufficient for the day. . . .

He suddenly jumped to another point, no doubt stimulated by observations made in the House of Commons about "provocation" and about "boycott" of the Canal. "But it is not our purpose to try to bring about a concerted boycotting of the Canal."

Was this confusion, or was it astute diplomacy? He had inveigled —it is the appropriate word—his closest allies into the trial of this SCUA scheme. Two feasible sanctions of its operation were available. One was force. This he almost altogether excluded *at this stage*. The other was economic sanctions. The chief sanction which he had recommended to his allies was for all the users, or as many as possible, not to use the Canal. His privately expressed intention was to make a "dry ditch" of the Canal. This kind of leverage over Nasser could come only if all or a substantial number of users took the Cape route. *This is what Dulles had intended and had promised his allies.* He now had disclaimed in public any intention of a joint boycott.

His statement was a direct falsehood, if, indeed, it had been his plan to boycott the Canal, and a betrayal of his promise to his allies if he had not meant to do so. He might, of course, have argued, though with some deviousness, that his purpose was only to get a rightful arrangement to go *through* the Canal. But, would this not be a rather too highly sophisticated equivocation? For his purpose in sending vessels around by the Cape *was* to be that of a boycott, as the means to impose a reasonable and rightful settlement of Canal passage, either by the eighteen-power proposals or by SCUA.

Dulles then gave some more attention to the oil resources that would be available to the Western nations if they should have trouble getting that fuel from the Middle East, and to the tankers owned by the American government that would be taken out of mothballs. He exerted a little pressure on Nasser when he said there were plans which would save the Western world from economic disaster if, "unfortunately, passage through the Canal should be physically interrupted by Egypt." Still, Britain and France were not asking America to save them from an economic disaster. They were asking for assurance that they could go their wonted and legal ways through the Canal with confidence in the future. Dulles went on to observe that, since some countries would be short of dollar exchange for oil supplies, there *could* be loans from the Export-Import Bank. But no commitments had been made as yet.

What if Egypt used physical force to prevent passage by the Users' Association? Would this be regarded as a violation of Egypt's treaty obligations and therefore as an act of aggression? Yes, if Egypt obstructed the organization or refused to insure the execution of the 1888 Convention, it would be a breach thereof. Then, the parties to or beneficiaries of the Convention would be free to take steps to assure their rights through the United Nations or through *other action appropriate to the circumstances.*

The questioner pounced on the italicized phrase. What did it mean? It was the acid test.

Dulles, of course, evaded it. "If you tell me the circumstances, I will try to tell you the appropriate action." This was as guarded, and as parrying, as Eden in Parliament was, at about that same time, to a similar question.

A reporter then asked:

> Would you regard the nation whose ships were stopped as entitled under the self-defense provisions of the United Nations Charter to defend itself against the violation of the treaty?

Dulles answered:

> Well, I would say if a vessel in innocent passage was attacked and if it had the means to defend itself, it would be entitled to use those means. I don't know whether that answers your question or not, because most of those vessels that go through are in fact unarmed.

Here was an admission of the right to use force, probably much more far-reaching than that which the British or even the French government had in mind. Had Dulles not considered the escalation of a fist fight into one with shovels or revolvers and so on up to machine guns and warships and planes?

It was becoming clear that the Secretary was improvising his way out of the most deadly crisis of NATO in relation to the Middle East he had yet faced or anticipated. He stumbled on from one fantastic idea to the other, as if by free and irresponsible association. He said there would be contact "not with the head of the Egyptian government," but with the people who were operating the Canal. So (this is almost too fantastic to repeat!) there would be a practical talk between the ship-users' agent and the Egyptian operating personnel, and the agent would say, "Now here we have got a vessel, Mr. X; you haven't got a good pilot to put aboard this vessel. We have got a pilot who is well qualified," etc., etc., etc. Dulles expected the Egyptian "operating people" (Nasser's appointees) to accept such overtures and say, "O.K., let's leave aside the question of legal rights. You go ahead and go through the Canal." Dulles concluded his explanation, "We hope that this is what would happen." This, it would seem, was to trifle. Had he the right to any but a guilty anger when his allies, nearly two months later, after much more of the same behavior, acted without first informing him?

He evaded a direct question at the press conference whether the users' association had originated in Washington. Why would he wish so to deceive by evasion? He wanted the benefits of a bastard without the onus of being known as its father.

A newspaperman was puzzled that "sailing round the Cape" was *not* a boycott. Dulles's answer, when plain speaking or plain silence would have been good diplomacy, demonstrated forensic genius, or something else:

> It is not a boycott of the Canal, as far as I know, to refrain from using force to get through the Canal. If force is interposed by Egypt, then I do not call it a boycott to avoid using force to shoot your way through. We do not intend to shoot our way through. It may be we have the right to do it, but we don't intend to do it as far as the United States is concerned. And to suggest that not to shoot your way through the Canal is a boycott of the Canal is something which I cannot understand. If we are met by force, which we can only overcome by shooting, we don't intend to go into that shooting. Then we intend to send our boats around the Cape. But that is certainly not a boycott of the Canal.

He was heckled on Israel's exclusion from the Canal by Egypt during the past eight years. Would the proposed Users' Association guarantee Israeli ships passage through the Canal? Dulles replied that he was afraid the Association was not going to be in a position to guarantee anybody anything. "We can't even guarantee anything to our own ships." (A light touch!) But he could not be oblivious to the fact that Egypt was already in violation of the 1888 Treaty so far as Israel was concerned. (No action was contemplated, apparently.)

The Secretary was confronted with Eden's hint that Britain would brook no interference with the Association when its ships sought transit. Was the United States in conflict with British policy when it said the United States would go by the Cape rather than try to force a way through?

> Well, I think that each nation has to decide for itself what action it will take to defend, and if possible, realize its rights which it believes it has as a matter of treaty. . . . I did not get the impression that there was any undertaking or pledge by him [Eden] to shoot their way through the Canal.

The tortuousness of that last sentence is worth remark. But Eden had not given a pledge *not* to shoot his way through! Nor had he been asked to undertake that he *would!*

Did not, Dulles was asked, Nasser remain with all the trump cards in his hands, since the United States had renounced force and since Soviet Russia was supporting Egypt?

The Secretary, of course, made out a case that he did not. It was specious.

> Well, what are the trump cards? Let's look at the situation from a moral standpoint! I do not feel that adequate appreciation has been given to the fact that great powers with vital interests at stake, possessed of overwhelming matériel and military power, have exercised so far at least, a very great measure of restraint. I think that, even if contemporary opinion does not judge it, history will judge it, that the exercise of that self-restraint, although possessed of great power, in deference to the obligations undertaken under the United Nations Charter, adds more from a moral standpoint to the so-called "great" nations who exercise that self-restraint than if they had used their force.

How ironic, to praise Britain and France so highly! So far the United States had lost *nothing* at all, and had not exercised any of these high virtues. And, to his allies' cost of being so spectacularly moral, Dulles had only contributed pressure not to go to the United Nations, which he in the same text extolled. As for history, it may be ventured that many of men's virtues are forgotten, and even more virtues are regarded by those who have an interest in doing so as vices.

It is highly probable that the Secretary had his last question planted in order to sound the note on which he wanted to finish. He had several astute assistants.

Would the United States support Britain in such a venture as an armed convoy through the Canal if the SCUA ships were stopped by Nasser?

> Well, I don't know what you mean by "support." I have said that the United States did not intend to try to shoot its way through the Canal. But if by "support" you mean would the United States then go to war—I don't know if that is the impact of your question—if so, I think that was answered very fully by President Eisenhower at his press conference this week.

On hearing these words by Dulles, Eden was dumbfounded. He says:

> It would be hard to imagine a statement more likely to cause the maximum allied disunity and disarray. The Americans [that is, Dulles, and Dulles alone] having themselves volunteered that the new arrangements would be less acceptable to the Egyptians than the eighteen-Power proposals, Mr. Dulles proceeded to make plain at this juncture that the United States did not intend to use force, even though it had the right to do so. The words were an

> advertisement to Nasser that he could reject the project with impunity. *We had never been told* that a statement of this kind was to accompany the announcement of the Users' Club. Had we known that they were to be used as an accompaniment to the American announcement, we would never have endorsed it.[11]

It is well attested that almost unanimously Dulles's own official entourage, let us say the top ten aides closest to him, whether in Washington or New York or in the Embassies in London and Paris, shared Eden's opinion, except that they ruefully or gleefully, according to the degree of their personal affinity for Dulles, were officially obliged to condone the Secretary's action. They were servants of the United States government bound by oath or interest to public silence. For the highest statesmen of Britain and France their nation's injury was the overriding concern.

Eden continued, that though an identity of statements had been established, Dulles's remarks on "not shooting our way through" and on the advisability of each nation's deciding on action for itself, and so on, had entirely submerged that identity of statements!

> To us, the emphasis had been that the Egyptians, having rejected reasonable eighteen-Power proposals, could not expect to do as well. To the public, the emphasis now was that, whatever happened, the Egyptians had nothing to fear. The Users' Club was an American project to which we had conformed. We were all three in agreement, *even to the actual words of the announcement*. Yet here was the spokesman of the United States saying that each nation must decide for itself and expressing himself as unable to recall what the spokesman of a principal ally had said. Such cynicism towards allies destroys true partnership. It leaves only the choice of parting, or a master and vassal relationship in foreign policy.
>
> In the House I had, in fact, said nothing to suggest that we would shoot our way through. I had used the formula agreed upon with the United States Government, which M. Mollet had also used, that we would seek our rights "through the United Nations or by any other means." This left the course of future action deliberately vague so as to strengthen pressure on behalf of the Users' Club. The whole purpose of the Users' Club had been, by a display of unity in association with the United States, to avoid having recourse to force. American torpedoing of their own plan on the first day of launching it left no alternative but to use force or acquiesce in Nasser's triumph.

Dulles's adroitness had produced a loss of confidence in his fidelity. One needs a very long sight and a true conscience in the affairs of nations, just as much as the dubious astuteness of a difficult day, and plain honesty is a mighty tool. Without doubt, Dulles's adroitness had also increased Nasser's arrogance and belligerence.

Within two days of Dulles's press conference, Nasser let him have it between the eyes.

If we like, we can call Eden and Mollet and their Foreign Ministers fools for falling for Dulles's tactics. In that case, seeing that they were loyal to their ally, what name would Dulles deserve? The trouble was that the punishment would fall on them and their nations and not on Dulles and Eisenhower. Even a left-wing writer in London, for whom I cannot have unqualified admiration, referred to SCUA as "Dulles's double-cross." [12]

Dulles, always dutiful, always energetic, always meticulously diligent, went from his press conference that had such disastrous consequences, to invent a way of repairing the situation with his allies and also of finding the most effective practical way of disciplining Nasser. For it should not be lost to sight in all the labyrinthine ways he trod that he detested Nasser personally and politically. Nasser was causing him and his nation more trouble than anybody else in the world except Bulganin and Khrushchev and his impulsiveness might yet incite a third world war starting in the Middle East.

In the next few days, Dulles worked in the office, he worked at home; he even worked on Sunday. All day on Monday, September 17, there were staff meetings. For he was preparing to launch SCUA at the second London Conference of Maritime Powers.

The week end after the press conference, that is, from September 13 to September 17, was not a quiet one. Nasser issued a diatribe; the Suez Company's pilots were withdrawn with only a momentary disruption in the normal flow of traffic; and Moscow, whose ambassador in Cairo had been in constant colloquy with Nasser, was virulently active. We must ponder these occurrences.

Nasser spoke at an Egyptian air force graduation ceremony on September 15. It was a long speech full of insults, malice, and militarism. He noted with pride that ships were being conducted through the Canal by Egyptian and Greek pilots. Thus he had "succeeded in foiling a conspiracy of Britain and France." He was in battle against imperialism, which wished to destroy the Egyptian economy, Egyptian power, Arab nationalism, and Gamal Abdel Nasser. "Eden also said [in the House of Commons] Egypt shall not be allowed to succeed because that would spell a success for Arab nationalism and would be against their policy, which aims at the protection of Israel." This, of course, the air force graduates did not know was a falsehood.

Alas for Dulles's repeated appeals for and belief in isolating the proposals for settling the Canal situation from emotions of colonialism and patriotism and pride!

> Today they are speaking of a new association whose main objective would be to rob Egypt of the Canal and deprive her of

> rightful Canal dues. Suggestions made by Eden in the House of Commons which have been backed by France and the United States are a clear violation of the 1888 Convention, since it is impossible to have two bodies organizing navigation in the Canal. . . .
>
> We instructed our Ambassador in Washington to tell America's Foreign Secretary that America is helping Britain excite people in Egypt and engage them in a new war. The American President has been speaking of maintaining peace, so why does America support this proposal for the formation of an association which they call an association for users of the Canal but which is in truth one for declaring war?
>
> They are threatening to use force against us. But we are fully determined never to surrender any of our rights. We shall resist any aggression and fight against those who attempt to derogate from our sovereignty.
>
> . . . Of 8 million Algerians, 10,000 are fighting half a million French soldiers. We have arms sufficient to equip those who can fight. We shall fight aggressors.[13]

And so on. Nasser had said, "They are threatening to use force against us." This was not strictly true, but forces were certainly moving into his part of the world. He may well have suspected that his actions merited chastisement. He had since July 26 told his henchmen he expected an attack.

The Egyptian government itself had rapidly recruited and trained enough men—about 160 in all—by this time to keep the Canal going, and had made plans for further training. This achievement had been made possible in part because foreign countries had rerouted many of their ships via the Cape, so reducing pressure on the working pilots. But the Egyptian government rightly considered its handling of the matter a substantial triumph of energy, planning, and diplomacy. On September 13, that government sent a letter to the United Nations' Secretary General informing him that the Universal Suez Canal Company had ordered the non-Egyptian employees to quit by Saturday, September 15, and that the governments of France and Britain had publicly endorsed the order. Egypt would do all in its power to assure passage through the Canal. But if passage were hampered, the responsibility would be that of those who had endeavored "to create conditions aimed at obstructing the so far unaffected normal passage of shipping."

Soviet Premier Nikolai A. Bulganin addressed almost identical letters to Prime Ministers Eden and Mollet on September 13 (and to the United Nations). The maximum harassment from the maximum number of power-sources is a well-known epigram of diplomacy, or deserves to be, for that is the practice. Another is, when a vehicle is going downhill under its own momentum or through the exertion of pressure from elsewhere, give it a push that will win you credit from those who will be gratified by its crash.

Bulganin denied that Russia was inciting Egypt. He declared that his country wished eagerly to contribute to a peaceful settlement with due regard to the interests of all states concerned. (The same stale and double-speak story as Shepilov had told at the London Conference.) The Soviet Union was bound to look favorably upon Egypt's defense of her sovereignty and national territory. Bulganin accused France and Britain of threatening force against Egypt's inalienable rights, and he mentioned official declarations in which, he alleged, these countries threatened to attack Egypt with their forces.

I am not in possession of the French reply,[14] but Eden's appears in his *Memoirs*. It was dated September 17. He denied the allegations that there had been official threats of force. He emphasized that the British aim was a peaceful solution, an aim that had been repeated in many official statements. He recited the steps taken to secure this end. As for the military measures about which Bulganin had complained, Eden answered that they were justified by the fact that the ruler of Egypt was a militarist whose book had said, for example, "Throughout my life I have had faith in militarism"; that he had employed militarism to hold the Canal personnel, occupy the premises, and seize the assets of the Company. "This act of force," which had created a state of tension in the Middle East, had not yet evoked any expression of disapproval on the part of Bulganin's government

Finally, Eden reminded Bulganin that, in 1946, the Soviet government had proclaimed its support for international control of the Canal. This was what Britain was seeking now. Such control was, he concluded, fully consistent both with Egypt's sovereignty and with the Charter of the United Nations.

It was the desire of Mollet and Pineau, for France, to employ force against Nasser by mid-September. They were almost ready to do so then. Continued open passage of the Canal, and Dulles's diplomacy, postponed the day of reckoning; but Dulles's diplomacy made it a day of force when it did come. Since actions have consequences in the diplomatic struggle, it is impossible to purge oneself of sharp dismay at the tactics by which Dulles had cleverly evaded a collective obligation when he had given the British and French Ambassadors a convincing and indubitable impression that he conscientiously intended it.[15] As soon as it appeared expedient, he abandoned them.

Dulles sorely needed another conference, for SCUA had been whittled down to almost nothing; and his principal allies, Britain and France, felt so cheated and exasperated that dire consequences must surely follow. A new meeting was set for London on September 19, where the eighteen powers were to contemplate the ashes of the Menzies mission and consider whether life could be breathed into them.

10. SCUA COLLAPSES

THE NATIONS (OTHER THAN BRITAIN AND FRANCE) WHO HAD SUPPORTED the eighteen-power proposals bitterly complained that Dulles had not consulted them before the announcement of a plan of action that contained in it an element of coercion. They were absolutely right. Dulles, in the full spate of his intellectual pride, and fearful of some incident if a stopgap were not furnished, had insensitively cold-shouldered the other nations. He had not measured the expensive consequences for them of his own proposals for detouring the Canal. They were shocked and they let him know it, so much so that when the British sent out invitations, by arrangement with Dulles, for another conference, it was touch-and-go whether they would even accept.

However, much more was at stake for them than mere pride at not being consulted, important as that must always be to sovereign nations, at least as sovereign as Nasser was declaring Egypt and its "dignity" to be. If Nasser retained unqualified control over the Canal, the power position of the "middle powers," Britain and France, in the whole world, the Middle East vis-à-vis Africa and of Russia and the Mediterranean, their communications with Australia and New Zealand and various possessions in the Red Sea and the Persian Gulf and the Pacific must be in jeopardy. But the other fifteen nations were not even "middle powers"; some of them, like Sweden, had pledged themselves to an almost total neutrality in the politics not only of the super-powers, but of any powers at all, anywhere. All they wanted was peace and prosperity. If they could pass through the Canal with low enough tolls, they tended not to worry about who managed it. A reaffirmation of the Treaty of 1888, especially if made solemnly before the United Nations in some special procedure, could satisfy them. They did not want a challenge that would close the Canal to them. Their Socialist Parties followed the lead of the British, and were nudged on by the Soviet Union. Dulles, with his grandiose ideas, had not sufficiently appreciated the position of the little fellows. He soon learned better.

Pakistan, especially, now entertained very grave doubts about the probability of the use of force, and protested to this effect. Nasser's vituperation and a feeling of solidarity with the Arab countries (because, like Pakistan, they were Moslem), as well as the "colonial" theme, became increasingly influential with the Pakistanis. Iran had her worries with the Soviet Union's menace to her north, and with the Voice of Cairo egging on her peasantry and proletariat with pro-Moslem slogans of a Holy War. The closing of the Canal would be even more onerous to Iran than the Holy War; it would reduce her sales of oil and her budget. West Germany expressed doubts at the thought that SCUA might be a club in a warlike as well as cooperative sense: she had an interest in the continuance of her trade expansion, her "economic miracle" since 1949. Even Australia was divided, for the opponents of Menzies, Liberals and Socialists, took a stand rather like Gaitskell's. Turkey murmured about the extent to which American handling of the dispute had played into the hands of the Soviet Union. Turkey was the strongest nation in the "northern tier," but she was also within easiest striking distance of the Soviet Union, which, now, by reason of the West's tactics, had an extra pincer on Turkey's southern border—Syria, which was being armed with increasing momentum by the Soviet Union with heavy weapons and with a Communist Party.

On the eve of the second London Conference, it looked as though the eighteen powers were dissolving their partnership. Pakistan rejected SCUA as it stood at the time of Dulles's explanation on September 13. Spain, Iran, Sweden, and Japan were decidedly cool towards it. Britain and France were strongly in its favor only *if* it had "teeth" in it. Germany, Australia, Norway, New Zealand, and Italy would go along with it, but Italy had payments agreements with Egypt involving serious reservations. The U.S.A. did not know what it wanted, excepting peace, and did not know how to go about achieving that—whether with SCUA, whatever it was in Dulles's mind by now, or without it.

By September 16 Dulles was smitten with anxiety that he had lost his hold on Britain and France, and on all but a handful of the rest. He began to speak of a "sufficiency of power" if even only the five chief users of the Canal went along with his scheme: the commerce of Britain, France, the U.S.A., Norway, and Italy ran about 75 per cent of all the Canal shipping. He let it be rumored that "he was not at all adamant about his plan," and would welcome amendments to it. He flew kites to the effect that "no concerted boycott was sought" by him. He let it be heard that the only condition he insisted on was that no *Russian* pilot should be employed on any *American* ship, and that the Canal was not to be managed by Egypt with unfettered rights. Also, the rumor got about that, if SCUA were refused transit, then the powers would go at once to the United Nations.

At this, the powers with whom Dulles was trying to do business became even more suspicious of his tactics and alarmed at his purposes. For, first, he had promised what was tantamount to a boycott of the Canal. But, now, Dulles was by-passing his by-passing boycott!

On one other matter Dulles aroused marked distrust about his intentions and his abilities as a diplomatic leader. Probably as the result of consultations with George M. Humphrey, Secretary of the Treasury, and certainly as the result of consultations with the Arthur Flemming Committee on Oil Resources, he was able to estimate what it would cost to the United States to supply oil to Europe—if, by the action of SCUA, that continent should be cut off from its oil supplies via Suez and the Mediterranean. Besides the thirty-five or forty tankers that would be supplied by the United States, the oil itself which Europe would need from Western Hemisphere sources (the U.S.A., Canada, Venezuela, and Mexico) was calculated at 450,000 barrels per day, plus 300,000 diverted from the Middle East and the U.S.A. (This amount, plus 850,000 from Middle Eastern pipelines, and 800,000 more from the Middle East via the Cape, would total 2,400,000 barrels per day, almost the usual requirement.) This total could, with organization, be provided. It would cost the British and French and the rest of Western Europe an extra $500,000,000 per annum.

Moreover, the European countries would have the additional costs of going around the Cape. The Bank had no authority to help meet those. Where would the $500,000,000 come from? Dulles said only that the Export-Import Bank would "stand ready to consider favorably applications by European countries for *loans to finance imports of oil* from the United States." Yet by the time he arrived at the National Airport to board his plane for London on September 17, though expectations had been aroused, he "denied knowledge of any *specific* plan to lend $500,000,000 to European countries to help them meet the economic difficulties that would occur if the Canal were closed." [1]

The *New York Times*, reporting events of September 16, stated that it had been given to understand Dulles was ready to find that amount of credits.[2] This he wished to do, the article continued, to maintain the policy of a boycott, "while he is said to dislike the term 'boycott.'" He was reported to feel that the American people would accept the burden of dollar loans willingly when it was explained to them that it was the price of keeping Britain and France out of a war with Egypt. When Dulles was asked by the *Times* reporter how much credit would be available for oil supplies, he turned the question by asking, "Well, how much oil do you want?" Such fractiousness may, conceivably, be forgiven in a Secretary of State caught in the toils of his own plausible but unworkable invention; but to his tormented allies it sounded flippant.

The *Washington Post* went so far as to say, "There would be a better reception for Secretary of State Dulles's plan to assist in the rerouting of oil traffic around the Cape of Good Hope, if the United States did not appear quite so much in the position of a flinty-eyed banker." [3] But, then, Secretary of the Treasury George M. Humphrey had played, was playing, and would continue to play an even more potent part in the making of American foreign policy in the Suez affair. He did *not* like that $500,000,000 commitment, any more than he had liked the idea of making a loan to Egypt for the Aswan Dam.

For the European countries, a boycott of the Canal would have meant higher prices in general, more taxes, and a raising of interest rates. On the other hand, Dulles could have put pressure on Nasser, had he willed it, by (a) causing Egypt to lose a large part of the Canal revenues, by some method other than a boycott; (b) dumping American cotton from surplus on the world market to cause a loss in Egyptian cotton sales; and (c) reducing American tourism in Egypt. As for (a), Egypt would be losing only what she had never yet received, to a large extent; as for (b), Dulles was afraid to risk United States popularity in "world opinion" by using it; and as for (c), it was a threat and only a long-run prospect. Such measures could have only a negligible effect on a country whose normal standard of living was so low and whose national fanaticism was so high.

Dulles arrived in London, with his usual hard-working entourage, at 10:30 A.M. on September 18, and soon met with Selwyn Lloyd, Christian Pineau (who was growing to dislike Dulles's policy and tactics vehemently), Ambassadors Aldrich and Dillon, Loy Henderson, and Herman Phleger.

The Conference was to open its first session at 11 A.M. on September 19. Dulles began conferring with his staff at the Embassy at 8:45 A.M. They surveyed the news from the United States, and from other principal areas of the world, which had especial bearing on the agenda of the Conference. The reports were not encouraging. Dulles was in very serious trouble. He was facing an increasingly hostile world, more and more united against the West—meaning Britain and France and the U.S.A.; or to put the countries in descending order of the hostility directed against them, France, Britain, and the United States.

Threats had been pouring in from the Soviet Union, not always couched in direct and outright terms of hostility, and thus the more slippery to deal with. The Cairo correspondent of the *Times* reported: "He [Russian Ambassador Kiselev] is in and out of the Presidency (Nasser's official headquarters) these days as often as any priest with a convert." At the very time that Dulles was emplaned for London, the Soviet Union was inciting all socialist parties throughout the world—that is, those that were non-Communist, democratic—to support Nasser and oppose Eden and Mollet, the latter, of course, denounced "unmasked," as a betrayer of the workers' cause. The Moscow press meanwhile showered praise on Gaitskell! It was all most vexing to Dulles, that the Soviet government should appear to be so peace-loving to the rest of the world, while the United States was vilified for keeping company with "colonialist" aggressors, though the will to peace of Dulles and Eisenhower was more intense and genuine than that of the Soviet Union.

Nasser's façade of strength seemed to be bolder and better shored up as day followed day. In only one respect did it sag. He had sent out invitations to forty-five nations to attend his own Suez Conference. The response was so feeble that the conference had to be abandoned. By the date of the SCUA conference in London, Nasser had only twenty favorable responses: from the Soviet bloc, India, Communist China, the Arab nations (not including Iraq)—and *Panama* (!). But, on the other hand, Egypt had been able to keep the Canal functioning with the Egyptian and newly recruited foreign pilots and was having ever less difficulty in doing so. India provided her with foreign exchange by a loan of some $10 million. Communist China promised credits against cotton. She could get wheat from Communist and neutral nations against credits, and various other kinds of assistance from the Arab states (again perhaps excluding Iraq). The personnel running the Canal—the Egyptians, at any rate—would work for less money than their predecessors, as a patriotic duty, and maintenance and improvement works could be postponed. The brunt of Dulles's potential economic war would fall on the victims of Nasser, especially if a boycott were invoked.

Britain and France could, of course, go to the extreme of instituting a complete economic blockade, including the repulsion of contraband shipments to Egypt. It is a course which, in the future, nations deprived of their rights by forcible seizures or other warlike but non-massive assaults may have to take, failing justice from the United Nations and the support of its sanctions. Short of this measure, however, which might have to be the peaceful arm of a declaration of war, Britain and France were in the weak position of victims who could not use their overwhelming power by the economic means then at hand.

Nasser was in continuous parley with the Arab nations, with the dissidents in Iraq, with Pakistan, with Tunis; and by September 18 he had begun a series of conversations lasting several days with Krishna Menon, who had come to Cairo to seek a way of getting Nasser to make some concessions. Indeed, it was reported that India had induced him to agree to some form of international *control* of the level of Canal dues, the factor in the dispute of most importance to India. But Nasser continued to receive Indian support. Nehru had written letters to Eden and Dulles counseling the inadvisability of force, the reassumption of negotiations, and a settlement rather on the lines of the Indian proposal to the first London Conference.

The forces of the Arab League were mustered to make various threats: that all the Arab countries would cease trading with the West and divert their imports to Soviet bloc countries; that, if force were used over the Canal, World War III might be precipitated. Against the conscience of Dulles in particular, and America in general, the Arabs concentrated their "anticolonialist" fire. Bandaranaike, Prime Minister of Ceylon, declared on September 18 that SCUA was "a giant step towards world war." At about the same time he asked Eden for a guarantee that if war came the British bases in Ceylon would not be used; and the assurance was given.

On September 16, the Egyptian government had exhibited its cleverness and its self-confidence in an interview which Nasser gave to a correspondent of the Press Trust of India.[4] "We shall not allow the Western-proposed Canal Users' Association to function through the Canal. We Egyptians shall run the Canal smoothly and efficiently and if, in spite of this, the Canal Users' Association forces its way through the Suez Canal then it would mean aggression and would be treated as such." He was putting Dulles and Eisenhower on the brink of war for a purpose they did not consider vital to American interests. He declared that Egypt was ready to meet aggression from whichever quarter it might come. She had the arms and heavy equipment necessary. As for the possibility of a shooting war, he said:

> As a responsible person I have to be ready. I cannot treat aggressive Western declarations as mere bluff. . . . The West is worried not so much about the Suez Canal as about its prestige in the Arab world. The West believes that if it loses the battle in the Suez Canal it might be ousted from the Arab world. This is what is worrying them most. I think the current Suez crisis has more than ever united the Arab world and the West is already feeling the pinch of it.

Nasser was asked about the Menzies mission, and he replied, as usual, with an untruth. It had come with a closed mind, and, in his opinion, it had had no intention of reaching a negotiated settlement; it had wanted Egypt to accept the Dulles plan blindly. But if this opinion was to him a truth so firmly held, then from Dulles's standpoint and on Dulles's theory of what might be hoped for as a settlement via SCUA, it was disastrous. There was no peaceful way out with Nasser short of surrender to his usurpation with some sweet frosting over it. When the correspondent asked what part the United States was playing in the Suez crisis, Nasser replied, "Really, the United States is a puzzle to me. I am not able to follow it." Dulles had a dubious reputation everywhere.

Nasser's defiance next took the form of an appeal to the United Nations. The Egyptian government, following the submission of the letter to the Security Council by the British and French, stated its attitude in the same form on September 17. It reiterated the legality of the seizure and of the measures since taken to honor the treaty of 1888; and all the rest. It declared that SCUA was incompatible with the sovereignty and dignity of Egypt, and that it was a flagrant violation of the Charter of the United Nations and the 1888 Convention. It would be "an organization with a self-granted jurisdiction within the territory of a sovereign State Member of the United Nations without the consent of the State. It will, moreover, constitute a threat to international peace and security. The 1888 Convention, while guaranteeing the freedom of passage through the Canal, does not in any way deprive Egypt from [sic] its right to administer the Canal." [5]

The letter repeated Egypt's contention that if SCUA were established, a complicated and contradictory situation would result from the existence of two opposing authorities, one legal, the other a usurper, with many dangers inherent in the situation. Therefore, any vessel wishing to pass through the Canal—let Secretary Dulles note!—should comply with the Canal regulations and duly pay the regular tolls and charges.

Thus, Dulles's problems were many and tough. Furthermore, the Presidential election was now only seven weeks away, and Adlai Stevenson was challenging the Administration's foreign policy powerfully (though discreetly as yet on Suez and the Middle East). The President as a man wanted peace, and as a candidate needed it. That was not all, by far. Dulles's chief furies were Britain and France, especially France. They felt that he was absconding from SCUA's attendant obligations. Both governments had come under severe popular pressure. Even Gaitskell was obliged to remonstrate with those in the Labour Party who were speaking openly as Nasser's supporters, and he himself trimmed his sails a little to avoid being classed among them, and to give responsible support to the Government, if it were on its way to the United Nations.

A speech by Christian Pineau on the Paris radio on September 14 expressed the hopes he had been led to entertain in regard to SCUA. He assured his listeners that it was not his Government's wish to use force, but, on the other hand, France would not bow to it. (That is, the act of force involved in Nasser's seizure of the Canal.) He repudiated those persons and those arguments that were putting France in the position of responsibility for the potential use of force. If the operation of SCUA were hampered by Nasser's officials, then "a military conflict can still be avoided *if* the users show their firmness and solidarity in such a way that Colonel Nasser will hesitate to sacrifice once again the interests of his people to his adventurous dreams." Pineau emphasized, no doubt for Dulles's benefit, that Nasser had counted on divisions among the Western allies. The setting up of SCUA showed, he thought, that the democratic nations were not bowing before the accomplished fact. It demonstrated the tightening of Western solidarity. It did not prevent the search for a final solution acceptable to all users and in conformity with the real interests of the Egyptian people.

Another motif now enters ominously into the irritant sounds that flocked in on Dulles's hearing. Dulles should have known that two days before this speech, on September 12, the leader of the Israeli nationalists, Menahem Begin, of the *Herut* party, had appeared before the Deputies and Senators of the French Parliament, and among other things had said:

> We must clearly say to Nasser's regime, You will be destroyed. Our alliance with France does not have to be written. France does not need to fight for Israel, nor Israel for France, but France and Israel can and ought to work together, and if necessary, fight together.

In Britain, the emphasis was rather different. Once Parliament had adjourned, the forces against the Government increased their activity in public meetings, parades, and so on. Various "Suez Emergency Committees," whether by that or other names, appeared all over the country, to agitate the public against the Government's policy. These groups, all tending toward the position of the left-wing Labour M.P.'s, expressed an attitude that was part not only of the Suez war that might come, but of the class war that had come long ago. The Government was not too well geared, given its social basis, to counteract this kind of propaganda. It could never match the energies and emotional appeal on a mass basis supplied by the left-wing socialists and their allies. To some extent stimulated and incited by a tiny minority of Communist sympathizers, these men exerted considerable influence by their work in certain political groupings and in the trade unions. Their propaganda techniques and their utter lack of scruples could always find converts and dupes for causes labeled Justice, the United Nations, Anti-imperialism, Ban the Bomb, Law not War, and so on. This nation-wide agitation was the more effective because the country was in the vacation or leisure period of the year, without adequate responsible discussion across the floor of the House. Supported by the mass-circulation newspapers of the center and left, the movement caused the public-opinion polls to show a slightly decreased support for the Government—a matter for increased mortification among the Government and its supporters.

The Government's response was wise: even more than before, it stressed the legality of its position, to persuade the masses of the rectitude of its course, and to engrave on Dulles's mind as well that it had a sound case. Lord Chancellor Kilmuir reiterated the legal case in the House of Lords' debate on September 12.[6]

On September 17, prior to taking his plane to London, Dulles issued a statement of intention. It ran:

> Let me make certain things quite clear:
>
> The United States is dedicated to seeking by peaceful means assurance that the Suez Canal will carry out the international purpose to which it is dedicated by the Convention of 1888.
>
> We are not, however, willing to accept for ourselves, nor do we seek from other nations acceptance of, an operating regime, for the Canal which falls short of recognizing the rights to Canal users by the 1888 Convention.
>
> We are not trying to organize any boycott of the Canal, but we cannot be blind to the fact that conditions might become such that transit through the Canal is impractical or greatly diminished. There must always be ways to assure the movement of vital supplies, particularly oil, to Western Europe. Accordingly, we are carrying out planning as a prudent precaution. But our hope remains that satisfactory operating arrangements can be worked out with Egypt.[7]

Dulles was in a far weaker diplomatic position than when he had crossed the Atlantic for the first London Conference. Then he had had with him a constructive and plausible plan that would have satisfied Britain and France; he had had excellent selling points and effective arguments. He had been in the position of a possible supporter of coercion against Nasser. But now he knew that his arguments and plans had come to nothing and that his allies and friends knew it, and, furthermore, that the substitute he now proffered was unworkable if it was robust and warlike if it was workable. He was bringing them trouble, not gifts. That *is* exactly the time to look the horse in the mouth, and they did.

Selwyn Lloyd, in the chair, began this second London Conference by asserting that the proposals rejected by Nasser still remained open.[8] The British must reiterate that "they could not accept the unrestricted control by one Government or one man over the vital waterway of Suez. There could be no compromise on that principle." To protect the rights of the users, some form of international *control* was essential. The British Government did not want to settle this matter by force, but would act in the spirit of the U.N. Charter. "There has never been in the minds of Her Majesty's Government any doubt as to the need to go, at some stage, to the Security Council." When, and with what constructive proposition, were questions *to be discussed at the present meeting.* Emphasis must be given this phrase because, later on, Dulles complained bitterly that he was taken by surprise when the British did go to the United Nations.

The area of damage done by Nasser's action of July 26 was extending. Painful adjustments would have to be made "in many countries" unless confidence could be restored in the operation of the Canal—decisions now had to be made about "not just its technical operations [*Dulles, take due note!*] on a short-term basis but also as to its future both politically and technically." Thus, Lloyd took immediate issue with the vague ruminations of Dulles, his listener, who had been hearing the same argument across the Atlantic cables and at meetings with the British and French ministers since he had stepped off the plane a day before.

Now an emergency salvage operation was called for, and Dulles addressed himself to this herculean labor not only in the full sessions, but especially outside and in between them. He moved to rally the other seventeen nations as soon as the chairman had ended his speech, whereas in the first London Conference he had waited until most others had had their say. But this was *his* scheme, more so than the previous one, in a sense; and in the prevailing mood of doubt, he had to talk early.

The government of Egypt had made no counterproposal, Dulles noted to the delegates when he took the floor: this attitude of Egypt had created a new and difficult situation. "Exercising the restraint enjoined by the Charter of the United Nations [he was now using the language of Britain and France of two weeks before, and the language exerted on him by the Scandinavians in particular], we continue to seek, by peaceful means, a solution of this difficult problem." He claimed that vessels had rights at all times to pass through the Canal. He claimed that those rights were jeopardized by the Egyptian government's action in usurping the functions of the Universal Suez Canal Company. Egypt's declaration that it would respect international rights would be tested by whether it would give the parties the facilities needed to exercise their rights.

The language and tone of the next passage of Dulles's speech require special concern, in order to appreciate the intellectual skill of the Secretary of State, and also to judge, at later stages of this crisis, whether Dulles and President Eisenhower were acting in the spirit of this declaration—always providing, of course, that the argument and posture were sincere commitments in the first place.

> I know that the Government of Egypt has argued that it can always, by the use of force, interrupt traffic through the Suez Canal, and that therefore transit must depend on Egypt's good faith and good will. But there are many sanctions against open and

> forcible interruption of free passage. The same is not true if any one government dominates and controls all phases of operation. The operation of the Suez Canal is a highly complicated, intricate affair. It offers infinite possibilities of covert violation and the practice, in obscurity, of preferences and discriminations. Lack of efficiency can be a grave hazard. It is against risks of this kind that the users can, and I believe should, protect themselves in the exercise of their rights under the 1888 Treaty. The economic well-being of many nations and peoples is at stake, and there are no adequate sanctions against the dangers I describe.
>
> The third point I would like to make is this: When vital rights are threatened, it is natural and elemental to join to meet the common danger.
>
> The Government of Egypt has warned us not to join together in association. It is natural that it should prefer the canal users to be unorganized and divided. I recall that in its Memorandum of September 10, 1956, to the Secretary General of the United Nations and to many governments, the Egyptian Government seeks the creation of a negotiating body that will reflect what it calls "different views." But for those endangered to come together and to harmonize their views is an elemental right, not to be foregone.

Then Dulles set out the main elements of his proposal for the association.

The eighteen nations should continue their association. The reason for doing so was freely to achieve a common will, not to have one or more of them impose their views on any of the others. *It was not to coerce Egypt.* (This is a change from the original form of the SCUA proposal as passed on to Eden and Mollet and even from its form as modified during and after the Commons debate by Dulles's press conference.) The purpose of SCUA was usefulness in the present necessities for the nations represented and for others which used the Canal. Its operation would also be in the interest of Egypt whenever she was "willing constructively to seek a solution with those who are chiefly concerned." And—"it is in the interest of world peace that we stand together."

SCUA would be based on the eighteen-power proposals, pending a permanent solution. A small operating staff would be needed, and it would hope for cooperation with local Egyptian personnel. In addition to performing the technical and organizational service needed for passage through the Canal, and providing pilots, this staff would collect dues and pay out expenses. A small governing board would be chosen from among the eighteen powers, for subordinate policy-making and executive functions, to be the employer of the staff answering to the eighteen. This governing board would keep in touch with the development of large tankers and new pipelines, and inform the eighteen of circumstances that might affect their economic life.

Now came the feature of Dulles's proposal that just managed to keep the eighteen powers together, but not to solve the Suez crisis.

> Membership in the Association would not, as we see it, involve the assumption by any member of any obligation. It would however be hoped that members of the Association would voluntarily take such action with respect to their ships and the payment of Canal dues as would facilitate the work of the Association and build up its prestige and authority, and consequently its ability to serve. This action, I emphasize, would be entirely a voluntary action by each of the member governments if it saw fit to take it.

The reader will have noticed the *voluntary* nature of the association. Now, the trouble with this provision was that the ships of various nations are in aggressive competition with each other, and so are the shipping lines within each nation. Unless there was a minimum common obligation, say, on the payment of tolls, or the detour by the Cape, then the nation or line taking the easiest way out in order to get and retain business would be best off. A fear that this kind of competition would cause the bottom to fall out of the scheme afflicted all who heard Dulles, and a fear also afflicted almost all of them lest an obligatory collective rule be established! One of those with the most fears was Dulles himself. For he had no authority to make a firm promise that American shipowners would pay tolls to the agent appointed by SCUA. Dulles could have delivered only by great exertions, and ultimately he was not willing to make such an effort: he would not go to Congress for powers to compel American shipowners to comply, nor would he persuade them to act voluntarily.

How could he defect in such a way from his own proposal? It depended on what he wanted SCUA to do. But on this he could not quite make up his mind, once the potential use of some kind of duress to make it work became known, or suspected, or imagined. He let others into the noose, and then wanted to escape it himself; so he cut it (making full participation voluntary) and this left him free. He had achieved the "gaining of time"—but to that matter we turn later.

Dulles was fertile in all sorts of expedients. Now, he concluded his address with one new idea: "SCUA might suggest a provisional solution which the United Nations might find it useful to invoke while the search for a permanent solution goes on." It was an afterthought, but it bridged, it seemed, the possible desires of several nations to do *nothing*, and the known desires of others to go to the United Nations immediately.

This speech was delivered about noon. During the rest of the day, with a break for lunch, the various delegates flung questions at the chairman for Dulles to answer, while Dulles listened, becoming more and more glum at the Frankenstein he had invented to frighten them. Not that he intended that effect—there was the rub. He was just being helpful to them and the world with all the inventive ability at his command. He ceased doodling, and when he stood up his stance was no longer so cocksure.

Sweden, Norway, and Denmark had issued a communiqué on September 16. They did not touch on the merits of the coming second London Conference. They simply went straight to the point that represented their best interests. "The Ministers were agreed that the problem had now come to a point when it should appropriately be referred to the United Nations. It was established that the three Scandinavian Governments were not prepared in advance to decide their attitude towards the proposed plan for a canal users' association." But they would come to the meeting, to explore all possibilities of a peaceful solution of the conflict.

Swedish Foreign Minister Unden, who had been a member of the Menzies mission, now suggested that there were indications of a basis for negotiation and that Egypt might be prepared to give guarantees. The best path was to bring the whole issue to the United Nations, at once, now that a serious attempt to find a solution had been made and had failed. This suggestion brought the fervent Christian Pineau to his feet with a question to Unden. Could he throw any light on the kind of international guarantees which Colonel Nasser would be prepared to give? Unden admitted that, as Colonel Nasser had not made any counterpropositions, he could not give an answer.

The Iranian delegate, Dr. Ardalan, who had also been a member of the Menzies mission, suggested that the mission had been restricted to explanation and had not had the freedom to negotiate. (This was a misunderstanding, or a formal and superficial interpretation of the mission's purpose, or a way to smooth the path, diplomatically, for future negotiations in preference to the establishment of SCUA. It was *not* true.) He suggested that the next step might be a negotiating committee within maxima and minima (my phrasing) set by proposals that the nations present might agree on.

The Spanish delegate moved quite a distance towards Nasser's approach. He did not say so, but the Spanish press had already made it clear, that Spain was not anxious to be other than friends with the Arabs of North Africa. He recommended that the Conference give close attention to the Egyptian government's offer of September 9 to negotiate (Chapter 7). "These offers should be duly considered, because they make it possible to continue the negotiations initiated as a result of the first London Conference." Thus, the Spanish delegate also bypassed SCUA.

It was with exceptional chagrin that Dulles heard his scheme controverted by the delegate of Italy, her Foreign Minister, Dr. Gaetano Martino. Italy that had been liberated from Mussolini and Hitler by American G.I.'s, and helped to rise to its feet by American gifts and loans running into hundreds of millions of dollars, and helped, also, to solve the Trieste conflict with Tito of Yugoslavia! But Martino challenged Dulles's scheme by a direct frontal attack on its legality. He did not agree that the treaty of 1888 gave user nations the right to run ships through with their own pilots. "This is juridically not exact." He interpreted the Egyptian decrees of 1854 and 1856 as explicitly requiring that ships seeking passage must accept the pilots supplied by the Canal administration. It was a logical position also, said the doctor learned in international and administrative law: the pilot is held responsible for the security of the Canal as well as of the ships!

He was joined in a resolution by the Netherlands, Denmark, and Norway. This severely limited the function of SCUA to be nothing but a negotiating body! The resolution provided that the members of the conference submit the present dispute to the United Nations and also that the users' association should be open to all nations without discrimination. (Dulles's concern was: Does this include the Soviet Union and all its cohorts, those atheistic Communist nations?) According to Martino's resolution, SCUA would merely establish with Egypt a new treaty guaranteeing freedom of transit through the Canal while preserving Egypt's sovereign rights. Gone, then, was the international managerial board of eighteen-power plan! Martino's idea of what exactly was to solve the conflict remained entirely vague. It could hardly be of any comfort to Dulles or his two chief allies in NATO.

Pakistan joined in urging negotiation as the sole purpose of SCUA; if the eighteen powers were rebuffed by Nasser, they should submit the dispute to the Security Council. The Japanese delegate, that country's Ambassador to Britain, Haruhiki Nishi, asked many pointed questions. Since Dulles attempted an answer to them later, they can be left to the account of the Secretary's speech.

During the lunch recess, which continued to 4:20 P.M., Eden entertained some of the delegates, including Dulles. At this gathering Dulles was confirmed in his feeling that he must exert all his moral power to hold the eighteen together, however minimal the purpose should be; to hold them together, even to do nothing, was itself an essential purpose. At noon, September 21, Dulles sent a note to the Pakistani Foreign Minister, personal and informal. He asked that he not reject SCUA out of hand, in view of U.S.-Pakistani relations through SEATO, etc., etc. He asked him to weigh the pros and cons of "precipitate negative action." It looked like threatening pressure.

When the meeting resumed, Dulles rose to speak once more. His speech was extemporaneous, that is, it had been worked out as the various delegates had presented their opinions. It fell into six parts. First, the Secretary answered those who wished the dispute to go to the United Nations. Second, he proclaimed the need to have SCUA as a *de facto* institution giving some reality to the justice of the eighteen-power proposals. Third came that stubborn and impossible figment of Dulles's limited imagination, the likelihood of getting Egyptian personnel running the Canal to cooperate with SCUA ships —the delegates shook their heads and some hid skeptical smiles that he could have continued to play them with, as they saw it, this kind of fiction. Fourth was the evocation of the grave possibilities if passage through the Canal should break down, so that a provisional operating scheme was essential. Fifth, Dulles answered the Japanese Ambassador's questions. And, finally, he made the appeal that SCUA would be useful while the U.N. handled the dispute.

His response to the Japanese Ambassador's questions went as follows:

Would Egypt's agreement be required for the operation of SCUA? Dulles hoped so, though not by treaty. "All it requires is *de facto* operating cooperation at the local level." Therefore, it *did* require agreement with Egypt. (Surely, this was something of a change in position in regard to SCUA?) He did not think of imposing any of the operations of SCUA on Egypt by force.

Would SCUA operate only on the water or would it establish facilities on land as well? It would not supersede the Egyptian personnel and authorities and facilities (e.g., signaling stations) on land.

What is the minimum cooperation asked of the Egyptian authorities? That which is practically necessary to keep the traffic going: any Egyptian pilots ("who are not there for the purposes of espionage," i.e., Russians); avoidance of discrimination in the pattern of passage through the Canal for the vessels of SCUA's members.

Suppose Egyptian law requires the use of her pilots exclusively? Well, then, SCUA's pilots would not have much to do, "and that part of the plan would have collapsed." (What a collapse of SCUA!)

Must the ships of SCUA members be forbidden to use Egyptian pilots? The United States had no authority to command this. He supposed that many other nations were in the same situation.

These Japanese questions left of SCUA hardly more than an inglorious shambles.

Turning to another point that had been raised in the discussion, Dulles argued that the United Nations had only limited powers. Among those it did not have was the power to require a nation, like Egypt for example, to make a new treaty—so as to replace the system of 1888. The eighteen-power proposals had been made to secure a treaty by conference. The Security Council could only call on nations to live up to existing treaties. Therefore, his SCUA proposal was in itself necessary if a substitute for the earlier proposal was to be found; and it was also necessary *as indicating a solution* to the United Nations whenever the matter should come before it. SCUA would be provisionally operative till then.

Then, in a panic-stricken attempt to salvage something for his scheme, his prestige, his substitute for open force and for immediate submission to the Security Council, Dulles turned to a much wider perspective and addressed an appeal to more general emotions.

> . . . There has been exercised, and is being exercised, a great restraint in the face of a great peril. But you cannot expect that to go on indefinitely unless those of us who appreciate the problem, who are sympathetic with it, rally our forces to try to bring about a settlement which is not only a peaceful settlement but a settlement "in conformity with the principles of justice and international law."
>
> Some may feel, although I do not think anyone here feels—it could be felt by some nations that are not immediately involved in this problem—that the only aspect of it that concerns them is the problem of peace, and *if you can just be sure that there won't be force used, you can just forget about the rest of it. That is only half of the problem, and you cannot solve the problem just by half-way measures which relate only to peace and which do not also put the full weight of our strength behind what we believe to be a solution in conformity with the principles of justice and international law.*
>
> Now, we agreed on what we thought were principles of justice and international law in relation to this matter. Our conclusions are reflected in the statement that we agreed upon in the month of August. I believe that we owe it to ourselves, to every one of the nations here involved, to stand together to try to work this thing out, not just in terms of peace but to work it out in terms of bringing about a just solution in accordance with the principles of international law and in accordance with the provisions of the Charter. I believe if we don't do that, if we scatter thinking that the problem is solved because perhaps the danger of war seems a little less than it did, then I believe we will have done a great disservice to ourselves.
>
> What we do in that respect—if that should be what we would do—would come back to plague us and haunt us in the days to come. So I say, let's stick together in this proposition and continue to work not only for "peace" but also for peace "in conformity with the principles of justice and international law."

At this point, a witness reports, a sympathetic hush fell on the conference. Dulles was almost in tears. His glasses were moist. His eyes blinked in bereavement. He was, says the observer, trying to line up with all the other nations who had urged going to the United Nations, and indeed, trying to re-enter the harmony with the other seventeen that had persisted until he had produced from his briefcase his awkward nostrum, SCUA. As he spoke these few last words his voice broke, and his voice choked with emotion. He tapped the table for emphasis, and he continued in a constricted voice:

> And I would like to point out, fellow Delegates, that *the United Nations Charter itself does not just say, "there must be peace."* What does it say? The very first article of the United Nations Charter says that the purpose of the United Nations is to bring about settlements by "peaceful means, and in conformity with the principles of justice and international law." And if that latter part of it is forgotten, the first part of it will inevitably come to be ignored. . . .
>
> We have to realize, when we have to deal with problems of this character, that we are not really in the long run furthering the cause of peace, even peace for those of us who seem remote from the particular problem, *if we don't feel that we have just as much a responsibility to try to seek a solution "in conformity with the principles of justice and international law" as we have a responsibility to try to prevent the use of force.* If we only put our emphasis upon one side of that problem and forget the other, then our efforts are going to be doomed. And the hopes represented by this Charter of the United Nations are equally going to be doomed.

When the Secretary arrived at this point in his throbbing but halting cadences, having wet his lips frequently because his mouth was dry from nervous tension, the onlookers were absorbed and silent, impressed by the inferences to be drawn regarding Nasser. Then, says the close observer who was sitting next to him, the Secretary resumed "with Lincolnian calmness"!

> We are dealing with one of the most significant aspects of post-war life. Upon what we do, in my opinion, will very largely depend the question of whether or not, in fact, we are going to build a peaceful world.
>
> Our problem is no less than that in its importance. Now, why do I say that? I say that because we all want a world in which force is not used. True. But that is only one side of the coin. If you have a world in which force is not used, you must also have a world in which a just solution of problems of this sort can be achieved. I don't care how many words are written into the Charter of the United Nations about not using force. If, in fact, there is not, as a substitute for force, some way to get just resolutions of some of these problems inevitably the world will fall back again into anarchy and into chaos.

To get his own way, that is, at this moment to prevent the seventeen other powers from flying each its own way, Dulles had given a tremendous moral hostage, a commitment he was later called on to honor. To ascertain how deeply he was now committed, one needs only look over the last few paragraphs again. Finally, Dulles was emphasizing the word that always appears in the United Nations Charter alongside *peace—justice*. (Some of the lines in which such emphasis was made most strikingly have been italicized.) Dulles clearly implied that peace would be lost if international law and justice were not served. He was using almost the very words with which Eden had answered the Labour Party and other opponents! And this time Dulles was right. But did his own rightness make an impression on *him?* Did it make an impression on Nasser? For this kind of plea was addressed to Nasser, with a certain tone of menace in it, surely?

The event would tell. At any rate, a British spokesman said of this part ("justice!") of Dulles's speech that it was "Admirable!" and congratulations were also extended to him by most of the other delegates.

He sat through the discussions the next day, whittling and taking down notes, always extremely alarmed lest matters should slip entirely out of his hands. The delegates wrote a declaration for the establishment of SCUA. Given the lack of "teeth" in it, and the voluntary and individual nature of the obligations it required, it meant very little even though its terms seemed to promise very much.[9] Since to join SCUA did not impose any such legal obligations on the members as would require the United States government to submit the matter first to the Senate, Dulles, in a short concluding speech, announced at once that America would subscribe to the declaration, that is, would be a member of SCUA.

* * * * *

On September 21, about 5:30 P.M., Dulles had a long conversation with Eden. Eden expressed disappointment that SCUA had not taken the expected shape of a truly effective organization. Dulles could not differ from this judgment, but expressed hopes that it would nevertheless help to solve the Suez problem. Eden responded that the British position would have to be reserved, that is, that he was not satisfied and he would have to ponder his next step. All aspects of the crisis were discussed at length. Dulles strongly appealed to Eden to keep the crisis out of the United Nations for the time being, on the ground that taking it there would not be a fruitful move. Then he asked that, if Eden should decide he must go to the Security Council, he consult with Dulles first.

It seems that, on this occasion, Eden had not definitely made up his mind to go to the Security Council, or perhaps he had decided to, but could not trust Dulles to cooperate with him. Whatever the reason, communication between the two failed. The older antipathies may have intervened to prevent frankness of disclosure or readiness to comprehend. To some colleagues, Dulles described this conversation of Eden's with him as "open": yet Eden had given him no inkling that he would now go to the U.N.

Dulles left shortly thereafter for the United States. He confided to one of his close associates on the way to the airport that Britain and France were not being frank with him, and that he was afraid they intended to use force against Nasser. Actually, Eden had already decided, or decided soon afterwards, to go to the United Nations. Dulles believed, or told people he believed, that Eden had lied to him —whether positively or by reticence; he believed it, resented it, did not forgive it. From the moment he discovered Eden's intention his suspicions grew blacker that he was not being taken into the confidence of his Western allies. He became more desperate; and at the end sought reprisals. The conversation with Eden was a watershed in the events leading to the Suez invasion.

Dulles arrived back in Washington at 3:08 P.M. on Saturday, September 22. As the plane stopped on the runway, Herbert Hoover, Jr., his Deputy Secretary, ran across to it and told him that *the British and the French were at once taking the dispute to the United Nations!* Dulles listened, and as Hoover gave him details, he became more and more angry, murmuring that he had not been consulted, that he had been kept in the dark.

Let us go back a little to examine the immediate circumstances behind the British and French decision. Eden and Selwyn Lloyd had realized by the end of the first day of the Conference that SCUA was about to fall apart, to become an obstacle rather than a help to their rightful claims. Hence, they conferred with the French, who were even more skeptical, actually contemptuous, of the Secretary's contrivance, which they said was ramshackle. The French had for weeks been in close conference with the Israelis. The British and French decided they must go to the Security Council at once.

Time was running out. This anxiety was in their minds and consciences as it was in Dulles's, but for different reasons. If they were to be compelled to resort to arms to wrest from Nasser what he had seized by arms, then it was essential that their legal way be clear. They could not know with certainty what the Security Council would do for them, but that body would undoubtedly serve either as a facilitator of their claims or as an impediment. If the latter, they would be able honestly to say, "We have fulfilled our obligations according to the Charter and we have not received justice, and therefore we shall take the alternative presented by the United States Secretary of State, John Foster Dulles: coercion to secure justice."

Selwyn Lloyd firmly claims that his remarks during the Conference were clear enough, and that Dulles should have expected recourse to the U.N. as the next immediate step that his allies would take. Eden and Mollet, Selwyn Lloyd and Pineau now said, "No further shilly-shallying: at once!" Dulles's real problem, they contended, was Nasser's lawlessness, or it was nothing. He refused to face it. Pineau especially felt that the SCUA conference was merely a device of postponement, not a genuine attempt to find a settlement. Dulles consistently underestimated his allies' abilities and necessities.

Eden found, during the conference, that it would be easier for the delegates to accept SCUA if an appeal to the United Nations were undertaken simultaneously. Especially was this point pressed at a lunch he gave on the last day of the Conference for the principal delegates from New Zealand, Iran, Norway, and Portugal. He felt it was not possible to delay action. He was afraid, also, that the Soviet Union might jump in and present the matter to the Security Council before the West did, getting the issue put on the agenda in its own embarrassing phraseology.

Now, by this stage of the conflict, Dulles had emasculated his own scheme which he had begun by advocating with such a bang. He could not give firm commitments that American ships, under American or foreign registry, would pay their dues to SCUA. He could not give firm commitments that the Export-Import Bank would make loans to his allies to meet the costs of American-supplied oil. He was incapable, beyond this, of finding some way of compensating these nations and any others which would suffer from having to make a detour around the Cape, for the losses of their other cargoes. As Eden said: "It became clear to us only gradually that the American conception of the association was now evolving so fast that it would end as an agency for collecting dues for Nasser. Perhaps this was not clear to the United States delegation themselves at that time." It was a tart criticism; it had a granite-like core of truth in it.

On arrival in Washingon, the Secretary told the waiting reporters: "The second Suez conference at London registered solid gains." [10] We know that the record of facts completely contradicts this tranquilizing bluff. A more astringent appraisal might have put Nasser on notice to his obligations. The statement is not candid. It was campaign time.

> The Conference expanded greatly the prospective role of the Users' Association. As now agreed, the Users' Association will not only help the vessels of the members to get through the Canal, but it will serve the United Nations in helping to work out a provisional solution; it will be a means of dealing with the serious economic problems that may arise for some of the member nations if the Canal were blocked; and it will study alternatives which might reduce dependence upon the Canal.
>
> There was a splendid spirit of fellowship at the Conference. It looked, not vindictively to the past, but hopefully to the future. The door to a peaceful and fair solution is kept widely open, if only the Government of Egypt will choose that way.

At 5 P.M. Dulles went to the White House to report to President Eisenhower. On Sunday, September 23, he rested and pondered in the morning, and then, in the afternoon, appeared on TV on the National Broadcasting Company's program *Meet the Press*. It is important to pay attention to what was now said in the view of millions and of what therefore was fully reported to London and Paris. I have verified the performance from the NBC videoscope.

Dulles made the point, in regard to the British and French war plans which had begun to take shape earlier in the affair, that the United States had been cautious. His military experts had informed him that involvement in these preparations might mean "getting bogged down into a war to which one could see no end," for example, as the French in Indo-China, "fighting a kind of hopeless operation." The SCUA idea did not include shooting a way through; and boycott was not contemplated—"if we can get through on decent terms." He then made a commitment of principle.

> *Question*: London reports this morning indicated that the British and the French feel they would have your tacit consent to shoot their way through the Canal if the United Nations failed to secure a settlement. Is there any truth in those reports?
> *Answer:* No, there are no truths in those reports. We have not discussed at all what might happen if the United Nations efforts should fail. I have pointed out in a speech I made last Wednesday night—that I do believe that peace and justice and international law are two sides of the coin, and you can't always count on nations not using force unless there is some alternative which conforms to international peace and justice. And I said there that unless we can work it out, some system here which is just, which recognizes the real rights of the users, then *I don't think you can expect to go on forever asking people not to resort to force*. And the United Nations really is based upon the assumption that these two things are two sides of the coin. And we have got to work just as hard as we can to get out of the United Nations a program here which will conform to what I believe are the rights under international law which arise from that 1888 treaty, and the just position of countries to depend upon it.

"*I don't think you can expect to go on forever asking people not to resort to force*." This was strong talk—but . . .

Although it is the fond opinion of some of Dulles's close companions in office that the Secretary of State had the character to grasp the nettle of danger, he had not done so, he was not doing so, on this occasion, unless the enemy was Britain and France. The nettle was from the beginning Nasser's action and character; the nettle continued to be that; Dulles was converting it into Britain and France, as being the less prickly and poisonous nettle. It was a mistake in foreign policy, although it could be masked by the plea of Peace!

On Monday, September 24, Dulles and his staff worked furiously. In these meetings he indulged in a disgruntled monologue against the appeal of Britain and France to the United Nations. The staff well knew the background of his grumbling, half-muttered ratiocinations and expostulation. The Afro-Asian nations, working in an informal but morally bound and interest-begotten alliance, had made Britain and France unpopular. They had developed an atmosphere at the United Nations sympathetic to the underdog—even if the underdog was vicious. All underdogs are noble, they claimed; they can do no evil; evil is not evil when underdogs do it. The Secretary now once again expressed his fear that he was placed between bad alternatives, not good ones. If force could be postponed and he could take Britain and France and Egypt along with him on a peaceful course, then in time "world opinion" might cure the wounds the Suez seizure had inflicted.

Then Dulles became less contemplative and more accusatory in his remarks to his staff. Why were the British now taking such *precipitous* action? He waxed resentful. Eden had been open about his position only two days ago—or three days ago—but he did not give the Secretary any inkling that he and the French were going to do this, to go to the United Nations. No! Dulles got it from neither of them, not Eden or Selwyn Lloyd, nor the French for all the spate of words always forthcoming from Pineau. Dulles wanted, he continued, to exhaust all other possibilities first, to consider all the alternative oil resources that could be brought in. *What relief did the British and French expect,* yes, what relief did they expect, from this move to the United Nations? What did they calculate they would obtain from their proceedings there? Surely, they could have discussed the move with the United States Secretary of State first, especially as he had conversed with them in such a way as to give them an opening to do so? Didn't they know that if they made a move in the Security Council, then Pakistan and some of the other nations would use the Security Council as an excuse to avoid participation in SCUA or would join with the intention of paying only lip service to it?

What eluded Dulles in his preoccupation with the voting tallies at the United Nations was the fact that he had dissuaded Britain and France from going to the United Nations earlier, had got them both into trouble with their own publics on that account. Furthermore, in pursuing a policy whose purpose, he told his staff, was to keep as many doors open as possible, to have the maximum of flexibility, he had, in SCUA, shaped a warped door from the wrong material, one that could not be opened. These defects had reduced his diplomatic flexibility because it caused his clients to lose confidence in the master builder. Britain and France sensed that Dulles's grasp at SCUA and an embargo was only in the nature of "alternative noises" (a State Department staff phrase) to frighten Nasser; actually, the device frightened them and the rest more than Nasser. Dulles had lost his credit.

The proposal of SCUA caused the allies still more misgiving, in that Dulles seemed to be playing fast and loose with the problem (and the charge) of the illegality of their position. If SCUA were legal, then it could be legal only under their rights according to the Convention of 1888. For this was a substitute "system" to that which had grown up since 1888. If the Convention were legal, then the basis of SCUA was legal; if SCUA were legal then the Convention ought to be preserved or supplanted by an equal substitute. In either case, what grounds had Dulles to question the legality of their basis, as he was from time to time inclined to do, when it suited him to depress their mood?

When Pineau returned to Paris late on September 21, he stated that since other nations were then postponing their decision about joining SCUA, especially where the payment of dues was concerned, France would do the same. It would eventually be necessary to take the dispute over the Canal to the United Nations. France's refusal to sign the SCUA declaration at once was based on the direct instructions of Prime Minister Mollet. Pineau told the Foreign Affairs Committee of the National Assembly that he had lost faith in SCUA when Italy had, at the London meeting on September 21, announced she would continue to pay tolls direct to Egypt.

In the French Cabinet, opinion was divided. Some members, led by Jacques Chaban-Delmas, a whole-hearted de Gaullist, wished the Cabinet to resign because it had not given Nasser the riposte it had promised to the National Assembly. Others urged Mollet to reject the declaration and resume France's freedom of action. Members of the National Assembly and other leaders of French public opinion saw that SCUA had again postponed the hope of inflicting on Nasser a brusque, humbling defeat. They feared an infinite ensnarement in debilitating and futile conferences or even in vacuity. On September 22, the Cabinet nevertheless did adhere to the SCUA declaration, to Dulles's satisfaction—his sardonic satisfaction, for he reasoned, "What else can they do?"

But later that day,[11] the Prime Minister, Guy Mollet, spoke with bitterness, which was the connected phenomenon of the sardonic twist in Dulles's smile. He spoke in the chief town of his parliamentary constituency, Lens, in the coal mine district of Pas-de-Calais. The united democracies, he said, had been able to halt Hitler's Pan-Germanism and Stalin's Pan-Slavism. Nasser was a much smaller man, but he nursed a similar dream of Pan-Arabism. Would it be possible for the democracies to stop this expansionism in time? (It, too, was a form of imperialism.)

> We shall succeed [in halting Nasser] only by our will and the unity of all free men. Why not admit our bitterness and our disquiet in noting that the free peoples are not aware as we are, of the danger, in noting that to our will there does not correspond adequate unity from our friends and allies? France is hurt by this conclusion, but is not discouraged. I can assure you that France's will has not changed. I know that the same is true of Britain's will. The coming to Paris of Sir Anthony Eden will show in a few days that French-British solidarity is complete.

This was the kind of speech which should have made Dulles beware. The days when he could insult France's politicians, as he had insulted Mendès-France in 1954, were now gone by. Such days dawn rarely, and when their evening has come the insulted are better prepared to avoid and resist a repetition.

The sulky declaration of the French government (on September 22) read:

> The Cabinet reaffirmed the will of the Government to establish the principle of international operation of the Canal, defined by the first London Conference, and to accept no compromise on this point [*transaction* is the French word: it can mean also bargaining]. It is with this express reservation that France accompanies her adherence to the Users' Association. The French Government regrets that certain countries sought immunities within the Users' Association hardly compatible with the principles of solidarity asserted by the Eighteen. It wishes to let it be clearly known that, such being the case, France intends to preserve its liberty of action and will refuse to cooperate in any measure it considers contrary to its essential interests and to the objectives previously defined by the Eighteen.[12]

In England, the Government's mood was quite firm, like that of any person with character after an experience which it believes to have been disillusioning and even deceiving. The Conservative newspapers exhibited sharp resentment towards Dulles, and asked to what limits a nation like Britain should go in following the lead of its ally America, and her representative, Dulles. The chauvinist *Daily Express* (which was the organ of Lord Beaverbrook, a native of Canada who espoused the conservatism of the Mother Country with a provincial's vehemence), headed its editorial on SCUA "*Fifty-seven Wasted Days*," days, it then said, of indecision and inaction. Dulles's former cheer leaders were now much more sedate. The *Daily Herald*, a highly peculiar organ of the Labour Party, declared that Dulles's plan for SCUA, "hailed by Sir Anthony Eden as a fiery sword at Nasser's head, turned out to be a blunt kitchen knife—safe, if not particularly useful." Other papers on the Left blamed Eden for being subservient to Washington; so did his own right-wing extremists.

No wonder that the NATO alliance was strained, and that Eden and Mollet felt the rise of desperation within themselves. Dulles's ploy and its failure were bound to have desperate repercussions. In view of what happened in the fifth act of this drama, let it be said that it was ridiculous of the Labour Party Opposition to plead that Dulles was not consulted by Eden and Mollet, and untruthful of Dulles and Eisenhower to give the impression that they were kept in the dark, except in the last few moments. Did they lack the sovereign quality of the statesman: foresight and prophetic inference?

A quite brilliant column appeared in the *New York Herald Tribune*, by Marguerite Higgins, headlined, "Nimble Diplomacy in London." Dulles's allies knew she was in the State Department's confidence. Her description of Dulles's "agility" could not have endeared him greatly to them in their bereft predicament.

> And although the rapid shifts in American tactics have had a "the-hand-is-quicker-than-the-eye" quality about them, it must be admitted that the situation has been extremely mobile. It called for nimble diplomacy. And nimble is what Mr. Dulles was as he juggled innumerable different courses of action in the air in the attempt to keep a steady balance, keep the favor of all spectators, and prevent a resounding international crash. He can scarcely be reproached if his performance was not considered absolutely perfect by absolutely everybody.[13]

Well, how did the commentary end?

> And in London even though Mr. Dulles's nimble tactics and conciliation of the majority may annoy the more belligerent, he should be credited with once again gaining time. At this stage, the hard realities may plunge beyond the high waves of emotional British and French resentment against Egypt to a calmer acceptance of negotiation as the only acceptable alternative.

The idea that the gaining of time will produce calm, that it will produce, as frequently claimed, a "cooling-off period," is not always true. In the politics of nations, Time is a neutral: whether Time produces calm or, to the very contrary, heats up the resentments and the passions, depends entirely on what the aggrieved party had been made to suffer and the treatment received from allies or enemies as the days pass into weeks and months. In this case, Dulles's nimbleness did *not* gain time for cooling off or calmness, even if it had deserved to. Perhaps he hoped that it would. But if this was, indeed, his hope, he had mistaken the adversaries, and to his friends he had not early enough acted with the necessary utter frankness of saying,

"Force will on no account be used. I cannot help you. I will hinder you, if you use it! Go to the United Nations!" But this would have required from Dulles an abjuration of his own cleverness, his conceit that he could handle any complicated railroad reorganization lawsuit in his own personal way, and win! One of his intimates, remembering his speech at the SCUA conference, said to me: "You could have heard a pin drop at that peroration! A pin! Here was the interpreter, the teacher, the advocate, the analyzer, and he was very emotional!" True, an observer might comment, Dulles was the interpreter, the teacher, the advocate, the analyzer . . . BUT—where was the Secretary of State? Wherever he was, Dulles did not put himself in the place his allies occupied; he lacked the empathy.

The news from Cairo was that when the reports about SCUA reached there, Nasser knew the battle was over. Dulles had, in fact, if not in outward manner, abandoned Britain and France. He had offered his maximum. It was a broken reed. Nasser had won. Even the tap on the wrist now safely administered by Nehru could be laughed off and laughed at. Nehru said to a mass meeting in New Delhi on September 23: "I would, however, say that the way Egypt took hold of the Suez Canal was not our way. We follow a different way, but who am I to criticize others? Our way is a little different. If they [the Egyptians] had followed a different way so many difficulties would not have arisen. But they had a right to follow their own method." Nehru was then of the opinion that the danger of war over Suez had receded.

Even at that moment, Nehru was in correspondence with Eden, and was party to Menon's journey to Cairo, and then later to London, to seek a concession from Nasser but a surrender by Britain and France. Nehru himself was on his way to make a three-day visit to Riyadh, the capital of Saudi Arabia. President Kuwatley of Syria was also on his way there, and so, too, was Nasser. Nasser was tenaciously pursuing his policy of Pan-Arabism, the union of all Arab countries, even of all Arabs within non-Arab states, under *his* leadership. But Saudi Arabia's welfare rested on its supplies of oil, and these were brought to the surface of the earth and distributed to consumers all over the world by American oil producers, ARAMCO. If the Canal were blocked, the sales of oil and the share of profit that went into King Saud's public budget and private pocket would decrease. Besides, Saud regarded himself as the leader of the true Orthodox Moslems and resented the secularism and Communist friendships of Nasser. And he especially rejected Nasser's claim to dominate all Arab lands, in whatever guise of nobility, including Saudi Arabia. Syria was rent by factions, military and civil, in so many directions that it is almost impossible to follow them; primarily, however, they produced a basic instability and a division of the nation between pro-Nasser and anti-Nasser forces.

On September 24, the conference of Saud, Kuwatley, and Nasser "adopted a single outlook, a fact which inspires confidence in a future in which the Arab nation with Allah's guidance will achieve its aspirations." Meanwhile it proclaimed the usual mortal enmity towards Israel. On the Suez Canal affair it made this unanimous pronouncement, most interesting in the light of later events, and of the State Department's erroneous judgment (as it turned out) of Arab solidarity:

> The problem and the conditions and circumstances surrounding it were of concern to all Arab countries. The conference therefore supports Egypt fully in every attitude she takes and also backs Egypt's declared readiness to reach a peaceful settlement that would safeguard Egypt's national interests and conform with the aims of the United Nations. The conference believes that the means of ensuring the interests of those concerned over navigation in the Suez Canal is to start negotiations with Egypt, the owner of the Canal, within the framework of the United Nations charter, the spirit of the Bandung conference resolutions, and free from pressure of any kind or intention to impose any unilateral solution.[14]

This was most pleasing to Nasser, and as disconcerting to the State Department, which means Secretary Dulles's career experts. They told him, "I told you so! Touch Nasser, and the whole place will go up in flames!"

After talking with Nasser during a stay of four days in Cairo, Krishna Menon went on to London, where he conferred with Selwyn Lloyd and Sir Anthony Eden. He was received with courtesy but neither total pleasure nor confidence. To the press he said: "I have come here to speak to people I know, friends of mine who have always treated me and my country in a friendly way, and to get some appreciation of various points of view."[15] Of course, he strongly urged the need for a peaceful solution. And he added that he had found Cairo peaceful in atmosphere and that Nasser had always said that a peaceful settlement was possible. The terms remained undisclosed.

Meanwhile, Britain had called a meeting of SCUA for October 1 and was preparing for the almost-simultaneous first round of proceedings at the Security Council on Wednesday, September 26. Sir Anthony Eden and Selwyn Lloyd visited Paris on September 25. Although the visit had been contemplated as far back as July, its occurrence at this moment was valuable in rallying French opinion behind its own government and offering some assurance that the

British were taking as firm a stand as their French colleagues in regard to Dulles.

This was the moment also when the criticism of NATO reached a new height. The French politicians of all parties and groups—except the Communist Party, which was to its heart's content enjoying French confusion and dismay over Suez—seriously questioned the value of NATO if the United States followed the principle of limited liability, and did not fully share the extra-European troubles of its allies. Pineau had concluded his answers to the Foreign Affairs Committee with the remark, "I cannot say that, whatever Nasser's attitude might be, we will never have recourse to force. That would, in any case, be contrary to the Charter of the United Nations." This made headlines and was under the nose of Eden and Selwyn Lloyd as of Dulles.

Thus, in his quest for peace and the avoidance of force, Dulles had made persistent and clever efforts. However, it is not skill but character that primarily governs the fate of nations. The summary of his diplomacy so far in the Suez affair amply demonstrates this principle (for such a summary, see Chapter 18).

Now the allies, Britain and France, were heartsick with Dulles's tactics of contrivances without sanctions, and suspected him of simply delaying justice so that they should surrender their rights. He had not succeeded in dispelling their intention to use force, if necessary. All he had done was to destroy their momentum and self-confidence, and to produce a dissipation of the support they had had at the time of the eighteen-power proposals and of a widespread resentment against Nasser's seizure of the Canal and culpable arrogance. He had damaged his allies' case and power to obtain redress.

They decided without first asking him that they were going to the Security Council, and they went, in spite of his dour objections.

11. THE ALLIED RIFT WIDENS

THE MAXIMUM COMMITMENT THAT DULLES COULD NOW SECURE FROM his allies was that they would make the proposals of the two London Conferences the basis of their appeal to the United Nations, and would defer the Security Council discussions until October 1, at least, when SCUA would actually be organized.

He seems to have exhausted his power of improvisation with SCUA. However, he joined (he could hardly help it) with Britain and France in the attempt to get the best out of their submission to the Security Council. The allies expected, at the least, that they would secure the moral support of a majority vote in the Council. Dulles conjectured he might serve the United States by helping his allies, while restraining them, or by being an honest broker between them and Nasser, while posing as their particular friend.

His incongruous purposes were soon put to the test.

The allies' letter of complaint was moderate.[1] It simply asked for a peaceful solution according to Chapter VI of the U.N. Charter, on the pacific settlement of disputes. But Egypt, in a counter-complaint,[2] took the offensive, accusing them of actions "which constitute a danger to international peace and security, and are serious violations of the Charter of the United Nations."

The British and French and their friends (not including the United States) were extremely annoyed that the evildoer was actually taking the offensive! Now the question became how these allied and Egyptian complaints were to be related to each other on the agenda. France declared immediately she would vote against the charges contained in the Egyptian complaint. When people like Henry Cabot Lodge, United States Ambassador to the U.N., and the officials concerned with United Nations affairs in the State Department counted the possible votes, they believed Egypt would be supported in its bid for space on the agenda by the U.S.S.R., Yugoslavia, Iran, Cuba, and perhaps Peru and China. Britain, France, Australia, and Belgium (under Paul-Henri Spaak, a stout friend of NATO), would possibly abstain.

Therefore, the decisive vote for Egypt's complaint would be that of the United States—to make the seventh affirmative vote the Charter required to place an item on the agenda.

Dulles, I think, owed it to his allies to let them know in advance of the actual proceedings whether that vote would be given, or whether, say, the United States would abstain. Henry Cabot Lodge, who usually made the United States decision on such matters, now publicly stated that this was so important a decision that Dulles himself would have to make it.

Now, it was clearly within the will power of Secretary Dulles and President Eisenhower to help administer a warning to Nasser at this point. They could have decided that Nasser could not expect the benefit of the Charter and the liberalism of free nations. He had acted (as Dulles had publicly and privately charged) in ruthless disregard of the rights of other nations, had violated the sanctity of treaties, and had maneuvered with cunning to extract the maximum he could from the scruples of the Charter while he himself craftily contributed the minimum loyalty. By merely abstaining, the United States could have caused Nasser's complaint to drop out of sight.

Dulles failed to admonish Nasser. He deliberately refused the British and French request to abstain. And the diplomatic reasons are interesting, even if they do not represent the inward motive, which no one will ever be able to extricate beyond a doubt. First, said Dulles and Lodge, in private, we always vote as a matter of form for any complaint to appear on the agenda. Every complaint by any nation should have the opportunity of ventilation, especially as the Soviet Union will aways take advantage of it if we do *not* keep open the right to appear on the agenda whenever we need to. We must open the way, whenever it should become convenient, to indict the atheistic, materialistic, anti-Christian conspirators, the Russians. Then, said Dulles in private, we have lost practically all influence with Nasser already, and if we knock the bottom out of his complaint we shall not retain even a shred of it. Finally, said Lodge and Dulles, in private: We will manage to abort the Egyptian complaint, for since the complaint of the British and French (our friends) will come up first, having been the first submitted, discussion will involve the Egyptian position, and the Council will never get around to the latter as a separate item!

Those tactics were no doubt astute, but they had two defects. In the first place, the Egyptians and their congeners knew exactly what the trick was. But, above all, Dulles had failed to exploit an available means of public rebuff in majestic halls. By abstaining, he could have called world attention (since he was incessantly concerned for a "decent respect for the opinions of mankind") to the United States government's disapproval of Nasser's policies and behavior, and have made Nasser himself realize that America resented his treatment of her closest allies. The very fact that a practice is usual means that acting unusually would be regarded as a manifest mark of feeling, possibly salutary when dealing with an unscrupulous culprit.

Now, another problem that faced Britain and France and the United States was that of the form their own resolution should take. A tug of war went on among the U.N. delegates of these countries in New York and among the governments in Washington, London, and Paris on this subject. The British and the French wished to press the issue of international operation of the Suez Canal in the form of the eighteen-power proposals. They were America's proposals just as much as theirs! This move would force Egypt to state its attitude to the proposals in open debate. Britain and France were not seeking the interpretation of the treaties in the first place: they were sure of their own interpretation. What they demanded was that the Security Council should redress the injustice done to them. Their legal position remained the same, it must be emphasized, as Dulles himself had expounded and advocated at the first London Conference.

Two ideas now spurted up in the fertile and suspicious mind of Secretary Dulles. First, were his allies sincerely seeking a solution *not* by force, or were they prescribing a formula for a settlement, so couched that it must be rejected, without an alternative in view that might be acceptable? He was now full of misgiving as a result of what he believed was Eden's deception on September 21, and of the military concentration on Cyprus that was developing at full speed!

He induced his allies to include in their resolution a reference to SCUA as well as to the eighteen-power proposals. He also softened their resolution by getting them to avoid terms like "international participation" in the management of the Canal or, worse, the word "control." This was definitely to retreat, as the shape of the resolution finally put to the vote demonstrates. Dulles simply would *not* try boldness in support of justice. He believed that justice would be unobtainable in the Security Council; he believed that it would fail against Nasser's determination; he believed that if it were tried successfully it might provoke a war, and that if it failed it would also provoke a war. Justice, therefore, took a distinctly subordinate place in his efforts, however stoutly his words rang from time to time. Indeed, had it any place at all?

On September 26, the Yugoslav friend of Egypt had moved to have the Egyptian complaint debated concurrently with the Franco-British complaint. The Soviet delegate had even proposed that the Egyptian complaint be given priority, but when this tactic failed, switched to the Yugoslav proposal. The proposal obtained only the votes of these two nations; all the other members of the Council voted against it or abstained.

On October 2, both Selwyn Lloyd and Christian Pineau flew to Washington to confer directly with Dulles, Lloyd coming almost directly from the opening of the SCUA organizing conference. The three then agreed on a resolution, which must surely be regarded as reasonable and fair and dispassionately phrased. It consisted of two main parts: the Suez Canal should be managed in accordance with certain principles, six in all, and there should be established an international system, on the lines of the eighteen-power proposal or SCUA, to carry them out. Dulles and his staff played a large part in this final shaping of the resolution, but also full credit is due to Britain and France (who, it must be solemnly repeated, were victims of an act of unscrupulous despoliation), for their amenability to peaceful and legal courses.

The British and French proposed, and they were unanimously supported in this, that Egypt be invited to take part in the coming discussions without a vote—Egypt not being a member of the Security Council. Henry Cabot Lodge made some most peculiar amends to the British and French. The United States' vote for inclusion of the Egyptian counterresolution, he declared, did not mean that his country agreed with Egypt's contention that Britain and France had acted inconsistently with their obligations under the Charter. The American action still left a bad taste in the mouth of the nations which opposed consideration of the Egyptian resolution and a sweet one in Nasser's. Dulles had not dared!

It was later decided to call the Security Council meeting for October 5, to give the various national representatives time to reach New York.

Before examining the proceedings of the Security Council, it is desirable to view the general scene. Ominous, even fatal, new factors were rising in strength. All through the year Israel had endured serious tension and incidents on her borders, caused by incursions and ambushes on her people, with many murders and arson and sabotage, the work of Syrians, Jordanians, and Egyptians. The Israelis from time to time retaliated severely. Both sides sporadically appealed to the officials of the Armistice Commission. During August and September, Nasser organized, trained, and let loose *fedayeen*, alleged volunteer infiltrators, who, mostly under cover of night, pressed marauding raids into Israel, reaching at least as far as Tel Aviv. The Israeli government complained again and again, as it had done for years, to the United Nations. It was suffering from the Arab economic boycott. Its Red Sea port of Elath could not be developed because Egypt had armed the Sinai coast at Sharm el-Sheik with six-inch and three-inch guns to forbid passage through the Straits of Tiran and the Gulf of Aqaba.

Thus the alternative, inferior as it was, to passage through Suez, was also illegally blocked.

Henry Cabot Lodge and the State Department knew very well that organized warfare was being carried on by the Arabs. The United States attitude toward this was bland, as though Israel were a troublesome beggar complaining of an occasional mosquito bite. The Arab assaults became one of Dulles's most serious diplomatic dangers. At any rate, when the Western nations and Egypt submitted their complaints about Suez against each other to the Security Council, Israel asked that she be invited to take part, without a vote, in the proceedings. As Ambassador Abba Eban's letter to the President of the Security Council said, Israel had a "special interest" deriving "from the restrictions placed on the passage of Israeli goods and shipping through the Suez Canal, which violate the central principle of the international convention (of 1888) under which the Canal is operated." But Australia (not without a thought for Britain's interest in the imbroglio of Israel in the Canal, the ignoring of her claims condoned by Britain as well as the U.S.A. and France and so many other countries, anxious for a quiet life) proposed and secured postponement of action on this request until the next meeting.

However, since the West knew that Russia and her satellites were sending considerable quantities of arms, especially jet fighters and bombers, to Egypt, Canada sold twenty-four Saber jet fighters to Israel, valued at $6,000,000, with the assent of the United States government. It was learned then that for some time France also had been shipping Mystère IV fighters to Israel—a total of twenty-four from this source, it is said.

IN FACT, AS WE SHALL SHOW LATER, WHAT WAS PRACTICALLY A MILITARY ALLIANCE BETWEEN FRANCE AND ISRAEL WAS IN ACTIVE MAKING, AND BETWEEN OCTOBER 5 AND OCTOBER 13 WAS SETTLED: ISRAEL WOULD INVADE EGYPT.

Naturally, on hearing the Canadian decision to sell fighters to Israel, the Egyptian Ambassador to Canada expressed in Ottawa his indignation, declaring that Canada's action "added fuel to the already inflamed situation in the Middle East" and mixed the Israeli-Arab dispute in with the Suez crisis. As though these were truly separable! As though Nasser had never concluded an arms deal with Russia in September of 1955! It was reported by Israeli officials that Dulles had actively been an influence in favor of the sales of Canadian arms to Israel. This is most probably true, and Dulles's action was taken with the intention of making Nasser feel the pinch; *but* the pinch was not sharp or long enough. All that the United States would itself ship to Israel was some electronics equipment and light arms. For United States policy still would not permit America to grant heavy armaments to Israel. The reason, as State Department spokesmen told news reporters, was to avoid making the Middle East another battleground of the "cold war." "You see," they continued, with sweet reasonableness, "you see, if the Soviet Union sends supplies to Egypt and then we ship American equipment to Israel, that would give a local conflict just too much of a Soviet-versus-United States flavor! Don't you see?"

Meanwhile, members of the British government were telling the world and Secretary Dulles unmistakably and vigorously that they expected redress.

Macmillan, the strongest advocate within the Cabinet of a punitive treatment of Nasser, arrived in America September 20, en route to a meeting of the World Bank on September 26. He went first to his mother's birthplace near Indianapolis and on September 21 spoke "off the record" at lunch. His remarks were published in the *Indianapolis Star*, September 23. Dulles therefore should have known the terms and temper of Macmillan's resolve as expressed on this occasion. Macmillan's theme was, "Nasser must be stopped!" If not, he vigorously exclaimed, the Middle Eastern oil resources might fall into Nasser's hands. This would lead to a sapping of the strength of the Western European economy and even to the collapse of NATO, which had been built by the U.S.A. as a bulwark against Red aggression. He said, "It would mean war in a matter of months," and by "it," he evidently meant the possibility of Nasser's not being stopped from consolidating his hold on the Canal. "I am confident," he declared, "we can stop Nasser without war, but he must be stopped somehow. There is no possible sign of any settlement yet. . . . If he gets away with his violation of treaties and contracts, Egypt will fall more and more under Nasser's and Russia's domination. We will not say exactly what our next move will be, what cards we hold or when we will play them." The British Government was determined not to travel the path of appeasement; it was determined that the kind of policy that had led to appeasing Mussolini and Hitler should not be followed again.

But Macmillan was giving Dulles a distinct warning. The latter's retreat from SCUA had convinced his allies that he had left them only one way towards tolerable redress, *force*. They intended to use it some day, not yet exactly determined, but to be arranged, and they were trying to tell him their resolve as expressively as they could. He did not or would not understand them.

Selwyn Lloyd was saying, on September 24:

> We are going to the Security Council in good faith. [The duty of the U.N.] is to preserve the rule of law and this, indeed, will be a test of the United Nations as to whether it has the will and the power to preserve justice and uphold international obligations. We maintain that Egypt has broken her international obligations by the

action she took on July 26, but I assure you we will do everything we possibly can to obtain a peaceful solution to this problem, of such importance to our people and many other peoples in Europe and Asia.[3]

It is, at this point, crucial to understand that *the passion* of the British and French peoples and, even more, of their political leaders, *was at a high pitch.* Foreign policy is psychologically not merely the product of the brain; its dominant ingredient is principles springing from conscience and appetite direct from feelings and instincts. This is what makes man. The British and French leaders felt bereaved, despoiled, abandoned, and denied justice. Dulles did not feel this, hardly at all.

In Britain even some Conservative politicians inside and outside the Eden Government (of course, the more extreme) were sharply criticizing that Government for its apparent lack of firmness in domestic as well as foreign policy. Eden was beset with a raging Greek rebellion in Cyprus simultaneously with the trouble in Suez. And the uncertainties produced by these crises, as well as the continual precariousness of British commerce, so dependent on all the hazards of foreign markets, were causing a slump on the Stock Exchange and a loss of sterling. Few politicians will in these circumstances exhibit an oversolicitous sympathy for the leader—even if they are his friends. They want results. If they are of extremer opinions than he is, especially if they own newspapers, they will turn upon him. That is what happened to Eden. He began to be called a "ditherer," and was accused of not showing firm and decisive leadership, of fumbling. Such attacks produce a reaction in a sensitive man at the helm, and the reactions do not entirely evaporate with the obscene epithets Oxford and Cambridge have taught their alumni to use for relief during moments of angry tension. Most exasperated with Eden were a group of extreme Conservatives known as the "Suez rebels," those most hostile to the Anglo-Egyptian Treaty of 1954.[4]

In addition to this opposition from members of his own party, Eden had given a very easily hit target to his Labour critics when he had, weeks ago, called up 20,000 reservists. The United States has had ample opportunity since that time to realize what partisan political mischief an ugly-mooded opposition may cause over such a necessary step. Each man who has been drafted says, "What am I doing here? Why was *I* called up?" The withdrawal of workers from their jobs causes a disorganization at their office or plant, since teamwork is disrupted and the special skills for which they have been drafted into the army are exactly what their job needed. Vote-covetous critics began to manipulate "near-mutiny" in the armed forces.

Among other acid observations on the Suez issue, British and French political commentators noted with some bitterness that Egypt, getting gradually into economic straits, had taken advantage of the International Monetary Fund to get relief. This organization had been established specifically to enable international financial cooperation, *without infringing any nation's sovereignty*. On September 27, the Fund lent Egypt $15,000,000, in "a routine transaction," to tide her over her foreign exchange and payments difficulties. It is true that Egypt had made her quota contribution to the Fund and was entitled to the assistance.

Avid also for sterling, and therefore forced to offset Britain's freeze on her sterling balances, the Egyptian government on September 27 advised all banks in Egypt that inward transfers of currency to Egypt must be in United States or Canadian dollars, free Swiss francs, or other currencies approved by the government's Exchange Control Board. This order hit at Sweden, Denmark, and Norway, who until then had paid their Egyptian debts in sterling. It also put pressure on British citizens living in Egypt and ordinarily in receipt of sterling remittances either to leave the country or to find other currencies. Also, the government required that henceforth all Egyptian goods exported to the United States must be paid for with American dollars —the United States was holding these frozen. It was assumed that Indian rupees would also be accepted, as hitherto.

About September 24 Macmillan arrived in Washington to explore the possibility of assistance from the International Monetary Fund for Britain, should her reserves fall below two billion dollars, regarded as the minimum then for her multifold international needs and services to other countries. She was now planning to seek a short-term dollar loan of $500,000,000 at the proper time to offset the damaging speculation against sterling caused by war scares. It was desired to prevent the pound from falling below $2.78. For this purpose Macmillan saw George M. Humphrey, U.S. Secretary of the Treasury: the American member's vote was required for authorization, although the amounts to which Britain was entitled from her support of the Fund totaled far more than she was asking. Humphrey, as we have already appreciated, played an important part in that disastrous episode of American foreign policy, the rescinding of the Aswan Dam loan, as well as in the hesitations on the financial underpinning of SCUA. He was later to exert financial leverage in the Suez crisis of an even more decisive kind. Macmillan subsequently saw Dulles, and he must on that occasion have reaffirmed the stern determination of his Prime Minister's policy in terms such as those he had used in Indianapolis. Dulles had *no* reason to complain afterwards, "They didn't tell me!"

Furthermore, it appears that around September 26, when Macmillan was in Washington, he told General Bedell Smith, one of Eisenhower's favorite friends, that England would go down against Egypt with flags flying rather than submit to the Suez despoliation.

Bedell Smith, perhaps as hoped, told this to the President. The President then asked Smith, and later repeated the question to Drew Middleton of the *New York Times*, "Now, what do you think Macmillan meant by that?" Was the President only displaying a sense of sardonic humor? Or didn't he really know? It is most possible that Dulles had not been candid with him, in full detail, or that Dulles, being essentially timid, did not face the reality himself. Someone was not relating facts to the public accurately. The President, it seems, was not certain that he was always fully or truthfully informed by the State Department. He had been heard to complain about the State Department, asking, "Do they believe the facts are too much for my dainty ears?"

President Eisenhower, at his press conference on September 27,[5] was not subjected to many queries on the Suez affair. He was politicking and so was everybody else, and therefore the questions were largely on domestic issues. While London and Paris burned, he was more good-naturedly pacific than ever. However, he was asked about the American protests that had been made for some five years, first by the Truman Administration and then by his own, over the blockading of American ships en route to Israel via Suez. If there had been no favorable response from Egypt on these protests, was there any reason to hope, "*if force is not used*," that Egypt would react favorably to the West's request on the administration of the Suez Canal now? Eisenhower's answer was:

> Well, of course, that is a black mark that has stood there for a long time, and I personally think it is most unjust, and I believe it is not in accord with the 1888 Treaty.
>
> Therefore? What ought to happen?
>
> Now, the great hope is this: that the users of the Canal, showing such unanimity in what they believe should be a proper, let's say, set of rules, the procedures to be observed, that Egypt will see that her own best interests lie in the same way. . . . Now if they [the eighteen nations] are successful in getting an *ad hoc* method, a provisional method of operation, and finally can get something that is at least similar to, or let's say, represents the principles made in the first proposal, I would think this particular thing should be cured at the same time.

If and *if* and *if*. . . . But the President either had not been faithfully briefed on the weaknesses of SCUA by Dulles, or he had accepted Dulles's blind faith, or open pretense, that all's well, or he simply did not understand what all the rest of the world was talking about, or he pretended he didn't, because confession would have required the effort and burden of remedial action. As this last would have involved leverage over Nasser which his Secretary of State could or would not entertain and contrive, he spoke as complaisantly as the date, forty days to election day, permitted.

On September 26, Dulles was heavily questioned on Suez.[6] He talked with knowing diplomacy, or with the self-deception that he called "faith," or with an escape from the burdens of mind and spirit, counseling patience, and hope, and some charity. He began with a statement.

> The purpose of the United States in relation to the Suez situation is precisely that which is set forth in the First Article of the Charter of the United Nations, namely to seek a settlement by peaceful means, and in conformity with the principles of justice and international law. Now, *this is not easy to do quickly*. There is not acceptance by all as to what is "just," nor as to the rights of the nations under international law. Therefore, a settlement in accordance with the provisions of the Charter calls for patience and resourcefulness. We are confident that with these qualities there will be an agreed settlement.

But could those qualities confidently be expected of Nasser, some might have asked? That doubt could not have been absent, surely, from Dulles's own mind.

So far the suggestion of a credit for Britain and France of $500,000 from the Import-Export Bank for oil supplies had been calculated only for one year. Supposing it took longer to settle the question of how the Suez Canal was to be run? Dulles did not tell the reporters what he meant by "not quickly." His statement continued:

> Some may ask what are the inducements for the kind of settlement that we seek *if force is not used*. How can a nation be brought to accept a settlement which recognizes the rights of others?
>
> The answer is that no nation can live happily for long or live well without accepting the obligations of interdependence.
>
> When a nation's conduct frightens others, there are inevitable consequences.

For example, tourists would not visit such a country; credit would not be extended to it; big tankers and pipelines would by-pass the Canal. Patience, and Egypt's realization of these penalties of ignoring interdependence, would cause Egypt to recognize *freely* the need of a just solution.

It will be seen that Dulles still had not said in public (as he had never said in private) that force was utterly excluded. But if it was not used, while it was not used, other pressures might apply. He was admitting that without pressure, serious enough to threaten the economic subsistence of Egypt, Nasser would hardly "disgorge." But could Dulles really believe that the appeal to "the obligations of interdependence" could favorably influence an atavistic character like Nasser, with his entourage of colonels as atavistic, as bigoted and egotistical, as he? Dulles stated that there was a "good chance" Egypt would cooperate. He must have known better from his Ambassador in Egypt and, via Eden, from Krishna Menon. Also, he referred optimistically to the proceedings that same afternoon in the Security Council as though he had not done his maximum to block them and then, when he had found this was not possible because of the determination of his allies, to enfeeble them.

If the Egyptian government refused to let SCUA's boats through, would the Secretary send ships around the continent of Africa?

His answer was, "We have no legal power to direct ships to particular voyages." But if they could not get through on "reasonable" terms (what a side-stepping!), they would in fact go around the Cape. If that happened, the U.S.A. hoped the Export-Import Bank "would be ready to play its *normal* role in helping to finance those exports." The meticulous use of the adjective "normal" is worth noting. The Secretary was not going to open up American financial resources except for oil supplies and those from the U.S.A. George Humphrey was watching!

He escaped from a direct question whether he believed that the Users had a legal right "to have a voice in the operation of the Canal." He had in his statement (above) uttered something that sounded like a disagreement over the legal rights in this case. Now he twice evaded the question, the second time definitely. The Users had the right to benefit from the easement across Egyptian territory by the treaty of 1888; and "we believe that they are also entitled to organize to exercise the rights of use and, generally, their rights under the treaty." But he did *not* answer whether they had or they did not have "a voice in the operation." His allies were being abandoned, and they eavesdropped.

As for the construction of alternative pipelines, yes, that might reduce dependence on the Canal. However, the United States *government* was not directly concerned, because the oil companies had the resources to accomplish this as they thought it necessary.

Dulles then was frontally engaged on the question of the payment of tolls. This was his answer: The United States would stop direct payments to Egypt and allow such payments to be made only through the Users' Association. It was intended that SCUA should pay moneys to Egypt to help maintain the Canal (so that, in a way, SCUA would act as agent for a vessel). Vessels flying the United States flag would not pay anything else to Egypt. But this prohibition could not be extended to American-owned ships under Panamanian, Liberian, or other foreign registry—that is, some one-half of all American-owned shipping. United States vessels would no doubt pay via SCUA (if the scheme worked!) and then part of the money would go to

Egypt. This is the basis of Eden's bitter comment that SCUA was to become the agent for collecting dues for Nasser! The condemnation is correct and just.

A question was asked concerning the Egyptian boycott of tankers (among them Norwegian, Danish, and American) and of ships carrying food to Israel, and concerning the incident in which the Egyptians had fired on an American ship in the Gulf of Aqaba a year or so earlier. The Secretary was urged to reply what, if Egypt had chosen to act with such stubbornness in the past, could be expected when a SCUA ship presented itself? It was a decisive question: on it turned peace or war.

Dulles once again laboriously explained that he didn't intend to shoot his way through. "I have excluded that, so far as that concerns any *present* United States policy." Was the inclusion of the word *present* expected to exercise an influence on Nasser's mind? Dulles retreated to the vantage point of his hopes, as stated earlier in his opening passages. "I believe if we are patient, resourceful, persistent, we can count on these pressures having some positive effect. But I do not believe that the situation is such *now* as to call for any drastic action like going to war." Not *now?* When, then . . . ?

He was trapped on the statement he had made on September 13 that if a ship was refused passage through the Canal and attacked it would have the right to defend itself. Well, merchant ships didn't carry arms; so drop the question!

Under interrogation, Dulles made it clear that SCUA had no powers of collective action of an obligatory nature. In joining it, a nation did *not* commit itself to acting in unison with other member nations—in using the Cape, for example. Each nation would exert pressure on its own shipping companies, if it wanted to. SCUA could not prevent vessels from using the Canal. "We cannot create, nor do we attempt to create, any universal boycott of the Canal." This was a radically different version of SCUA from its original form. The nonobligatory (that is, the useless) character of the organization was now confirmed.

Yes, Dulles thought out loud, yes, "but because one ship was diverted wouldn't necessarily mean that all would be diverted. Any ships that couldn't get through the Canal would *presumably* go around the Cape." "I suppose. . . ." If a master of a ship wanted an Egyptian pilot, well, that was that, you could not make him take SCUA's pilots, *but*, mind you, something could be done about prohibiting a ship's master from paying dues. But, answered the news reporter, doesn't it amount to very little money, since you could not control ships of Panamanian or Liberian registry? "That is a fact." Then Dulles added a comment that produced dismay: "But, bear in mind, that the amount of money which Egypt gets out of the Suez Canal is *not* a major factor in the Egyptian economy, and the pressures which could be exerted by going around the Canal would be relatively little."

What, then, was all the vaunting of SCUA about, if detouring the Canal would make so little difference to Egypt's economy? Also, the Secretary suddenly gave birth to another idea, why, again it is impossible to fathom, unless he wished to show how strong, even invulnerable Nasser really was: ". . . ships will be transferred maybe to a registry which makes it easier for them to go through the Canal, and there always will be as long as the Canal is open—there will always be a certain amount of revenue to Egypt from that source. Perhaps, it won't be quite as much but, on the other hand, the burden on Egypt will not be quite as much either."

If Egypt "got away with it" would Nasser's victory be followed by the nationalization of the oil concessions and then the abrogation of Western bases in the Arab countries?

Dulles rejected the possibility of Egypt "getting away with it." What were his reasons? He merely repeated the inadequate opinion that Egypt would find it not to be good business to deny the implications of "international interdependence."

Let us reflect on this answer for a moment. A commonly observed and marked propensity of the Secretary was to procreate rather glittering, brave-sounding words instead of an effective policy. "Massive deterrence"; "targets of our own choosing"; "liberation"; "disgorge"; "boycott"; "unleashing"; "on the brink"; and now he flourished "interdependence."

He was unable under questioning by the reporters to propose any effective practical way of bringing Nasser to task except "in the long run," and by the consequences we have already listed.

> We live, all of us, in an interdependent world, and you cannot deny the principle of interdependence in one respect without suffering from that denial in a whole lot of other respects, and the consequences in the long run, of persistence in this course, to Egypt would be very bad.

He could not possibly tame Nasser by his reasoning; nor could it possibly any longer beguile his allies. They were then saying among themselves, "What is he talking about? He has not taken our hardships to heart. He has merely made them the occasion for sermons. We had better go our own way, whatever the path of justice happens to be as we see it. It is really no use talking to him any longer about it." Surely, in a world where the Soviet bloc would help Nasser, Dulles had lost his bearings?

When he was asked whether Israel was not qualified for participation in SCUA, he was at once ready with a practical answer. "The provisional view" taken in London was that membership was based on "one million net tons or more of shipping through the Canal during the prior calendar year, or a pattern of trade which showed approximately 50 per cent or more dependence on the Canal. If those are adopted, as seemed to be forecast by the talks of the second London Conference of the eighteen, *then Israel would not be eligible to be a member*." Of course not! Thus, the problem had been soberly and judiciously thought through even down to the specific use of the adjective *calendar*, in case anyone should be mistaken about what a year meant—e.g., fiscal year, or some other kind of year. The joker was, of course, that SCUA was not going to have *any* facilities!

It was the performance of a mind exceedingly troubled, one that had stumbled into a thicket of forces too many and too thorny to disentangle without forceful pressure at a likely point. In considerable agony of mind, by now, Dulles could not find that point. It would not be fortunate for the Secretary's permanent reputation if the reason for this failure were wholly or in part a preoccupation with the results of the coming Presidential election.

The last question in this conference may be given verbatim with the answer.

> *Question:* Mr. Secretary, there has been a new outbreak of border incidents between Jordan and Israel. Do you see in this new situation any danger of an adverse impact on the efforts to get a Suez Canal settlement?
>
> *Answer:* Well, I deplore and regret the outbreak of additional border incidents. They seem to indicate the non-acceptance of the principles for which the Secretary General of the United Nations strove when he undertook his recent mission to that part of the world. At the moment I do not see any likelihood of a direct relationship of nationalization [*this situation?*] * to the Suez Canal situation. Conceivably, one might develop, but, so far, the two issues have been rather independent of each other.

Conceivably! Distinctly so. For about this time Ben Gurion of Israel saw his nation's existence threatened by Egypt, Syria, Jordan, Iraq, and Saudi Arabia. He did not intend to wait as long to save his people as Israel had waited and pleaded for the United Nations to implement its own 1951 unanimous resolution on free transit through the Suez Canal.

Eden's judgment that he was right to go to the United Nations was at this point reinforced, according to his own account, by two events. Macmillan reported from Washington about September 21 that little could be expected from Panama and Liberia on the withholding of Canal dues, especially since Panama had virtually lined up with Egypt. Also, he reported, the State Department was convinced that

* Transcript unclear as Dulles's articulation unclear.

six months of economic pressure on Nasser would squeeze him into compliance with British and French requirements. Eden's experts didn't believe it.

Furthermore, Britain regarded support of its own national policies by the countries of the British Commonwealth as a cardinal, if not always a totally indispensable, principle (the support was not necessarily required to be unanimous either in number or degree of acceptance of policies). Thus Eden derived encouragement from a speech given by Prime Minister Menzies in the Australian House of Representatives on September 25. Menzies had concluded a remarkable survey of the Suez issue in these words, words that deserve careful pondering by the student of international politics.

> First: Negotiation for a peaceful settlement by means of an honourable agreement. So far, we have tried this without success. Our failure, let me repeat and emphasize, has not been due to any unfairness or illiberality on our side, but to a dictatorial intransigence on the other. Should we continue to negotiate on a watered down basis in a spirit which says that any agreement is better than none? I cannot imagine anything more calculated to strengthen Colonel Nasser's hand or weaken our own.
>
> Second: Putting on of pressure by a co-operative effort on the part of user nations. Colonel Nasser must be brought to understand that his course of action is unprofitable to his country and to his people and that he is abandoning the substance for the shadow. This is one of the great merits of the Users' Association now established by the second London Conference. The more canal revenue is diverted from the Egyptian Government the less will the Egyptian people believe that it pays to repudiate.
>
> Should the United Nations, by reason of veto, prove unable to direct any active course of positive action, we may find ourselves confronted by a choice which we cannot avoid making. I state this choice in stark terms:
>
> (a) We can organize a full-blooded programme of economic sanctions against Egypt, or
>
> (b) We can use force to restore international control of the canal, or
>
> (c) We can have further negotiations, provided we do not abandon vital principles, or
>
> (d) We can "call it a day," leave Egypt in command of the canal, and resign ourselves to the total collapse of our position and interests in the Middle East with all the implications for the economic strength and the industrial prosperity of the nations whose well being is vital to ours.
>
> This, I believe, is a realistic analysis of the position. It has been for me an astonishing experience to find that there are people who reject force out of hand, reject economic action on the ground that it is provocative and so, being opposed to action of either

> kind, are prepared to accept new tyranny with regret, perhaps, but without resistance. Such an attitude is so inconsistent with the vigorous tradition of our race that I cannot believe it commands any genuine and informed public support.

Of course, when Eden and Lloyd visited Paris on September 25 and 26, they were almost overwhelmed with recriminations against Dulles, the United Nations, and the Users' Club. The French as a corporate personality of masses, parties, and leaders are generally more skeptical about world international justice than the British and much more so than the Americans. Also, they had more to lose, Algeria, than either, by any false trust they might repose in international institutions. And the Frenchmen talking, by the way, were Socialists; but they were Socialists in office, not like their British counterparts filling a role of opposition, without responsibility for action to preserve and enhance their people's welfare. Eden countered the French desire for "action at an early date," with the admonition that "we must first have recourse to the United Nations and do our best there." Eden has summarized as follows the agreement reached:

> The Foreign Secretary and I undertook, however, that, if the Security Council showed itself incapable of maintaining international agreements, Britain would not stand aside and allow them to be flouted. If necessary we would be prepared to use whatever steps, including force, might be needed to re-establish respect for these obligations. The French ministers agreed, though with some reluctance, to try out all the resources of the Security Council, on the strict understanding that there should be no abandonment of the original proposals approved by the eighteen Powers. This was an attitude with which we were ourselves in full agreement.[7]

This meeting was also the scene of a Franco-British show-down about Israel, of crucial importance; it is analyzed later (Chapter 13).

When Eden returned to London, he received another disquisitious letter from the ever-just Soviet Prime Minister. It repeated the usual spurious arguments about the eighteen-power proposals, Egypt's sovereignty, and Britain's course of action since July 26. The letter prompted Eden to cable President Eisenhower at length, on October 1, 1956. Eisenhower and Dulles should have known from this message that if they had hitherto been "nimble" about the gaining of time (while their allies were losing it) time was now fast running out. With this cable in their hands they had no cause whatever to be ignorant of the fact that their allies intended something drastic and were beseeching them for help—even help in abolishing the necessity for it.

Eden's cable ran:

> You can be sure that we are fully alive to the wider dangers of the Middle East situation. They can be summed up in one word —Russia. . . .

There is no doubt in our minds that Nasser, whether he likes it or not, is now effectively in Russian hands, just as Mussolini was in Hitler's. It would be as ineffective to show weakness to Nasser now in order to placate him as it was to show weakness to Mussolini. The only result was and would be to bring the two together.

No doubt your people will have told you of the accumulating evidence of Egyptian plots in Libya, Saudi Arabia and Iraq. At any moment any of these may be touched off unless we can prove to the Middle East that Nasser is losing. That is why we are so concerned to do everything we can to make the Users' Club an effective instrument. If your ships under the Panamanian and Liberian flags would follow the example of those under your flag that would greatly help.

I feel sure that anything which you can say or do to show firmness to Nasser at this time will help the peace by giving the Russians pause. As usual I send you my thoughts in this frank way.[8]

To this Eisenhower, I am directly informed, replied by a letter—but not until October 11. The lapse of time was unconscionable, when time meant so much to the allies on both sides of the Atlantic. Perhaps Dulles found it expedient to stall, to "see how the dust would settle" as the Security Council went into session, to keep his cards close to his chest, to act in accord with all those metaphors men invoke when they wish to hide their thoughts or avoid making up their minds to assume responsibility for action. When he did reply, Eisenhower merely said that he deeply deplored Bulganin's letter to Eden; it was forbidding, and hardly the kind that should be sent from one Chief of State to another. He also deplored the suggestions in the press both in the United States and abroad (meaning London and Paris) that the allies were working at cross purposes.

I can report, on evidence from one of the most honorable diplomats in international politics since 1945—and he is *not* American or European—that *the Administration then knew or could have easily inferred (if it had wanted to stop playing Pollyanna) that, failing redress at the United Nations, America's allies would fall on Nasser at a convenient time.*

I re-emphasize what I have just reported, regarding Eden's warning, his appeal, and the Administration's attitude of tinkering, trifling within the aura of Faith.

But the day after Eden's cable was dispatched, on October 2 (this allowed ample time for colloquies between the President and Dulles), Dulles, of course, obeyed his compulsion to appear before another press conference—the second in less than a week.

It should be remembered that Eden's cable of October 1 to the President (and thus indirectly to Dulles too) was private. Eden had surrendered himself to their judgment without the public's being brought in to redress any unfairness the President and the Secretary might show to his cause. Another pertinent fact is that the Security Council, to which the British and the French looked for justice, was to meet on October 5, only four days after the cable was dispatched. And Britain and France had been assured all along of American support for their case on the basis drafted in conference with Dulles, in agreement with Dulles, and composed of proposals which he himself had declared were not only just, but the alternative to a probable and even just use of force.

It is uncertain whether Dulles's pedagogic loquacity overcame his prudence, or whether he now spoke out deliberately in public retort to Eden's private cable and even more private suspicions that war was afoot. But Dulles at this press conference practically committed a declaration of hostility towards his allies—at the wrong time, in the wrong forum, in the hearing of envoys who would make wrong use of it. The words as spoken and immediately published were a massive axe sundering the ties that held America and its Western allies in cooperation and mutual help. At once, Dulles caused a most intense international agitation; his ideas, without any doubt at all, added gasoline-soaked fuel to the gathering tinder of war.

Now, Dulles's answers to questions at press conferences were not entirely spontaneous and improvised. He had worked for most of October 1 on the probable questions and the answers to be given at this conference. It is also highly possible that his Assistant Secretary for Public Affairs planted questions, much as this is done from time to time at Presidential news conferences.

The press conference was held at 11 A.M. October 2, or 5 P.M. London time.[9] Dulles was asked:

> There have been rather widespread reports since the ending of the second London Conference, where there was a decision to set up the users' association, that there is a split on the one hand between the United States and the British and the French on the other, or at least a difference in degree of approach. Now could you comment on that and tell us how you view it at least?

The Secretary's answer was in two parts: one referred to SCUA and the difference on that plan. His answer on SCUA will be reported later. For the second part had to do with wider and far more serious differences.

Let us first look at the answer Dulles gave as taken down verbatim by the *New York Times* correspondent at the news conference. It ran:

> There is some difference in the approaches to the Suez Canal problem. That difference relates perhaps to some rather fundamental things. In some areas the three nations are bound together by treaties, such as the Atlantic pact area, the three nations are bound by treaty to protect. In those the three areas stand together.

> Other problems relate to other areas and touch the so-called problem of colonialism in some way or other. On these problems, the United States plays a somewhat independent role.[10]

As soon as this was uttered, the scoop-pursuing reporters dashed off to the telephones and teletype machines, so that the world might soon know that *à propos* of the Suez question, differences of a "fundamental nature" split the United States from its European allies—and the world was reached by the Secretary's words.

Dulles's intimates, sitting in the conference room or nearby, immediately realized the trouble he had gotten himself into, especially when they saw the English newspaper correspondents taking special notice. Within an hour or so after Dulles had reached this point in the conference, the State Department had prepared its revised version of his observations. It was disseminated at once, particularly fast to Ambassador Winthrop Aldrich in London, in the hope that it would supersede the original reports.

Now, Dulles and his editorial associates had made his observations read:

> Now there has been some difference in our approach to this problem of the Suez Canal. This is not an area where we [the United States, Britain, and France] are bound together by treaty. Certain areas we are by treaty bound to protect, such as the North Atlantic Treaty area, and there we stand together and I hope and believe always will stand absolutely together.
>
> There are also other problems where our approach is not always identical. For example, there is *in Asia and Africa*, the so-called problem of colonialism. Now there the United States plays a somewhat independent role. You have this very great problem of the shift from colonialism to independence which is in process and which will be going on, perhaps, for another fifty years, and there I believe the role of the United States is to try to see that that process moves forward in a constructive evolutionary way and does not either come to a halt or take a violent revolutionary turn which would be destructive of very much good.
>
> I suspect that the United States will find that its role, *not only today but in the coming years*, will be to try to aid that process, without identifying itself 100 per cent either with the so-called colonial powers or with the powers which are primarily and uniquely concerned with the problem of getting their independence as rapidly as possible. I think we have a special role to play and that perhaps makes it impractical for us, as I say, to identify our policies with those of other countries on whichever side of that problem they find their interest.

Thus, the original words and tone of antagonism were wrapped in a cocoon of silken exculpation. The present tense was changed to the past tense. The reference to "Africa and Asia" as I have italicized it, was added to claim the severance of the Secretary's remarks from the present Canal dispute and to add an air of generalization; in all, a kind of speculative mood was invoked, as, for example, in the phrase, "not only today but in the coming years." "Fundamental things" was dropped.

The *New York Times*, as well as other American newspapers, was incensed at the Secretary's tactics. In its issue of October 3 (page one), that newspaper showed that he could not pull the wool over the eyes of everybody. It accurately observed that up to that time, the formal United States position had been to chastise Egypt for raising a false alarm, whenever the latter country charged that proposals for international management of the Canal was a new form of colonialism. Now the United States appeared to be supporting that very point of view.

Dulles had had no reason to do anything more in answering the reporter than to stick to the question regarding SCUA. Why had the colonial issue been dragged in? To suggest that the Suez conflict was a colonial matter? This implication would, of course, bring warm comfort to the Arab nations, to Nasser, to nations like Indonesia and Ceylon. But—would it help a just solution of the Suez dispute? What had colonialism to do with a violation of international law, with the rape of what, according to the Secretary himself on so very many solemn occasions, was an international institution? The Suez controversy was not a dispute between a power exerting imperial rule and a colony seeking to free itself from such rule, any more than refusing a loan for a dam was. It was a dispute between a sovereign nation, Britain, and another sovereign nation, Egypt, about the violation of a treaty made long ago, made multilaterally, and without duress, for the common benefit of all nations in the world. If it was "colonial," how far back in history were modern nations to go in the revision of their treaties? Did "colonialism" include the Panama Canal?

Why did the U.S. Secretary of State himself drag in the kind of ideological theme which he had repeatedly begged should be avoided by all parties because it would jar the practical examination of the problem of Suez in itself? Now, gratuitously it seemed, he was intruding it. Was it an election stroke by a man who normally claimed that it was improper for the Secretary of State to make American foreign policy the football of party strife? Why should he not vie with the Democratic campaign leaders and say that he and the President were just as ardent anticolonialists as they were?

Or was Dulles pursuing that obsession of his, to vie with the Soviet Union on every possible occasion? Was he preparing the way for an attempt to win over the Afro-Asians at the coming United Nations proceedings? Was he bowing to the incessant drumfire of accusation by many former and present colonies that Israel was a "beachhead of colonialism and imperialism" in the Middle East, serving Britain, France, and the U.S.A.?

Was it tit-for-tat because his allies had appealed to the United Nations against his will? This could be. Is the explanation of this diplomatic *gaffe* that it suddenly came into his head during the news conference? It was not in America's national interest to blurt out his prejudice against colonialism *then*, when, as he claimed, he was seeking conciliation.

Moreover, the minimum courtesy expected of an ally is that he be fair. Dulles may well have been irritated by French action in Algeria, and by British fighting against the Greek Cypriotes in Cyprus (there was a substantial Greek lobby in New York and Washington, D.C., and big Greek communities in those and other large cities, all votes!). But how could he not add, in fairness to the British, mention of the remarkable advances they had made since 1945 in decolonization, leaving their colonies in every case far better educated, far better able to govern and administer themselves, far better off economically, than they might have been had the British never settled in those lands? Dulles had not breathed a word about British withdrawal from Palestine; Malaya; the Gold Coast; India; Burma; Ceylon; the British preservation of Sudanese independence against the claims of Egypt.

Eden and Britain irked the sick consciences of many State Department officials. Indeed, one of Dulles's closest assistants tried to defend the Secretary's folly by blaming the European allies for "behaving like schoolboys" in "brewing the elements of trouble" in showing chagrin at Dulles's talk. But who had supplied the grapes for the brew? How could they know Dulles was not serious in his charge, if, indeed, he was not serious? And what a charge, that the British and French press were merely "self-serving"! What a boomerang accusation to make!

The harder State Department officials strained to smooth over the blunder, the more furious its victims grew. They were especially angry when these officials, leaving out the reference to "fundamental" differences, and so on, told them that all Dulles had meant was that the Suez canflict was *one* example of a "somewhat different approach" and "colonialism" was another.

It might seem that men who debate so furiously over the words used by one of their colleague-statesmen are trifling. But a war over a word is a war over an idea and that kind of war is a struggle for power, prestige, honor, and interests. As Justice Oliver Wendell Holmes said in *Gitlow* v. *State of New York* in 1925, "Every idea is an incitement. . . . Eloquence may set fire to reason." The American Ambassador in London was overwhelmed by the resentment that welled up throughout Britain. Dulles's observations exacerbated anti-

Americanism where it existed in that nation; it sowed it where it did not; it impaired future cooperation between the two countries. Those in Britain who were pro-American suffered the deepest offense. Labour Party leaders said in private that the British could not found their foreign policy on the leadership of the United States because American foreign policy was unpredictable.

The question was naturally asked by political leaders and publicists whether the Western alliance was one of only limited liability on the part of each of the partners for the security of the others? They doubted, if so, whether the United States deserved assistance in Europe against the U.S.S.R. That assistance, they excitedly argued, was a holding operation favoring the American position in the Far East against Communist China and Russia's eastern Siberian lands. Why should America's allies shoulder her burden, if they were treated so shabbily by her Secretary of State when their vital interests were involved—outside Europe, to be sure, but close enough (Turkey, Greece, etc.) to be an integral part of the single defense area?

In Paris, *Le Figaro* on October 3 protested, "If the Suez crisis has taken a bad turn, it is because the support of our American friends has been completely denied us from the beginning." (This statement shows how one exaggeration produces another.) The respectable opinion of the Netherlands bitterly observed that it was the leaning of Dulles towards the nationalism of men like Nasser that had actually helped to foment the seizure of Suez. The Washington correspondent of the *Times* of London (also on October 3) correctly noticed that the official emendation of the Dulles speech heightened the impact of his implied association of the Suez dispute with the issue of colonialism. He emphasized, as we have already done, that these observations of Dulles came "dangerously close to disavowing the whole course of American reaction to the Suez crisis in which Mr. Dulles was the first to deny that his efforts to retain some semblance of international control over the Canal could be seen as a new form of colonialism."

On that same day, the *Times*, representing by now (in contrast to its very early stand) a policy of peaceful if stern demand for international management, not force, took Dulles to task quite grimly in an editorial called "Distorting the Issues":

> Some of his words at yesterday's Press Conference can hardly claim the indulgence of that understanding [the imminence of the Presidential election] any longer. They will be deeply and bitterly resented by America's friends this side of the Atlantic.

In a listing of Dulles's errors at his conference, the editorial demurred that

> . . . the issue is not an issue of colonialism but one of elementary international law and order affecting a waterway which is many

> times as important as the Panama Canal is for North America. . . . To speak of it [the cleavage between colonial powers and those seeking independence] in this context is to misrepresent the Suez issue itself. Such gross misrepresentation at such a moment, with the Security Council debate imminent, is a grave disservice to Anglo-American unity.

Let us turn back a moment, and look at Dulles's responses on the Suez Canal Users' Association to the newsmen on October 2. (We have noted earlier that this was one part of his statement at that time.) The reader has facts enough to judge whether the Secretary was being candid. His answer, unadulterate, but paraphrased by the *New York Times* reporter present, was this:

> There is no detectable change in the formula for the users' association between what it now is and what was planned, at least as far as the United States is concerned, and, as was made known to the British and French before the project was publicly launched. In private consultations a charter of the users' association was drafted and what is coming into being today is almost exactly what was planned then. There is talk that the teeth were pulled out of it. There were no teeth in it.[11]

When this was amended, and some would say doctored, it appeared in this more sophisticated form:

> As far as the formula for the users' association is concerned there is no detectable change, *at least not detectable to me*, between what it now is and what was planned, at least as far as the United States is concerned, and, as *we* made it known to the British and the French before the project was publicly launched *in any way*. There was drawn up a draft of the charter, so to speak, the articles of the users' association, and what is coming into being today is almost exactly what was planned at that time. There is talk about the "teeth" being pulled out of it. There were never "teeth" in it, *if that means the use of force*.

The italics, especially the last-applied, demonstrate Dulles's dexterity. His allies did not find it to their taste or advantage. And where was the boycott?

It should be added that at this news conference one more rumor of the power the United States might exert over Nasser was dispelled: the report that American cotton surpluses would be put on the world market and so depress the Egyptian prices. It was now explained by the Secretary that the length of the American cotton staple differed from that of the Egyptian, so that the former could not really compete with the latter. Besides, said the Secretary, "We are not now engaging in any economic war against Egypt." What had happened to the "inexorable" consequences of not admitting "interdependence"?

The actual breaking point between France and Britain on the one hand and the United States on the other over the ultimate action to be taken against Egypt, failing a decent settlement by negotiation, most probably occurred between the end of the SCUA meeting in London, September 22, and the news conference held by Dulles on October 2. This circumstance marked the low point of desperation, futility, and loss in the whole affair. (Perhaps the break was delayed until some time during the proceedings at the United Nations; but as the *Economist*, so eminently fair in its outlook, thought, the news conference was the height of ambivalence in American policy.)

A reasonable judgment seems to be that, when the matter came to the United Nations on October 5, peace was hanging only by a thread. It could still be secured, but only by the most powerful pleas of Dulles, the most extraordinary, even miraculous endeavors by him and Henry Cabot Lodge. Perhaps it could not have been achieved even by these means, given the forces arrayed against the West.

Here let us assess the effects of Dulles's folly at the press conference. First, the occasion offers a prime example of what may be termed Dulles's deficiency in imagination. Here was he in supreme, almost unqualified, charge of America's vital interests, in which perhaps the most important was the preservation and even the strengthening of the NATO alliance. He was, moreover, as so many observers of his behavior have remarked, deficient in empathy: the instinctive ability to enter into the feelings of others, to see the matter from their point of view, and so make his point, if it needed to be pressed, as to avert the loss of their readiness to confide in him.

Once again, one reflects on the seeming impossibility of the avoidance of miscalculation, not merely among enemies or rivals, but among allies and friends, and, at that, nurtured in the same mother tongue.

It was difficult for anyone to know where, actually, the Secretary of State stood. When Drew Middleton had visited Washington a few days earlier, on September 27, and talked with Dulles, the latter was breathing fire and slaughter against Nasser (privately), threatening, among other things, that he would even stop CARE packages going to Egypt, and use SCUA to bring him down. Then, as we have seen, within a few days, just over the weekend, he had shifted from this ground, assuming that this *was* his ground.

The truth is, I think, that Dulles was now losing his personal moral assets and resources fast. He was about to come up against the real crunch in the Security Council. He would be compelled to speak up and be counted. He used two tactics, and both of them were very clever, although not necessarily in his nation's interest in the long run, or even in a run just beyond a month or two.

The first tactic was the one he had just adopted, perhaps instinctively, as a man grasps at any straw; or perhaps (as Machiavelli advised) craftily—hoping either not to get found out, or if found out, to have so muddied the waters that others might drown, but not he. This tactic consisted of side-stepping the true issue, which was the search for some way to coerce Nasser (the subject he had discussed with Drew Middleton) in order to exact a fair settlement. Dulles brought up another issue, colonialism, by which he could divert men's minds from the true one, and simultaneously throw a certain odium on his allies, who were demanding so much from him and from his President by contemplating war.

The second tactic was to get the Security Council meetings held *off* the record. This arrangement had marked advantages: the most bellicose feelings could be expressed in private rather than shared with an onlooking and inciting world spurred on by the news media. But, from another point of view, one so often advocated by Dulles himself, keeping the hearings confidential extinguished the possibility of molding "world opinion" on the issues. He had all along been in favor of promoting the allies' claims by bringing in the whole world to witness the protracted conferences on the issue, in the hope that this would help to bring Nasser to his senses. Of course, he was mistaken about the nature of "world opinion"—its composition, its advent, and its effect. But this was a cause he had espoused. Now he hastened to abandon it; he put all his energies and intellect behind assuring a discussion in private. For this move he can hardly be criticized. If he had to choose between his evaluation of world opinion as a "moral force" or "power" on men with consciences like Nasser's (it had proven totally ineffective for this purpose), and an attempt to solve the problem in quiet and privacy, he was supremely right in choosing the latter.

War and peace now hung in trembling balance. Could the United Nations render justice to Britain and France, could it restore the international rights disrupted by the Egyptian government's illegal violation of treaties?

12. THE UNITED NATIONS FAILS

TWO THRUSTS OF HUMAN PURPOSE AND POWER NOW CLASHED IN IMMEDIATE and desperate struggle—an attempt at the United Nations to find an answer to the British and French requests for justice, and active French arrangements to make war on Nasser if justice should be denied. French and British patience and self-control were running out fast. During the week beginning October 5, while the United Nations was at work, the French were formulating a military agreement with Israel, at French urging and in consideration of Israel's mortal necessity, to be put into effect if the United Nations should fail. The French did not bargain at the United Nations in bad faith; they bargained with consuming doubt about Dulles and with a waxing finality of trust in the eventual use of arms. By October 10, the military agreement had been established, and by that time, Selwyn Lloyd and Eden knew that war was in the wind. During these days, Dulles strongly suspected that war was being contemplated, partly because he privately felt that his own efforts so far had failed, and partly because his allies had talked war to him ever since July 31. But he could get no firm information, because Mollet and Pineau had not yet made the ultimate resolve; and Eden and Lloyd were still not yet engaged, even if they were talented at guessing. The Western allies were not yet beyond the point of no return, but they were close to it and prepared to face it. All three, Dulles, Selwyn Lloyd, and Pineau, tried desperately for a peaceful outcome in the U.N. proceedings that followed, but, as all along, their interests were different, and the significance of their objectives were far from the same.

By October 3, the Foreign Ministers of the principal nations were in New York. Dr. Mahmoud Fawzi, Egyptian Foreign Minister, now represented his country, wearing suits of English pinpoint cloth as well tailored as Dulles's. Fawzi was one of the subtlest of intelligences among all the foreign offices of the world, and one of the ablest debaters.

Henry Cabot Lodge, Jr., now advanced into the center of the stage with Secretary Dulles. He had long worked closely with Dag Hammarskjold on attempts at easing tensions in the Middle East, most especially during April and June of 1956. Neither Hammarskjold nor Lodge relished the prospect of the Soviet's intervention in either open debate or private negotiations to follow. The object of Hammarskjold's diplomacy was to make a bridge of the United Nations on which Fawzi's influence with Nasser, and America, Britain, and France could meet, for he realized the desperate nature of the situation by this date. He did not look with any joy on the possibility of a crisis which might endanger Western positions in the Middle East.

Dulles at once urged on Selwyn Lloyd the usefulness of private meetings between the principals. Lloyd finally proposed to the United Nations closed meetings of the Council and private meetings of the principals. In return for his pliancy he obtained Dulles's assurance of American support of the British-French resolution. On October 5, Dulles discussed the various issues individually with Lloyd, Pineau, Shepilov, and Fawzi. He announced to the Security Council America's support for the British and French resolution, basing himself on the position to which he had committed himself at the first London Conference. He talked to newsmen: he was sarcastic about the "buzzing about" of Menon; he did not think that if the United Nations now failed violence was the only result possible; he still entertained the idea that if Nasser was recalcitrant, many sanctions would fall on Egypt, but he did not state precisely what these might be.

He did not speak again until October 9; but Lodge kept him fully informed of all transactions.

In these, Selwyn Lloyd, who introduced the British and French resolution [1] in an hour-long speech,[2] firmly and clearly reiterated the position of the two nations as it had been all along—before, during, and after the first London Conference and the eighteen-power proposal. The determination he expressed was, also, perhaps, not new, but it was firm determination, as can be seen from the peroration:

> In the face of a problem whose features are so clear and so unequivocal, no half measures will do. No admissible settlement can be arrived at on the mere pretext that it would keep the peace for the time being. The United Nations Charter considers that there is no genuine peace without the maintenance of justice and international law; it thus recognizes that circumstances may arise where weakness is more perilous than firmness. We are eager for a peaceful settlement, but we can accept no solution which

would enshrine the accomplished fact and recognize a chief of state's right to free his country from international undertakings to which it had freely subscribed.

Pineau followed Lloyd, speaking in the same resolute vein. (He was in the President's chair, since, for the month of October, it was France's turn to occupy it.)

The private meeting behind closed doors was a modern and deliberate recourse to secret diplomacy. It had the characteristic benefits of secret diplomacy, that the men could be candid with each other without being almost immediately punishable or subject to pressure by an uninformed, short-sighted, and emotional public, under the tutelage of editors and commentators or of skirmishing political adventurers, the latter usually concerned with the passions of the moment and oblivious to long-range consequences. Partly at Dulles's prompting, partly on his own initiative, the Secretary General of the United Nations, Dag Hammarskjold, played a considerable part as informal chairman in the private discussions.

Dulles and Selwyn Lloyd conversed often. On October 7, Lloyd again urgently pleaded with Dulles to take immediate action to stop American ships from paying tolls to Nasser. Such a move on the part of the United States would influence the private talks with Fawzi, and make Nasser realize that he was faced by harsh possibilities. Dulles's answer was the parrying and inconsistent one: the same result could be obtained by accelerating the activities of SCUA; so far as his allies was concerned he was bent on putting teeth into it—not tolls! The weakness of Dulles's countersuggestion was that SCUA at that time possessed no strength, and never acquired any later on, and in the nature of the situation, could not. (It had held its organizational meeting in London, October 1.)

Meanwhile, it may be noticed that Nasser had not slackened his efforts to exert pressure on the West. For one thing, he sent Ali Sabry to New York with Fawzi to make sure the allies looked beyond Fawzi to the actual grimness of their situation in the Canal. For another, in case there should be room for misunderstanding, Nasser announced in Cairo on October 7 that "the United Nations would collapse if it supported the British and French plan for international operation of the Canal." When Israel, on October, charged at the United Nations that Egypt had blocked the passage of a total of 103 ships serving her interests, Ali Sabry's answer was immediate: "Israel is a belligerent state and it is only a *matter of logic* that a nation in a state of war with Egypt would be denied the use of the Canal." Thus, it was not a matter of law that Israel would be barred; the Egyptian representatives knew only too well that they were skating on the thinnest ice in such an interpretation of the 1888 Convention; it was *a matter of logic.*

In other words, Egypt's individual nationalist needs commanded the situation. It was not a propitious sign for a settlement with justice and without force. In the background of the U.N. fight to keep the Canal open was Israel's claim to its use. All knew that! Furthermore, host at a reception at the Egyptian United Nations Embassy in New York, Sabry mockingly explained to a reporter that Egypt would agree to international supervision of the Suez Canal only if all the waterways of the world were brought under a similar world organization—but, it would have to be at somebody else's suggestion!

On October 8, Fawzi, whose contribution to a settlement so far had been extremely small, confined mainly to listening and waiting matters out, searching for the weakest joints in the allies' positions, made his first principal speech in the Security Council. It was the speech of one of the most skillful diplomats of our time, and it was made in English that was not only impeccable, but distinguished.

Fawzi set Nasser's tone early by saying that the question of the Suez Canal was "deeply rooted in the struggle between domination and freedom." Those who had expressed approval of the nationalization of the Canal represented no less than two-thirds of the world's population! What was the tactic of the *entente* between Britain and France, except "to see to it, of course, that the now slipping grab of the nineteenth century, when time was slumbering and the sky was dark, should be retrieved, to see to it that the Suez Canal should be finally amputated and severed from Egypt, as if it belonged to anybody or any group, whichever it might be, to deprive any state of a part of its territory."

He then reiterated his government's assurance that "without prejudice to Egypt's sovereignty or dignity, solutions could be found for the critical questions." He proposed that a negotiating body be set up, consisting of representatives of the different views held by the states using the Canal, and that discussions should take place at once to settle the composition, the venue, and the date of such a meeting.

Fawzi was thus virtually saying that, at the moment, he had no concession to make in the direction of the eighteen-power proposals or SCUA, but wanted only to negotiate about negotiation. This was not what Britain and France thought they had come to New York for. As we have seen, they especially realized (as Dulles did not realize or pretended not to realize) that time was *not* on their side.

Fawzi then denounced British and French aggressiveness, and boasted of Egypt's orderly and lawful handling of Canal traffic. He descanted at some length on the legality of nationalization—of course, with all the precedents that favored his case stressed and those that did not thrust out of sight. Most mortifying to the allies was the slick use of legal terminology and argument to gloss over the act of force by which Nasser had seized the Canal. It was slick, truculent, and dangerously defiant. It could have been paraded only by agreement with the Soviet Union which was displaying a faithfulness to Nasser not matched by Dulles's loyalty to Britain and France. Did Fawzi, so self-confident and actually disdainful, almost contemptuous, not reflect that his attitude might very well have dire consequences? If he did, and it is not beyond him and Nasser's henchmen, then the elegant baiting could have been performed with impunity on two grounds: that Russia would support whatever Nasser did to the hilt (and the hilt was what suited Russian interests, even if not Egyptian); and that, as the Egyptians sensed, when it came to the crunch Dulles would *not* be on the side of Britain and France. They had made a fool of Dulles's SCUA by warning him that the arrival of ships at the Canal in the terms he had used would mean war. He then decided to divert the ships!

Fawzi then let Dulles have it with both barrels, on his most sensitive spot: the rescinding of the offer of the Aswan loan.

> The sudden withdrawal, without any notice whatever to Egypt, of all the arrangements which had initially been agreed upon, was accompanied by a vicious campaign against the reputation of the Egyptian economy, aimed at shaking the confidence of the world in it. We thoroughly understand that a bank, for example, has the right to change its mind in relation to the extending of a loan to one firm or the other, although it is questionable that such change of mind should be made in a sudden way which would upset the expectations and the planning of that firm. What would be infinitely worse, nay unthinkable, for the bank to do would be to go around the market telling everybody how bad the books of the firm in question were. Even if such a claim were true, the bank in that case would be suable for defamation and liable to damages.[3]

He concluded by throwing cold water on the resolution introduced by Britain and France, with the promise of American support. He offered for purposes of negotiating further this guidance: the negotiating body should work out a plan that would (1) guarantee for all and for all time freedom of navigation in the Canal; (2) institute a system of cooperation between *the Egyptian authority operating the Canal* (note: the grand question raised by the eighteen powers, led by Mr. Dulles, is not only begged, but is rudely answered in the negative!) and the users of the Canal, taking into full consideration the sovereignty and rights of Egypt (notice the ambiguity of this phrase, as hitherto demonstrated!) and the interests of the users of the Canal; (3) establish a system for the tolls and charges which would guarantee for the users of the Canal fair treatment free from exploitation; (4)

provide for a reasonable percentage of the revenues of the Canal to be allotted especially for improvements.

Fawzi was followed immediately by the Soviet Foreign Minister, Dimitri Shepilov.[4] As forecast by all connoisseurs of the Soviet Union and the United Nations and the small suppliant nations, and by Secretary Dulles especially, the spokesman for the Soviet Union inveighed against the Canal company, "the thoroughly corrupt, imperialist, colonial system." The line of argument, almost the words, certainly the sequence of phrasing, was identical with that of Egypt. What was being sought by the West? "The United States monopolies are seeking to take over the Suez Canal, to establish *de facto* control over its administration. . . ."

Shepilov then introduced a theme which has proven dear to the heart of the new nations. They have swallowed it whole, and recite it whenever it is necessary for them to squeeze out financial assistance from the democratic governments and peoples of the world. They are aided in keeping their own masses loyal to them by such inflammatory vituperation against "foreigners."

> It should be recalled that acts of colonialism are often, nowadays, cloaked in the snow-white robes of disinterested financial and technical aid to economically backward countries. Such acts are often called "non-political," and are supposed to be the product of pure altruism. Experience shows, however, that no matter what form foreign domination may take—whether it appears as a political and military dictatorship or under the disguise of financial control—the essence of colonialism remains the same.

Why had the Western allies appealed to the United Nations? Shepilov supplied a sarcastic parody of the pleas of Britain and France:

> You have urged us to appeal to the United Nations. We have done so. We have appealed to the Security Council. But, as you see, it is powerless, it can do nothing. Negotiations with Egypt are useless. Other steps must be taken. Egypt is guilty. Crucify it!

After this deliberate barrage of provocation, Shepilov affected a reasonable regard for the interests of Britain and France—and the other powers using the Canal. It was essential to enter upon negotiations, and in these Egypt must have full equality of status. The principles would be those which Egypt and India had at various times suggested. Then he added an extremely clever new condition: "The Canal is never to be the theater of hostilities or subjected to blockade." This would have removed the possibliity of any coercive sanction on Egypt and given the Soviet Union a much freer hand in politics concerning the Canal.

Dulles and Lodge were vexed beyond control by the whiplash

sarcasms of Fawzi and Shepilov. Shepilov, in particular, had exhibited an insolence and an arrogance, indeed, a malice, beyond toleration. The Americans issued statements, lodged with the Security Council for the record, protesting the stabs that gave them most pain. Dulles's statement rejected Fawzi's version of the rescinding of the loan for the Aswan Dam. Lodge (Dulles's spokesman) replied thus to Shepilov:

> Having been here almost four years and heard the speeches of the late Mr. Vishinsky, of Mr. Gromyko, Mr. Zorin, and Mr. Sobolev [successive Russian representatives on the Security Council], I can only conclude after hearing Mr. Shepilov's speech today, that the man who writes the speeches is still the same. Even during the most active days of the cold war, no speaker ever attacked the United States from so many angles, all of which are unfair and unjustified, and none of which can be substantiated.
>
> It is a pity that Mr. Shepilov carries the cold war into these delicate Suez negotiations. Let us hope that his better judgment will prevail.

This mild and decent rejoinder could only, of course, give the Russians cause for the heartiest laughter. But the spirit in which the Soviet Foreign Minister approached the Suez conflict, and in the end, finished with it, became etched into the resentment at the injustice felt by the British and French leaders. The Communist Party of the Soviet Union, in Shepilov's parody, had made its own brutal prophecy of what the British and French would attempt to do to secure redress. Its Suez policy thereafter helped to make it come true.

If the Soviet Union could block the way of justice within the United Nations, armed by a veto that had been designed for a nation's own self-protection, but not, surely, for the fulfillment of all policies anywhere in the world deemed pleasant and valuable to the Soviet Union, what, but force, was left to the Western allies—force, or surrender? The fear was freely circulating in the United Nations that if any one country, namely Egypt, had unqualified control of the Canal, then that country could be dominated by the Soviet Union, which would in fact have acquired a stranglehold over the West. Were Secretary Dulles and President Eisenhower afraid to stand up to Russia?

Dulles took the floor on October 9.[5] Before he spoke, he had listened to the speech of Popovic, the Yugoslav Foreign Minister. Dulles asked the members of the Council to remember their obligations: to seek by peaceful means a settlement in accordance with the principles of justice and international law. "We have thus a two-phased responsibility; one aspect relates to peace; the other aspect relates to justice and conformity with law."

He inferentially rejected the charge of aggressive action and intentions made against Britain and France (and others among the users). Two and a half months had gone by since they were deeply aggrieved and endangered, and still they had made no forcible response, but had sought scrupulously under the Charter a peaceful settlement. He listed the various steps already taken (as we have witnessed), six of them: (1) the meeting in London at the beginning of August; (2) the first London Conference; (3) the choosing of the Menzies mission; (4) the mission to Cairo under Menzies' chairmanship; (5) the second London Conference, to establish SCUA—"That was the fifth peace move"; (6) the submission of the conflict by Britain and France to the Security Council.

> Rarely, if ever, in history have comparable efforts been made to settle peacefully an issue of such dangerous proportions. This Council knows it is not dealing with Governments bent on the use of force. Even the most aggrieved have shown their desire to bring about a just solution by peaceful means.

Dulles then turned to the problem of finding a just and legal solution. He insisted on the legality of the treaty of 1888 and of Egypt's concession to the Suez Canal Company of the responsibility of providing the "definite system destined to guarantee the rights of passage under the treaty."

The reader may notice once again Dulles's voluntary interpretation of the treaties and concessions made to establish the rights of the users and the rights and obligations of Egypt. It is essential to realize that if Nasser were not compelled to live up to these rights and obligations, he would be violating what Dulles himself, unprompted by anything but his voluntary study of the instruments, did say were treaty rights. Nasser would be a breaker of a treaty; he would be sinning against the sanctity of international obligations, of international law, in letter and in spirit, in regard to the positive law and to the essential justice of the situation. Moreover, if the United Nations did not uphold this view, then, it too, in spite of the noble terms in which its birth and growth might be eulogized, or the optimistic affection lavished on it, or the claims that it was the best hope the world had for peace and justice—it, too, would be a violator of international law.

Dulles continued with increasing strength and fervor to stress the extent to which Egypt was under international obligation. He quoted from a statement made by the representative of Egypt—again voluntarily, never under duress—before the Security Council, nine years before, in August, 1947, relating to British treaty rights abutting on the Canal. The Egyptian representative had then said:

> The status of the Suez Canal is quite different from that of other artificial waterways which serve as arteries of international communication, for it is fixed by that multipartite international

> agreement to which I have just referred [the Convention of 1888]. The Suez Canal was an international enterprise from the very beginning, and within a few years after it was opened all the principal Powers of Europe joined with the Ottoman Empire, acting for Egypt, to regulate its traffic, its neutrality and its defence.

Seven years after this statement another Egyptian representative, defending Egypt against a charge by Israel that one of her ships, the *Bat Galim*, had been illegally seized by Egypt in the Canal, had said (October 14, 1954):

> The Canal Company which controls the passage, is an international company controlled by authorities who are neither Egyptian nor necessarily of any particular nationality. It is a universal company, and things will continue to be managed that way in the future.

This, emphasized Dulles, was the law. Now, what of the justice of the matter?

He stated the four principles previously enunciated by the eighteen powers as the basic ingredients of the "definite system" required by the treaty of 1888 for freedom of passage: (1) efficient and dependable operation, maintenance, and development of the Canal as a free, open, and secure international waterway in accordance with the principles of the Convention of 1888; (2) insulation of the operation of the Canal from the influence of the politics of any nation; (3) a return to Egypt for the use of the Suez Canal which would be fair and equitable, and would increase with the enlargement of the Canal's capacity and its greater use; (4) canal tolls as low as consistent with the foregoing requirements, involving, except for Egypt's share, no profit.

These principles would be carried out with due regard for the sovereign rights of Egypt. How could anyone, Dulles asked, seriously dispute them? In fact, only one of the principles had been seriously disputed and that by only a single power at the London Conference, the Soviet Union. The principle was the second one, that the operation of the Canal should be insulated from the politics of any nation. But, Dulles now asked, *is this not the essence of the matter?* The economies of a score or more nations were vitally dependent on the Canal.

> If such a waterway may be used as an instrument of national policy by any Government which physically controls it, then the Canal is bound to be an international bone of contention. Then no nation depending on the Canal can feel secure, for all but the controlling nation would be condemned to live under an economic sword of Damocles. That would be to negate the 1888 Convention and to violate both justice and law.

> If, as the United Nations Charter commands, we are to seek justice, we must agree that the operation of this international utility shall be insulated from the politics of any nation.

The four principles themselves were therefore not subject to alteration. But Dulles showed a willingness to bargain *on the mechanism* by which they might be carried out. A variety of means existed for this; none of the eighteen powers regarded any one method as sacrosanct; the Council ought not to close its mind to any alternative suggestion.

He cogently recalled that the smaller nations of the world had rebelled at San Francisco, when the Charter was being established on the basis of the original Dumbarton Oaks draft made by the three great powers—the U.S.A., Britain, and the Soviet Union—because the organization's purpose was only peace. They had insisted that the big powers could club together to impose peace *without justice.* They successfully demanded safeguards to ensure that peace should be made always "in conformity with the principles of justice and international law." Among the most forceful claimants of this fundamental change was the representative of Egypt! He had pleaded then:

> If we want to keep peace and security only, we would not differ much from Hitler, who was also trying to do that and who, as a matter of fact, partly succeeded. But where the difference lies, is that we want to maintain peace and security in conformity with the principles of international law and justice.

The Secretary of State then moved towards his conclusion. All parties said they wanted peace. The situation was governed, as it rarely was, by clear principles of law and justice. If with all these assets the Council should find itself impotent, "then our failure would be a calamity of immense proportions."

All seemed to recognize this—but NO! One power at the Council table did not: the Soviet Union. Dulles rebuked Shepilov for the monstrous remarks he had made on "monopolies." He ironically analyzed Shepilov's proposal for a more representative committee.

> Mr. Shepilov obviously believes it very unfortunate that 18 nations, representing over 90 per cent of the traffic and of diversified user interest, could agree upon a solution. So he wants to make a fresh start by establishing a committee which is so constituted that we can know in advance that it will never agree.

Dulles wound up this satirical and diplomatically quite unnecessary teasing of the Soviet Union with a reference to the proverb about fishing in troubled waters. "But it is usually considered respectable to veil such purpose. Rarely has a scheme to perpetuate controversy been so candidly revealed." In the light of events to come, those of October

29 onwards, Dulles's wounding if truthful attack on the Soviet Union is most ironic.

If Egypt, Dulles continued, accepted the principle that there should be a system to "ensure that the Canal cannot be used by any country as an instrument of its distinctly national policy," then the subsidiary problems could be resolved. If the principle were repudiated, then a negotiating body could hardly be useful. Indeed, one could hardly look forward to a settlement according to international law and justice, and the Charter would have been undermined.

He concluded on a dove-like note: how all peoples wanted a vista of new hope for an area of the world too long oppressed by alarms of war and the economic burdens of preparation for war; a new hope for all humanity, too, "which has begun, I fear, to lose confidence in the capacity of this Organization to secure peace and justice." The United States intended to vote for the British and French resolution, because it embodied the basic principles to which he had referred.

"Who can doubt what our choice will be?" he asked.

It was nearly time for lunch.

What effect had this speech on Selwyn Lloyd and Christian Pineau? Dulles's speech convinced *them* more than ever that their claims were just and legal; that they were right and Nasser wrong; that the practical way of redress which they were seeking, and which would be of benefit also to all other maritime nations, was right and sensible. Under these circumstances, they were entitled to say to their Prime Ministers and peoples, "We are right; Dulles is on our side; no one has expressed more forcibly and cogently than he that if the United Nations does not do us justice then we shall be in the position of suitors before a court unjustly abandoned. In that case, the other side of Dulles's most powerful and valid argument—force—must surely be used, to remove the sword of Damocles from our heads, to vindicate our rights and interests which have been ignored, even derided by some, in the United Nations."

Dulles had, in reality, talked as though he did not see that the sword of Damocles was precisely what Nasser had gone out to seize, to be used as a menace over the head of the Western powers whenever it should be in the interest of his own country and of the Pan-Arabism he fomented to do so. Dulles talked and acted as though this were a law case *within* a nation. Apparently President Eisenhower had not shown in private, or in his public utterances, any serious appreciation of the gravamen of his Secretary's argument: that what was involved was not merely interference with an international public utility and the rights of easement (Eisenhower did understand this part), but the violation of international law, *the breach of treaties freely made.*

After Dulles's speech, the private talks began between Lloyd, Pineau, Fawzi, and Hammarskjold. They did not begin in favorable circumstances—favorable, that is, for Egypt's submission to the point of view of Dulles, Britain, and France. Nasser by this time was practically free of pressure, Dulles having postponed the tolls question. According to rumors from Cairo, Nasser had even proposed that the African and Asian nations which had attended the Bandung Conference in April, 1955, should form an economic alliance to free themselves from dependence on Western trade and financial assistance.

This proposal appeared in a Cairo newspaper, *Al Messaa*, and was reported by the *New York Times* on October 9, 1956. It was probably an extension of the search by Egypt for markets and currency outside her trade patterns established hitherto, and of a new economic and trade agreement signed between Egypt and Communist China, giving the former long-term credits and setting up a barter-trade arrangement.

The principal representative of the *New York Times* in London, Drew Middleton, had access to the highest echelons of the Government, it may be to Sir Anthony Eden himself. He reported that Dulles (once the hero of the man in the London streets, especially during his "finest hour" of the first London Conference) had become the "whipping boy for the national feeling of frustration over the Suez crisis and a focus for the rising anti-Americanism." He quoted the remark of "a senior Government official" on Dulles's speech: "It was a useful speech all right. But how can we be certain, on the basis of past performances, that Mr. Dulles won't shift his position overnight?" Middleton estimated that anti-American sentiment (I add, shared by all classes and parties by now) was "80 per cent mistrust of Mr. Dulles." Eden himself had done, and was doing, his utmost to quiet the resentment against Dulles and the United States for fear that the alliance with America might suffer harm. The *Daily Telegraph*, Conservative and pro-American, complained that Dulles thus far had "led them [the allies] to expect greater support than he was able or willing to give. . . . The United States Administration has shirked risks inherent in her loyalty to her Allies and her leadership of the West."

By October 10, the state of spirit among the allies had become so morbid and so divided that Dulles asked the President to take up the matter in his press conference of October 11. The President's most pathetic response on that occasion concerned the news of dissatisfaction in Britain with American policy. He had, he said, that morning questioned Dulles on this, asking him:

> . . . whether he had even had any intimation from anyone in British officialdom whom he met that they were dissatisfied with our stand in this thing or thought that we have been vacillating and not carrying forward as we started out. He hasn't and I assure you I haven't.[6]

The reader has now in his possession ample authentic facts, for example, Eden's cable of October 1, to know that this phrasing is in substance quite untrue.

In the private talks at the United Nations between Britain, France, and Egypt, with Dag Hammarskjold as moderator, Dulles was not present. It would have been most useful if he had joined them, at any rate, after the first or second of such preliminary contacts, but his inclusion would have required the inclusion also of Shepilov and Menon. The chief difficulty experienced by Lloyd and Pineau was the impossibility of getting a counterproposal from Dr. Fawzi.

At the very moment that the Security Council was in open and in private session, and as the three-party talks were proceeding, the Israeli-Jordanian frontier was aflame with hostilities instigated, assisted, and spurred on by Cairo, which had made a nest for its *fedayeen* in the Gaza Strip. On the night of October 10-11, the Israelis had conducted a severe reprisal on Jordan at Qalqilya, of which more later.

At the end of the day's talks on October 11, the Western powers claimed that Fawzi had made no commitments, though Fawzi himself held out hope that something could be accomplished. But he, and Ali Sabry and Omar Loutfi in the corridors, had just listened. Selwyn Lloyd in a "constructive" and "friendly" way had tried to bring matters to a settlement by mentioning that time was short. Fawzi had no time limit: he would stay as long as was necessary. On October 11, a private meeting had been held of the eighteen powers who had fashioned the London proposals, and here Selwyn Lloyd and Pineau reported the progress of their talks with Fawzi. Dulles was present. His return from Washington had given rise to speculation that something important was imminent. Dulles announced he would be in New York indefinitely.

The general report given to the eighteen was related at a private meeting of the Security Council afterwards. It appears that the British position was now that Egypt might be the manager of the Canal, provided that there were an advisory committee to supervise and participate in establishing Canal policy on tolls, development, patterns of shipping, discrimination, and so on, and provided that this committee could take "*automatic*" action if there were any violations of the accepted rules on the part of Egypt. That is to say, in case of infractions, the committee would be self-executive, and would not need to wait for the United Nations or the World Court to clear up a disputed point. The British proposal was a major concession, praiseworthy as a step toward a peaceful settlement.

Dulles was very well informed of the turn the talks were taking at each moment. He knew all about the British plan, and about that put forward by Krishna Menon: Egyptian management, a consultative committee, as suggested above, with recourse to the World Court in the event of disagreement between Egypt and the committee. It leaked out through Indian sources that the talks were not going well, and Menon let it be inferred that some compromise might be found if India and the United States were now admitted into the sessions to exert influence on both sides.

Also on October 11, the private talks in Hammarskjold's apartment between Britain, France, and Egypt had come to an end. Six meetings had been held by the three ministers and the Secretary General. Hammarskjold had been able to induce the three to accept Six Principles that should govern the cooperation of the Canal. They had long been in the air and on paper: he had formulated them as possibly expressing a consensus. They will be stated in a moment. The British and French were, however, worried about the *implementation* of these principles: how would they be carried out, who would interpret them? They had made a tremendous concession now that they had agreed to give up the full international management of the Canal (as a substitute for the Suez Canal Company system) and be content merely with some kind of supervising, consultative board, which would, of course, be of international composition. But they required that this board must have the power to act whenever the principles might be violated. They had been cheated once, and badly; they could not again submit themselves to the chance that Nasser was an honorable man. Was this not a decent and courageous request, if the "definite system" that had been broken by Nasser's rape was to be conceded? Both countries had a thousand years of constitutional experience in which they had well learned that principles without administrative institutions are valueless. They could not, however, prize out of Fawzi, which means out of Nasser and his henchmen, an acceptance, in any precise form at all, of their proposal for such automatic, self-executory fulfillment of the Six Principles. They intended to propose means of implementation as well. When they did, members of the Egyptian delegation expressed resentment that this had not been agreed by them in the private talks.

Dr. Fawzi, it is reported, strode out grimly from a Security Council meeting held on the evening of October 11, because the allies were firm in rejecting the idea of an international body that would have merely the power to *advise*, with appeal to be made, in case of trouble, to the United Nations or the World Court (or both). Above all, Egypt had insisted that *no* body that might be set up would be allowed to deal with "discrimination against users"—in other words, "sovereignty" meant excluding any nation (such as Israel) from the Canal, whenever this action suited Egypt's views of her foreign policy and defense of "vital interests," of which she would be the sole interpreter. Now, what was to happen?

The issue was taken back into the Security Council on October 13. The open session began at 5:30 P.M.; after a recess, it met again at 9:30 P.M. The debate, which is recorded in the *Security Council*

Official Record,[7] revolved around the resolution put by the British and French and supported by the United States, with the original accusatory preamble taken out to please the United States. The members of the Security Council at this time were Australia, Belgium, China, Cuba, France, Iran, Peru, the Soviet Union, the United Kingdom, the United States, and Yugoslavia.

Selwyn Lloyd reviewed the request his nation had made for justice to relieve a "dangerous situation." As at Cairo, so now, Britain hoped for negotiation, the proposal being the same as in August and September. The private conversations, said Lloyd, had made a beginning toward discovering a basis for negotiations. But no *great* strides had been made. Although the talks had not been entirely negative, the hard problems lay ahead "and they demand urgent solutions."

The third requirement of the Six Principles, the insulation of the Canal operation from any nation's politics, was "the essence of the matter," Lloyd continued. But this required that the means for carrying out the principles be specified. If the government of Egypt still rejected the eighteen-power proposal for supplying this, then it ought to show how the basic requirement *could* be met. Thus, Nasser was put into the box of international responsibility: so far, in spite of all the talks, nothing "sufficiently specific" had been offered by Egypt. The British government hoped, conciliatorily, that progress could be made by the voting of its resolution, including the Six Principles and the means of their implementation, "in face of a situation about which we felt strongly and still feel strongly."

Pineau's speech retraced and supported Lloyd's. But he was more adamant on the lack of progress: "It is plain that we are still very far from seeing eye to eye on many points." But the envoys would continue to converse, and meanwhile SCUA was necessary.

Fawzi accepted the Six Principles—BUT, especially referring to "what it [the text of the Principles] calls the insulation of the Canal from the politics of any country," he rejected the means proposed for implementation.[8] Even the principle was an "unfortunate" as well as a "misleading expression"; it "allows for various and contradictory interpretations." So much for Dulles's "essence"! Fawzi would go only so far as to reaffirm or renew the treaty of 1888 as the sole guarantee of the principles.

He claimed therefore to be ready to negotiate a settlement, and to have put forward concrete proposals. That is all he had to offer. For the sting in his argument and position was now exerted to the full, though in sparse words:

> *This* [Fawzi's proposals and suggestion for negotiation on their basis]—this, I submit, is the logical and practical way in which the Suez Canal question can be dealt with and in which the Suez Canal itself can be insulated from politics, whereas such

an approach as that outlined in the second part of the joint draft resolution [that is, with the eighteen-power proposals and SCUA as a basis] would do exactly the contrary and would throw the Suez Canal violently into the fray of the politics not only of one nation, but of a great number of nations.

Fawzi concluded his speech with a rather too suave, too obviously unctuous, reference to a most optimistic speech made the day before by President Eisenhower.

Eisenhower's speech had been given in the course of an election-campaign television conference, October 12. It came almost with the abruptness of "I will go to Korea!" It ran:

I have an announcement. I have got the best announcement that I could possibly make to America tonight. The progress made in the settlement of the Suez dispute this afternoon at the United Nations is most gratifying. Egypt, Britain and France have met through their Foreign Ministers and agreed to a set of principles on which to negotiate, and *it looks like here is a very great crisis that is behind us*. I do not mean to say that we are completely out of the woods, but I talked to the Secretary of State just before I came over here tonight, and I will tell you that in both his heart and mine at least there is a very great prayer of thanksgiving.[9]

Dulles had evidently, the evening before, repeated his performance of optimistically informing the President rather in the manner he had originally presented the Suez Canal dispute as hardly anything more than one of "eminent domain" and had told the President only the easy side of the SCUA proposition, omitting or softening down the harsh problem of fulfillment.

After Fawzi had completed his remarks before the Security Council, Shepilov moved in to give the coup de grâce to any peaceful settlement except at the expense of the West. He was all praise for the Principles; for the United Nations; for Egyptian good will. BUT—

Most unfortunately, however, and I should like to say, completely to the surprise of many members of the Security Council, there is a second part to this draft resolution which in no way stems from the conversations which have taken place or from the work done by the Security Council in recent days.

There were no legal or moral grounds why the Council should force on Egypt the institution of the self-executive advisory committee. If this were done now, then negotiations in the future would be impossible.

Then Shepilov threw SCUA out of court. Only a *few* nations (in SCUA) were going to claim particular functions in the Canal, functions that belonged to the Egyptian Authority. All this was not the province of the Security Council, for the Canal was functioning well. Since the United Nations had the dispute before it, a genuine safeguard existed for the fulfillment of Egypt's treaty obligations regarding the Canal. Therefore, he could not support the second part of the resolution.

Dulles, speaking next, expressed gratification at the progress made in the talks, at the constructive and calm proceedings that had produced "important agreements." A solution "all at once" could not be expected, but an important stage had been passed by the agreement on principles—"realistic and concrete." This agreement would permit the future proposals and conduct of the parties "to be judged by this Council and the world." These were the "just principles" he had forecast as being the right ones.

However, the second part of the resolution, dealing with the implementation of the Principles, was still in question. Dulles emphasized that he had not excluded "alternative suggestions," in place of the eighteen-power proposal. The draft resolution now contained language to this effect and asked Egypt to submit any such suggestions "which would *equally* accomplish the desired results." (Notice the term *equally!*) Dulles seized on the statement, made earlier by Dr. Fawzi, that Egypt had made a certain concrete proposal in the confidential talks. He hoped for more of the same. The proposal in the resolution that Egypt, France, and Britain should continue the interchanges was of particular importance. "Important positive results" had issued from those already undertaken. The procedure ought to be pursued. Therefore, the United States intended to vote for the resolution.

Then the crisis began, the beginning of the end: Popovic of Yugoslavia found the second part of the resolution, the implemental part, unacceptable. He proposed more negotiation on this.

Selwyn Lloyd was compelled to take the floor again, especially nettled by the Soviet jibes and fallacies. With some feeling, he reminded the Council members that a breach of an international obligation had been perpetrated. Britain and France had not insisted that this charge be made in their preamble. They had acted with great restraint. (How true, if one makes a sober judgment about the action the Soviet government would probably have taken if Turkey had suddenly closed the Dardanelles to the Russian fleet!)

> But we, the Governments of France and the United Kingdom, took the initiative in informing the Security Council about the situation. We took the initiative in coming here to the Security Council to discuss it. We took the initiative in suggesting private meetings. We took the initiative in suggesting private conversations in the presence of the Secretary General. There has been an idea put about in some quarters that we would come to the

> Security Council simply as a formality. I think our actions during these discussions have shown how utterly unfounded such a suggestion was. I believe we have done everything possible in a difficult situation to promote a peaceful solution, and we have done it of our own volition.

Lloyd claimed that the British and French position was temperate and conciliatory. He was not asking for action on the Canal, but for agreement on the proposals that might bring about a peaceful and just settlement. He repudiated Shepilov's accusation that the second, implemental, part of the resolution was "coercion." He had accepted an Iranian amendment, to make the draft even more flexible ("equally accomplish . . ."), and to make it plain that there should be no iota of coercion involved.

> But we believe that at the moment the international community is suffering from a wrong, from a course of action which —and I do not want to come into undue controversy—was embarked upon without notice, without negotiation, as a unilateral act. And we believe, as I say—I do not want to be too controversial, because that is quite contrary to the spirit in which we have introduced this draft resolution—that Egypt is in breach, and we can really accept the continuation of that situation during discussions only if there is a genuine attempt to establish, *ad interim*, a system of cooperation between the users and the competent Egyptian authorities.

He did not want to define what this system must be; he thought the discussions might have made such cooperation possible. "But that, I think, is really the very least which we can ask." He requested the Council to accept the Six Principles and "our ideas" as to how they might be implemented.

> I really believe, and I say this with all the emphasis which I can command, that the best contribution the Security Council can make to a reduction in the tenseness of the situation is to vote our draft resolution as we have put it forward.

Robert Walker of Australia spoke in support of Britain's position.

It was also supported by Paul-Henri Spaak of Belgium. The resolution, Spaak declared, was not a condemnation of the Egyptian government, but an invitation to it: for clearer information, for a clearer picture. It would be unwise for the Council to disperse without enacting provisional measures (which someone had called "conservatory" measures). This was practical wisdom, and moreover it conformed with Article 40 of the Charter, which went on to specify that "Such provisional measures shall be without prejudice to the rights, claims, or positions of the parties concerned."

> Who can reasonably oppose the application of such a provision? How is it possible in such a delicate and serious situation, *where unintended incidents may break out at any moment and embroil the parties in measures far exceeding their real wishes*—not to feel the absolute necessity of applying this same Article 40 and of adopting by common accord such provisional measures "without prejudice to the rights, claims, or positions of the parties concerned."

Why not, asked Spaak, add the other 10 per cent of the nations to SCUA, if, as the Soviet representative impressively argued, 90 per cent was insufficiently representative; why not, that is, bring all nations into SCUA? This suggestion neatly turned the tables on Shepilov and his destructive purposes. But the Soviet Union could still destroy the voice of reason and justice by its vote. It possessed the veto. Spaak's speech was masterly; Shepilov's vote was also masterly—and decisive.

The Peruvian Foreign Minister, Belaunde, proceeded to support the British and French resolution in a cogent speech, even lauding the eighteen-power proposals.

Next Shepilov, conscious of his decisive power, conscious, it is certain, of the determination of the chiefs of the Communist Party of the Soviet Union, and its satellites and allies, took the floor for what was virtually a demand for a vote. His spade was drawn; he wanted the kill: one ear to Egypt, one ear to Yugoslavia.

Pineau, as President of the session, put the resolutions.

The first part, that is, the Six Principles, was adopted unanimously. The second part was voted for by: Australia, Belgium, China, Cuba, France, Iran, Peru, the United Kingdom, and the United States, *nine nations.* Two nations voted *against:* the Soviet Union and Yugoslavia. The vote of the Soviet Union, a permanent member of the Security Council, was a veto, and so killed the second part as an effective, legal resolution of the Council. The unanimous vote for the Principles was a legal victory as well as a moral one; the nine-to-two support of the proposal for implementing them was a moral victory, not a legal decision. But the moral victory was of no effect on the mind or conscience of the rulers of Egypt, led by Nasser.

What was to happen from this point on? Dulles still maintained a public posture of optimism. He could not forego the valedictorian comments of a good loser:

> I regret that it has not been possible for the Council to agree on more than the principles, the requirements of a settlement; but that is already much. I think, of course, that it is understood that the Council remains seized of this matter and that the Secretary-General may continue to encourage interchanges between the Governments of Egypt, France and the United Kingdom—a procedure which has already yielded positive results.

The Security Council may have remained seized of the dispute; but Nasser remained seized of the Canal. Pineau concluded the meeting at shortly before midnight on October 13 with the observation that "we have been able to achieve results which, while incomplete, are, nevertheless, positive. . . ."

Secretary Dulles, after a few desultory words with some of the Ministers and with his intimates, went off to his suite at the Waldorf-Astoria. He did not go to bed at once. After a short time Selwyn Lloyd joined him in the living room. Dulles called for drinks. His favorite was some special brand of rye. He went through his almost invariable ritual when he lifted the glass; he sniffed at it, and then he put his right forefinger in it, stirring a little, until his finger got well wetted with the liquor, when he put it to his nose and took in the aroma in a few deep and appreciative whiffs.

He said he was very happy that the Russians had vetoed "only" the operative part of the resolution and not the Six Principles! Perhaps he felt that with the Security Council agreeing unanimously on the Principles, he could still somehow shape world opinion so that justice would be achieved for the British and French claims, and Nasser's conscience and behavior would be reformed. Selwyn Lloyd responded, in the course of the conversation, that the West had come out of the debate very well indeed with a victory on the Six Points, and he congratulated Dulles on his tactics that had contributed to this result.

Presently, Pineau opened the door and came in to join the story-telling. Disgust with Russia was uppermost in the thoughts and words of the three men. Then Dulles, conscious that France's attitude was more furious than Britain's, at any rate on the surface, wagged a warning finger at Pineau (as though he *knew* something!) and admonished: "I know you think that if you use force *after* the Presidential election we will take no action, but let me tell you now, we will!" In the conversation, Selwyn Lloyd once again pleaded with Dulles to hurry with the activation of SCUA and above all to see that American-owned ships ceased paying tolls to Egypt: Could Dulles and Eisenhower, *would* they, bring to bear on Nasser at least this relatively minor instrument of pressure? It was very far removed from war or force; it might make all the difference. Selwyn Lloyd knew how far the French had gone with Israel.

Nations on every possible occasion test the loyalty and determination of their friends, linked to them by ties for defense or offense or mutual assistance. An ally, after all, is another sovereign nation, and all peoples are very considerably strange to each other. The policy, intentions, and capability, above all the durable sincerity, of any nation's allies are always the object of anxious guesswork. For the British and the French, the question they had put to Dulles—"Will you stop paying dues to Nasser?"—became their ultimate test of American policy and will. They found that Dulles failed them on this. They said to themselves, "Where there is a will there is a way! If he cannot do this by Executive action, he can by asking Congress for a law. If he can or will do neither (partly because he and the President do not want to call back Congress so late in an election year, though earlier it would have been possible), then we are abandoned to our own devices, for all of Dulles's eloquence and for all his and Eisenhower's press conferences breathing optimism more than determination, and for all of Eisenhower's letters to 'My dear Anthony.' "

Selwyn Lloyd tried to make Dulles understand that Britain would go to all lengths with Nasser unless the vetoed part of their resolution were restored in an acceptable manner *in fact.* No one can now, or perhaps ever, say whether Dulles let this sink in through his illusions.

This was the second time in a week that Lloyd had asked Dulles for this means of help: not war, not force, not the condonation of these things, but a relatively minor means of pressure, along the very lines that Dulles himself had repeatedly advocated. And for the second time in a week he got a dusty answer. Last time it was, "Wait until SCUA is organized!" and this time it was, "Wait until I take it up with you through diplomatic channels!" *If* Dulles had said "Yes! We will do this at once!" then, with the withdrawal of the total American tolls, making up 30 per cent of all, and the British and the French, Nasser would have been running his Canal while losing about 70 per cent of all normal Canal revenues!

SCUA had met a few days before, but had not yet been able to find the proper man to be administrator. The organization was looking for a Dutchman or a Swede, some man who had had substantial experience as a shipping executive. Was Nasser to be left in possession of the Canal, without any exhibition of a will opposed to his, till such things were settled? Dulles's allies had hoped he would join them in immediate action. But he merely said, "Wait!"

It was rather unfortunate that Dulles, Lloyd, and Pineau met as friends at the Waldorf-Astoria suite of the United States government, in spite of so much that is said hopefully of face-to-face meetings. Their confrontation was very painful and awkward, full of malaise. Dulles labored under the constant foreboding that something ominous was being kept from him, especially since he considered he had been deceived by Eden about the appeal to the Security Council. Hence his cautionary (and probing) remarks to Pineau about French military action after the election.

Pineau's hints about October 10 to Selwyn Lloyd, intended to advise him that France meant business, and that Israel would be party to a chastisement of Nasser, did not reach Dulles. But during the New York meetings Dulles did tax his allies with his information about their concentrations of troops on Cyprus. They answered that their actions were deterrent, launched to protect British citizens in the Middle East against attack by native mobs. But Dulles observed that their supply of long-range wing-tanks for the F-86's could not be merely "precautionary." He talked to his State Department associates as though he realized that, unless something definitely constructive were established by the Security Council, the allies were going down the slope to war. He even went so far as to confess a feeling (to a high career adviser) that allied military action in the Middle East would set that region on fire, with the gravest repercussions on the Atlantic alliance. Perhaps the CIA now fed his misgivings.

Dulles did not find Selwyn Lloyd warm and confiding between October 5 and 13. On the other hand, Lloyd seriously distrusted Dulles by this time. He very firmly reminded the Secretary that at the annual conference of the Conservative Party, to meet October 11 to 13, Eden would have no unlimited latitude to surrender British interests in the Çanal and the Middle East. Neither the party leaders (of which Lloyd was one) nor the British people were in a mood for surrender. Dulles tried to probe Lloyd's mind and intentions. But the British Foreign Secretary had been open with Dulles for about two and half months already, without reserve. Dulles used intermediaries, his career officials and their friends who knew Lloyd, to try to fathom British thinking. All he got back was the news that both the British and the French found Dulles obtuse and insensitive and unable to comprehend his allies' necessities or Nasser's threat. Dulles remained unconvinced that war was not intended.

Those who were present at these private talks at the Waldorf-Astoria, and have served more than one Secretary of State, believe that a greater degree of frankness and urbanity would have prevailed had someone other than Dulles been the U.S. Secretary. It was evident that Selwyn Lloyd and Pineau resented, and were antagonized by, Dulles's attitude of detachment from allied loyalty and his overbearing and disputatious personality. Above all, at this moment, they were literally revolted by the fact that Dulles had not forbidden American citizens to take jobs as pilots through the Canal. Nasser had seized allied property, yet Dulles was building up an organization, SCUA, which could assist Nasser to obtain tolls, and the American pilots would be of assistance to him in doing so.

Dulles entertained some curious but interesting ideas as he reflected on his colloquies with Lloyd and Pineau. By October 12, he told a well-known reporter for a favorite weekly magazine that "All Pineau is doing is sitting there and saying 'no good' to everything that comes up," while the British and the Egyptians seemed to be getting closer together on the issues. He was worried over the fact that Pineau had several times threatened to quit and go home, abandoning the attempt to settle the issue in the Security Council. Dulles even speculated that the French might abandon their British allies—or if they should join with them on some solution short of war, then they would do so reluctantly. He reiterated his anxiety that the French were steadily in disagreement with the various conciliatory moves that were being made. He saw the interest they would have in war: they were already at war in Algeria, so that if war started in Suez, it would be to their advantage since then they would have the British as indirect allies in the Algerian struggle.

On October 13, Eden appeared before the annual conference of the Conservative Party. He had learned about the Soviet veto at about midnight. He had heard also that Dulles had made no severe response, but had delivered a Pollyanna benediction. Eden made up his mind to take hold of the least optimistic of the President's phrases of October 12, emphasize this, and conclude once again that force could not be excluded. He also requested that Lloyd should talk again plainly to Dulles, to express concern at the consequences to Britain (and France) of "these [the President's and the Secretary's] repeated and unjustified flights of hopeful fancy."[10]

He gave his speech on this basis. It had a mixed reception. A few in the Conservative Party had now become faint-hearted over the prospect of a break with the United States; this group included one senior Minister, R. A. Butler. On the other hand, the right wing of the Party, and it was a very large right wing (one of its factions, the Suez Rebels, was truly extreme), was solidly and hotly in support of a policy of imminent action. It seems certain that Eden himself, for reasons we shall examine later, experienced within himself the varieties of feeling within his Party. His lifetime reputation had been as a formulator and maker of peace. In his speech, he rubbed in hard the President's statement that peace must be coupled *with justice* or it is not peace.

Dulles was by now bankrupt of ideas regarding British and French concern with Suez, though he was still replete with power and will. One can pay due and sober respect to the Secretary's skill, craft, and forensic talents, and sympathize with the awful burden that oppresses a man who by his single word can call down upon himself and his nation a rain of atomic fire, and who may also inflict it. But Dulles was the man who had breathed fire and slaughter against the Soviet Union for years. He was now in a curious position. Now all was a-boil: Lloyd's and Pineau's hard demeanor; Eden's speech of October 13; the Egyptian protest against that speech lodged by Fawzi with the United Nations Security Council almost at once.[11]

On the next morning, Sunday, October 14, Dulles flew back to Washington. He told newsmen on his arrival that, in spite of the Soviet veto, there were good grounds for hope of a peaceful settlement of the Canal dispute, and that "negotiations would go ahead just as though there had not been a veto." Dulles's determined but baseless optimism pervaded the President's view of the issue as well. October 14 was his birthday in a year fraught with sore trials. On leaving church he offered the public the blessing: "It looked a little bad last night, but things look better again today."

Dulles was, once again, under compulsion to hold a press conference.[12] Eden's speech had especially worried him. In fact, one of his *alter ego*'s in the State Department, preparing for the press conference, expressed the neighborhood view: "It was very stupid of Eden to make a speech just when Lloyd and Dulles were getting together!" The speaker of these words seems not to have reflected that perhaps by now Eden did not trust Dulles; that Britain's interests were, according to Dulles himself, vital, while America's interests in the Canal were *not;* and that perhaps over the trans-Atlantic cable the alleged getting-together of Washington and London was not evident.

(Eden had learned through Lloyd in New York of the association between France and Israel; he was so surprised by this that he exclaimed, "What, Israel to attack Egypt? Don't be stupid!")

Dulles's press conference, held on October 16, began with a statement to the effect that the adoption of the Six Principles marked progress towards a just and peaceful solution of the Suez crisis. Substantial "moral support" had been obtained when nine votes out of eleven had affirmed even the vetoed second part of the resolution. But Dulles did not emphasize or even seem to notice the corollary: the British and French thought their moral position to have been affirmed also. "Thrice is he armed that has his quarrel just," they believed. Dulles believed that no one could say with certainty there would be a peaceful solution. But, "each difficulty overcome means one less difficulty remaining to be overcome," and he took satisfaction from the United Nations attainment.

However, in foreign policy difficulties are of different kinds. We often hear such phrases as, "The powers agreed on 95 per cent of the issues," giving the impression that the conflict is over. No! There are difficulties and difficulties, some being less tractable than others. The difficulty that still remained in the Suez crisis at this moment was the difficulty that had existed from the moment of Nasser's seizure of the Canal; he had taken possession of it, forcibly, against law and against justice and against his pledges to the United Nations. Could he be made to give it up so that the claims of the British and French could be satisfied? This was *the* difficulty; it was almost 100 per cent of the difficulty; all the rest was commentary.

Dulles was asked whether he had caused any sort of regulation to be issued compelling American ships to pay tolls to SCUA, and whether he had such authority. He did not answer the second half of the question. The first part was answered by a prevarication. "The

British and the French have not shifted to require their ships to pay into SCUA nor have we." And just prior to that, "and in all cases, in the cases of those three countries (Britain, France, and the United States) or the ships *with those flags*, we have been carrying on as before." In other words, the U.S.A. was still neglecting to deprive Nasser of the revenue from American tolls. But, again, a good-natured practical man's optimism: "And we are trying to work out a common procedure in that matter, but, so far, the payments are being made by the three countries, and indeed, other countries, precisely as they were made before." This suave answer directly misrepresented the facts! Actually, Britain and France were not paying tolls to Nasser and—and this *was a difference from before*—American-flagged ships were paying, "but under protest." To have admitted the latter would have been to admit the feebleness of Dulles's position. For combining "protest" with payment of the tolls to Egypt was all he had actually *done*, except, as we have said earlier, for the freezing of past accumulated Egyptian government assets. Pilots with American passports were helping to run the Canal!

In answer to another question, the Secretary said that the transit of Israeli shipping through the Canal had not been specifically settled, but it was "generally understood" that the Principles covered Israeli ships. (Mikoyan had that morning in Moscow expressed that that was the Soviet Union's understanding of the resolution also.) "But we did not seek and receive any explicit assurances of Egypt in that respect."

Dulles declared that though Fawzi said he would have voted against the resolution (Egypt then had no vote on the Council), Dulles thought that "there were *indications*, perhaps *not formally given*, which led us to *believe* it is *not beyond* the realm of *possibility* that there *could be* developed practical cooperation with" SCUA. This tortuous sentence of hypotheses and conditional clauses merits grave contemplation, in order to appreciate what Dulles's allies and opponents had to suffer in (a) understanding whether he understood what was occurring, and (b) apprehending what he meant by any given assertion. The suppositious language has been underlined by the writer. Which nations could risk their vital interests on such uncertainties?

The Secretary was invited to explain the meaning of "insulating the Canal from the politics of any nation." His observations were almost the last he made in the piping times of peace. The one defect of his pronouncement was that he could not make his own begotten principles and policy effective on the culprit, Nasser.

> Now every nation—and Egypt is no exception—has policies which from time to time make it want to favor some country or perhaps to put pressure to bear upon some country. Now the essential thing is that the Canal should not be an instrument of that kind of policy.

Overt defiance of the Convention of 1888 could be overcome by moral and even, perhaps, practical sanctions.

> Now, the problem, as we see it, and as I described it in London and elsewhere, is the danger of what I call covert violations. That word "covert" is used, you will notice, in the six principles, the danger that in various ways the ships of certain countries, let us say, against which Egypt wants to exert pressure may fail to get pilots in time, might get unqualified pilots, might be put at the end of the traffic line that goes through the Canal. Now I think that there should be sufficient participation, such a close contact with the practical, day-by-day operations of the Canal that nothing of that sort could go on without being promptly detected and brought to light.

A reporter pressed him whether "a supervisory board" as well as "an operational board" could secure insulation from political pressure?

His answer, reasonable and flexible, must, however, have seemed rather too defeatist for his allies, for he talked of "a score or more of practical methods which would accomplish the same result." But they had already seen several of these invented by him, only to fail, each in its turn. They had also noticed that every time a new one was invented to be a substitute for the one that had just failed, it was a weaker guarantor of their rights than the one before. Especially had this been the case when Dulles declared that Nasser, having rejected the proposals of the eighteen powers, would not get terms as *good:* in fact, SCUA was far easier on Nasser in its plan and principle.

But, for what it is worth, this is what he answered:

> Well, words have so many different meanings that it is awfully hard to express our ideas in words without danger of misinterpretation. The word "supervisory" is a word which has a whole gamut of meaning. If you were actually supervising an operation you may be right there on that spot watching it and, indeed, directing it. So that I do not attach any magic to the word "supervision," as against other words that have been used, like "participation," and so forth. I think the practical problem is to have enough of an international contact with the day-to-day workings of the Canal so that there could not go on the type of covert preferences or discriminations to which I refer.

* * * * *

From the moment this press conference ended, according to the closest American associates of Dulles and of the President concerned with the Suez affair, a "blackout" of information from London ensued. A "blackout" was indeed organized. But, as we shall see, not so long after a fateful and decisive meeting between British and French leaders began in Paris, about the time on October 16 when Dulles was in Washington ambling with his hands in his trousers pockets towards his rostrum in the State Department auditorium, *the State Department was informed by two official sources that France and Israel and probably Britain were about to make trouble in the Suez Canal area. Someone in Washington knew.*

Dulles did not realize it in hard fact at once, but his allies had almost severed the strands that bound them to America, because for them America then happened to be Dulles and—behind him, preoccupied with his own re-election and domestic policy, often far behind him—Eisenhower. Britain and France pondered the events of three months. They had lost the Canal, largely through Dulles's diplomatic clumsiness. They had been persuaded by Dulles not to use force at once or as soon as they could assemble their forces, which might have been by the end of August. They had been persuaded to evade the United Nations after the Menzies mission had failed. They could have been told that force would in *no case* be tolerated by the United States, and then left to make their own decision: whether to let Nasser keep his ill-gotten gains, or to exert sanctions, economic or physical, on him, to embark on a full economic blockade or an invasion.

Now, we must make due allowance for the fact that the United States has numerous obligations throughout the world, and is, therefore, in its initiatives, like Gulliver in Lilliput, tied down by a multitude of threads. This predicament may give the giant the appearance of timidity when called on to move; quiescence may be a sensible caution. Any strong tearing at the threads of peace anywhere may have effects everywhere: war may seem to be indivisible.

Yet the record seems to lead to the conclusion that Dulles was a timid man: he had little nerve. He was *not* a brinkman, in fact, not that it is always a credit to be one or to boast about it. Above all, he was terrified of Russian power. His hatred of Moscow was shot through with the fear of Moscow, though not necessarily because of specific threats, such as those Moscow was about to make. He was simply mortally afraid of the Soviet Union, and his verbose bravado against the Kremlin was a symptom of his fears as much as of his moral detestation.

It is true, of course, that Dulles and Eisenhower were bound to be affected more or less consciously by the fact that the latter was up for election within three weeks and the former for continuance of office stemming from the success of his candidate—that is, popular opinion had to be taken into account, even if other nations were moving through severe stresses and anxieties. But Eden and Mollet, too, were subject to democratic dependence on their electorates. Eden performed in a political system where he met his opponents—and his political friends—day by day in a face-to-face small forum. His country was an extremely small island with a dense population and a metropolitan press of some eight or ten newspapers, one of which was on the breakfast table of every reader in Britain every day, so that the waves of public opinion beat upon him incessantly and intensely. The situation was rather similar in France, with the added democratic difficulty that the Prime Minister of the day (and the phrase is used advisedly!) must hold together more than the members of his own party, a rather fragile coalition of ill-assorted parties. Mollet and Pineau had to satisfy the Socialists, the de Gaullists, the Radicals, and a very small group to their left, not to speak of the center and right wings in the Assembly. Some few members of the Socialist Party were already critical of a warlike policy. The British and French leaders also felt a moral responsibility for the security and vital interests of their country, a conscientious obligation toward the national interest, beyond the pressure on them exerted by the public and the political leaders.

Later, but with the events of the Suez controversy vividly in mind, Sir Anthony Eden thus summed up his sense of frustration with Dulles's diplomacy from the seizure of the Canal to the point we have reached in this narrative:

> I soon learnt that the Soviet Government regarded the proceedings at the United Nations as a victory for Egypt and for them. In this they were undoubtedly right. I was not surprised when messages from our friends in the Middle East showed dismay at Nasser's swelling success. . . . It was clear enough to me where we were. The powers at the London Conference had worked out, with care and forethought, a scheme which would have made the Suez Canal part of an international system giving security for all. The United States had put its whole authority behind the scheme and her Secretary of State had introduced the proposals himself before the London Conference.
>
> Now all this was dead. It was no use to fool ourselves on that account. We had been strung along over many months of negotiation, from pretext to pretext, from device to device, and from contrivance to contrivance.[13]

This feeling was for Eden and Selwyn Lloyd, for Mollet and Pineau, a justification for pursuing their nations' interests and claim for justice in their own way, without further appeal to or consultation with the United States. For those, everywhere, who supported Dulles's and Eisenhower's peace at any price, the "stringing along" was a masterpiece of protractive diplomacy. But Eden had correctly described the toils in which British and French leaders had been ensnared by Secretary of State Dulles.

13. COLLUSION BRINGS A HOT WAR

ON OCTOBER 10, FRANCE AND ISRAEL REACHED AN AGREEMENT TO MAKE war, as the French said, in "orchestration" with each other. On October 16, Eden, Mollet, Lloyd, and Pineau had a long and private meeting to consider their course regarding Nasser. On October 22, Prime Minister Ben Gurion of Israel made a secret visit to France, where he conferred until October 24 with the top French government leaders—and Selwyn Lloyd. On October 25, the British Cabinet met in long and serious session on their next dealings with Nasser and on the aggravated troubles brewing between Egypt, Jordan, and Israel. On October 29, Israeli forces attacked Egypt, via Sinai, in strength. On October 30, Britain and France requested that Israel and Egypt keep their armed forces away from the Suez Canal, threatening sanctions if they did not comply in a short time. On October 31, Britain and France joined in an assault on Suez. Dulles's attempts to settle the Suez conflict, and his shying away from the Israeli-Arab disputes, had ended in a "hot" war. We have now to trace the diplomacy of the three Western nations and of Israel by which this event came about.

* * * * *

The Franco-Israeli arrangement had been developing over the past few weeks, as will be explained presently. The accord committed France to supply airplanes to Israel, and to provide air and naval cover for the invasion of Egypt that Israel would launch; it also included an expectation or assumption that France would land forces in Egypt. When military action was started by Israel on October 29, events proceeded to unfold much in the fashion and sequence envisaged. British cooperation, including eventually even military leadership, was involved, too, although this was settled later than October 10. October 10 was the day when Simon Peres, Israeli career chief in the Ministry of Defense, came to Paris to confer with French leaders, and when the talks between the two governments resulted in the formulation of the accord. In its preparation to that date, and in its consummation two weeks later, Christian Pineau played a leading role for France, instructed by Defense Minister Maurice Bourgès-Manoury, both authorized and supervised by Prime Minister Mollet.

It will be recalled that after the conclusion of the Egypto-Soviet arms deal in September, 1955, Israel's Foreign Minister, Moshe Sharett, had toured all Western capitals asking for arms. He was turned away from each with very little. Israel could not at that time persuade anyone to relax the Western solidarity against a Middle Eastern armed conflict. In this unspoken common front, the Soviet Union was associated with the West. Encircled and immediately and heavily threatened, Israel was fortunate in securing on October 10 the promise of France's friendship. An Israeli attaché who returned to Israel for a visit before this date unrelievedly gloomy, came back to Washington on October 11 radiating confidence. France was an ally of Israel. Selwyn Lloyd knew it; so did Eden, and a handful of other British leaders. Early on October 16, Selwyn Lloyd arrived in London from New York by air, and went directly into a Cabinet meeting at which the Chief of Staff was present. The Cabinet, now fully informed of the talks between Lloyd, Dulles, and Fawzi, was forced to face the problem whether the proceedings in New York left the British and French any effective hope of action by the United Nations or the United States. It was decided that the Egyptians would never agree to the eighteen-power proposals or anything like them. As Eden has explained in his memoirs, he could have gone on to hold further negotiations with the Egyptians, and have brought back to Britain a piece of paper that might look reasonable, but would actually throw the British people off their guard against a predatory dictator. Thirty years of foreign-affairs experience had convinced him that this was a false tactic. The Canal must be insulated from Nasser's control. The Cabinet must therefore, now, pursue two simultaneous courses: await the Egyptian proposals for a settlement which Dag Hammarskjold was promoting, and align its policies with those of France. Eden does not say, at this point in his memoirs, that he knew by now that France and Israel were virtually allies in an imminent offensive against Egypt.

Lloyd and Eden went to Paris that afternoon, October 16, for long and private conversations with Mollet and Pineau, with no other person present. They talked for nearly six hours. There has been much suspicion and speculation about this meeting. It is alleged that here some form of collusion was arranged bringing Britain into the accord already existing between France and Israel, though no firm knowledge has been divulged except what appears in Eden's memoirs (considered below). There *was* collusion, and of the kind suspected.

According to Eden's account of the discussions, the topics were the Security Council's action; the progress of SCUA; and, "in particular, the growing menace of hostility by Egypt against Israel." [1] For, as soon as Nasser's anxieties had been relieved by Russia's veto, he had reinvigorated the *fedayeen* raids into Israel. The British and French leaders concluded that the Six Principles could not be regarded as a serious commitment. Therefore, they would take their stand on the Dulles-advocated eighteen-power proposal. Egypt was expected to make a precise offer. SCUA was hopeless, because Dulles had rejected the idea that American ships should pay tolls to it rather than to Egypt. As Eden complained to his friends, Dulles had even charged that, whereas his proposals on SCUA were a means of cooperating with Egypt, the British and French regarded them as a method of punishing Nasser!

The statesmen turned to the Arab-Israeli scene. They knew that an Arab joint command was in the making. Britain's point of view was, in Eden's words:

> Unless Israel was prepared just to sit and wait until it suited her enemies to strangle and finally destroy her, it was clear that before long she would have to take some counter-action, at least to put an end to the *fedayeen* raids.

We may add to this the testimony later given by Pineau in the National Assembly.[2] France, he said, found in the second fortnight of October a vast emptiness: but "the new fact around this period was the great disquiet manifested by Israel. . . . The phrase 'preventive war' has not the same meaning in Israel as for other countries. . . . Many have spoken in the British House of Commons of collusion between Israel, France, and Great Britain. I do not quite see what the practical meaning of this term can be." Both France and Britain knew about Israel's precarious situation. "It was therefore quite normal that the two countries, which had been perfectly united in their diplomatic action during last summer, should consult each other on what was to be done." Britain and France had made joint plans of a military nature to deal with the Canal situation; "the situation due to the Israeli intervention was of another order and required a modification of previous plans." That "modification" Pineau, Mollet, and Bourgès-Manoury had already set up by the date of this meeting.

In considering the British position, some weight must be given to the evidence in Beal's biography of Dulles, since the bulk of it was based on material supplied by Dulles, some privately and some in background briefings to which other journalists were privy. He says (p. 269) that in Eden's conversation with Dulles on September 21 in London, Dulles "urged Eden again to play it so that Nasser would be the one to take hostile or obstructive acts against the users before attempting to carry the Suez dispute to the United Nations." So advised, Eden was entitled to think that in the last resort the United States would at least play the part of a neutral. He could also believe that *if* the Canal were obstructed, or was likely to be obstructed by an event like that which occurred, the Israeli attack on Egypt for *cause*, then the U.S.A. in the United Nations would remember Dulles's state of mind revealed to Eden, and even if Dulles were not happy with the situation he would at least not turn against his allies. (But one thing Dulles did not explain in detail in that conversation was the course of action he would take at the U.N. if Britain and France did go to war.)

Eden's worry was lest Israel attack Jordan, for Britain had a defensive agreement with the latter, and this situation opened up the horrible possibility of the Royal Air Force helping Jordan while French *Mystères* fought them in aid of Israel! There would be no worry if Israel acted against Egypt, for Nasser had organized the horror of the *fedayeen.*[3] Eden and Selwyn Lloyd had it confirmed to them October 16 that Israel's move would be against Egypt, not Jordan. "Now," says Eden, "Nasser's policies were provoking Israel beyond endurance and this also we had to prepare for." Specifically, "the safety of the Canal" was at stake.

A communiqué [4] was issued declaring British and French agreement on adherence to the Six Principles; it noted that these were already being questioned in certain Egyptian quarters. The two nations were ready to consider together any proposals Egypt should make, as requested by the Security Council, on the basis of the eighteen-power proposals or equivalent guarantees to the users. They had exchanged views on the problems of the Middle East and had decided to maintain constant contact on these in the spirit of the closest friendship.

A British Cabinet meeting reviewed these matters two days later, on October 18. No decision, says Eden, was taken for action then, though the situation was serious. But Britain would await the Egyptian proposals.

On October 16, then, Eden and Selwyn Lloyd knew the main lines of the Franco-Israeli plan of assault on Nasser's Egypt. They knew, as the *Americans also knew* about this time, even in numbers, how France had considerably exceeded the number of aircraft and other arms Dulles and Eisenhower had sanctioned for supply by France to Israel.[5] The date of the assault was to be as soon as militarily feasible, say, some two weeks from October 16, since Israel did not feel she could risk her existence beyond that time. The French urged an even earlier date. On the other hand, assuming that the target date was October 30 or thereabouts, the British held back a little, insisting on November 2 or 3, for reasons of military organization. In the final shape of the plan, the British command would head the expedition, and it wanted a little more time for full preparation and movement of the extremely complicated supplies and of the troops by ship from Marseilles, 1,200 miles distant, and from Malta, 900 miles away.

Contrary to some rumors, the French and British assault was not timed for *after* the Presidential election, November 6. It would have been undertaken two days earlier than it actually was had the British command not delayed. The date was the product mainly of Israeli fears and French vehemence against Nasser, the former for survival, the latter over Algeria and the Canal.

It is possible that Eden and Lloyd gave no commitment to the assault until October 24. Between October 16 and that date, the Israelis and the French political leaders and military chiefs worked on the timing and the stages of the assault. By October 24, on which day (or the day before) Selwyn Lloyd saw Ben Gurion in France, all were set to attack, the British included. However, the British decision awaited the actual *casus belli*, which would be signaled to them by the French, before commitment. Eden himself was not anxious to know too much about the arrangements, because he wished to be in a position (a) of freedom not to go forward if he should later decide not to do so, and (b) of innocence of any "collusion" with Israel, since this would discredit him with the Arabs at a time when he was seeking a settlement of the Canal dispute and wished to retain the friendship of Iraq and the curious liaison with Jordan.

Hence, let us return to the action of the French leaders, for it was they who forced the pace. The following account is based on the Brombergers,[6] and on J.-R. Tournoux, *Secrets d'État*[7] (Pineau has observed to me that Tournoux is pretty accurate but not the Brombergers). Useful also are some observations by Lord Randolph Churchill,[8] the latter employed with caution. Above all, much oral evidence has been pieced together in the attempt to comprehend the situation.

It amounts to this. By September 20, the day after Dulles's emotional appeal for unity within SCUA, Mollet and Pineau decided that he was unreliable and that they would use force against Nasser. An embryonic plan had even been sketched shortly after the failure of the Menzies mission. On the same day, having also realized that SCUA not only had no teeth but even no face, Bourgès-Manoury and his close administrative and military associates visited Israel to propose that France assist Israel in attacking Egypt. The French would supply jet fighters to cover the Israeli cities against attack by the Russian jet fighters and bombers supplied to the Egyptians. The French suggested that the British might join in if the Israelis and France attacked Egypt, though the evidence does not show that the British were consulted on the matter at this time. On September 23, Prime Minister Ben Gurion told the Mapai Party that "Israel at last has one true ally."

In fact, these circumstances had been preceded by the development of unusual diplomatic ties between France and Israel. France had given more help to Israel, since July, 1956, than has yet been made public. Since August there had been much coming and going. Menhaem Begin, leader of the Israeli extreme nationalist political party, *Herut*, had been welcomed by French Deputies and Senators on September 12.[9] Colonel Yehashafat Harkabi, director of Israel intelligence, had also visited France, in early October.[10] It was at this time that the military officers of Israel and France began to develop a plan of cooperation with immediate vigor. Officials of the French Ministry of Defense conferred in Israel with that country's representatives. Twice in October, Moshe Dayan, Israeli Chief of Staff, visited Paris. On October 8, Ben Gurion postponed an important speech, which was to have been given in the Knesset that day, until October 15. As we have already noted, the Israeli career Secretary of Defense held talks with French military officials, especially Abel Thomas, in Paris on October 10.[11] Before and after the United Nations meeting in New York, Pineau drove to and fro in his private car to meet the Israeli visitors, so that no one would discover what was afoot. Meanwhile, a direct radio connection had been installed between the Ministry of Defense in Paris and Tel Aviv, and in the former's office an Israeli officer was interpreter so that French preparations would remain secret. The French Foreign Office was kept ignorant of these preparations, lest foreign diplomats should deduce too much.

On October 22, Ben Gurion himself arrived in Paris.[12] He appealed to Mollet for assistance against annihilation by the Arab armies under a single command. Particularly did he dread attack from the air on Israel's cities, for example, Tel Aviv, hardly more than seconds away from the Arab air bases. He also needed naval protection for Haifa and Tel Aviv, both on the coast. He could expect no help from the United Nations; "*its resolutions were dead letters.*" Israel's existence was at stake. France was the only friend Israel had in the world.

Mollet replied that he would not allow such a crime to be perpetrated. Now, it is well known that statesmen, as we have seen in the career of Dulles, and shall see in that of Eden, sometimes say one thing but mean another. Mollet may have said this to Ben Gurion while thinking that France, by this same help that he promised, would destroy the extreme Arab rebels in Algeria by overthrowing Nasser, who gave them all possible aid. But it is still possible to have the two motives, quite sincerely, the former as well as the latter, when they come into juxtaposition by the force of circumstances. Mollet, in talking with me on this subject (*not* on his meeting with Ben Gurion) certainly insisted passionately that he, as a democratic Socialist, had for *long* been determined to assist Israel to survive against Arab and especially Egyptian attack, because Israel was a democracy, and he did not wish once again to see democracies destroyed as they had been by Communists or Fascists without an attempt at rescue by France, itself a democracy. Still less did he wish to see a repetition in Israel of the crime the Fascists and Communists had committed in Spain. At any rate, it was the emotional appeal of Ben Gurion for help against annihilation that caused the French ministers in the know—Mollet, Pineau, and Bourgès-Manoury—to begin to provide help at a swift pace. The rest of the Cabinet was kept in the dark, except as they could make their inferences from clues and hints and exceptions to routine.

It must not be thought that Israel approached France for help with no qualms. She would not be able to obtain help without giving something in return. The French national interest was focused on the overthrow of Nasser, especially after the empty-handed return of Pineau from his visit to Cairo in March, 1956. As a matter of fact, the *chef de cabinet* of Prime Minister Mollet had invited a very high-ranking U.S. diplomat in April to a private luncheon, where he had asked: "How would the United States react if the Israelis with the help of France gave Nasser a sound thrashing?" The American diplomat sent news of this prospect to the State Department. It was evidence of the fact that France and Israel had some important interests in common, and that they had ideas. Thenceforward, France gave Israel substantial help. When Israel did approach France seriously, some time in August, 1956, it was only after the rift between Foreign Minister Moshe Sharett and Prime Minister Ben Gurion had become firm and decisive. For Sharett had wished to continue the conciliation of the Arabs and the West. Ben Gurion's judgment was, on the contrary, that if Israel waited for Arab appeasement, while Egypt was training her armies with Russian weapons and inciting all Arabs to attack Israel, his country would be crushed. He therefore appealed to France for arms. As soon as the French realized that the quantity and type of arms he asked for implied a heavy attack on Egypt, they asked to be let in on the plans, and later on a joint intervention. The French were already fighting the Arabs; to fight Egypt was a relief and a salvation for them. Israel trusted the French, but not the British. They thought that in certain circumstances the British might even bomb Israel, not Jordan nor Egypt!

The secret of what was being planned was kept to the Prime Ministers and the Foreign Ministers and the Ministers of Defense of Britain and France. In Britain, the circle of those who knew was rather larger than in France, but it did not by any means include the whole Cabinet, even a normal "inner Cabinet": Selwyn Lloyd, Macmillan, Salisbury, and R. A. Butler were *au courant* as to intentions and as to ways and means. Crossing the Channel often with Bourgès-Manoury was his close confidant, Abel Thomas, who was well aware of what was going on.

It is not my purpose here to detail the ingenious devices used by the French to assist Israel, including the doctoring of the sales contracts for arms officially made on the basis of the agreements with the United States. The French support amounted to a deliverance for Israel, of course, when added to the Israelis' resources of brains, courage, morale, and resolution to fight for their lives against superior numbers.

In a masterly survey, Ben Gurion has told the history of French help.[13] In almost the last of the Parliamentary proceedings (October 15, 1956) in Israel before the attack on Sinai, October 29, Ben Gurion was calm and confident. He defended his earlier policy of refusing a "preventive war," because he was solicitous of the young people who would be killed and the old people who would be bereaved. Israel had sought arms; she had knocked on many doors, but had found them closed. England had sold heavy tanks to Egypt, but refused them to Israel. The policy of reprisals against Egypt and Jordan had been unavoidable, because the United Nations was helpless. Israel had used her right of self-defense under Article 51 of the Charter—"until the Security Council could act. . . ." Ben Gurion ended his speech with the words:

> It is our desire and our right to live, work and produce in our homeland in tranquillity and security, for our aim is peace; but we must not close our eyes to the disturbing developments in the area —we must stand guard with open eyes, with goodwill, and foresight, with determination and increased military capacity. *We are compelled to make a supreme effort for security*. It is forced on us by external and hostile forces. *We are perhaps facing momentous decisions and events*. Let us stand ready and united, and the Rock of Israel will not fail.

These italics are official. They are designed to indicate that the Prime Minister was prophetic, and was saying a word to the wise. He spoke as a man who had made a supreme decision and had assurance that his decision would be successful.

Now, in the months since Nasser's seizure of the Canal, it had not been easy for the French to persuade the British to accompany them in assisting Israel to overthrow Nasser. For as the reader may have gathered from previous pages in this work, the British Conservative Government were not friends of Israel: they were friends of Iraq and Jordan, and would have been friends with Nasser if he had not made life impossible for their Middle Eastern policy and positions of strength. From January, 1955, to June, 1956, the British sold £27 million of arms to nations of the Arab League, and to Israel £3.26 million. When Israel searched for an ally against what she believed, *with justification*, was the prospect of an Arab attack on her by the fall of 1956, with Soviet weapons, she sought it in France, not Britain, after having been refused help by all other countries. Britain needed to keep her vestiges of influence in Jordan. It is said that Eden believed he might still bring Nasser down after another try, this time, successful, he hoped, in persuading Jordan into the Baghdad Pact. This would be accomplished by helping Jordan to resist the pressure of the pro-Nasser elements within that country. Thus was born the policy of working with Nuri Es Said to lend Jordan Iraqi troops, which would cross the Jordan frontier and bolster Hussein. But the Israelis strongly opposed the entrance of Iraqi troops into Jordan: for they would be that much closer to Israel, and Iraq had not signed the armistice agreements of 1949!

At the meeting with the French in Paris on September 26 already mentioned (Chapter 12), Eden raised this matter with the French. The French rejected the policy, arguing that Israel could not and ought not to accept the idea of Iraqi help to Jordan, and that Nasser could not be toppled even if Jordan did enter the Baghdad Pact. On the other hand, Eden was afraid that if he went along with the French and the Israelis against Nasser, Iraq would quit the Baghdad Pact. But it was noticed that *after* September 26, the British government pressed, as never before, Israel's right to Canal passage as a test case of Egyptian intentions!

Eden continued in his Jordan-Iraq policy down to the retaliatory raid by Israel against Jordan at Qalqilya, October 10-11. He believed this Israeli move would overthrow Hussein. Nuri Es Said was about to move his troops Jordanwards. The French protested—now publicly! Israel, on October 14, practically threatened war if Nuri Es Said persisted. The move was abandoned.

On October 13 came the Soviet veto of the implementing instrument for the Six Principles at the United Nations. It was after this that Eden, further dynamized by the Conservative Party Conference on October 13, resolved that force must in all probability be used, and approximately on the basis of the French arrangements with Israel that he recently heard had been formulated on October 10.

The Brombergers report, with close accuracy, that General Maurice Challe, of the French General Staff, went to London on October 15 to explain further to Eden the Israeli plan to attack Egypt and the course of French cooperation once it should begin. Eden was already well acquainted with the arms and training assistance France was giving to Israel. It was in these circumstances that the Paris meeting of the British and French leaders occurred, actually one or two days before it had been originally scheduled. On October 15, Ben Gurion spoke in the Knesset with the confidence we have already noticed, for he had been fully apprised of developments in French policy since the return of Pineau from New York (he left there October 14, in the afternoon), as well as of Pineau's last-minute consultations with Selwyn Lloyd in New York, when the latter had stayed on trying to get Dulles to commit himself on Canal tolls, in vain.

On October 17, Ben Gurion spoke again in the Knesset, and made even more of Egyptian aggression than before: he especially focused his remarks on the dangers Israel suffered from Egypt's "Fascist dictator," the violator of the armistice.[14] He was speaking after having been told by the French leaders that the British could now be relied on to cooperate. Also, on October 16, Pineau had told the National Assembly, in the course of a speech on the fiasco at the United Nations, that "We have some very considerable trumps up our sleeve." This was shortly before Eden and Selwyn Lloyd arrived at Le Bourget. The game, he said, was far from over. He explained that he had prodded Dulles at the United Nations to have the Six Principles drawn with precision to include Israel's rights in the Canal.

On October 18 Sir Walter Monckton, British Minister of Defense, had been replaced in that position by Antony Head, till then Secretary for War. The *Manchester Guardian Weekly* of October 25 interpreted this change as weakening in the British Cabinet the position of those members who were on the side of moderation in the Suez dispute. Head was not one of these. The newspaper commented that Sir Anthony Eden had assumed personal responsibility for Britain's policy "probably to a greater extent than is usual in a country with Cabinet government. Sir Anthony seems to have been acting rather in the manner of Sir Winston Churchill at critical periods of the war . . ." and it added, because it did not, as we have amply shown, like his policy, ". . . although his judgment has not been so sound."

All the memoirs dealing with Churchill that have appeared since that time tell what insiders well knew: that Churchill's judgment was not *always* sound. It is pretty certain that the *Guardian* would have been happy to have Sir Anthony act most tyranically had his judgment happened to coincide with its own principles and prejudices.

* * * * *

In Washington, Dulles was more worried about Suez than he had admitted to the President and the American public. He and his staff had frequent meetings on October 15 and 17 and 19.

By October 19, somebody in his Department, perhaps also his brother Allen Dulles, should have known that the French and Israelis would most probably attack Egypt—but the date given them was directly after election day! [15] For both the State Department and the CIA had been apprised by October 18 or 19, at the latest, of the Franco-Israeli intention. The State Department was in possession of information of the kind I have mentioned from one of its unimpeachable sources by October 18 or 19. It was volunteered by a French Cabinet minister, but not any of those I have mentioned, and not by the Minister of Defense, Bourgès-Manoury. Furthermore, on October 20, in the lobbies of the Assemblée Nationale in Paris, French deputies were whispering rumors of an Anglo-French invasion of Egypt, and some phoned the U.S. Embassy.

It may have been given to American channels for either of two reasons. First, the purpose could have been to make Dulles understand he had better, now, at the very last moment, put pressure on Nasser to respond to the second part of the Security Council resolution (the part vetoed by the Soviet Union). Secondly, it could have been to mislead Dulles about the date of an attack. It could have been the two motives together. The date suggested was not, of course, absolutely certain. For one thing, an invasion X-Day cannot always be rigid, since military preparation cannot be forecast with absolute accuracy when the factors involved, as in this area, are very many, very complex, and highly interdependent. For another, to reveal accurately is to expose one's life to a leak of information, unless the revelation is intended to be leaked.

It was alleged by the French informant that he was, in some way, authorized to pass on this information to the American government, so that the French government might receive some response in a similar clandestine way, without the usual diplomatic confrontations and possible publicity. This method of informing was intended as a safeguard and cover for Dulles and Eisenhower, as well as a convenience for the French government.

As for the second source of information, it was the French Secret Service. It passed the news, I am told, to the American "Secret Service"—which presumably means to the CIA. What is not comprehensible, if these reports are true, is the apparent apathy of the CIA and the State Department when the information was received. Perhaps, since the leak indicated the attack would take place *after* election day, November 6, the recipients shelved it while they concentrated on the election campaign. It is highly possible that Dulles, knowing what was in the wind, may have deferred diplomatic action, rather than take it immediately, because (a) it would have stirred up warlike trouble (through Press leakage on both sides of the Atlantic) in the closing days of the election campaign, and (b) he would have been obliged to recommend strong action to the President and take it himself. He did not do anything about the news, partly out of fear and confusion, and partly because, as I shall suggest in another connection presently, he was torn between God and Machiavelli. He may well have harbored for a few days, too long a time in the circumstances, the feeling that it would be well if the detestable Nasser were toppled, and therefore have waited. Or, he may have been too confident that France and Israel (and certainly England) would not *dare* act without telling him formally, and that if they should do that, he could tie them up as he believed he had done in early August and (possibly) in mid-September. For he had overweening self-confidence.

Yet—he began to smell a rat! When he scanned the cables with his staff each morning he noticed, beginning on October 16, that something was missing—the regular reports from London and Paris. "What's going on?" he asked. "Something's going on," he muttered. He looked suspicious and cross at his close associates and the security officer who brought in the cables and news digests. The British Ambassador, Sir Roger Makins, had left for Britain some days before (the change had been gazetted in May and had nothing to do with the Suez crisis), and the new Ambassador, Sir Harry Caccia, had not yet arrived. Hervé Alphand, France's new Ambassador, was not in Washington. It all looked very suspicious, especially after the curious behavior of Pineau and Lloyd at the U.N. Usually, communications between the United States, Britain, and France were very frequent, almost daily, giving considerable civil and military data. The three were allies, and their connections were tied in together through at least three switchboards: information came from the British and French Embassies to the State Department; from the military liaison and mission officers of the European allies to the Pentagon, via NATO and other allied arrangements; from their Secret Services to the Central Intelligence Agency and the State Department. The men of the three countries who were engaged in comparable official business knew each other; went to parties together. Now the information mills were turning out no grist and were taking none in. (On the other hand, if it is argued there was a blackout from October 16, information of intention before that was ample.)

Also, was it not fishy that, when all the trouble was occurring in Israel and among her Arab neighbors, Abba Eban, Israeli Ambassador to Washington, should suddenly have been recalled to Israel along with the Ambassadors in Moscow, London and Paris?

On October 15, Monday, Dulles conferred at length with Eban before he left. The officially well-primed Washington correspondent of the *New York Herald Tribune* said (October 18) that Dulles had sent a personal plea to Ben Gurion for moderation. For Middle Eastern developments in the ensuing few days (the approaching of October 23 elections in Jordan) posed the greatest danger to peace since 1948. But this warning, which apparently contained a message from President Eisenhower to Ben Gurion within it, does not seem to have arisen out of anything that might have been guessed about British and French intentions. Nor does it tally in date with Dulles's reaffirmation in his press conference of October 16, the day after he had seen Eban, of the Tripartite Declaration, to the effect that "within constitutional limits" the United States would go to the aid of any victim of aggression, whether it should be an Arab state or Israel.

It is noteworthy that State Department fears of Russian intervention in the Middle Eastern imbroglio in this period were already most acute. President Eisenhower (he later recalled) had said to Eban (later still this was amended by the President to "said to him *through* Dulles") this:

> I hoped he would not allow any misinterpretation of sentiment in [the United States] to sway him, and particularly because of possible Jewish sympathy for what seemed to be an intention to building up around the mobilization of Israel at that time—I hoped he would not allow this to sway his judgment as to what this Administration would do in doing the very best to prevent any outbreak of hostilities and the, you might say, settlement of international issues by force. And I told him that if he thought that this would have any . . . iota of influence on the [U.S. Presidential] election or that that would have any influence on me, he should disabuse his mind of it.[16]

President Eisenhower, in talking to Dulles before the Dulles-Eban meeting, had made the firm request, "Foster, do not soften my words!"

Soon after this, Dulles sent to Ambassador Winthrop Aldrich in London and to Ambassador Douglas Dillon in Paris (who knew quite a good deal) to ask, "What's going on?" Aldrich was kept at arm's length, to his sadness, because he liked the English and was on very good terms with the members of the Government and English society. He was the representative of the United States on the nascent SCUA at this time. He knew that there was talk, perhaps around October 20, that Israel was getting ready to mobilize. He knew what the American military attaché knew, and that the latter was not being entertained by his British military counterparts as usual. It was all very baffling. Dillon was kept at arm's length also by the French Foreign Office—but he learned important secrets elsewhere and he passed them on, for whatever they would be worth, to the State Department.

Furthermore, the CIA, which had been monitoring the allies' radio communications, found that from October 15 or thereabouts onward, the communications between Paris and Tel Aviv became remarkably frequent. (The code was apparently not broken.)

In Dulles's own office there was a sense of something brewing, a sense of foreboding. Dulles's anxious concern, and that of his immediate advisers (say the top eight men in State and the liaison men in the White House), was lest any of the three possible belligerents

(France, Israel, and Britain) should start an incident without telling the United States.

Dulles did not improve matters with his allies by the tenor of a press conference he held on October 16. He was challenged by correspondents about his revision of the transcript of his press conference on October 2, when he had talked of "fundamental" differences with his allies over Suez—and other matters. He now responded in a furious tone, that he had the right to revise his remarks if he thought he had committed a *blunder!* Perhaps his anger was merely a theatrical act for diplomatic effect; perhaps it was sincere. But the trouble was that Marguerite Higgins, the State Department confidante, had in the *New York Herald Tribune* but recently defended Dulles's policy of "differences with our allies" too truly to Dulles's state of mind for the allies to be mollified by the outburst. It only increased their distrust of him.

The fate of the Atlantic alliance now came strongly into the foreground, causing grave concern. In the last analysis, some in the State Department were saying, America is not going to be happy to preside over a defeat for Britain and France. The Secretary was seriously worried, but he was also, it seems, paralyzed into immobility. As one of his intimates has put it (imputing the blame to Britain and France): "It was the hell of a way to run an alliance!" But this official and Dulles and their associates (with the probable exception of the head of the European section and of Robert Murphy, Deputy Under Secretary of State) were looking at the matter rather too selfishly, if the sentence just quoted describes their mentality accurately. The question could be asked, how had Dulles run the alliance till now? No tolls withdrawn from Egypt; no boycott; no economic pressure on Nasser; Americans allowed to become Canal pilots!

The information offered in Erskine Childers' *The Road to Suez,*[17] and in Lord Randolph Churchill's polemical biography of Eden, indicates that Eisenhower had sent Eden a letter on October 16, saying his hands were tied until election day, and promising strong cooperation to settle the Canal issue after it. These reports are *false*. President Eisenhower did not send any letter of this kind at any time, and resents the suggestion that he could have done so.

While Dulles was bothered with the question, "What's going on?" and just about the time, surely by October 19, when he should have taken very seriously the warning from Paris, dramatic news came from Hungary. It distracted his attention from the Middle East: no longer could his attention be undivided. Probably stimulated by the half-success of the Polish government's defiance of Soviet domination that had begun with the first of the Poznan Riots on June 28, and that had resulted at least in the rescue of the Polish people from the extreme Stalinists and communization, the Hungarian people had begun to rebel actively against the detested government of Erno Gero, successor to Matyas Rakosi, and the Soviet iron hand that guided and supported it. On October 14, the Communist Party of Hungary was forced to rehabilitate Imre Nagy! The insurrectionary passions and nationalist and economic demands that had led up to this surged on more massively until, on October 20, the State Department got wind of moves toward an uprising in Hungary. At the same time, Dulles's mind was involved in events currently taking place in Poland. The steadfastness of the Poles had forced the Russian General Rokossovsky out of the Polish Communist Party's Politburo, had brought back Gomulka as the head of the Party, and was compelling the Soviet Union to remove its troops from Poland. On October 21 (a Sunday), when his mind should have been exclusively on the Middle East, Dulles had appeared on the CBS television program, *Face the Nation*, spent time preparing for it, time in getting to it, time at it, and time in recovering from it.[18] It was mainly about Poland. Dulles's chief point was that the United States (in spite of his strident pronouncements two years before about a "roll-back" of the Soviets) would not become involved in Poland: that though he approved of the Polish revolt, he could offer *no* military assistance to it whatever. At best economic aid might be forthcoming. At any rate, he had obtained a pledge from the American Red Cross that it would give aid!

Questioned about Suez, Dulles said:

> Well, we have developed a common policy, and I think it's just amazing the degree to which we have had a common policy. We have now had what you might call four Suez conferences, that I personally have attended, over the last three months, and while we have sometimes started out with somewhat different points of view, we have ended up together, and the fact that there are certain minor superficial differences as to details about just how you handle tolls or how much is going to get paid to Egypt and how much isn't, doesn't detract from the fact that basically we do have a common policy.

Was this, once again, merely a brave front? Was it a deliberate electioneering pose? Was it Dulles's true belief? Was he deceiving himself? How could he possibly square this statement with his conversations with Eden and Selwyn Lloyd and Pineau and his anxieties that they had decided to use force? Would it not have been better, given the circumstances, for Dulles not to make such public appearances, in which, even if his faith in his own perceptiveness was sincere, he risked misleading the public he constantly claimed he needed to educate?

He evidently relished this appearance at a moment of difficulty for the Soviet Union, since it gave the United States the propaganda advantage. Dulles used the opportunity to assert again that "our job is to keep alive the concept of freedom. That is a contagious thing and if anyone will catch it, it will be the Poles."

As a matter of fact, there is a most curious air of utter unreality about the days between October 16 and October 29, when one surveys from hindsight the march of affairs *on the surface* concerning the Suez crisis and the attempts at settlement. Dulles seems to have moved through it like a somnambulist towards the unsuspected brink of a steep staircase.

In the first place, it was reported in London on October 19 that the United States would press American owners of ships flying Panamanian and Liberian flags to pay their dues to SCUA. Then, within four days after that, news came from the United States that the State Department favored passing on to Egypt 90 per cent of the dues collected! The Foreign Office and 10 Downing Street could hardly regard this proposal as anything but folly or naïveté, either of which would be dangerous to their interests. On October 20, SCUA at last found an executive officer.

On October 21, an Egyptian newspaper, *Al Gomhouria*, published an Indian plan for a Suez compromise, developed apparently through Menon's efforts with Nasser.[19] Menon reported that, "If other forces do not get in the way, the talks are getting on." The plan was a renewal and revision of the treaty of 1888, and included many ideas similar to those set forth in Dag Hammarskjold's letter to Fawzi. It proposed changing the number of members of the implementing body to sixteen—Britain, France, the United States, Egypt, Russia, India, and Japan, and representatives of the various regions of the world. This revised SCUA would hold regular meetings with the Egyptian Canal Authority, but would not be allowed to interfere in its everyday administration or authority. It would be merely consultative and cooperative, a funnel for suggestions and complaints. Increases in dues would have to be submitted to it, and, failing approval, would then go to the World Court, or other arbitral body. Other matters in dispute would go first to the Egyptian courts, and subsequently be the subject of a decision in a joint meeting of the Egyptian Authority and SCUA. If the result in the joint meeting was unsatisfactory, the issue would go to the World Court or to some United Nations agency.

The renewed or revised treaty would be registered with the United Nations, which would have authority to appoint three experts to serve on the Egyptian Canal Authority for three-year terms in the first instance. This was Menon's plan; but Nasser had not committed himself to it. It was not even an Egyptian proposal such as had been envisaged at the Security Council.

About this time, the date of October 29, proposed by the Security Council[20] for further talks on Suez to be held on the basis of firm proposals from Egypt, had been shifted by Egypt. According to diplomatic rumors from Cairo, that country wished the talks delayed to the opening of the United Nations General Assembly on November 12! Nasser had just told an American journalist that he would be willing to go to Geneva himself to meet other heads of government if it would contribute to a peaceful settlement. But this was regarded in London and Paris only as a use of a well-known tactic of getting favorable notice while committing oneself to nothing.

Talks between Dr. Fawzi and the British Ambassador in Cairo, Sir Humphrey Trevelyan, on October 22 and thereafter, and a conference between Fawzi and Nasser did nothing to settle the matter of the U.N.-sponsored meeting. Fawzi announced that still no date or place had been fixed. Also on October 22, the British Foreign Office asserted that no official proposals had yet been received from the Egyptian government for implementing the Six Principles. "It is felt that if Colonel Nasser genuinely wants a negotiated settlement he will offer some clear-cut proposals." The Security Council had given Egypt the responsibility of producing proposals. But the *Christian Science Monitor's* correspondent in Cairo, the well-informed Geoffrey Godsell, reported that the "highest level" in the Egyptian government regarded it as "extraordinary" that the British insisted on "more concrete proposals before talks can be resumed." The government of Egypt thought the explanatory notes exchanged by both sides during the talks in New York should be enough to bring the parties together for further discussions leading to negotiations.

In order that the facts do not get lost to sight, we may note here that no basis exists for the contention by some onlookers that the Suez Canal dispute was at this point close to a settlement, the path towards which was being cleared by the correspondence between Hammarskjold and the government of Egypt. Some perennial critics of British Conservative Governments, such as Paul Johnson of the London *New Statesman*,[21] contend that because some alleged offer of negotiation was not accepted by London and Paris, they were manifestly not interested in getting a peaceful settlement. But this is nonsense. The Egyptians did not reply to the Secretary General of the United Nations *until November 2*, that is, twenty days after the ending of the crucial Security Council meeting. Their official spokesman proffered the reason for delay before October 29 to be the need for careful study by Egypt of what it was going to propose and her demand for clarification of what the allies wanted. But all of this was concocted long after the events of October 29.

By this time, the fire was ablaze, and so the reply might never have been sent at all except as a ploy to gather support for Egypt's case for protection now that force was being used against her. Egypt had not produced proposals to satisfy the minimum allied demands.

In the meantime, disturbing events had been occurring, as we have narrated, between Israel, Jordan, Syria, and Egypt; all these events were instigated and assisted by Egypt. Then the tensions were sharpened on October 16 and October 22. On October 16, the French captured the Egyptian munitions-carrier yacht, *Athos*, en route from Egypt to Algeria with war materials for the Algerian rebels. The *Athos* was also found to hold diplomatic documents, a discovery that caused a rise in temper in the French Cabinet and Assembly. On October 22, French feelings were further exacerbated by the French Algerian military command's interception of a plane from Tunis carrying the five top leaders of the Algerian rebellion to Morocco, apparently against the orders of Paris. They were headed by Ahmed Ben Bella, who had long been a guest of Nasser's in Cairo.

On October 23 (with Ben Gurion already in Paris at Villacoublay, near Sèvres, for some 24 hours), Prime Minister Mollet declared in the National Assembly that the matter of the transport of arms would be taken to the Security Council and that the French Ambassador to Cairo had been withdrawn. He declared, also, that Franco-British solidarity on Suez was complete and that both countries were resolved to accept no solution not providing for international administration of the Canal. In the light of what I have reported about the current meetings between the French leaders and Ben Gurion, not so many miles from the Place de la Concorde and even London, it is not surprising that Mollet spoke in this sense. He continued that Egypt must now come forward with acceptable proposals. He made it clear that the Menon scheme was so involved in legal gadgets as itself to threaten to be a cause of friction and conflict. The British and French expected a "precise" offer promising effectively that Egypt would not be absolute mistress of the Canal.

Prime Minister Mollet was most belligerent. The game has only begun, he said; it is not yet over; Nasser knows he cannot win; we are in complete agreement with our British allies on the measures to be taken in all circumstances; we are not prepared to accept a Munich; we will not accept half-measures to maintain peace! He repeated Dulles's two-sides-of-the-coin argument.

The capture of the *Athos* was used to justify the movement of French warships to cover Alexandria—although, in fact, the naval patrols moved to cover the coast of Israel. At this same time (with Ben Gurion and his aides in communication with Jerusalem), Israeli forces, already alerted and assembling to counter any threat from Jordan, if she accepted the entry of Iraqi troops, continued to concentrate, though that threat receded.

On Tuesday, October 23, Pineau made a sudden and swift visit to London to consult with Selwyn Lloyd and Eden: he arrived and departed by air between 8 P.M. and 11 P.M. He had been in conference with Ben Gurion and Bourgès-Manoury and Mollet. Lloyd was shortly to be in conference with the Israeli Prime Minister in Paris also; he probably joined Pineau on his return flght, made for that very purpose.

It seemed as though the military forces of France, Israel, and Britain would be in motion very soon—not *after* November 6.

Earlier on October 23, before Pineau's visit, Selwyn Lloyd announced to the House of Commons [22] that Egypt had not yet put forward any proposals. "But there seems to be a gap between Egypt's acceptance of the principles [the Six] and definition on her part of the means to apply them . . . we need proposals, not the mere acceptance of principles. We still await these proposals." When asked by Robens, the Opposition's specialist in foreign policy, whether the next step ought not to be the opening of direct talks, Selwyn Lloyd replied that he had spent four days in New York with Hammarskjold, Pineau, and Fawzi, "having *precisely* those direct talks to see whether it is possible to achieve a basis for negotiation. I think it is better for definite proposals, which could constitute a basis for negotiations, to be put forward." (The word *precisely* is underlined here because the Foreign Secretary emphasized this word.)

Moscow's intelligence services seem to have been alert and well-connected, for the Franco-British movements of October 23 were noted. On October 27, *Pravda* reported that, "On October 23 a decision was taken in London by the ministers of foreign affairs of France, Pineau, and England, Lloyd, about the start of military intervention in Egypt in the nearest future." Yet it may have been only a guess.

President Eisenhower made a campaign appearance on October 24 on a television program called "In the Afternoon," at a time usually devoted, as a reporter said, to "soap-operas, give-away shows and old movies," to answer questions asked by a panel of seven women. One response he gave could only have brought further distress and determination by the British and French to go it alone against Nasser. Actually, the Suez question "went off the air" because the time allotted was at an end; but the question and answer were published in the press. In answer to the question, "Can you give us a picture of this unrest that we are now having with the Suez Canal?" Eisenhower replied:

> Now, on top of this [the Jewish-Arab conflicts], we have this Suez Canal, which we thought was all settled until 1968 because the treaty of 1888 says that until 1968 it is going to be done this way. I think no one can challenge the legal right of Egypt to nationalize the Canal, but unquestionably there is involved in it the point, not only the point of national prestige but the point of personal prestige.
>
> So here you have got this great waterway on which so much of the economy of the world depends, particularly all shipping nations.

. . . Well, now, when these nations all see that passageway is sort of threatened, and their economy is threatened, which would mean a depression of some kind for them, they get very excited. We are not as heavily involved as are most, but still I think we have about two and a half per cent of that, so it is a very complicated question. You can talk on it all afternoon, I assure you.[23]

Where was the President's mind at this critical time, when war was possibly brewing? On October 25 he was to speak at Madison Square Garden; on October 29, in Miami and Jacksonville and Richmond; on October 31 in Dallas and Oklahoma City; on November 1 in Philadelphia, returning to Washington each night—in order to keep in touch, said Press Secretary Hagerty, with "the fast-breaking developments in the satellite nations."

From October 20, day after day, Dulles plodded away in staff meetings all day long, working to understand events in Poland, the Middle East, and above all, Hungary! At 7 P.M. on October 23, the news was brought in to him of the actual outbreak of rebellion in various cities of Hungary, including Budapest! Now and again, he stood up and walked around the room, his hands in his trousers pockets, especially cocksure when he pronounced his views on Poland and Hungary. "Did I not tell you," he reminded his associates, "that our financial aid to Yugoslavia would be like bread cast on the waters, that it would come back tenfold? See how the helping hand towards Yugoslavia kept that country independent of Soviet domination entirely, even made it a thorn in the side of Moscow! Of course, the people of Poland and Hungary, their leaders, have seen that it is possible to be independent of Moscow! We kept alive the yearning for freedom. It worked in Yugoslavia; it will work in Poland and Hungary. The great monolith of Communism is crumbling!" He could not restrain his joy. But neither would he help the rebels in Budapest.

But his mind slipped off Israel. It was bent on two essays, one to be the material for a note by Eisenhower on Hungary, and the other a speech he must give in Dallas, Texas, on Saturday, October 27, before the Council on World Affairs. Considering the critical state of world affairs, this latter appearance was not at all necessary at that time.

On October 25, the Jordanian Government arraigned Israel before the Security Council for the heavy reprisal of Qalqilya, on October 11.[24] Abba Eban had by now returned from Tel Aviv and presented Israel's defense and countercharge. He reviewed the history of the *fedayeen* gangs, and observed that every thirty-six hours, on the average, during the last three months, someone in Israel had been killed or wounded by Jordanian attacks. He reproached Britain, Iran, and the Soviet Union for their observations of a week earlier praising Jordan's restraint and expressing sympathy for her casualties without mentioning Jordan's persistent assaults on Israeli civilians.

He turned the tables on Eisenhower and British and Australian leaders (though he did not mention the French), by quoting remarks from their various speeches on the Suez crisis to the effect that *the use of force in the last resort was recognized fully in other situations.*

He pledged: "If we are not attacked, we shall not strike; if we are attacked we fully reserve the inherent right of self-defense." He said that on September 11, Eisenhower had spoken of circumstances (in another Middle East context) "where self-defense itself would indicate some quick response" and "where we would recognize that Britain and France had no other recourse than to continue to use [the Canal] even if they had to be more forceful than merely sailing through it." Eban also referred to Menzies' speech of September 25, and to Selwyn Lloyd's of October 4.

In the background, the State Department must have known, were facts driving Israel towards an outbreak. The United Nations had not been capable of compelling Nasser (or the previous regime) to carry out the unanimous U.N. resolution of September 1, 1951, that the Canal must be kept open to Israeli ships. The members of the organization knew that this defiance was only one item in an Arab, and especially an Egyptian, policy of smothering the state of Israel. The others were: the refusal of passage to ships and cargoes going to and from Israel; the boycott of all business firms everywhere which did business with Israel; the denial of Israeli access to the world by sea via Elath on the Red Sea, accomplished by collusion between Saudi Arabia and Egypt (the islands of Sanafir and Tiran off the coast and Sharm el Sheik on it, had been mounted for this purpose with Egyptian long-range cannon); a plan of continuous aggression, by night and day, against the 591 miles of Israeli border. In spite of the armistice agreements, freely signed, with all professions of honor by the Arab countries (except Iraq), and the supervision thereof by the U.N. Mixed Armistice Commission, the assaults continued. By October 29, 1956, there had been no less than 11,873 cases of Arab sabotage and 1,335 Israeli casualties, some of them horrible in their bestiality, most of them of civilians, large numbers of the victims being women and children.

The Israeli policy of reprisals was mostly directed toward Arab military personnel. The Israeli government, hemmed in by 40 million Arabs, believed that such action, and a parade of military strength close to the Arab borders, were essential to Israel's survival. They could see that they would soon be attacked in an Egyptian-inspired "second round," the purpose of which would be Israel's extermination, and they were well aware that appeal after appeal to the United Nations and the United States had brought them no help or dependable guarantee. As we have seen, Dulles's policy was to keep out of the Israeli-Arab conflict, leaving it to the U.N. and Hammarskjold to find some way out.

Indeed, Israeli-Arab relations had begun a crescendo of fatal tension in the early months of 1956. In late March, Hammarskjold had been sent on a mission to seek peace. It was to no avail: the Soviet Union was by now fully supporting and inciting the Arabs. That nation and Czechoslovakia were reported to be training Egyptian officers in Poland. The United States government reaffirmed its role in the Tripartite Declaration. Again, on the very day that Dulles was rescinding the offer of the loan for Aswan, Hammarskjold had to be sent on a pacifying mission to Israel, Jordan, and Egypt. Even he, detached as an international administrator, could not avoid denouncing, on August 16, a particularly horrible group-murder of Israelis by Jordanians.

By the end of September, 1956, Nasser had the Canal well in his grip. He and Hussein of Jordan pursued their offensive against Israel. Israel retaliated with severe reprisals. The United Nations condemned the reprisals. But Nasser and Hussein were not compelled to behave peacefully: Britain had a mutual defense treaty with Jordan, while Nasser had proved to be too tough to discipline, and, curiously, the Anglo-Egyptian Treaty of 1954 was still in effect.

Jordan was being shaken most violently by propaganda from Nasser and by the maneuvers of his followers. On October 21, she was to hold Parliamentary elections. Emotions were becoming intense and highly unstable. To assist the King in maintaining order, the British arranged that Iraqi troops should enter Jordan; Dulles and Eisenhower were persuaded of the wisdom of this action. But the Israelis warned that if Iraqi troops made the move, they must take measures to counterbalance them: Iraq had never signed the armistice agreements with Israel. The Israeli government rejected British assurances that they would not suffer by the arrangement—indeed, rejected stern British threats. The pother was so great that Iraqi troops did not move at all. On October 21, the Jordanian election took place: the pro-Nasserite forces won a considerable victory.

Israeli military intelligence in the Arab countries was singularly competent. Its information on Egypt's growing strength and the deployment of Russian weapons and other supplies in Sinai led it to the measures of self-defense and reprisal we have touched on, especially the seeking of French aid. Other actions were symptomatic of timing and intention. On October 3, Israel withdrew from the Mixed Armistice Commission on the grounds that it was ineffective and often unfair to Israel. On October 8, her Foreign Minister, Golda Meir, declared that since the U.N. was incapable of compelling the Arabs to respect their pledges, Israel would meet force by force. The Israelis had become more fearful that the Arabs were about to attempt to overwhelm them. Their raids on Jordan increased.

On the other side, Israel's growing activism spurred the Arabs towards military union. In twos and threes, the Arab states arranged financial assistance for each other and vowed their mutual loyalty. Then, on October 24, a joint Egyptian-Syrian-Jordanian command was announced, with the Egyptian commander in chief to be at its head if there were major fighting with Israel. This was, for Israel, the public signal for mobilization.

On this same day, October 25, in New Delhi, a French correspondent asked Nehru whether the plan put forth by Menon did not lack the guarantees desired by the West. He replied: "In the ultimate analysis there are no guarantees, except the normal guarantee when two nations agree to come to terms; when the United Nations also comes into the picture the guarantee is a very powerful one. Any other guarantee will really be a restriction on the sovereignty of a country."

This philosophical pronouncement was palpably specious, even though Prime Minister Nehru may have believed it to be sound. But his queer pacifist ideas were markedly divorced from harsh nationalist and power realities. At about that very moment Israel (for whom the government of India did not care a fig compared with her egoistic interests in the Arab nations) was saying in the United Nations, "You have not helped us; you cannot help us; you will not help us."

Nehru did not protest the Arab joint military command or the explicit threat to annihilate Israel. For Indian ships did not pass through Israel; they passed through the Suez Canal. The correspondent asked him about the right of Israeli ships to pass through the Canal. His noble, dispassionate answer was that Israel should go to the World Court about Egypt's claim that she was at war with Israel and so entitled to block transit. He was as calm as a marble god about Israel's troubles. Of course, Egypt could say she was at war if she wanted to do so: and *that* took away Israel's rights to pass through the Canal!

Matters were coming to a head, the fearful raging head of Mars. Through United States Ambassador Winthrop W. Aldrich, British leaders were still trying to obtain Dulles's agreement to withhold tolls from Nasser. They had no luck. Nor had Nasser replied to the opportunities presented to him by the publication of the Indian plan of compromise. Christian Pineau told the press on October 26 that it would take a long time to get results from the efforts for negotiation being made by Hammarskjold, because Nasser had vetoed his own Foreign Minister, Dr. Fawzi, when the latter had suggested Egyptian cooperation with SCUA.[25]

All eyes were now focused on Jordan and Hungary. (In London, SCUA, under the chairmanship of Lord John Hope, and awaiting its manager, was taking its routine course. On October 26, the news was announced that £50,000 per year was needed initially for its administration, and it was explained how this would be divided among the various nations. It was all very lawful and peaceful, like a Christmas Day that happens to fall on a Sunday. This money would go into one account; another account would receive, hold, and disburse Canal tolls paid to SCUA.)

The three-way liaison between Dulles, Eisenhower, and Henry Cabot Lodge on Hungary at the United Nations was especially intimate and absorbing. They were in continual conference with the British and French over the tactics to be used in the United Nations to denounce the brutal action in Hungary of the old-guard Communist leaders and the Russian commanders, as well as the formidable troops and weapons the Russian army was bringing into action there. Resolutions and speeches were being carefully formulated.

October 25 was a particularly glorious day in Dulles's office at the State Department. Meetings were held frequently on the news and reaction thereto from Hungary. Statements were prepared. Yes, he had told one of his special critics, Senator Fulbright, only a little while ago (Chapter 1) that the Soviet empire was on the decline. Faith had been justified. The sinners were being whipped at last. God was not mocked!

It is most important to realize that Dulles and Eisenhower were now, under the impact of these stirring events, especially the barehanded heroism of the men and women and youth of Budapest, working themselves into applauding excitement and exultant moral elation. Their emotions could easily be transferred to another situation, if Hungary and the Soviet Union did not offer them full release and gratification—the gratification of satisfied desire to catch the criminal, indict him, and punish him. It could not be done to Russia, for Russia could hit back.

We are thus brought to British policy as decided in the Cabinet meeting of October 25, described with studied care by Sir Anthony Eden.[26] The Franco-Israeli plan to invade Egypt and the agreement of the British to join in its accomplishment were decided in general principle on October 16, and polished and fully affirmed in the three days, October 22, 23, and 24, when Ben Gurion was in France. Eden's account of the October 25 Cabinet meeting is written as though he had definite foreknowledge of all that occurred from October 16 onward. So he did. But his memoirs do not make the explicit point that he did; they do, however, give the impression that something substantial underlay the Cabinet's foreconsciousness of events soon to occur, in the order in which they occurred.

Eden asserts that, on October 25, a report came that Israel was about to mobilize. He does not admit that he knew beforehand that this was about to happen; but he *did* know it. With his knowledge now on the table, the Cabinet was not prepared to condemn Israel "if he [the marked victim of the garroter] strikes out before the noose is round his throat." This being so, British military experts expected Israel to win against Egypt. The chief peril to Britain, then, was not in this conflict itself, but in its potential extension if other Arab states should enter the hostilities. The best way to stop that was by the intervention of Britain.

Eden says: "Ministers had already considered at several meetings the ways in which the situation might develop. These had also been canvassed with the French." This statement may be read as covering that *a* minister, the Foreign Minister, had canvassed these matters with Ben Gurion as well as Pineau and Mollet. It is, therefore, now not difficult to comprehend how the British Cabinet on October 25 discussed "the specific possibility of conflict between Israel and Egypt and decided in principle how it would react if this occurred."

How? (1) Britain and France would at once call on both parties to stop hostilities and withdraw their forces a certain distance from either bank of the Canal. (2) If one or both did not comply, allied forces would temporarily intervene to separate the combatants. (3) Britain and France would occupy key positions at Port Said, Ismailia, and Suez; the purpose was to safeguard free passage through the Canal if it was threatened by war, and to arrest the spread of fighting in the Middle East.

On Thursday, October 25, the State Department received news from U.S. military intelligence in Israel that Israel was apparently beginning a military mobilization. Indeed, at 3 P.M. on October 25, preparations to mobilize were ordered at a top-level meeting in Ben Gurion's office. From that time a special State Department official was given the assignment of keeping in contact with Reuben Shiloah, political counselor in the Israeli Embassy in Washington. On October 26, further communications from the United States military attaché in Israel confirmed the previous day's report and judged that the mobilization was total. Moreover, the British and French diplomatic and military personnel apparently knew more about what was happening than the Americans did, but evaded talking about it to them. Israeli officials merely answered that the mobilization was not general, only partial, and gave none but the (by now) usual reasons for it. William M. Rountree of the Near East Department disclosed to Dulles the alarm he felt over events in Israel and their association with Britain and France, and suggested Dulles investigate.

On Saturday, October 27, in circumstances we have related (Chapter 1), Dulles was to leave at noon by air for Dallas, Texas, to speak to the Council on World Affairs. The President was to enter Walter Reed Hospital for a pre-election check-up. Before the President left for the hospital, he had a message to Ben Gurion dispatched at 12:25 P.M. It has not hitherto been made public.

It said this. It recalled a message sent by the President to Ben

Gurion on October 20, to calm Israeli apprehensions over the entry of Iraqi troops into Jordan. So far no such entry had occurred. Thus, the suspension of such a movement was a contribution to peace. Now, the President was concerned about the heavy mobilization of the Israeli forces, because it was increasing the tension. The world was under great strain these days. Self-restraint and statesmanship of a high order were needed to control tensions in the Middle East and to stop a breach of the peace and prevent any extension of trouble to others who would be affected by the ramifications. The President told Ben Gurion, then, that he remained confident that only a peaceful and moderating will to peace would improve the situation. He renewed Dulles's plea that no action be taken, no forcible initiative by Israel be taken, to lessen the peace and friendship between Israel and the United States.

Israel was now seething with military activity, with a concentration of forces opposite the Jordan frontier. Since the Israelis calculated that the best-trained troops in the Arab countries were in the Jordanian army, its core being the Arab Legion, they must make sure that Israel should not be cut in half at its narrow waist, where it was only fifteen miles across from the Jordan frontier to the Mediterranean.

The next day, October 28, Eisenhower was still in Walter Reed Hospital. Dulles did not get back to Washington from Dallas until 4 P.M. In the meanwhile, as it was now late afternoon on October 28 in Israel, an urgent and very serious cable from Ambassador Edward B. Lawson in Tel Aviv, who now reported total mobilization in Israel, had to be run around to the hospital by Herbert Hoover, Jr., Under Secretary of State. He was given a second message from Eisenhower to Ben Gurion. This was dispatched at 3:32 P.M. Washington time, or about 10:30 P.M. in Israel, where as the Bible so often says, "the evening and the day were one"—that is, almost October 29. The decision had been taken to attack the very next day.

This second message carried an "extra urgent" mark to Ambassador Lawson. It is made public for the first time here. Yesterday, it said, I sent you a message voicing my grave concern. I renewed the previous plea of Dulles that no forcible step be taken to endanger peace in the Middle East. Now I hear that this morning additional information shows that your mobilization is complete and continuing. I therefore draw attention again to the gravity of the situation. Because of the wide repercussions that might result in a wide state of tension, and the intervention of the United States according to the Tripartite Declaration of 1950, I have given instructions that this situation be discussed with Great Britain and France, parties thereto to make all efforts to ameliorate the situation. I have also appealed to other countries in the Middle East to stop any hostile actions. I am compelled to emphasize the degree of apprehension I have about the present situation and the hope that you do nothing to endanger the peace.

This letter, like the President's message to Ben Gurion of the day before, was also communicated to London and Paris.

Eisenhower could not have been very well coached by Dulles on Arab aggressions against Israel. For he now spoke to his staff as though the reason why the Israelis were going to make war was solely for expansion, deliberately so.[27] The Israelis, the President was saying, want more land, whereas to survive they need peace with the Arabs. As though Ben Gurion and all political chiefs, excepting the *Herut*, had not been begging for it for years, and asking America to help to achieve it!

At Dallas, Dulles spoke as though his eyes were looking inward and not to the clash of arms outside. It was like an academic lecture, touched with complacent self-praise.[28] His first reference was to Suez: "an unfinished drama of suspense, which illustrates the kind of an effort, often called 'waging peace,' which will be required, day in and day out, for many years, in many matters, as we seek a just and durable peace." Back to the terminology of his chairmanship in 1941 of the Interchurch Commission on the Christian Bases of a Just and Durable Peace!

His principal theme was the need for military power of an atomic kind, plus conventional forces and tactics, to be employed against "nibblings" by the Soviet, that "vast military power in the hands of a dictatorship unrestrained by moral principles." We need allies, he said, to balance the military power of the Soviet bloc. The United States has something over and above what its allies have, however, "a capacity to retaliate on a scale which is sufficient to deter aggression."

Now, the talent of a Secretary of State does not reside alone or chiefly in how he formulates his principles, but in his sufficiency of wisdom or artistry to recognize exactly in what circumstances and by what means the principles shall be applied. "We must have that capacity [nuclear power to deter aggression from the Soviet bloc], not in the expectation of having to use it, but because if we have that capacity we shall probably never have to use it." When the issue arose during the events that were now moving in like doom upon him, this doctrine proved wrong: the Soviet bloc was to triumph against right in the case of Budapest.

Dulles continued. He applauded the spirit of patriotism of the captive peoples of Europe, the victims of the Soviet government. And today, that very day, "their longing for freedom of thought and of conscience and the right to mold their own lives, are forces which erode and finally break the iron bonds of servitude."

> And all who peacefully enjoy liberty have a solemn duty to seek, by all truly helpful means, that those who now die for freedom will not have died in vain. It is in this spirit that the United States and others have today acted to bring the situation in Hungary to the United Nations Security Council. The weakness of Soviet imperialism is being made manifest. Its weakness is not military weakness nor lack of material power. It is weak because it seeks to sustain an unnatural tyranny by suppressing human aspirations which cannot be indefinitely suppressed and by concealing truths which cannot indefinitely be hidden.

No man can kill a strong enemy by a mere expression of disgust couched in a Biblical simile—unless he is clever enough to know the enemy through and through and use the right strategy and tactics. Even as Dulles spoke a conflagration had started, and he *did not* see it. But he did label the Soviet Union a "whited sepulcher."

He then launched into a repetition of the six steps to peace he had made in the Suez crisis, because "it is of great immediate importance" and "illustrates the ever-present task of 'waging peace.' " As quoted in the first chapter of this book, Dulles asserted that, in the conditions that prevailed before the advent of the United Nations, "we would almost surely have had war before now. The future is still obscure." For three months peace had been waged "with intensity and imagination." Imagination? Impeding the British and French appeal to the United Nations?

He repeated the solution he hoped would prevail: "Egypt should not be in a position to exercise such arbitrary power, open or devious, over the operations of this international waterway that the nations dependent on the Canal will in effect be living under an economic sword of Damocles." (To insert this smart word "economic" was again willfully to blind himself to the situation in the Canal. It was once again also to mislead the American public, by omitting Nasser's geopolitic-cum-military sword of Damocles over America's allies, about whose strength only a few strophes earlier in his prose-poem Dulles had said, "Fortunately, it is not necessary for the United States alone to possess all of the military power needed to balance that of the Soviet bloc. We have allies, and they contribute to the common defense.")

The Foreign Offices of Britain and France must truly have thought themselves not one whit beholden to Dulles after he said:

> The second basic proposition is that *economic* interdependence between Europe, Asia and Africa, such as is served indispensably by the Suez Canal, cannot be made truly secure by coercion and force.

Faithfully or faithlessly he had stacked the cards again by the word "economic." The issues were *even more* strategic-power, and the sanctity of international treaties. He did *not* say this.

> I cannot predict the outcome. The situation is grave. There are complicating and disturbing factors, unrelated to the Canal itself. But if the Governments most directly concerned, those of Britain, France and Egypt, with help from the United Nations, do come to agree, they will have written an inspiring new chapter in the age-long struggle to find a just and durable peace. They will deserve the praise which world opinion and history will surely bestow upon them.

Why could he not, after three months, predict the outcome? Because he had not been willing to face reality earlier. He had produced schemes which needed an element of power over Nasser to make them prevail. Surely he wished them to prevail if he thought they were just, and he had argued at length that they *were* just. What was the "complicating factor"? Israel's demand for survival. It had been in Dulles's well-equipped hands nearly four years, and he had not been able to make the Arab nations understand that they must make peace with Israel. He had not been able to stop the murder of Israelis by *fedayeen* gangs. He had not armed Israel. He had not mustered the power or tactics to ensure that the Security Council's resolutions requiring Egypt to open the Canal to Israel, as the treaty of 1888 required, be respected. Vigor and imagination are inefficacious without power. Is that not the meaning of one of the Secretary's favorite quotations from Admiral Mahan: "Force gives the time for moral ideas to grow"?

As Dulles's plane came to a stop on the Washington runway, Herbert Hoover, Jr., told him what had happened. He explained also that on the President's instructions the State Department was arranging to encourage and facilitate the evacuation of Americans from Israel and its neighboring states. "My God!" Hoover had exclaimed as the cables arrived from Tel Aviv, "Look at what those Israelis are doing!"

By now, let us say towards midnight in Israel, and say 5 P.M. in Washington, D.C., the State Department and the CIA and the Pentagon had put the scraps of information and "blackout" phenomena together, and perhaps someone also remembered what had been authentically foretold by French sources around October 18 or 19. The United States was a party to the Tripartite Declaration. What were they going to do about an Israeli outbreak? Dulles and Eisenhower a short time later became painfully worried about the intentions of Britain and France.

Dulles issued instructions to his staff to let the American Ambassadors in the Arab capitals know of the President's and his appeal to Ben Gurion. He also warned the Arab nations by cable and through the embassies against military action, arguing, as he had to Israel, that there was nothing in the situation that justified hostilities.

Dulles then called in Israeli Ambassador Abba Eban, told him what he knew and suspected, and asked him to explain what was going on on Israel's Jordanian frontier. He said that Ambassador Lawson had reported that a mobilization was being undertaken, although the situation in the neighboring states was apparently not so unusual as to call for it. The Israeli Ambassador truthfully told Dulles that all *he* knew was that any such mobilization could be only of a defensive nature against Jordan.

Dulles's nervousness was unabated. He sent for the chargés d'affaires of the British and French Embassies, J. E. Coulson and Charles Lucet, respectively, because there was then, as we have observed, no British Ambassador in Washington, and Alphand, the French Ambassador, was out of town. Dulles told them that if fighting broke out the United States would ask the United Nations to stop it. He warned that the use of force would blacken the West's reputation all over the world. It would be completely illegal under international law. It would damage the Western case against Moscow regarding Hungary. He wanted the support of the British and French governments. The chargés d'affaires could only reply that they would communicate what he had said to their Foreign Offices and wait for a reply.

The Israeli armed forces struck against Egypt at Sinai at 4 P.M. on Monday, October 29, or 9 A.M. Washington, D.C., time, and they moved with increasing momentum. Their first official communiqué, perhaps to hide their real plans, declared they intended merely the liquidation of *fedayeen* bases in the Sinai Peninsula. It mentioned various hostile actions committed by Egypt against Israel, including the blockade of the Canal and the Gulf of Aqaba. It said that Israeli forces had attacked Egyptian commando units at Kuntilla and Ras El Akab and had taken up positions west of the Nakhl road *in the vicinity of the Suez Canal.* The italicized words represented a situation that was very premature; they have been regarded as the signal France and Britain were awaiting.

The Israeli Ambassador was in Dulles's office at about 2 P.M. on October 29, to see Assistant Secretary William Rountree (who had replaced George V. Allen as head of the Near Eastern Bureau), to talk over Middle Eastern and, specifically, Israeli problems that had arisen since his recent return from Israel. He had not previously visited the State Department because he had been engaged at the United Nations in defending Israel against Jordan's charges of aggression.

Rountree had Fraser Wilkins, a specialist in Arab-Israeli affairs, with him. Eban explained that the mobilization in Israel was defensive and pointed out the well-known facts, as he had just recited them for the *n*th time at the United Nations. The discussion went on until nearly 3 P.M. (or 9 P.M. in Israel). A secretary opened the door and called Wilkins out. She gave him a report that had just come in on the busily throbbing news-ticker: Israel had invaded the Sinai Peninsula! Wilkins took the flimsy sheet into Rountree's office. As Rountree finished his current sentence, he read the message. War! Eban protested that he knew nothing of what had occurred; and then, needing urgently to know at once what was happening in his own land, he took his leave for the Israeli Embassy. Indeed, when Eban said he did not know, he was entirely truthful: his government had deliberately kept him in the dark, to avoid exposure and diplomatic complications. The practice is far from unusual in many foreign-policy situations. (For example, possibly, the U-2 flight of June, 1960.) The moment Eban left, Rountree sped to Dulles's office and broke the very serious news to him: Israel had invaded Egypt!

At once, Dulles called a staff conference. His face and neck were flushed with anger. These Israelis! It was an Old Testament appellation as well as one often used in Wall Street. What could be done? The whole business must be stopped at once! For this was the one good opportunity, a *casus belli,* which Eden and Pineau had been hoping for! A picture now took on clear lineaments in his mind: made up of his suspicions and forebodings since September 21, and especially from October 2 to October 13. Meanwhile, Henry Cabot Lodge reported from the U.N. that it was impossible to pry any information out of the French and British delegations.

At ten minutes after 5 P.M. Dulles again summoned the British and French chargés d'affaires to his office. He told them that an immediate appeal to the United Nations was necessary. But they were unable to answer for their governments, only being able to say, as before, that they would make the proper inquiries as soon as possible. They left within less than twenty minutes. Their demeanor and observations had been well scrutinized in order to discover whatever might be gleaned from their faces and even silences. The conclusion of State Department officials like William Rountree and Robert Murphy was that they had been kept in ignorance of whatever was to happen.

From the State Department, after a time for further consultation and reflection, Dulles went to the White House, where the President had called an emergency meeting for 7 P.M. Besides Dulles and the President, there were present Admiral Radford, chairman of the Joint Chiefs of Staff, Defense Secretary Charles E. Wilson, Allen W. Dulles of the CIA, and Sherman Adams, as well as various Presidential assistants. Apparently Henry Cabot Lodge was not present. The meeting, refreshed and sustained by sandwiches and drinks, lasted about an hour. Radford played an important part in giving information on the armed strength of Israel, Britain, and France. He and his officers had long watched the gathering forces in the Mediterranean. He had believed, as some in the State Department said *afterwards* they had believed (or they may have followed Radford's expert opinion *then*), that the "Israeli boys" could beat the Arab armies, all of them together, some even said with one arm tied behind their back, and that they would move against Egypt.

Radford hoped that *if* the British and the French came in, they would roll Nasser over, for Radford's business was the maintenance of United States strength, and therefore the maintenance of the power of America's principal allies, Britain and France. Allen Dulles added his information—but he was rather in a fog about the concentrations of the British and French at Cyprus. He told his brother that the British and French had kept the secret confined to so few top leaders that he had not been able to get his usual information.

The question was: What shall we do? The meeting resolved on snuffing out the fire the Israelis had started (in their bid for survival), and on snuffing it out as fast as possible, before complications could arise. Therefore, two parallel lines of action were undertaken: the United States would go to the United Nations to stop the fighting, and simultaneously would issue a statement reasserting America's intention to utilize the Tripartite Declaration of 1951, to assist any victim of aggression in the Middle East.

Neither the President nor Dulles was finished with his labors for this fateful day. J. E. Coulson, the British chargé d'affaires, was once again called in to see the President, along with Dulles—at 8:15 P.M., shortly after the emergency meeting had broken up. The President, in an extremely angry state of mind and demeanor, used unwontedly strong language, especially considering that he was speaking to a younger member of the diplomatic corps, who could hardly be held responsible for events not, in any possible way, of his making. But the President and Dulles wished thus, by personal confrontation, to let Eden and Selwyn Lloyd know that they suspected cooperative action by Israel and France, in which Britain was very probably involved too, and that they hoped to make second thoughts prevail. As a matter of fact, the next day, October 30, when the President cabled to Eden, he repeated most of the substance and some of the tone he had poured upon Coulson (this communication will be quoted presently). The President's message reached London and Paris by 3 A.M. their time. They did not make acknowledgment until late in the morning.

Ambassador Winthrop W. Aldrich, as soon as the gravity of the Israeli mobilization had been appreciated in Washington, was urgently instructed by Washington to discover in London what was happening in the Middle East. He arranged to have dinner with Selwyn Lloyd on Sunday evening, October 28. Each brought with him a political counselor. Aldrich asked Lloyd what Britain believed to be the significance of Israel's mobilization. Lloyd answered that he did not know; that the British were in the dark about it; that the British government had warned the Israelis not to attack Jordan. Then Aldrich asked: May I ask you specifically whether Israel is going to attack Egypt? To this, Selwyn Lloyd's reply was: I have no information at all! (*Later*, after the Suez and Sinai campaigns were in full swing, a British Foreign Office witness "threw up his hands and eyes to Heaven" at the ignorance alleged by Selwyn Lloyd.)

No doubt by that time the Foreign Secretary, like his Prime Minister and the other Cabinet ministers in the know, regarded themselves in a state of war. In war, not all of everyday morality is thrown out of the window, but nearly all is. As far as the British and French point of view was concerned, the proverb applied: All is fair in love and *war!*

Then, Aldrich saw that on the evening of October 29, English time, the Israelis attacked Egypt. He immediately asked for an appointment with Selwyn Lloyd on the subject, especially after he had cabled to the State Department, that is, Dulles, detailing his conversation with Lloyd on Sunday night, October 28. He was given an appointment at the Foreign Office at 10 A.M. London time (in Washington, 4 A.M.), October 30, and kept the wires to Dulles open. The same two pairs, English and Americans, met. Aldrich asked Selwyn Lloyd, "Now that Israel is clearly fighting against Egypt, what do you intend to do?" Lloyd answered that in his judgment, Her Majesty's Government *must charge Israel with being an aggressor against Egypt!* But, he added, Prime Minister Mollet and Foreign Minister Christian Pineau were at that very moment on their way to London for conversations, and before taking any action, the two nations would consult together. The British and the French would have to be very careful what steps to take, and they were anxious about events, *because they had shipping in the Canal.* Therefore, he could not say just what the British and French would do until he had talked with the French Ministers at lunch. He would see Aldrich after lunch and give him the answers to his questions then.

Aldrich returned to the American Embassy and at once (say 11 A.M. London time) reported what he had been told to the State Department. By about 6 A.M. on October 30, Washington time, this is all the State Department knew: Something is going to happen. Dulles reached his office at a little before 8:30 A.M. and at once went into conferences with his staff. By this time, about 2 P.M. in London, the lunch of Eden, Lloyd, Mollet, and Pineau at the Foreign Office was nearing its end.

Aldrich was at the American Embassy, awaiting his appointment with Selwyn Lloyd. He received a telephone call from the Foreign

Office. It was Lloyd's secretary. He explained to the Ambassador that the situation was developing in such a way that Selwyn Lloyd must go down to the House of Commons immediately, and Lloyd therefore regretted that he personally could not see Aldrich at the time previously arranged. But—Sir Ivone Kirkpatrick, Permanent Secretary of the Foreign Office, would see him rather later in the afternoon, at 4:45 P.M. London time. This would be about 11 A.M. Washington time. Everyone was on the alert in the State Department, and Eisenhower was on his way back from Florida to Washington.

As Aldrich arrived, Sir Ivone Kirkpatrick gave him two sheets of foolscap paper. They were formally "requests," but diplomatically "ultimatums," to Israel and Egypt. Aldrich rushed through the text, and exclaimed, "There is something absurd about what I am reading! Both of these texts say 'Stay clear ten miles *east* of the Canal!' But Egypt is west of the Canal. Egypt could stay west, but not east! And by the way, are the Israelis at the Canal? If not, what is the sense in telling them to stay ten miles east? Another thing, how do you expect Egypt to accept this ultimatum?"

Sir Ivone explained that his government had aimed strategical strokes at both Egypt and Israel. (Pineau was in the room, an interested observer.) Kirkpatrick had given the ultimatum to Egypt's Ambassador at 4:20 P.M. and to Israel's at 4:30 P.M. And Aldrich reflected that *he* had not been given the news until 4:45 P.M. to pass on to his government. He felt most distressed. He asked whether the ultimatums were public. The answer was that they were being made public at that very moment. Aldrich took his leave on the note that "All I can do is to transmit what you have told me. But I suppose it will already have arrived by the news services." He noticed that Kirkpatrick and his colleague were extremely upset. Aldrich, at once phoning the State Department, was told that the President had already heard the news.

We must retrace our steps a little. On Saturday, October 28, a statement was issued by President Eisenhower. Of course, it was drafted by State Department officials in eventual editorial consultation with the President and his speechwriters. It embodies the thoughts and fears and hopes we have noticed expressed in the letters of October 27 and 28 to Ben Gurion.[29]

I will not repeat that part of the material which appears in another form in the letters to Ben Gurion. I merely wish to add one or two parts of the statement to indicate the progress being made by Dulles in formulating plans to deal with the threat of imminent war. Instructions, said the statement, had been given that recent developments be discussed with Britain and France, partners in the Tripartite Declaration of May 25, 1950. Also, Eisenhower's concern had been communicated to other Middle Eastern governments, asking them, too, to refrain from action which could lead to hostilities. He drew attention to the fact that the Security Council at that moment already had before it "various aspects of the maintenance of peace in the Middle East." The statement of the President concluded, "I earnestly hope that none of the nations involved will take any action that will hinder the Council in its efforts to achieve a peaceful settlement." Privately, the President was fuming at the possibility that Britain and France would side with Israel and balk him on their pledge in the Tripartite Declaration.

The State Department itself issued a statement about the same time, reiterating these views. It added that the United States "earnestly hopes that a high order of statesmanship will be shown by the governments involved, and that the peace will not be violated." [30] Then, when Israel was actually attacking Egypt, a statement was issued by the White House Press Secretary, after the meeting held from 7 to 8 P.M. on October 29 that we have already described.[31] This said that at the meeting the President had referred to the pledge made by the United States to assist the victim of any aggression in the Middle East. Then: "We shall honor our pledge." The statement related that the United States was consulting with the British and French governments, partners in the Tripartite Declaration; and that the United States plans, *as contemplated by that Declaration*, were to take the situation to the Security Council the following morning, that is, October 30.

That very same evening, October 29, Henry Cabot Lodge wrote a letter to the President of the Security Council—who happened to be a Frenchman, Cornut Gentille, requesting the convening of the Security Council *as soon as possible*, to consider "The Palestine Question: Steps for the Immediate Cessation of the Military Action of Israel in Egypt." The grounds for this request were treated in the first part of the letter: violation of the 1949 armistice agreement, since the armed forces of Israel had penetrated deeply into Egyptian territory; this agreement was a responsibility of the Security Council, which further had primary responsibility for the maintenance of international peace and security.

From 10:30 P.M. until 2 A.M. on the night of October 29-30, the British Cabinet was in session. Eden stayed on at work until 4 A.M. The Cabinet met again at 10 A.M. on October 30. The French ministers were on their way from Paris. The Cabinet deliberated on the terms of the requests to the combatants, a matter to be settled with Mollet and Pineau on their arrival. It also examined the statement to be made by Eden in the Commons that afternoon. It discussed the attitude of the United States. It hoped that that country would remember the warlike intentions of Egypt and its aggressions against Israel, take account of these, and "*be watchful of Soviet moves.*"

Then the first message from Eden to Eisenhower, embodying the Cabinet's invitation for general support, was sent off.

Above all, it was felt, the trouble must be localized. It was decided that Jordan and Syria could be kept quiet if Israel won a swift success and if it were known that British and French forces were on the way. Eden says:

> If that restraint was to be effective it must be applied at once. Twenty-four hours might well be too late, forty-eight certainly would.
>
> The choice for us was stark and inescapable, either act at once to bring about the result we sought, the localization of the conflict, or involve ourselves in consultations. This would mean the same inaction as in the last three months. We chose to act.

That Cabinet meeting was a long one: it lasted from 10 A.M. until 12:45 P.M., when the French Prime Minister and Foreign Minister arrived from Paris. It was not easy to arrive at the decision, "We chose to act." For some of the Ministers in the Cabinet, this meeting was the first intimation of the scope of the commitments already made by the five top Ministers over the last three weeks. There was opposition and there were regrets. These factors plagued the action. The opposition within the Cabinet was carried by Eden and Lloyd into the discussions with the French leaders in the form of misgivings and stings of conscience and military requirements. For this reason, the meeting between the two nations also lasted long: from 12:15 P.M. until 4 P.M. By then, and only then, the decision was joint and final.

The next phase of the action in Washington is best learned from *a hitherto unpublished cable* from Eisenhower to Sir Anthony Eden sent on October 30, just before 11 A.M. Washington time.

The President addressed Sir Anthony as his "long-time friend and believer in Anglo-American understanding." He explained that Coulson (the British chargé d'affaires) had visited him the preceding night and that Eisenhower had told him much that was on his mind, and this he was going to repeat to Eden. The President was very much disturbed by his impressions of the march of events. He did not wish to dwell for the moment on military matters, but to clear his understanding about the relations between the United States, Britain, and France. He asserted that France had provided Israel with arms in excess of the amount specified in the agreement among the allies. He had seen the need at the end of the past week to send letters to Ben Gurion, and he had informed Eden and Mollet about them.

Therefore, on Monday, October 29, that is, the day before this letter to Eden was dispatched, the United States government had gone to the United Nations about the situation, on the basis of the

Tripartite Pact of 1950. That evening Henry Cabot Lodge, the United States Ambassador to the United Nations, had met with Sir Pierson Dixon, the British Ambassador to the United Nations, to consider the problem of proceedings before the United Nations. At this meeting of Lodge and Dixon, Dixon announced that the Tripartite Declaration *had lost its value and had no current validity*. (The italics are supplied by the present author.)

The President's letter continued, saying that this statement was quite incomprehensible to Eisenhower, Dulles, and Lodge. If it was the intention of the British government to denounce the Pact in spirit, then why did it not tell the United States government, since it was a signatory of the Pact? The United States, in accordance with the Pact, had denied arms to both Israel and Egypt. The President expressed the hope that Britain would *not* repudiate the Pact, because the consequences in the Middle East would leave America and Britain in confusion.

If the United Nations should find Britain to be an aggressor, then the Soviet Union would come into the affair and the fat would be in the fire, the letter warned. The *de facto* situation then would make the American and British position look pretty indecent. Therefore, the two countries and their leaders had better be completely open with each other and concert their ideas and plans. Their peoples needed to understand their common concern.

The President's letter ended there.

Now, this letter, cabled over to London, reached Eden at about 5 P.M. on the same day, perhaps somewhat later, London time—that is to say, after he had spoken to the Commons on British policy, after the lunch with Mollet and Pineau. But he himself had already sent two messages to Eisenhower, the first *before* the lunch with Mollet and Pineau, at the conclusion of a decisive meeting of the British Cabinet that morning. This message, then, was sent about 6 A.M. October 30, before the President wrote; and the second was dispatched at about 4:45 P.M. London time, or 10:45 A.M. Washington time, after the delivery of the notes to the Israeli and Egyptian Ambassadors. This second message perhaps arrived in Washington for processing when the President's letter referred to was already on its way by cable to London.

These two telegrams from Eden are important and must be cited. Eden and the Cabinet had before them, at the time the messages were being drafted, Coulson's story and observations from Sir Pierson Dixon on the American intention to go to the Security Council with the purpose of having Israel accused of aggression.

The first message read thus:

> We have never made any secret of our belief that justice entitled us to defend our vital interests against Nasser's designs. But we acted with you in summoning the London Conference, in

despatching the abortive Menzies mission and in seeking to establish SCUA. As you know, the Russians regarded the Security Council proceedings as a victory for themselves and Egypt. Nevertheless we continued through the Secretary-General of the United Nations to seek a basis for the continuation of the negotiations.

Egypt has to a large extent brought this attack on herself by insisting that the state of war persists, by defying the Security Council and by declaring her intention to marshal the Arab states for the destruction of Israel. The latest example of Egyptian intentions is the announcement of a joint command between Egypt, Jordan and Syria.

We have earnestly deliberated what we should do in this serious situation. We cannot afford to see the canal closed or to lose the shipping which is daily on passage through it. We have a responsibility for the people in these ships. We feel that decisive action should be taken at once to stop hostilities. We have agreed with you to go to the Security Council and instructions are being sent this moment. Experience however shows that this procedure is unlikely to be either rapid or effective.

To this telegram, the President sent a short reply, just after midday on October 30. He said that he had already sent off a long cable about his attitude (the letter just described). He said he would await a further message, but repeated that the United States and Britain differed on the Tripartite Pact, and asked how could "we" violate our pledged word? He said he would watch the unfolding situation anxiously.

Then Eden's second message was on its way. The version immediately below is that given in his memoirs, *Full Circle* (page 587); certain passages he does *not* there reproduce will follow. All that Eden records of the cable is this:

My first instinct would have been to ask you to associate yourself and your country with the declaration. But I know the constitutional and other difficulties in which you are placed. I think there is a chance that both sides will accept. In any case it would help this result very much if you found it possible to support what we have done at least in general terms. We are well aware that no real settlement of Middle East problems is possible except through the closest cooperation between our two countries. Our two Governments have tried with the best will in the world all sorts of public and private negotiations through the last two or three years and they have all failed. This seems an opportunity for a fresh start.

. . . Nothing could have prevented this volcano from erupting somewhere, but when the dust settles there may well be a chance for our doing a really constructive piece of work together and thereby strengthening the weakest point in the line against communism.

Eden added, in his memoirs, that the message went on to inform the President of the "requests" (called by others "ultimatums") issued to Egypt and Israel to stay away from the Canal.

Some passages of Eden's letter were not published in *Full Circle*. They were as follows, in close paraphrase:

> We met with Mollet and Pineau. Of course, Israel could be accused of *technical* aggression. But she *could* argue that her action is in self-defense. But we do not wish to support or condone what Israel has done.
>
> When we received news of Israel's action we told our Ambassador to warn Tel Aviv not to attack Jordan. We warned them about our obligation to Jordan. But we had no obligation to help Egypt.
>
> We must stop the fighting at once. Therefore, we have made certain requests of them; copies have been given to Winthrop [Aldrich, the U.S. Ambassador]. I shall communicate this to Parliament shortly. [The gist of the requests or ultimatums was then given.]
>
> We must have a physical presence in the area, because we know what these people are. Our presence will be temporary, *pending a settlement of all these problems.* We are happy to go to the Security Council, for either Egypt or Israel might have done so before us—so also the Soviet Union might have made a charge against us.
>
> Why do we act so *fast?* [Then followed the first paragraph of the passage published by Eden.] . . .
>
> We must cooperate for Middle East peace. We have tried for two years, but we have failed. We must make a fresh start. [The second paragraph of the above-reproduced passage about a "volcano erupting somewhere" ended the letter in its original form.]
>
> The present conflict is not one of colonialism.

The "communication" or "request" or "ultimatum" delivered by Britain and France to Egypt must now be reproduced *in toto*.[32] Except for one detail (noted below), it was identical with the one sent to Israel.

> The Governments of the United Kingdom and France have taken note of the outbreak of hostilities between Israel and Egypt. This event threatens to disrupt the freedom of navigation through the Suez Canal, on which the economic life of many nations depends. The Governments of the United Kingdom and France are resolved to do all in their power to bring about the early cessation of hostilities and to safeguard the free passage of the Canal. They accordingly request the Government of Egypt:
>
> (a) to stop all warlike action on land, sea and air forthwith;
>
> (b) to withdraw all Egyptian forces to a distance of ten miles from the Canal; and

(c) in order to guarantee freedom of transit through the Canal by the ships of all nations and in order to separate the belligerents, to accept the temporary occupation by Anglo-French forces of key positions at Port Said, Ismailia and Suez.

The United Kingdom and French Governments request an answer to this communication within twelve hours. If at the expiration of that time one or both Governments have not undertaken to comply with the above requirements, United Kingdom and French forces will intervene in whatever strength may be necessary to secure compliance.

The communication sent to the government of Israel required the forces of that country to withdraw ten miles east of the Canal.

Thus, to part the combatants and so maintain free passage of the Canal, was, then and later, the British government's official justification for its intervention. *BUT*—the publicly announced justification in the ultimatums was also a limitation on the British and, therefore, on the French, in their ulterior purpose, which Eden does not openly acknowledge—the overthrow of Nasser. Not the overthrow of Egypt; not the overthrow or harm of the nation and its people; but the overthrow of Nasser. Not the establishment of some other ruler in his place; but Nasser's overthrow, leading to another agreement on the management of the Canal. This agreement would be made with whatever people should emerge from among the Egyptian leaders themselves who could give the guarantees of the Six Principles and an acceptable means of their fulfillment, as provided in the Security Council Resolution of October 13.

The question has frequently been asked whether the date of the attack by Israel, October 29, was the date settled in the famous meeting in Paris of October 16. My own view is that the date had been set for a little before the election of November 6, say about November 2 or 3. This was for British military convenience. The Israelis had good reasons for jumping the gun. First, they knew that the French would at some time invade the Canal area. They expected the British would do so as well. But they, the Israelis, had a great political interest in achieving a clean-cut defeat of Nasser's Egypt by their own forces exclusively before that—though they did not mean to exclude the air support and defense the French had supplied. They had taken the measure of British national interests over too many unhappy years, above all, with a Conservative Government in control, and could expect to be bilked of a victory. They might believe, for example, that the British ultimatum to them was, in spirit, really intended, and would always be intended, for the benefit of continued Arab ties with the British.

Secondly, the Israelis probably realized that the Presidential election campaign would tend to slow down retaliation by the United

States government if they made their assault before election day. Theirs was *not* a calculation that the Jewish vote would cause the President to waver. It was rather the Administration's practical preoccupation with election campaigning that caused the Israelis to believe that the time was as propitious as any, and probably better than after the election. Just think of Dulles's moral thunder after winning a second term!

Thirdly, the Israelis believed themselves immediately threatened, for day by day the planting of Soviet arms throughout the Sinai Desert proceeded, and day by day the Soviet and Czech technicians were teaching the Egyptian armed forces how to use the planes, tanks, and anti-aircraft guns they had been given. They acted on Churchill's aphorism, "If it is to be done eventually, why not now?"

Fourthly, the Hungarian revolt had flared up since Israel's military understanding with France, and had broken openly into the field of East-West diplomacy. It would, to this extent, enable Israel to achieve a victory without interference either from the United States or from the United Nations. Moreover, the total impotence that the United Nations could be expected to display, in any attempt it might make to apply a civilized standard to the brutalities of the Soviet in Hungary, might result in some understanding and condonation of the action of Israel. If the United States could not apply the moral law and the Charter to Russia, could it fairly apply them to Israel? One law for both; or no law for either?

However, the French also were interested in as early an attack as feasible. In early October, Pineau was urging the advisability of action in late October on the theory that election preoccupations would impede any unfriendly tactics by the State Department and White House. The date was, according to this account, deferred little by little, until around November 2 or 3, for various technical reasons, and perhaps because the British were hesitant politically.

As a matter of fact, when, at the Cabinet meeting of October 25, the British virtually decided to join in, November 1 was held tentatively in mind as the date they would take action. But then they, and therefore the Israelis, who were ready to move by October 27 or 28, were delayed for two days. The delay occurred because Lord Mountbatten, First Sea Lord (that is, the highest naval career expert in the advisory body to the Admiralty), demurred at Eden's intention. He therefore pleaded with Queen Elizabeth, whose uncle he is, to inquire of Eden into the justification for the military action contemplated. But the cables of Eisenhower to Ben Gurion on October 27 and 28, and the earlier admonition by way of Eban, spurred the Israelis to take action sooner than planned, and the French military leaders encouraged them in this. Hence, October 29 was a few days earlier than the British expected. It was eagerly seized upon by Pineau and Mollet, who feared the hesitations of the British Cabinet, and especially of Eden, who was a seriously sick man and much concerned for Anglo-American friendship. This is why there was such a rush from Paris and so much tension in London on October 30.

Eden made a grave diplomatic mistake in not informing President Eisenhower beforehand of the decision to deliver an ultimatum to Israel and Egypt in terms which meant that intervention would follow. It is equally correct to attach blame to the President for not being *absolute* regarding his attitude toward the employment of force by his Western allies in the Suez affair, and for not having kept adequate control over Dulles's many transactions with them which led to their distrust and desperation. Eden cannot be exonerated on the grounds that he had been conducting correspondence with an unjustifiably optimistic President and negotiating with a devious Dulles, and that they *should* have known what he might do.

What expediency could have recommended this secrecy? Was there reason strong enough to offset the anger, mistrust, and retaliation thus caused in the White House and the State Department, first in Dulles, and then even more so, unfortunately, in his Deputy, Herbert Hoover, Jr.? Eden thought that if Eisenhower knew in advance, he would issue a direct command (that is strong language, but not too strong) to Eden not to do what he intended. It is perfectly possible. But if the vital interests of Britain required this action, the Prime Minister merely had to say so to Eisenhower: "We are going ahead, just the same!" Now, it is a certainty that if Eden had communicated his intentions to the United States, within an hour or so they would have been leaked to a White House or State Department reporter or ferreted out by him. The safety of Israel and of British and French action may then have been altogether at the mercy of some forceful action by Russia, or the Egyptians might have at once begun raiding the towns of Israel or flying off their planes to safer air fields. A military appreciation might have shown that these fears, if, indeed, ever entertained, were unwarranted in the degree of trouble that secrecy vis-à-vis the President brought down on the British and French enterprise. The resentment lasted until they ignominiously left Suez, defeated, not by the United Nations, but by the United States government.

Mollet later (December 20, 1956) explained in the National Assembly [33] that the Americans were not informed lest they impose additional hindrances to action; during such delays Israel would have taken the risk of being destroyed. He says he told American officials afterwards frankly that France did not want to wait for American help as it did from 1914 to 1917 and from 1939 to 1942. Had his country done that, he added, "we should have been weeping for Israel annihilated, as we today weep, impotent, for Hungary martyred."

Christian Pineau, in the same post-mortem debate in the National Assembly—post-mortem in order that the Mollet-Pineau Cabinet might continue to live by the vindication of its action in the Suez affair—explained the problem of "informing" the United States government. "For three months," he declared, "the Americans knew perfectly our feelings, our disillusionment, our military preparedness, and our efforts to secure a pacific settlement of the problem," and he meant Israel's problems as well as France's. On the eve of the Israeli operations, Eisenhower, Pineau continued, had sent a message to Ben Gurion asking him to stop the mobilization: "Everything, therefore, allowed our reaction to be foreseen. As regards our methods [of reacting], it is perfectly accurate that we did not tell our friends, but we never had the impression that we acted *against* our friends, although we now and then resented the bitterness of certain speeches and certain votes in the U.N.O." [34]

Thus, war began: Israel, Britain, and France in Sinai and Suez; and the United States versus Britain and France and Israel in the United Nations and by diplomatic pressure outside. And Moscow was no passive or innocent bystander.

14. DULLES IMPEACHES HIS ALLIES

THE BRITISH AND FRENCH NEVER CAME ANYWHERE NEAR TO SENSING THE fearful degree of anger generated in the White House by Israel's entry into battle. They did not foresee the missionary zeal, efficiency, and speed with which the American leaders would press action in the United Nations. Eden and Lloyd asked Sir Pierson Dixon, when he called London on the evening of October 29, to request a delay of the Security Council meeting. But the very next morning after the conversation of October 29 between Henry Cabot Lodge and Dixon about the Tripartite Pact, Lodge was instructed to open proceedings in the Security Council. Perhaps this conversation stimulated the convening of the British Cabinet and the dash to London of the French leaders, as we have narrated, on October 30. At any rate, when, on October 30, at 9:30 A.M., Ambassador Aldrich conferred with Selwyn Lloyd in London about the draft resolution which the United States was composing to put before the Security Council, Lloyd demurred at the State Department's proposal that Israel be named an aggressor. He argued that this was one-sided, in favor of Egypt. He succeeded in modifying the charge to "violation of the armistice agreements." But Dixon was unable to secure any delay of proceedings on October 30: only one hour of respite was conceded. For Lodge was "carrying the ball" for Dulles and Eisenhower. When the allies and their friends protested about the lack of notice, the American answer was, "Well! You did not tell us at all!"

Although, by the time he presented the matter before the Security Council, at 11 A.M. on October 30, no member had been able to receive instructions, Lodge moved in with celerity, relish and animus. He recited the President's response to Israeli mobilization and action. He called on the Council to find a breach of the peace, to order a cease-fire, and to instruct the Israeli forces to withdraw behind the frontiers as established in the armistice agreements. The demands of General Burns (head of the Mixed Armistice Commission) for a cease-fire were being ignored, and the United Nations truce observers were not being permitted by Israel to perform their duties!

Lodge concluded (and the mind behind the words was the mind of Dulles):

> We, as members of the Council, accordingly should call upon all Members of the United Nations to render prompt assistance in achieving a withdrawal of Israel forces. *All* Members, specifically, should refrain from giving assistance which might continue or prolong the hostilities. *No one, certainly, should take advantage of this situation for any selfish interest.* Each of us here, and every Member of the United Nations, has a clear-cut responsibility to see that the peace and stability of the Palestine area is restored forthwith. Anything less is an invitation to *disaster* in that part of the world.[1]

To say "disaster" was extremely overrhetorical. This choice of language represented the loss of temper and diplomatic good sense in the White House and State Department—more especially the latter, which had all along given guidance to the former and had initiated the actions undertaken in Middle Eastern affairs.

The Soviet representative, Sobolev, dropped two bombs. The first was the demand that, as the Israeli action was "aggression," it must be quashed as such. He offered the United States an orchid that should have put the American government strictly on guard about the wisdom of the foreign policy it was now following and about to intensify: "May I add," he said, "that the initiative of the United States in bringing this extremely serious matter so rapidly before the Security Council is warmly welcomed."

The second Russian bomb was far more sensational. The Associated Press, Sobolev announced, had just distributed the report that Britain and France had, but moments ago, issued ultimatums to Israel and Egypt. Lodge had not yet heard this. The Russian made apt use of the news. It proved that Israel must have been encouraged to attack by "those aggressive circles" who were trying to find some pretext to move their troops into the Middle East. He demanded instant action to get Israel to withdraw from Egyptian territory. "This applies also to the United Kingdom and France." He was on Lodge's side—or rather *in* it, a poisonous thorn.

Now it would have been perfectly possible for Dulles and Eisenhower to have handled the transgressions of Egypt against Israel, and of Egypt against Britain and France concerning the Canal, together and constructively or separately and constructively. It would have entailed all of Dulles's ingenuity, but it was far from beyond him and his legal and political experts. In this way, Nasser could have been levered into a situation where, possibly, peace with Israel would have been made, but, more surely, the Canal passage would have been settled on the terms laid down by Dulles in the eighteen-power proposals which he had devised and advocated with such fervor. Dulles could have practically applied all his own pleas about the "two sides of the coin"—peace with justice. This approach would have been a constructive one, of far reaching present and future benefit to the whole world. He could have advised the President that the moment had come for a showdown—not with Eden and Mollet, not with the allies of the United States, but with Nasser.

Their policy could have been formulated in something like these terms: Israel must go back to the armistice lines, but the United Nations must equally implement the resolution freeing passage for Israel through Suez, must open up the Gulf of Aqaba to all nations, and must compel Egypt and the other Arab nations to participate in negotiations at the peace table. Egypt must also *forthwith* (three months had passed since the rape of the Canal!) produce the practical equivalent of the eighteen-power proposal, or otherwise suggest a plan for Canal management acceptable to Britain and France. If Egypt failed to meet these requirements, the United States would abstain from voting against Israel, Britain and France; or would even, if necessary, use its veto in support of this policy of elementary justice. The United States government had trusted the United Nations to achieve peace and justice in the Middle East, and had assisted that body and the various nations involved: it now sought justice and peace in return from them. If the U.S.A. failed to get valid majorities in the Security Council or the General Assembly, so be it: it would still stand tenaciously by what its Secretary of State had declared all along was the just solution. It would not be a party to the two injustices, Egypt's belligerency against Israel, and Egypt's forcible violation of the universal and perpetual rights established by the treaty of 1888 and attendant documents. Though unpopular with small nations, it would stand staunchly by these two policies, its own policies so frequently proclaimed and advocated. It would be hoped that justice would be eventually seen to be on the side of such an approach, and that the strength of Britain, France, and Israel would continue to be exerted until Nasser's violence was appropriately disciplined. The American statesmen did not take this stand. It required courage to take a firm initiative and so set the mood and tone and temper of the behavior of the many nations in the U.N. and other diplomatic channels.

Such a policy and strategy, of course, would have been vociferously contested by the Soviet Union and Yugoslavia. The former would have used the veto where its national interests required it, quite callously. But, then, that would have been the demonstrable fault of the Soviet Union, *not* of the United States, and would have opened up many propaganda opportunities for the U.S.A. Action such as that suggested, and as various thoughtful American publicists at that time also suggested, would, further, have incurred the hatred and scorn of many, perhaps all, of the new nations. All of the Arab world would have raged and vociferated against it and most of the Asian nations as well, with Nehru and Menon at their head. For the scene was now a perfect set from Lenin's *Imperialism*. But such passion and rancor could not then, and in all probability could never thereafter, have done the slightest practical damage whatsoever to American interests or reputation. A resolute strategy by the United States government, on the principles of the eighteen-power proposal, providing for justice for Israel and peace between her and her neighbors, might, if consistently and eloquently stated and ingeniously and resolutely pursued, have been of constructive benefit. America's resistance to the clamant new nations would eventually have required them also to confront their own unjust egoisms and their many vindictive illusions. They could not be more open to Soviet infiltration than they were, and Korea had taught them to beware lest they, too, should become Koreas.

This course was *not* tried by Dulles and Eisenhower, not even attempted or considered. Lester Pearson believes there was a time when it was feasible: at the start.

By 11:30 A.M. on October 30, the State Department and White House seethed with a terrible anger, while pandemonium reigned, the on-the-spot observers report. We have already referred to the "mad as hell" passions that overwhelmed Dulles and Eisenhower. All close participants in both offices testify to this. It must be added that one of the observers, a good, loyal, just, above-the-average career State Department official, a man of equable temper and one rarely given to superlatives, said that he had in long years never seen Dulles in a fit of temper more than once or twice, but that on this occasion of hearing the news of the British and French ultimatums, he was "close to apoplexy." "How could people do this to *me?*" asked Dulles of his nearest relatives. "How could they pull a stunt like this on me, when I've been working with them all these weeks? They seemed to accept my lead all along!" he complained in the office. "Why put me on a spot just when election day is due? Why give the Russians cover for their crimes in Hungary?" The observations are revealing and most significant. Dulles and Eisenhower momentarily lost their heads. They allowed resentment and personal vindictiveness to overcome their judgment of what to blame and what to seek, of who was the friend and who the enemy of their country. They lost their grip, their judgment, and their perception of advantageous constructive alternatives. And, once having taken their stand, they felt thereafter that it must be justified by moral and legal argument, and carried out with impolitic moralizing fury. It became increasingly difficult and then impossible for them to retrace their steps; for, among other reasons, the Soviet Union outwitted them.

To Dulles, as he told the French Ambassador, Hervé Alphand (Chapter 1), the action of the British and French was a personal disappointment and affront, deeply felt as such. Of course—for he had misunderstood Nasser; he had advised the President imprudently on Nasser, on the legal situation of the treaty of 1888, on SCUA, and on the possibility of a settlement in the U.N. Dulles had hitherto felt that he had Britain and France thoroughly in his grip. Vice President Nixon, a very close witness, testifies to Dulles's dismay when he found his self-confidence had betrayed him. He felt like a cuckold. He now had to justify his faults—for the fact that war had broken out or was imminent exposed many faults of his—to the President. And the President feared a loss of the election, because war was about to explode in the final days of his first term.

Those closest on the scene in the White House, men with a high sense of responsibility, have tried to sort out the elements in the punitive vehemence that gripped and shook the chief actors at this point. Certainly the news of the British and French action intensified the resentment over the Israeli assault on Egypt; in some this resentment was elevated, in others petty. "Here," men heard the highest of the nation cry, "are two of our great allies and one small and almost insignificant nation, all of them being assisted by us, militarily and economically, and they are *flouting* us, showing contempt for us by their actions or speeches. They have *betrayed* us!" They were heard to exclaim further, "It's criminal that Britain and France and Israel should involve us without our permission or concurrence. Of course, they think, no doubt, that if they get into trouble the United States would come to their help and bail them out!" And, furthermore, when they began to rationalize, they uttered the profound conviction that if the fighting were not stopped at once, a world war would break out. Russia was the specter before which they quailed, in spite of "massive retaliation," and all of Dulles's other boasts and claims, realist or idealist. They could not stand up to Bulganin and Khrushchev: these men had The Bomb.

Understandably, President Eisenhower was rather out of his depth. In contrast to his position in the days when he swerved away from capturing Berlin (April, 1945), *he* was now fully responsible for the inseparably interwoven strands of the political relations between his nation and his allies and their enemies. He could not, in this maelstrom, take refuge in the thought that political responsibility belonged to someone higher in authority over him and vested with final responsibility, while his only concern was with a military decision about soldiers. Now he had to weigh long-term forces affecting the balance of power in the world, in all their complexity, and assume responsibility for the results, without alibi. He did not, as we have already reported, truly understand Israel's need to defend herself; or perhaps he did not care. He did not understand the action of the British in particular, largely because he had not studied the details, the ins and outs, of all the conferences with them conducted by Dulles. He believed that once the British heard how sternly he had rebuked Israel and understood that he intended to keep his Tripartite Declaration pledge, they would not enter the war. He thought the Israelis would stop fighting as soon as the British ultimatum reached them. He vacillated a little between keeping the tripartite pledge, and abandoning it on the ground that the other two powers had done so, as he might do with the excuse that Egypt had bought arms from Russia. In a pinch, Eden should have guessed, Eisenhower would be pacifist.

On November 5, probably, perhaps a day or two before, Arthur Flemming went to Eisenhower's office at the White House to confer about the mobilization of oil supplies. Eisenhower said to him: "I'm a poor person to talk about organizing an oil lift this afternoon! This is the first time in my experience where a democracy has committed its forces to a military operation and a large percentage of its citizens opposed it." It was clear that the President was puzzled and baffled by events. "Good lands!" he continued, "I'm a *friend* of theirs [the British and French]. I'm not going to make life too complicated for them!" No, but his acquiescence in the policy of Dulles and Henry Cabot Lodge had already done so, irrevocably. As the French proverb says: "Only the first step really counts!" Once that is taken it is one more force adverse to any alternative line of action. Also, the President's historical knowledge in matters of this kind did not reach back very far. Thus, he should have known that France was deeply divided in 1939, divided to death. Britain was to a large extent divided in 1939. The U.S.A. was divided even after Pearl Harbor. The British and the French were divided in entering World War I. The U.S.A. was divided in entering World War I. When a man is out of his depth he usually falls back on his prejudices or stereotypes, and he may believe they are "principles." It is a psychological process known as "reductionism." The President was keeping his pledges on a theory relevant to military operations but not to diplomacy. Diplomacy is not a salute to the flag or a superior officer. In military operations the pledge is an oath of allegiance and the exercise of professional honor to capture the enemy's cities and armies. The objective is specific and the directives are imposed on the commanding general. The fulfillment of a pledge in international relations is of a radically different nature: it admits of and requires creative flexibility and options in interpretation and execution.

Dulles saw everything he had worked for, and expressed optimism about, crumbling. He saw the NATO alliance and the containment of Russia collapsing. He saw that ruin was likely in the Middle East. He saw the triumph of the Soviet Union's mischief-making. He saw men as clever as he—Eden, Mollet, Ben Gurion—taking action, perhaps successfully, without his participation, men defiant as well as clever. World War III might break out. All his potential philippics against the Russians over Hungary were deferred or entirely aborted as a result of having his own friends act, in his opinion, as lawbreakers. He saw the United States impotent and shamed at the United Nations, and the United Nations itself in danger of collapse—the regular cry of leaders of all member nations then and since when they cannot get their own way. (Nasser had said it, too, only a few days before.)

The President's anger was rather simpler, less sophisticated—as damaging, but more forgivable and forgiving. He knew that the people of Britain were very fond of him: he had been their commander in chief as well as America's on D-Day, 1944, and beyond, to victory in Europe. Now Eden seemed to be repudiating him. He *thought* he had made it clear to Eden that force was not to be used *in any circumstances* except an incident provoked by Nasser. Now the British and French had practically provoked one themselves in the onslaught of Israel towards the Canal. They had gone to war without consulting him or even informing him of their intentions. It was a snub. Who did they think he was?

Prime Minister Eden admits quite openly that he miscalculated the attitude of President Eisenhower—and of Dulles. On the other hand, the President misunderstood the position of Eden and Mollet. Eisenhower believed *they* believed that, if they persisted in their invasion of Suez and opposition to American resolutions in the United Nations, he would, at the last moment, yield to their point of view. They may have hoped this; they certainly had the right to do so, considering Dulles's record of diplomatic zigzags over three months during which they had been cooperative and even pliant. They did not *believe* it fully. They acted when they found their vital interests, their rights in their "life line," as the President had acknowledged it really was, not supported by the United Nations, especially jeopardized by the Soviet Union (not for "justice," but for Russia's nationalist and imperialistic purposes), and not upheld, as Dulles had promised, by the U.S.A. They did hope, of course, that the United States would in some way find a tactic, while remaining neutral, of coping with "the Bear" if that should be necessary, in pursuance of American obligations under the NATO Pact. Even Winston Churchill, who was from time to time consulted by Sir Anthony Eden, and who at other times invited himself to advise Eden, believed that their ally, the United States, would "hold the ring"; her leaders, he felt, even if they thought Britain wrong, would nevertheless find a way in the interstices of the Charter to preserve her vital interests. Neither thought, as Churchill shortly afterwards confided to Eden, that the United States would not merely prove to be no good player on their side, but would actually lose the game for them by kicking the ball into the allies' own goal! They could calculate interests, but they miscalculated temper and evangelism. Yet they may, also, have underestimated the extent to which Dulles intended to subordinate them as "middle" powers to his preoccupation with Russia.

Eden did not sufficiently appreciate that Eisenhower, since he had become President, at any rate, was affected by a self-esteem that was simple, naive, and charming, but enormous, a tacit sense of total faultlessness. How could it be expected that a man so endowed with pride, and advised by Dulles, would tolerate an independent action by these lesser nations, England and, even more difficult to endure, France? *Israel?* Why, it was *lèse-majesté*, and it was insubordination! Hence his terrible anger. These men for whom America had done so much, Ben Gurion, Eden, Mollet, had disobeyed, yes, and had done it behind *his* back, when he and Foster had for months tried so hard to be reasonable! They knew he was all for Peace and the United Nations and the Rule of Law, and yet they were rejecting his advice and appeals, and they were not keeping their Word. He could not tolerate it. He was a man of Principle. The more the President insisted on his own immaculate respect for Principle, as he did, the more did he throw on his staff, for example, Dulles, the onus of doing the necessary dirty work of politics. In compensation, such men needed the solace of righteousness.

Israel must quit fighting and get out of Egypt. Britain and France must stop helping Israel, and had better not get into Suez themselves or there would be the devil to pay. The proper forum was the United Nations, after and along with the cabled appeals from the President (already quoted).

A statement was issued from the White House on October 30, 1956. It ran:

> As soon as the President received his first knowledge, obtained through press reports, of the ultimatum delivered by the French and United Kingdom Governments to Egypt and Israel, planning temporary occupation within twelve hours of the Suez Canal Zone, he sent an urgent personal message to the Prime Minister of Great Britain and the Prime Minister of the Republic of France.
>
> The President expressed his earnest hope that the United Nations Organization would be given full opportunity to settle

> the items in the controversy by peaceful means instead of by forceful ones.
>
> This Government continues to believe that it is possible by such peaceful means to secure a solution which would restore the armistice conditions between Egypt and Israel, as well as bring about a just settlement of the Suez Canal controversy.[2]

There is obvious sarcasm in the phrase "knowledge, obtained through press reports."

Henry Cabot Lodge's personality played a considerable part in the evolution and climax of American action at the United Nations against Israel, Britain, and France. He never had anything like the massive intellect of Dulles. He himself privately thought that Dulles was a very good man to have in "the back office" where his legal ingenuity would be most useful, but not in the front office where *decisions* were made—that is, where forces were weighed and estimated and a course of action formulated. Lodge has ability, but it is not originality, not vision; it is in the fifth or sixth order of quality below that of a Winston Churchill. It is the ability of a top career expert; a tactician with the objectives prescribed for him by those higher in authority. His close associates agree that it takes him time to grasp an idea. The corollary of that judgment is, surely, that it takes him time to discard it for a new one.

Lodge normally took his orders from Dulles and carried them out faithfully even if he did not like them. But, in the main, he did like them, because he could not think of anything else that was better. He was, however, also a politician, and this inclination gave him rather more drive and emotion than representatives to the Security Council usually have. Furthermore, being on the spot in the forum of the United Nations, he had become "the Lyndon Johnson of the United Nations," the maker and manipulator of majorities for the U.S.A. He was more sensitive to the feelings of the foreign delegates than the officials who worked from the White House and the State Department.

A Bostonian, he cherished a sense of public virtue, brimful with moral indignation, hitherto poured, boiling or iced, over the Russians. He did not intend the British and French to triumph over the United States of America. He did not intend to allow aggression to damage the United Nations, for fear people might think he was infected with the narrow-mindedness that had caused his grandfather, Henry Cabot Lodge, in 1919, to reject the Treaty of Versailles and prevent the entry of the United States into the League of Nations. People might have asked of him (as they had asked a similar question of his grandfather), "Who killed the United Nations?" To the contrary, many people had recently said, "Lodge *is* Mr. U.N."

That was not all. Just as Dulles and Eisenhower felt that they had been *duped* by the British and French (*without any fault on their part, of course!*) because they had not been informed about or consulted on the ultimatums and the intervention in Suez, so did Lodge feel deceived. He had adopted this attitude in spite of his astringent private criticism of Dulles's fumbling negotiations with America's allies, his leading them up a blind alley, and the ludicrous contraption (as Lodge thought it) of SCUA.

One thing more: Lodge was hypersensitive about the "anti-colonialist" stand of the Afro-Asian bloc of nations in the United Nations. They had dinned it into him, day after day, for years, that Israel was a guilty offspring of American paternity, a beachhead of imperialism, the embodiment of a more corrupt form of colonialism. They had angered him into the feeling that a terrible stain lay on America's conscience. He was also suffused with the deep prejudices of 1776: the British and French were colonial nations, and the Boston Tea Party must be repeated *à propos* of Suez. American high official testimony is totally convincing: Lodge was excessive in his prosecutions in the Suez affair, and very vain. He always claimed, and often made good, the right to make policy, with considerable independence of the State Department. This attitude arose partly because he had preceded Dulles as a friend of Eisenhower; because he had direct access to the White House on easier terms than other officials; and because he made much of his membership of the Cabinet.

Thus, American action at the United Nations burst upon the British and French with the power, momentum, and brightness of a rocket—to the delight of Africans, Asians, Indians, and Russians. The United States on this occasion, as the Presidential statement we have quoted indicates, invested all its faith in the United Nations, ostensibly, at any rate, in its public claims. This was the forum where the issue was to be debated, fought out, and decided. Whatever decision the United Nations made was to be the law for all nations, and no force outside it was permissible, even in self-defense under Article 51 of the Charter.

On October 30, at the U.N., it was time for the representative of Britain, Sir Pierson Dixon, to make his contribution to the discussion of Israel's attack. He merely said that he had not yet heard the contents of the speech then being made by Eden, his Prime Minister, in the House of Commons. He felt the Council would wish to know them in considering the very grave situation with which it was confronted. It is a fact that he had not yet been informed of the events in London that morning, the Cabinet meeting, the lunch with Mollet and Pineau, the delivery of the ultimatums. The United States had rushed the Council so fast that communications had not been able to get to him.

The Egyptian spokesman, Omar Loutfi, a most impassioned partisan of his nation's cause, demanded that Israel be branded as an aggressor and that sanctions and the rest be applied according to Chapter VII of the Charter. He also demanded the expulsion of Israel from the United Nations.

The other members were not prepared to go to this length. They all had a feeling that Egypt bore considerable responsibility for the state of affairs. They preferred to deal with the attack as a violation of the armistice, an unusually large-scale reprisal raid, rather than as a war.

The U.S. resolution therefore read:

> The Security Council, expressing its grave concern at this violation of the Armistice Agreement:
>
> 1. Calls upon Israel immediately to withdraw its armed forces behind the established armistice lines;
> 2. Calls upon all members (a) to refrain from the use of force or threat of force in the area in any manner inconsistent with the purposes of the United Nations; (b) to assist the United Nations in insuring the integrity of the Armistice Agreements; (c) to refrain from giving any military economic or financial assistance to Israel so long as it has not complied with this resolution;
> 3. Requests the Secretary General to keep the Security Council informed on compliance with this resolution and to make whatever recommendations he deems appropriate for the maintenance of international peace and security in the area by the implementation of this and prior resolutions.

The Council adjourned until the afternoon, at 4 P.M., at which time it convened again, for its 749th Meeting.

In considering the deliberations of the Council that ensued, we must examine the principal tactics and arguments of the chief contenders: Britain and France; the United States; and the Soviet Union. (The British and French tactics and arguments will be collated here, since they were similar.)

The clear purpose of the British and French was to delay any decision in the Council, and later in the General Assembly, condemning *their* action. They sought the maximum delay so that if Egypt and Israel, and this in reality meant Egypt, did not accept their ultimatum, they would have a legal basis (interference with passage in the Canal) to invade Egypt and bring down Nasser. For this they needed time—say ten days or two weeks from October 30.

A summary of the British arguments follows, drawn from that nation's representations in the Security Council or General Assembly, and from the vindications made by Eden and Selwyn Lloyd in the House of Commons at various times.

The fighting between Israel and Egypt must be stopped at once. If not, free passage through the Canal would be jeopardized, with damage to so many nations. The United Nations Security Council had no effective military arm to achieve this, and, furthermore, any action on its part was blocked by "persistent misuse of the veto." Therefore, the Security Council ought to support the British and French in their action in Suez almost as though those nations were its agents.

The British linked the extinction of the fighting with safeguarding free passage through the Suez Canal. "In our mind," said Sir Pierson Dixon, "they are intimately bound up." [3] They (Eden in the Commons, for example, October 30, 1956) argued that an ultimatum could not wait until the United Nations came to a decision. They (Eden and the Cabinet) took a calculated risk that there was a reasonable chance the ultimatums might be accepted. Therefore, at the afternoon meeting of the Council on October 30, Dixon expressed the hope that Lodge would not press his resolution *that day*.

The British, furthermore, took the attitude that America's purpose of having Israel condemned *without* setting up the constructive bases of a general Middle Eastern settlement was wrong in itself. They also held that the United States resolution of condemnation made their ultimatum ineffective, for it supported Egypt by indirection, at least, and also took the initiative away from the allies. The resolution would merely condemn Anglo-French action, and substitute nothing for it. The British firmly contended that they were acting within the Charter, and that they differed from the United States not in purpose, but in method only. They were at pains to be purged of the accusation that they had the ulterior purpose of imposing a Suez settlement. The method used by the United States government, that is, the attempt to have a resolution passed by the Security Council, could not be helpful, as events were moving far too fast. The situation was one of the utmost urgency.

After the British and French had cast their vetoing votes on the evening of October 30, against the American resolution, Sir Pierson Dixon, seeing the unraveling of events, and American remorselessness and zeal, went further in the argument supporting the actions of the European allies.[4] He claimed that Britain and France had the right to defend their *vital interests*, which were also the interests of so many other countries. But this was not the express reason for the ultimatums and intervention: this was to stop the conflagration. He did not condone the action of Israel. In the House of Commons on October 31,[5] Eden claimed the right for Britain to discharge its "national duty" without necessarily waiting for the agreement of the United States. To have waited thus

> . . . would have been to ignore what everyone here and in the United States knows to have been the different approaches to some of the vital Middle Eastern questions. They know it. We

> know it. Of course, we deplore it, but I do not think it can carry with it this corollary that we must in all circumstances secure agreement from our American Ally before we can act ourselves in what we know to be our own vital interests.

The American leaders had long ago said that the Canal was not vital to them; but it was vital to Britain.

The Foreign Secretary, Selwyn Lloyd, in the course of the Commons debate from which the immediately preceding excerpts have been taken, further argued that the Charter permitted the use or threat of force lawfully on the express authority of the United Nations or in self-defense. He argued that self-defense "undoubtedly included a situation where the lives of the state's nationals abroad are in imminent danger." [6] Lloyd went on to question the authority and strength of the United Nations in such a case as this dispute between Israel and Egypt. By implication he noted, too, that the assurance of free passage through the Canal was threatened by the hostilities. Thus:

> The United Nations is not yet a world government and, therefore, it has not the power to take action and produce practical results on the ground in a particular situation rapidly. We know that in one case—the case of Korea. . . . We have a strong suspicion that that would have happened whatever the United Nations said about it, and that *the United States would have acted in that situation*, and I think, rightly. We in the present situation are, I believe, taking the right course to achieve peace, in order to protect British lives and interests and contribute to a final settlement.[7]

The Prime Minister next advanced the argument that "great wars were avoided by preventing small ones." This was the lesson of the 1930's, when the lesser wars were *not* undertaken.[8] The experience of the League of Nations, in which Eden had for fifteen years been immersed, during almost all of its existence, had shown that without its own "police force," a world organization must sooner or later fail. In the absence of such a United Nations police force, then, the alarmed and anxious countries must assume the responsibility of extinguishing a war before it got out of hand, and this is what Britain and France were doing.

It is now useful to turn to a consideration of the American tactics and argument.

The United States plan was to subject Britain and France to the United Nations in the interest of preventing the use of force, or if it were to be used before preventive action could be taken, of stopping it. It was not the American wish to do this by consultation with those allied governments, now that they had declared, as we have observed, that the Tripartite Pact of 1950 had no current validity for them.

Henry Cabot Lodge deliberately brushed Sir Pierson Dixon out of his way when the latter sought to converse with him.

Dixon, however, had already pleaded with Lodge *not* to press the United States resolution on October 30. Lodge now turned all his personal wrath on Dixon, with whom he had for months been transacting the friendly business of the Atlantic allies, often in opposition to Russia. When it came to Dulles's and Eisenhower's and Lodge's turn to be rude, these had no compunction about it at all, as the British and French leaders had had since July 26, even when they realized Dulles's trickiness. Lodge actually forced the pace after Dixon's request for a delay: the Security Council must deal with the invasion first, and then, only after that was settled, could it take up the Canal question. No member of the Council, not even Russia, was so fanatical in zealous leadership as Lodge for the U.S.A.

> We believe that the draft resolution, if promptly adopted and carried out, would effectively meet the situation created by the present military penetration of Egypt. This is given as the reason for the twelve-hour ultimatum which the Governments of the United Kingdom and France have given to Egypt and Israel which, in the case of Egypt, calls for the occupation of the Canal Zone. If this draft resolution is adopted and complied with by Israel, then the basis for the ultimatum will have disappeared.

The resolution must be adopted *without delay*.

The Soviet representative would have liked to add to this resolution the explicit condemnation of Israel as an aggressor. For to the Soviet Union, Israel was quadruply satanic: it was a bourgeois state, it was democratic, its people were religious, and Israeli workers exercised all the rights of a free people and at the same time made an economic success of an unfertile land without a Stalin! However, Arkady Sobolev did not press for an amendment to the American resolution or seek to substitute such a phrase. Matters were going only too well! The United States was deeply embroiled with its allies, and was injuring these two bastions of NATO, Britain and France, who were the shield of Europe and America against the U.S.S.R. Moscow had, so far in vain, been trying for years to split, destroy, or expel this Western alliance. Sobolev said he would support the resolution.

In any case, the condemnation of Israel as an aggressor, and so liable to sanctions, economic and military, by all the members of the United Nations, was not then feasible. Members of the Council within the meeting room and outside in the humming corridors—the bazaar of national egoisms and personal egoisms—understood too well that the United Nations had failed to assist Israel to obtain peace and tranquility or even passage for her ships and goods through the Canal, in spite of the Security Council resolution of September, 1951. If Egypt were a victim, then she was a victim *provocateur*, as some publicist wrote at that time. Ambassador Eban was permitted to appear and justify the Israeli action by detailing the wrongs she had suffered at the hands of Egypt, including imminent destruction—and everyone knew where Egypt's arms had come from. One amendment, proposed by Britain and France, was made in the resolution now before the Council. *Egypt as well as Israel* was called on to cease fire. The European allies refused to support a resolution that condemned Israel only.

"The Council," Lodge argued revealingly, "is somewhat like a doctor who faces a patient with a ruptured appendix, in whose abdomen gangrene has set in. A clean, quick operation is needed, and that is what our draft resolution seeks to do." Analogy is a desperate guide to political decision: every analogy is ultimately fallacious.

The Australian delegate asked for a delay. The Nationalist Chinese representative was a little ambiguous (he had to remember the rights of small countries like Israel—and his own), but he came around to Lodge's side, for he also remembered Formosa's interests in the United Nations and the United States. Sir Pierson Dixon tried to avert an immediate vote.

Lodge pressed it: "I do urge an immediate vote." The Russian Ambassador fully agreed with him: "The hands of the clock are rapidly bringing us closer to the hour of expiry of the ultimatum." [9] Only another four hours to go. The French representative, with dignity and clarity and restrained passion, recited the French and Israeli wrongs at the hands of Egypt. The Egyptian spokesman objected to this. The French member then tried to delay a vote by asking for time to consult his government about the form of the resolution as amended. The Soviet representative refused to hear of this.

Lodge's resolution, including the amendment on Egypt, was submitted to a vote. Australia and Belgium abstained. For it were: the U.S.A., China, Cuba, Iran, Peru, the Soviet Union, and Yugoslavia. Against it were: Britain and France. Thus, though there was a majority in favor, seven out of eleven, the British and French votes were each of them *vetoes* (this was the first time that Britain had ever cast a veto in the United Nations). This outcome had not been premeditated by Britain; it had not been thought that such a situation could possibly arise. The allies had miscalculated Washington's pressure, political, electoral, and moral.

What carried most tragic consequences for the future of American relations with Europe was that the American spokesman did not privately approach the British and French to attempt, even by tenaciously annoying persuasions, to find a way out that would at least save their pride. Instead, Lodge ostentatiously evaded them. The reverse is not true.

The Soviet Union competed with the United States in zeal to crush the British and French. Since the whole resolution could not pass, having been vetoed, it at once proposed to substitute, instead, the preamble to the effect that Israel had entered Egyptian territory, *plus* the demand that Israel alone be called on to withdraw. The suggested revision said nothing about a cease-fire, thus leaving Egypt free of blame and not enjoined in any way to stop its own shooting. Since the Soviet delegate must have known that the Soviet arms supplied to Egypt were overwhelming in quantity and quality and were cached in the Sinai Peninsula, this was a pretty piece of familiar deceitfulness.

The Chinese delegate moved, however, to reinstate Egypt as a recipient of the command to cease fire also. Upon this the French proposed that the Council adjourn until 9 P.M., since a new element had entered into the proceedings; they needed time to reflect and consult. Thus, for the moment, Lodge, like the Soviet representative, was thwarted. The motion to adjourn was adopted by a vote of 8 to 1, the lone dissenting vote coming from the U.S.S.R., with two nations abstaining, the U.S.A. and Yugoslavia (the special friend of Nasser).

At 9 P.M. the Council reassembled. The item on the agenda was the Soviet resolution. To circumvent the British and the French, and perhaps even to win over Lodge, their new-found friend, the Russians had, *during the recess,* amended the command to cease fire so that it applied to "*all* parties concerned." The Australians and British objected to this gambit: sensing that it was directed against the British and the French.

The Soviet Union, poker-faced and always unabashed in the frigid, callous game of power politics, then offered to amend its own amendment from "all parties" to "Israel and Egypt." Finally, its resolution read:

> The Security Council,
> Noting that the armed forces of Israel have penetrated deeply into Egyptian territory in violation of the General Armistice Agreement between Egypt and Israel;
> Expressing its grave concern at this violation of the Armistice Agreement,
> 1. Calls upon Israel and Egypt immediately to cease fire;
> 2. Calls upon Israel immediately to withdraw its armed forces behind the established armistice lines.

The vote on the Soviet Union's resolution was 7 in favor and 2, Britain and France, against. Belgium and the U.S.A. abstained. Thus this resolution was also vetoed. The French member had definite instructions from his government to veto the resolutions. Therefore, for the sake of allied solidarity, the British went along with the French. The French had some time before promised Israel the use of the veto, if necessary. During the recess, although it was then about 2 A.M. in London, Sir Pierson Dixon had phoned to London for instructions.

The Soviet delegate called it a black day for the Security Council. It had proved incapable of action, he complained! Making full use of a letter of complaint sent in by the Egyptians, he abused the British and French and insinuated that Israel, France, and Britain had acted according to a prearranged plan.

It must not be thought that matters were other than catastrophic for Secretary Dulles. For the last forty-eight hours, Dulles had been, and he now continued, in a state of the most intense mental anguish and torment of conscience. All his fears had intensified. Also, the President might be injured in his election prospects. His own faith, so long clung to, might not be justified. His prayers were not being answered. Above all, his allies, to go back to the beginning, might abandon him and all his fabric of policy. His lids drooped; his shoulders were now bent; he did not, as before, stride about confident and dominant.

When the British and French vetoed the Security Council's resolutions, the anger of Dulles and Eisenhower was all the more intensified. The European allies were *not* going to get away with it! But why should Dulles and Eisenhower and their serried confidants have been so shocked? Even up to 1950, France had voted No 23 times and Britain 29 times and the United States 34 times—the votes not being counted as vetoes, because they were cast alongside each other; and twice France had vetoed resolutions on her own.

When State Department officials received the news of the British and French vetoes, they cried out: "The *veto*—used against the United States of America by Great Britain! Her oldest and strongest and firmest ally! We went to England's help in two World Wars! No! England has not vetoed anything the Russians and their satellites have ever proposed—but, America! They vetoed us! It's a dirty business!" They denounced Eden's statement to the Commons that a "request" had been made to Israel and Egypt, with the bitter phrase, "The hypocrisy of it!" Inferentially, it was as though they expected each of these nations to be, in Eden's phrase, "a vassal" of America. Perhaps they had not had access to the papers which would have revealed Dulles's earlier deviousness to them; and, of course, many times the true motive and purpose of policy is not even the subject of a written memorandum, or if it is, the evidence is thrown into the incinerator.

By this time, British and French forces were moving on Suez, for Egypt had rejected the ultimatum. Naturally Egypt had done so, because the ultimatum had been so drawn that if Israel merely stayed ten miles away from the Canal, she would still be occupying almost all of the Sinai Peninsula. Nasser always played with death, for the highest stakes he could extract by the unlawful use of violence, as in the seizure of the Canal, or the maximum he could extract from peace-loving people by the exploitation of the law to its utmost confines, as in the United Nations—while violating his pledges to the United Nations (e.g., on his *fedayeen* murders and his closure of the Canal to Israel). He could be moved to do justice only by the exertion of force: the British and French as well as the Israelis now intended to get justice from him. The United States government flinched. Even if Nasser had violated a treaty, the United States would not make a stand against the African and Asian nations.

According to General Charles F. Keightley, Commander in Chief of the Allied Forces in the operations in Egypt, it was on October 30 that he was warned to start operations. This meant, he wrote, that "instead of ten days' interval between the executive order and the start of operations I was liable to get about ten *hours* [from the warning from London about the ultimatums to the end of the ultimatum period], and our operations might well be quite different to those for which we had planned." [10] But he did at once set about sending off some assault forces from Malta and the Western Mediterranean (French), and follow-up forces from these places and Britain, and he alerted all other forces, e.g., navy and land forces (paratroopers) at Cyprus, etc. It has been said (by the Brombergers and other journalists) that, the day before, some of the navy vessels had sailed already on "exercises." All forces began a movement at 4:30 A.M. on October 31, to occupy Port Said, Ismailia, and Suez.

There is an apparent note of complaint in the Commander in Chief's dispatch, in his implication that he should have had ten days in which to mount the attack. This observation fortifies judgment that the date originally planned for the descent by Israel on Suez was about November 3 or a little later.

An extremely grave and untoward event occurred at the termination of the Security Council proceedings. The Yugoslav member, the Soviet Union's faithful and abiding ally on foreign policy against the United States and NATO, prompted, it has been rumored, by the Indian representatives, suggested that the Security Council call an Emergency Session of the General Assembly under the terms of the "Uniting for Peace" Resolution of November 3, 1950. This move refreshed the zealous impetuosity of the United States government.

In the Korean crisis the issue had arisen of what should be done if the great powers could not agree on action, in a situation where aggression was manifest and dangerous. It happened by the sheer chance of a Soviet political mistake that the United Nations was able to take prompt action, and only just in time, on the outbreak of hostilities by the North Koreans. The Security Council passed resolutions on this matter on June 25 and 27, 1950, under the impulse of the United States, and *validly*, because the Soviet representative had stalked out of the meeting and thus the resolutions were not vetoed. It was also possible to act because the United States happened to have considerable forces, air, navy, and land, in Japan, and in the Ryukyus and nearby waters, without which the North Koreans would have overwhelmed all Korea long before the Security Council could have acted in accordance with its normal procedure.

It even happened on that occasion that President Truman jumped the gun, or rather that his guns jumped the moment of the passage of the resolution of June 27, 1950. The North Koreans invaded South Korea on June 25. On June 25, the Security Council voted 9 to 0 that the North Koreans had committed a breach of the peace, and it ordered them to withdraw and cease fire. Instead, they intensified their drive, and South Korea began to crumble. On June 26—before the U.N. voted for *action* by its members—Truman, to his everlasting credit, ordered General MacArthur to use U.S. air and naval units at once, south of the 38th parallel. Simultaneously, Formosa was put under protection of the U.S.A., not, be it noted, of the United Nations.

Later in the year, under the inspiration of Dean Acheson, U.S. Secretary of State, the General Assembly accepted the "Uniting for Peace Resolution." It provided that, in the event the Security Council should fail to exercise its "primary responsibility," then the General Assembly should take immediate consideration of any situation that involved an act of aggression or other threat to the peace. If the Assembly were not then in session an emergency meeting could be held within twenty-four hours.

Now, some hold the Uniting for Peace Resolution is of doubtful legality, for it amends the Charter of the U.N. without using the procedure established in that document for amendment, the *only* way of legal amendment. To be legal, an amendment needs endorsement by the Security Council, and here the veto applies. The new Resolution was never subjected to that legal procedure. The Soviet delegates did not altogether resist the Resolution: but they opposed, with their bloc, the most important part, namely, that which we have described above. The five who voted *against* the Resolution in the General Assembly were: the Soviet Union, Poland, Czechoslovakia, the Ukraine, Byelorussia: one mind, five voices. This mind was definitely opposed to the extension of the power of the General Assembly as also of the United Nations in general. On October 31, 1956, the Russians and their supporters, being professional *realpolitiker*, and not amateurs and idealists like Henry Cabot Lodge and his bosses, exuberantly rejoiced in exploiting the resolution offered by Yugoslavia against Israel, Britain, and France. For they, as distinct from Dulles, could *not* forget that these countries were allies of America.

Let us for a moment turn to the scene in Washington. The rancorous indignation in the State Department and White House was not yet appeased. Dulles and Eisenhower, who had to suffer the sacrifice of his campaign trip to Texas and Oklahoma City on account of the gravity of international developments, conferred together again on the morning of October 31. At this time Dulles recommended that Eisenhower should call his friend Anthony (Eden) on the telephone. He did so at 10:43 A.M. This was just after 4:30 P.M. in London, and it caught the Prime Minister in his room at the House of Commons. The President, rather in the terms of the latest of his messages of October 30, but in less official and rougher, army-life, tongue-lashing language, told the Prime Minister of his "deep concern" over the drastic action implied by the ultimatum and its probable consequences. The Prime Minister burst into tears. He had been extremely, debilitatingly ill since October 5. His present policy, not entirely happily for the milder elements of his conscience, was facing dreadful hostility from many quarters as well as his ally, was now confronting not only the strength of a giant, but of a giant turned from friendship to bitter and prosecuting enmity.

On that same day, President Eisenhower spoke on television on the Middle Eastern situation, at 7:00 P.M. Washington time. By this time, British bombers had been attacking Egyptian airfields for some eight hours. By this time also, the President's election tacticians were greatly rejoicing that the British and French invasion of Suez would put the election of Eisenhower for a second time "in the bag." He stood for PEACE; and horses must not be swapped in midstream. They were right about the result, but not for the reasons they supposed.

It is necessary and instructive to review the President's speech. For, having taken precipitate action in the U.N., it now became necessary for the United States government to collect principles to give it moral respectability, to salve the conscience of its perpetrators, and also to tell the American people where they stood. The ideas in the President's speech are of the gravest significance in the material and moral commitment made for the American people by their leaders, even if they were pieced together just to satisfy the necessities of an awkward and unexpected moment. What was the relevance of the reasoning of the President and the Secretary to this particular conflict?

Two pertinent matters had better be mentioned now, in reference to Dulles's policy and the President's speech, especially their publicized full reliance on the United Nations and intention to regard as

Justice whatever that organization voted. First, the United States distributes about $4 billion per year in military, economic, and technical aid, directly, *not* through the United Nations, for purposes of its own exclusive national policy. It does not, correctly, trust the United Nations to administer all this wealth. It seeks, outside the United Nations, to affect the balance of power in the world in its favor, and by this means indirectly to affect the voting strength at its disposal within it. Dulles and Eisenhower had continued this policy, which had been established by President Truman, General Marshall, and Dean Acheson.

Secondly, in taking their present attitude of opposition to British and French vital interests, the Secretary and the President cast doubt on their own stated principle at the end of the Eisenhower speech under consideration that there must be "only one law for all, friends and enemies." For Dulles had already made it public, more than once, that he regarded America's interest in Suez as comparatively *unimportant*.

There were therefore *not* two equally important interests before the United Nations' judgment. It is all very well to claim one law for friends and for enemies before an independent and impartial court of justice, and quite otherwise for oneself to appear with unequal and less important interests contending against those which are acknowledged as "vital." The United States' interest in the matter was that peace should not be broken: but she had no specific immediate interests to defend.

In addition, specifically in the opposition to Israel's policy of self-defense, there was an implication for American foreign policy that runs through the policies of most nations: casualties among *American* G.I.'s, if it came to war, were more deplorable, and therefore more to be avoided, than casualties among other nationals. For example, the losses the Israelis had been suffering without redress from the United Nations or the United States. This was the principle implicit in the almost mathematically calculated decision in 1945 to use atom bombs on "the Japs," to save American casualties. Law and justice are very different within a nation from so-called law and justice between nations, whether or not before the bar of the United Nations. Within a nation all men's lives are equal; all men's property interests are equal (assuming that conditions of feudal privilege and other vestiges of exploitation of race, creed, color, and class have been straightened out). Not so in contemporary foreign policy.

Eisenhower's speech on October 31 [11] was a long one, and therefore it cannot be reproduced. Here we shall merely examine the bald propositions, and immediately after each, observe its error—that is, what the American electorate was *not* told (this commentary in each case appears in italics).

1. America's allies had wished to use force, but had desisted under American influence. *But they had desisted on a promise of justice by Dulles, part of it spurious. Nasser was not pressed, for fear of the Soviet Union.*

2. It "seemed" that an acceptable accord had been reached on the Six Principles. *But acceptable to whom? Dulles would not use leverage on Nasser to make "seem" become effective.*

3. Eisenhower recognized the danger to Israel's life from Nasser. *But he did not scale the casualties, comparing Israel's population with America's (1.7 million to 170 million), that is, multiplying the loss of life, etc., by 100. Thus, the gravity of Israel's plight was not brought home to the American people he was addressing.*

4. He complained that the United States was not consulted about the invasion, or informed in advance. *But Dulles and he had been constantly and continually warned for twelve weeks, almost day after day, in close conference, as the record has shown. More recently, Eden's letters to Eisenhower had assumed a desperate urgency.*

5. These nations had "the manifest right" to make their own decisions, but he believed they were in error. *But did he expect Israel to wait to be "garroted"? Those who fought the American War of Independence had waited only so long, and had then taken up arms against "a long train of abuses and usurpations . . . to provide new guards for their future security." The United Nations had been a failure as a shield; the Tripartite Pact, under Dulles, had not been tooled for timely and preventive action.*

6. Eisenhower rejected force as a wise and proper means of settling international disputes. *But his nation had entered the Korean War to protect its interests, with the recommendation and support of Dulles—rightly. It had defended Formosa—rightly. It had used its fleet to protect Quemoy and Matsu—rightly. It had secured the forceful overturn of a Communist government in Guatemala—rightly. Hence, it appeared there was one law for America's national interests, but another for Israel's, and those of France and Britain. Eisenhower's principle was thus a double standard, the advantageous one for the United States. He should not have led the American people to believe that other nations would see the truth this way.*

7. He knew these nations had been subject to "grave and repeated provocations," and did not wish to minimize his determination to maintain friendship with them. *But to "know" of provocations is not enough; provocations must be* felt, *to the point of doing something to relieve them. Dulles and Eisenhower had refused to grasp the nettle: Nasser. They left it to "Dag," that is, to the United Nations, which they knew to be an agglomeration of interest-begotten prejudices,*[12] *without power. Merely "knowing" is an evasion of responsibility. Dulles had surely learned the Biblical lesson: Resist evil!*

8. The action of the three nations could not be reconciled with the principles and purposes of the United Nations "to which we have all subscribed." *But neither had the United States always acted, as we have seen, only as the authority of the United Nations expressly allowed, where her national interests were concerned. Furthermore, the Charter requires justice to go along with peace. No one was so sententious and vociferous about this principle as Dulles. He did not seek justice with all the modalities at his disposal, because it did not suit America's national interests, as he interpreted them. As for whether war can serve the interests of a people in the long run, the war against Hitler is a case in point and America's hold on Okinawa is another. And how long is the long run?*

9. Eisenhower intended to bring the power of the United Nations to bear on the conflict in the General Assembly, where there is no veto—where the opinion of the world can make itself heard. *But he had now slipped away from "justice" to "the opinion of the world." And why, in the existing egoisms of nations, should that opinion prevail? What does it represent? Polyglot masses? Illiterate billions? One hundred and eleven sovereign nations, each intent on its own way of life, ranging from the highest civility to the lowest debasement? The personal wishes of the Sukarnos and Nkrumahs, exerted against their more humane countrymen for their own personal power? A majority of 111 states, or 3 billion people? And, above all, is the majority sacred in the relationships of nations? Dulles did not conscientiously think so, if America were to be outvoted. Nor did Russia, when it came to her actions in Hungary. Nor did the President leave Britain and France and Israel to the United Nations: he was about to exert unilateral sanctions of dollars and oil supplies on them.*

10. Eisenhower did not believe that the "injustices" suffered by the three powers could be solved by war—"another injustice." *But the word "injustice" is an evasion. The three nations had suffered from* injuries. *Those can be put right by war; American action after Pearl Harbor had demonstrated that. Also, the use of the word "injustice" here is tricky: one justice is what the United Nations says it is; another justice is the international right of reprisal in self-defense. The United Nations Charter does not abrogate this.*[13] *With modern methods of war (missiles from afar, infiltration by guerrillas in an undeclared war), the interpretation of "self-defense" has changed—to America's benefit in the case of Cuba at the moment this page is being written. Surely, the President was not inferentially committing the U.S.A. to accept whatever the United Nations prescribes, without exerting craft to keep the issue out of the United Nations or disregarding its resolutions when the United States believes that substantial injustice has been done to it?*

11. *So we come close to the dynamic principle of the President's*

course of action. "And there can be no law, if we were to invoke one code of international conduct for those who oppose us—and another for our friends." *This abysmal fallacy and evasion has already been dealt with.**

This speech, the discovery and exploitation of principle, *after* the fact, had a most curious gestation. Dulles sent a draft to the White House at 3:15 P.M. But, tired and agonized by the collapse of his hopes and ventures, Dulles had produced merely a garrulous narration about Communism, Russia, Hungary, and the Middle East, without any energetic principle of forward action. The President and the men around him were also in an extremely emotional condition, though one of a somewhat different nature; they were frightened and sentimental. They felt the nation must be found a justification of American foreign policy.

The President and his chief speech-writer, Emmet Hughes, talked over the points the address should include. They discarded Dulles's attempt as bankrupt of ideas. The President accepted Hughes's slogan (it was now 4:15 P.M. and TV time was 7 P.M.) of "one law for all—friends as well as enemies." It was a slogan taken, because of the pressure of time, from a speech already prepared for the President's delivery a day hence at Philadelphia, and in that form it was directed against "the strong," that is, against the Soviet Union for its behavior in Hungary and Poland.

At 6 P.M. Dulles was sent for, and he listlessly let the newly dictated pages go with hardly a change. While the speech was being put in its final form, the President, like Sir Francis Drake, who played bowls while the Spanish Armada was sailing up the English Channel, did some putting on the White House lawn. Then, while dressing for TV, the President had the advantage of hearing the speech read aloud. At any rate, he had insisted on including (as Dulles had not) that the British were still America's right arm, and that America needed her allies. The speech was copied in extra large characters and handed to the President page after page as each was finished, as he was going to his reading desk.

Of course, it must be asked: Was this speech, so conceived, a thoughtful and pondered formulation and commitment of principle? Could it be said to have followed from Eisenhower's general commitment to the United Nations? Had the President time in which to cogitate the logical consequences of its several themes, above all for the problems of Suez and Israel? The answer, surely, is No! But the main principle seems thereafter to have helped make his attitude

* In contrast to the loftiness of the President's allocution, one of Dulles's close representatives observed, on hearing of Prime Minister Eden's struggle in the House of Commons, "*We taught Anthony a good lesson!*"

towards his allies a rigidly punitive one, and especially to have had this effect on his subordinates. If he and they did not stick to this principle of action, what could they stick to?

We return to the Security Council. On October 31, the meeting having started at 3 P.M., the Yugoslav delegate moved a resolution to call an Emergency Session of the General Assembly. Sir Pierson Dixon, the British representative, asked for some time to consider this resolution and study the actual text. Every member of the United Nations is entitled to examine a proposed action, to see whether it conforms to the terms of the Charter (a treaty of immense complexity), and to discover whether the obligations which other members are proposing to subject it to are warranted by its own interpretations and the Charter's own evolution over the years.

After a half-hour recess, Sir Pierson Dixon made two objections to the resolution: The Security Council was not, in fact, at that moment seized with a resolution concerning a threat to the peace, breach of the peace, or act of aggression. The resolutions of the day before were not in these terms; but constituted a call on Israel and Egypt to cease fire. Therefore, a lack of unanimity of the permanent members of the Council on the substance mentioned above had not yet been manifested. No resolution of this kind had been circulated or voted on. The two draft resolutions voted on the day before did not come within the Uniting for Peace conditions. In the second place, the resolutions were less effective than the British and French action.

Dixon requested that the resolution be ruled out of order. He was overcome by 6 votes to 4, China abstaining: that is, Australia, Belgium, France, and Britain were overruled by Cuba, Iran, the Soviet Union, the United States, and Yugoslavia. No juridical answer had been offered to Dixon's legal objections by anyone, not even Hammarskjold.

When the resolution itself was put to a vote, seven nations voted in favor: China, Cuba, Iran, Peru, the Soviet Union, the United States, and Yugoslavia. Britain and France voted against. Australia and Belgium abstained. Sir Pierson Dixon then expressed doubt, on behalf of the British government, of the legality of the Council's resolution. The French representative endorsed this comment.

Dulles had grasped lightning-like at the opportunity opened for him by the forthcoming meeting of the Assembly. All the morning of November 1 he was at work with his aides on a plan of action and argument that Lodge would carry out. But when the time came, the President asked Dulles personally to go before the Assembly to represent the United States.

On that morning also, Israeli Ambassador Abba Eban called on

Dulles, in view of the approaching Emergency Session. By that time the Israeli forces had been in action for about forty-eight hours. A curious conversation occurred. Eban told Dulles he had just received a telephone call from Jerusalem: We have won a complete victory! Dulles looked astounded and anxious, but not unhappy. He knew it was true, in spite of the deliberately lying claims of Nasser that *he* had annihilated the Israeli army and air force by October 30! Worried, Dulles answered Eban: "Are you thinking of *staying* in the Sinai Peninsula then? You know, it would be bound to affect our relations. We could hardly continue economic aid, and all the other kinds of assistance you get from us!"

Eban answered, "Sir, a more fundamental event has occurred as a result of this total victory. This is the first time an aggressive dictatorship has been resisted. As a result of what Israel has done, Nasser is going to lose all his credit. A more moderate government will replace his. Possibly Israel and other countries will be able to make peace at last in the Middle East. Another thing: Russia's influence in Egypt will be reduced. The victory might cause a total change in the map of political power!"

Dulles thrust his hands deeper into his trousers pockets and wrinkled his brow, as he strode around the office. Eban's were big conceptions, and he liked them. "Look," he answered, "I'm terribly torn. No one can be happier than I am that Nasser has been beaten. Since spring I've had only too good cause to detest him."

The Ambassador thought Dulles looked tempted by the opportunity.

"I'm torn," Dulles finally repeated. "*Yet:* can we accept this good end when it is achieved by means that violate the Charter? Look here, we could improve our position in the world if we used force, say in Korea, or Quemoy, or in Germany. But if we did that, the United Nations would collapse. So I am forced to turn back to support international law and the Charter. I have to work on the basis that the long-term interests of the United States and the world are superior to these considerations of self-benefit. Another thing: if the invaders do not evacuate and go back behind the armistice frontier, Secretary General Hammarskjold would resign!"

On this note of potential bereavement, the Ambassador and Dulles went their separate ways towards the Emergency Session of the General Assembly.

Dulles, his Legal Counsel, and the Assistant Secretary for Public Affairs were airborne for New York at 3 P.M. out of Washington. On the plane, the tactics to be adopted were carefully considered. The weather became very bad, bumpy, and all the area around New York City was shrouded in heavy fog. The pilot found a swooping way to ground at Newark. Dulles arrived in the auditorium as Sir Pierson Dixon was speaking, and had to take his seat just opposite him over the aisle, as the United States and the United Kingdom are alphabetically contiguous.

With the exception of the Egyptian spokesman, the consensus of the Assembly at this point was that something like, but not quite, aggression was being committed; and the members were shaken that Britain had a share in it. But since Egyptian victimization of Israel was understood even better by this time than earlier, the Assembly tended towards a cease-fire and withdrawal of forces rather than a condemnation of aggression, in spite of the Soviet bloc's denunciation of the "aggressors," or even perhaps because of it.

Some reaction against American severity was experienced at the United Nations and by the public also against the rather brutal proposals in Washington made by some minor members of the United States Administration, haters of Britain and France, surely: that military aid from the United States to them be stopped! That some redisposition of the Sixth Fleet in the Mediterranean be so arranged as to hamper and thwart French and British action! The Pentagon soon put a stop to such vindictive dreams, and its observations on this score began to have weight with the President. As a matter of fact, some of the career and political personnel in the State Department and the Pentagon and around the White House, those to whom the Western alliance and civilization were precious, spoke quietly but hoped ardently that Nasser would be overthrown before the pressure of the U.N. could thwart their attack on him.

Dulles spoke to an American draft resolution.[14] It noted the many violations of the Israeli-Arab armistice agreements, and observed that Israel had now again disregarded them by her invasion. It also noted that Britain and France were conducting military operations against Egyptian territory, and that traffic through the Suez Canal was interrupted. It, therefore, urged that as a matter of priority all parties involved in hostilities agree to an immediate cease-fire and halt the movement of arms and military forces into the area. It urged that the parties to the armistice agreements promptly withdraw all forces behind the armistice lines, desist from raids across them, and scrupulously observe the agreements. The resolution continued with the recommendation that all member states refrain from introducing military goods into the area of hostilities and refrain from acts which would delay or prevent the implementing of the present resolution. It urged that when the cease-fire became effective steps be taken to reopen the Canal and restore secure freedom of navigation. It asked that the Secretary General observe and report compliance with the resolution to the Security Council and the General Assembly, for such further action as they might deem appropriate according to the Charter. The General Assembly would remain in emergency session pending compliance with the resolution.

Dulles said:

> I doubt that any delegate ever spoke from this forum with as heavy a heart as I have brought here tonight. We speak on a matter of vital importance, where the United States finds itself unable to agree with three nations with whom it has ties, deep friendship, admiration, and respect, and two of whom constitute our oldest, most trusted and reliable allies.
>
> The fact that we differ with such friends has led us to reconsider and reevaluate our position with the utmost care, and that has been done at the highest levels of our Government. Even after that reevaluation, we still find ourselves in disagreement. Because it seems to us that that disagreement involves principles which far transcend the immediate issue, we feel impelled to make our point of view known to you and through you to the world. . . .
>
> To be sure, the United Nations perhaps has not done all that it should have done. I have often pointed out, particularly in recent weeks, that our charter by article 1, paragraph 1, calls for the settlement of these matters in accordance with the principles of justice and of international law, and it calls not merely for a peaceful solution but a just solution. The United Nations may have been somewhat laggard, somewhat impotent in dealing with many injustices which are inherent in this Middle Eastern situation. But I think that we ought, and I hope will—perhaps at the next regular meeting of this General Assembly—give our most earnest thought to the problem of how we can do more to establish and to implement principles of justice and of international law. We have not done all that we should have done in that respect, and on that account a part of the responsibility of present events lies here at our doorstep.[15]

"Somewhat laggard"! "Somewhat impotent"! "We have not done all that we should"! "On that account part of the responsibility for the present events lies at our doorstep"!

The cleverness of the Secretary shines out. "Our doorstep" means the doorstep of the United States as well as that of all nations he was addressing. In this homely metaphor, he both admits contributory negligence and spreads the negligence, thereby *diminishing it*. For if he had been more realistic in portraying the situation, terming it, let us say, as unwillingness to meet his nation's obligations to the United Nations in respect to the Middle East, he could hardly have pressed on with his resolution, or with his eulogy to the majesty of the United Nations.

"If . . . whenever a nation feels that it has been subjected to injustice it should have the right to resort to force . . . then I fear we should be tearing this Charter into shreds. . . ." And world wars might follow!

Informed publicists thought they discovered a considerable difference between this attitude and Eisenhower's point in his speech that it was the allies' "manifest right" to act as they did.

We who live in the aftermath of the Suez crisis and the action of the United States and the United Nations in it, know that it did not deter the continuation of acts of force by nations who were in that episode the accusers of Israel, Britain, and France. Egypt continued to preach assassination, and in Iraq she succeeded; while the United States, WITHOUT BENEFIT OF THE CHARTER, or of international law, intervened by force in Lebanon in June, 1958. India hung on to Kashmir *against* the Charter. India made war on Portugal in Goa, *against* the Charter. The Soviet Union fomented war wherever it was able, *against* the Charter, and refused even to permit a United Nations mission to visit Hungary, *against* the Charter. Indonesia gained New Guinea from the Netherlands by the threat and the use of force; this time the Charter was distorted by its own officials, with the assistance of the United States, against the will, interests, and rights of the Netherlands and of the natives.

Dulles went on to recount once again what we already know about the successive conferences. He concluded by defending the policy of *not* trying to settle the main issues involved in the two disputes, that between Israel and Egypt, and that between his allies (those "oldest and most trusted and most reliable" allies) and Egypt. Instead, he maintained, a cease-fire must first be achieved, and only then should the attempt be made to settle the substantial issues.

He did not say it was impossible to do both together. If he had not, through anger and excessive moralism, started on the course which had brought him to this point, and which by now seemed irreversible, and if he had had the nerve and the imagination, he could have found the way to give a constructive lead to the nations assembled. *But he was afraid* of a world war, a figment of his own trepidation, and especially of the hostility of the Arab-Asian peoples, much of it delinquent, unless the military actions were stopped at once. This was his true motive; but his rhetoric and tactics appeared in the guise of devotion to the Rule of Law through the United Nations. Let us see.

> . . . I believe that the first thing is to stop the fighting as rapidly as possible lest it become a conflagration which would endanger us all—and that is not beyond the realm of possibility. . . .
> . . . I fear that if we do not act and act promptly, and if we do not act with sufficient unanimity of opinion so that our recommendations carry a real influence, there is great danger that what is started and what has been called a police action may develop

> into something which is far more grave. Even if that does not happen, the apparent impotence of this organization to deal with this situation may set a precedent which will lead other nations to attempt to take into their own hands the remedying of what they believe to be their injustices. If that happens, the future is dark indeed.
>
> We thought when we wrote the charter in San Francisco in 1945 that we had seen perhaps the worst in war, that our task was to prevent a recurrence of what had been, and indeed what then had been was tragic enough. But now we know that what can be will be infinitely more tragic than what we saw in World War II.

It is often difficult, as we have discerned several times in this study, to judge whether Dulles was speaking out of conviction or merely to persuade his listeners to an interest-begotten policy. Did he *really* fear a world war? Was the electoral prospect affecting him? Was the apologetic and pathetic quality of his words the product of a feeling of guilt towards his allies? Did he really bother about Israel? But how about his NATO allies, on whose importance Admiral Radford had had a few important observations to make during the past few days? Was Dulles exercising his *personal* emotions, reinforced by those of the President and Henry Cabot Lodge, when a more democratically *representative national* approach was needed? And again, it must be asked, did he really fear a world war? But the Chairman of the Joint Chiefs of Staff had made it perfectly clear to him that Russia was in no position to do anything militarily in the Middle East, even by way of a dispatch of "volunteers." Was he afraid of the very Red Specter he had himself so substantially built up in his own mind? If that were so, then except for continental self-defense, the United States could not use its enormous armament to correct abuses in the world, because the Soviet Union would prohibit it, while within the United Nations, any injustice, even to "our oldest and most trusted and most reliable allies," could be done with impunity, because the Soviet Union had the power to veto any proposed counteraction!

Dulles himself believed he had made the most notable as well as the most noble contribution of his whole life to policy and eloquence in his speech. When later, recovering from his bout with cancer, he recounted the thoughts he had had as he was wheeled into the operating room, he delighted in telling officials or his intimates among churchmen: "If that had been my very last act on earth, it would have been exactly as I would have wished it; I would have liked it for my epitaph."

The meeting recessed after Dulles's speech at shortly before 8 P.M. About 9 P.M. he went to have dinner, having had nothing to eat since noon. The meeting started again at 9:50 P.M. Many speakers followed. Dulles was feeling very tired. He asked an assistant, "Shall we leave?" The answer was: "If you stay, the majority for our resolution will be bigger than if you leave, though in any case there will be a majority." He stayed. The proceedings were unexpectedly prolonged, because the Italian delegate insisted on introducing a resolution condemning the Soviet Union for its brutalities in Hungary.

The vote on the American resolution was taken at about 3 A.M., and was adopted by 64 votes against 5. The 64 represented almost the entire world of nations, with the United States and the Soviet Union in the van. The minority was made up of Britain, France, Israel, Australia, New Zealand. Abstaining were 6 nations: Portugal, South Africa, Belgium, Canada, Laos, the Netherlands.

At this point, a small but relevant connecting thread in the process of diplomacy may be revealed. Vice President Richard M. Nixon made a campaign speech on November 2. It was ostensibly in answer to criticisms of the Administration's Middle East policy by Adlai Stevenson. The remarks Nixon made on this occasion caused one of the President's speech-writers to muse that here, once again, was one of "Dick's improprieties." The passage relating to Suez ran thus:

> This vote [for the cease-fire, in the General Assembly] constituted a world-wide vote of confidence, the like of which has never been known before [since sixty-four nations have given their unqualified support to the President's position on the Middle East conflict]. It is significant that only five opposed our resolution.
>
> In the past the nations of Asia and Africa have always felt we would, when the pressure was on, side with the policies of the British and French Governments in relation to the once colonial areas.
>
> For the first time in history we have shown independence of Anglo-French policies toward Asia and Africa which seemed to us to reflect the colonial tradition. That declaration of independence has had an electrifying effect throughout the world.

This part of the speech was written by Dulles and sent to Nixon for delivery. Nixon enjoyed delivering it. He worked in constant harmony with Dulles.

At the U.N., Dulles still could not leave the Assembly, since the condemnation of the Soviet Union was now to be discussed. He could hardly condemn the Western allies without also voting to condemn the Soviet Union. He stayed on and expressed his gratification that his resolution had been adopted, and also that the Hungarian situation was being watched by the Assembly. He left for the Waldorf-Astoria at about 5 A.M. He took off his coat and had a drink, remarking how satisfactory had been the outcome of the meeting. An assistant asked when they were returning to Washington. He answered, "Wheels up at 8:30 A.M.!" The assistant quipped: "If you're not careful they'll get you for a breach of the peace against your staff." Dulles yielded: "Make it 11:30 A.M.!"

Actually, Dulles was up at 9:30 A.M. on this Friday morning, November 2, and almost immediately was on the telephone to the President and State Department. He arrived back in the capital at 2:30 P.M. and drove directly to the State Department to work. He had said on the plane that now that the resolution was passed it was necessary to devise ways of getting it carried out at once. He laughingly chided a close associate who left at 5:30 P.M. because he felt tired.

Dulles arrived home in the evening of November 2, and after dinner and some conversation went to bed. At 2:30 A.M. on Saturday morning, November 3, he suffered a severe attack of abdominal pains. By 5:30 A.M. physicians were in attendance on him, and at 7:30 A.M. he was in Walter Reed Hospital, soon to be on the operating table for over three hours. It was cancer.

For some days, let us say until November 6, matters were entirely in the hands of other people, chiefly Herbert Hoover, Jr., Henry Cabot Lodge, and President Eisenhower. The staff meetings at the State Department were conducted under the chairmanship of Hoover, although the regular march of American policy on the Suez and Israeli affairs was dictated by the principles Dulles had formulated and had initiated on October 30 and November 1. Meanwhile, other more flexible and less confined minds than Hoover's saw to it that America's foreign policy was not exclusively dictated by him. However, his personal character and limited experience, allied to Eisenhower's new-found principle of "one rule," sharpened rather than tempered the prevalent persecuting and idealist attitudes, and also the hatred and fear of Russia.

It was significantly detrimental to the NATO alliance and the future of the Middle East from a Western point of view that Herbert Hoover, Jr., was Acting Secretary in the absence of Dulles. Of all his colleagues not one denies him the character of a gentleman and pleasant colleague. Unanimously they testify to his remarkable comprehension of the oil business. Without dissent his many associates praise his industriousness. Yet, also unanimously, they doubt that he possessed either the degree of knowledge, the experience, the judgment, the finesse, the imagination, or the decisiveness required in the highest position charged with the conduct of America's foreign affairs during a world crisis. They declare he had certain disabilities: that his deafness made him suspicious of his associates; that it made him unable to follow a multi-party conference; that he had considerable difficulty in making up his mind; that he shared his father's very strong anti-British prejudices; that his Middle East oil transactions made him powerfully pro-Arab. It cannot be accounted a responsible act of prudence by Dulles, that he had a major hand in Hoover's appointment in October, 1954, to a post, where, in the absence of Dulles, decisions of high policy would devolve upon him. And Hoover particularly disliked Eden.

Something more must be emphasized. The first splenetic outburst of anger among Washington officials had given place to a steady, stern, cold determination to liquidate the Suez affair at the earliest possible moment. This objective necessarily involved driving the British, French, and Israelis out of their positions, *at any cost*, including the calculated risk that they might break with NATO. This American policy was based on a general attitude in the Administration, as expressed by some of its members, including the President and George M. Humphrey, that Eden had made a terrible mistake. This, they felt, was due to his military misunderstanding of the Suez problem; to his lack of bloody decisiveness to carry through the expedition to success within twenty-four or forty-eight hours, cost what it must cost; to his lack of foresight and planning to "take care of his backdoor," that is, to provide for oil reserves and financial support for sterling, which linked Britain to half the whole world's economy. Hence, in addition to the original ire, other feelings entered: especially the desire to clear up a mess quickly, even, in a sense, as an act of good will towards the British, "to bail them out," as the saying went. At any rate, each time the British demurred to being hustled out of Suez, the angry emotions blazed up again. And there was no doubt at all that the harshest bulldozing sanctions would be applied against them by the Administration if they put up any opposition to withdrawing from Suez.

From about November 4 until the end of the month, when American policy fully triumphed, Herbert Hoover and George M. Humphrey, with a group of staff aides, enacted that policy, conferring with the President from time to time. *Of course, Dulles was in the background*. Humphrey entered substantially because the provision of money was a key element in the inducement-compulsion tactics with Britain (centered on oil and support of sterling), and because he was greatly trusted by the President for his character and judgment.

Yet quite soon Dulles was once more in command of the main guiding lines of policy. By November 6, election day, he telephoned to the State Department saying he would be back shortly, "cracking the whip—so don't let any of the boys get any ideas!" His hand was back on the tiller after that telephone call, as no one dared take action without getting his concurrence and advice. By November 9, Dulles asked that the cables be sent to the hospital; William

Macomber, his private secretary, was already installed there. On Saturday, November 10, he looked at the TV showing of the Princeton-Yale football game and Eisenhower and Nixon visited him.

Now we return to American tactics in the General Assembly and elsewhere. Israel had agreed to a cease-fire in response to the British and French ultimatum. But by now, say November 3, 4, and 5, two more problems needed solution—to get her to withdraw from Sinai, and to get the British and French to cease fire. For while Israel remained in Sinai she was in defiance of the resolution of the General Assembly, even though a resolution of that body is but a recommendation, without legal effect. But now that Nasser's military forces were shown to be utterly ineffective under battle conditions, he could rely only on the United Nations to eject Israel from her victorious positions. Krishna Menon, the Soviet Union, the Arabs, the Asian nations who followed Nehru's lead, all of them gave loud tongue in the chase. The United States was on the same side; she could not relinquish her championship of "a decent respect for the opinions of the world." Henry Cabot Lodge had to be conspicuously more zealous than Arkady Sobolev; and President Eisenhower and Herbert Hoover, Jr., too: "One Law." Moreover, the votes were not yet in, either at the United Nations or at the Presidential polling stations.

In these circumstances, Herbert Hoover, Jr., on Sunday, November 4, tried some personal diplomacy. He sought out Maxwell Rabb, secretary to President Eisenhower's Cabinet, haunting the White House, in and out, in a state of tetchy anxiety until he found him. He asked Rabb what he could do to have the Israelis withdraw and so prevent further trouble in the Middle East (he was terrified by Russia and anxious about his Arab friends), by appealing through other than formal diplomatic channels to Ben Gurion. Could some intimately informal contact be established to present the American view and policy to the Prime Minister and other leading Israelis? The idea was to get Israel to give up fighting, and that, it was hoped, would lead to a cease-fire by Britain and then by France.

Rabb recommended approaching General Bedell Smith, who, since he had witnessed the Nazi concentration camps, was sympathetic to the Israelis, and suggested that Bedell Smith might talk with Reuben Shiloah, Political Counselor of the Israeli Embassy. Not relishing the role of intermediary, Bedell Smith nevertheless assumed it, in the expectation that the American view would be conveyed by Shiloah to Ben Gurion. Sherman Adams and Hoover then went to the President and explained what was being attempted. The President exhibited intense worry—the peace of the whole world depended on Israel's action! The atmosphere in the White House was highly emotional, and Hoover again and again cried out that Britain and France had gone behind America's back. "Would they like us to go behind their backs? Just think what would happen if we did!"

Shiloah was called to the White House to see Rabb and Hoover; Bedell Smith was also present. An earnest discussion, full of tension, occurred between Shiloah and Bedell Smith, Hoover intervening. The spirit of Hoover's interventions was altogether coercive in regard to Israel, and Shiloah conveyed this circumstance to Ben Gurion. The latter has revealed the substance of Hoover's remarks thus:

> A senior official of the State Department—Mr. John Foster Dulles, the Secretary of the State [sic], was ill at the time—summoned the Israeli Minister in Washington (our Ambassador was at the Assembly), and said to him: "We are on the brink of war. Israel's refusal to comply with the Assembly's decision is endangering the peace of the world. Israel's attitude will inevitably lead to grave consequences, such as the stoppage of all governmental and private aid to Israel, sanctions by the UN, and perhaps even expulsion from the United Nations Organization." [16]

Yes, the United States threatened even to stop *private* aid! This constituted Dulles's, Eisenhower's, and Hoover's own form of direct American sanctions on Israel. They would do to Israel directly what they had forbidden Britain and France to do to Egypt!

Since our present interest is in the use and misuse of American power, it may be added that an examination of Dulles's resolution of November 1, at the General Assembly, demonstrates several advances towards realism, although it remains far from realistic. It did not use the term "aggression" at all. It did not condemn any nation. It resembled the earlier and frequent resolutions concerning armistice violations. It did not fix the responsibility entirely on Israel, but took the course that had been suggested in earlier speeches in which various delegates referred simply to "parties." And a further concession was the omission of the point in the vetoed Security Council resolution, as introduced by Henry Cabot Lodge on October 30, that all members deny military, economic, and financial assistance to Israel until she had accepted a cease-fire and made a retreat. In fact, Lodge, excited by the smell of Battle for the Right, and badgered by the Menon-led African and Asian nations, had wished to use his original resolution.

This more moderate approach in substance, though it was still fiery in drive, gained the support of most countries, among them some of Latin America, those of Western Europe, and the Philippines. These nations were rather afraid of the Assembly's appearing to assume the power of imposing binding decisions (binding therefore on them, then, and at some future time, when such a power might be highly inconvenient to their interests). Moreover, they refused to consider the remote possibility of invoking sanctions. That would impose even more serious moral and material strains on them. Of course, the Arab and Asian countries, especially that witness to hot-blooded justice, Ceylon, the satellite of India, looked to condemnation and would have applied sanctions. Not that some Arab leaders would not have rejoiced at the spectacle of a debacle for Nasser.

Almost out of the blue, a new and creative element entered the melée. The Canadian Foreign Secretary, Lester B. Pearson, was in a painful dilemma. For Canada was bound to the United States by more than a century and a half of good neighborliness, and bound, too, by strong ties of culture and economics. On the other hand, the bonds of the British Commonwealth, bonds of blood, history, tradition, language, and literature, and again, economics, were powerful, vital, and omnipresent. Britain was not to be humiliated, especially by being voted an "aggressor." Pearson attempted to make the resolution of the United States more generally agreeable by the contention that the Assembly had passed a resolution which was only in the nature of a recommendation, *not* a command. For it to be effective it would need the compliance of Israel, Britain, and France. He lamented the fact that the three allies had not found time for full and perhaps private discussion of how to bring about a cease-fire. He, like some others, especially the Israelis, British, and French, protested that Dulles's resolution did not embody any constructive procedure for settling the basic causes of the present troubles: that is, Palestine and Suez.[17]

However, the Dulles and Eisenhower approach, ardently manipulated by Lodge, was (1) to show that aggression does not pay, and (2) to secure a cease-fire at once, if possible. It would not tolerate simultaneously the ordering of the cease-fire and an attempt at arranging a constructive and permanent settlement, for fear the Afro-Asians and Russia would blame the United States for not hotly enough pursuing the principle that "aggression does not pay."

When, on Saturday, November 3, 1956, at 8 P.M., the General Assembly met again, Loutfi of Egypt, the other Arabs, some Asians, and all the raucous and virginal Soviet chorus were demanding immediate withdrawal and sanctions.

Bowing to criticism by some of the more important columnists and American and European political organs of opinion and leadership, and endeavoring to meet also the cogent criticism of the contributory negligence of the Administration to this Middle East conflict, Henry Cabot Lodge now changed America's diplomatic stance. "We must not lose sight of the problems and conditions which gave rise to the present conditions." [18] He now belatedly recited what we have heard in these pages before, that the United Nations was to blame; that Nasser was to blame. He submitted two draft resolutions to the Assembly. "With these draft resolutions we hope that we may begin to lay the foundation for the constructive action which must follow the cessation of hostilities. . . ." He was now doing what the U.S.A. should have done, sincerely, and unyieldingly, at the very outset.

He proposed the establishment of a five-member committee to take the place of the old Palestine Conciliation Commission; its purpose would be to survey the entire problem of the relationship between the Arab states and Israel. For the Commission had failed—after eight years of existence! Justice delayed is justice denied! The new committee would also try to solve the Arab refugee problem. The second resolution was designed to set up a three-member committee that would assume responsibility for clearing the Canal of obstructions; it would also draw up a plan, in consultation with the three nations involved, for implementing the Six Principles.

At once, the Afro-Asian nations and the Soviet Union assailed Britain and France with scathing and scornful accusations of murder, aggression, slaughter, colonialism, and Fascism. The Assembly turned its contemptuous back on Lodge's resolutions. Iraq's representative called for sanctions under Chapter VII of the Charter. He denounced the American resolution concerning Israel and the Arab countries as "ample evidence" that the aggressor's interpretation of the law and actions were being accepted. He aimed a most lethal and adept blow at Ambassador Lodge's proposal: it bore all the "elements of appeasement"! The Indian delegate, Lall, joined the majority in calling for immediate attention to a cease-fire.

At this point, the constructive intervention of Lester Pearson played a decisive role in bringing hostilities to a close. He proposed a course of action that would support the British and French morally and juridically while enabling them, above all Britain, above all Eden, to cease fire. His plan was that a United Nations Peace Force should be established to stand between Israel and Egypt and to secure freedom of transit as soon as possible through the Canal.

The genesis of this proposal needs some notice. Even by October 31, Pearson had hoped to be able to take the British and French at their public word that they had merely intervened to part the combatants and open the Canal. Why not, then, convert their forces into a United Nations force? Then, with some other national forces added later, the action in Suez could proceed under the aegis of the United Nations, and so the very character of the enterprise would have been changed. Pearson worked with his government without bringing this idea into the open from October 31 to November 2, because the fury of all those nations opposed to the allies would have condemned it then to instant death, beyond resurrection. He was at that point consciously using the tactics of delay, with the hope of bringing the Assembly's influence to bear on *all* the hostile parties.

Pearson personally approached Dulles on November 1, during the "heavy-heart" discussion at the Assembly. It had been his responsibility in the first place to make such a proposal. But Dulles was in no mood to listen then to any proposal for an immediate attempt at a constructive solution. He did, however, express his sympathy for the idea of a United Nations force, but did not wish to have his resolution for an immediate cease-fire delayed. Dulles was again obsessed with what the Soviet Union would do: it would take over the leadership of the Assembly if the United States did not persist in its present course. (But why not a clash with Moscow with America taking her own independent *constructive* course?)

Lester Pearson adopted, because he thought and felt, a wiser and more prudent and steadier and more far-sighted policy than that pursued by Dulles, Eisenhower, and Lodge. The Canadian government had expressed its "regret" at British action, but in a friendly way. When the American resolution of November 2 had been passed in the small hours of that morning, he spoke from the rostrum, regretting that there had not been more time for consideration of the best way to bring about the kind of cease-fire which would have enduring and beneficial effects. He thought that "we" (the Assembly, the parties to the dispute, and so forth) were entitled to that time.

> The armed forces of Israel and of Egypt are to withdraw or, if you like, return to the armistice lines, where presumably, if this is done, they will once again face each other in fear and hatred. What then? What then six months from now? Are we to go all through this again? Are we to return to the *status quo ante?* Such a return would not be to a position of security, or even a tolerable position, but would be a return to terror, bloodshed, strife, incidents, charges and counter charges, and ultimately another explosion which the United Nations Armistice Commission would be powerless to prevent and possibly even to investigate.

In this attitude, Pearson had been much influenced by Abba Eban.

Pearson went on to suggest the establishment of a United Nations force large enough to keep those borders at peace while a political settlement was being worked out. Before Dulles left the Assembly near dawn on November 2, he spoke in support of Pearson's proposal in principle, and added, "The U.S. delegation would be very happy indeed if the Canadian delegation would formulate and introduce as part of these proceedings a concrete suggestion along the lines that Pearson outlined."

How much more creditable it would have been for American diplomacy if Dulles himself had initiated the policy earlier, or if

Henry Cabot Lodge had developed it as America's basic and indispensable demand from that moment!

Pearson and the Secretary General, who was cautious and suspicious, at once began to confer on Pearson's idea. When later, in mid-morning on November 2, it was realized that the British and French and the Israelis would not obey the cease-fire recommendation, more serious talks began between them and Andrew Cordier, executive assistant to Hammarskjold. The sound juridical basis, Pearson said, was that the British had asserted that a police force was one of the preconditions of a cease-fire.

Pearson conferred with Sir Pierson Dixon, who promised to see what the response might be to the idea in Whitehall and Downing Street. Now, in the Commons debate on November 1, at about 5:20 P.M. London time (midday in New York and Washington), Sir Anthony Eden, in the course of his reply to a debate marked by disgraceful hooliganism by Labour M.P.'s, had said this:

> We do not want to stay [in Suez], and we do not intend to stay, one moment longer than is necessary. But effective action to re-establish peace will make easier an international solution of the many problems which exist in that area.
>
> Israel and Egypt are locked in conflict in that area [Suez]. The first and urgent task is to separate these combatants and to stabilize the position. That is our purpose. *If the United Nations were then willing to take over the physical task of maintaining peace* in that area, no one would be better pleased than we. But police action there must be to separate the belligerents and to prevent hostilities.

Eden takes credit for originating this suggestion of a United Nations force. He tells in his *Memoirs* [19] that he had long held that idea, and had even proposed it to the Russians as far back as 1945. Nevertheless, with the deepest respect and admiration for Sir Anthony, this suggestion made in the Commons was no more than a casual part of his argument for British and French intervention, and apparently he did *not* intend it then as a serious suggestion for immediate application.

However, the fact that Eden said what he did gave Lester Pearson some encouragement in the course he was already pursuing. On November 2, London was reached by Pearson and clarification and *approval* given by London. The United States and Norway were consulted on phrasing and tactics. Lodge participated in the drafting of a resolution, providing, in particular, legal advice. Pearson then lobbied among delegates for the support of his resolution. The Indian delegate, Lall, promised to support Pearson's new draft. Pearson compensated him, however, for his promise by Canadian acceptance of an Indian draft resolution calling in stronger terms for a cease-fire. The two together, a powerful cease-fire resolution *and* the proposal for a

United Nations police force, would make a forceful vote-getting combination. Pearson's draft was as follows:

> The General Assembly, bearing in mind the urgent necessity of facilitating compliance with the cease-fire resolution adopted by the Assembly on 2 November 1956,
> Requests, as a matter of priority, the Secretary-General to submit to it within forty-eight hours a plan for the setting up, with the consent of the nations concerned, of an emergency international United Nations force to secure and supervise the cessation of hostilities in accordance with all the terms of the aforementioned resolution.[20]

Lodge, perhaps relieved to be momentarily free from the pressure of hounding his NATO allies, postponed his own resolutions. After all, they were for constructive efforts for the *future*, and now, before him, he had just what the President needed: a cease-fire resolution along with a proposal for a police force that would undercut the British and French arguments before the Assembly and "world opinion." The existence on the agenda of his resolutions, of course, gave the Soviet representative the opportunity to demonstrate in acid terms the United States' attempts to "smother the main issue, the halting of aggression"—remarks made to the tremendous jubilation of the Asians and Arabs.

At any rate, the Canadian resolution was adopted by 57 to 0. Among those who abstained were the Soviet bloc (seven nations, including Hungary!); Egypt; Israel; Australia and New Zealand—and Britain and France! Sir Pierson Dixon explained that the text was inappropriate, going too far and also not far enough, and that he had not had time to submit the proposal in *textual* form to London.

This vote came at about 3 A.M. Sunday morning, November 4. Nearly forty-eight hours afterwards, Krishna Menon arrived at a meeting of the Afro-Asian bloc and attempted to upset the whole plan of a United Nations police force. It was, he clamored, not pleasing to Egypt. It might be a kind of "collective colonialism" that could be used against other such nations also. (Suppose somebody had proposed such an arrangement for Kashmir, for example!)

Then, the cease-fire resolution, sponsored by nineteen powers, was voted on: and adopted by 59 to 5, with 12 abstentions.

The British and French strategy was now to delay implementation of the resolutions as long as possible, so as to be able to complete their hold on the Canal. Whatever may have been said on the cables or in telephone conversations between Sir Pierson Dixon and the Foreign Office and the Prime Minister and Lester Pearson and Ottawa, a night or so ago, Dixon held to the position now required of him by London. The United Nations Emergency Force must be of a composition and specific purpose to satisfy Britain and France that it would fulfill their main political end. It must give promise of settling "the root of the problem." The British and French would not *withdraw* (at that moment, it was actually only a question of whether they should cease fire) until they felt there was some probability that the basic questions, that is, of the Canal and of the Israel-Arab peace, would be properly solved.

Lester Pearson and some United Nations officials still believe that the British were glad that the force was being established, since it helped them to extricate themselves from a position that was proving to be impossible, politically and militarily. This opinion is most probably exaggerated.

At this time, that is, November 3 and 4, it would seem that the State Department and White House might have considered it their conscientious obligation, as well as a prudent course of action, to consult with their two NATO allies. It is true that Britain and France would be America's grave liabilities if Russia should attack them. Even more, then, should Lodge consult with his nation's allies, seek them out, try to win them over, especially on the United Nations Emergency Force (UNEF) and the aftermath of its arrival in Suez. But the apostles of Dulles and the President would not touch pitch, lest they be defiled!

The United Nations' twelve-hour deadline for the cease-fire passed, ignored by the allied forces. Lodge, taking his cue from Hammarskjold's report on proposals for the UNEF, and making retort to Sir Pierson Dixon's remark that Britain was consulting with France, once again put the pressure on America's friends.[21] "The Assembly's call for a cease-fire was unconditional. The States concerned—and, above all, those engaged in attack—must stop their military operations. . . . Silencing of the guns is the necessary prelude to the solution of any—I repeat any—of the problems which beset the Middle East." (The Israeli and allied successes in Sinai and Suez were now known; they must be stopped!) Thus, Dulles's original impulse had re-acquired its original irate momentum and Lodge's hortatory forefinger!

The Secretary General was to present his full plan early on Tuesday, November 6. The session of November 4 ended half an hour after midnight, that is, early on November 5. Lodge had promised American help for the UNEF, when ready, in aircraft, shipping, transport, and supplies.

Sir Pierson Dixon asked for a delay in the voting, because it was the middle of the night in Europe, and consultations were therefore difficult. But Lodge, with uplifted arm and admonitory gestures, would brook no delay. The resolution in the name of Canada, Colombia, and Norway, for UNEF, was adopted by 57 to 0. There were 19 abstentions, including Britain, France, Egypt, Israel, and the Soviet bloc. Britain's reasons we have suggested. Egypt's reasons are very simply inferable. And the Soviet bloc wanted no precedent for a UNEF in Hungary, at that moment the scene of Russian carnage.

Neither Dulles nor Lodge nor Eisenhower would turn his attention away from accusing, prosecuting, and condemning the allies or the democratic nation of Israel to the horrible tragedy that was being inflicted by the Soviet Union in Hungary. Although the Security Council had taken up the Hungarian affair as early as October 27, and had accused the Soviet Union of "violently repressing the rights of the Hungarian people," the Council had passed no resolution. It let the repression go on without intervening. It was another *five days* before the Council again met on Hungary, although Britain and other nations had pressed for a meeting. Lodge even suggested that the British were urging attention to the Hungarian situation in order to divert attention from Suez. "We must not do *that!*" Hungary would be taken care of, but the Suez conflict needed to be quashed *at once*. However, on November 2, when Lodge believed that the Suez and Sinai affairs were being reined in, the Security Council went into session at 5 P.M. on Hungary. Here Lodge most vehemently indicted the Soviet Union.

Nevertheless, it was not Lodge, but Sir Pierson Dixon, who had the words with which to typify the Russian attitude, now that the U.S.S.R. was revealed, once again, as the remorselessly brutal aggressor. "I was astonished," Dixon said, "to hear Mr. Sobolev dismiss the situation in Hungary in a few words as an armed uprising of criminal elements of a Fascist type against the legal Hungarian Government."

The debate on Hungary dragged through November 2 and November 3, the Yugoslav representative acting as the Soviet Union's protector and delayer, while the Soviet Ambassador pretended that it was too difficult for him to take part because he did not have enough up-to-date information from Hungary. And, naturally, he could not accept that provided by Britain and the other governments. Australia, Belgium, China, Cuba, France, and Britain voted to continue on November 4 at 5 P.M. The one country voting against this was the United States of America. Therefore, if the Soviet Union abstained with Yugoslavia, and they were joined by only one other nation, there would be less than 7 votes for a meeting the next day. That is exactly what happened, with Peru providing the other abstention. Lodge thus stopped a meeting on Hungary arranged for the very next day. *He* did not intend to be deflected from disciplining Britain, France, and Israel! But everybody did vote for a meeting on November 5, except Australia, abstaining because its government had wanted the earlier meeting. But events moved with such ruthlessness in Hungary that Lodge had to call a meeting of the Council at 3 A.M. on Sunday morning, November 4. It had now been borne in on him that it would have been too vile a disgrace to wait until Monday. Sobolev had the infernal insolence to suggest that Britain, France, *and the*

United States had brought the Hungarian situation to the Council in order to distract attention from the Middle East!

At about 5:25 A.M. on November 4, then, an American resolution on Hungary was put to a vote.[22] Its executory phrases required the Soviet Union to stop forthwith its intervention and withdraw all its forces, and requested the Secretary General and all nations to render humanitarian help to the Hungarian people. The Soviet Government immediately vetoed the resolution. Its friend Yugoslavia exhibited the minimum grace in not voting. Thereupon Lodge called for a vote on a resolution to take the matter to the General Assembly. The Soviet representative answered that any U.N. action in Hungary would be interference with the *domestic* affairs of another nation! Again, he accused the allies and others of obstructing action against "the aggression committed against Egypt." [23] The resolution of the Security Council was nevertheless taken before the General Assembly, in substantially its original form; it was approved by 50 to 8, with 15 abstentions, including India, the saintliest nation of all. The Russians completely ignored the resolution. The Secretary General and the United Nations observers were refused admission into Hungary. (Again on November 9, to anticipate, the resolution was passed. India was on that occasion the only non-Soviet-bloc nation to vote with Russia.)

The question arises: Was this calculated Soviet murderousness in Hungary a corollary of the acceptance by Dulles and Lodge of the Soviet Union and Yugoslavia as partners in their chastisement of their democratic allies? Justice requires the recognition of differences between the morality of the claimants, especially in the world of states, where each has its own might and its own interests (above all the Soviet Union, which wished that other nations should have none of their own) and each remains a judge in its own cause, whatever may be its pledge to the United Nations Charter. Every foreign office chancellery in the world has its own national commentary on the Charter, and the essence of that commentary is how to exploit the Charter to maximize the advantages to be obtained from it, while rendering to the U.N. the least possible—up to the point where condign punishment would fall on the nation by the might of one or more hostile nations. But, "One law . . ."?

The British and French attitude to the UNEF arrangements was clearly embodied in a statement made by the Prime Minister in the Commons on November 3.

> They accepted only on conditions. They maintain their view that police action must be carried through urgently to stop the hostilities which are now threatening the Suez Canal, to prevent a resumption of these hostilities and to pave the way for a definite settlement of the Arab-Israel war. . . .[24]

The allied conditions for acceptance of UNEF were (1) that Egypt and Israel would accept a U.N. force to keep peace; (2) that the U.N. would maintain such a force until an Arab-Israel peace was reached and satisfactory arrangements regarding the Canal were agreed on, the U.N. guaranteeing both; (3) that, until the U.N. force was established, Egypt and Israel would agree to having limited numbers of Anglo-French troops stationed between the combatants.

Even on November 5, Foreign Secretary Selwyn Lloyd was impressing it on the House of Commons[25] that military operations must continue, because "to return deliberately to the system which has produced the continuing deadlock and chaos in the Middle East is not only undesirable but impossible. . . ." Until the UNEF was in actual being the Anglo-French military presence was the surest guarantee that the objectives—namely, Israeli withdrawal, the prevention of a recurrence of fighting, and the restoration of the operation of the Canal—would be fulfilled. Lloyd went further (was it an olive branch to Dulles [in the hospital] and the President and Henry Cabot Lodge?): let there be a Security Council meeting now with all the Foreign Ministers present to find a settlement. For a handful of United Nations officers would not be able to establish peace.

Those whose hand held a birch rod would not discard it to make room for the olive branch. They had committed themselves unwisely. The most curious symptom of Dulles's Suez policy, at first sight pathological, was that it led to United States partnership with the Soviet Union, which according to Dulles was a despicable and hateful "atheistic" and "anti-Christian materialistic society" under murderous Kremlin rulers. How could the United States side with that government against the best representatives of the civilization of the West? Yet it did.

Eleanor Lansing Dulles, Secretary Dulles's sister, for long herself a State Department official, affectionately recalls that Dulles told reporters that the decision to condemn the allied attack on Egypt was one of the hardest the President and he had ever had to make.[26] It was, however, not the hardest he could have taken in the Suez affair. The course he took was easier than the more just course open to him but forsaken. Dulles may have felt badly about his decision and policy, but it was easier to browbeat Britain and France than to discipline Nasser and face the Russian challenge, and that is what he elected to do.

15. DULLES YIELDS TO RUSSIA

IT WAS THE INTENTION OF THE BRITISH AND FRENCH TO CAPTURE THE whole of the Canal before the United Nations and the United States could end their military action prematurely. They expected, with a *fait accompli*, to secure a just, practical settlement of the Canal dispute and, hopefully, thereby to overthrow Nasser.

They failed to achieve either. What were the reasons? Dulles and Eisenhower, facing a challenge from the Soviet Union, which was acting as the champion of Nasser and Arab nationalism, were so afraid of Moscow's power and intentions that they yielded to their fears. To make good their retreat before Moscow's fancied might they exerted fierce pressures on Sir Anthony Eden which his physical condition and conscience were unable to bear. Unwilling to contend against Russian pressure, they forced Eden to capitulate. The history is a little complicated with chains of action and reaction, but it is possible to unravel and present the salient truths. We begin with the Anglo-French military venture, then move to Russian diplomatic pressure on the United States, and finally show their repercussions on Prime Ministers Eden and Guy Mollet. It should be remembered all along that Dulles was fully informed about the forces in England that opposed Eden's policy of war in Suez. He could take satisfaction in and full advantage of this. Eden could not do likewise regarding the United States, because it has no coherent parliamentary or even national opposition that can be appealed to: the Chief Executive in such circumstances as those of Suez has it all his own way.

The Anglo-French assault, under General Keightley, could not even be commanded to start until the ultimatum to Egypt expired, for otherwise it would have been inferred that Britain had acted in collusion with Israel. Moreover, given the intense divisions in the House of Commons and nation, the military action must be of the "bloodless surgery" type. Such tactics might perhaps mollify opposition in the United Nations as well. It required the minimum casualties among the British forces—as also the minimum number of killings, zero, if possible, of Egyptian soldiers and, above all, of Egyptian civilians. The tactical consequence of this objective was that the military action must be psychological and slow. It was thought, in the first place, that a long period of aerial bombardment of Egyptian military airports would become known to the Egyptian population and military and, besides smashing the Egyptian air force (as it did completely), would perhaps cause a rising against Nasser. As a matter of humanity, the bombs to be used were twice reduced in size. The air assault was to be accompanied by the quick destruction of the Voice of Cairo and a deluge of anti-Nasser broadcasts from an allied transmitter in Cyprus. This also worked. But these influences needed time, time that was not available if the condemnatory action of the United Nations and the United States should be pressed fast—as it was, far faster and incomparably more effectively than United States action against Soviet behavior in Hungary.

The French constantly demanded a far quicker assault against what they calculated to be an enemy who would cave in at a touch. They wished also to forestall any action by the Egyptian government to obstruct the Canal by the sinking of blockships. But by the evening of October 31 the Egyptians had sunk one of these; later they engaged in a veritable orgy of sinkings, which they, blatantly lying, blamed on the British and French. The falsehood was designed to justify the claim that Egypt had preserved the freedom of the Canal, as provided by the treaty of 1888, while their Anglo-French attackers had destroyed it.

The French, in despair, begged the British to permit immediate paratroop assaults. Pineau and Bourgès-Manoury even rushed more than once to London to beseech Eden to speed up the action. Eden was appalled by the task he had undertaken, and vacillated, hoping against hope that public opinion in the United States and the United Nations would become less hostile toward it. The French appeal for intrepidity failed also against the stolidity of the British Generals Keightley and Stockwell. These pursued their methodical course of waiting for the paratroop drop from Cyprus until they were assured of immediate ground support by an invasion with troops and armor, then still far away at Malta and at Marseilles.

They could not take the chance of failure for lack of mass support, the mistake made by Montgomery at Arnhem. There was an alternative, which the French would have accepted, but which the British, least of all Eden, could not. They could have obtained the support of the Israelis who were lodged on the east side of the Canal. The British could not accept this assistance for fear they would lose the friendship of Nuri Es Said of Iraq, an enemy of Nasser, but also an enemy of Israel, and with it lose the diplomatic center of the Baghdad Pact and a point of influence throughout the Middle East. They were willing to have Israel as "an indispensable momentary associate," but not as a "fully accepted partner." This had its military effects. The British Embassy in Baghdad even had to explain to the Iraqi leaders that Britain had intervened in Suez to prevent Israel from winning a humiliating victory over Egypt, a Moslem state!

The limiting factor of this expedition, according to the British view, was stated in Keightley's dispatch: "At full speed for Port Said, a distance of 936 miles by the shortest route. At the maximum speed of the landing craft this trip must take 6 days." By this calculation the reinforcements could not be available for landing until November 5. On November 3 and 4 Egyptian armored concentrations were bombed and the defenses of the beach (consisting of mines and anti-aircraft guns) were reconnoitered. The United States Sixth Fleet, which had caused the British and French "real difficulties . . . and great inconvenience" by its presence for the purpose of evacuating American nationals from Alexandria and the Levant, withdrew on the night of November 4/5.

Suddenly, from the Prime Minister's office, at 8:15 P.M. London time, on November 4, the Commander in Chief at Suez was asked to state what was the latest time a decision could be made to postpone the airborne assault for twenty-four hours for *political* reasons? Meanwhile, Pineau was at hand to beg Eden not to go back on his commitment. For the chief Ministers in the British Cabinet had been intensely reconsidering the effect of the UNEF resolution and of the one calling for a cease-fire within twelve hours. A choice had to be made quickly between invasion as soon as the ships arrived, postponement of the paratroop drops while the combatants moved to accept the UNEF with the allied forces recognized as its advance guard, or abandonment of military action for the time being on the grounds that allied action had put an end to the Arab-Israeli conflict. It was decided that since it was entirely uncertain whether the UNEF would be accepted by Israel or Egypt, the action must proceed. Eden sent a telegram to President Eisenhower expressing the Cabinet views. It is important in view of the harassment to which the British and French were later subjected by Herbert Hoover, Jr., and his associates, and by the White House. He said:

> If we drew back now chaos will not be avoided. Everything will go up in flames in the Middle East. You will realize, with all your experience, that we cannot have a military vacuum while a United Nations force is being constituted and is being transported to the spot. That is why we feel we must go on to hold the position until we can hand over responsibility to the United Nations. . . .

Keightley answered Eden, "at the latest, by 11 P.M."; he and the French commander, Admiral Barjot, explained that such a postponement would have serious consequences and must be avoided at all costs. He was then told that there should be no postponement! The war was on again. On November 5, the airborne assault took place with remarkable success, though not without resistance and some casualties. By 3 P.M. Port Fuad was surrendered. At 3:30 P.M. Port Said's Egyptian commander began to haggle over surrender.

At this point, the Russians entered the war on Egypt's side. The Soviet consul in Port Said supported the local Egyptian commander's action in withdrawing the surrender offer. He had Russian arms distributed to all and sundry, especially the adolescents. Loudspeaker vans ran through Cairo blaring out that Russian help was on the way, that London and Paris had been bombed (inference: by the Soviet Union), and that World War III had started. Since communications with Cairo had not been altogether broken (a military error) by the allied aerial bombardment, Nasser was able to order the local commanders to continue fighting.

As a result, the British and French were delayed in their attempt to press up the Canal to Suez. Also, there was fighting the next day, November 6, by the seaborne forces, with the British and French taking risks in order to minimize Egyptian civilian casualties and damage to property. Port Said is a big city in comparison with the forces landed, and numerically superior defenders in the built-up areas made its capture difficult in any *short* time. Street-by-street fighting, house-by-house attacks were sometimes necessary. Time was dragging, especially because the regular Egyptian troops had discarded their uniforms and put on civilian *gallabiyahs,* while many civilians were armed and fighting. Nevertheless, by dusk of November 6 (or midnight in Washington, when President Eisenhower had just been re-elected by the greatest landslide in American political history), Port Said was completely in British hands.

Then, at about the same time, 5 P.M. London time, the British government informed General Keightley that a United Nations Force would take over from him: he was to cease fire at one minute before midnight that day, and no further move of forces would take place after that time. The leading allied forces, particularly paratroopers, had by that time arrived at El Cap, twenty-three miles further up the Canal. The European allies needed no more than forty-eight hours, even twenty-four hours, to occupy the whole Canal length, and virtually to ensure the overthrow of Nasser. Yet, even if they had gained the Canal, even if Nasser had fallen, even if their military victory had been greater (and it was very considerable, in spite of the loss of most of its political fruits), Dulles, Eisenhower, and Lodge were committed by their initial moralistic, legalistic attitude, and their merely immediate fire-extinction policy, to crush that military victory. For the British and French were still in possession of the Canal. *That was the inacceptable, even iniquitous, thing!*

America's allies now had a gage. They, like Nasser, were lodged in Suez. Who could get them out before they had obtained a just settlement—a Dulles-advocated, two-sides-of-the-coin, justice-with-peace settlement? Only Dulles and Eisenhower. And they did it. But, in doing it, Dulles and Eisenhower themselves bowed before Russian will and might.

Within the British Cabinet some were now afraid for two consequences of the Anglo-French intervention, the loss of American friendship, as had not been made sufficiently clear to them earlier, and the loss of Arab friends, now antagonized. Some were also affected by being in defiance of the United Nations. But, above all, anxieties arose over some domestic consequences of continued fighting: the rapid loss of sterling and the swiftly approaching need for petrol rationing. The body of the nation supported Eden's policy in substantial measure. Thus, the opinion polls, making inquiry between October 30 and November 3, showed that the Labour Party's attitude was not given hearty support by their own Labour voters, and that the Conservative Government was being strongly supported by the people who had an opinion. Thus, of *all* voters, 48.5 per cent supported the Suez invasion, 39 per cent opposed. In polls taken between November 5 and 6, 51.5 per cent supported it; only 36 per cent opposed it. Eden's leadership satisfied 47 per cent on November 1-2, dissatisfied 41 per cent, and on November 10-11, the figures were 57 and 35, respectively. The deficit represented No Opinionites.

However, there remained some within the Cabinet who had misgivings. When action is in the planning and propaganda stages some men are all fervor, but blench and fail in the "imminent deadly breach . . . ," as Shakespeare put it. It is said that among those dissenting was R. A. Butler, then second to Eden in the Cabinet, or perhaps vying with Macmillan there for the succession to the Prime Ministership. He could not be accused of want of courage. But he had been privy to every move and thought of Sir Anthony from July 26 onwards, and at the Conservative Party Annual Conference had said on October 11 this of his Prime Minister:

> I have served under at least five Prime Ministers, and sometimes in difficult times. I have seldom known times more difficult than they have been this summer, and I have never known under any Prime Minister I have served, the qualities of courage, integrity and flair more clearly represented than in our Prime Minister who is about to address us.[1]

Butler stayed in the Cabinet, but, when the sterling situation was aggravated, he advanced reasons for stopping at whatever point the British and French had reached. The U.S. Secretary of the Treasury, George M. Humphrey, with whom he had been on friendly terms since January, 1953, had telephoned him; the sense of Humphrey's words had been, "Don't invade!" and then, "You had better stop it fast!"

By November 5, the crisis had caused the Cabinet to suffer two losses, of not particularly important men: one was Anthony Nutting, Minister of State in the Foreign Office. His *volte face* was incredibly extraordinary. Only on October 11, he had extolled the Cabinet's policy in the strongest terms to the Conservative Party conference, more fervently than any other speaker. On November 3, he resigned. On November 5, Sir Edward Boyle, Economic Secretary to the Treasury, and a favorite of Harold Macmillan's, followed suit.

Now, however, the Soviet Union brought all its diplomatic force to the front to affect the forces in collision. The rulers of the Soviet Union base their international strategy on one basic and never-never-forgotten principle: the attempted subversion of all nations not already under their sway. This is the fundamental and abiding ethic of Moscow. It is to be fulfilled with the minimum of cost to the Soviet Union. But it is to be fulfilled at every opportunity, and where opportunity does not arise spontaneously, by chance or by the rest of the world's folly, then opportunity is to be fabricated and then exploited. No loyalty to a universal rule of law modifies the Communists' pursuit of their national interests; no mercy, no decency; no respect for the opinions of mankind; no faithfulness to their pledge to the United Nations, except the pledge as they understand it, with the veto as its instrument and symbol.

The Soviet Union, its hands deep in the blood of Hungarian men, women, and children, and impotently denounced by a vote of the Security Council and the General Assembly, now used its usual tactic, diversion and counterattack. Its leaders, who had an acute perception of what was happening within the United States government, in regard to the chastisement of Britain and France, and of the division of public opinion in Britain and France, made a series of atomic blackmail threats. These they conveyed through their press agencies and by letters direct to the Prime Ministers of the attacking governments and to the United States. It is essential that we examine these tactics more closely. The boldness, the insolence, the irresponsibility are awe-inspiring; and that is what the show of it was no doubt intended to be.

Dulles's policy had undoubtedly spurred the Soviet leaders on to take liberties. His behavior towards his allies was so strange that the Kremlin first believed that he was playing a deep conniving game with them. But after the "heavy heart" speech was delivered, and

Lodge continued the chase with encouragement from the press, it dawned on them: the Administration intended to wound its own allies! Then the Russians leapt in against Israel, France, and Britain, with a cool insolence that even seemed lunatic. It worked! They entered to push down what was already toppling, and they played their part with magisterial nobility, claiming to act in behalf of the United Nations and Peace!

On November 5, 1956, Prime Minister Bulganin sent a cable to the President of the Security Council.[2] It demanded an immediate meeting of the Security Council to discuss "new aggression" and the noncompliance of Israel, Britain, and France with the General Assembly's resolutions. It also submitted a draft resolution calling for a cease-fire in twelve hours (the time span of the Anglo-French ultimatums!) and the withdrawal of all foreign troops from Egypt within three days. If, it said, the parties failed to comply, then

> . . . all members of the United Nations, especially the U.S.A. and the U.S.S.R., as permanent members of the Security Council having powerful air and naval forces at their disposal, should give military and other assistance to the republic of Egypt, which has been the victim of aggression, by sending naval and air forces, military units, volunteers, military instructors and other forms of assistance, if the United Kingdom, France and Israel fail to carry out this resolution *within the stated time limits.*

What an astute gesture: together *with* the United States. Is not a joint action pure in heart?

Simultaneously with this letter, Bulganin sent notes to the governments of the United States, Britain, France, and Israel.

> The Soviet Union and the United States are . . . the two great powers which possess all modern types of arms, including atomic and hydrogen weapons. . . . The United States has a strong navy in the zone of the Mediterranean. The Soviet Union also has a strong navy and a powerful air force. The joint and immediate use of these means . . . would be a sure guaranty of ending the aggression against the Egyptian people, against the people of the Arab East.[3]

This message reached President Eisenhower at the White House at 4 P.M. on November 5, the eve of election day. It was a critical —indeed, the decisive—moment in the President's mind. Herbert Hoover, Jr., and Herman Phleger represented the State Department, at a meeting called in the President's office to answer the note. *They were all terrified!* Alarm pervaded the entire group that the Russian leaders might undertake serious aggression, afraid that the West might assist or at least encourage the rebellions in Eastern Europe, and noting also that the allies were now divided. The President even went so far as to think that the letter was a kind of *ultimatum;* he even expected an attack, and even counseled the need for readiness for an all-out war the moment such an intention became evident. Into the midst of this discussion, Ambassador Charles E. Bohlen sent a message from Moscow frantic in tone, recommending the quickest possible cease-fire in the Middle East, to undercut the Russian threat of a considerable military action. The President was greatly affected by this message: he regarded Bohlen as "one of the ablest Foreign Service officers I had ever met." [4] Bulganin's letter and Bohlen's message, as we shall see, decided the issue. Britain, France, and Israel must be brought to heel immediately. No suggestion arose of *daring* the Russians.

The answer [5] to Bulganin was that joint action was "unthinkable," in Emmet Hughes's apt phrase. It went on to draw Moscow's attention to the brutalities for which the Russians were responsible at that very moment in Hungary, and which they had perpetrated in defiance of the United Nations. Herbert Hoover, Jr., lived in permanent fear of war from miscalculation by the Soviet Union.

Bulganin's message had said:

> The piratical war was launched with the aim of restoring colonial order in the East, an order which had been overthrown by the people. If this war is not stopped it carries the danger of turning into a third world war.

Bulganin's argument, save for the word "piratical," had become Dulles's own argument, to the very last point! Herman Phleger, in a sense Dulles's momentary *alter ego,* told the President that the issue was that of which was to tumble from office: Eden or Nasser? It did not suit American policy that it should be Nasser.

As a tactic of terrorizing overwrought government leaders, and as a means of bringing to the boil the peoples' fears and suspicions of their own governments, the Soviet Union, slightly earlier than these letters, made more direct threats of force through its news agency, *Tass.*[6] The purpose was to develop such a state of fear throughout the world that, when the Soviet's official communications to governments were published, gratification would be felt that the Soviet government was not, after *all,* as villainous as it was painted!

The note from Bulganin to Prime Minister Eden recited the Suez affair from the Soviet and Egyptian point of view; Britain and France and Israel were aggressors. The threat to use atomic bombs was implied in the form of an hypothesis.

> In what position would Britain have found herself had she been attacked by more powerful states possessing all types of modern weapons of destruction? Indeed, such countries, instead of sending to the shores of Britain their naval or air forces, could have used other means, as, for instance, rocket equipment.

> If rocket weapons had been used against Britain and France, you would certainly have called it a barbaric action. Yet, what is the difference between the inhuman attack perpetrated by the armed forces of Britain and France against almost-unarmed Egypt?

The note requested the British government to heed the call of common sense and stop the war in Egypt, and it also called on Parliament, the Labour Party, the trade unions, and the people of Britain to stop the aggression, the bloodshed. It threatened that a third world war might result, and that Russia was "full of determination to crush the aggressor and re-establish peace in the East by using force."

A similar letter was sent to Prime Minister Mollet, with some variations in its pungent nosegay of vilifications. To Mollet Bulganin could address the reproach, "What has the bandit-like attack against Egypt, which looks like an open colonial war, to do with socialism?" For Mollet, leader of the Socialist Party of France—that is, of the democratic socialists, or half- or quarter-socialists—had met Bulganin in Moscow the preceding May, and had spoken to him of his actions as being inspired by socialist ideals! The threat now uttered by Bulganin to Mollet was:

> What would be the position of France had she been attacked by other states which had at their disposal the modern terrible means of destruction?

The Bulganin letter to Prime Minister Ben Gurion was of the same general vituperative and denunciatory nature as the others: "all peace-loving mankind indignantly brands the criminal actions of the aggressors." Israel was "acting as a tool of foreign imperialist powers" and "continues the foolhardy adventure," etc., etc. These circumstances, it was alleged, showed "what all the false assurances of Israel's love of peace and its desire to co-exist peacefully with the neighboring Arab states were worth." The note omitted mention of the Soviet arming of Nasser since 1955.

Thus, "the Government of Israel is playing with the fate of peace, with the fate of its own people, in a criminal and irresponsible manner; it is sowing hatred for the State of Israel among the peoples of the East which cannot but affect the future of Israel and which will place a question upon the very existence of Israel as a state." The Soviet Union demanded that the State of Israel come to its senses before it was too late. To frighten the leaders and people of Israel, Moscow immediately recalled its Ambassador from Tel Aviv.

Prime Minister Eden decided not to reject Bulganin's offensively worded letter, but to answer him with "counsels of reason." He recited the British view of the crisis and his Government's grounds of action. He invited Bulganin to participate and make use of the UNEF to settle the issues that had arisen in the Middle East, including the Canal dispute. He emphasized his policy of having the U.N. assume the physical task of maintaining peace in the area. He deeply regretted the casualties, but the Franco-British attacks had been "conducted with the most scrupulous care in order to cause the least possible loss of lives." They could in any event not be compared with the casualties still being inflicted by the Soviet forces in Hungary: "ruthlessly crushing the heroic resistance of a truly national movement for independence, a movement which, by declaring its neutrality, proved that it had been no threat to the security of the Soviet Union." [7]

Ben Gurion replied on November 7. He narrated coolly and factually the exploits of Nasser's *fedayeen* in their organized campaign against Israel, and the threats of annihilation, and the Egyptian determination of October 13 that discrimination against Israel in the Canal would continue. Thus, Israel's action was one of self-defense. Yet in response to the General Assembly's appeal, Israel had ceased fire, and for several days past there had been no armed conflict. Israel was willing at once to enter into peace negotiations. Ben Gurion expressed his "surprise and concern at the threat against Israel's existence and well being" contained in Bulganin's note. "Our foreign policy is dictated by our essential needs and by our yearning for peace. It is not and will not be dictated by any foreign factor."

Mollet answered on November 7, with an argument similar to that of Eden. "The present situation could not be," he maintained, "improved by the menace and the potentialities of long-range weapons. If the U.S.S.R. had exercised a moderating influence in Cairo events would have taken a much different turn. If the U.S.S.R. intended respect for the United Nations it could cease spilling blood in Hungary." France had already accepted a cease-fire, definitely, as soon as the UNEF was able to accomplish the tasks assigned to it.

The impact of the threats by the Soviet Union may be illustrated by a curious episode that now occurred.

On November 6, the day of the Presidential election, at about 8:30 A.M. Washington time, a message was flashed from the Supreme Headquarters of the American Command in Europe (NATO) to this effect: "Jet planes are flying over Turkey. The Turkish air force has been alerted." In Washington, Arthur S. Flemming, who was in charge of mobilizing American oil resources in the event of such hostilities as were then taking place, and who was therefore briefed by the CIA every morning on world events, became worried about something he noticed in the report handed to him. He consulted Sherman Adams, asking, "Do you know about this?" Adams advised him to go and tell Eisenhower. When Flemming arrived at the White House office, Allen Dulles of the CIA was already there with the President. Having learned the disturbing news, the President queried, "I wonder if I dare go to Gettysburg to vote today?" His advisers counseled him to go, and he drove off. An hour later, the CIA reported a flight of Russian planes over Turkey. Flemming returned at once to Andrew Goodpaster, Eisenhower's Special Assistant for Defense. He was worried that the report might trigger off all the NATO operations plan. The President was called back at once. The National Security Council and the Joint Chiefs of Staff, with all their various experts, were immediately called into the Cabinet room. After a little hurried and anxious discussion the President put the United States on a limited alert.[8]

What worried the President, and Headquarters in Europe, and also Sir Anthony Eden and Prime Minister Mollet, given the newscasts from Moscow about atomic bombs and the letters of November 5, was the belief that Russian planes were en route from the Caucasus —to somewhere in the Middle East. After all, the U.S.A. had radar in that region, and apparatus that could even overhear the conversation inside Russian planes! Other information added up to the fact that a large supply of military weapons, including 100 MIG-15's, had arrived in Syria. A British high-flying plane, a Canberra, at 45,000 feet, had been shot down over Syria, and only MIG's could do that! "Volunteers" were being promised or threatened for the Middle East from Moscow and later Peking; they soon would be on the way. Other terrifying rumors circulated: one concerned a Russian fleet, surface and submarine vessels, en route through the Dardanelles. Result: the NATO alert, and the American semi-alert; naval vessels from the United States towards Europe, including the U.S. *Forrestal* carrier with atomic weapons; *the fear of a Pearl Harbor*, with Allen Dulles giving credence to the rumors.

All the "facts" were false! The Soviet jets were nothing but swans! As mythical as Swan Lake! No movement was detected at the airports of Syria. The crew of the Canberra who had parachuted said, in a Beirut hospital, that they had come down to 15,000 feet by mistake. No Soviet submarines were about: some had left discreetly as soon as the British and French moved their ships and planes on Suez. The Soviet planes spotted, allegedly fighters or bombers, were bringing back Syria's President Kuwatley and party from a brief trip to Russia.

Bulganin's notes to Britain, France, and Israel were issued at 11:30 P.M. on November 5, that is, Paris and London time (or about 5:30 P.M. November 5 in Washington, D.C., and New York). By this time, the British and the French governments were caught in their own juridical toils concerning cease-fire between Egypt and Israel. Now, at a moment of maximum diplomatic weakness, that is, when the juridical principle of the UNEF had been accepted by the United Nations, Eden was trapped by his own publicly announced reason for moving on Suez. And at this same moment came the maximum manipulation of fears by the Soviet Union; meanwhile, the pressure of the good Mr. Lodge at the United Nations did not relax. The intrusion of the direct Russian threat was the occasion for a cruelly severe offensive by the White House and the State Department against Prime Minister Ben Gurion. He was told plainly that if Russia attacked him he would not be assisted by the United States!

On November 5, the President sent Ben Gurion a letter, which for technical reasons [9] was not received until November 7. It was courteous, but it had a clear tone of threat. It must be read in conjunction with the American Ambassador's verbal threats uttered to the Israeli Political Counselor on November 7. It said that the highest priority was the withdrawal of foreign troops—"*after* which new and energetic steps should be undertaken within the framework of the United Nations to solve the basic problems which have given rise to the present difficulty." The letter continued:

> I need not assure you of the deep interest which the United States has in your country, nor recall the various elements of *our policy of support* to Israel in so many ways. . . . It would be a matter of the greatest regret to all my countrymen if Israeli policy on a matter of grave concern to the world should in any way impair the friendly cooperation between our two countries.

Israel was being ordered to withdraw at once and make its decision known *immediately*. If it did not intend to withdraw from Egyptian territory this "could not but bring about the condemnation of Israel as a violator of the principles as well as of the directives of the United Nations."

The Israeli government knew well what it was risking. Ben Gurion and his Cabinet were just as determined as George Washington and his Founding Fathers that his nation should keep its independence and survive. He, therefore, answered on November 7 that neither he nor any other authorized person in Israel intended to annex the Sinai Peninsula. *When* the UNEF was satisfactorily established and Israel and the United Nations had come to an agreement on its entry into the Canal area, Israel would withdraw her forces. He required that Egypt's declaration of a state of belligerency with Israel be renounced; that it abandon the policy of blockade and boycott; that it cease sending murder gangs into Israel; and that it enter into peace negotiations with Israel. He thanked the President for America's support of Israel. Israel would always be ready to make its humble contribution at the side of the United States in its efforts to strengthen justice and peace in the world.

The pressures on Prime Minister Eden became irresistible. They would not have overwhelmed Sir Winston Churchill, who wrote to Prime Minister Mollet: "I would have gone on!" Nor would such pressures have affected General Charles de Gaulle, who said at that time, to those who came to him for counsel, roughly this: "I approve the principle of intervening at Suez; I don't like British predominance in the conduct of the operations; at last we are *doing* something; it is a difficult operation. As for the American government, I would have said, 'Here! This is what we wish to do, and if you don't agree, well . . .' And the Americans would have agreed. Now [that is, November, 1956] they threaten us with not supplying petrol. Very well, I, I would have said . . ." M. J. R. Tournoux, who reports this disquisition,[10] can be believed. The gaps are left for diplomatic reasons connected with de Gaulle's advent to the Presidency of France in 1958 and for good taste.

A Churchill or a de Gaulle would have continued, in the conviction that their course of action was *right* and in the expectation that *success* (as de Gaulle ventured) would have produced compliance by Dulles and Eisenhower. *Success*, yes; but not the too-slow half-success of Prime Minister Eden. Nothing succeeds like success, according to an old proverb. Show weakness, and those who look on, especially when they suffer from evident weaknesses of their own (and Dulles and Eisenhower had abundant weaknesses in foreign policy and in diplomatic tactics), improve their own public appearance and magnify their self-satisfaction in their own believed-in strength, by taking it out on those who have shown weakness.

From the standpoint of war-making, Eden's physical and spiritual misfortunes were for Eisenhower and Dulles and the Kremlin very valuable assets. And some attention must now be focused on this aspect of the Suez affair. Eden had committed himself to a military enterprise which he considered just, but the justice of which was spurned by his strongest and most preferred ally. In this policy he was challenged by a majority of nations, including the Asian and African members of his own Commonwealth, and criticized in every edition of the nation's press, and denounced by the Established Church and universities (both divided),[11] and called to account in face-to-face debates in Parliament. All this required a sheer physical fortitude, a robustness of body and nerves, which Eden may never have had, and certainly did not have now. Military experts estimated that this enterprise would need two weeks or more in the first substantial crunch, and then perhaps some months of military and diplomatic mopping up.

Two weeks is a crucifyingly long time to have one's nerves and physical being on the rack, even when one is in the best of health. The statesman needs to keep under control, and according to plan, all the many diverse forces that have been set in action—the economy, the morale of the people, Parliamentary support, the movement of army, navy, and air forces. He needs to be inspired by successes. He is also wracked by the anxieties and tensions that tomorrow may bring. It is difficult for any foreign student and even for Englishmen outside their Parliament to understand the agonizing nature of the constitutional compulsion that a Minister *must* face his opponents in the Commons day after day. This human pressure, this immediate impact of man on man, almost of body on body, the reaching out of the eyes and the ears and the voices, the expressions of the many faces, the sometimes inarticulate surges of disapproval, are at their most intense in the British Parliament—unparalleled anywhere else in the world, even in those Dominions which have imitated English ways and means of imposing daily responsibility on their Chief Executive, that is, Prime Minister and Cabinet. The Opposition can go berserk and become entirely cynical in advancing from the attitude that "We must show reasonable alternatives of policy to those of the Government," to a position that can be summed up, "Let it rip! Get the bastards out!"

This is what happened in the Suez affair. Seizing on the pretext that he had been informed only a quarter of an hour before Eden made his statement about the ultimatums in the House, Gaitskell decided not merely to divide the House, that is, to take a vote by roll call against the Government, but he declared (October 31) that he would use "every constitutional means . . . to save the country from the disasters which we believe will follow the course set by the Government."

At that moment and from that moment, Eden was harried, booed in the House, subjected to demonstrations outside the House and outside Downing Street. Enormous crowds, incited by Gaitskell and Aneurin Bevan, took up the chorus "Eden must go!" and "Law not war!" Though Eden could take some comfort from the fact that the opinion polls showed that more and more of the population, whether Conservative or Labour, approved of his military action, figures are less palpable than shouts from the Opposition.

But he was terribly ill. Eden says, and his closest assistants confirm, that he suffered from "recurrent bouts of weakness." He had a history of grave trouble with stoppage of the bile-duct. He had been on the diplomatic rack since July 26. On October 5, another attack of fever, perhaps connected with the effect of the earlier malady on the liver, had most debilitating effects. His temperature soared to 106 degrees. He was kept in the hospital until Monday, October 8. The process of auto-intoxication would to some degree respond to rest. But at this time rest was out of the question. The grip of his sickness on him was graver than he himself recognized or would admit. Hugh Gaitskell, who watched him from across the floor of the House and occasionally negotiated Parliamentary business with him, and Mollet and Pineau and their press secretary, were shocked by the drastic physiological and nervous sickness that was overcoming him. His own press secretary, returning on October 30 from a vacation that had started on October 16, testifies to the physical disaster to Eden that he then witnessed.

Cabinet sessions in Britain are not cosy like Cabinet sessions in the United States: in Britain they are a war of wills, for responsibility is collective and each Cabinet member is popularly elected like the Prime Minister and has his own political career as well as character at stake in all the important Cabinet decisions, not least, of course, in war. No man can expect mercy or gentleness from his rivals when office and high policy may be the fruits of their denunciation and brutality. Sir Horace Evans, physician to Queen Elizabeth as well, urged him to take some days off. This was impossible. He was headed for a breakdown.

In addition to his physical weakness, Eden was afflicted from within by his own conscience. War demands that a man have a stomach and not a conscience. But Eden's conscience was especially vulnerable and tortured about war. All his political career, especially the some thirty years of official responsibility for foreign affairs, had been founded on and involved in seeking a way to preserve or restore peace. In the furtherance of this purpose he had sought just solutions, or feasible solutions in which the concepts of justice as held by the contenders could be brought into settlement without bloodshed. Above all, he had grown in office and reputation by action in and for the League of Nations and, since then, the United Nations. The moralistic and over-pious objurgations of Dulles or Eisenhower were never needed to make him realize vividly and painfully, yes, even with agony, what it meant to be opposed to the Rule of Law in the world as it happened to be then embodied in the United Nations Charter, or to dash the hopes of so many millions who, too often in ignorance, believed that that body was already the world government that outlawed war and ensured peace and justice.

This, then, is what happened. November 5 had been a very trying day for all the British Cabinet Ministers, and especially for the Chancellor of the Exchequer, Harold Macmillan, who was in charge of Britain's economic responsibilities, and above all of sterling supplies. It was much more so, of course, for the Prime Minister. Eden spoke in the debate in the Commons on November 5. The session was one of the most disgraceful witnessed since the early 1920's. Labour members accused the Government of having caused Russia's murders in Hungary by the action it had taken in the Middle East. Their utterly stupid cry of "collusion"—with France or with Israel—again echoed in Parliament. The word *stupid* is used advisedly, because if a Government is resolved on war for the preservation of the interests of the nation, that is, of the whole people (even if Labour members regarded Conservatives as working only for *their* class), then to associate with others, to plan with others, to take advantage of actions useful to one's own cause, to "orchestrate," as the French publicists put it, is desirable and necessary. The issue is not collusion, but the expediency of a war of which "collusion" is a useful instrument. Once the circumstances make war necessary as a last-resort policy, the method, assuming it does not violate civilized restraints, is secondary. The British Government was in a weak position in regard to these issues only in its claim that it had not preplanned the actions of October 31, above all with Israel.

But the proceedings in the Commons became so bitter and so rowdy, with cries against the Cabinet of "fascists," "cowards," "murderers," that the Speaker was compelled to suspend the session, for the first time in over 20 years, for a cooling-off period of half an hour. The Prime Minister had gone to bed the day before, Sunday, knowing of the violent demonstrations arranged against him by the Labour Party in Trafalgar Square. (Christian Pineau, who had come to London to plead and at the same time to offer moral support, was inside No. 10 Downing Street as the angry, belligerent cries rang out.)

Eden participated in the conclusion of the debate. During it a Labour member reported to the *New Statesman* this: "The Prime Minister sprawled on the front bench, head thrown back and mouth agape. His eyes, inflamed with sleeplessness, stared into vacancies beyond the roof except when they twitched with meaningless intensity to the face of the clock. . . . The whole personality, if not prostrate, seemed completely withdrawn." [12] Eden had taken abuse of the most malicious kind, especially about some leaflets that had been dropped from the English planes over Egypt. These leaflets were bloodcurdling indeed; but they were intended to avert actual bloodshed by frightening the Egyptians to surrender without fighting. The Opposition made wicked use of these—wicked because they made the pretense that the threats were serious, while forgetting that some day the Opposition, if in Governmental responsibility, might also, for their own people's just claims, be obliged to make frightful faces at their enemy to avoid frightfulness in deed.

The *Times,* which had eloquently supported Eden's policy hitherto and had had very sharp words for Secretary Dulles's behavior, had several days ago (October 31), acknowledged "deep disquiet." The *Economist,* which had, at least, found the left wing of Labour repugnant and also had had the most serious misgivings about Dulles's actions since July 19, could offer "no confident support" of the Government since the attack on Egypt had been undertaken "against the reasoned urging of the world." (We have seen too much of the evidence to accept the adjective "reasoned.") It had taken exception (November 3) to the "obfuscatory statements" with which the Government covered its activities. The *Observer,* a Sunday newspaper highly regarded as sensible and liberal, had charged (November 4) that Eden was "internationally discredited" and ought to resign: this newspaper had connections which made some official secrets of importance open to it, even if it was not fully specific about its sources.

Also, Eden must surely have heard through the Chief Whip, Edward Heath, of an abortive yet mortifying and pending threat by about forty or fifty of what might be called the "good" and "sensible" Tories, people like Nigel Nicolson and Robert Boothby.[19] They had drafted a letter to the Prime Minister asking for a cease-fire, since the objective of separating the combatants had been achieved, and they *hinted* that they might abstain (that is, not vote *with* the Government) if the House divided. But the letter was never sent. It was believed by some that the Government had secret war information which required it to persist in its course, and among Conservatives especially the desertion of their Prime Minister, in the course of such an action as in Suez, is anathema. Yet, though the letter was never sent, the Prime Minister undoubtedly knew of it; it is reported that even Gaitskell, the Opposition leader, had information about it.

Eden, after the very, very shattering day of November 5, went to bed at 1:30 A.M. Almost immediately his private secretary brought into his bedroom the brutally threatening letter from Bulganin whose contents we have already noted. No sooner had Eden absorbed the menace of this than the phone rang: Prime Minister Mollet was calling from Paris about the letter he also had received from Bulganin. Men responsible for the safety of their nations and of the world in a time of nuclear weapons and rocket delivery cannot sleep on such threatening letters. (Britain was the first nation in history to have been the target of long-range missiles, fired by Nazis stationed in France, Belgium, and Holland!) Almost upon this phone call, too, a message from Hammarskjold, saying that both Egypt and Israel had agreed to a cease-fire, was brought to the bedroom. Eden then got out of bed and called his principal Ministers and advisers. He did not get back to bed until 5 A.M.

He was up again at 9 A.M. (November 6) ready for work, and soon afterwards a Cabinet meeting was in session. It continued throughout the morning. A long debate ensued on whether to cease fire. R. A. Butler, the most moderate member of the Cabinet, recommended the cease-fire in some such terms: A substantial part of the Canal was now occupied. Could much more be gained politically by continuing further up the Canal? Perhaps whatever could be achieved if the whole Canal were taken could still be obtained diplomatically on the basis of present gains? He believed that the additional potential political gains were not sufficient to offset the losses in the opposition of the United States and the world in general. Furthermore, there was *just* a chance that Russian volunteers would arrive. It looked as though Butler, and Heathcote-Amory, Minister of

Agriculture, a Conservative worthy, and Sir Walter Monckton, Paymaster-General, were prepared to quit the Cabinet if a cease-fire was not ordered.

In addition, Harold Macmillan was compelled to report the very serious dollar-sterling situation. Financiers, sober as well as speculative, had been acting on the assumption that the pound must surely be devalued, considering the financial drain of war and of fear among all the nations which used sterling as their world-wide currency. On November 6 alone, $300 million was needed to supply those who had titles to sterling balances.

Since the arrangements for the intervention in Suez had been more than usually, for affairs of this sort, kept secret by the Prime Minister in the hands of only four or five other Ministers, and the career officials had been rather less than usually consulted for their expert advice, the operations found Britain unprepared for the drain on sterling. Had the operations not been challenged by the United States at the United Nations, or had they been more swiftly carried to military success, the flight from the pound would have been less massive and more easily retrieved. But the military preparation had been surreptitious. And, perhaps, it had at the very last moment been impulsively decided: this statement applies to the period between about October 18 and October 20, and especially to the final decision on October 30. Thus, the financial strain became unbearable,[14] for sterling finances about one-half of all the world's trade. An enormous number of separate business accounts are interested in the value of the pound, officially and normally $2.80 per pound sterling.

The flight that had been mild since the SCUA conference accelerated on October 29 and became feverish by October 31. Great amounts of pounds were being sold in New York (blocks of $5 million), and, since the pound was sagging to $2.78, the Bank of England was buying in blocks of one million pounds to offset the weakening. On November 5, the U. S. Federal Reserve Bank was selling some of its sterling to avoid losses of its holdings. There is no doubt that State Department officials, now headed by Herbert Hoover, Jr., and advised by George M. Humphrey at the U. S. Treasury, suggested that the Federal Reserve Bank do this, as a means of avoiding loss, but also as a leverage over British-Suez operations. Those in the State Department and the White House, in the absence of Dulles, wanted an immediate cease-fire. The British Treasury advised the Chancellor of the Exchequer, Harold Macmillan, that the Bank of England needed *one billion dollars* to stop the devaluation of the pound by buying it.

Early on Tuesday morning, November 6, Macmillan phoned to Washington seeking substantial support, including help in making a call on British quotas in the International Monetary Fund. It was then about 4 A.M. in Washington, and no answer could be obtained at once. But the answer did come during the British Cabinet meeting that started at about 10 A.M. London time. A loan would be available, but on the imperative condition that a cease-fire be announced by Britain by midnight of November 6, that is, that same day!

Faced with a disastrous loss of the reserves needed to sustain all Britain's economic activities, the Cabinet was compelled to agree to a cease-fire. It was in America's power to sustain the British finances without asking for a cease-fire; it was America's policy to use her control over British finances to dictate the cease-fire, to exact it. Macmillan was taking astute and heroic measures to ferret out every resource to meet the obligations and stem any panic. HIS VIEW, BASED ON AMERICAN AND OTHER SPECULATIVE OPERATIONS AGAINST THE POUND, PREVAILED. Eden agreed to a cease-fire.

In the night of November 5/6, that is, probably early morning on November 6, Eden was called on the telephone by Eisenhower. Later, Christian Pineau (December 20, 1956, in the National Assembly) declared that American pressure had been "formidable." The gist of the phone call to Eden was: "I demand that you give the order to cease fire at once, if you want to preserve Anglo-American solidarity as well as peace. I cannot wait any longer." It was in the nature of an ultimatum: the deadline was not later than November 6, midnight.[15]

At 1 P.M. London time on that day, Eden had succumbed to arguments, pressures, forces—with the confidence in America that, with so much of the Canal in allied hands, the British and French could thenceforward exploit this diplomatic advantage to get their Suez claims fulfilled in a reliable way. He called Mollet in Paris, and told him, "We must have a cease-fire. We've almost won what we went after. Nasser cannot last long now!" Mollet, with tears in his eyes, begged Eden to be tenacious for another few hours so that the forces could reach Suez. "We are in a posture for success. We don't want the expedition to have been useless. How can we abandon the Israelis?" But Eden, on the telephone, said, "I am cornered! I can't hang on. I'm being deserted by everybody. My loyal associate Nutting has resigned as Minister of State. I can't even rely on unanimity among the Conservatives. The Archbishop of Canterbury, the Church, the oil businessmen, everybody is against me! The Commonwealth threatens to break up. Nehru says he will break the ties. Canada, Australia are no longer following us in our policy. I cannot be the grave-digger of the Crown. And then, I want you to understand, really understand, Eisenhower phoned me. I can't go it alone without the United States. It would be the first time in the history of England. . . . No, it is not possible."[16]

We are going to stop, to cease fire, Eden announced to Mollet, asking for understanding. Mollet countered with his point of view. Eden continued trying to persuade him to join in the cease-fire. If Eden had had his way, the cease-fire would have been effective at 7 P.M., London time. Mollet convinced Eden that the fighting should be prolonged until 11:59 P.M. that day, November 6—but, Eden insisted, "Not one minute more!" The French government was not eager to comply with Eden's appeal. A tense struggle took place in the Cabinet. But, clearly, France could not go on unless in combination with Britain, for their forces were intermingled, quite apart from the political consequences of separate action. The French had accepted British military leadership because they needed to overcome British reluctance to enter the Suez enterprise at all, though some among the French leaders, more especially their generals and admirals, realized that British leadership made full collusion with Israel impossible and therefore threatened a sure and swift victory. They also had to yield the condition that a cease-fire could be ordered only with the consent of both Britain and France. France also owed much to and needed much from the United States government: they were allies in NATO. But an order to cease *fire*, if issued to the French forces from Paris, would not forbid *movement* of forces. The French wanted the maximum territory gage they could get. Let it be clearly understood, Eden meant to cease fire, even if the French had not consented. This time there was no meeting in Paris or London to concert policy. The British and French ceased fire, at that moment, in part because they believed they were further up the Canal, past El Cap, than they, in fact, were: communications with Keightley were at fault.

One other matter is involved in the diplomacy of the cease-fire on November 6. It is the part played by United States obligations under the NATO treaty. This consideration gave a very keen edge to the President's telephone call to Eden early on the morning of November 6.

Neither the government of Britain nor that of France feared the threats of Russia as much as Washington did. They did *not* take them seriously, regarding them (mainly) as a diplomatic maneuver to demonstrate to the Arabs that they, the Soviet leaders, stood by their friends and had the power to impose a cease-fire. The attitude of the governments, however, was not the same as that of the *peoples* of the democratic countries. Their newspapers could not possibly miss such a sensational opportunity, available on November 5, of stirring public opinion (and selling newspapers, since war and sex are the two most powerful newspaper sellers), especially, of course, when they happened to be newspapers hostile to the government's policies.

All the evidence indicates that the threat of the Soviet Union hit Washington with more terror than it did London or Paris. The members of the Administration, especially such inexperienced and unsophisticated politicians as Herbert Hoover, Jr., and some members of the Policy Planning Committee, were terrified of nuclear war, and actually talked of the world being "fried to a crisp!" It has always been so, and is so now, at the date of this writing. It is to be expected that fears should be more vivid and timidity more widely evinced in Washington, in spite of the fact that threats have been made against European peoples rather than the United States. For, in the end, it would be the power of the United States that would be engaged to avert a Russian attack on Britain and France or, if that had already occurred, to go to their rescue. Dulles and Eisenhower did not possess the tenacious nerve to dominate the Russians and make them back down by confrontation.

Now, the NATO Pact demanded American action, if a Russian attack should take place on any other signatory nation. But where? At Suez, or in the Mediterranean, or only in their homelands? Clearly, the diplomatic hesitation of the State Department and the White House in giving its word that NATO obligations would be honored forthwith could be a leverage in compelling the allies to cease fire and withdraw. The issue became somber and immediate when the Bulganin letters were delivered, and when the *Tass* agency of the Soviet Union had made public, that is, circulated to the press of all nations, its more brutal threats. This it had done by the early hours of November 6, when the decisions to cease fire in any case were already being formed in the minds of the British Cabinet.

A rumor still persists that Herbert Hoover, Jr., gave London to understand that the fulfillment of America's NATO obligations could not be taken for granted. I have not been able to trace the truth of this.

When the French Ministers considered Bulganin's threat in the early hours of November 6 (about the time that Mollet and Eden talked on the telephone in regard to the same matter), they formed two conclusions. (1) The guarantees of the NATO alliance, that is, help from all of the members of the alliance, above all the United States, would be forthcoming, even if for the moment they had not specific confirmation of this from Washington. (2) In any case, even if the United States "ultimatum" were not a mere maneuver of intimidation (as they assessed it to be), nothing irreparable was to be feared for the forty-eight to seventy-two hours immediately before them. In that time, they believed, consultations with Washington would be feasible, while the Russian deployment of forces and the troubles in Hungary would make it impossible for Russia to undertake any form of intervention, whether with rockets or volunteers. Meanwhile, the Anglo-French forces in Suez could continue to move up the Canal.

While the French Ministers were in session, let us say at about

1:15 A.M. on November 6, Ambassador Douglas Dillon arrived at the Hotel Matignon and asked to see Prime Minister Mollet for a few minutes privately. Dillon came with a written note from Washington. Its gist was this: "If you continue in your wrongful action, do not count on the United States. The only proper action is through the United Nations. You must stop your intervention in Suez, and if you do not, you cannot count on our support."

This was an extremely violent shock to Mollet. His Ministers, to whom he immediately reported Dillon's message, suffered the same blow. Mollet was especially disturbed by the threats in *Tass*, at any rate, so far as the effect on the French public was concerned. And governments want even remote risks to be insured. "We are members of the Atlantic Alliance," he said. "Are we going to be helped?" He was given the official answer, "Of course, we will help you!" Mollet then asked whether he could get the assurance direct from Washington. Would the Ambassador ask his government? What Mollet wanted was a *public* announcement, so that the Soviet government would know quite clearly that it could not use the blackmail threat it had made. The American Ambassador demurred, and not as an alibi, since he had considerable sympathy with the allies' plight. He pointed out that it was too late at night in Washington, so he could not act at once. However, the private assurance was there. When the Ministers did shortly thereafter continue their discussions, it was a matter of moment to them that Washington had *not*, in answer to Bulganin's note, already declared *publicly* that, if America's allies were attacked by atomic weapons, America would retaliate in kind against the attacker—that is, Russia. These considerations were part of the conversation at 3 A.M. between Mollet and Eden on the cross-Channel telephone.

It was not until *after* the cease-fire that, through Ambassador Alphand, a *privately conveyed* message went to France (and through channels also to Britain) that the Atlantic Pact guarantee was in operation. But even then, the allies were left in some vagueness as to the area of its applicability, probably by deliberate American policy. For when the assurance arrived, it was in the form, Yes, the United States government will respect its obligations and will come to the immediate help of its European allies, if these are attacked. It did not specify whether the promise applied only if they were attacked in Europe; or what the United States considered its obligations if its allies' expeditionary forces in Suez and in the region around it were attacked.

In fact, it was not until November 13, when the talk was still of Russian and Chinese volunteers, that the American government responded to its allies' wishes and the Russian threats categorically. It did so then for its own sake, its own power and security and interests. The spokesman was General Gruenther, Commander in Chief of the NATO forces in Europe. Also by this time, UNEF had committed the Allies to withdrawal: they would not start fire again!

Gruenther declared:

> If the Soviet Union carried out its threat to use guided missiles against Western European countries, we should immediately retaliate and the Soviet Union would be destroyed. That is as certain as that night follows day.

In Washington, on November 6, Alphand had been sent to the State Department to get from the American government the desired *public* assurance of guarantees of support against an attack on London and Paris. He arrived in Hoover's office at noon. He apprised him of his government's wish. But Hoover replied, "Oh! Haven't you heard? Only a couple of minutes ago, London announced a cease-fire!" Thus, the timing shows that, though the problem of a Soviet attack weighed substantially on French minds, and a little less on British minds, it did not play the vital part in London and Paris some have claimed for it, and certainly not the part the Russians claimed—in its crude form. The worry over NATO came, it is apparent, when London's decision to stop was already in an advanced state of ripening.

But—Russian power, in spite of Admiral Radford's advice that the Soviets could do nothing of what they had threatened, did play a decisive part in the general thinking and diplomacy of Washington. It was not so much the immediate threat of action, as fear because the military potential to cause trouble was in Russian hands, and awareness of the likelihood that the brunt of any actions against the Soviet Union would fall on the United States. It is most probable that the very fears of Russia which had been developed for several years by Dulles, and promoted by him throughout the Administration, inhibited Administration boldness, made Eisenhower and Dulles and their aides tougher with their own allies, more tender with the Arabs and especially Nasser than they might have been otherwise. Thus, America did not come forward spontaneously with a public announcement that the American NATO obligations would be honored. Indeed, Israel was specifically warned that she would *not* get protection! Dulles and Eisenhower bowed to Russian atomic might, or to what they had portrayed it to be.

What was the Suez situation, then, at this stage? Britain and France held the Canal up to El Cap. Who could get them out, failing a settlement of the Canal dispute on their terms? The Israelis held the whole of the Sinai Peninsula. Who could cause them to withdraw except with a peace treaty and a guarantee of *their* rights in the Canal?

The United Nations attempted only to persuade these nations

to withdraw from Suez and Sinai, in vain. The United States, by supplying actual direct economic force and threats, achieved this goal. America conceded nothing at all to her allies. She diminished their power and prestige. But in some respects, Dulles was forced to yield to Israel's patriotic determination not to be robbed of the right to survive.

About the time of the order to cease fire, Nasser and his henchmen were in fear of the imminent fall of their regime, and had already made plans to retreat or retire to some distant background. President Eisenhower knew this, but did not use it to the advantage of the United States, Britain, France, and Israel, then, or for the future.

The American policy that led to the submission of her allies in Suez was excellently summarized by former French Prime Minister Mendès-France in a debate in the French National Assembly on December 18, 1956. He observed that "The political constellation was not characterised by the old opposition of three (America, France and Britain) against one (Russia), but by a new formula . . . the two biggest (America and Russia) against the two less big, and it is from that fact that the quashing of the Suez action occurred." [17]

Dulles suffered extreme displeasure a month or so later when the U.S. Ambassador to France, who had been an intimate party to the transactions leading to the cease-fire, declared that he thought neither moral suasion nor the pressure of dwindling oil supplies nor American diplomacy had caused it, but "these Soviet threats which were very strongly phrased." [18] Dillon was compelled to amend his remarks at Dulles's insistence.[19] However, the truth remained the truth. Dulles had panicked before the Russian threat.

16. DULLES SANCTIONS HIS ALLIES

THE ELECTION WAS OVER, WITH A COLOSSAL VICTORY FOR EISENHOWER. In a charming note he sent to "Foster" in the hospital on November 12, he said that he thought Dulles would have, "as do I, a feeling of gratification that the verdict of the American voters supported in such large measure both the foreign and domestic policies of the Administration." [1] Thus, all was well in the Republic and its relations with the world.

The Administration, now comprising the President, Herbert Hoover, Jr., and Henry Cabot Lodge so far as foreign policy was concerned, cooperated almost obsequiously, almost beseechingly, to the very letter, with Hammarskjold in his interpretation and application of the Charter. It was very astute to do this. For such action exhibited the United States as the pioneer of the Rule of Law in the world; the champion of the Charter; the pious venerator of the Secretary General. The Administration was astute and zealous in manner, but it was feeble in policy. It was savage in its sustained determination to force Britain and France and Israel to their knees in surrender to its policy. However intense the hostility of the United States to its Western allies before the cease-fire of November 6, it was still moderate compared with the raging and continuous bullying after that date: the Rule of Law required unconditional surrender. In Dulles's lawyer's terms, once applied (regarding SCUA) to Nasser, unsuccessfully, of course, the other party could not expect better terms than those they had rejected.

The essence of the Secretary General's position was embodied in two tenets, which had emerged again and again since the Suez dispute had come before the United Nations. The first was the unqualified preservation, down to the utmost jot and tittle, of Egyptian sovereignty, which had been violated. The Charter's essence was the preservation of national sovereignty. And, secondly, no atom of advantage must be gained as a result of aggression. Hammarskjold had no care for the victims of Nasser; he was heart and soul and single-mindedly, as also narrowmindedly, concerned for the principles of the Charter—he personally placed all weight on peace and *not* on the term "justice" in its paragraphs. At that moment it suited the leaders of American policy to side with him, and in a sense to transfer all their troubles of conscience and power to him.

Now, Eden had expected that, having consented to the cease-fire, Britain would be back in the good graces of Eisenhower and Dulles. He therefore assumed that the constructive parts of the resolutions moved by the United States Ambassador to the United Nations, concerning a settlement of Middle Eastern problems, including that of Suez, would be implemented with as much energy as the demand for a cease-fire and a withdrawal. The cynical French may not have expected such fair treatment, voluntarily, from Washington, but they hoped to get it, if, with the British, they could remain entrenched in Suez long enough. In their own interests, the British had begun by November 3 to veer sharply away from their association with Israel. Eden in a broadcast that day promised that Britain would make sure Israeli forces withdrew, and two days later, in the Commons, Selwyn Lloyd repeated this assurance. The French dissented.

The post-cease-fire action now developed along two fronts, as it were. Britain and France attempted to resume solidarity with the United States. The UNEF resolutions regarding Suez and Sinai needed to be carried out.

Shortly after Eisenhower had heard the news (on November 6) that the British and French had ordered a cease-fire, he acted on a friendly personal impulse, indeed, and telephoned to Eden. Eden was in his room at the House of Commons, for it was the afternoon shortly after he had told the House that he had ordered a cease-fire. He had received assurances from Hammarskjold of Egypt's and Israel's unconditional acceptance of a cease-fire, as well as the Secretary General's assurances regarding the objectives of the UNEF as set out in the General Assembly's resolution. A witness in the Prime Minister's room during Eisenhower's call noted the genuine good will in the President's voice on the phone, as he exclaimed, "My dear Anthony! How are you?" He was, of course, extremely pleased about the cease-fire. He said that Eden had accomplished what he had set out to do, namely, stop the fighting, and it was good, too, that it had not spread. Eden, in turn, congratulated the President on the election returns which were so overwhelmingly in his favor. The President suggested that Eden keep in touch with him on the telephone: a new cable had just been opened up.

Eden then telegraphed Mollet optimistically that friendship with the United States had been restored, that Soviet plans in the Middle East had been exposed by the joint action of Britain and France, and that the allies were "physically holding a position which can be decisive for the future."

The next day, November 7, after a bedside consultation with Dulles and Hoover that morning, the President sent Eden a telegram. In this he urged that the UNEF should be carried into effect immediately to prevent (in Eden's reporting of the telegram), "what he [Eisenhower] considered to be developments of the greatest gravity in Egypt." [2] Eden interpreted the President's phrase as referring to the possibility of Soviet intervention in some form. For, at that time and thereafter, the Russians were making tremendous propaganda gains with the claim that they had forced a cease-fire, and they were now clamoring for the further diplomatic successes they could achieve by means of a speedy withdrawal of British and French forces. Once again the talk of volunteers from Russia (50,000, said *Tass*!) and Communist China was circulating on the international grapevine. In fact, some hours earlier Ambassador Dillon had assured Prime Minister Mollet that the United States would resist any "new forces," meaning Russians, in the Middle East. Furthermore, the Egyptian Ambassador had the effrontery to ask Hoover, formally, for *American* help against Britain, France, and Israel, by volunteers, arms, or otherwise! The President was certainly in a vexing situation.

The President asked, in his telegram to Eden, that in order to expedite the establishment of the UNEF Britain (and France) consent to the exclusion of "contingents from the great powers" from that force. (For Egypt refused *absolutely* to permit Britain and France to participate and Hammarskjold totally supported Egypt in this prohibition. The reasoning was this, for Egypt and the Secretary General: if allied troops were included in the UNEF, it would be admitting the forces of the aggressors into a legitimate collective occupation of Suez. Also, Egypt knew that until the allies were out, Nasser would be in continuous danger. Their forces, continuing to build up, might resume fighting. The Canal could not be cleared. A settlement could still be imposed on Nasser, or Egypt could be kept in an uproar, making routine government operation practically impossible.) The President's telegram presented this urgent suggestion as a means of keeping the Russians out. If it were accepted, *the Soviet Union would have no excuse left for an intervention.* Furthermore, said the President, any attack on the UNEF would meet with resistance from the United Nations.

Eden asked for time to consider. He consulted the Cabinet. It concluded that the lower levels of the State Department (including Henry Cabot Lodge) did not truly understand the political consequences in the Middle East, and specifically Suez and Sinai, if the allies did withdraw. Nor the dangers of Soviet penetration, in spite of the arms caches that had been found by the Israelis, and the more recent arming of Syria. It was most desirable to consult with President Eisenhower personally.

Hence, at about 8 A.M. Washington time (2 P.M. London time), November 7, Eden phoned the President. He explained the need for a meeting, for a full discussion. The President at once agreed on the wisdom of a meeting. He asked what date Eden might have in mind. Eden answered, "The sooner the better; why should not I and Mollet come over this very evening?" The President immediately agreed, suggesting that Eden phone Mollet and bring him over, and said that Mollet would get a confirming telegram from him. Eden phoned Mollet. In spite of some inconveniences, Mollet said he would gladly join.

One hour later, the President telephoned Eden again. He now asserted he wanted it understood that Eden would not be making the trip simply to argue about the United Nations resolutions. Eden replied that this was not what he had in mind, and that he did not even know what the said resolutions might be at that moment. The President responded that he was glad of this, because it would be awkward if he and Eden were to argue about the United Nations resolutions and then disagree. Eden told the President again that such was not his purpose.

Some little time after this conversation, the President, who had begun the day so fairly and magnanimously, telephoned Eden once again. He explained that he would be busy in the next few days consulting with Congressional leaders. Therefore, the visit should be deferred, without ruling it out for a later date. This was a severe shock to Eden, who was on the verge of departing rather happily for the Commons to announce the visit as agreed.

A substantiation comes from the other side of the Channel.[3] Eden had phoned Mollet, as just recounted. "At last we can breathe again. President Eisenhower just phoned to let me know that he expects both of us, tomorrow, November 8, in Washington. We shall have to leave without any publicity, with one associate each, because our host is counting on the effect of surprise and does not wish our journey to be announced before our actual arrival. The spectacular re-establishment of a united Anglo-Franco-American front will offset the effect of the cease-fire. Our policy was sound." Eden meant that the cease-fire decision was sound.

An hour after this call from Eden to Mollet, Eden called him again: Eisenhower had changed his mind. He had given Eden to understand that it was impossible to consider a meeting "before the complete fulfillment of all the decisions of the General Assembly of the U.N." Any other attitude would be misunderstood in the United

States and "in certain countries." This about-face was confirmed by a visit by Ambassador Dillon to Prime Minister Mollet soon afterwards.

What had happened in Washington? The history comes from several participants. But it is well summed up in the account of this episode in diplomacy in Sherman Adams's *First Hand Report*.[4] Adams recalls that the President was pleased to have had Eden's call, as it was difficult for him "to take an aloof or diffident attitude and he was too anxious to restore the traditional friendship between the Americans and the British to let pride or the nursing of hurt feelings keep him from eagerly accepting Eden's offer to get together again."

According to Adams, the proposal was passed along to the State Department by the President, "with his own view that it would be good for the world to see that even with our differences our firm friendship with Britain was unaffected." The proposal was handled in the first place by Herbert Hoover, Jr., Herman Phleger, William Rountree, and a few other career officials, in consultation with Henry Cabot Lodge. The prospect of a visit by Eden was thoroughly ventilated by these men. Dulles had been consulted on the problem. Hoover informed Sherman Adams the consensus was that the visit was premature and should be discouraged. Would he tell Eisenhower? The reason for the postponement was "that the State Department was opposed to him [the President] inviting Eden to this country until after the British Government withdrew its forces from the Suez Canal. I pointed out to him [Goodpaster, Eisenhower's principal special White House assistant] that if he [Eisenhower] received Eden now the visit might be misunderstood as an approval by the United States of the stand that the British had taken in the Middle East."[5]

"Who touches pitch shall be defiled."

Ambassador Dillon, in Paris, at that time did not agree with this decision. He thought: "What could possibly be wrong in just talking?" This was Eisenhower's personal spontaneous view, and he was right. In this situation it was right, *if* the policy at the beginning was right, to continue it—namely, to insist that the British and French must withdraw. But it was also right and even essential that the earliest possible Anglo-American conversations should be held. If news of such a meeting should hurt the Arab and African and Asian feelings, if it should give pain to Nehru and the Ceylonese, then they must bear the pain; they and the world must be told that such consultations were desirable even in their own eventual interests. Nothing in this situation, except wrong-headedness, required the President to be pressed to forego consultations with America's closest allies.

The final comment on this maladroit diplomacy is made by Sherman Adams. "Eisenhower understood the State Department's thinking and accepted its decision, but he accepted it with reluctance and impatience. He told me that turning down Eden's request for a personal talk did not seem to him the right thing to do. He felt that this was no time to be so concerned about appearance and propriety." Here the generous spirit of the President was shiningly right compared with the petty fearfulness of the vendetta-minded tacticians—recently lawyers or oilmen in parochial practice—of the State Department, and of the United Nations.

The British and French, as we have seen, had consented to a cease-fire for two main reasons, (1) fearful pressure from the United States and (2) the promise from the United States, as leader of the United Nations, that the UNEF would be the means of securing justice to Israel and to the allies in the Canal dispute. The conditions on which they had agreed with Hammarskjold to cease fire were very clearly stated: [6] the cease-fire was *not* unconditional.

At this point of American-British diplomatic strategy, the following observation by Anthony Eden may be accepted as true: "We [the British Cabinet] would have taken a second, and maybe a third look at the problem [of ordering a cease-fire] had we understood what was to come." [7] As Eden explains:

> We were ashore with a sufficient force to hold Port Said. We held a gage. Nasser had received a humiliating defeat in the field and most of his Russian equipment had been captured or destroyed by the Israelis or ourselves. His position was badly shaken. Out of this situation intelligent international statesmanship should, we thought, be able to shape a lasting settlement for the Arab-Israeli conflict and for the future of the Canal. *We had not understood that, so far from doing this, the United Nations, and in particular the United States, would insist that all the advantages must be thrown away before serious negotiation began.* This was the most calamitous of errors. Had we expected this to be perpetrated, our course might have been otherwise, but we could not know. As it seems to me, the major mistakes were made, not before the cease-fire or in that decision, but *after* it. I did not foresee them.

The underlined phrases are of most significance. United States policy was now not primarily engaged in solving Middle Eastern problems. It had engaged itself (the American policy makers persuaded themselves) in the supposed salvation of the United Nations and in building a world "without war," a world in which all conflicts between nations were to be solved by the Rule of Law. So much in foreign policy depends on timing; this emphasis, at this stage in human evolution, seems to have been premature.

Here was the cease-fire. Where was the constructive settlement? The British and French governments' attitude and their understanding of what was owed to them, as well as what they had promised the United Nations, amounted to this.[8] First, their forces would not be withdrawn until "the international force to be set up will be competent to secure and supervise the attainment of the objectives set out in the operative paragraphs of the resolution passed by the General Assembly on November 2." Secondly, the permanent members of the Security Council must be part of the UNEF, if that were to be effective. Thus, Britain and France would be included. Thirdly, Britain and France, extremely anxious about the reopening of the Canal, which had been deliberately blocked by Egypt (some forty ships having been sunk in it, many filled with cement), demanded of the General Assembly, through Secretary General Hammarskjold, that they be allowed to undertake the clearing of the Canal, since that was a nonmilitary operation. Fourthly, *they would not complete their withdrawal from Suez until the conclusion of a settlement of the Canal dispute and a peaceful arrangement of Arab-Israeli conflicts.*

They still hoped, it is plain to see from this, and from their speeches in London and Paris, to overthrow Nasser, and to get their settlement, as months ago Dulles had advocated and pledged it, on the basis of the eighteen-power proposals. In the House of Commons debate of November 8, the Minister of Defence, Antony Head, who had visited the Suez battle headquarters on November 5, observed that "the whole point is that the Canal cannot and must not be solely the concern of the Egyptian Government. That is what this has all been about."[9] That night, Selwyn Lloyd had been able to stave off a defection of right-wing Conservatives only by the promise of no withdrawal until the UNEF was in being.

Meanwhile, Secretary General Hammarskjold was intensely busy solving the problems of the emergency nature of the force, its functions, its size and organization, its financing, its recruitment.

The General Assembly went into session again at 10:30 A.M. on November 7. The Secretary General had answered some of his crucial and most difficult questions, in every instance to the unqualified advantage of Egypt and Nasser. The onus and the odium were all thrust on the shoulders of the European allies.[10] The United States had now abdicated its own initiative to that of Hammarskjold. From this move it might claim some present and long-term advantages: it could claim that it was heart and soul behind the majesty and strength and legitimacy, even the sacrosanctity, of the United Nations. The Soviet Union, in Hungary, was in brutal defiance of the United Nations and the Rule of Law! In the very long run, would not the Arabs, and Asians, and all other peoples, be attracted to the U.S.A. and away from the U.S.S.R. if the United States were conspicuously law-abiding? Also, the attitude had tremendous immediate advantages for the material interests of the United States. It relieved Dulles, Lodge, and Eisenhower from the burdens of war and preparations for war. It relieved the Administration of having to think about the future of the Middle East *now.* It permitted the earliest pacification, and this would be favorable to the resumption of oil production on a normal basis. Middle Eastern oil output had undergone and would yet undergo a marked diminution, accompanied by (a) a decrease in profits to the American firms engaged therein and (b) a loss of revenue by countries like Saudi Arabia—important to the United States both as the country in which its strategic base of Dhahran was located, and as an offset to the strength of Nasser. The quicker the pacification, the more serene and stable the relationships of the United States with Iraq and Iran and Jordan and Lebanon, relationships already much shaken by the present hurricane of fire.

As for the NATO alliance, that, in the rejection of the visit by Eden and Mollet, had just been risked for the moment. And, *for the moment*, it appeared to be a good risk. They, the European allies, would have to come crawling back. Did not their anxiety about Russia's threats and their request for assurances about America's atomic protection of Western Europe clearly demonstrate this? So, *for the moment*, NATO could be put on the shelf. The allies could be treated roughly, cavalierly, and no harmful consequences would ensue. *For the moment*, however, was hardly enough. The problem before the State Department and the White House was not only the present moment but the long run: the long run was sacrificed, with the most serious consequences to the security and burdens of the United States.

Thus, the U.N. Secretary General, the agent not only of the voiceless terminology of the Charter but also of the vociferousness of its members, was exploited by those who made the clamor and had the votes. His policy was as follows. The forces of Britain and France were *excluded* from the UNEF. How could it be expected that Egypt would tolerate their inclusion, or the rest of the Afro-Asian bloc endorse it? Secondly, the Secretary General interpreted the resolution of the Assembly as meaning that there was *no* intention in setting up the UNEF "to influence the military balance in the present conflict and, thereby, the political balance affecting efforts to settle the conflict." [11] Thirdly, Hammarskjold was adamant that the general political control of the force be left in the hands of the Secretary General, that is, in *his hands*. The UNEF was not to be an agency of enforcement, but merely the supervisor of the cease-fire. Even then, whether the UNEF could even enter the area at all was left to the consent of Egypt, since the action of the General Assembly (so mandatory on Britain and France and Israel!) was only a recommendation! Finally, he rejected the use of the UNEF to secure freedom of navigation, and the demand by the allies that they be empowered to clear the Canal.

By a vast majority, the Assembly adopted a resolution embodying these conditions.[12] But its Afro-Asian members wanted more than this: the immediate and unconditional withdrawal of all forces from

Egyptian territory. The Secretary General was to report compliance or noncompliance to the Assembly.

The U.S. Ambassador to the United Nations, Henry Cabot Lodge, strongly supported the Secretary General's resolution (submitted by seven powers, Argentina, Burma, Ceylon, Denmark, Ecuador, Ethiopia, and Sweden), and the additional one (sponsored by Afghanistan, Burma, Ceylon, Ethiopia, India, Indonesia, Iran, Iraq, Jordan, Lebanon, Liberia, Libya, Nepal, Pakistan, the Philippines, Saudia Arabia, Syria, Thailand, and Yemen).[13] It will be appreciated, from an inspection of the names of these nineteen sponsor nations, where American interests lay—whether over and above, or under and beneath, the American delegation's conscientious embrace of a transcendent faithfulness to the United Nations as an entity and conception distinct from its diverse individual members. Lodge announced: "If we are to accomplish our purpose, we must move quickly to carry out the plan embodied in the draft resolution. We must not hesitate, we must not falter at the last moment, and thus make possible new and even more serious complications. Speed is vital." [14] He praised the Secretary General's competence, speed, intelligence, and determination. He lamented the victims of the military actions in Egypt. Could anyone lean back upon a more serene and comfortable conscience than this?

Meanwhile, regional and ethnic interests in the Middle East were playing their role. The Moslem members of the Baghdad Pact, that is, Iran, Pakistan, Iraq, and Turkey, publicly demanded the immediate and unconditional withdrawal of Anglo-French forces; the application of the original 1947 resolution on the Palestine question to settle the Israeli-Arab dispute; and the settlement of the dispute over the Canal within the United Nations by negotiation with Egypt.

The Assembly swept aside the British representative's plea that the cease-fire had been accepted under stipulated provisos. What on earth, they thought, could he be talking about: Provisos! He had had no business ever to have started fire! Their interests and their sense of injury demanded only one thing: Get out at once!

Some suggestion had been made by the Swiss government that the Chiefs of State of the U.S.A., France, Britain, the U.S.S.R., and India meet at Geneva to find a settlement. But this was not American policy at all. Why should the United States face its allies directly, when the U.N. would give the U.S.A. all the cover it needed for the success of its policy? Nor did the United States find acceptable the suggestion, made by Sir Pierson Dixon, that a Ministers' meeting in the Security Council should negotiate an international settlement.

The Secretary General's resolution (the seven-power one) of November 3 received 64 votes for, 0 against. But the Soviet bloc, plus Egypt, Israel, and South Africa, abstained. It did not suit the interests of any of these nations that either the principle or the practice of a U.N. force should be accepted—*if* it seemed to imply an imposition of peace *conditions* on a sovereign nation. Israel's abstention was based on a policy of survival: the number of Afro-Asian nations was rising to a figure where, one day, they might, to please Egypt and their own ethnic rancors and interests, combine to vote the rescinding of the actions of the U.N. in 1947. She had immediate reasons not to admit the U.N. to undertake actions inimical to her survival. That organization had shown little effectiveness in securing her safety during the past few years. Moreover, strong suspicions were entertained by some people in Israel that Hammarskjold, finding he was up against a very tough customer in Nasser, wilted, and had lost some of his impartiality in fact if not in intention. He was favoring Egypt all along the line. Egypt, of course, presented herself as an exploited victim and wanted no possible limit to her own frantic policies: hence her abstention. South Africa was alienated from United Nations action since it resented interference in its internal affairs concerning the policy of *apartheid*. But it will be inferred that Britain and France, of course, were in the majority for the resolution. On the resolution (of November 7) for an immediate cease-fire and withdrawal, the Assembly vote was 65 in favor; Israel voted against, and ten nations abstained, among them France and Britain, the smaller NATO countries of Western Europe, Australia, New Zealand, and South Africa.

The British and French tried desperately to get the Administration (which by now, say November 8, 9, and 10, included Dulles) to come to some arrangement to recognize their claims. In vain! In the poker game, they had let themselves be cajoled into throwing away the only factor that could possibly have changed Dulles's policy: obstinacy and fortitude in continuing military operations. But, against any British and French determination, Dulles, Eisenhower, Henry Cabot Lodge, and the Secretary of the Treasury, George M. Humphrey, had two trump cards: they could withhold oil supplies from Western Hemisphere sources, and they could see to it that no dollar support of sterling was available, either directly or from a drawing on the International Monetary Fund.

It was not American policy, as established by Dulles, to use the United Nations as an agency which would teach Nasser and rulers like him everywhere in the world then and yet to come, that they had obligations that must be fulfilled. As Dulles observed in January, 1957, "the entry [of allied troops] had been illegal, and it was *not proper* to say that they could stay until they had gained certain political objectives." [15] It was a specious argument.

The day of the complete American capitulation to the forces that opposed Britain and France, and not for the sake of what was noblest in the United Nations but for the sake of what was most opportunistic in it, was November 10. Then Lodge moved that the Emergency Session be adjourned and its work be transferred to the regular annual meeting about to begin shortly. To win over the British and French, he moved that the Assembly take up the *permanent* problems of the Middle East and Suez according to the resolutions he had moved at the beginning of the proceedings (November 2). But this gesture at a constructive effort was opposed by Egypt. Out, at once, demanded the Egyptian representative! Lodge was afraid to stand up to him! On hearing the Egyptian's tirade, he immediately retreated. His paragraph requesting "urgent consideration to" his constructive resolutions was *surrendered.*

Shortly after the telephone conversation of November 7 with Eisenhower, Prime Minister Eden had sent him a telegram. He hoped that a meeting would come about soon. He felt that the troubles that had recently occurred between the two countries regarding the Middle East had resulted from the lack of a clear understanding between them. Stability would not be attained unless they were working towards common objectives.[16] This message was almost identical, ironically, with that which the President had sent to Eden on October 30: the situation was now reversed, Eisenhower having been the suppliant earlier (Chapter 13). Eden still, in this same telegram, hoped to be able to come to Washington "within the next few days," as correspondence on such matters did not supply the proper medium for considered conclusions.

The President replied that an early date was agreeable to him. BUT—the United Nations resolutions must first be carried out, that is to say, the Anglo-French forces must be withdrawn from Egypt without delay. A meeting would be possible only when this was done.

It is not worth pursuing the same tale stage by stage as it proceeded down towards the third week in November. Once Nasser realized that almost everybody's national interests, when combined, favored him, he grew more and more intransigent. Britain and France were surrendering one by one the conditions that they had established as necessary for fulfillment before they would cease fire and withdraw. Nasser would not admit the British and French forces to be part of the UNEF; they conceded this. He would not allow the clearance of the Canal by British and French equipment; they were forced to concede this—no matter how tenacious they were with Hammarskjold and his assistant, Andrew Cordier, down to the end of January, 1957 —because Nasser would not allow any clearance operations until all the troops were withdrawn. He flatly refused to enter into any negotiations for a settlement of the problems of the area at that time. Hammarskjold and the United Nations and the United States conceded this also. The original idea of including Canadian personnel in the

UNEF was rejected by Egypt; the rejection was conceded.[17] The Soviet Union raised the question of reparations by France and Brittain to Egypt; ultimately such payments had to be made as a key to open the Canal and keep it open.

At a Press Conference on November 14, President Eisenhower seemed to hold out an olive branch to Britain and France. It was just after the President's reception of the new British Ambassador, Sir Harold Caccia (when he had told the Ambassador that he shared Eden's views on Nasser!). The President said:

> There are still some differences with our Allies. They all boil down to one specific point, and until this point is settled, because the United Nations has taken it over, I think that any meeting of ours, would appear, make it appear, that we are going off to some other subjects, when this important one is still ahead of us . . . our friendships with these two countries are going to be stronger than ever, if I can bring it about.[18]

When Eden heard this, and also the news that the new Ambassador had been received with a certain graciousness, he thought that there still might be some chance of securing a constructive solution to Britain's and France's Suez problem, and also to the Arab-Israeli conflicts. He at once sent Foreign Minister Selwyn Lloyd to the United Nations, and asked him and the British Ambassador to make as close contact with the leaders of the United States as was possible.

They were coarsely rebuffed. The British Foreign Minister could not get to see the President. He could not at first even get to see Herbert Hoover, Jr. He could make no headway when he tried to get Bedell Smith to be his intermediary. He tried this connection because on November 9, the President, in difficulties owing to Dulles's illness and Herbert Hoover, Jr.'s want of aptitude, had appointed Bedell Smith to be his special White House assistant on foreign policy. The President, having burned his fingers over the invitation to Eden and Mollet, now kept his distance. The obduracy of the allies in not immediately withdrawing, and also, especially, the obstinacy of Ben Gurion, cumulatively annoyed him. Indeed, his manner, once angry and emotional, was now colder; he was set in his course. He had suffered and was suffering from shock over Russia's threats. He would not even see Australian Foreign Minister Casey, who was bringing a message from Menzies, Australia's Prime Minister.

Finally, Selwyn Lloyd did see Hoover, and on November 17, he and Sir Harold Caccia visited Dulles in the hospital. Dulles came forward in his easy clothes, slacks, sweater, slippers, with his shirt collar open—and shook hands. He said, *seriously*, "Well, once you started, why didn't you go through with it and get Nasser down?" Selwyn Lloyd answered, "Foster, why didn't you give us a wink?" Dulles

answered, "Oh! I couldn't
to say that this observation
This is not true. *Dulles was*
clinical exhibition, by dread
Nasser all along, evil Dulles
ning. He did not like it. Bu
from "going through with it
serious misgivings about the
his pet "colonial" statesmen.

Moscow would not let
unteers into the area of ho
partment and the White H
apprehension. On November
France and Israel, to the la
On November 16, therefore,
at the General Assembly of
about Russia's threats:

> Introduction of external forces into the area of hostilities would clearly hamper the efforts that are now being made and in fact would be a threat to the United Nations force now entering the area. The United Nations would be obligated to take appropriate action. President Eisenhower has announced that the United States would fully support such action.

It had become critically necessary to speak with force to the Soviet Union, because Moscow was extracting the maximum prestige advantage from the posture of being the only sincere friend of the Arabs, and also because a press statement of November 5 had given a first impression that when the Soviet Union said "we" would take action in Suez, "we" meant the Soviet Union alone. It was later explained by the Soviet Foreign Office that "we" meant the United Nations. Now, the United States wanted it to be clear beyond miscalculation that Russian action would be resisted.

As regards withdrawal from Suez and Sinai, Hoover urged immediate compliance. But it is almost sickening to hear the familiar refrain, in words which continued to be an escape from action calculated to give them any effect: "We must now act with equal promptness and unity to facilitate a settlement of the problems which gave rise to this emergency."

The rude answer to such facile talk came from the Indian delegate, Krishna Menon, on November 23, 1956. It was also the answer to the British contention,[21] that which had been much ventilated since November 7, that the word "immediately" in that day's Assembly resolution that forces should be withdrawn did not, and could not, mean "instantaneously." Lester Pearson had interpreted the word

ickly as *possible*"; that is, "there is an
n the withdrawal of the forces and the
f the UNEF." Lodge had used the inter-
drawal"; that is, with each phase of the arrival
here would occur a phase of withdrawal of the

oon put an end to this kind of tergiversation, and in
e provoked a violent convulsion within the U.S. delegation
United Nations, which, under Lodge, consisted of Dulles,
ors William Knowland and Hubert Humphrey, Paul G. Hoff-
an, and Elsworth Bunker; with, as alternates, former Ambassador J. J. Wadsworth, Richard L. Jones, Frank C. Nash, Edward S. Greenbaum, and Mrs. Oswald B. Lord. Some in this delegation resented the fact that the General Assembly could do nothing effective about the Russian atrocities in Budapest, but was in a hurry to bully America's allies. Senator Humphrey, the leading Democratic figure, became increasingly restive with the Lodge-Dulles-Eisenhower policy of yielding to Nasser, above all when the brunt of policy came more and more to be hostile to Israel. The Democratic Party leaders were well informed and briefed by him in the subsequent rally to the support of Israel.

For Menon led twenty Afro-Asian nations in presenting a resolution on November 23 to change the word "immediately" to "*forthwith*," that is, at once, or instantaneously; or, as one supporting Middle East politician put it, the British and French were to get out as swiftly, by plane and sea, as they had arrived!

Paul-Henri Spaak of Belgium, after days of behind-the-scenes conversations, had put an amendment to this resolution, to eliminate "forthwith," thus leaving the "phased" withdrawal interpretation in. He tried to influence Lodge, and succeeded in momentarily doing so, to such effect that Lodge, also influenced by the other members of the U.S. delegation (some of them strongly anti-Soviet), thought of voting for the Belgian amendment. At noon that day, a victorious vote seemed possible. The NATO countries pressed for such a vote and some Latin American countries asked why it was thought necessary to inflict another humiliation on America's allies. But the State Department was consulted. This meant that the President was consulted. This meant, further, that Dulles was consulted. And this resulted in Henry Cabot Lodge's being told to do what he had it in his heart to do before the nations of the Western world had begun to trouble his mind and conscience about justice and Russia and Western power. He led the abstentionists. The vote was 37 against the Belgian amendment and 24 for it, with 18 abstentions, including the United States. The French delegates judged that if the U.S.A. had voted against, so, too, would the Latin Americans.

Ambassador Abba Eban, appearing before the Assembly, pleaded against the "forthwith" resolution, and submitted how unrighteous it would be if all the events that had preceded October 29 in the Middle East were ignored, and if the Assembly declined to look beneath the surface "to the long and deep and tormenting story of a siege and state of belligerency which no other member of the international community has been called upon to endure." [22]

It was to no avail. Menon tried to have the question put even before all the delegations, some of whom had been waiting two days for their turn, had spoken. But for once Menon, after twenty years in the left-wing wilderness of London, was master in an arena where he could demonstrate that he was a world statesman of a virtue far superior morally to those who had so long ruled Britain and India, and to the Americans, also, and in parliamentary tactics, as "floor manager" of the Asian and African countries, a maestro. He said:

> It gives me no pleasure—on the contrary, it gives us much pain—to take up this position in regard to the United Kingdom, but they leave us no option. Time after time the Foreign Ministers have come forward and said, "We will move out when you do this and when you do that." That is not the language of a person who has committed a crime of aggression upon a people who had given *no provocation* in this respect.

The "forthwith" motion was adopted by 63 votes against 5, with 10 abstentions. The five were Britain, France, Israel, Australia, and New Zealand. The abstainers included the NATO countries of Italy, Holland, Belgium, and Luxembourg, plus China, Cuba, South Africa, the Dominican Republic, and Canada. It will be noticed that Australia and New Zealand were members of the British Commonwealth; as also Canada and South Africa. It throws serious dubiety on a far-fetched rumor that if the British had persisted at Suez, the Commonwealth would have been dissolved. This is nonsense. Even India would have receded from her veiled threats.

It was within the option of the U.S.A. at least to have abstained from voting. It did not, because it could be bullied by men like Menon. Furthermore, the original animus of American policy, Dulles's animus by which the President was affected, resumed its sway, and the reasoning prevailed among Lodge's circle that by voting for "forthwith" withdrawal, the United States would acquire greater influence with Nasser when it should come to a general Middle East settlement! Though his speech of November 24 tended to weaken the interpretation of "forthwith" [23] by harping on "phased" action, he nevertheless voted for the resolution, thus carrying water on both shoulders, as though this was not observed by the combatants for future use. It even gave Selwyn Lloyd some hope of not being hustled out of Suez!

It was one thing to vote this resolution and another to get it carried out. And in all probability it would not have been fulfilled for a very long time, perhaps not even until the toppling of Nasser, had not the United States exerted its power *outside* the United Nations, and unilaterally at that, and without any specific assignment of authority to do so by the United Nations. France and Britain would not have moved a man without this American coercion. The British and French governments and many of their leading politicians and citizens were especially antagonized by the United States, because Dulles and Hoover, pushing Lodge and inspired by his semi-hysteria, accepted the "forthwith" resolution before obtaining any compensatory pledges from Nasser through Hammarskjold, or even private assurances from Nasser that the clearance of the Canal could start at once.

Egypt gave abundant trouble at this point, true to its frenzied intransigence that had started all the trouble on July 26. The Secretary General was concerned from November 7 with getting the UNEF in place in Suez. He authorized General Burns to negotiate with Nasser for the immediate installation of the UNEF.[24] But Burns could not supply the answers to Nasser's insistent and conditional questions: How long was the force to remain? Where was it to be located? Was it going to operate the Canal? Therefore, Hammarskjold himself had to visit Nasser. It took him several days of negotiation, and it was November 20 before he could report the results to the U.N. Then he announced that Egypt had declared it would be guided by the resolutions setting up the UNEF and calling for withdrawal of the foreign military forces. Nasser imposed on Hammarskjold the condition that no Canal clearance could be started until the non-Egyptian forces were gone. This put the pressure on all nations who urgently needed passage through the Canal. Furthermore, he had imposed on Hammarskjold the idea that an international force would not be needed *in the Canal Zone*. Forces from New Zealand, Pakistan, and Canada were rejected by Nasser, who was supported in this also by Hammarskjold; two were British Dominions, while Pakistan was no friend of India and had been one of the supporters of the eighteen-power proposals.

No tyrant ruling a great power has ever surpassed Egyptian Foreign Minister Mahmoud Fawzi in his recalcitrant determination to do with the Canal what he, and he alone, wished. Interrogated by an NBC panel on *Meet the Press*, on November 25, he said: "All that the world is entitled to know about it [the control of the Canal by Egypt] is that we have no intention of exploiting anybody. What we do with the Canal is our own business." Having force on his side, there was not a millimeter of give in his position. "Intact" and "entire" were the words he had used in an earlier debate at the U.N. And now, he asked, if Egypt was right hitherto, why should she change her position?

The allied position was extremely difficult, also, because all pipelines from the oil fields to the Mediterranean, especially the one from Iraq through Syria, had been sabotaged by government-sponsored, and, it is rumored, Russian-instructed, agents, acting under cover of indignant labor unionists and such—excepting Tapline, which ran from Saudi Arabia to Lebanon.

A tense struggle now occurred behind the scenes in Washington. It was waged relentlessly and callously against Britain and France by President Eisenhower, Herbert Hoover, Jr., and Treasury Secretary George M. Humphrey, assisted from his convalescent home in Key West by Dulles, and encouraged and paced by Henry Cabot Lodge.

First, it is interesting to note Dulles's *ave* on emerging from Walter Reed Hospital on November 18, 1956, to fly to Florida. He said:

> As regards the Near East, we are, I think, on the right track. If the countries concerned show respect, as they have promised, for the opinions of mankind as expressed through the General Assembly of the United Nations, that will give reason for hope for further progress towards stable peace in that troubled part of the world. It would, however, be a great mistake to believe that stability and tranquility can be permanently established merely by emergency measures to stop the fighting. It is necessary to attack the basic problems of the area. The many nations which want peace must also be prepared to struggle for the conditions necessary for a just and durable peace.[25]

How harsh, however, the reality! Let us examine it.

Sir Winston Churchill must have sent President Eisenhower a letter about November 19 or 20, for the President replied to him in a long letter on November 23. It appears that Churchill was asking his old comrade in arms not to press so cruelly on the British government and especially on Prime Minister Eden. He pointed out, it seems, the damage being done to the NATO alliance to the benefit of the Soviet Union, and also Nasser's opening of the Middle East to the Russians. Could not the troubles be repaired, and the United States and the United Nations take advantage of the British presence in Suez to achieve a constructive settlement?

The President answered Sir Winston at some length, justifying his policy. He said: I tried earnestly to make Eden understand our position. For example, in my letter to him of July 31 (Chapter 4),

I asked him to avoid the use of force until it was proved to the world that the United Nations could not achieve a settlement. We must be especially aware of the position that Russia would take in a world situation if we invaded Egypt. It would be power politics, and we are not in favor of that. Nasser is an Egyptian Mussolini and we shall have to curb him somehow. But force, invasion, is not the way to correct the situation. Now I was given the news of the ultimatum by the newspapers. At once, we resolved to support the United Nations. Our policy was that the real enemy is the U.S.S.R. Nothing would please the United States government more than to see Britain restored in the Middle East, and we would not want the Soviet Union there. Furthermore, we shall help you with fuel and money. All we want is for Britain and France to let the UNEF in. We are not hostile to Britain and France, and there are people in Britain itself who resent the actions of the Government in relation to the United Nations. We want to be friends. It is bad that Britain has acted against the principles of the alliance—and bad also, that it has all been done so inefficiently. It is a sad thing that even from the angle of expediency the action has been so mismanaged. I think it is a sad matter that our friends are in trouble.

To this talk, straight from the heart, although not necessarily historically valid or politically justified, considering the extremely sorry role played by Dulles since July 26, Churchill merely answered: "Thank you! I agree with your main theme. I'll write more later." But the present author has not been able to find out whether he did, and it does not matter.

Both Britain and France were about to introduce gasoline rationing in order that the drain on supplies for industry and commerce should not become seriously damaging. The run on the pound and the franc was still grave. By November 15, Macmillan in an economic conference in Paris and Sir Harold Caccia in Washington had publicly pleaded for oil supplies, without which the industry of Europe would grind to a halt in a matter of months. Britain's gold reserves were dwindling at a rate for the whole month of November that amounted to one-eighth of the total.

By November 23, the date of the General Assembly debate when Krishna Menon had driven through his "withdrawal forthwith," with the support of Henry Cabot Lodge, serious misgivings had come over the Administration. They had begun to worry about the debilitating effects of their policy on their allies in NATO, and about the strength they were adding to Nasser's capacity for performing mischief in the Middle East. Indeed, both of these matters became grave concerns to the convalescent Dulles. For one item on the agenda of the very near future was the regular December meeting of NATO Ministers in Paris!

Eden was forced to take a vacation from his office by reason, his physician announced (and we know) of "serious overstrain." He transferred the duties of presiding over the Cabinet to R. A. Butler, associating Harold Macmillan with him in the leadership. On November 23, he left for Jamaica.

The President and his closest advisers, among them Admiral Radford, were now extremely anxious to repair the Anglo-American friendship in America's interests. For one thing, this anxiety was strongly urged on the White House by Robert Murphy and also by William Tyler of the European Division of the State Department. The latter all along had tenaciously, if disappointedly, striven to present the point of view of America's European interests. He had been unable to make any impression on Herbert Hoover, Jr. Pineau and Selwyn Lloyd had put the position of the British and French in Suez temperately but firmly at the United Nations meetings and in private to intermediaries since their arrival for the current session. Pineau had even tried to get in touch with Admiral Radford about November 15 in Washington. The State Department, that is, surely, Hoover, had at first forbidden the contact. But Pineau was persistent, and the State Department relented to the point of approving a visit by Radford to the French Embassy. Pineau then reported on the enormous stocks of Soviet war matériel that had been found by the Israeli army in Sinai, and argued it must have been deployed there to be ready for Russian volunteers. He promised to supply details.

However, the President was, as Sherman Adams puts it, "caught in a squeeze." He had committed himself to a position in the United Nations from which extrication was now hardly possible. A point of no return had been reached on November 2, one that should never have been created. Thereafter, it became harder and harder for the United States to conduct an alternative policy there of heroic import and dimensions and requiring a heroic character to accomplish it: that is, to mingle blame on the allies with blame on Nasser so that the Charter could be sustained in *both* of its pillars: justice *and* peace, if these were the formal terms in which the Charter demanded that one must *speak*. By now, it was hardly possible to effect a reversal. The President was on vacation in Augusta, Georgia. But in going forward, the President, moving along the lines Dulles and Lodge had rooted firmly in his mind and conscience (not without the ground itself being yielding), was obliged to humiliate further British and French pride and honor, and aggravate their loss of prestige and friendship in the Middle East and the rest of the world. Of course, they were holding on to Suez as long as possible. The President and his State Department associates were caught in the very awkward paradox of rebuking the allies in public, but trying to find ways in private of averting a disaster to them and winning back their intimacy in NATO. Even the

American Ambassadors in London and Paris were most anxiously involved in this process, and they even pressed Washington to act with good sense.

On November 26 and 27, Sir Harold Caccia called on Secretary of the Treasury George Humphrey. The British government, Caccia said, needed American support for withdrawing a substantial amount of money from the International Monetary Fund. Humphrey's answer was dry and rough. "You will not get a dime from the United States government if I can stop it, until you have gotten out of Suez! You are like burglars who have broken into somebody else's house. So get out! When you do, and not until then, you'll get help!" The Ambassador demurred to this rather too vivid portrait of his government's foreign policy, and politely observed that the British were in Suez, *where they had treaty rights that had been violated by Nasser;* that they were asserting their rights; and that, if they asserted them successfully, it would be not only to their benefit but to the benefit of the rest of the world as well. Humphrey scorned Caccia's explanation. He gruffly replied that all this was mere talk. "A moral issue is at stake, and even from the standpoint of my own personal morality, what the allies have done is morally wrong, and until the situation is righted, I personally could give no help whatever to them." Humphrey probably maintained the resentments of the days in which he had displayed "white-hot flashes of anger" (as described by a Washington reporter). To make quite sure that the British government understood the Administration's determination, Humphrey telephoned to London, to Deputy Prime Minister R. A. Butler.

All this was painful and heavy leverage, in spite of the fact that the lusty and pungent Secretary Humphrey himself would argue that he and his colleagues were only trying amicably to help the British out of a grave political and military mistake, which was especially the sick Prime Minister Eden's. In spite of the fact that he had claimed warm official "friendship" with Butler and Macmillan since 1953, the leverage is as plain as a pikestaff, and its purpose was, naturally, to implement *American* foreign policy, in support of her national interests, as fast as possible.

The American Embassy in London drew State Department attention to the tremendous anti-American feeling engendered by the latest phases of American policy in yielding to the passions of the United Nations. After the U.N. voting on November 24, no less than one-third of the Conservative Party, 110 M.P.'s, gathered together to draft a motion to be placed before the Commons condemning American policy and diplomacy. It was a protest also against the signs of yielding by Selwyn Lloyd and Macmillan and Butler to American pressure. The motion, drafted by November 26, read:

> That this House congratulates the Foreign Secretary on his efforts to secure international control of the Suez Canal and deplores both the resolution of the General Assembly calling for an immediate and unconditional withdrawal of British and French troops from Egypt and the attitude of America, which is gravely endangering the Atlantic alliance.[26]

If this attitude and temper persisted, then it seemed that the Conservative leaders would be repudiated if they submitted to America's policy, and that when the time should come for those leaders to ask the House for support in such submission, they would be abandoned by their followers.

Sherman Adams attended two meetings in "late November." Adams represented the President.[27] The others were Herbert Hoover, Jr., Admiral Radford, George Humphrey, Arthur Flemming, Secretary of Defense Charles Wilson, and some oil experts from the Department of the Interior. The President now wanted action, in the form of American support of her allies, as quickly as possible without violating his role at the United Nations. This is one of the reasons why Lodge pressed forward the arrival of the UNEF in the Suez area. Eisenhower still feared complications with the Soviet Union and perhaps Chinese volunteers. But, also, he could not supply oil to Britain and France while Hammarskjold's negotiations with Nasser were not yet concluded.

By about November 24, Hoover was ordered to press for the delivery of oil within a day or two, instead of holding out for a longer delay for strategic purposes. The ratiocinations at these meetings were interminable, puerile and amusing. The participants worried about the anger of the Arab world if the U.S.A. supplied the oil. They worried about Hammarskjold's displeasure for the same reason. Radford was obsessed with the fear that the Syrians would blow up Tapline: transport charges for oil from its Mediterranean outlet to Marseilles were ten times cheaper than oil from Galveston to Marseilles. The United States (through Aramco) had induced King Saud to keep open the Tapline from Saudi Arabia to the Mediterranean only by the promise that none of the oil would be supplied to the British or French. The group heard, privately, that the British had told Hammarskjold they would withdraw, but wanted Nasser to accept the UNEF first. Hoover now advocated furnishing supplies to the British,[28] who would induce France to withdraw, and claimed that the Israelis had told him they would also withdraw. But Humphrey feared that once Britain was assured of 75 per cent of the supplies, she might stay on in Suez. He held on to the last to the idea that there must be either an allied withdrawal or clear-cut pledges of withdrawal—the U.S.A. could not run out on its word.[29] Then Radford began to quake about the effects on NATO of being too rough with the British and French, yet he did not wish it to be thought they were forcing America's hand. Humphrey saw Nasser's point of view: [30] he should not be kept waiting another two weeks before the British gave assurances they would leave. And so on, and so on.

The group met again on November 29. Because Eden had physically collapsed, the men in the State Department were afraid the Conservative Government would fall; so was Eisenhower. The Conservative rank-and-file motion had an effect. Again and again, the members of the group rehearsed their fixed ideas. Now, Hoover pressed for a settlement: after all, NATO was to meet on December 10! They decided to tell the British that supplies of oil and dollars would be available on November 30, so that Selwyn Lloyd and the Conservatives could make political capital with this "good news" [31] over the week end. The Admiral thought that the U.S.A. was over a barrel,[32] since the Russians were calling the tune in Egypt. Finally, the plan of supply received approval at that day's meeting of the National Security Council, of which the group were members: 200,000 barrels a day would be added to the daily quota of 300,000 being shipped from the Gulf of Mexico and South American ports to Western Europe.[33] As Sherman Adams says, having, like his colleagues, so meager an understanding of the functioning of the Constitution of Britain: "Its Conservative Government remained in office."

Thus, the allies were to get their oil. After Lloyd's announcement in the House of Commons on December 3 that a phased withdrawal was being undertaken, the way was open for financial help as well. The government had little difficulty in carrying its supporters with it. On December 4, the British government requested permission to buy, with sterling, $1.3 billion in dollars and other currencies, to be paid back over three years. On December 10 permission was given. Secretary of the Treasury Humphrey was as good as his word: the burglar having left the premises burglariously entered, or having pledged to do so to Hammarskjold's satisfaction, he assisted the British in their currency difficulties with all energy and good will. Immediate interest payments on the debt owed to the U.S.A. were waived.

On December 8, *Tass* announced that the complete withdrawal of the British, French, and Israelis "naturally eliminates" the departure of Soviet volunteers for Egypt.

Dulles's policy to October 29 had failed to preserve the peace or secure justice. He used sanctions unilaterally against Britain and France to force them to bow to his policy. His power was exercised in part through and for the United Nations. The avowed purpose was to prevent the spread of a dreaded war—which, almost certainly, would *not* have come about. The opportunity to defeat Nasser was present. Neither the State Department, under Dulles and his substitute, Herbert

Hoover, Jr., nor the White House possessed the fortitude or the sagacious, realistic approach to the immediate problem and its inferential commitments which would have been necessary to solve it. They fled, instead, to the United Nations and a utopian view of its present and future possibilities, with what sincerity it is truly difficult to divine. The Administration was soon to regret what it had done, and some of its principal members were to admit explicitly they had been mistaken.

Dulles returned to Washington on December 3, restored in health, after two weeks at Key West. He had been kept *au courant* by Hoover, and had visited the President at Augusta, Georgia, on December 2. On December 5, 1956, the *New York Times* published an article by its distinguished foreign affairs commentator, C. L. Sulzberger, containing facts of immense portent for the future of American-European relations. He said that the effect of the Suez affair was to make it almost inevitable that *the French would seek independent atomic power*, so as never again to have to surrender to atomic blackmail as they had had to do when faced by the attitude of Moscow and Washington toward their national rights.[34] But independent nuclear capacity is intimately linked with and serves a more general independence of policy whether in Europe or outside it, and especially in regard to Russian demands all over the world. The morale of NATO was enfeebled: it was a very big price to pay for American obeisance to Dulles's righteousness concerning "colonialism" and the passions of Arabs and Asians, and all his mistaken beliefs and misjudgments about these, shared so zealously by the President.

Dulles now had to face his allies at the NATO meeting set for December 10. Its agenda included a subject unpleasantly relevant to the recent trouble, the report of the Committee of Three on Nonmilitary Cooperation in NATO: the members were Gaetano Martino, Halvard Lange, and Lester B. Pearson, the Foreign Secretaries of Italy, Norway, and Canada. The report dealt with the subjects of consultation among allies, and the ignoring of allies' interests, when convenient, by others of the allies.

Dulles carefully prepared the ground for his advent among the Europeans. The major effort in this direction, apart from the consultations with George M. Humphrey, Secretary of Defense Wilson (both of whom were to attend the NATO meeting), and the rest of the staff, was the drawing up of an elaborate, full-scale state paper in the form of a speech to be delivered by the chosen instrument, Vice President Nixon, on December 6.

This speech [35] consisted of a comprehensive and prideful claim of American victory, morally, tactically, and in knowledge and wisdom, in the "great events of the last forty days." It contained many patent errors of fact, full discussion of which would be out of proportion here. Its main theme was the One Law, established so curiously on October 31. "Lesser men would have sought easy vote-getting solutions on the eve on an election. They [Eisenhower and Dulles] chose statesmanship and high moral principle." However, the point of the speech (Dulles's composition), besides the fervent and uncompromising vindication of the American position, was to extend an olive branch to the down-trodden allies. This part was hardly consistent with the superior self-approval of the rest:

> First, with regard to our alliances, it is essential that we recognize that history may record that neither we nor our allies were without fault in our handling of the events which led to the crisis in which we now find ourselves. Our friends believe that we did not appreciate adequately the provocation which brought about their action and that we did not assume our proper responsibility in working out a settlement of the basic problems existing in that area.
>
> We, on the other hand, felt that we had some legitimate criticisms to make of their policies during this period.
>
> Now is the time for us all to recognise that recriminations and fault-finding will serve no purpose whatever. The cause of freedom could suffer no greater disaster than to allow this or any other incident to drive a wedge between us and our allies.

And so on. "Provocation," is surely a vast understatement of "vital interest" and "lifeline" and "Sword of Damocles."

Once again words were uttered that we have shown by the narration of the facts to be false. For Nixon said:

> It is to their lasting credit that they [Britain and France] accepted the decision of the United Nations when they agreed to a cease-fire and to a withdrawal of their forces even when they believed that this decision was not in their best interests.

They withdrew, in fact, because the United States privately manifested its direct and bitter hostility against them, as well as making use of the United Nations to beat upon Eden's conscience. Dulles knew this, and so did his allies. Another statement in Nixon's speech was almost as dubious:

> Inevitably, if a friendship or alliance survives a period of adversity, it is stronger in the end than it would have been otherwise.

Actually, the meeting of NATO that began on December 10, 1956, was extremely painful to the leaders of the Western allies, America, Britain, and France, and to the European friends of the latter two. The military commanders, like Admiral Radford, could more easily forget the recent rift among allies than could the political leaders, for they regarded those rifts among "two or three" men as nothing fundamental, since the military "hardware" and military comprehension was for them the truly basic matter, and here there was solidarity. As for Dulles, Lloyd, and Pineau, they avoided Suez and talked about other things. All of them were hit, and surely Dulles most of all, whether he felt it sensitively or not, by the report of the Three. It said:

> Interallied relations have also undergone severe strains. The substance of this report was prepared . . . in the course of its meetings and intergovernmental consultations last September. Subsequent events have reinforced the Committee's conviction that the Atlantic Community can develop greater unity only by working constantly to achieve common policies by full and timely consultation on issues of common concern. Unless this is done, the very framework of cooperation in NATO, which has contributed so greatly to the cause of freedom, and which is so vital to its advancement in the future, will be endangered.
> . . . An Alliance in which the members ignore each other's interests or engage in political or economic conflict, or harbour suspicions of each other, cannot be effective either for deterrence or defence. Recent experience makes this clearer than ever before.[36]

Although it was open to Dulles to regard these admonitions, in his self-righteousness, as directed not against him, but his allies, it was borne in on him by the lesser powers that he was mainly to blame for the current tension. He was most resentful and angry at the suggestion. Now, after the trauma of his sickness and of his failure to avert war, and with the gnawing and increasing realization that Nasser had won not only over his allies but over *him,* his feelings were hard to contain. He was even more hostile to Selwyn Lloyd and the English than before. He therefore assumed what flowed straight from his character: a very high-handed, almost contemptuous, manner of exclusive rectitude.

The Secretary threw his weight about at the meeting, taking the stance of a moral and military victor. The *Times* (London) of December 12 reported that he admonished the European members of NATO; he pointed out that grave injustices were not grounds for the resort to force, that restraint under great provocation was a proof of moral strength and "created a moral climate which stimulated and encouraged the forces which were destroying the Soviet system." This attitude of Dulles's hurt the allies badly. For Nasser had been allowed to seize the Canal and to violate a treaty. Some British politicians and some Cabinet members were revolted at being "lectured" to, being "bullied," and having "sermons" addressed against

Britain and France. The man could simply not stop! In the *New York Times* of December 3, he must surely have read the article that began with the Biblical quotation: "Thou hypocrite, first cast out the beam out of thine own eye; and then shalt thou see clearly to cast out the mote of thy brother's eye."

Moreover, Dulles was adamant in maintaining that NATO had only limited claims on United States foreign policy. From behind the closed doors, the *New York Times* and the *Times* (both of December 14) were able to report that Dulles had told the Committee of Three the United States would not subject its policies or actions, in the defense of Taiwan, for example, to prior consultation with its Atlantic pact allies. He was driving home the lesson that America would shape her policy outside Europe as it suited her interests, even if European interests and tranquility were harmed.

In spite of the pleasant remarks that Nixon had made, Mollet and Pineau responded in terms that foreshadowed the loosening of the bonds between France and the United States. The alliance was not being destroyed by Moscow, but by Dulles's driving egoism—of course, in the name of America.

A close intimate surely goes too far when he says that, like his allies, Dulles ignored the recently inflicted wounds, but, transcending their magnanimity, he sought to bind up their wounds with Lincolnian tenderness! From the European point of view Dulles attended the NATO meeting as either a clumsy meddler or a clever deceiver and outwitter. He spoke on December 11 in the spirit of a draft paragraph (unpublished) that remains in his papers at Princeton.

> Heretofore the concept of the "just war" has been deeply rooted even in religious belief. But there is a growing tendency to doubt that modern war can, in fact, eliminate more injustices than war inevitably inflicts. Both morality and expediency now reject deliberate resort to war as an instrument of national policy. That, indeed, is our engagement.

This, even from a mighty country that is well satiated, is hardly a sympathetic, and therefore hardly a prudent, understanding of nations who are less mighty; and considering American military presence in Formosa, Okinawa, Korea, and South Vietnam, and considering the U.S. Marine landings in Lebanon to come within eighteen months, and control of the Panama Zone, the pontification leaves a sour taste.

Selwyn Lloyd was obliged to raise with Dulles a most serious development. The British and French had promised to evacuate Suez without specific conditions. But, soon, under the prompting of Russia, Nasser threatened reprisals for injury done him, against British property and persons in Egypt, and decrees were already issued to put this threat into effect by the time NATO met. Selwyn Lloyd did not intrude this British worry on Dulles until the NATO meeting was over. Then he explained the difficulties, suggesting that British troops remain until they were settled. All of Dulles's overbearing rancor was now evinced. If the British did not go, it would be regarded as a breach of faith "on the part of the Administration with Congress and United States public opinion." He maintained that [British] action had caused revulsion throughout the United States. "Throughout," even allowing for the data of the Gallup polls, was a vast exaggeration. And even the antipathy of those in America who disapproved of the Suez invasion was to a large degree produced by the Administration's own shaping of the facts, not least through a press that was, in any case, and for every other political reason, loyal to President Eisenhower. Actually, Hammarskjold was more comprehending than Dulles and Hoover about the deliberateness of the allied evacuation of Suez! At this time Nasser subjected French and British citizens and especially Jews who lived in Egypt to brutal persecutions, so bad that the French and the Israeli Governments appealed to the United Nations.[37]

The withdrawal was complete by December 23, 1956.

After his return to Washington, at a press conference on December 18, 1956, the Secretary reiterated his attitude towards his allies and towards NATO. He strongly defended U.S. policy in the Suez affair, and particularly the action taken by him in the United Nations, but not on the basis that the British and French had failed to consult with him on the Suez attack. He admitted that they had been consulting for three months, on three occasions in London and then at the Security Council meeting in October. He now introduced a theme that had apparently never entered into any of the documents or voiced communication that passed between him and the President and the allies from July 26 to the day of this press conference. It was this:

> We considered that such an attack under the circumstances would violate the Charter . . . , and would violate Article 1 of the North Atlantic Treaty itself, which requires all parties to that treaty to renounce the use of force, and to settle their disputes by peaceful means.[38]

But Britain and France were not making war on the U.S.A. or any of the other parties to NATO; and Egypt was not a member of NATO. The interpretation, even if it had been offered during the process of negotiation since July 26, would have been an overstrained one. How difficult, therefore, Britain and France found it to accept an observation Dulles made about the meeting in Paris.

> I would not go so far as to say that there are still no scars that remain—no differences about past performance. But the best way to forget the past is to be planning for the future. . . . As we think about the future, and plan for the future together, there tends to be a healing of the old wounds and I think that process is under way.

But that was not the answer, it was only the question; for the wounds were not superficial and the scars were not merely on the skin. It was in the cards that as soon as their nations were economically stronger, some of the European leaders would not ever again expose themselves to the tactics and morals of another power with the subservience they had been forced to show in the summer and fall of 1956.

As usual, Dulles was perfectly briefed about the contents of Article 1 of the NATO Treaty. Its provisions had not, however, deterred President Truman from going to war in Korea in advance of his allies' approval or the U.N.'s consent, and he had done so with Dulles's previous support of the policy. Nor had Article 1 been allowed to stand in the way of Dulles's threats of force against Communist China and in Indo-China. This sudden charge, made in public, against America's NATO allies was hardly calculated to increase their affection for Dulles, their trust in the U.S.A. as an ally, their degree of loyalty to NATO itself. The recrimination was in timing and manner exactly what they regarded as hitting below the belt: it was legal, but it was not fair. It is so reminiscent of the previously-quoted observation made by one of America's Ambassadors during this episode, specifically *à propos* of the rescinding of the Aswan loan: "He kicked them in the teeth with a missionary twist." It could not be surprising if proud men in proud nations resolved never to submit to a similar indignity in the future if they could help it.

Moreover, Dulles's allies were possessed of a truth which neither Dulles nor Eisenhower revealed to the opinion of the world. It was exposed by Sherman Adams.[39] On February 20, 1957, Eisenhower met with Congressional leaders because he had to contemplate sanctions against Israel to secure the evacuation of Sinai. Disarmingly, the President disclosed that ". . . THE UNITED STATES HAD APPLIED SANCTIONS ONLY THREE MONTHS AGO AGAINST THE UNITED KINGDOM AND FRANCE FOR EXACTLY THE SAME PURPOSE WHEN OIL FROM THE GULF OF MEXICO AND THE CARIBBEAN WAS WITHHELD UNTIL THESE POWERS AGREED TO WITHDRAW FROM EGYPT." But the public had been led to believe by the President and Dulles that the moral power of the United Nations and the Christian commitment of the United States had done the job. It was not a truthful education for the American people or the leaders and masses of Britain and France: they felt cheated.

* * * * *

This chapter deserves a colophon to the capitulation of British and French leaders under the pressure of American sanctions induced by Dulles's and Eisenhower's retreat before Russian power. It concerns two facets of the Suez affair. The first is the errors made by the British and French, the second is the respective fates of Nasser and Eden at American hands.

British writers hostile to British and French war on Egypt believe that their statesmen made four errors. The first was to think that Russia's troubles in Poland and Hungary would prevent her from action in the Middle East. It is, however, doubtful whether the allied statesmen ever entertained such a belief. The second error alleged, was not to let Israel win the military victory over Nasser alone. Israel would have soon brought down Egypt and have caused such a loss of face on Nasser's part that he must have fled. But this contention assumes that the United States would have allowed Israel to win such a triumph, and it fails to weigh the allied concern that other Arab nations, driven to Pan-Arab desperation and assisted by Moscow via Syria, would have felt compelled to make war on Israel. The third alleged error was to mount an attack on Suez so massive and complicated that it dragged until overtaken by hostile forces inside and outside the U.N. This point is sound. If the allied claim was self-defense, then the possibility of "bloodless surgery" should have been discarded and a swift and heavy assault undertaken. The fourth error was the allied failure to inform Eisenhower that they were going to attack. It was an error.

At the emotional climax of President Eisenhower's meeting in his office on November 5, when the message from Ambassador Bohlen in Moscow was read that fighting in the Middle East must be stopped to avert Russian intervention, Herman Phleger, Legal Counsel to the State Department and Dulles's very intimate confidant, made a pregnant observation. He said: the situation was now such that either Nasser must fall—or Eden. The President, on this note, brought the discussion with his advisers to a close with the tart commentary: "All I can say is—it's one hell of a way to conduct a *world* election." (He had in mind next day's election for the Presidency.)

He and Dulles were not, however, engaged in an election, but in a selection, the selection of the values that were to prevail in the world. And what was the choice that had been presented to them? They all knew that Nasser had been an assassin and that he still suppressed the native Egyptian opposition to him by naked force and practiced assassination vicariously in all the Arab lands by encouragement and funds. They also knew that he had meant it when he had said: "And now I go back to the wandering role for a hero to play it." But Eden? Aneurin Bevan, his bitterest opponent, by social class and political creed, could not help but pay him the grudging tribute: "They [the Cabinet] have been synthetic villains. They are not really villains. They have only set off on a villainous course, and they cannot even use the language of villainy." [40]

It was between two claimants, both crystallizing their national positions, that Dulles and Eisenhower had had to choose, and they had chosen Nasser.

17. ISRAEL RESISTS THE "DOUBLE LAW"

ISRAEL HAD TWO ASSETS WHICH PROTECTED HER TO A CERTAIN EXTENT from Dulles's United Nations policy and American economic threats. The nation was fighting for sheer survival, whereas Britain and France had only sought their vital interests. Important as vital interests may be, the world recognizes the difference. Moreover, the nation that fights for its survival feels that difference, and so, with the exception of the small number of Israeli Communists, Israel was not only united, but united by a spirit of the highest militant morale. It intended to endure, whatever the political or moralistic necessities and casuistries of Eisenhower and Dulles, whatever the threats of its enemies in the United Nations, the legalisms of Secretary General Hammarskjold, or the heroic delirium of Lodge.

The Israeli case in the United States and the United Nations was represented by an exceptionally gifted delegation. It was headed by Abba Eban, a talented diplomat especially known for his distinguished oratory. All of the members of the delegation were imbued with the vitality and reveringness of the Old Testament, its promises, its proverbs, its Psalms, its Commandments. They demanded the respect for their national independence that the Arabs were demanding and getting. They defied Eisenhower and Dulles to the last point. Fortunately for them, they were able to appeal to Congress to redress the overimpetuous and irrational loyalty of the State Department and the White House to Secretary General Hammarskjold and the clamor of the Arabs and Asians. Israel, of course, obtained no support or sympathy from Nehru or Menon.

Yet Ben Gurion was under *force majeure* to bend to a great extent to Washington's pressure. In the first flush of victory, on November 7, he had spoken in strong victorious terms to the Knesset. But, crossing this speech on the same day, was the letter from Eisenhower (Chapter

16) and a message to be delivered by the American Embassy. Both were in the severest terms, the message especially so, even though Israel was demonstrating she intended no further military action. They threatened the cessation of "friendly cooperation between our two countries." Ben Gurion changed his public tone. He answered (November 8) that Israel would withdraw after a UNEF had entered the Canal region. However, as previously indicated, the pressure that brought about this sharp change was not merely economic or American: it was Russian. Rumors of Russian encouragement of Syria, including a considerable arming of that country, had reached Israel; she faced attack from the north. The American message, delivered orally, made it clear that if a Russian attack or a Russian-assisted attack came, Israel could not count on American help.

It appears also that Paris and London (especially London), by now at Washington's mercy, forcefully indicated that they would not be able to assist Israel against such an attack either. Selwyn Lloyd put the maximum pressure on the Israeli Ambassador to London, Eliahu Elath, in a long and tenacious conversation on the afternoon of November 8. The Ambassador tried to get assurances of a nonaggression treaty with Egypt; a peace treaty guaranteed by the powers; a defensible frontier; the end of the Arab boycott; free passage for Israeli ships and foreign ships bound for Israeli ports through Suez and Aqaba. Lloyd and his officials were more interested in Israeli withdrawal to "save Nuri Es Said" of Iraq. These foreign interventions caused a paroxysm of reconsideration in the Israeli Cabinet meetings and in a conference that was called of all Israeli political party leaders except the Communists. But Ben Gurion did not intend to lose all the fruits of war; some guarantees of his nation's security, he regarded as indispensable.

On November 8, Israeli Foreign Minister Golda Meir sent a letter to the U.N. to inform the Secretary General that Israel would willingly withdraw its forces from Sinai. She noted in this, however, that in accepting the withdrawal and the arrival of the UNEF, "we must repeat our urgent request to the U.N. to call upon Egypt, which has consistently maintained that it is in a state of war with Israel, to renounce that position, to abandon its policy of boycott and blockade, to cease the sending into Israel of murder gangs, and in accordance with its obligations under the U.N. Charter to live at peace with Member States, to enter into direct peace negotiations with Israel." [1] Ben Gurion's letter to President Eisenhower of November 8 reiterated this point.[2] The Israeli spokesmen insisted on guarantee of Egypt's policy and intentions with respect to belligerency toward or peace with Israel.[3]

During December, 1956, and January, 1957, the Israeli forces were pulled back almost entirely, with the exception of those located in two places.[4] One was the area of Sharm el-Sheik, the strip on the western coast of the Gulf of Aqaba which controls the freedom of navigation through the Straits of Tiran and in the Gulf. The Israeli government was prepared to enter into conversations with the Secretary General on this matter. Furthermore, Israel still held the Gaza Strip, overseeing its military and civil administration. This issue, again, the Israeli government wished to discuss with the Secretary General. Israel was also asking for protection against raids across the original armistice lines.

Hammarskjold's policy was complete surrender of Israel to the dictates of the U.N. resolutions and of Hammarskjold's arrangements and interpretations of the Charter and of the merely cease-fire arrangements of the UNEF. The Israelis were to withdraw without conditions. He could not protect them from Arab raids, except by admonitions. He once again paraded the promises of "constructive tasks" after the UNEF had fulfilled its function "to help maintain quiet." [5]

The problem of getting Israel to quit Sharm el-Sheik and the Gaza Strip became, at this point, entangled in a pattern of policy that Dulles was forced to weave for the handling of Middle East problems, called the Eisenhower or Middle East Doctrine. He was under this compulsion because his policy and behavior had allowed Nasser to grow in power and to swell in the head. The Doctrine was before Congress from early January, 1957, until its acceptance and financing on March 9, 1957, The Congressional resolution that embodied the Doctrine declared that the United States regarded as vital to the national interest (that is, America's) and world peace the preservation of the independence and integrity of the nations of the Middle East. To that end, if the President determined the necessity thereof, the United States was prepared to use armed forces to assist any such nation or group of nations requesting assistance against any country controlled by international Communism. (The United Nations was not consulted on this declaration of American national interest.) This idea had begun to agitate Dulles on his return from the NATO meeting, December 17.[6]

By this time, State Department staff meetings were hard at work on the problem of creating a Middle East counterweight to the swollen Nasser. For the Israeli army had uncovered Russian arms, and the most terrible shocks had been given to American policy makers by Russia's insolent, bold, clever, and successful activity in the Suez crisis. Dulles meant to counteract that threat to the United States (as the British and French had begged him to do earlier), if not to extirpate it. Russian action had robbed the American exhibition of practical Christian nobility of any meaning for the Arabs—who thought their practical savior to be the Soviet Union, as it was.

The policy, translated from Dulles's Latinized lawyer's English into the vulgate of his immediate entourage, ran almost verbatim as follows. "We must create a counterweight to Nasser, because he is so heady. So Ibn Saud ought to come over here for friendly talks. We can ask him: Why do you not take a more commanding lead in the Arab world? Nasser will raise hell! And he did. So King Saud stuck to the idea of the visit. Because after the wreckage of Suez, Dulles was not going to let Nasser get ahead. A motive of the Middle East Doctrine was to get a lever against Nasser. Just because we [*sic*] had forced Britain and France and Israel *out*, we were not going to let him be the tin god of the Middle East. [How strange and exact an echo of the arguments of Eden and Mollet!] Therefore, build up Saud; curb Nasser."

King Saud arrived January 29, 1957. After many talks, a joint communiqué was issued on February 8; it was quite subtle. The two governments would try to settle justly Middle East problems within the framework of the United Nations Charter. They opposed force from any source as a means of settling international disputes. Independence, peace, economic freedom, and prosperity were the aim of the Middle East peoples; and any aggression against their political independence or territorial integrity, or intervention from any source in their affairs, would be opposed in accordance with U.N. principles and purposes. The King intended to cooperate closely with the United States, and carried the express wishes of other Arab states to do so also. As for the Middle East Doctrine, the King "received this exposition with satisfaction and assured President Eisenhower that he welcomed every step that promotes the United Nations principles respecting independence, sovereignty of States, and self-determination of peoples."

The U.S.A. would provide military and economic assistance to Saudi Arabia, and would be permitted the use of the Dhahran airfield for another five years. And what a status was assigned by the communiqué to Saudi Arabia!

> Saudi Arabia, by virtue of its spiritual, geographical and economic position, is of vital importance in the Middle East. It is in the interests of world peace that this kingdom be strengthened for the maintenance of its own stability and the safeguarding and progressive development of its institutions.

After he left the United States, King Saud attended the conference of heads of Arab states held in Cairo on February 25; and in the meanwhile he had sent his brother to see Nasser in Cairo, for political reinsurance. Nasser's star was far too high in the ascendant, placed there and burnished by Dulles's policies, to be outshone by Saudi Arabia, and the King knew it.

However, while he was in the United States, he insisted, of course, on the prompt and full exit of Israel from Sinai. Therefore, Dulles and Eisenhower exerted ever greater pressure on Israel. As the Israeli forces withdraw, the areas they had held were occupied by UNEF forces, for instance, El Arish by Yugoslavs; southern Sinai by Indians. Again and again the General Assembly also repeated its resolutions and speeches: Israel must quit forthwith. The Secretary General demanded that the original *status juris* be restored. Egypt denounced any such settlement as Ben Gurion requested. Out, they cried, without conditions!

It was noticed that in the resolution of January 17, to this effect, 74 votes against those of Israel and France, *Britain was suddenly missing from the supporters of Israel.* The French privately very much deplored this grim, cold egoism of the British government. As for the United States, Henry Cabot Lodge, still hotly pursuing peace, supported the resolution as reasonable and moderate. But he *hoped* that in the two areas in contention, which had been "major sources of tension in the past," UNEF forces would be deployed in such a way as, "to be in a position to prevent a recurrence of hostile activities." This hope was endorsed by the British spokesmen. But Israel was still insisting on January 17 on satisfactory assurances regarding the questions she had asked as far back as November 4 at the U.N. Did Egypt still maintain she was at war with Israel, as she had declared over the years? Was Egypt prepared to enter into immediate peace talks with Israel? Did Egypt agree to cease her economic and Suez blockade against Israel? Did Egypt undertake to recall *fedayeen* under her control in other Arab countries?

On January 23, 1957, Ben Gurion declared in the Knesset that Israel would *not* withdraw from either Sharm el-Sheik or the Gaza Strip until it had the guarantees it demanded. Israel, further, was ready to sign a nonaggression pact with Egypt! Ben Gurion's detailed proposals were presented by Ambassador Eban to Hammarskjold and circulated to all member nations. At this Lodge, Dulles, and Eisenhower, growing more impatient and angry day by day, called on Israel to withdraw, using the choice word found by Krishna Menon for Britain and France, "forthwith." Lodge then used the language of oblique threat: "I cannot predict the consequences if Israel fails to comply with the resolution." Dulles and Eisenhower had committed themselves to Saudi Arabia; they had to deliver. The Israeli Cabinet on February 3 persisted obstinately in its attitude: no withdrawal without guarantees. Israel was determined to develop her Red Sea port of Elath, her link with the world by sea otherwise than via the Suez Canal, and for this purpose she needed free passage through the Gulf of Aqaba.

At this time, the drive of American policy, especially in relation to Israel, ran through two intermingling courses. One was represented by Hammarskjold, Lodge, and Eisenhower. This was emotional, moralistic, and legalistic. Its very insistence on the letter of the law *now*, without any insistence on the letter of the law for Egypt in the Suez or Israeli-Egypt conflict, could have led, in Israel's judgment, to two things: (a) a repetition of Israel's danger, for Russia would surely replace Egypt's lost armaments; and (b) the extinction by political and legal means of Israel's great military victory and of the consequent loss of face for Nasser. The other current was represented by Dulles, Herman Phleger, and Robert Murphy. The first two had been compelled by bitter experience to recognize the need for some elasticity towards Israel's needs and demands, in order to produce stability: Murphy's wisdom had always understood that. Dulles had gone through many injuries to his pride, in personal affronts and in the collapse of his meticulously built house of cards, with its flimsy walls of peace and justice leaning on each other's weakness. He was also being chastened very severely by the Senate Foreign Relations Committee and by the House Committee on Foreign Affairs. Here, all his mistakes in the Middle East were dissected from every side with skillfully used scalpels, not by the Democratic Party only.

Until the end of January, the first of these courses, that of Hammarskjold, Lodge, and Eisenhower, prevailed.

Meanwhile, the Israeli Embassy and its press officials undertook a steady and persuasive campaign of public enlightenment of its position. The prestige of Israel was high because its military victory had been truly brilliant, and the American public—"throughout," in Dulles's phrase—was glad that Nasser had been given two black eyes. Israel's effective argument was that only two points of explosion in the Middle East, so far as Israel was concerned, existed: Aqaba and Gaza. Surely they ought to be solved? Democratic Party leaders, Lyndon B. Johnson, Hubert Humphrey, and J. W. Fulbright, had considerable sympathy for Israel's pleas. Delay assisted Israel's appeals for her security.

Dulles advised the President to bring pressure to bear on Prime Minister Ben Gurion. This, *in paraphrase*, is what President Eisenhower wrote to him on February 3, 1957:

> I attach the greatest importance to the United Nation's resolution on the ending of hostilities in Egypt. In your [Ben Gurion's] letter of November 7 you said you would withdraw to the armistice line according to the U.N. resolution of November 2. I was gratified by your reply. Now nearly three months have passed. The British and French have gone, but Israel has *not*. This delay in implementing the U.N. resolution has resulted in continuing tension in the Near East and has impaired our efforts to find a settlement with lasting solutions of peace. On February 1,

two further resolutions were passed by the U.N. . . . Provision has been made for the UNEF to enter on the demarcation lines, to achieve peaceable conditions, according to Hammarskjold's report of January 25, etc. Other nations have joined in sponsoring these resolutions. I believe the Secretary General's report lays the foundation for a sound peaceful conclusion in the area of former hostilities regarding Gaza and Sharm el-Sheik. The essential first step is that Israel must withdraw behind the demarcation line. I earnestly hope that that will be done without delay.

We wish friendly relations with Israel and the cooperation that has contributed to Israel's development to continue. I feel warranted in urging most seriously the compliance with the United Nations steps to secure tranquillity and justice regarding Egypt and the neighboring lands.

The continued ignoring of these views will result in the invocation of further United Nations procedures which will disturb relations between all nations and the U.S.A. The United Nations has tried constructive action and I hope you will do the same. We have done much to settle matters fairly and I hope you too will make contributions.

This letter seemed to foreshadow the possibility of sanctions against Israel: the Arab countries and their supporters in the Asian lands and the Soviet bloc were raging. But, apart from the political difficulties of getting a two-thirds majority for sanctions, there was the legal difficulty that the General Assembly had only the power to recommend, not enact.

Dulles was affected by the possibilities currently retailed to him by Eban of renewed hostilities in the Middle East if a basic change were not made in the conditions that had contributed to bringing on the friction in the first place. He was also caught on the other horn of his dilemma: the imposition of sanctions was highly unpopular in the United States and abroad; and uncertainty in the Middle East continued. However, he was not unwilling to threaten physical pressure against a weak opponent.

Hence, Dulles and Eisenhower, in public, manipulated the threat of sanctions. Dulles spoke as follows at his news conference of February 5, 1957:

> . . . We would not take any action in the way of sanctions unilaterally. If there was action by United Nations calling for sanctions, we would of course have to give them very serious consideration. . . . We have good ground to hope, at least, that this resolution will be complied with and we have not gone on to think what would happen if it did not. Ambassador Lodge made the statement if it was not complied with it could not be predicted what would happen. I would prefer myself not to make that prediction.[7]

Sanctions were not directly threatened, but unmistakably insinuated, with Dulles's verbal craft at its best.

Prime Minister Ben Gurion replied to the President on February 8.[8] He was most courteous and firm. He explained the enormous extent to which Israel had already evacuated the Sinai Peninsula, and noted that the only place still held there was the narrow strip at the Gulf of Aqaba. It would be evacuated also as soon as the United Nations could guarantee Israel freedom of passage through the Gulf. He reminded the President of the eight years during which Egypt had disregarded the armistice agreement, the Charter, and the U.N. resolution regarding passage through the Canal, and of the pledge (broken) by Egypt to respect freedom of passage at Aqaba (to the American Ambassador, Cairo, January 28, 1950). As for the Gaza Strip, Israel would leave it if a civil administration and police force were set up so that they would remain in a suitable relationship with the U.N. This arrangement would certainly benefit the local population, largely Palestinian refugees, *not* Egyptians. Ben Gurion deplored the fact that different standards were applied to Egypt, a violator of United Nations resolutions, and to Israel. Why? "Are we not, like other States, entitled to security from attack?" He went on to ask the President, with deepest respect, why "*no effective action was taken by the government of the United States*" and the U.N. to give Israel such security?

The Israeli Prime Minister then took up the implied threat about "procedures" to be undertaken in the U.N. against Israel. Such procedures had never been invoked against Egypt! "Is it conceivable that the United States, the land of freedom, equality and human rights, should support such discrimination and that United Nations 'procedures' should be invoked to force us back into a position which would again expose us to murder and blockade?"

His peroration was remarkable, and deserves full quotation.

> Mr. President, in the Law which we received more than three thousand years ago on Mount Sinai and which has become part of mankind's heritage, the message went forth that there shall be no discrimination between man and man and between nation and nation. Throughout millennia of persecution our people have not lost faith in ultimate justice, peace and human equality. It is unthinkable that now that we have recovered our independence in our ancient homeland we should submit to discrimination. Our people will never accept this no matter what sacrifice it may entail. Israel though small is entitled to security, freedom and equal rights in the family of nations. Like any other independent nation Israel is free as of right and our people are determined to defend their independence.

> The question is not a legalistic one. It affects the very foundations of international morality: will the United Nations apply one measure to Egypt and another to Israel? . . .
>
> More than any man now living, you, Mr. President, may be able to help in putting an end to all this hostility and establishing peace between our neighbours and ourselves.
>
> Permit me in conclusion to thank you for your kind interest in my well-being, which I deeply appreciate.

The letter had not the slightest effect on the President. His advisers had led him to prefer the Arab case and he had just sat at a state banquet with King Saud. He, personally, could by his own judgment and discretion not act flexibly towards Ben Gurion's just plea. Furthermore, voices in the State Department repeated: "If Israel had not joined France, there would have been no Suez affair!"

Dulles was now subjected to a battering by a number of warring forces, the diversity and weight of which the President did not comprehend. In various guises and manner of expression they tenaciously continued through until March, 1957.

Dulles desperately needed the speedy withdrawal of Israel from Sinai. For this Israel asked a price. If an injustice were done to Israel, then he would find it difficult, perhaps impossible, he did not know, to secure Democratic support and Republican votes for the Middle East Doctrine. But if he pressed Nasser to yield something to Israel, he would only stir Nasser's resentments, and these, as Ambassador Raymond Hare well knew by now, would include an exacerbation of the rancor which obstructed the clearance of the Canal. Here again, his allies pressed him hard: they wanted the Canal open to passage: they were losing wealth because oil supplies were not coming through. Nasser offered every kind of fake reason for obstructing General Wheeler's clearance force. Dulles bitterly resented the brutality of Nasser towards him and the U.N., as well as the protraction of the period necessary for nursing NATO back to health. Meanwhile, the Russians made capital out of Israel's refusal to quit without conditions and American reluctance to subject Israel to sanctions.

It was necessary to work behind the scenes. On February 11, 1957, Dulles in consultation with the Israeli Ambassador prepared an *aide-mémoire* on Aqaba and Gaza. He was extremely firm with Eban that on the response to this offer would turn the question whether American-Israeli relations would become much better or worse. Eban even wondered whether Dulles was threatening him with some kind of *force*. Dulles persisted with the contention that had so frightened him and was used by him to frighten others: World War III might break out if the Israelis persisted. Then, further, Dulles argued with Eban, Egypt would some day recuperate; she might fight again; and she might very well be helped by the Soviet Union. What would happen to Israel then? Hence, Dulles concluded, with his own mixed metaphor, "The United States was at the rock bottom of its concessions, as the Soviet Union was on a good wicket internationally."

The *aide-mémoire* [9] recognized that Gaza had been the source of armed infiltration into Israel. Therefore, the U.S. government believed that the Secretary General of the U.N. should seek to have the UNEF move into the area and stand on the boundary between Israel and the Gaza Strip. The U.S.A. also declared its belief that the Gulf of Aqaba constituted *international* waters and that no nation had the right to prevent free and innocent passage in the Gulf and through the Straits giving access thereto. It reiterated (at this late stage) the Egyptian government's pledge (of January, 1950) that the occupation of the islands of Sanafir and Tiran was not designed to obstruct passage and that this would remain free as in the past, in conformity with international law. (Hitherto, the U.S.A. had not lifted a finger to secure the fulfillment of the pledge.) Now, unless the International Court of Justice should decide to the contrary, the U.S.A. would, on behalf of vessels of American registry, be "prepared to exercise the right of free and innocent passage and to join with others to secure general recognition of this right."

The *aide-mémoire* went on to an even firmer declaration. The U.N. had called for more than prompt and unconditional withdrawal of Israel behind the armistice lines—it had called "for other measures." Then, on such withdrawal, the U.S.A. would be prepared to use its influence, in concert with other United Nations members, to the end that "these other measures should be implemented." The U.S. government believed that its views and purposes were shared by many other nations. Israel's tranquillity in the future would be best assisted by relying on this fact rather than by occupation of the disputed area in defiance "of the overwhelming judgment of the world community."

Ambassador Eban went to Israel February 18 to learn whether Ben Gurion could be persuaded into some additional flexibility. He argued there that the land captured was of value not in itself, but only as a counter which could well be traded for a concession on free passage at Aqaba. If Israel remained in Sharm el-Sheik, there would be no free passage.

Before his journey to Israel to see Ben Gurion and between that time and his return to Washington, a strong movement for sanctions against Israel whipped up the passions of the United Nations Assembly. By February 11, 1957, Israel had defied the sixth request of the clamoring U.N. to withdraw her forces. Alongside Lodge's veiled threats, Dulles was simply unable to divest himself of an ecclesiastical appeal to morality and of his belief in the power of a mobilized world opinion. He claimed good grounds to hope that Israel would comply with the U.N. resolutions, because:

> I have those hopes [that Israel would comply] because Israel is a country which, like most of the free nations of the world, has what we call in our Declaration of Independence "a decent respect for the opinions of mankind," and I would think that a country like Israel, which naturally has that respect and which also depends very largely for its continued existence upon the good will of many other nations, that it would pay a respect to the overwhelming verdict of the world community. After all, you had a vote there with only two negatives—that of Israel itself and of France—and that is a pretty impressive thing. I am not basing myself on any special inside information as to what Israel would do but merely on the fact that I would think a country which has the traditions of Israel, the democratic instincts of Israel, which is itself the creation of the United Nations, would have a decent respect for such an overwhelming verdict of the U.N. as was expressed last Saturday night.[10]

It may be remembered that Dulles had never hitherto exceptionally exerted himself to preserve this country, and that the passage from the Declaration of Independence was written by a nation not surrendering but fighting for its rights! If Israel had depended on Dulles alone, it would by now have been on the list of victims of the crimes of which he accused the Soviet Union.

In this atmosphere of threats to Israel, a popular revulsion of feeling against unfairness to Israel erupted in the United States, remarkably widespread throughout the nation. It was first expressed with force by the Republican Majority Leader of the Senate, Senator Knowland, on February 6. Knowland was not an admirer either of Dulles or of Eisenhower, some of his reasons being good and some not so good. But now, after Dulles's latest remarks, Knowland, who had an obstreperous temper but a strong sense of right and wrong, demanded in public that the U.S.A. should not support sanctions against Israel unless the United Nations was also prepared to take similar action against the Soviet Union for persistently ignoring the U.N.'s condemnation of Soviet aggression in Hungary. Knowland declared that to punish Israel while "sidestepping the larger aggression" of the Soviet Union would be both "immoral and insupportable." It would mean the application of a "double standard." Where now was the "one law . . ."? To this, behind the scenes then and since that time, the Administration's defenders made the jejune retort: "The standard was the same, equal for both: BUT in the Soviet case it could not be enforced!" The inferences to be drawn from this state of mind are truly disastrous for United States foreign policy.

Other Republican leaders joined Knowland, for example, Senator Styles Bridges. The nation was in an uproar, to the credit of its sense of fair play and common sense about power and ethical realities in the world of nations. The Democrats had been strongly expressing such criticism of the Administration already. Meanwhile, Dulles and Eisenhower needed Congressional support of their resolution and money for the Eisenhower Middle East Doctrine, then undergoing skeptical and scathing hearings before the Senate. Furthermore, on February 15, Eban, instructed by his government, refused to accept Dulles's proposals of February 11 without conditions, including that Egypt be forbidden to return to Gaza. In this event, Israel would make a contribution towards the resettlement and compensation of its refugees.

Consequently, a White House statement was made on February 17, 1957 (from Thomasville, Georgia, where the President was vacationing), making public the *aide-mémoire* of February 11, and justifying its contents and the pressure being exerted on Israel to withdraw. It reiterated the principle that undertakings at the United Nations "*seem*" (why "seem"?) to "preclude using the forcible seizure and occupation of other lands as bargaining power in the settlement of international disputes."

Of course, this assertion diplomatically ignored the causes of the "forcible seizure" of other lands. But Dulles and Eisenhower appeared still bent on worshipping the immaculate conception of the United Nations. It was difficult for them to do otherwise, for if they had, their whole legal case based on the Charter for their action hitherto would have been jeopardized. The statement explained that Britain and France had "deferred to the overwhelming judgment of the world community"—and had withdrawn their forces without conditions. This attribution of the cause of their withdrawal is substantially false, as we have amply seen: direct American intimidation with oil, and dollars, and cold-eyed bullying accomplished the withdrawal, and behind these circumstances was United States government fear (justified or not) of Russian action. Whether the purpose was expedient is another question: the means is not in doubt, as the record shows.

The United States, the President's (that is, Dulles's) statement continued, "is aware of the fact that Israel has legitimate grievances and should, in all fairness, see a prospect of remedying them." The *aide-mémoire* gave her an assured prospect of this.

Upon this, Senator Lyndon B. Johnson, Democratic leader of the Senate, sent a letter to Dulles, protesting against the threat that sanctions might be used against Israel. He questioned the Dulles-Eisenhower principle of "one-law-for-all," and turned the tables on the President's policy:

> The U.N. cannot apply one rule for the strong and another for the weak; it cannot organize its economic weight against the little State when it has not previously made even a pretence of doing so against the large States. I have seen no suggestions in the U.N. of the application of economic sanctions against the U.S.S.R. Israel has in large part complied with the directives of the U.N.; Russia has not even pretended to be polite. . . .

Israel had a right to guarantees from the United Nations, Johnson maintained, as soon as she withdrew her troops. On February 19, the Senate Democratic Policy Committee unanimously approved Johnson's statement, and called on President Eisenhower to resist any United Nations attempts to impose sanctions on Israel. Meanwhile, Dulles sought to placate Nasser, through Fawzi and Ambassador Hare, on his plans for Aqaba and Gaza.

A serious and imminent crisis threatened the President and Dulles. At this point Dulles grasped at an additional device to ease his own way and to ease Israel into compliance, by exerting influence on Zionist leaders and on Ben Gurion. Someone in the State Department, or in the President's offices, had furnished Barney Balaban, the motion-picture magnate, with a list of eight American Jews prominent in Jewish philanthropy and cultural life (but none of them associated with the Zionist movement in the United States!). They were invited to meet with Dulles, and perhaps later with the President, for a frank discussion of the Eisenhower-Ben Gurion exchanges. The State Department proposed February 19 or February 20 for the meeting with Dulles. But, in order that they might themselves confer beforehand, they asked for this meeting to be held on February 21.

While this conference was pending, Dulles and Lodge flew to Thomasville to concert measures for a hard line against Israel and for the U.N. Then, President Eisenhower flew back from Thomasville (cutting short his vacation) in order to discuss the crisis with Republican and Democratic leaders. On February 20 he met with twenty-six of them, and, in addition, Dulles, Nixon, and Lodge. They assembled at 8:30 A.M., for a discussion that lasted two and a half hours. Sherman Adams, who was present, says, "The Vice President [Nixon] sat through the whole two and a half hours of serious, and sometimes heated debate without joining the argument." [11] For *his* interest was not Israel or the United Nations or the Rule of Law: it was "his reluctance to become involved in a battle between Eisenhower and Knowland." [12]

The President explained why he was putting strong pressure on Israel for unconditional withdrawal. Of course, as his listeners might have expected, it was being done for Israel's own good! You *see*—Israel would soon be in a dangerous financial crisis. It would need help from the U.S. Export-Import Bank. Such help would be possible only if peace were restored. Another point: if the "brawls" between Israel and Egypt did not end, the resumption of full-scale traffic in the Canal would be retarded. Furthermore, the Russians would increase their influence among the Arabs, and the interruptions in the oil supply from the Middle East would continue to harm the European and British economy. And—the whole thing might end up in a general war!

Now the President was talking the language of Dulles not to the masses but to canny political leaders. They looked at him quizzically and with impatience. "Disarmingly," says Sherman Adams, "the President told the legislators that he was well aware of their opposition to sanctions against Israel and that he could understand their attitude." Whereupon, he made that confession, perhaps self-praise, that he had applied oil sanctions successfully against Britain and France [13] (as quoted in Chapter 16).

The President then mixed his argument a little. He confused American interests with the status of the United Nations in the world. For he made this appeal:

> Then Eisenhower stated flatly that he did not know how to protect American interests in the Middle East except through the United Nations.[14]

That was one thing. Now the other, that followed on directly.

> If the United States failed to support the United Nations on the Israel issue, he declared, it would be a lethal blow to the principles of the world peace organization.

"Nobody likes to impose sanctions," the President concluded, "but how else can we induce Israel to withdraw to the line agreed on in the 1949 armistice? The Arabs refuse to discuss a permanent settlement until that move is made." The President did not tell the Congressional leaders that King Saud had only a few days previously exacted from him and Dulles the pledge that Israel would have to leave unconditionally. Nor did he refer to the indignation that Ben Gurion had felt, when, in behalf of American interests in the Middle East, the President at the suggestion of Dulles had invited King Saud to Washington. Saud, in a frenzy of bloodshed at the time when Nasser had seized the Suez Canal, had actually urged the annihilation of Israel and had made Nasser a gift of $10 million as a mark of encouragement.

As the meeting continued, Dulles added assurances about the neutralization of the Gaza Strip and American exercise of free passage at Aqaba. This was a benefit for Israel. Therefore, either it was sanctions, or some other forceful alternative. The United States could not give the world the impression that on such a matter as this Israel could control America's policy! Otherwise, the Arabs would feel compelled to turn to Russia!

Lodge, Dulles, and Eisenhower were adamant. Lodge said,[15] that since November there had been a steadily increasing respect for the United States among the Arab people. (This was a most dubious proposition—they just did not vilify the U.S.A. with the same Levantine curses as before, and they were playing the U.S.A., and especially Lodge, for all they could get.) "Now," said Lodge, "they won't understand it if we abandon our position on the Israeli withdrawal. Unless the Israelis withdraw, the Canal will not be reopened." He thought that even a postponement of United Nations action on sanctions could not be obtained, as Knowland suggested (while further attempts at settlement with Ben Gurion were made), because it would appear as though the United States were opposing sanctions. The element of fear as also of spirited flagellation in Lodge is astounding. He declared that the United States would be as "tough" with Israel as with such old allies as Britain and France.

The President's attempt to obtain a unified statement (what a Dullesian tactic!) from the Congressional leaders supporting immediate withdrawal by Israel was repulsed. As Senator Fulbright said: "I am not sure all would agree unless it could be made certain that Israel would get justice after she withdraws." *And that was really the point.* The leaders did not believe the action the President and Dulles contemplated was *just.* In the course of the Senate hearings on the Eisenhower Doctrine, their general review of Dulles's long course in the Middle East had convinced them that he had for years been a clumsy muddler in his handling of America's relations with the region. This was especially true, they felt, of the Suez affair since July 19, 1956. They believed that the present course being proposed to them was unjust and inexpedient, and that American interests outside and inside the United Nations could be served better by a fulfillment of Israel's requests.

The President was left, properly, to make his own decision, as Dulles and he had made it all along. He determined to announce his chosen course in a speech on television and radio that evening. One important newspaper was given a long list of all the ways in which Israel could be ruined, mainly by American punitive economic pressure. Cairo expressed pleasure at the President's firmness.

On February 18, Abba Eban had left for Tel Aviv, to find how much give there was in Israel's Cabinet. On the same day, Ben Gurion had sent an urgent last-minute appeal to Dulles asking him to get the United Nations discussions adjourned for a short period so that an impartial committee could come to Israel—and, if need be, to Egypt—to try to get an agreed settlement on Aqaba and Gaza. He observed what a historic wrong would be committed if the United Nations voted sanctions against Israel: he thought it would strike a fatal blow at the moral foundations of the organization. Such a move, too, would be an act of discrimination against Israel.

Eban arrived in Israel on February 20. He had been outraged at the statement made by the President from Thomasville, Georgia, on February 17, since it contradicted the agreement he had reached with Dulles, expressed in the *aide-mémoire* of February 11. Eisenhower's statement was made after consultation with Dulles and Lodge, and therefore constituted a deviation by Dulles himself from the assurances in his own *aide-mémoire*. What were the differences? They lay in the condemnatory tone of the statement; the harsh manner in which it put Israel in the wrong about "using forcible seizure of other lands as a bargaining power"; the brusqueness with which it said that the United Nations resolution of February 2 and the *aide-mémoire* of February 11 "provide Israel with maximum assurance that it can reasonably expect at this juncture, or that can be reconciled with fairness to others." Dulles could always wind up the President with the argument that the United States was being pressured from strength in a matter involving principle. Lodge, post-haste from the U.N., added petulance and agitation to the theme.

Eban, very disturbed, took counsel of Bedell Smith. The latter recommended: "Go ahead with what they have offered, and be a little more flexible than Ben Gurion has been till now!" Perhaps on February 18, Eban saw Dulles at his home with Christian Herter (who had replaced Herbert Hoover, Jr.), Herman Phleger, Robert Murphy, and William Rountree.

On February 19, Dulles held a news conference. In this he reaffirmed that the U.S. would expect, of course, to be able to pass through the Aqaba waterway. He did not anticipate search by Egypt for contraband to stop innocent passage. He was in some difficulty about the meaning of "innocent passage": perhaps it meant traffic not designed to do injury to anybody? Still, he thought it probable that the Egyptians would not restore their interpretation of "belligerent" ships—meaning those of Israel, though the phrase was theoretically applicable to any nation. Israel had not modified its position on its conditions for leaving Aqaba and Gaza. He still had hopes that it would do so, on the assurances of the United Nations and of the United States.

Dulles then launched into one of his "exhaustive" explanations, which were quite sophisticated in their diplomatic intention: namely, to bring pressure on a nation to change its course. He discoursed on sanctions, thus:

> I would, however, just like to make one observation: The word "sanction" is sometimes used as though it had a precise meaning. Of course, there are all kinds of sanctions. There is a wide variety of action which can be called a sanction—moral sanctions, economic sanctions—as to which, again there is a variety—military sanctions. So, the word "sanction" just used in the abstract does not have any clearly-defined content.
>
> . . . There are certain types of sanctions which would probably require Congressional action: there are other types of sanctions which can be done by the Executive without any participation by Congress.[16]

One can deduce from this comment why Congressmen, and foreign diplomats as well (especially from the nations doing contentious business with Dulles), were convinced they were facing a devious person. They could not be sure what he was saying or to what he had pledged his word.

He further said, at this news conference, that the United States would not shoot its way through the Straits of Tiran, but, also, that it would probably never be necessary to do so. Dulles now proceeded to vocalize that vaguest kind of irrelevancy known as cant, which, as the dictionary says, is "affected or unreal phraseology; especially language implying goodness or piety which does not exist." But, now, too, Dulles felt that in all probability, though he was restored to health and vigor, he could hardly at sixty-nine expect the length of days that might have been his if he had not been attacked by deep-seated cancer. He had need more than ever to justify his recent policies in the noblest, most religious, terms. As he said: "I think we will have made one of the great forward steps in history in the development of an international order."[17] That is, "if the world can get through this present stage by liquidating the armed attack. . . ." He reproduced his "two sides of the coin" argument. He expected that for the future there would be a greater effort to secure compliance with United Nations decisions, like the Security Council's resolution of 1951 requiring that Israel be permitted free passage through the Suez Canal.

On the evening of February 20, after the conference with Congressional leaders, President Eisenhower made his broadcast to the nation. He stood by the insistence that Israel withdraw unconditionally, relying on the United Nations and the United States to see that she obtained the two conditions that she required, *afterwards*. He noticed that Israel could hardly insist on the condition that it be entrusted with the civil and police administration of the Gaza Strip in association with the United Nations. But she ought to get guarantees about future administration in Gaza and safeguards against attack from that place.

He repeated the totally specious assertion that Britain and France had withdrawn from Suez because "of a respect for the opinions of mankind as expressed almost unanimously by the eighty member nations of the U.N. General Assembly." [18] Did Dulles believe that Ben Gurion, Eban, Shiloah, and the Israeli Commander in Chief General Dayan and his officers did not know that it was spurious?

An ominous note now entered the speech. "We are approaching the fateful moment when either we must recognize that the United Nations is unable to restore peace in this area or the United Nations must renew with increased vigor its efforts to bring about Israeli withdrawal." The United States, as a member of the United Nations, would support some participation of the United Nations in the administration of the Gaza Strip. It would exercise the right of passage of Aqaba and join with other nations to secure general recognition of this right. But, the President continued, Israel was seeking "firm guarantees" as a condition of withdrawal. This raised the basic question of principle. The United States could not countenance the use of force as a means of settling international differences and thereby gaining national advantages. (He had that very morning rather boasted in the White House that *sanctions*, which constituted a kind of force perhaps more severe than physical, *had been used* to support America's policy.) Force could not be reconciled with the Charter. So we would face the disaster that the "best hope of establishing a world order" would have been destroyed. (Every word of this proposition with the exception of the indefinite article "a" is of dubious validity.)

Where now was the coin with *two* sides? It was discarded for *force majeure*. Now came a far too clever plea, too clever to be ethically and politically good for America.

> I do not believe that Israel's default should be ignored because the U.N. has not been able effectively to carry out its resolutions condemning the Soviet Union for its armed suppression of the people of Hungary. Perhaps this is a case where the proverb applies that *two wrongs do not make a right.*

Even in the nursery such reasoning would rightly be questioned. Israel's demand for justice had nothing to do with the horrors that Russia had perpetrated in Hungary. Her demand for justice stemmed from the aggressions committed against her, the United Nations and the United States having failed to live up to their obligations to stop them and remedy them. These aggressions were the one obvious and gross wrong, and it was the one that the President did not touch on at *this* point at all. No one had said that Israel's default should be ignored because the U.N. had not been able to call Russia to account.

In reality, the two actions were not the same kind of wrong, if

Israel's was a wrong at all. *Once again:* the wrong committed by Russia was the brutal massacre of many thousands of people in a land not her own, for purposes of dominating that foreign country, while the action of Israel was self-defense in the strictest and most vital sense, occurring after years of murders of her citizens within their own land by Arab invaders, who had been organized most recently by Egypt. The two actions were as different as night is from day, as evil is from good. Both Israel and Russia were in default against the United Nations: this was a wrong by both, but their substantial actions were diametrically different. Even the action of the Soviet Union in the United Nations was a wrong in a different and nefarious sense from that of Israel: the Soviet Union had a veto with which to protect the wrongs it did and wrongfully to inhibit justice being rendered to those, like Israel, to whom wrong had been done.

If it was Dulles who supplied the President with the proverb that two wrongs do not make a right, then it was he who was guilty of misconceiving the truth about political reality and the moral relationship between human beings. It was a simplistic attitude: intellectually dishonest; pathological in its imagination; misleading on foreign-policy realities to the American people, upon whom so many responsibilities had yet to fall in the twentieth century. It disarmed America herself when her own self-defense should come in question (as, for example, in the case of Cuba), or required her to enter into tortured and hypocritical arguments to sustain the plain justice of her own defense there, or, say, in Panama.

Was it for Israel's sake or for America's own anti-Soviet policy that the President then made his contrast between these two nations, whose wrong-doing he had just equated? Dulles's characteristic kind of appeal?

> There can, of course, be no equating of a nation like Israel with that of the Soviet Union. The people of Israel, like those of the United States, are imbued with a religious faith and a sense of moral values. We are entitled to expect, and do expect, from such peoples of the free world a contribution to world order which unhappily we cannot expect from a nation controlled by atheistic despots.

"We are entitled to expect. . . ." But who is "We"? How could such an Israel possibly have committed a wrong identical with the Soviet Union's? "We are entitled to expect . . ." but *not*, "We are morally obliged to *give*. . . ." !

By February 21, Ben Gurion had learned the contents of this address, and he had conversed with Ambassador Abba Eban. He answered the President on February 21, saying that Eban would be in

Washington again within a day or so and would inform him of Israel's considered attitude. He wanted to cooperate to the maximum in order to arrive at a reasonable solution. He asked for further opportunity for clarifications.

The Prime Minister of Israel answered the diverse moral contentions of Dulles and Eisenhower in a powerful speech in the Knesset, also on February 21. He posed this issue:

> The controversy is over a decisive moral question in international relations—whether the United Nations, with the aid of the United States, shall apply different standards of justice, one for dictatorial Egypt and one for democratic Israel; whether those who desire to destroy us shall be allowed to disregard every international undertaking and promise, violate the U.N. Charter and the resolutions of the General Assembly and the Security Council . . . while Israel is not allowed to defend itself or to protect its rights, sovereign equality and security . . . whether the U.N. with the aid of the United States shall impose sanctions on us because we do not accept the double moral standard of the Egyptian dictator who demands that others fulfil everything that benefits him while he violates every bilateral agreement and international obligation which benefits others.

He pledged loyalty to the United Nations, though it was in its infancy, and needed much improvement to approach perfection. He praised the United States for its democratic basis and its immigrant pioneers. He praised President Eisenhower, for his illustriousness in his command of the forces that had defeated "the most monstrous and terrible regime in human history." He felt the moral pressure of the President's messages. The heritage of the Bible was a common approach between the Israeli and American peoples. BUT—"The people of Israel cannot submit to discrimination in international relations." He appealed for justice from the United States.

Dulles did not intend to give justice as asked for by Ben Gurion in his appeal based on fact and law and on the Charter. For Nasser had taken Dulles to the brink, and he had flinched; and the Soviet Union had manipulated before him and the President a vista of the brink, also, and they had flinched. They would not allow the heavens to fall simply for the sake of Justice. They had committed an injustice, and they felt they must persist with their original attitude, lest, in any change, critics would find material for accusing them. But their behavior made their appeal to the One Law and the Charter ring hollow, and in that ring cynicism is nurtured. They were deficient in nerve.

The Balaban group of eight representative American Jews denied themselves the pleasure of seeing the President, as they had been invited to do on February 21. They were outraged by his speech of February 20; in their opinion, he had in tone and words put the blame on Israel, and made her subject to sanctions, which he had paraphrased as "pressure." But they did talk with Dulles for an hour and a half. He explained the American position to them. Above all he expressed the wish to be understood as meaning no harm to Israel. He protested his resentment over the suggestion that he could possibly be anti-Jewish: how could it be possible, considering his religion, that he was a Christian?

He was listening to their questions and responses. Even as the voices rose and fell, Ben Gurion's answer to the speech of February 20 was brought in to Dulles and them. Dulles was terribly, visibly disappointed at the impasse which that speech revealed. One of his visitors expressed the mood of all of them when he said: "I don't know anything about politics or diplomacy. But I do know that for our country to try to bludgeon Israel against its own vital interests is morally wrong." This point, I am told, Dulles did not argue. He offered to take them over to see the President at once. They declined, in view of the President's speech. They dispersed.

In this impasse, Eban consulted Ralph Bunche. He also asked Arthur H. Dean, Dulles's long-time law partner, to talk to Dulles on the telephone.

Bunche, with long experience and diplomatic genius, advised Eban he might get better treatment from the United States government than from the U.N. General Assembly—and, perhaps, Hammarskjold. For men maddened with nationalist fervor, like Krishna Menon, supplied with briefs, and expert in exploiting the Charter and international law for their own interests, were setting up fiery roadblocks to any settlement based on the recognition by Egypt of her obligations. The issue seemed never-ending. On February 22, Iraq, Lebanon, the Sudan, Afghanistan, Indonesia, and Pakistan laid a "sanctions" resolution before the U.N. It would call on *all* states to deny to Israel "all military, economic or financial assistance or facilities." A spokesman threatened that the Arabs would turn to Moscow if their rights were not satisfied. "As lethal as bullets" was the *New York Times* description of the suspension of American economic aid to Israel.

Finally, Eban asked Dulles, privately, "What action would the United States take if Egyptian guns halted *American* ships from innocent entry at the Gulf of Aqaba?" This was Dulles's divine meat. "Mr. Ambassador," he answered quickly and certainly, "it is the policy of the United States to defend its shipping rights anywhere in the world."

Hence, Dulles and Phleger had a very long discussion with Eban about the details of a settlement on February 24. Rountree, Under Secretary of State Herter, Francis O. Wilcox, Assistant Secretary for U.N. Affairs, and Reuben Shiloah, Israeli Embassy Minister, also participated. They drew up a memorandum. In writing, these American answers were given to Eban:

1. Will the United States send a ship through Aqaba and will you react if stopped? Answer: Yes.
2. Will you support the idea that the UNEF should stay at Sharm el-Sheik for a long time? Answer: Yes.
3. Will you send a ship with the UNEF flag through the Gulf of Aqaba? Answer: This depends on Hammarskjold's assent.
4. Will you open an oil route for us from Iran? That is, through the Red Sea and the Gulf of Aqaba? Answer: Yes.
5. Will Gaza be a United Nations-administered enclave? Answer: We will try our hardest to persuade the United Nations and Hammarskjold to make such an arrangement.

Dulles, it will be noted, held back on some points, saying the answers depended on the United Nations. Therefore, Eban went to see Hammarskjold about these issues, and explained what Israel wanted and what Dulles would like to concede.

Hammarskjold was extremely annoyed that the United States and Israel were getting along so very well! The hair at the top of his skull, towards the back of the head, stood on end. He absolutely and indignantly refused to send a ship through Aqaba bearing the UNEF flag. Then he said, "As regards Gaza, Egypt has her rights. What you arranged with Dulles does not suit me or Egypt!"

Eban was bound to report home this impasse. This is why Ben Gurion says, "It was made clear in New York and Washington that the two problems [getting out of the Gaza Strip and freedom in the Gulf] could not be separated and we were again faced with deadlock." [19] Eban simultaneously wrote to Dulles: "I'm less optimistic now than yesterday! The Gaza proposal is not working out! I thought after talking with you that it would be O.K."

Eban next saw Dulles on February 26. The question arose, What shall we say in public, for the press is clamoring and the nations are watching? Dulles said, "Supposing we say that the question of Aqaba is settled, and that we will turn to Gaza later?" Eban answered, "No! It cannot be done that way! There is an interconnection between the two, as our claim on Aqaba is based on our being nonbelligerents, whereas Nasser is maintaining a claim to belligerency against us all-round and in Gaza, which we want pacified."

Dulles then asked, "What do the French feel about it?" For Mollet and Pineau were in Washington at that time. "Why not go and see them?" France had stood by Israel all along since October 29. The British had sided with the other nations, including the United States, when it came to enforcing the withdrawal of Israeli forces from Sinai, since they wanted to get the Canal cleared, and to show their respect for the Rule of Law.

When Eban followed Dulles's suggestion, Pineau recommended: "Ask that as the Israelis leave the two areas so the UNEF enters; then the Israelis leave in expectation of no commando raids and hostilities—and stipulate that if these conditions are not fulfilled, she will exercise her legitimate rights of self-defense, that is, she will reoccupy Gaza!" Mollet entered the room at the French Embassy a little while later and added: "Demand that the United Nations must go into the disputed areas or another outbreak of war is to be expected!" Eban answered, "But we can never get a United Nations resolution to this effect!" Mollet suggested: "Then get the United States and other countries to back you on it, in their individual and joint capacities, and you will have nothing to fear."

Eban took these proposals back to Dulles. The crucial point was that if Israel were attacked in Aqaba she would act in self-defense. BUT—Dulles added, say, rather, "in self-defense under Article 51 of the Charter," as this would give any defensive action a legal basis. The suggestion of legality gave Dulles inordinate pleasure. This formula became the basis of an agreement between Israel and the United States, and Israel and the United Nations. It was formulated in a speech that Golda Meir would give at the United Nations General Assembly on March 1, 1957, and it was drafted by Eban, Shiloah, Phleger, and Rountree, so that the United States and Israel would each know to what it was committed and what it could expect of the other.

The speech was taken in finished form by Eban to Dulles's house, and Dulles supplied the main lines of the speech that Lodge would make at the same session. The French retailed what they would say. Sir Harold Caccia and Lester Pearson were let in on the arrangement. Caccia was pleased that the freedom of Aqaba incidentally gave Britain free sea access to Britain's ally, Jordan. Eban said to Pearson, who had been a most valiant friend of Israel's during this trying period, "The United States and France and thirteen or fourteen maritime powers would employ their maritime law to secure the freedom of Aqaba."

Thus, it seemed that the rights of Israel in Aqaba and protection against attack from Gaza were gained by Dulles's guarantees and the movement of the UNEF into Sharm el-Sheik and the Gaza Strip. This statement was made in the Golda Meir speech of March 1. It was supported by the United States, France, Argentina, Costa Rica, Cuba, Panama, Holland, Norway, Belgium, Australia, New Zealand, Sweden, Britain, Canada, Portugal, Italy, and other countries.

The speech made by Henry Cabot Lodge, in response to Golda Meir's, was so curious in tone, although he repeated the words of the assurances Dulles and Eisenhower had specifically and verbally authorized, that Ben Gurion held up the withdrawal pending assurances from the President. Lodge stressed very strongly, indeed, that if either party committed hostilities or violations of international obligations including the armistice agreement (a provision which could be applied to Israel's action against Gaza or against a reoccupation of Sharm el-Sheik), then the United Nations would deal with the matter! He also reread the terms of the Charter which had so long been ignored by Egypt and neglected by the United Nations to the danger of Israel. It had been expected, as a result of the Eban-Dulles conversations and agreements, that Lodge would make it clear that the U.S.A. would support a U.N. administration of the Gaza Strip and oppose Egypt's return to the area. Lodge omitted such an assertion from his speech. This omission by implication contradicted what had been believed to be the assurances of Dulles that there should be "international rule in Gaza without the Egyptians." Moreover, Israel was disconcerted by Lodge's stubborn use of the phrase "not unreasonable" when talking about Israel's "assumptions"—that is, the bargain struck with Dulles.

On March 1, Dulles saw representatives of the nine Arab nations in Washington, and assured them that the U.S.A. had made "no promises or concessions whatsoever" to Israel to secure her agreement to withdraw from Gaza and Aqaba. An announcement by the State Department shortly afterwards said that Israel's withdrawal would be wholly predicated upon the decisions of the General Assembly, the reports of the Secretary General, and the public position of the United States, notably the position expounded by the President in his address of February 20. The Arabs needed much soothing.

Ambassador Eban appealed to Dulles. Their colloquy at Dulles's house was assisted by the presence of Robert Murphy. Dulles said he would get a letter from Eisenhower to Ben Gurion, saying, "We truly mean what we say about Aqaba; and we even intend to try to open up Suez!" Having written out what the message should be, Dulles went to the Presidential phone. James Hagerty, the Press Secretary, was on the receiving end of his call to the White House. Dulles read out the message and asked, "Can I put Ike's signature on this?" There was hardly an instant's pause, and the answer came back, "Yes!"

The President, urged thereto by Dulles, sent a letter to Ben Gurion on March 2. Its core was this:

> I believe it is reasonable to entertain such hopes and expectations [of more stable, tranquil conditions and welfare than existed before], that had been voiced by your foreign minister and others and I want you to know that the United States as a friend of all the countries of the area and as a loyal member of the United Nations, will seek that such hopes prove not in vain.

One spokesman maintained his partisan prejudices to the very last: Krishna Menon. He tried to prevent the Aqaba settlement by a long and learned discourse on international law regarding such narrow straits, attempting to prove the straits were an internal waterway.

In spite of heavy opposition in Israel—for the disappointment after military victory was tremendous—especially from those who feared for the future of peace in the developing Negev, Israel's southernmost area, Ben Gurion issued orders on March 4 for full and prompt withdrawal and for arrangements for the entry of the UNEF troops. Ben Gurion later told the Knesset that the concern aroused by Lodge's speech had not been entirely erased by the President's letter of March 2. What he thought of Dulles's and the President's assurances can be deduced from his remarks in the Knesset on that day (March 5):

> The President of the U.S.A. and the representatives of other States approved this assumption [that the U.N. Administration would remain in Gaza until a peace settlement was concluded] in various terms. But in spite of all this, I must state that there is no certainty and no clear and authoritative undertaking that the Egyptians will not return or be restored, whether as a civilian administration or through military occupation, relying on the excuse of the Armistice Agreement.

What he feared would happen, happened, in spite of all the orations of Dulles about justice and peace. By March 7, the Israelis had evacuated the Gaza Strip totally. The frontier settlements returned again to their night guards and searchlights against *fedayeen*, pruning hook in one hand and gun in the other. The UNEF took over Gaza at once. Pro-Egyptian demonstrations were immediately fomented, with Egyptians and Arab refugees making physical attacks on the UNEF. On March 11, the Egyptian government appointed a civil administrator for the Gaza Strip, and falsely accused the UNEF of firing at its inhabitants. On March 13, the Egyptian civil administrator took over. No finger stirred at the United Nations. All hands were inhibited by Hammarskjold's interpretation of the Charter, as Egypt wanted it. Gaza belonged to Egypt, though she had seized it by force in 1948 against U.N. resolutions! Nasser threatened that if Israel returned to Gaza, Aqaba would be closed and the *fedayeen* would sow terror through Israel.

Ben Gurion affirmed to the Knesset that if *fedayeen* attacks began again, Israel would take military action. So long as the UNEF remained there, however, peace would reign. On March 18, Golda Meir raised the question with Dulles whether the advent of an Egyptian military staff in Gaza was consistent with the assurance and expectations on which Israel had evacuated Gaza. At this stage, the Israelis being gone from the Sinai Peninsula, and therefore having no power over Dulles, he could be rather less assuring and looser in language than in earlier exchanges with Ben Gurion. He had got what he wanted for the time being. The immediate fire was out, even if his promises were not fully kept. Could he be expected to keep totally all "hopes and expectations" he had delineated? He announced in a joint communiqué (March 18, 1957) with Mrs. Meir [20] that matters stood as in the Lodge speech and the President's letter of March 2 and the "hopes and expectations" the U.S. had expressed about Gaza and Aqaba, and the Six Principles for the Suez Canal! [21]

Except for the messy mopping up, as any army commander might say, the Suez affair was over. At least, it was over for Dulles. Not for Israel.

On Israel's Independence Day, April 28, 1963, Prime Minister Ben Gurion spoke to the *New York Herald Tribune:*

> I know that he [President Eisenhower] is not in the habit of giving promises that he and those he represents do not intend to keep, and I have not the slightest doubt that all his statements, whether by word of mouth or in writing, were made with complete sincerity. But I must point out with deep regret, that the United Nations did not fulfill the hopes placed in it by the United States, through President Eisenhower, and it cannot be said that the hopes and expectations voiced by our Foreign Minister, Mrs. Meir, at the U.N. Assembly at the beginning of March, 1957, have been realized. The sword of Damocles hangs over our heads as before. . . .

18. SUMMING UP: Suez and Beyond in American Foreign Policy

DULLES'S MERITS

Dulles's Suez diplomacy must now be appraised by the standards of America's national interests and of the moral obligation which she, like every person or nation, owes to civilization.

At the very outset, it must be emphasized that it was not Dulles who waged war in Suez and Sinai, but Britain, France, and Israel. The losses in world power and economic well-being suffered by Britain and France as a result of their military action were not Dulles's direct fault. But that does not by any means end the lesson. For their action was from the beginning, to a very substantial extent, demonstrably impelled and shaped by Dulles's foreign policy and diplomatic methods. His allies trusted him to work for their reasonable benefit. Considerable blame for the injurious results of the Suez affair is clearly imputable to Dulles, because, from July 19, 1956, he was of his own will a principal, even *the* principal, decision-making person in the train of events leading to war.

Dulles is entitled to credit for certain of his announced purposes, even if they were failures in practice. He persevered for weeks to find a just and viable solution to the specific conflict over the Suez Canal seizure. His ingenuity, forensic gifts, diplomatic eloquence, and tenacious moral character almost succeeded, but Nasser's despotic ambitions and aggressive imperiousness defeated his efforts. He sought to fortify the Rule of Law in world politics (or in "world opinion"), and therefore employed his talents in upholding the U.N. Charter. Some applaud Dulles for having avoided an atomic war with the Soviet Union, one that might have begun with a mere clash of ground forces and then have been "escalated." Others laud him for his befriending of the anticolonial forces, so, it is suggested, attracting to the U.S.A. the gratitude and good will of the Afro-Asian peoples. Finally, it is claimed, he compelled the British and French to realize their position of subordinacy in world politics—as interpreted by the United States, which must be the principal, even the dominating, power throughout the world.

THE DEFICIENCIES OF DULLES'S SUEZ POLICY

If, for the sake of argument, we accept the wisdom and nobility of Dulles's purposes, the question arises how serious he and President Eisenhower were in espousing them and what they were sincerely prepared to pay to secure their fulfillment. Another consideration is the weight they attached to each purpose in relation to the others. Dulles's actual policy and personal conduct largely contributed to his allies' desperation and political and military defeat and to the magnification of Nasser's power.

Dulles first erred in not protesting with adequate vigor against the Egypto-Soviet arms deal of 1955. Without a single stern word, he indulgently allowed Nasser to open to Russia a foothold in the world of the Arab and African nations, when he well knew that one of the motives for Britain's wish to remain in the Suez base was precisely to block an enemy's road into Africa.

Then, if Dulles had not offered the Aswan loan, would Nasser have had occasion to seize the Canal? It would have been better to signal the displeasure the Administration felt at Nasser's dangerous ambitions. Dulles again erred in revoking the offer of a loan in so brusque and insulting a manner. He lacked the foresight—the sovereign talent of the statesman—to apprehend an act of violence by Nasser, well known to be a desperado. The ignorance or, perhaps, want of concern certainly demonstrated insensitivity to the dangers that threatened his allies. He gave Nasser an excuse to seize the Canal in hot blood.

The Canal seized, Dulles was without a policy to follow through and make Nasser "disgorge." When he rather belatedly realized that Nasser had contemptuously dragged him, through his allies, to the "brink of war" (supposed to be a favorite location of Dulles's), Dulles acted swiftly to avert a possible military retort by Britain and France. These nations were the victims who bore the brunt of Dulles's myopia and Nasser's radical violence. They could, Dulles knew, invoke the right of self-defense to make war against Nasser's kind of delict. He exaggerated the imminence of military action, to indulge his own conceit as a potent maestro of world political savoir-faire, and to secure leverage over the American public and Congress and President

Eisenhower. He tried to defer the approaching First London Conference, but Eden and Mollet insisted on an early session: they, not Dulles, had invented the idea of such a conference, although he tried to claim sole credit for it.

Thenceforward, Dulles did not tell his allies, precisely, candidly, or comprehensively, what America's Suez policy was, above all, whether it absolutely excluded their use of force. He and Eisenhower, in public and private utterances, left open the corollary that if all the peace-seeking conferences failed, force could not be excluded, indeed, would be justified. At the end of July, Dulles became what he had been denouncing as immoral in June, a neutral. He avoided the exertion of any available nonviolent pressures on Nasser to enforce just restitution on him, and he was terrified by the destructive possibilities of any act of war. War outraged his moralism on this occasion, if not when he had proposed it over Indo-China in 1954. War threatened him and the President with a loss of reputation as the vindicators of the United Nations and as men of peace. These pacific feelings were acutely intensified because the President was a candidate for a second term in the election of November 6, 1956. While Dulles in public paraded the idea of the economic attrition of Egypt, he was acknowledging in private that it could not possibly be effective in view of the primitiveness of the Egyptian economy. At any rate, he did not even try it.

From the instant Britain and France showed fight, Dulles was fear-stricken by two factors in the situation: the military power of the Soviet Union, and the impact that internationalizing Suez might have on America's status in the Panama Canal. About the first, he was misled by his own prejudices regarding Soviet politics in the world arena; he was overterrified. About the second, Panama, he preferred to deflect to his allies the anger of "colonial" nations by pampering these so that they temporarily forgot Panama. However, his allies were bitterly antagonized by his sermons against their "colonialism." For they knew quite as well as Dulles what he was hiding about Panama, and the Suez issue was not colonialism, even if it suited Dulles to pretend that it was while he was abandoning them. The Suez conflict was due to the rapacious violation of treaties for reasons of Egyptian national grandeur, as Dulles himself repeatedly asserted. But, taken to the brink of war, Dulles puffed out an iridescent smoke screen, false and irrelevant, about "anticolonialism." It was good for votes in the U.N.; it outbid the Soviet Union; it obscured Panama; it depressed his allies. But Panamanians were absorbing his arguments.

His diplomatic virtuosity was at its brightest at the First London Conference. But his triumph, the eighteen-power proposal, was bought by public, specific, and clear official American commitments to uphold British and French legal and political rights in Suez against Nasser. His allies were entitled to believe he intended to honor these commitments. He then made the critical mistake of refusing to lead the mission to Cairo which was to present the proposal to Nasser.

When the British and French, and especially Sir Anthony Eden, sincerely and urgently proposed to appeal to the United Nations, while there was still some fluidity in Nasser's *fait accompli*, Dulles obstructed the move. Instead, he constrained them (because he had *force majeure*) to accept a kind of stopgap, the Suez Canal Users' Association. He was fully conscious of the fact that the plan was unworkable, because it contained no means of compelling Nasser to accept it. Dulles promised it would make a "dry ditch" of the Canal. He knew quite well that to boycott the Canal was the only "teeth" the Association might have, but when Nasser threatened war if the Association tried to have its ships pass through the Canal, Dulles, in panic, dropped the "teeth." He had no genuine plans to help his allies economically on his avowed road to peace and justice. The allies concluded that Dulles had beguiled them by prevaricating persuasions into the morass of SCUA to win time and deflate their expectations of justice, and so they further lost faith in his sincerity, friendship, and clarity of mind.

Dulles had never entirely excluded the use of force by his allies; but neither had he clearly explained to them the actions the U.S.A. would be compelled to undertake to carry out the Tripartite Declaration or the stand it would take in the United Nations, if they did use force. Nor did he ever suggest that the Administration would arraign them or impose direct American economic punishment on them. He and the President negligently left them guessing with far too much room for miscalculation. This is not a wise practice for the strongest party in an alliance.

Dulles more and more came to look like a friend of Nasser's and an enemy of his allies. His Ambassador to Cairo advised and encouraged Nasser to keep the Canal operating smoothly. Dulles repeatedly refused to stop American-owned ships from paying tolls to Nasser, though he simultaneously made lusty announcements that Nasser must be made to feel the economic pinch. He did not prevent American citizens from taking jobs as pilots for the Egyptian Suez Canal Authority, the legality of which he had denied.

When the delays and detours used by Dulles to edge his allies into renunciation of their just claims had made them unbearably heartsick, they appealed to the United Nations. He still tried to obstruct their appeal, rather than bring discipline to bear on Nasser. Desperation forced them to override his objections. He could hardly do other than support their Six Principles regarding the future status of the Canal, for they were substantially his very own, pronounced by him in public for weeks. But he almost simultaneously subverted the moral strength of his allies by denouncing "colonialism" and linking the smear to the Suez dispute! He then pretended that his inimical slur was only a "blunder" of the tongue, but they suspected and very soon after verified that his hostility was deliberate.[1] He was buying prestige and an easy life at their expense.

Dulles still pretended optimism when the Soviet Union vetoed the Six Principles and their administrative-political implementation. His oft-proclaimed injunction that without justice there could be no peace was derisively flouted before his very nose, by Nasser and Nasser's friends.

During all these weeks, and in the preceding years he had held office, Dulles neglected to cope firmly with the imperialistic mischief perpetrated by Nasser's agents in Jordan, Syria, Iraq, and Israel. He pretended reliance on the United Nations, while knowing it was unjust and powerless. He failed to concert, with Eden, planned prophylactic measures, before a hot-war crisis should occur, to implement the Tripartite Pact.

Whatever one may think of the wisdom and expediency of making war on Egypt, there was hardly left to Britain, France, and Israel any alternative to such a course except surrender to Nasser, once Dulles's timid and tortuous diplomacy had delayed, confused, and weakened them. He underestimated their tenacity and undervalued their national interests and their concern for their national dignity, while overindulging Nasser's corresponding interests and concern. The Suez war having broken out, because his own proposals had been flouted by Nasser (with Moscow and Belgrade in support), Dulles allowed his personal indignation and his personal moral proctorship to govern the foreign policy of America. He totally abandoned a feasible insistence on a constructive settlement of the issues that had caused the outbreak of war. He was abjectly intimidated by the seething passions of the Afro-Asian nations, transmitted to him by Henry Cabot Lodge, whose own personal susceptibilities amplified their hysteria. Dulles's intellectual and spiritual pride and colossal self-righteousness drove him into a morally indefensible role, for he evoked the Rule of Law as the world's hope while he and the President (the latter soon with some reluctance) clandestinely subdued Britain, France, and Israel with mortal economic sanctions. Behind his public appeals for "a decent respect for the opinions of mankind," Dulles was motivated by overt and covert panic before Russian power. He seems, also, to have been intimidated by Dag Hammarskjold's even more powerfully pious personality, as though he, too, was Dulles's confessor.

British writers who are hostile to Eden's policy on moral or military grounds are far from being enamored of Dulles's diplomacy and character. I quote only five among hosts of them, all moderate persons. One says: "It is difficult to see how any British Foreign Secretary could have dealt better [than Lloyd did] with an ally so uncertain, equivocating, and unreliable as Mr. Dulles." [2] Another believes, as we have already noted, that at least one action of Dulles's (SCUA) came "perilously close to prevarication." [3] Another says: "Possibily it was his training as a lawyer that had habituated him to maintaining separately but simultaneously in his mind the arguments that may be made for one side of a case, the arguments that may be used for the other side, and the arguments that may be used in rebuttal of either side. . . . This tendency of Dulles to shift his ground and his arguments to suit the case he was making for the moment was particularly prominent during the Suez crisis." [4]

Still another writer, who had unusual opportunities to know what was going on at the United Nations from October 5 to October 13, 1956, and who was a castigator of Eden, says: "Eden was not the first to have called Dulles a liar [he did not do so!], for his skill with words enabled him to make rings round cleverer men than the British Foreign Secretary, and gave him a complete dominance over his nominal master. . . . Now, Dulles was one of the most unattractive figures in modern history. . . . There is no doubt that Eden had a great deal of personal prevarication and evasion to contend with." [5] To conclude this sample anthology one may add the advice given by an English reviewer of Eden's memoirs, who remains anonymous. He said, *à propos* of Dulles's Middle East policy, and it seems in respect of "anticolonialism," that those who conduct American foreign policy should learn to include in their principles this old aphorism: No people do so much harm as those who go about doing good.[6]

Whatever the genuine or feigned nobility of Dulles's objectives in foreign policy, his deeds in the Suez conflict were inept, and eventually the United States was compelled to pay for them. We must presently look at the consequences in two related perspectives, the immediate aftereffects of the Suez war, and then, the politico-strategic ramifications.

THE IMMEDIATE AFTEREFFECTS OF SUEZ

The principal immediate aftereffects of Suez and Sinai were these. The United States weakened on the Six Principles. The British and French were forced to pay compensation for war damage to Egypt. The Canal was finally cleared of Egyptian blockships. The United Nations Emergency Force was established. The Canal was established as fully within the politics of one nation—Egypt.

In March, 1957, the government of Egypt addressed to all foreign diplomatic missions a unilateral declaration of its obligations regarding the administration of the Canal,[7] followed by another to the U.N. on April 24, 1957, after much pressure by Dulles through

Ambassador Raymond Hare. Eventually, Henry Cabot Lodge declared that the United States believed the declaration was very far from confirming the Six Principles. But he prudently added that it should be given a try.[8]

By May, 1957, the British and French governments withdrew the boycott of the Canal they had hitherto imposed on the shipping operations of their nationals. By early 1958, the claims and cross claims for war damages caused by the allies and for the "Egyptianization" of the installations on the Canal Base and of allied business firms in Egypt were settled, and Egypt's sterling balances were unfrozen. All tolls thenceforward were payable to the Egyptian Suez Canal Authority.

To test her rights and the sincerity of Dulles's promises, the government of Israel was compelled on March 13 to declare she would resume fighting if Aqaba were again blockaded by Nasser. Then, on March 17, an Israeli freighter sailed through the Gulf, and was not molested. A wild, acrimonious storm of protests issued from the Arab countries. Dulles was caught in the embarrassing fix of trying to get his Eisenhower Doctrine accepted both in Washington and in the Middle East, and especially in the continuing attempt to ingratiate himself with Saudi Arabia. Fear of an Israeli resumption of fighting, as well as recognition of the justice of her case, and the admission that he had made a distinct pledge about Aqaba, compelled him to stand by his pledge and to tell the Arab claimants that if they wished to contest it, they could ask the International Court for a ruling. At the beginning of April, 1957, a U.S. tanker chartered to Israel arrived at Elath, the first American ship to do so since 1950. The storm of protests from the Arab countries reached hurricane violence, with the threat that such vessels would be blacklisted. Further such sailings were not undertaken while the State Department and Cairo were discussing the forthcoming Egyptian declaration on the future management of the Canal. The negotiations were tense and trying: Nasser was a brutal customer after having been presented with a political victory of world-political proportions by the U.S. But on May 8, after Nasser's Canal declaration to the United States, and Henry Cabot Lodge's swallowing hard but not protesting at its inadequacy, a second U.S. tanker reached Elath, to confirm the internationality of the passage. But, again, on June 29, the State Department was forced to administer an exceedingly sharp rebuke to the Arab countries for their threats against freedom of passage. The Administration was then also annoyed by the passage of Russian warships, surface and submarine, around and through Suez, and their cruising in the Red Sea, a typical example of Nasser's contemptuous provocation and connivance. He was merely exploiting every atom of power his nation possessed.

In July, 1957, Egypt, being now in total possession and control of the Canal, enacted a law forbidding its Canal Authority to discriminate against the passage of any ship, *except* Israeli vessels. It announced that the Authority would accept compulsory jurisdiction before the International Court in legal conflicts concerning the Canal's operation. Of course, the Egyptian government could cancel that law whenever it saw fit. Thus, the Canal was entirely subordinate to the politics of one single nation, Egypt. This is the situation Dulles had repeatedly inveighed must not be allowed to take shape. Of course, as was to be expected, Nasser abrogated the Anglo-Egyptian Treaty of 1954. The winner takes all!

Yet, ask the intimate collaborators of Dulles, now, after seven years, their judgment of Dulles's Suez policy, and they will claim it was a success. For this belief they advance two reasons. First, they argue, the Suez Canal has been free for passage and has been efficiently operated, and the increase in the tolls has not been unreasonable. Secondly, the Russians have been kept out of the Middle East. With an eager expression of pride in their handiwork, they demand what more could be expected?

This self-satisfaction is far from justified, and is fairly easily countered. For, first, the Canal has until now been open and its operation efficient largely because Britain and France made war in 1956. We are entitled to doubt whether if they had not descended on Egypt and terrified Nasser he would have kept the Canal open to them at all times. Might not passage have been closed or impeded in order, for example, to help the Algerian rebellion against France? Might not the threat of obstruction have been used to assist the "fraternal" Soviet Union to exert its pressures on Berlin and Cuba and thereby on the United States? Might not the Canal have been openly or surreptitiously mismanaged to counter Western assistance to Jordan, Lebanon, Iraq, and Saudi Arabia against Nasser's subversive activities? Could it not be expected that help by the West to Israel against the *fedayeen* would be estopped by the threat of Nasser to close the Canal, as Dulles himself feared? It is a valid point that the trauma and military disgrace Nasser sustained at Israel's hands has forced him, so far, to honor his unilateral declaration that the Canal passage would be kept open even if not to Israel. The shock of physical force has compelled him to keep his promise lest force should be used again. Yet, even so, Israeli ships and the ships of some nations, *not* Israeli but doing business with Israel, have been hindered in their innocent passage by the Canal Authority, to assist Egypt's policy of enmity to Israel.

Secondly, Moscow lost influence, by degrees, in the Middle East, not so much because the United States had opposed Britain and France over Suez, as because experience before and after Suez caused fear among the Arabs that once the Soviet Union is allowed into a country as an ally, it or its local agents usurp the government of that country once and for all. Furthermore, the infiltration of the Soviet Union and China into Cuba, with the former's building of missile sites and weapons there, between 1959 and 1962, seems to justify the sinister interpretation of Britain and France: they believed that the Communist deliveries to Egypt of arms and other military supplies, which were then deployed in the Sinai Desert, were intended eventually to win control over the Middle East.

Thirdly, following from the considerations already set forth, if the Canal had been allowed to stay in Nasser's hands in 1956 by mere complaisance on the part of the despoiled allies, who knows what adventures he, rabid to be a Hero, and Moscow, bent on acquiring world hegemony wherever the cost is cheap, might not have undertaken in the Middle East, according to their own conveniently planned timetable? Certainly, the approaching war against Israel would have come fairly soon, and America would have been brought into that war in spite of herself—or would Dulles and Eisenhower have found a way to evade their word to Israel? Until Suez, the United States had not developed a practicable scheme to quell Nasser or to acquit its pledge to Israel under the Tripartite Pact. And the promises of Dulles, Eisenhower, and Henry Cabot Lodge, during the actual uproar over Suez at the United Nations, have not been kept.

THE POLITICO-STRATEGIC RAMIFICATIONS OF SUEZ

The Eisenhower Doctrine for the Middle East. By the middle of December, 1956, Dulles took fright that Nasser's unbridled incitements from Cairo would precipitate the overthrow of the Arab governments in the Middle East, disintegrate the Baghdad Pact, and open the door fully to the power of the Soviet Union. On January 5, 1957, the President asked Congress to associate itself with his Middle East foreign policy by a resolution. This would endorse the giving of aid to any Middle East government that asked for help against an overt attack by a government "dominated by international communism"; the supplying of arms to these governments for use against internal threats; and the furnishing of special funds for immediate disbursement in order to strengthen such governments.[9] Before, during, and after the President's request, the press was saturated with pleas by the Administration, that is, Dulles, that a "power vacuum" existed in the Middle East. The Senate Foreign Relations Committee was literally assailed with this demand for endorsement, either by panic or by shock tactics, with the plea that every minute counted.

The Doctrine was promulgated in the name of "collective self-defense," which was a perfectly prudent and legal reason. But the striking feature of the Doctrine was that America's own national interest was deemed to justify American armed intervention in the Middle East at America's exclusive discretion. The United Nations was not in any way consulted on this United States threat to use force so far away from the American homeland. Yet in this, Dulles and Eisenhower were justified and wise: they had created a Frankenstein in Nasser; he now needed to be curbed. Nevertheless, it caused the British and French political leaders to claim wryly that the moral rules Dulles had applied in the Suez affair, to their discomfiture, were cynical and hypocritical. They also validly pointed out that Dulles was now asking for authority to enter the Middle East with arms because, since Suez, there was a "change in the possible deterrent role of certain Western European nations." He had dealt that role a fatal blow.

After the Doctrine and the money had been trundled about the Middle East for some time by Ambassador James P. Richards, a special envoy (a former Democratic Congressman, appointed to demonstrate bipartisanship), Dulles, with improbable humor, observed that the Doctrine was "nothing that is sufficiently tangible to be 'embraced,' you might say. (*Laughter from the reporters.*) It is an attitude, a point of view, a state of mind." [10] Iraq, Lebanon, Libya, Turkey, Iran, Pakistan, Afghanistan, and Saudi Arabia officially accepted the Doctrine. Yemen and the Sudan received the Ambassador, but not the Doctrine. He did not expect to be received on the subject by Egypt, Syria, and Jordan, and his expectation was fulfilled. The main utility of the Doctrine was as a public warning to Moscow not to go beyond a certain trip-wire.

In April, 1957, Hussein of Jordan, beset by Jordanian political enemies who were instigated by Nasser, indirectly asked for help against "international communism." Dulles and Eisenhower could warrant that Egypt and Syria were the instruments of the menace. Eisenhower declared Jordan's independence "vital" to the United States. Hussein's regime was saved by the young king's intrepidity as well as United States diplomatic support.[11] Yet by this support America laid itself open to the charge of meddling in a purely inter-Arab conflict, and its action looked like an example of what had been vituperously condemned as "gunboat" diplomacy during the Suez crisis by those hostile to Britain and France. Indeed, a little earlier Dulles had declared that he would take whatever action he thought necessary in the Middle East without first asking the U.N. for its endorsement. How much better it would have been to have disciplined Nasser during October and November, 1956, when he was very weak and conspicuously culpable! Even Tunisia, Libya, Ethiopia, Iraq, Lebanon, Jordan, and Saudi Arabia felt it necessary by mid-June to expel Egypt's military attachés in order to put an end to their subversive scheming on Nasser's orders.

Dulles's policy had nourished a monster. During the Jordanian crisis, the Sixth Fleet had had to be ordered to maneuver in the Eastern Mediterranean. When the Anglo-Jordanian Treaty was abrogated by Jordan in March, 1957, and the British subsidy of $30 million a year thus came to an end, the United States was forced to become the regular subsidizer of Jordan. The United States was in the Middle East up to the hilt, and Moscow became an ever more shrill and menacing enemy there.

In the late summer of 1957, Syrian collaboration with the Soviet Union reached almost a hot-war level. In particular, Turkey, the anchor of the Baghdad Pact and the east flank of NATO, feared a Syrian-Russian attack. For separate and for common reasons, Lebanon, Jordan, Iraq, Saudi Arabia, and Israel also were frightened. President Eisenhower was compelled to issue a strong warning to Syria and Russia and to send Loy Henderson to the spot to appraise and appease local fears and to manipulate the Eisenhower Doctrine. As soon as Syria was warned, all the other Arab countries turned against the United States! Some of them had already received their American money or a commitment that they would do so.

The vaunted rise in American prestige in the Middle East, expected by Dulles and State Department officials as the reward for the Administration's enmity towards the allies' attack on Suez, was dissipated (if it had ever existed). In June, 1957, Nasser, while slightly reducing the credit to Russia for her support, also attributed the Anglo-French cease-fire to other causes: that the allies had not obtained a quick victory; that the Egyptian people were prepared to continue to fight; that the Egyptian army was still in being, though in retreat; that world opinion foiled the allies. Some of these claims were deliberate political lies or illusions. The omission of thanks to Dulles and Eisenhower was the grossest ingratitude.

In January, 1958, Nasser obtained some reward for his everlasting plotting and intrigues. Syria joined Egypt to form the United Arab Republic. It did this because the Syrian National Socialist politicians now feared the capture of their nation by the Syrian Communists.

A graver crisis involved the United States more dangerously in July, 1958, in the Middle East. In the most extreme brevity, the facts need to be noticed.The internal political system of Lebanon is based on a free and highly precarious balance of diverse Moslem and Christian sects. Its stability was imminently menaced in mid-1958 by a Moslem reaction against the attempt of President Chamoun, a Christian, to seek a further term of office. Lebanon and Iraq went to the Security Council for help against "massive, illegal and unprovoked intervention" by the United Arab Republic. The Security Council was unhelpful, since the Soviet Union supported Nasser, so offsetting the help given Lebanon by the U.S.A. and Britain. Eisenhower, advised by Dulles, alerted the Sixth Fleet and had the Marines in the Eastern

Mediterranean reinforced, without the blessing of the United Nations. This was analogous to the allied move on Suez.

In the midst of the poised violence in Lebanon, the Iraqi government was overthrown by a joint assault of pro-Nasser and "nationalist" Communist groups (July 14, 1958). Nuri Es Said and King Faisal and many in their government and among their political supporters were bestially murdered and their bodies desecrated. General Abdel Karrim al-Kassim's followers, the victors, were so fanatical and violent that a war of all against all in the Middle East, Arabs versus Arabs, and Arabs versus Israel, was rightly feared. The American and British governments acted at once by joint arrangement in response to appeals for help by Beirut and Amman. The U.S. landed Marines as soon as this was physically possible, without asking the U.N. for permission first, dispatching them, indeed, long before it even notified the U.N. The decision and speed were praiseworthy. But the action did stir derogatory comments about Dulles's philippics against the British and French, about the sanctity of the "one law" as established by the U.N., and about his preachments against the use of force. Dulles's justification was the need for swift action to exercise the right of collective self-defense; to satisfy the call of a freely elected government subjected to indirect aggression; to protect American nationals; and to uphold the principle that "the independence and integrity of the nations of the Middle East [are] vital to the American national interest and to world peace." [12] Some of these pleas were not so very different from the British and French pleas regarding Suez—Britain and France had, according to Dulles, been actually despoiled of their international rights by illegal violence.

We lack the space in this context to pursue the American adventure further. President Eisenhower (he told me) lived through a period of sharp agony after ordering the Marines to land: he feared that Russia might set the Middle East, and maybe the world, ablaze. This was one more miscalculation of Russian tactics and strength. All American forces were appropriately deployed throughout the world. The Russians moved only the muscles of their mouths. The Marine landing was, of course, unopposed, and was far from being the efficient exercise the Administration claimed.[13] But the Middle East simmered down, and the troubles of Lebanon were resolved by domestic negotiations assisted by the good offices of Robert Murphy.

Dulles's policy in Lebanon resolutely cold-shouldered the U.N. in the early and decisive stages—and rightly so. Eventually, American forces left, mainly because it was learned that they were unwanted, unneeded, and ineffectual. The United States gladly accepted the U.N. resolutions for their withdrawal.[14] The venture was politically sound, as, in the end, the British, French, and Israeli action had been. For it showed Nasser and the Syrian politicians and Moscow that the

United States meant business. It was also a deed of the most doubtful legality,[15] perhaps more so than that of Britain and France had been in the much more complicated legal circumstances of the Canal's seizure. (Israel's action, based on self-defense, had been legally pure.)

Thus, United States armed intervention in Lebanon called the Russian bluff about sending "volunteers." Nasser learned, with shock, that if he went too far in his revolutionary trouble-making, or committed an act of war himself, the United States could act effectively and quickly. Once engaged, he would have to retreat, or lose face, or be overthrown.

He also learned the lesson of dressing up his personal ambitions to be a Hero in a more highly colored and deceiving mantle of Arab nationalism, Arab socialism, and Arab independence. Thereupon the United States returned to its former "impartiality" and bolstered Nasser's economy, during years of severe strain for him, with economic help. Since the beginning of 1959, this has totaled more than the amount for the Aswan Dam that in the 1956 scheme would have had to come from the United States and Britain and the World Bank together: to mid-September, 1963, Nasser had received a total of $671.3 million, of which $147.2 million was in grants, the rest loans.[16] None of this aid was military, but Egyptian budgetary diversions have enabled it to support Nasser's continued military strengthening. He has even employed nearly 30,000 men from 1962 onwards in a war in Yemen to impose his hegemony through a "rebel" and "republican" government. (During the years 1959 to 1963, Israel has received from the U.S.A. $356.5 million, of which $56.6 million has been in grants. The military assistance within this has been $3.2 million.)

In some recess of the State Department there seems to reign an impregnable concern for the Arab nations, and especially Egypt, that triumphs over any change in the party in power. What is behind this concern? Is it oil? It it strategic location? Is it containment of Russia? Is it pro-Arab romanticism? And once again, is it oil, and the businessmen who deal in oil? The pro-Arab interest is abiding; it is occult; it evades full daylight and tractability.

In Chapter 17 we quoted Ben Gurion's reproach to President Eisenhower that the sword of Damocles, in spite of American promises, still hangs over Israel's head. The sword of Damocles, in 1963, included the employment by the Egyptian government of foreign (mainly German) scientists to develop missiles, capable, as Nasser has boasted, of reaching as far as Syria, which means Israel as well. The standard American State Department defense for refusing to obstruct such help to Nasser's capacity to make the war that all the Arab nations fearfully promise is that if the scientists were not German then they would be from the Russian bloc! There are certainly more potent answers to Nasser available to the State Department than such facetiae. One is the sale to Israel of the Hawk, a ground-to-air missile. But there are others even more peremptory and effective.

The British remain in the Middle East: in Kuwait, Bahrein, the Trucial States, and Aden; and they have important interests in Iran. They are more determined spiritually, and better equipped militarily, as a result of being jockeyed so injuriously by their American ally in 1956. Yet the brunt of maintaining peace in the Middle East falls on the United States. When Kassim's Iraq broke away from the Baghdad Pact, in September, 1958, Dulles found it imperative to make separate bilateral security agreements with Turkey, Iran, and Pakistan (consummated in March, 1959), and fully to enter the military committee of the Baghdad Treaty organization, thenceforward, with the exit of Iraq, called the Central Treaty Organization.

Most of the Arab nations, including Egypt, have drawn back from the Russian embrace, realizing that it is fatal. It was Dulles's grave misjudgment to believe they would ever have succumbed to it, Dam or no Dam, Suez or no Suez. The Russian intrusion into Egypt remains strong, however, for all sorts of arms still flow from the Russian bloc, and (since 1959) Russia is building the Aswan Dam. But the more crucial and enduring grip that Russia has over Nasser derives from another power-political factor altogether. At any moment, Moscow could allow a quarter- or half-million Russian Jews to leave the Soviet Union for Israel, by opening the possibility to them and supplying the exit permits. Nasser prefers to have these potential emigrants remain imprisoned in Russia rather than have them in Israel to help guard Israel's borders and repel the assault of Arab soldiers. Since Khrushchev's ignominious retreat with his missiles from Cuba in October, 1962, most of the confidence his Arab friends, like Nasser, had in the Soviet Union has evaporated. It was, therefore, only funny when Syria and Iraq, in August, 1963, expressed their confidence in the Soviet Union because its Ambassador at the United Nations vetoed a resolution that condemned Syria's wanton murder of two Israelis. The West, after Suez, and especially after Cuba, is no longer to be frightened by Arab appeals to Moscow, as Dulles and Eisenhower were frightened in October and November, 1956. It is also wryly amusing that after all of Dulles's support to Jordan, Jordan in October, 1963, established, for the first time, diplomatic relations with Moscow.

"*Colonialism.*" Dulles failed in fortitude and sound reason when he submitted to Arab and Asian accusations of his allies' colonialism. A justification can always be found for breaking a treaty when the culprit is sufficiently unscrupulous to pretend to have acted from nationalism as the world's highest good. The violator of treaties has only to allege, for example, that his nation happened to be in a weak bargaining position at the moment the treaty was made. But such self-serving justification opens up a radical and unending era of revision, driving all nations back to the dawn of history. As Ernest Renan said in *Qu'est-ce qu'une nation?*, "Everybody would demand what is strategically convenient to him, and a war without end would ensue . . . to reach some mountain or some river, to which one credits a kind of a priori quality." And in our time, a dictator's own personal creed, his own ambitions for power and place, can easily be made to appear in the guise of his nation's necessity. If the corollary of nationalism is a permanent state of change, with every country having the right to tear up treaties upon any new whim or caprice of a patriot or a party, then the right of resistance to maintain one's own achieved position in the world of competing and rebelling nations is equally justified. Nations should not restrain their allies who try hard to keep their heads above water. For *they*, like the alleged liberators, may well argue: "This present revolt against us is only a temporary change in order to amend a former temporary change in the administration of a given area. Why should we tolerate it, if we have the power to stop it?"

And why should it be expected that newly arrived dictators in Africa, Asia, the Pacific should be satiated when they have made gains like those of Nasser's in Suez? As soon as the British inducted Kuwait into nationhood, Kassim of Iraq laid claim to Kuwait. The India of Nehru and Menon had no compunction about seizing the province of Goa (belonging to Portugal) by *force*, although Menon had pontificated to the United Nations during the Suez proceedings before the General Assembly, November 26, 1956, "We deny the right to wage war." Sukarno, tyrant of an Indonesia with a population of 100 million people, still used force to jockey the Netherlands and the United States government in 1962 into giving up Dutch New Guinea to him, and, his *arriviste* imperialism still unappeased, threatened force to prevent the establishment and peaceful operation of the federation of Malaysia, founded in September, 1963. He did this despite the United Nations' acquiescence to his (and the Philippines') demand that it send experts to ascertain the wishes of the inhabitants, and the fact that the United Nations had certified the popular consent after proper inquiries in which his representatives participated.

The lamentable truth is, as Eden foresaw, and as he has recently reiterated, that the appeasement of such men does not mean peace over the long run, but only the relaxation of tensions for a while.[17] We have learned since Suez that to such men as Nasser anticolonialism does not merely mean exemption from being governed by foreigners, but the freedom to oppress, imprison, exile, or execute native political opponents without any control, legal or otherwise, from inside or outside the nation, as well as to be imperialistic.

The Rule of Law and the United Nations. The Suez and Sinai episodes throw a searching light on the United Nations. They once again expose the futility of a weak nation's seeking justice from it; for Egypt received not justice, but indulgence, and Israel got not justice, but injury, as did Britain and France. The Charter, it seems, may be a sanctuary for the users of illegal violence, the violators of morality, peace, and international law, if they are strong and unscrupulous and can collect interest-begotten votes. In such situations, injury can be inflicted on the more conscientious and law-abiding parties to a dispute: the international desperado goes free. The *total* factors in an injustice, that is to say, all the elements that created it, were not, in the Suez and Sinai affair, brought into the account at the U.N. For example, Menon refused to include consideration of the kind of government that rules Egypt, that is, Nasser and "mob rule," as he called it (lenitively, not punitively). Yet this happened to be quite a significant element in the seizure of the Canal and the dispatch of *fedayeen* to perpetrate murder and arson in Israel.

In the Suez affair, Dulles, acting for the United States, played a dubious game at the U.N. Either he was insincere in his pronouncements that he was pursuing the Rule of Law, or his moralism overcame any prudent assessment of the national interest of the United States. Or, perhaps, his tactics were a mask for his physical fear of the Soviet Union. The outcome of his policy was a signal injustice for Britain, France, and Israel. It made American policy look cynical and neither noble nor Christian. The ardent pursuit of the "one law" and of "justice" was tarnished by America's use of economic sanctions and bullying against its friends, and the Middle East Doctrine and the descent on Lebanon demonstrated the superiority of national interests to the "one law." Such behavior is hardly conducive, when the public gets to know about it, to the enhancement of the moral validity of the U.N. and "world opinion." [18] Of course, the public attitudes of the U.S. government did not, in the slightest, persuade Moscow to let down its guard or cease manufacturing bigger nuclear weapons and missiles or mollify its egocentric actions in the U.N.

Dulles knew very well that a General Assembly in which all the unequally strong or unequally advanced nations had an equal vote is bound to vote unjust resolutions or obstruct just ones. But, in order to get his own way in the case of Suez and Sinai, he glossed over this deficiency, attributing to the General Assembly a supreme moral right, even imputing to it the representation of "world opinion"—

a notion, surely, replete with fallacies. Not to heed Dulles's critics on this ground—and the Soviet Union happens to be one of them—may lead to putting the United States on some very awkward occasion (as that of Lebanon or, possibly, of Panama) in a moral predicament, indeed, a legal mess, extrication from which will require chicanery or humiliation. This occurred in the matter of Cuba in April, 1961, and in October, 1962, though justice was never so much on the side of the United States as then. And justice was on the side of Britain, France, and Israel in 1956.

The Atlantic Alliance Devitalized. Dulles's tactics as much as his policy marked a decisive hour in the weakening of the NATO alliance. If the allies had lost the battle against Nasser, so long as they had had the support of Dulles and Eisenhower, even by neutrality and silence, NATO would have been strengthened. Suez tore NATO apart and it has never been possible fully to restore its corporate morale. France had strong reason to be annoyed with Britain. Germany glowed in self-righteousness that it was not she who had used force! The new British Prime Minister, Harold Macmillan, superseding Eden in January, 1957, conferred amicably with Mollet, and each of these with Eisenhower, and Macmillan and Lloyd in Bermuda in late March, 1957, with Eisenhower and Dulles.[19] Britain stretched out her hand toward the United States and France towards West Germany. But the warmth had vanished, even though Dulles tried his best to pretend it had not. On January 16, 1958, at the National Press Club, he claimed he had supported the rights of Britain, France, and Israel in the Suez Canal. But he still insisted that he would have advised the President to act as he had done in November of 1956. He continued:

> But I have never yet in public office—and I do not think I ever shall—try to explain the reason or defend myself for that, because I cannot do that without reopening old wounds, old controversies, which we are trying to heal and which, in my opinion, have been healed, for which I thank God.[20]

His self-assurance, as so often, was wrong.

The considerable increase in the economic strength of the European nations and in their inner cohesion from 1956 to the present, and the advent of de Gaulle as quasi-dictator of France in May, 1958, would have been expected to cause some relaxation of the postwar state of dependency of Europe on the United States. But Suez produced NATO's calamitous debility. This was Dulles's doing, blessed by the authority of President Eisenhower. De Gaulle was privy to every incident of allied relations during the unfolding of the Suez affair. Whatever objections Dulles might have made to de Gaulle's action, had he then been Prime Minister of France, de Gaulle would have gone on to the end, despite them, and thrown on Dulles the full onus of withholding dollar support and oil supplies from his allies, and of maintaining his chaste and prim procrastination in the clearing of the Canal. Why, the political leaders of France and Britain were bound to ask, why should their nations accept the subordinate fate to which they had momentarily been consigned by Dulles's hectoring, guile, desertion, and sermonizing moral rebukes? Their misgivings were not appeased by Dulles's suggestion to their envoys that it was a pity they had not finished Nasser, or by his concession that (as he soon admitted to Vice President Richard M. Nixon) he himself had been *too hasty in his promotion of anticolonialism*, or by his naked appeal to national interest in the affair of Lebanon.

At Nassau, in late December, 1962, Prime Minister Harold Macmillan impressed President John F. Kennedy with the plea that Britain must have her own nuclear weapon, Polaris, in her own control, to be used "where the Briitsh would be alone and would need this force." The specific reference of Macmillan and Kennedy was to the Suez situation, in which the former suggested that the British had been isolated, and threatened with the bombardment of their island. "We hope," said President Kennedy, "the situation will not come again where they are isolated that way again. But I think they are conscious of that history." [21] On January 14, 1963, de Gaulle reiterated his intention to build France's own atomic force, as America and Britain were doing, for purposes of the "supreme national interest." [22] On September 23, 1963, the policy was specifically related to the French plight during the Suez crisis by Ambassador Hervé Alphand in a public speech in Chicago.

The essential truth is that when a nation has allies it is because it needs them in its own interests, and not because it is doing them a charitable favor. It must expect to pay something for an alliance. But, in the Suez affair, Dulles was not even prepared to relax his personal righteousness and hauteur and discover a way for justice for his allies by putting a curb on Nasser. It was for them to make renunciations and so be "great and noble" by his standards, but he was to yield nothing, hardly even oil and dollars. It is not at all surprising that when in 1963 the United States asked its Western allies to stop their freighters from carrying goods to Cuba, in order to force that country to loosen its Communist ties, the allies refused with the same arguments used by Dulles when he refused to stop U.S. vessels from paying tolls to Nasser.

The fact is that Dulles would not acknowledge the classic principle of the "balance of power" and its subordinate device, *divide et impera*, divide and rule, according to which he should have attempted to weaken the power or potential power of men who were hostile to the West. Nasser has pursued this policy to prevent a union of Arab nations outside his personal domination, and he carries the principle even to subverting Arab states from within—Jordan, Lebanon, Yemen, Saudi Arabia, Iraq, Syria—and to disrupting the Arab League. The Soviet Union exploits the policy in keeping Germany divided. "Divide and rule" does not imply internal and deep rulership of the territories that have been kept more or less divided; it can be implemented as no more than the power to regulate relationships between the associated states or parts of states (if the country is not yet a mature nation) to assure one's own safety and peace. Thus, in 1958, the U.S. Marines were landed in Lebanon to prevent a mob-enforced union of that country with Nasser's regime.

Why should one build up one's potential enemies? Once the weak have been assisted to strength, their gratitude cannot be counted on. For example, consider the Egyptian reaction when, in November, 1963, the U.S. Senate moved to restrict American economic aid to Egypt, because it was "engaged in or preparing for aggressive military effort against the United States or any country receiving its aid." The government-dominated Cairo newspaper *Akhbar Al Yom* warned that "the natural answer would be the nationalization of the oil of the whole Middle East." [23] Another paper truculently mentioned the case of the withdrawal of the Aswan Dam loan offer. The Middle East News Agency had the audacity to denounce the proposed Senate prohibition as having been taken because Egyptian military action in Yemen "had shown gigantic developments in United Arab Republic military potential and that progress realized in the U.A.R. in the field of rockets will allow her to put an end to Israel in hours."

Dulles's failure in the Suez affair to discipline Nasser, because the Secretary adhered to some supposed principle of being kind to "Pan-Arab nationalism," has resulted in Nasser's arrogant aggressions all over the Middle East. There have been worse consequences. If Nasser had been shown that petty dictators, holding strategically located territory, would not be allowed to violate treaties with impunity, a Fidel Castro would never have dared defy the United States in association with Moscow or betray his own people by his treacherous megalomania. He would have known from Nasser's fate that he faced punishment by boycott, quarantine, blockade, and even rougher measures. Instead, what he witnessed was that intransigence *à outrance* was rewarded by brute success and heroic applause. And this was a bad example to Sukarno also, in respect of West Irian and his imperialistic threats against Malaysia.

These considerations pose the question Nasser opened for Britain, France, and Israel, namely, the right to self-defense. Thus Eden had implored that Britain's lifeline be not left unguaranteed in the hands of men like Nasser. Dulles had responded that the "sword of Damocles" ought not to be left in the hands that seized it illegally.

In his justly famous, even classic, speech of October 22, 1962, announcing a quarantine around Cuba on all offensive military equipment, and promising to defend America and her allies and Latin America against nuclear attack by the Soviet Union, President Kennedy said: "The 1930's taught us a clear lesson: aggressive conduct, if allowed to go unchecked and unchallenged, ultimately leads to war." [24] This was almost verbatim the burden of the pleas and cables and phone messages from Eden to Dulles and Eisenhower in the Suez affair. President Kennedy's action and principles were right. It is a pity that Dulles and Eisenhower did not take the necessary measures against Castro in 1959 and 1960. But since the United States did not defend its allies in principle or practice against Nasser (and its own interests, therefore, in alliances that stretch all the way to Pakistan and Australasia), on what principle could it move against Castro while there was time? It had swallowed the pretensions of Arab nationalism, as personified in Nasser—his claims to his own sovereign system of rule, his demands for self-defense, his acquisition of offensive weapons regardless of the terrible consequences for his neighbors. Anything, almost, Dulles and Eisenhower were saying, for a quiet life! Were Cuban nationalism and the Cuban dictator any less deserving of indulgence?

The United Nations Charter does not take away from sovereign nations their right of self-defense: even Article 51 accepts this as an "inherent" right. But international law gives wide latitude to nations to defend themselves in situations far less provocative than "armed attack" of a direct kind. It even extends to abrupt and hostile deprivation of one's economic resources, in the nature, surely, of a deliberate stranglehold. And certainly it permits retaliation against weapons at a distance "to which their guns would carry their shot." [25] The British and the French had a good, solid case against Nasser, and it is a pity that they did not act upon it forthrightly. The Israelis had an even better case, and did so act.

In an age of absolute thermonuclear weapons, with a supersonic speed of delivery, the accumulation of small losses of national power can end by being an irretrievable loss of power. Why did not Dulles help his allies and Israel? Partly from a congenital want of empathy. But that is not the only answer. He had been nurtured in a country that had never known, as these allies had known, the agony of occupation by a foreign enemy: the wars of 1870, 1914, 1939, and in Israel, 1948, and the incessant war of commandos. The United States had not, fortunately, suffered the atrocities, devastation, loss of life brought by war as had France and Britain in World War II. Nations whose very existence has been at stake conceive of their self-defense more realistically than those who have so far been spared the horror. But it is the profession of a statesman to understand horrors without having experienced them. If he does not, he commits the errors that Dulles committed. It is also the profession of a statesman to make an innocent people understand the terrors they have not personally experienced. If he does not, they also commit mistakes and can call him to account for the payment they must eventually make for his and their errors. Had Dulles had the appropriate imagination about reality in far-off lands, he might have advised his President to put inescapable pressure on Nasser, to face down the Soviet Union then and there in November, 1956, and allow Britain and France to topple Nasser or obtain the redress he himself prescribed for the undoubted wrongs done them. It was his responsibility to discover a better formula between the extremes of isolationism and domination.

The War of Nerves in the Twentieth Century. The foregoing observations suggest a final question: the posture the United States is to assume in the era of thermonuclear weapons. The present author foresaw in 1946 that the Superpowers would be so fearfully intimidated by nuclear weapons that they would be compelled to avoid war.[26] Yet the various causes impelling to war in different parts of the world still exist. America everywhere suffers a ceaseless and remorseless confrontation with Soviet Russia's power and Soviet Russia's friends. In the atomic age it is necessary to maximize the territory within which one can find friendly places over which to distribute one's military sites, on land and ocean, to insure against the total loss of strike-back power after an enemy has made his first and second atomic assaults.

No Communist encroachment can be accepted, whether direct or indirect, on American soil or in other lands, for example, Egypt or Syria or Turkey or Britain, which may give Moscow an atomic purchase over the United States. The risk must be run that apparently small disputes, such as Suez, may rise to atomic strikes. This dynamic geo-strategic situation imposes a war of nerves, in the first place, on the President of the United States. He needs the nerve to champion America's necessities and claims against the obstruction or aggressiveness of the Soviet Union, the nerve to make demands and threats as well as to act with prudence and conciliation. The example was set in the week of October 22, 1962, when the blockade was mounted around Cuba (directed against the Soviet Union). It was completely successful in its aims. It was the first time that anyone had had the courage to say No! to Khrushchev, inside or outside the Soviet Union, and to make the prohibition effective.

President Kennedy's daring and poise had the most salutary effect on the balance of power in the world. The ignominious withdrawal of Russia's missiles, the unmasking of the Soviet Foreign Minister's falsehoods to the President, the Russian submission to President Kennedy's demands with all signs of panic in Soviet political and military circles, all dealt a mortal blow to Khrushchev's global presumptuousness. No matter what boasts or threats he or his associates have subsequently uttered or may utter, they have irredeemably lost any substantial credibility. In the supreme trial of nerves, Khrushchev and his Communist Presidium were exposed as hollow, and too many nations know of this for Moscow's comfort.

This puncturing of the Soviet balloon could have been achieved in October and November, 1956, six years earlier, during the Suez affair. How healthy an event that would have been for the whole world! It is the principal tragedy of Dulles's role in the Suez affair, of Dulles over Suez, that for all his moral preachments, he was deficient in the nerve to challenge Bulganin and Khrushchev to remain passive while the United States or her allies acted. Indeed, Dulles's failure of nerve before the frown of Moscow contributed to the increase in Soviet strength and audacity, to additions to her friends and admirers, to the enhanced ability of small nations to harass and injure the United States and her allies, and to the nurture of homicidal subversion in the Middle East.

The full price has not yet been paid for Dulles's deficiency of nerve in not standing fast at the Suez brink created by Nasser and Moscow. He let himself be outbluffed, and the debts he so incurred are still coming to light. In public speeches and in the remoteness of the State Department and White House offices he truculently talked a forward-spirited, domineering, and all-too-crafty foreign policy. But involved in the real war of nerves, where the real bullets fly, he proved ineffective. For his vision of the national interest and the world-full of tough nations was confused by an unmanageable number of nebulous notions and fancies of a too-distant world with-
to the enhanced temptation of small nations to harass and injure the
out. It was simultaneously bedeviled by his own hyper-intense religious passions deep in the recesses of his ego. All contradicted each other even as they were contradicted by reality. These sentimentalisms and *idées fixes* were functionally disabling. And, furthermore, faced with reality in Suez and Sinai, his action was stultified by a want of courage.

Sources: The authoritative sources for this work fall into three categories: Personal Interviews, noted immediately preceding Chapter 1; Notes to the Text; Publications.

Notes

CHAPTER 1: DISASTER OVER SUEZ AND SINAI

1. John Watson Foster, *Diplomatic Memoirs* (2 vols., Boston, 1919).
2. Robert Lansing, *The Big Four and Others of the Peace Conference* (Boston, 1921), and *The Peace Negotiations: A Personal Narrative* (Boston, 1921); and Julius W. Pratt, in Vol. X of *The American Secretaries of State*, ed. Samuel Bemis (New York, 1929).
3. Cf. News Conference, U. S., Department of State, *Press Release*, 543, October 16, 1956.
4. Speech, "World Forum," given in Dallas, Texas, October 27, 1956, and appearing in U. S., Department of State, *Bulletin*, November 5, 1956, pp. 698 ff.
5. U. S., Senate, Foreign Relations Committee, *Hearings*, February 24, 1956, p. 19. "The fact is, they [the Soviet Union] have failed, and they have got to devise new policies. . . . Those policies have gradually ceased to produce results for them. The free nations have banded together, shown their strength, shown their unity to an increasing degree so that policy was not producing any positive results. The result is, they have got to review their whole creed from A to Z. . . . But one thing that is absolutely certain is that the unity and firmness of the free nations during the past few years have caused the old Soviet policy to fail, and today they are trying to figure out how they are going to get a better one."
6. *New York Times*, November 4, 1956. The story in Lord Randolph Churchill, *The Rise and Fall of Sir Anthony Eden* (London, 1959), p. 294, that on October 30, 1956, President Eisenhower summoned the French Ambassador, etc., etc., is untrue. M. Alphand did not see the President that day. There are other errors in the book.

CHAPTER 2: DULLES AND THE MIDDLE EAST

1. For a brief but excellent introductory study, see J. C. Campbell, *Defense of the Middle East* (New York, 1960), especially for its valuable expository bibliography. Mr. Campbell served in the State Department and in the Middle East.

2. Computation from Chase Manhattan Bank, *Petroleum Industry Annual Survey* (1955), pp. 7-9; Benjamin Shwadran, *The Middle East, Oil and the Great Powers* (2nd ed., New York, 1959); Robert Engler, *The Politics of Oil* (New York, 1960). The figure named in the text is the book value; of course, many billions were spent for research and development, etc., for which see J. Hartson, *Oil Companies and Governments* (London, 1962), especially Chapter VII.
3. This work was first published in an Arab newspaper, *Akher Sa'a*, in December, 1953. In April and May, 1954, it was translated by the British and American Embassies for their use, when it was published again. There are various English translations. A current one, translation by the newspaper *Dar Al-Maaref* (Cairo), is published by Economica Books (Buffalo, 1959). It is too civilized. More representative is the translation by Richard H. Nolte, in *Institute of Current World Affairs Newsletter* (April, 1954). The Public Affairs Press (Washington, D. C.) published a translation in 1955, under the title *Egypt's Liberation: The Philosophy of the Revolution.*
4. Dulles bitterly resented his defeat in the United States senatorial election of 1949 at the hands of Herbert H. Lehman. This was after Dulles had served four months in the Senate on his nomination by Governor Thomas E. Dewey to the vacancy for New York left by the death of Robert F. Wagner. The campaign was bitter. During it Dulles made some charges that left him open to the accusation of anti-Semitism. He said to farmers in upstate New York: "If you could see the kind of people in New York City making up this bloc [various political groups, including quite unsought-for fellow-traveling leftists] that is voting for my opponent, if you could see them with your own eyes . . . you would be out, every last man and woman of you, voting on Election Day." *Time*, November 7, 1949, pp. 22-23. He was widely accused of bigotry by minority groups, including Negroes.
5. Cf. Harry S. Truman, *Memoirs*, Vol. II (New York, 1956), pp. 93 ff., for these moves.
6. See U. S., Department of State, *Bulletin*, June 5, 1950, p. 886, for text.
7. Cf. text in U. S., Department of State, *Bulletin*, October 22, 1951, pp. 647-648; and Great Britain, H. M. S. O., *Anglo-Egyptian Conversations on the Defence of the Suez Canal and on the Sudan*, Egypt No. 2, Cmd. 8419 (1951).
8. Report on Near East, by Secretary Dulles, in U. S., Department of State, *Bulletin*, June 15, 1953.
9. The pressure is hardly evident in the account given by President Eisenhower in his memoirs, Vol. I, *Mandate for Change* (New York, 1963), p. 150 *et seq.* But the pressure was very strong, and insistent.
10. Cf. Wilton Wynn, *Nasser and Egypt* (Arlington, W. Va., 1959); and Robert St. John, *The Boss: The Story of Gamal Abdel Nasser* (New York, 1960).
11. It stirred memories of the Anglo-American tensions of the Iran oil dispute. Herbert Morrison, *An Autobiography* (London, 1960), pp. 281 ff.; and L. P. Elwell-Sutton, *Persian Oil: A Study in Power Politics* (London, 1955) (rather overwrought). See also Norman Kemp, *Abadan: A First Hand Account of the Persian Oil Crisis* (London, 1953). Members of the Conservative Party took the displacement of Britain from exclusive exploitation rights in Iran very badly, and the result became a legend for rancor among them.
12. For full terms of the protest, see Royal Institute of International Affairs, *Documents: 1955*, ed. Noble Frankland (London, 1958), pp. 300 ff.

CHAPTER 3: A LOAN REFUSED: THE CANAL SEIZED

1. Cf. Richard Goold-Adams, *The Time of Power: A Reappraisal of John Foster Dulles* (London, 1962), p. 100.
2. For Caffery's views on the Middle East, see U. S., Senate, Committee on Foreign Affairs, *Hearings,* Part II, 85th Cong., 1st Sess., February 5 to February 11, 1957, pp. 769-826 ("The President's Proposal on the Middle East"), but especially pp. 775, 776, 788, 797, and 799. Henceforward these Hearings are referred to as *Middle East Doctrine Hearings,* or *M. E. D. Hearings.*
3. *M. E. D. Hearings,* p. 773.
4. *Ibid.,* pp. 703-768. Byroade expected this evidence to be given in executive session, not to be published. Dulles was very disquieted that Byroade was to appear before the Committee, as Byroade had evidence that did not in every particular suit Dulles's own version or policy. But Dulles could hardly prevent him. Byroade would have responded to questions differently had he known that his answers were to be published, for some of his remarks were deleted. He felt Nasser and Dulles had, each in his own way, unfairly harmed his career.
5. Cf. Caffery's statements, *M. E. D. Hearings,* pp. 776-777; and *Egypt's Liberation: The Philosophy of the Revolution* (Washington, D. C., 1955), on Nasser's confession that he was an assassin. The word "assassin" derives etymologically from "*hashshasheen,*" used during the Crusades to denote Arab warriors who worked themselves into fighting dementia by eating a hemp called "*Hasheesh,*" an intoxicant. There are other methods of political murder all over the world, and other homicidiacs. Nasser was in the great tradition.
6. Cf. Hussein, *Uneasy Lies the Head* (London, 1962).
7. *M. E. D. Hearings,* p. 764, and *passim.*
8. See Lieutenant-General E. L. M. Burns, *Between Arab and Israeli* (Toronto, 1962), pp. 18-22. This is an excellent account of the work of the United Nations Truce Supervision Organization under General Burns, and most important testimony on Arab-Israeli relations. It is excitingly written. It is marred by a bias unmistakably hostile to Israel's point of view.
9. The policy and strategy of "massive retaliation" was expressed in two phases. The first was in an address before the Council on Foreign Relations in New York, January 12, 1954, then somewhat amended by an article in *Foreign Affairs* (April, 1954). See U. S., Department of State, *Bulletin* (January 25, 1954), pp. 107-108. In gist this was the point: Economic strength was necessary over the long haul; therefore America must not spend herself into bankruptcy; therefore American geo-strategy, given nuclear weapons, needed a "new look." This "new look" led to the conclusion that the United States, to keep its commitments around the globe, must rely upon "massive retaliation" by nuclear weapons. In case of attack on her interests or her allies, she would retaliate on "targets of our own choosing." Cheap, and effective, it was thought. It underestimated two factors: that some "brush-fires," e.g., Indochina, could hardly be treated by nuclear warfare for topographical and moral reasons; and secondly, that the policy gave Dulles's allies the sense that they were being abandoned, *as indeed they were.* The businessmen in the Administration were principally responsible for urging this new look, and among the businessmen was Dulles, formerly of Wall Street.

10. Cf. Matthew B. Ridgeway, *A Soldier's Memoirs* (New York. 1956); Maxwell D. Taylor, *The Uncertain Trumpet* (New York, 1958), *passim.*
11. U. S., *Statistical Abstract* (1955), p. 892, Table 1112, and p. 896, Table 1114.
12. U. S., Department of State, *Bulletin*, February 20, 1956, pp. 285-286.
13. *M. E. D. Hearings*, Part I, p. 264.
14. Cf. Robert St. John, *op. cit.*, p. 210.
15. Sherman Adams, *First Hand Report* (New York, 1961), pp. 245 ff.
16. Robert J. Donovan, *The Inside Story* (New York, 1956), p. 371.
17. Sir Anthony Eden, *Full Circle* (Cambridge, Mass., 1960), p. 373.
18. *Ibid.*, Chapter VIII.
19. My discussion of Aswan relies heavily on oral information. It is augmented by the discussions in *M. E. D. Hearings*, 2 vols., *passim;* M. L. Cooke, *Nasser's High Aswan Dam* (Washington, D. C., n.d.), by the Public Affairs Institute; Gamal Abdel Nasser, "The Egyptian Revolution," *Foreign Affairs* (January, 1956), pp. 204-207; C. H. Seager, "Elements of Hope in the Middle East Economic Relations," in U. S., Department of State, *Bulletin*, March 26, 1956, pp. 508 ff.; U. S., Department of State, *Bulletin*, December 26, 1955; U. S., Senate, *Congressional Record*, August 17, 1957, pp. 13394 ff.; and, another view, James E. Dougherty, "The Aswan Decision in Perspective," *Political Science Quarterly* (March, 1959), pp. 21-45; *The Economist* (London), November 19, 1955, p. 664; February 18, 1956, p. 445 *et seq.;* July 28, 1956, p. 295; U. S., Senate, Committee on Foreign Affairs, *Hearings: Mutual Security Program*, April and May, 1956, specifically Dulles's testimony; and Royal Institute of International Affairs, *Survey: 1955-1956* (London, 1960), pp. 302 ff.
20. U. S., Department of State, *Bulletin*, December 26, 1955, pp. 1050-1051.
21. *Ibid.*, January 2, 1956, pp. 11-12.
22. Royal Institute of International Affairs, *Documents: 1956*, ed. Noble Frankland (London, 1959). For Nasser's speech of July 26, 1956, see pp. 108 ff.
23. For this episode, cf. Hussein, *op. cit.*; Eden, *op. cit.*, pp. 388 ff.; Sir John B. Glubb, *Soldier with the Arabs* (London, 1957); and Erskine Childers, *The Road to Suez* (London, 1962), pp. 144 ff. This last is in large part the tissue of wishful thinking and guesswork of a strong Pan-Arabist romantic.
24. *New York Times*, May 23, 1956, p. 14.
25. The passages are from *Papers of the President* (1956), pp. 533 ff.; and U. S., Department of State, *Bulletin* (1956), p. 999.
26. U. S., Department of State, *Bulletin*, July 19, 1956, p. 188. In my text, I have not given special weight to the problem of Sudanese rights to Nile waters, but the point made in the communiqué was very important. For it, see Dougherty, *op. cit.*, pp. 24 ff.
27. Cf. Senator J. W. Fulbright, in U. S., Senate, *Congressional Record*, August 17, 1956, pp. 13394 ff.
28. U. S., Department of State, *Bulletin*, April 22, 1957, p. 642.
29. J. F. Beal, *John Foster Dulles* (New York, 1957), pp. 258 ff.
30. Field Marshal Bernard Montgomery, *Memoirs* (paperbound, London, 1960) p. 364.
31. *M. E. D. Hearings*, Part I, p. 266.
32. *The Times* (London), July 23, 1956.
33. *New York Times*, July 25, 1956.

34. Cf. Edmund Taylor, *The Real Case Against Nasser* (Washington, D. C., 1956); Josep Broz Tito, "The Roots of Recent Events," *Vital Speeches*, December 15, 1956, p. 138.

 The French language Lebanese newspaper printed in Beirut, *L'Orient* (courtesy of Library of Congress), contained on July 13, 1956, a most interesting article on the politics of the Suez Canal. It observed that discussions had begun at the Revolutionary Officers' Club shortly after the overthrow of Farouk, tending to the acquisition of the Canal by Egypt. They were stimulated by Professor Moustapha Hefnaoui, then Professor of Geopolitics at the Military Academy. The point was to find a legal basis for overthrowing the Concession agreements. Hefnaoui had written a law doctorate thesis at the University of Paris on the legal problems presented by the Canal. His view, much admired by the officers, was that the Canal was a strategic key in world politics, that it gave Egyptian leaders a power of veto over the policies of other countries could they get sole control over it. In August, 1955, Nasser set up a committee of experts, with eminent jurists as members, to find a hole in the Concessions. Students agitated for the release of their report after it had been pigeonholed for some time. They thought they saw two possible quibbles which would give them a legal claw to snatch the Canal. One was a failure of the Suez Canal Authority to build a port at Lake Timsah; another a challenge of the interpretation of "the right of innocent passage." The foremost Egyptian newspapers, run by close associates of Nasser, were, in mid-1956, nagging at the Company for its earnings out of which Egypt received so little; that the employees of the Company were so much wealthier than the Egyptians who lived in the vicinity; that so few Egyptians were employed by the Company. Some harassment of French vessels going through the Canal, allegedly by labor unions, was reported, out of sympathy for the Algerian rebels. Indeed, at the annual meeting of the Company in Paris, June 12, 1956, its president had complained about the holding up of ships in transit because of Egyptian insistence that nonexistent Egyptian pilots be employed. The Company had made substantial concessions to train Egyptian candidates. The Company also assigned more of its assets to holdings in Egyptian pounds and arranged for additional investment in Canal improvements.

35. In *Life*, January 16, 1956, pp. 70 ff. Told to James Shepley, chief of *Time-Life* Washington Bureau. Referring to action to make peace in Korea, to stop Communist success in Indochina, to hold Quemoy and Matsu. Dulles is actually quoted, on page 78, as follows: "You have to take chances for peace, just as you must take chances in war. Some say that we were brought to the verge of war. Of course we were brought to the verge of war. The ability to get to the verge without getting into the war is the necessary art. If you cannot master it, you inevitably get into war. If you try to run away from it, if you are scared to go to the brink, you are lost. We've had to look it square in the face—on the question of enlarging the Korean war, on the question of getting into the Indochina war, on the question of Formosa. We walked to the brink and we looked it in the face. We took strong action."

36. Two other theories have been advanced about the seizure of the Canal, both very farfetched. Jon Kimche, in *Jewish Observer and Middle East Review*, January 11, 1963, pp. 7-8, suggests that Nasser and the Soviet Union knew full well by June, 1956, that Dulles would not make the loan, and that the seizure of the Canal had been planned for 1956 in

any case, the Soviet Union being party to a premeditated plot with Nasser to make 1956 "the year of the Canal." The other theory, equally fantastic, is set forth in Erskine Childer's *The Road to Suez,* that the withdrawal of the loan was carefully plotted between Dulles, Eden, and Mollet, Eden being the instigator of Dulles, in order to overthrow Nasser by causing him to lose face—each Government for its own purposes. My own facts are well substantiated. Childers wallows in fantastic guesses and plunges of the imagination so long as the results make Dulles, Eden, and Mollet—but especially Eden—look villainous.

CHAPTER 4: DULLES'S FIRST CRUNCH OVER SUEZ

1. See Sir Anthony Eden, *Full Circle* (Cambridge, Mass., 1960), pp. 470 ff.
2. U. S., Department of State, *The Suez Canal Problem* (Documentary Publication No. 6392, October, 1956), p. 32. Hereafter cited as *S. C. P. Docs.*
3. July 28, 1956.
4. Eden, *op. cit.*, p. 476.
5. *S. C. P. Docs.*, p. 34.
6. Assemblée Nationale, *Journal Officiel: Débats,* August 3, 1956, pp. 3868 ff.
7. Reservists were recalled to duty; units of the fleet were moved towards the eastern Mediterranean and Malta; paratroopers were conveyed to Middle Eastern staging locations; British and French citizens were advised to leave Egypt; and both Britain and France blocked Egypt's sterling balances. Cf. *The Times* (London), August 6, 1956.
8. Cf. Norman A. Graebner, ed., *An Uncertain Tradition* (New York, 1961); also an extremely interesting essay by Alexander DeConde, *The American Secretary of State* (New York, 1962); and Don K. Price, ed., *The Secretary of State* (New York, 1960) ; Norman L. Hill, *Mr. Secretary of State* (New York, 1963); and, of course, Samuel F. Bemis, ed., *The American Secretaries of State* (10 vols., New York, 1927-1929). See also U. S. Senate, Sub-Committee on National Policy Machinery, Vol. I, *Hearings*, pp. 619-1333.
9. J. P. Tumulty, *Woodrow Wilson as I Knew Him* (New York, 1927), p. 444, for the circumstances. The text is supplied by Professor Alexander DeConde.
10. On page 142 of *Mandate for Change*, his memoirs (Vol. I), President Eisenhower notes that in six years of office the cables and memoranda exchanged between Dulles and the President "made a stack more than four feet high." He does not say what area the stack covered. I shall assume it was that of a legal sized page. I shall also assume that all of the material was Dulles's, none the President's. If this is so, it means that in six years there were forty-eight inches of paper, that is, eight inches per year. A ream of typing paper is five hundred pages of average weight. It is also nearly two inches high. So in a year some two thousand pages were sent by Dulles to the President. This is some forty pages each week. This calculation is the maximum favorable estimate of the quantity of information, etc., etc., Dulles supplied in this form. It does not, of course, include the many other sources of fact and inspiration focusing on the President, such as the National Security Council, his personal assistants, Dulles's phone and personal conversation, and so on. However, with double line spacing, and much of the

pages of the cables, etc., empty margin, it does not seem to be too large an amount of written material to ponder and digest.

11. For example, to go to the "summit" meeting in 1955; to make the Open Sky proposal there; to reject Dulles's readiness to make war in Indochina in April, 1954; the policy of caution in the Quemoy and Matsu crisis of 1955. Dulles discouraged the invitation to Marshal Georgi Zhukov to visit the United States in 1957.
12. A more extensive survey is in J. F. Beal, *John Foster Dulles* (New York, 1957); and better still in Raymond E. Platig, "John Foster Dulles: A Study of His Political and Moral Thought Prior to 1953" (unpublished Ph.D. dissertation, University of Chicago, 1956). I take this opportunity to commend two unpublished Ph.D. theses: Earl Oliver Kline, "The Suez Crisis: Anglo-American Relations and the U. N.," Princeton, 1961, and Walter Goldstein, "The Labour Party and the Middle East Crisis," Chicago, 1956.
13. Cf. Sherman Adams, *First Hand Report* (New York, 1961), p. 110: "Granted that Dulles was a man of great moral force and conviction, he was not endowed with creative genius that produces bold, new ideas to gain hitherto unattainable policy goals . . ." See also Chapter VI.
14. He attended two conferences in 1937. One was held in Paris: the Conference on Intellectual Cooperation under the auspices of the League of Nations. Shortly afterwards he went to Oxford for a conference of the clergy on Church and State. He was astounded by the difference between the two approaches: the first, the legalistic approach to "peaceful change," a cardinal theme of the 1930's; and the second, where the moral force of religion, exercised by men of religion, offered the most credible way towards necessary change, peacefully accomplished. Joseph Chamberlain, writing for *Life*, August 21, 1944, p. 92, after being privy to Dulles's confidences, actually called Dulles's experience at the Oxford Conference one that compared with St. Paul on the road to Damascus. He said that Dulles came away from that Conference realizing that "the ideals of his minister father were no less important than the worldly wisdom of his grandfather."
15. Roswell Barnes became Associate Minister at the Park Avenue Presbyterian Church in 1928, and then moved upwards in the ministry, becoming associated with the executive office of the Federal Council of Churches to reach the highest office in the American section of the World Council of Churches in 1958. His pastoral relationship with Dulles was most intimate, of a confessional nature, especially regarding the conduct of foreign affairs.
16. *Memories of a Catholic Childhood* (New York, 1957). Dulles greeted the employees at the State Department (Department of State, *Bulletin*, January 28, 1953, p. 239) with the observation that he did not suppose there was any family in the U. S. which had been for so long identified with the foreign service and the State Department as his own family. He listed his great-great uncle, his grandfather, his uncle, his brother, his sister. Quite an estate.
17. For a discussion of "reductionism," see G. A. Miller, E. Galanter, and Karl H. Pribram, *Plans and the Structure of Behavior* (New York, 1960).
18. Roscoe Drummond and Gaston Coblentz, *Duel at the Brink* (New York, 1960), pp. 45 ff.
19. *M. E. D. Hearings*, Dulles's testimony, *passim;* H. D. Van Dusen, *The Spiritual Legacy of John Foster Dulles* (Philadelphia, 1960);

Coral Bell, *Negotiation from Strength* (London, 1962); and Richard Goold-Adams, *The Time of Power: A Reappraisal of John Foster Dulles* (London, 1962), merely by way of extra indication. An elaborate thesis has been composed of this; cf. Ole Rudolf Holsti, "The Belief System and National Images: John Foster Dulles and the Soviet Union" (unpublished Ph.D. thesis, Stanford University, 1962), or Holsti, "The Belief System and National Images: A Case Study," *Conflict Resolution*, VI (September, 1962), 244 ff., an abstract of the thesis.

20. *Diplomacy* (London, 1939), p. 110.
21. Of course, I do not refer to an utterly unproven charge by Harold L. Ickes, *New Republic*, January 16, 1950, p. 130, that Dulles had helped to organize the New York branch of America First. There is not the vestige of support for this in the best study of the organization (all records open) in Wayne S. Cole, *America First* (Madison, Wisc., 1953).
22. Cf. Frank Gotham, "The Inconsistency of John Foster Dulles," *The Nation*, October 18, 1952, p. 353; and Richard H. Rovere, *The Eisenhower Years* (New York, 1956), pp. 58 ff.
23. This is inferrable from the argument, and the feeling behind it, in *War, Peace and Change* (New York, 1938); and the report of a debate between Senator Burton K. Wheeler, James D. Warburg, and Dulles on March 22, 1939, in *New York Times*, September 3, 1944, section 4, p. 3.
24. Herbert Morrison, *An Autobiography* (London, 1960), p. 280, on the Japanese Treaty: "I may be forgiven if I resolved there and then not fully to trust Dulles again." Bernard C. Cohen, *The Political Process and Foreign Policy: The Making of the Japanese Peace Treaty* (Princeton, N. J., 1957), pp. 148-154.
25. Drummond and Coblentz, *op. cit.*, p. 165.
26. Cf. Eden, *op. cit.*, Chapters IV, V, and VI; and Chalmers M. Roberts, "The Day We Didn't Go to War," *The Reporter*, September 11, 1954, pp. 11-12. Also, Sherman Adams, *op. cit.*, pp. 123-130; also, of course, Eisenhower, *op. cit.*, Chapter XIV.
27. Harold Nicolson, *The Congress of Vienna* (New York, 1946), p. 166.
28. R. I. I. A., *Documents* (1956), pp. 120 ff.
29. Eden, *op. cit.*, p. 486.
30. *Ibid.*, p. 512.
31. *Ibid.*, p. 483.
32. Cf. Dwight C. Miner, *The Fight for the Panama Route* (New York, 1940).
33. Cf. John Foster Dulles, *War or Peace* (New York, 1957), p. 99. Also, Shepley on Dulles, *Life*, January 16, 1956, p. 70: "In the singular lifelong preparation for the job he was about to undertake, he had probably devoted more thought to the subject than any other man alive. He believed he had isolated one of the major underlying causes of war: in a word, *miscalculation*."
34. Eden, *op. cit.*, p. 487.
35. *Ibid.*, p. 71. Said not merely apropos the Suez Crisis, but of the Berlin Conference, January, 1954, "the first occasion when I negotiated with him as a partner."
36. *S. C. P. Docs.*, pp. 34-35.
37. *New York Times*, April 2, 1956.
38. *S. C. P. Docs.*, p. 34.

39. *Ibid.*, p. 37.
40. *Ibid.*, pp. 37-42. Dulles is reported by one of his intimate counselors to have expressed superlative esteem for Syngman Rhee and Chiang Kai-shek as two gallant Christian gentlemen maintaining a Crusader's defense against the atheistic Communism of Red China and the Soviet Union. Of course, the Christian contentment with Chiang did not prevent Dulles from restraining his Mainland ambitions later on.
41. As to the financial possibilities of the Suez nationalization for assistance to the building of the Aswan Dam, they were meager, according to the very careful and knowledgeable analysis made in *The Economist* (London), August 4, 1956, p. 422. Over and above the annual cost of operation, plus upkeep plus improvement, only about £10 million to £12 million sterling per year would be available, comprising the dividends paid annually, or $28 million to $33.6 million, BUT, this amount ignores the compensation to be paid out of the annual profits. Furthermore, these figures are high.

    The Universal Suez Canal Company had built up, out of past profits, assets of £19 million sterling short-term investments, and £16 million longer-term securities, held outside Egypt in various countries, all or nearly all being beyond the reach of the Egyptian government.

    The total share value of the Company on the Paris Bourse on July 26, 1956, was £70 million, sterling. It could, theoretically, have been paid out of the Egyptian funds held in the sterling accounts in London.

    The application of the putative annual dividends of, say, $27 million a year, to the building of the Aswan Dam could not be effective: it was far too little. The American-British-World Bank arrangement called for a total investment of $1.3 billion: $70 million as a grant from the U. S. and U. K., $410 million in loans, by annual installments, with $760 million to be found by Egypt herself. Thus, critics of Nasser in British politics (and this included the Labour Party) drew the conclusion that Nasser could build the Dam with the profits of the Suez Canal only if he raised tolls. This would be an added charge on British industry and its standard of living. Some British people were prepared to accept such added charges for the sake of peace. One member of Parliament thought it worth the price of "peace" to accept tolls at five times their height.

    In his wild tirade of July 26, 1956, Nasser had declared to the crowds that he would take the whole £35 million sterling of the Company's annual income for the benefit of Egypt. He did not tell them what the working expenditures were, or the amounts needed for improvements, or for reserves. Nor did he help them to understand that even the amount of dividends paid out annually already included £1.5 million sterling.

    The financing of the Universal Suez Canal Company was regulated in the Concessions in 1854 and 1856. The Company was organized as an Egyptian corporation, but its legal and administrative headquarters were in Paris. The profits were to be distributed thus: 75 per cent to the Company, 10 per cent to the founders, and 15 per cent to the Egyptian government. The British did not enter administratively, financially, or politically (except as obstructionists) until 1875. The Board was originally French, Austrian, and Italian. The original capital was 200 million French francs, divided into 400,000 shares. They were sold to a wide variety of customers. The chief holdings were 207,160 to French shareholders, and 177,642 to the Egyptian Khedive (the viceroy). Assignments had been made available for fifteen principal countries, but the purchases did not match the proportions of the total made available. The British could have had 80,000 shares; they bought none. But in 1875, the British bought Khedive Ismail Pasha's shares for £4 million, since he had been so profligate in his expenditures (some on Egyptian resource development) as to be bankrupt. The French had an option on the shares but did not take them up. Although the British shares were a minority they were a large minority, and, because the French shares were scattered among many shareholders, the British bloc was dominating, and furthermore British shipping was by far the largest single amount passing through the Canal. In 1924, a two-for-one stock split was voted; thus the British held 353,204 shares out of 800,000. The Egyptian government's share of the profits, as arranged in the original Concessions, that is, 15 per cent, was sold to a French syndicate. Thus, between 1924 and 1949, the Egyptian government, as distinct from any Egyptian investors, obtained very little from the Canal. In 1949, the Company and the Egyptian government made some significant amendments. The number of Egyptian directors was increased from two to seven in a membership of thirty-two. An annual payment of 7 per cent of the gross profits per year, with a minimum of 350,000 Egyptian pounds, was established. Substantial Egyptianization of the technical and administrative staff was undertaken; and priority in the filling of vacancies for pilots was given to Egyptians.

42. Cf. Platig, *op. cit., passim;* and Van Dusen, *op. cit.*

CHAPTER 5: DULLES STUDIES THE FORCES

1. Lord Randolph Churchill, *The Rise and Fall of Sir Anthony Eden* (London, 1959), gives a reasonably good sketch of the successive plans and operations.
2. August 10, 1956.
3. Assemblée Nationale, *Journal Officiel: Débats*, August 2, 1956, p. 3847.
4. *The Times* (London), August 9, 1956.
5. *S. C. P. Docs.*, p. 46.
6. Sherman Adams, *First Hand Report* (New York, 1961), p. 250.
7. R. I. I. A., *Documents* (1956), p. 156.
8. *S. C. P. Docs.*, pp. 47-52.
9. We have preferred to have the law regarding Suez stated in Dulles's speech of August 16, 1956, made at the First London Conference, and reproduced in this work on pages 150 ff., below, rather than seek here to offer an independent interpretation. The law of Suez is to be elicited from the Egyptian Concession for Construction and Operation of the Suez Maritime Canal, November 30, 1854; the Definitive Egyptian Concession for Construction of the Suez Maritime Canal, January 5, 1856; the Convention Between the Viceroy of Egypt and the Universal Suez Maritime Canal Company, February 22, 1866; the Convention Respecting the Free Navigation of the Suez Maritime Canal, made at Constantinople, October 29, 1888, and therefore referred to by the present author, as convenience dictates, as the Constantinople Convention of 1888; and, finally, the Anglo-Egyptian Agreement Regarding the Suez Canal Base, October 19, 1954.

   Whoever wishes to attempt to penetrate the forest of treaties may refer to the following principal authorities: Paul de Visscher, "Les aspects juridiques fondamentaux de la question de Suez," *Revue generale de droit international public*, XXIX, 3 série (1958), pp. 400-443; T. T. F. Huang, "Some International and Legal Aspects of the Suez Canal Question," *American Journal of International Law*, LI (1957), pp. 277-307; M. D. Generales, "Suez: National Sovereignty and International Waterways," *World Affairs Quarterly*, XXIX (1958), pp. 177-190.

10. *New York Times*, August 8, 1956, pp. 1, 3.
11. R. I. I. A., *Documents* (1956), for U. S. S. R. acceptance, pp. 162 ff.
12. *Duel at the Brink* (New York, 1960), p. 157.
13. *New York Times*, August 9, 1956.
14. Cf. D. W. Bowett, *Self-Defense in International Law* (New York, 1958), Chapters VI and IX on the nature of self-defense.
15. Cf. *Text of Secretary-General's Statement in Security Council*, April 4, 1956, United Nations Office of Public Information, etc., etc.; *Statement by Secretary-General at Airport on Return from Middle East*, United Nations Office of Public Information, etc., etc., May 6, 1956. Also, *Report of U. N. Activities, 1956*, Secretary-General, *U. S. Participation in the UN*, Report by President to Congress for the Year 1956, released December, 1957, U. S. Government Printing Office.
16. Mr. Gaitskell mentioned in debate (House of Commons, September 13, 1956) that the cost of a gallon of gasoline would be raised by about 1½ pence, if tankers were obliged to take the Cape route to Britain rather than passing as usual via the Canal. He based himself on the analysis made in the *Financial Times* (London), September 13, 1956, of the factors in the cost of a gallon of gasoline to the consumer. The cost of transportation was about 2¾ pence via Suez. What then would be the total added cost per year to the consumers, or it can be put, to the British economy? I use the amount of 2 pence per gallon additional, since some other politicians claimed it would be much more than 1½ pence. Also I use the figure of 590,000 barrels consumed per day (of crude oil, that is), the figure given in *Petroleum Industry: 1955*, a report published annually by the Chase Manhattan Bank of New York, on p. 22. I allow forty-two gallons to the barrel. (The size of barrels varies from country to country; the quotations of quantities are often in tons and metric tons. The order of magnitude in the present calculation does not substantially affect the argument.) The amount is circa £74 million sterling, or about $207 million; and it compares with the British gross national product for 1955 of about £18 billion sterling, or $50 billion. Nobody in England would actually starve if the gross national product were cut even by 50 per cent; and £74 million sterling is far from that. But the question for the government of a "middle" power like Britain (and France, which consumed 395,000 barrels a day) is: Why accept any diminution of national wealth inflicted by a hostile power by an illegal seizure?

    The *United Kingdom Annual Abstract of Statistics* (1962), Tables 176 and 177, gives the imports and use of petroleum products for 1955, with analysis of the kinds of products made from crude petroleum.
17. Sherman Adams, *op. cit.*, p. 253.
18. Gallup polls; British Institute of Public Opinion, in *News Chronicle* (London), August 6, 1956; and "L'Affaire de Suez," *Sondages: Revue Française de l'Opinion Publique* (1956), covering France and Britain especially, and, secondarily, other countries.

CHAPTER 6: DULLES'S FINEST HOUR—AND STRANGE DEFAULT

1. *S. C. P. Docs.*, p. xiii. This volume contains many pertinent documents and texts of the verbatim record of the First and Second London Conferences. Significantly, it does *not* include the communiqué on the withdrawal of the offer of the Aswan loan. We frequently use this source, but sometimes the Department of State *Bulletin*, as cited, according to convenience.
2. *S. C. P. Docs.*, p. 65.
3. *Ibid.*, p. 71.
4. *Ibid.*, pp. 159 ff.
5. *Ibid.*, p. 248.
6. *Ibid.*
7. *Ibid.*, p. 172.
8. Cf. *Political Science Annual*, ed. E. Asirvatham (1962), Jabalpur, M. P., India, especially pp. 42-55, 85-96.
9. *S. C. P. Docs.*, p. 164.
10. The Security Council had, September 1, 1951, unanimously (that is, including Russia) resolved that the practice could not be justified as necessary for Egypt's self-defense, and, most importantly: "That since the armistice regime, which has been in existence for nearly two and a half years, is of a permanent character, neither party can reasonably assert that it is actively belligerent or requires to exercise the right of visit, search, and seizure for any legitimate purpose of self-defense." *SCOR*, 558 Meeting, S/2298/Rev. 1, para. 5 *et seq.*
11. *S. C. P. Docs.*, pp. 178-182.
12. *Ibid.*, p. 191.
13. *Ibid.*, p. 250.
14. *Ibid.*, pp. 250 and 293. The Spanish proposal was that if the negotiation along the lines of Dulles's resolution should not succeed, an Egyptian Board should operate, maintain, and develop the Canal, and there should be adequate representation of the community of nations using it.
15. *Ibid.*, p. 251.
16. *Ibid.*, pp. 264-265.
17. *Ibid.*, p. 155.
18. *Ibid.*, p. 235.
19. *Ibid.*, p. 64.
20. *Ibid.*, p. 89.
21. *Ibid.*, p. 238.
22. *Ibid.*, p. 91.
23. *Ibid.*, p. 130.
24. *Ibid.*, p. 132.

CHAPTER 7: DULLES'S SOLUTION FAILS IN CAIRO

1. Sir Anthony Eden, *Full Circle* (Cambridge, Mass., 1960), p. 549.
2. *The Times* (London), August 28, 1956.
3. *Ibid.*, August 25, 1956.
4. *S. C. P. Docs.*, p. 295.
5. *The Times* (London), August 29, 1956.

6. *S. C. P. Docs.*, p. 296.
7. *Ibid.*, pp. 296 ff.
8. *Ibid.*, pp. 297-298.
9. *Ibid.*, p. 300.
10. *Ibid.*, p. 301.
11. *New York Times*, August 30, 1956.
12. *Ibid.*, August 31, 1956.
13. *Ibid.*, September 1, 1956.
14. *The Times* (London), September 1, 1956; September 3, 1956; and September 4, 1956.
15. Dispatch from Cairo of September 2, 1956, in *New York Times*, September 3, 1956.
16. Frank Moraes, in *The Times of India*, September 2, 1956.
17. *S. C. P. Docs.*, pp. 306-307.
18. *Ibid.*, pp. 309 ff.
19. Cf. Wilton Wynn, *Nasser and Egypt* (Arlington, W. Va., 1959), p. 174.
20. *S. C. P. Docs.*, p. 323.
21. Robert St. John, *The Boss: The Story of Gamal Abdel Nasser* (New York, 1960), p. 253.
22. *S. C. P. Docs.*, pp. 316-317.
23. In a treaty of 1929 between Britain and Egypt, the division of the waters between the Sudan and Egypt had been effected, and both countries were benefited by the building of Owen's Falls, faithfully administered by Britain. Cf. Officials of the Sudan Government, *Equatorial Nile Project and its Effect on the Anglo-Egyptian Sudan* (Oxford, England, 1954).

CHAPTER 8: THE POISONED APPLE: THE USERS' CLUB

1. Sir Anthony Eden, *Full Circle* (Cambridge, Mass., 1960), p. 509.
2. *Ibid.*, pp. 513-514.
3. *Ibid.*, p. 516.
4. *Ibid.*, p. 517.
5. *Ibid.*, p. 518.
6. *Ibid.*, pp. 518-519.
7. Cf. the memorandum to the State Department by the Egyptian Embassy at Washington, and to other governments and the Secretary General of the United Nations, in *S. C. P. Docs.*, pp. 327-330.
8. *Ibid.*, p. 327. Following is the text of a letter sent September 12, 1956, to the president of the United Nations Security Council, by the United Kingdom and France:

   "In accordance with instructions received from Her Majesty's Government in the United Kingdom and from the French Government, we have the honor to address you . . . with regard to the situation created by the action of the Egyptian Government in attempting unilaterally to bring to an end the system of international operation of the Suez Canal which was confirmed and completed by the Suez Canal Convention of 1888.

   "1. Since the action of the Egyptian Government created a situation which might endanger the free and open passage of shipping through the canal without distinction of flag as laid down in the abovementioned convention, a conference was called in London on Aug. 16, 1956. Of the twenty-two states attending that conference, eighteen, representing between them over ninety per cent of the user interest in the canal, put forward proposals to the Egyptian Government for the future operation of the canal. The Egyptian Government have, however, refused to negotiate on the basis of the above-mentioned proposals, which, in the opinion of Her Majesty's Government and of the French Government, offer means for a just and equitable solution. Her Majesty's Government and the French Government consider that this refusal is an aggravation of the situation which, if allowed to continue, would constitute a manifest danger to peace and security.

"2. We have the honor to request that the contents of this letter be brought to the notice of the members of the Security Council." *New York Times,* Sepember 13, 1956.

9. Paul Johnson, *The Suez War* (London, 1957), p. 67; also, Randolph Churchill, *The Rise and Fall of Sir Anthony Eden* (London, 1959), p. 250. I am informed by President Eisenhower's archivist that Johnson's statement (*The Suez War*, p. 72) that the President phoned Eden on September 13 or 14, 1956, is false.
10. *S. C. P. Docs.*, p. 330.
11. Eden, *op. cit.*, p. 533.
12. *Ibid.*, p. 534.
13. *S. C. P. Docs.*, pp. 331 ff.

CHAPTER 9: EDEN VANQUISHED

1. Great Britain, *Parliamentary Debates* (Commons), September 12, 1956, col. 6.
2. *S. C. P. Docs.*, pp. 335 ff.
3. Great Britain, *Parliamentary Debates* (Commons), September 13, 1956, col. 291.
4. *Ibid.*, col. 298.
5. *Ibid.*, col. 306.
6. *The Economist* (London), p. 864.
7. The British Public Opinion Institute, in polls taken September 5 and 6, 1956 (No. 472a), showed 69 per cent of the sample favored the government's military precautions, with 21 per cent hostile and 10 per cent "don't know-ers." This was actually an increase in the support for the government over the poll results of August 16 to 24, 1956 (No. 470).
8. *New York Times,* September 14, 1956.
9. *Ibid.*, September 12, 1956, p. 1.
10. *S. C. P. Docs.*, pp. 335 ff.
11. Sir Anthony Eden, *Full Circle* (Cambridge, Mass., 1960), p. 539.
12. Paul Johnson, *The Suez War* (London, 1957). This is the title of one of his chapters.
13. *New York Times,* September 16, 1956.
14. However, the meticulous and judicious reports on French governmental and press attitudes in *L'Orient* (Paris), January, 1957, pp. 179 ff., 260, and 262, convey the lines of response the French government must have adopted.
15. In a survey of the Suez crisis, Professor Geoffrey Barraclough, Royal Institute of International Affairs, *International Affairs 1956-1958,* offers a most painstaking and intelligent epitome of the newspaper and periodical reports. BUT—it does not research below the newspaper surface and it seems bent on proving that Britain and France were legally and politically in the wrong. Even so, Professor Barraclough is compelled

to say of Dulles's advocacy of the SCUA plan, "In doing so, it is probably fair to say that he came perilously near to prevarication . . ." (p. 34). It is the maximum blame of, and I think the only point in which Professor Barraclough finds something to criticize in, Mr. Dulles's policy and diplomacy. Moreover, Professor Barraclough recounts the First London Conference not directly from the verbatim record but from the epitomes that appear in *L'Orient, loc. cit.* note 14, *supra.*

CHAPTER 10: SCUA COLLAPSES

1. *New York Times,* September 18, 1956, p. 1.
2. *Ibid.,* September 17, 1956, p. 1.
3. September, 18, 1956.
4. *New York Times,* September 17, 1956.
5. Royal Institute of International Affairs, *Documents: 1956,* ed. Noble Frankland (London, 1959), pp. 231 ff.
6. Great Britain, *Parliamentary Debates* (Lords), col. 706 ff.
7. *S. C. P. Docs.,* p. 350; also, Royal Institute of International Affairs, *Documents: 1956,* p. 234.
8. Ensuing epitome and quotations from *S. C. P. Docs.,* pp. 353 ff.
9. "Declaration Providing for the Establishment of a Suez Canal Users Association, September 21

"I. The Members of the Suez Canal Users Association (SCUA) shall be those nations which have participated in the second London Suez Conference and which subscribe to the present Declaration, and any other adhering nations which conform to criteria to be laid down hereafter by the association.

"II. SCUA shall have the following purposes;

(1) to facilitate any steps which may lead to a final or provisional solution of the Suez Canal problem and to assist the members in the exercise of their rights as users of the Suez Canal in consonance with the 1888 Convention, with due regard for the rights of Egypt;

(2) to promote safe, orderly, efficient and economical transit of the Canal by vessels of any member nation desiring to avail themselves of the facilities of SCUA and to seek the co-operation of the competent Egyptian authorities for this purpose;

(3) to extend its facilities to vessels of non-member nations which desire to use them;

(4) to receive, hold and disburse the revenues accruing from dues and other sums which any user of the Canal may pay to SCUA, without prejudice to existing rights, pending a final settlement;

(5) to consider and report to Members regarding any significant developments affecting the use or non-use of the Canal;

(6) to assist in dealing with any practical problems arising from the failure of the Suez Canal adequately to serve its customary and intended purpose and to study forthwith means that may render it feasible to reduce dependence on the Canal;

(7) to facilitate the execution of any provisional solution of the Suez problem that may be adopted by the United Nations.

"III. To carry out the above-mentioned purposes:

(1) the members shall consult together in a Council on which each member will be represented;

(2) the Council shall establish an Executive Group to which it may delegate such powers as seems appropriate;

(3) an Administrator, who shall, *inter alia*, make the necessary arrangements with shipping interests, will be appointed to serve under the direction of the Council through the Executive Group.

"IV. Membership may at any time be terminated by giving 60 days' notice."

10. *S. C. P. Docs.*, p. 369.
11. *Le Monde*, September 24, 1956.
12. *Orient* (Paris), January, 1957, p. 219.
13. *New York Herald-Tribune*, September 24, 1956, p. 11.
14. *Ibid.*, September 25, 1956.
15. *Ibid.*, September 24, 1956, p. 8.

CHAPTER 11: THE ALLIED RIFT WIDENS

1. Royal Institute of International Affairs, *Documents: 1956*, ed. Noble Frankland (London, 1959), pp. 226-227, 230, and 241.
2. *SCOR*, 11th year, Supplement, July, August, September, Document X/3656; and *New York Times*, September 26, 1956, p. 2.
3. *The Times* (London), September 25, 1956.
4. For an interesting discussion of one aspect of this, see Leon D. Epstein, "British M. P.'s and Their Local Parties: The Suez Cases," in *American Political Science Review* (June, 1960), pp. 374 ff., and see also the same author's "Partisan Foreign Policy: Britain in the Suez Crisis," in *World Politics*, (January, 1960), pp. 201 ff.
5. *Papers and Speeches of the Presidents*, 1956, pp. 806 ff.
6. U. S., Department of State, *United States Policy in the Middle East: September, 1956, to June, 1957*, Documents 6505, pp. 87 ff. This set of documents, an official sequel to *S. C. P. Docs.*, is henceforward referred to as *U. S. P. M. E. Docs.*
7. Sir Anthony Eden, *Full Circle* (Cambridge, Mass., 1960), p. 554.
8. *Ibid.*, pp. 555-556.
9. *U. S. P. M. E. Docs.*, pp. 100-104; and U. S., Department of State, *Bulletin*, 1956, p. 577.
10. *New York Times*, October 3, 1956, p. 8.
11. *Ibid.*

CHAPTER 12: THE UNITED NATIONS FAILS

1. *SCOR*, 11th year, 735th meeting, October 5, 1956, pp. 3-4, U. N. Document S/2666, S. C. Supplement for October, November, December, 1956, pp. 5-6.
2. Selwyn Lloyd, *ibid.*; October 8, 1956, 736th meeting, pp. 3-13.
3. *Ibid.*, p. 13.
4. *Ibid.*, pp. 14-27.
5. 738th meeting, pp. 6 ff.
6. *Public Papers of the Presidents* (1956), pp. 234 ff.
7. 742nd meeting, pp. 3 ff.

The principles and the guaranteeing resolution were as follows: "*The Security Council* (S/3675, October 13, 1956): . . .

"*Agrees* that any settlement of the Suez question should meet the following requirements:

(1) there should be free and open transit through the Canal without discrimination, overt or covert—this covers both political and technical aspects;

(2) the sovereignty of Egypt should be respected;

(3) the operation of the Canal should be insulated from the politics of any country;

(4) the manner of fixing tolls and charges should be decided by agreement between Egypt and the users;

(5) a fair proportion of the dues should be allotted to development;

(6) in cases of disputes, unresolved affairs between the Suez Canal Company and the Egyptian Government should be settled by arbitration with suitable terms of reference and suitable provisions for the payment of sums found to be due."

This was adopted unanimously.

The principal parts of the resolution that were vetoed said:

"*The Security Council* (S/3671): . . .

"*Notes* that the Egyptian Government . . . has not yet formulated sufficiently precise proposals to meet the requirements set out above;

"*Invites* the Governments of Egypt, France and the United Kingdom to continue their interchanges and in this connexion *invites* the Egyptian Government to make known promptly its proposals for a system meeting the requirements set out above and providing guarantees to the users not less effective than those sought by the proposals of the Eighteen Powers;

"*Considers* that pending the conclusion of an agreement for the definitive settlement of the regime of the Suez Canal on the basis of the requirements set out above, the Suez Canal Users' Association, which has been qualified to receive the dues payable by ships belonging to its members, and the competent Egyptian authorities, should co-operate to ensure the satisfactory operation of the Canal and free and open transit through the Canal in accordance with the 1888 Convention."

8. *Ibid.*, pp. 8 ff.
9. *Public Papers of the Presidents*, TV appearance October 12, 1956, pp. 241 ff.
10. Sir Anthony Eden, *Full Circle* (Cambridge, Mass., 1960), p. 567.
11. U. N., *Document* S/3679, October 15, 1956.
12. *U. S. P. M. E. Docs.*, pp. 122-127.
13. Eden, *op. cit.*, pp. 563-564.

CHAPTER 13: COLLUSION BRINGS A HOT WAR

1. Sir Anthony Eden, *Full Circle* (Cambridge, Mass., 1960), pp. 569 ff.
2. December 19, 1956, *Débats*, p. 6157.
3. Eden, *op. cit.*, p. 572.
4. *Ibid.*, p. 573.
5. The State Department had information towards the end of August that instead of twenty-four Mystère jet fighters provided by France to Israel, the number was sixty. There were subsequent newspaper reports that the number was even higher. Other supplies were being delivered also. Cf. especially *France-Observateur* (Paris), November 15, 1956.
6. M. and S. Bromberger, *Secrets of Suez* (London, 1957), an English translation, with slight changes, of their book *Les Sécrets de l'Expedition d'Egypte* (Paris, 1957).
7. J.-R. Tournoux, *Sécrets d'État* (Paris, 1960),
8. Randolph Churchill, *The Rise and Fall of Sir Anthony Eden* (London, 1959).

9. It is mentioned in Assemblée Nationale, *Débats*, of December 6, 1956.
10. Early October, 1956. Communicated privately.
11. Cf. *France-Observateur* (Paris), November 29, 1956; *Manchester Guardian*, November 29, 1956; *The Times* (London), November 21, 1956.
12. Tournoux, *op. cit.*, pp. 156-157. But Tournoux does not know the date precisely, as authoritatively communicated to me, nor more remarkable details. Bromberger, *op. cit.*, has a close guess: October 22.
13. *Israeli Government Yearbook, 1959-1960*, pp. 26 ff. But the Prime Minister is almost totally silent on the subject of France in his book, *Israel: Years of Challenge* (New York, 1963).
14. On October 17, 1956 (translation from the *Knesset Record*), he re-emphasized that the most dangerous and mighty enemy was the "usurper Nasser," and that Israel had friends.
15. Allen Dulles claims that the CIA foresaw and accurately estimated the actions of Israel, Britain, and France, and gave the information to the proper authorities. Cf. Allen Dulles, *The Craft of Intelligence* (New York, 1963), p. 168. But he does not say when the estimate was made, at what date the information was given, the solidity of the information, or, above all, what use was made of it. His claim is dubious.
16. *Public Papers of the President*, January 21, 1960, p. 128, and February 3, 1960, p. 144.
17. Erskine Childers, *The Road to Suez* (London, 1962), p. 238; and Randolph Churchill, *op. cit.*, published earlier, p. 295.
18. Mimeographed transcripts kindly supplied by the Columbia Broadcasting System.
19. Text from *The Hindu*, October 25, 1956, reprinted in Royal Institute of International Affairs, *Documents: 1956*, ed. Noble Frankland (London, 1959), pp. 257-259.
20. Text of Secretary General's letter to Fawzi, *SCOR*, Supplement, October, November, December, 1956, Document S/3728, in which no date is mentioned.
21. Paul Johnson, *The Suez War* (London, 1957), pp. 80-81.
22. Great Britain, *Parliamentary Debates* (Commons), October 23, 1956, cols. 491-496.
23. *New York Times*, October 25, 1956.
24. *SCOR*, 744th meeting, October 23, 1956, regarding Qalqilya, pp. 15 ff; and 745th meeting, pp. 1-20.
25. Harold Callander, in *New York Times*, October 27, 1956, p. 5.
26. Eden, *op. cit.*, pp. 584 ff.
27. Emmet Hughes, *The Ordeal of Power* (New York, 1963), p. 212.
28. U. S., Department of State, *Bulletin*, November 5, 1956, pp. 695 ff.
29. *U. S. P. M. E. Docs.*, pp. 134-135.
30. *Ibid.*, p. 135.
31. *Ibid.*, p. 137.
32. Royal Institute of International Affairs, *Documents: 1956*, p. 261.
33. Assemblée Nationale, *Débats, Journal Officiel*, December 20, 1956, p. 6175.
34. *Ibid.*, p. 6157.

CHAPTER 14: DULLES IMPEACHES HIS ALLIES

1. *SCOR*, 748th meeting, 1956, pp. 1 ff.
2. *U. S. P. M. E. Docs.*, p. 142.

3. *SCOR*, 748th meeting, p. 24.
4. *Ibid.*, pp. 7-9.
5. Great Britain, *Parliamentary Debates* (Commons), cols. 1449-1451.
6. *Ibid.*, col. 1565.
7. *Ibid.*, col. 1571.
8. *Ibid.*, cols. 1648-1649.
9. *SCOR*, 748th meeting, p. 25.
10. General Charles F. Keightley, dispatch on Suez operations, completed June 10, 1957, published in *Supplement* to *London Gazette*, September 10, 1957, p. 5330.
11. *Public Papers of the Presidents*, October 31, 1956, p. 1060.
12. My phrase. But see John Foster Dulles, *War or Peace* (New York, 1957), p. vii, for his acknowledgment.
13. Cf. D. W. Bowett, *Self-Defence in International Law* (Manchester, 1955).
14. Draft resolution, A/3256, November 1, 1956, *or*, A/RES/390, General Assembly, 1st Emergency Special Session, and A/3354. It ran:

    The General Asesmbly,

    Noting the disregard on many occasions by parties to the Israeli-Arab armistice agreements of 1949 of the terms of such agreements, and that the armed forces of Israel have penetrated deeply into Egyptian territory in violation of the General Armistice Agreement between Egypt and Israel of 24 February 1949,

    Noting that armed forces of France and the United Kingdom of Great Britain and Northern Ireland are conducting military operations against Egyptian territory,

    Noting that traffic through the Suez Canal is now interrupted to the serious prejudice of many nations,

    Expressing its grave concern over these developments,

    1. Urges as a matter of priority that all parties now involved in hostilities in the area agree to an immediate cease-fire, and as part thereof, halt the movement of military forces and arms into the area;

    2. Urges the parties to the armistice agreements promptly to withdraw all forces behind the armistice lines, to desist from raids across the armistice lines into neighbouring territory, and to observe scrupulously the provisions of the armistice agreements;

    3. Recommends that all Member States refrain from introducing military goods in the area of hostilities and in general refrain from any acts which would delay or prevent the implementation of the present resolution;

    4. Urges that, upon the cease-fire being effective, steps be taken to reopen the Suez Canal and restore secure freedom of navigation;

    5. Requests the Secretary-General to observe and report promptly on the compliance with the present resolution to the Security Council and to the General Assembly, for such further action as they may deem appropriate in accordance with the Charter;

    6. Decides to remain in emergency session pending compliance with the present resolution.
15. *ORGA*, November 1, 1956, Emergency Session, pp. 10 ff.
16. *Israeli Government Yearbook, 1959-1960*, p. 35
17. Cf. W. P. Frye, *A United Nations Peace Force* (New York, 1957). My account comes directly from Lester Pearson and Andrew Cordier.
18. Resolutions in *ORGA*, documents A/3272 and A/3273, November 3, 1956, pp. 6-7.
19. Sir Anthony Eden, *Full Circle* (Cambridge, Mass., 1960), pp. 599 ff.

20. *ORGA*, November 3, 1956, A/3276, Annexes, p. 8, and fuller plan in *ORGA*, First Emergency Special Session, Annexes, Agenda Item 5. 2nd and final report of Secretary-General on plan for an emergency international United Nations Force requested in resolution 998 (ES-1), adopted by G. A. November 4, 1956, document A/3302, November 6, 1956, pp. 19-26.
21. *ORGA*, *Ibid.*, p. 88.
22. S/3730/Rev. 1.
23. *SCOR*, 752nd meeting, p. 13.
24. Eden, *op. cit.*, pp. 606-607.
25. Great Britain, *Parliamentary Debates* (Commons), November 5, 1956, cols. 1956-1958.
26. E. L. Dulles, *John Foster Dulles: The Last Year* (New York, 1963), p. 45.

CHAPTER 15: DULLES YIELDS TO RUSSIA

1. *Report*, Annual Conference, Llandudno, 1956, p. 124.
2. U. N., *Documents* S/3736, November 5, 1956.
3. White House news release, November 5, 1956; *U. S. P. M. E. Docs.*, pp. 182-188, for messages to Britain, France, and Israel.
4. Dwight D. Eisenhower, *Mandate for Change* (New York, 1963), p. 212.
5. *U. S. P. M. E. Docs.*, p. 182.
6. Cf. Hans Speier, "Soviet Atomic Blackmail," *World Politics* (April, 1957), p. 322.
7. Sir Anthony Eden, *Full Circle* (Cambridge, Mass., 1960), p. 622. *U. S. P. M. E. Docs.*, pp. 197-198.
8. Another account of this episode appears in Charles J. Murphy, "Washington and the World," *Fortune Magazine* (January, 1957), pp. 78 ff.
9. *Israeli Government Yearbook*, 1959-1960, p. 35.
10. See Tournoux, *Sécrets d'État* (Paris, 1960), p. 177.
11. Cf. Max Beloff, "Suez and the British Conscience," *Commentary* (April, 1955), pp. 308 ff.
12. November 10, 1956, p. 576.
13. Nigel Nicolson, *People and Parliament* (London, 1958), pp. 129-134.
14. Cf. *Financial Times* (London), November 1 to November 8, 1956.
15. Tournoux, *op. cit.*, p. 37. Here, Tournoux, Nutting is misspelled "Nut*l*ing."
16. *Ibid.*, confirmed in lecture by Maurice Schumann, Chairman of the Foreign Relations Commission of the Assemblée Nationale, before Institut des Hautes Études de Defense Nationale, February 4, 1957, private communication.
17. *Débats*, December 18, 1956, pp. 6109 ff.
18. *Washington Post*, December 12, 1956, p. 4.
19. *New York Times*, December 13, 1956, p. 20; and President's Proposal on the Middle East, *Hearings*, I, p. 163.

CHAPTER 16: DULLES SANCTIONS HIS ALLIES

1. From Dulles's papers at Princeton University.
2. Sir Anthony Eden, *Full Circle* (Cambridge, Mass., 1960), p. 628.
3. Maurice Schumann, as previously cited, Chapter 15, note 16, *supra*, semi-classified document.

4. Pp. 259 ff.
5. *Ibid.*, p. 260.
6. Great Britain, *Parliamentary Debates* (Commons), November 5, 1956.
7. Eden, *op. cit.*, p. 625.
8. U. N., General Assembly, *Documents* A/3293, A/3306, A/3307.
9. Great Britain, *Parliamentary Debates* (Commons), November 8, 1956, col. 262.
10. E. L. M. Burns, *Between Arab and Israeli* (Toronto, 1962), pp. 274 ff.
11. U. N., *Document* A/3302, and Add. 1-16, Annexes, Emergency Session, p. 20.
12. E. S. Res. A/3308.
13. *ORGA,* p. 95, First Emergency Special Session, November 7, 1956, Resolution A/3309.
14. *Ibid.*, pp. 112-113.
15. U. S., Senate, House, Foreign Affairs Committee, *Hearings,* p. 70.
16. Eden, *op. cit.*, p. 630.
17. Burns, *op. cit.*, pp. 198 and 200.
18. As in *U. S. P. M. E. Docs.*, p. 4, where the transcript differs from that in the *New York Times* report, November 15, 1956.
19. *New York Times,* November 16, 1956.
20. *ORGA,* November 16, 1956, pp. 91 ff.
21. *ORGA,* November 23, 1956, p. 258.
22. *Ibid.*, p. 274.
23. *Ibid.*, p. 290.
24. Detachments of Colombian and Norwegian troops arrived at Abu Sueir November 16, 1956, the Secretary General in the same U. N. E. F. airlift. See Burns, *op. cit.*, Chapter XV.
25. U. S., Department of State, *Bulletin,* November 26, 1956, pp. 838-839.
26. *New York Times,* November 28, 1956, p. 1; *The Times* (London), November 29, 1956, p. 11.
27. Cf. Sherman Adams, *First Hand Report* (New York, 1961), p. 262.
28. *Ibid.*, p. 265.
29. *Ibid.*, p. 266.
30. *Ibid.*, p. 267.
31. *Ibid.*, p. 268.
32. *Ibid.*
33. *Ibid.*, p. 269. Cf. P. H. Frankel, "Oil Supplies During the Suez Crisis," *Journal of Industrial Economics* (February, 1958), pp. 85 ff. See also U. S., Congress, *Joint Hearings on the Emergency Oil Lift Program and Related Oil Problems,* 85th Congress, Sen. Res. 57. The several volumes of *Hearings* and *Memoranda* offer a rich field on policy and the relationship between Congress and the Presidency so far as the foreign policy of the United States involves oil resources.
34. Cf. Lloyd A. Free, ed., and Herbert Leuthy and David Rodnick, *French Motivations in the Suez Crisis,* Institute for International Social Research (Princeton, N. J., November, 1956).
35. *U. S. P. M. E. Docs.*, pp. 5-15.
36. Reprinted in *M. E. D. Hearings,* I, pp. 84-98.
37. Cf. *ORGA* documents A/3398, A/3392, and Israeli letter, December 13, 1956.
38. *U. S. P. M. E. Docs.*, p. 361.
39. Adams, *op. cit.*, p. 281.
40. Great Britain, *Parliamentary Debates* (Commons), December 5, 1956, col. 1282.

CHAPTER 17: ISRAEL RESISTS THE "DOUBLE LAW"

1. U. N., *Document* A/3320, 1956.
2. *Israeli Government Yearbook, 1959-1960,* p. 37.
3. U. N., Secretary General, *Report,* Document A/3384, November 21, 1956. The chief documents concerning Israel's claims in and withdrawal from Sinai are, of course, in *ORGA,* and they are also collected for the most part in *U. S. P. M. E. Docs.*, pp. 211-347.
4. E. L. M. Burns, *Between Arab and Israeli* (Toronto, 1962), pp. 233 ff.
5. Cf. Statement of Israeli Foreign Minister, *ORGA,* U. N., January 17, 1957, pp. 886 ff; and Secretary-General's Report, A/3500, January 15, 1957.
6. U. S., Department of State, *Release,* no. 624, December 18, 1956.
7. *U. S. P. M. E. Docs.*, pp. 290 ff.
8. *Israeli Government Yearbook, 1959-1960,* p. 45.
9. *U. S. P. M. E. Docs.*, pp. 38-39.
10. *Ibid.*, pp. 41-42.
11. Sherman Adams, *First Hand Report* (New York, 1961), p. 280.
12. *Ibid.*, p. 281.
13. *Ibid.*, p. 282.
14. *Ibid.*
15. *Ibid.*, p. 284.
16. *U. S. P. M. E. Docs.*, p. 302.
17. *Loc. cit.*
18. *Ibid.*, p. 302.
19. *Israeli Government Yearbook*, 1959-1960, p. 50.
20. U. S., Department of State, *Release,* March 18, 1957; *U. S. P. M. E. Docs.*, p. 347.
21. On December 22, 1959, the Foreign Secretary of Israel revealed that the Secretary General of the United Nations and the Egyptian government had entered on some private arrangement whereby Israeli goods carried in foreign vessels to a purchaser abroad, f.o.b., and goods imported into Israel in vessels through the Canal under ownership by the seller, c.i.f., would not be obstructed. The Government of Israel entered this arrangement most reluctantly, yielding to U. S. recommendation to try this method of easing the situation, for this might lead eventually to further access of vessels via the Canal. The reluctance stemmed from the unwillingness to concede Israeli rights under international law. A Greek ship sent quietly to test the gentleman's agreement with Hammarskjold and Nasser was turned back. Hammarskjold's appeal to Nasser to let the ship through, as agreed on, was rebuffed. By this date, Nasser had been assured of a loan from the International Bank of Reconstruction and Development for widening the Canal.

CHAPTER 18: SUMMING UP: SUEZ AND BEYOND IN AMERICAN FOREIGN POLICY

1. Cf. the article by Marguerite Higgins in *New York Herald-Tribune,* October 8, 1956, offering a defiant defense of Dulles's press conference of October 2, 1956.

2. Professor Martin Wight, "Brutus in Foreign Policy," *International Affairs* (July, 1960), p. 307, a review of the memoirs of Sir Anthony Eden.
3. Professor Geoffrey Barraclough, Royal Institute of International Affairs, *International Affairs 1956-1958* (London, 1963), p. 34.
4. Coral Bell, *Negotiating from Strength* (New York, 1963), p. 90.
5. Alistair Buchan, "Le Chevalier Mal Fet," *Twentieth Century* (March, 1960), p. 237, a review article of Eden's memoirs.
6. "Anglo-Saxon Attitudes," *Times Literary Supplement* (London), March 4, 1960, p. 138, a review of Eden's memoirs.
7. *U. S. P. M. E. Docs.*, pp. 371-390.
8. *Ibid.*, pp. 390-392.
9. Cf. J. C. Campbell, *Defense of the Middle East* (New York, 1960), Chapters IX and X; and *M. E. D. Hearings,* 1957.
10. *U. S. P. M. E. Docs.*, p. 69, April 23, 1957.
11. Royal Institute of International Affairs, *Survey of International Affairs 1956-1958.*
12. *Ibid.*, pp. 374 ff., and U. S., Department of State, *Bulletin*, August 4, 1958, pp. 181-182.
13. See Peter Braestrup, "Limited Wars and the Lessons of Lebanon," *The Reporter*, April 30, 1959.
14. Campbell, *op. cit.*, pp. 142 ff., and Royal Institute of International Affairs, *op. cit.*, pp. 369 ff. See also, Great Britain, *Parliamentary Debates* (Commons), July 17, 1958, cols, 1506 ff., on Jordan.

    I am glad to see that Robert D. Murphy, *Diplomat Among Warriors* (New York, 1964), Chapter XXVII, amply confirms my estimate of the disciplinary power of the U. S. landing in Lebanon over his adventurism.
15. Quincy Wright, "The United States in the Lebanon," *American Journal of International Law,* LIII (January, 1959), pp. 112-115.
16. Statistics provided by the Agency for International Development, Department of State, Washington, D. C., on private request. On Nasser's "Arab Socialism" see Leonard Binder, "Nasserism: The Protest Movement in the Middle East," in Morton A. Kaplan, ed., *The Revolution in World Politics* (New York, 1962).
17. *New York Times,* September 29, 1963, p. 31, 25th anniversary of Munich. Cf. Margery Perham, *Colonial Reckoning* (New York, 1962); and S. C. Easton, *Rise and Fall of Western Colonialism* (New York, 1963).
18. Cf. Paul-Henri Spaak, "The West in Disarray," *Foreign Affairs* (January, 1957), especially p. 185.
19. Royal Institute of International Affairs, *op. cit.*, pp. 209-210.
20. Cf. *Near East Report*, February 3, 1958 (Washington, D. C.), p. 67.
21. *Public Papers of the President,* 1962, p. 914, being a press conference of December 31, 1962, made public mid-January, 1963.
22. President Charles de Gaulle, press conference, January 14, 1963, supplied by the French Embassy, Washington, D. C.; see also Robert E. Osgood, *NATO: Entangling Alliance* (Chicago, 1962); and George Liska, *Nations in Alliance* (Baltimore, 1962).
23. *New York Times*, November 10, 1963, p. 9.
24. *Public Papers of the President,* 1962, p. 807.
25. Bowett, *op. cit.*, p. 74, concerning the *Kearsage Case.*
26. Cf. Herman Finer, *America's Destiny* (New York, 1948), pp. 316 ff.

Publications

The following list of printed authorities is not intended to be exhaustive. The books listed have been particularly useful, but the Notes to the text refer to additional ones where specific citation was appropriate. So, also, with the list of government and United Nations official documents.

NEWSPAPERS AND PERIODICALS

New York Times; New York Herald Tribune; Washington Post; Christian Science Monitor; Times (London); *Manchester Guardian* (London); *Neuer Zuricher Zeitung* (Zurich); *Le Monde* (Paris); *Le Figaro* (Paris); *France-Observateur* (Paris); *Economist* (London); *Spectator* (London). *Orient* (Paris, quarterly, from January, 1947); *Middle East Journal* (Washington, D.C., quarterly, since 1947); *Jewish Observer and Middle East Review* (London, weekly, since 1952).

GOVERNMENTAL PUBLICATIONS

United States. Congressional Record; Department of State Bulletin; Public Papers of the Presidents; Report, President to Congress, U.S. Participation in the United Nations, 1955, 1956, 1957, 1958; State Department, *The Suez Canal Problem, July 26 to September 22, 1956; United States Policy in the Middle East, September 1956 to June 1957;* the relevant reports and hearings of the U.S. Senate Foreign Relations Committee and House Foreign Affairs Committee, and sundry Hearings on the Mutual Appropriations 1955 and 1956, Security Act and Middle East Doctrine, 1957.

Britain. Parliamentary Debates, Commons and Lords.

France. Assemblée Nationale, *Journal Officiel, Débats.*

United Nations. Official Record of the General Assembly Emergency and Ordinary Meetings; Security Council Official Record, and annexes and supplements thereto; *Annual Report of Secretary General of United Nations,* 1953 to 1958.

DOCUMENTARY COLLECTIONS AND COMMENTARIES

Survey of International Affairs, especially 1954, by Coral Bell; 1955-56, by Geoffrey Barraclough and R. Wall; 1956-58, by Geoffrey Barraclough (also of special importance), all published for the Royal Institute of International Affairs, London, by Oxford University Press. *Documents on International Affairs,* especially volumes for 1953 through 1958, published annually for Royal Institute of International Affairs, London, by Oxford University Press. Those for 1953 and 1954 edited by Denise Folliot, and those for 1955, 1956, 1957, and 1958, by Noble Frankland.

BOOKS AND ARTICLES

Adams, Michael. *Suez and After*. Boston, 1958.
Antonius, George. *The Arab Awakening*. London, 1938.
Avram, Benno. *The Evolution of the Suez Canal Status*. Geneva, 1958.
Beal, John R. *John Foster Dulles*. New York, 1957.
Bell, Coral. *Negotiating from Strength*. London, 1962.
Berger, Morroe. *The Arab World Today*. New York, 1962.
Birdwood, Lord. *Nuri as-Said*. London, 1959.
Bloomfield, Lincoln M. *Egypt, Israel, and the Gulf of Aqaba in International Law*. Toronto, 1957.
Bromberger, Merry and Serge. *The Secrets of Suez*. London, 1957.
Campbell, John C. *The Defense of the Middle East*. New York, 1960.
Childers, Erskine B. *The Road to Suez*. London, 1962.
Churchill, Randolph S. *The Rise and Fall of Sir Anthony Eden*. London, 1959.
Connell, John. *The Most Important Country*. London, 1957.
Drummond, Roscoe, and Coblentz, Gaston. *Duel at the Brink*. New York, 1960.
Eden, Sir Anthony. *Full Circle: Memoirs*. Cambridge, Mass., 1960.
Elwell-Sutton, L. P. *Persian Oil: A Study in Power Politics*. London, 1955.
Foot, Michael, and Jones, Mervyn. *Guilty Men, 1957: Suez and Cyprus*. New York, 1957.
Glubb, J. B. *A Soldier with the Arabs*. London, 1957.
Goodhart, A. L. *Tensions in the Middle East* (Ed. P. W. Taylor). Baltimore, 1958.
Goold-Adams, Richard. *Time of Power: John Foster Dulles*. London, 1962.
Hartshorn, J. *Oil Companies and Governments*. London, 1962.
Henriques, Robert. *A Hundred to Suez*. New York, 1957.
Hourani, A. H. "The Middle East and the Crisis of 1956," *Middle Eastern Affairs*, No. 1. New York, 1959.
Hurewitz, J. C. *Diplomacy in the Near and Middle East*, Vols. I and II. Princeton, N. J., 1956.
Hussein. *Uneasy Lies the Head*. New York, 1962.
Issawi, Charles. *Egypt in Revolution: An Economic Analysis*. London, 1963.
Khadduri, Majid. *Independent Iraq: 1932-1958*. London, 1960.
Kimche, Jon and David. *Both Sides of the Hill*. London, 1960.
King, Gillian. *The Future of Aden and British Defence Policy in the Indian Ocean*. London, 1963.
Kirk, George E. *Short History of the Middle East*. New York, 1959.
———. *Contemporary Arab Politics*. New York, 1961.
Laqueur, Walter Z. (Ed.) *The Middle East in Transition*. New York, 1958.
———. *The Soviet Union and the Middle East*. New York, 1959.
Leeman, W. A. *The Price of Middle East Oil*. London, 1961.
Lenczowski, George. *Oil and State in the Middle East*. Ithaca, 1960.
Longrigg, S. *Oil in the Middle East*. London, 1961.
Marlowe, John. *Anglo-Egyptian Relations, 1800-1953*. London, 1954.
———. *Arab Nationalism and British Imperialism*. London, 1961.

———. *The Persian Gulf in the Twentieth Century*. London, 1962.
Marshall, S. L. A. *Sinai Victory*. New York, 1958.
Monroe, Elizabeth. *Britain's Moment in the Middle East*. London, 1963.
Murphy, Robert. *Diplomat Among Warriors*. New York, 1964.
Nicholas, Herbert. *Britain and the U.S.A.* Baltimore, 1963.
Nimer, Benjamin. "Dulles, Suez, and Democratic Diplomacy," *Western Political Quarterly*, September, 1959.
Nutting, Anthony. *I Saw for Myself: The Aftermath of Suez*. New York, 1958.
O'Ballance, Edgar. *The Sinai Campaign, 1956*. London, 1959.
Polk, William R., Stamler, David M., and Asfour, Edmund. *Backdrop to Tragedy: The Struggle for Palestine*. Boston, 1957.
Royal Institute of International Affairs. *British Interests in the Mediterranean and Middle East*. London, 1958.
Safran, Nadav. *The United States and Israel*. Cambridge, Mass., 1963.
Shwadran, Benjamin. *The Middle East, Oil and the Great Powers*. New York, 1959.
———. *Jordan: A State of Tension*. New York, 1959.
Wheelock, Kenneth. *Nasser's New Egypt*. New York, 1960.
Wint, Guy, and Calvocoressi, Peter. *The Middle East Crisis*. London, 1957.

Index

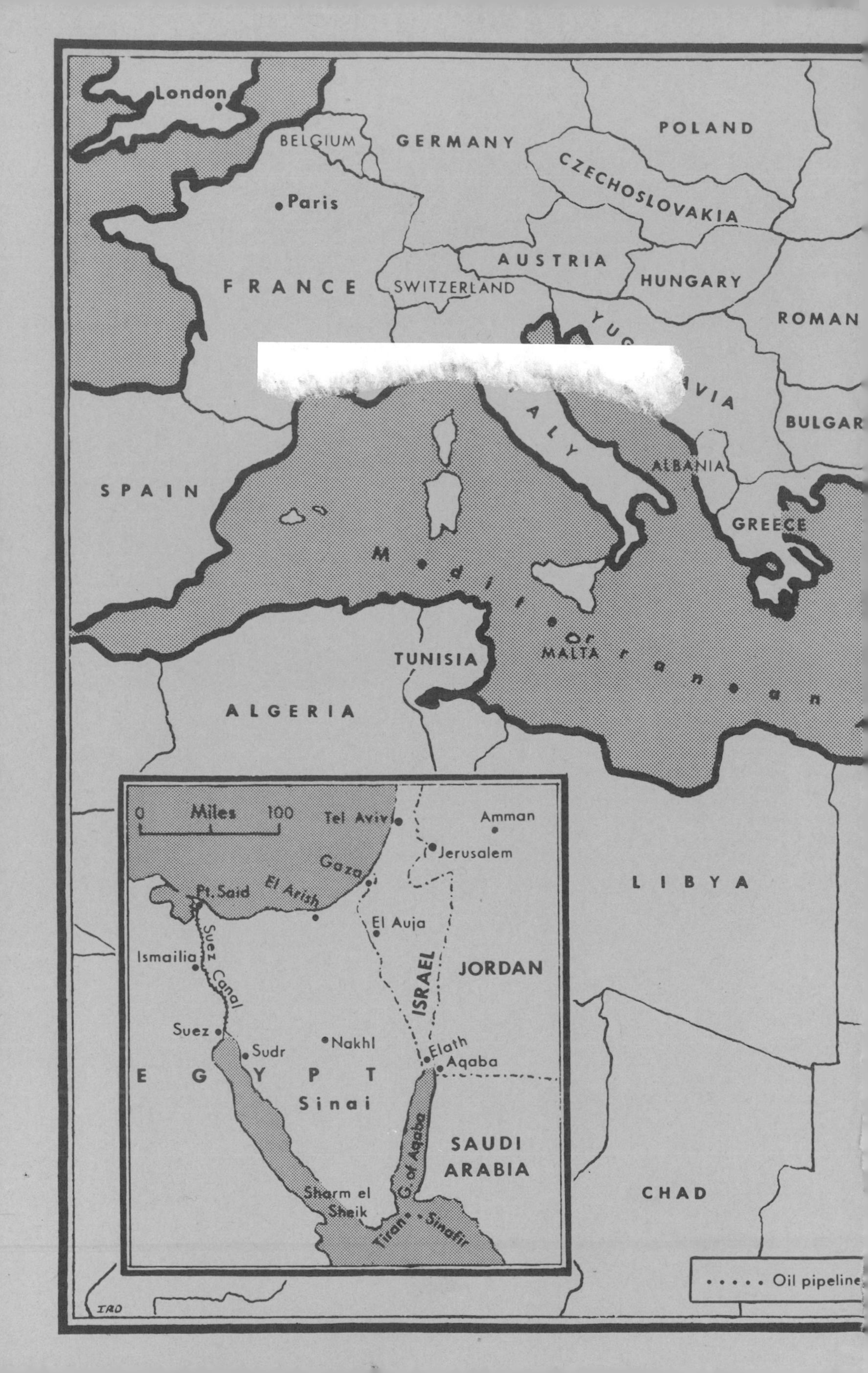
London
BELGIUM
GERMANY
POLAND
CZECHOSLOVAKIA
Paris
AUSTRIA
HUNGARY
FRANCE
SWITZERLAND
ROMAN
ALBANIA
BULGAR
SPAIN
GREECE
Mediterranean
MALTA
TUNISIA
ALGERIA
LIBYA
CHAD
0 Miles 100
Tel Aviv
Amman
Jerusalem
Gaza
El Arish
Pt. Said
El Auja
Suez Canal
Ismailia
ISRAEL
JORDAN
Suez
Sudr
Nakhl
Elath
Aqaba
EGYPT
Sinai
G. of Aqaba
SAUDI ARABIA
Sharm el Sheik
Tiran
Sinafir
Oil pipeline
IRD